HAWAI'I 2025

By Jeanne Cooper
& Natalie Schack

FrommerMedia LLC

Frommer's Hawai'i 2025

Published by:
Frommer Media LLC

Copyright © 2025 by Frommer Media LLC, New York City, New York. All rights reserved. No part of this publication may be reproduced, stored in a retrieval system, or transmitted in any form or by any means, electronic, mechanical, photocopying, recording, scanning or otherwise, except as permitted under Sections 107 or 108 of the 1976 United States Copyright Act, without the prior written permission of the Publisher. Requests to the Publisher for permission should be addressed to Support@FrommerMedia.com.

Frommer's is a registered trademark of Arthur Frommer. Frommer Media LLC is not associated with any product or vendor mentioned in this book.

ISBN 978-1-62887-607-9 (paper), 978-1-62887-608-6 (e-book)

Editorial Director: Pauline Frommer
Editor: Melinda Quintero
Production Editor: Heather Wilcox

Cartographer: Andy Dolan
Page Compositor: Lissa Auciello-Brogan
Photo Editor: Alyssa Mattei

For information on our other products or services, see www.frommers.com.

Frommer Media LLC also publishes its books in a variety of electronic formats. Some content that appears in print may not be available in electronic formats.

Manufactured in Malaysia

5   4   3   2   1

HOW TO CONTACT US

In researching this book, we discovered many wonderful places—hotels, restaurants, shops, and more. We're sure you'll find others. Please tell us about them, so we can share the information with your fellow travelers in upcoming editions. If you were disappointed with a recommendation, we'd love to know that, too. Please write to: Support@FrommerMedia.com

FROMMER'S STAR RATINGS SYSTEM

Every hotel, restaurant and attraction listed in this guide has been ranked for quality and value. Here's what the stars mean:

★   Recommended
★★   Highly Recommended
★★★ A must! Don't miss!

AN IMPORTANT NOTE

The world is a dynamic place. Hotels change ownership, restaurants hike their prices, museums alter their opening hours, and buses and trains change their routings. And all of this can occur in the several months after our authors have visited, inspected, and written about these hotels, restaurants, museums, and transportation services. Though we have made valiant efforts to keep all our information fresh and up-to-date, some few changes can inevitably occur in the periods before a revised edition of this guidebook is published. So please bear with us if a tiny number of the details in this book have changed. Please also note that we have no responsibility or liability for any inaccuracy or errors or omissions, or for inconvenience, loss, damage, or expenses suffered by anyone as a result of assertions in this guide.

CONTENTS

LIST OF MAPS

ABOUT THE AUTHORS

Jeanne Cooper grew up listening to songs and stories of Hawai'i from her mother, who lived on O'ahu as a teen. She began writing about Hawai'i and its diverse cultures for the *San Francisco Chronicle* and SFGate.com in 2002. Her travel stories have also been published in numerous U.S. and international newspapers, magazines, and websites. Before the relaunch of *Frommer's Hawaii* in 2015, she contributed to guidebooks for San Francisco, Boston, and Washington, D.C., her previous hometowns. She now lives on Hawai'i Island with her triathlete husband, two mutts, and two cats, and always enjoys learning more about Hawai'i's lovely islands with visiting family and friends.

Natalie Shack is a writer and editor lucky enough to be born and raised on the island of O'ahu, Hawai'i. Her career in journalism began as a student in Boston but brought her back to her beautiful home turf. Her work has appeared in *HONOLULU Magazine, Curbed, Hawaii Business Magazine, Green Magazine, Hana Hou!, Flux Magazine,* and many more. When she's not penning articles about the many marvelous facets of Hawai'i's unique culture, food, art, and business scenes, you'll find her rambling through the Ko'olau mountains, swimming O'ahu's south shores, and enjoying Honolulu city life with her husband and young son.

1

THE BEST
OF HAWAI'I

No place on earth is quite like this handful of sun-drenched Pacific islands. Here you'll find palm-fringed blue lagoons, lush rainforests, cascading waterfalls, soaring summits, two active volcanoes, beautiful beaches—and a culture that celebrates preserving them for future generations. The rich variety of dining and shopping reflects the multiethnic heritage of communities shaped by the plantation era and more recent immigrants, attracted by the islands' easy-going lifestyle and their abundant inspiration for chefs and artists. Each of the six main islands possesses its own unique mix of natural and cultural treasures—and the possibilities for adventure, indulgence, and relaxation are endless.

THE best BEACHES

o **Lanikai Beach** (O'ahu): Too gorgeous to be real, this stretch along the Windward Coast is a postcard-perfect beach—a mile of golden sand as soft as powdered sugar bordering translucent turquoise waters. The waters are calm year-round and excellent for swimming, snorkeling, and kayaking. Two tiny offshore islands complete the picture, functioning both as scenic backdrops and bird sanctuaries. See p. 109.

o **Kauna'oa Beach (Mauna Kea Beach)** (Hawai'i Island): The palest, purest sand of the island and generally gentle, clear waters here famously attracted Laurance Rockefeller to build the island's first resort, the Mauna Kea Beach Hotel, on the slope above the beach, back when there was nothing but rocky lava and scrubby ranchland within miles. Manta rays are known to hover under the light mounted on its northern point, while green sea turtles often bob around the submerged rocks at the southern point. It's often so calm that the hotel puts up floating platforms for swimmers to relax on—and so popular that you need to arrive early (and now pay) for a public beach access spot. See p. 223.

o **Keawakapu Beach** (Maui): On the border between bustling Kīhei and opulent Wailea but hidden from the road, lies this typically uncrowded, soft, golden strand, nearly three-quarters of a mile long. Intriguing tidepools await at the northern end and snorkeling sites in clear waters at the southern end; restaurants and beach gear rental

PREVIOUS PAGE: Regenerative tourism in Hawai'i starts with the *pono* pledge (p. 4).

2

options are close at hand without disturbing the serenity. The views are stellar, especially at sunset, and weekday parking is usually easy. See p. 337.

Along the beach in Poʻipū, Kauaʻi.

o **Pāpōhaku Beach** (Molokaʻi): The currents are too strong for swimming here, especially in winter's pounding surf, but the light-blond strand of sand, nearly 300 feet wide and stretching for some 3 miles can be great for picnicking, walking, and watching sunsets, with Oʻahu shimmering in the distance. See p. 444.

o **Hulopoʻe Beach** (Lānaʻi): This large sprawl of soft golden sand is one of the prettiest in the state. Bordered by the regal Four Seasons resort on one side and lava-rock tide pools on the other, this protected marine preserve offers prime swimming and snorkeling (in calm conditions), tide-pool exploring, picnicking, and the chance to spy on resident spinner dolphins. See p. 472.

o **Kēʻē Beach** (Kauaʻi): Now that visitors need a parking permit or shuttle reservation to access this North Shore beach at the end of the road, its beautiful crescent of sand bracketed by forest and steep green cliffs can be enjoyed in relative tranquility. In summer, conditions are often ideal for snorkeling on the teeming reef, but check with lifeguards here before venturing out, especially in winter. See p. 497.

o **Poʻipū Beach** (Kauaʻi): This popular beach on the sunny South Shore has something for everyone: protected swimming, snorkeling, bodyboarding, surfing, and plenty of sand for basking—just ask the green sea turtles that haul out at twilight. They're joined every so often by an endangered Hawaiian monk seal (admire both from a distance). See p. 530.

THE best AUTHENTIC EXPERIENCES

o **Eat Local:** People in Hawaiʻi love food. Want to get a local talking? Ask for her favorite place to get poke or *saimin* or shave ice. The islands offer excellent fine-dining opportunities (see the examples below), but they also have plenty of respectable hole-in-the-wall

DO THE RIGHT THING: pono pledges

The Disney movie *Lilo and Stitch* also taught many people that *'ohana* means "family" ("and family means no one gets left behind"). Now local authorities are trying to persuade visitors to behave as if they are indeed family, meaning everyone has a *kuleana* (responsibility) to act *pono* (righteously)—not only for their safety, but so that residents will continue to share aloha with visitors, whose post-pandemic numbers have neared the record 10 million in 2019.

Most suggestions sound like common sense: Don't trespass, don't litter, don't go out in unsafe water or hike unprepared, don't take anything but pictures from the natural landscape, respect cultural sites and local customs, avoid unpermitted vacation rentals (plenty *do* have permits), and so forth. Sadly, these reminders appear necessary, due to a combination of "vacation brain," where excitement about being in a dazzling new environment can cloud judgment (hey, it happens to the best of us), and widespread encouragement of risky or illegal behavior on social media. Just because someone on YouTube was able to swim at a place where people drown every year does not mean you will be immune from harm.

To help promote this more responsible mindset, Hawai'i Island tourism officials launched the **Pono Pledge** (www.ponopledge.com), with principles applying to all the islands: "I will mindfully seek wonder, but not wander where I do not belong...I will not defy death for breathtaking photos...I will mālama (care

for) land and sea, and admire wildlife only from far." In 2021, state tourism authorities began **Mālama Hawai'i,** encouraging visitors to participate in environmental and cultural activities with the incentive of an additional hotel night or other perks.

Responsible tour operators, including **Fair Wind** (Hawai'i Island, p. 231) and **Holo Holo Charters** (Kaua'i, p. 534) also formally ask participants to model pono behavior, such as using only mineral-based sunscreen (to avoid reef damage), not touching or standing on coral (which is easily damaged and takes decades to grow), and recognizing one's physical limits.

Traveling *pono* also means respecting local traditions, such as chatting with store clerks, waving cars into traffic, and being patient—island life is full of surprises and occasional delays as well as delights. And in the words of Clifford Nae'ole, cultural advisor to the Ritz-Carlton Maui, Kapalua, to travel *pono* is "to accept the concept of aloha by giving even more than you receive."

joints and beloved institutions that have hung around for half a century. On O'ahu, eat poke at **Ono Seafood** (p. 146), enjoy true Hawaiian food at **Helena's Hawaiian Food** (p. 151), and join the regulars at **Liliha Bakery** (p. 151) for a loco moco, coco puff, or poi mochi doughnut. On Kaua'i, slurp *saimin* and shave ice at **Hamura's Saimin Stand** (p. 577).

o **Feel History Come Alive at Pearl Harbor** (O'ahu): On December 7, 1941, Japanese warplanes bombed Pearl Harbor, forcing the United States to enter World War II. Standing on the deck of the **USS Arizona Memorial**—the eternal tomb for the 1,177 sailors trapped below when the battleship sank—is a profound experience. You can also visit the USS *Missouri* Memorial, where the Japanese signed their surrender on September 2, 1945. See p. 82.

o **Experience Hula:** Each year the city of Hilo on Hawai'i Island hosts a prestigious competition celebrating ancient Hawaiian dance: the **Merrie Monarch Festival** (p. 175), held the week after Easter. Year-round, local *hālau* (hula troupes) perform **free shows** at several shopping centers on several islands. On O'ahu, head to the Halekulani's **House Without a Key** (p. 166), where the sunset functions as a beautiful backdrop to equally beautiful hula. On Maui, the **Old Lāhainā Lū'au** (p. 427) is the real deal, showcasing Hawaiian dance and storytelling nightly on a gracious, beachfront stage.

o **Ponder Petroglyphs:** More than 23,000 ancient rock carvings decorate the lava fields at **Hawai'i Volcanoes National Park** (p. 209) on Hawai'i Island. You can see hundreds more on a short hike through the **Puakō Petroglyph Archaeological Preserve** (p. 193), near the Fairmont Orchid on the Kohala Coast, or an even easier walk through the **Waikoloa Petroglyph Preserve** (p. 193), near the Kings' Shops in Waikoloa Beach Resort. Go early in the morning or late afternoon when the angle of the sun lets you see the forms clearly. On Lāna'i, fantastic birdmen and canoes are etched into rocks at **Luahiwa** (p. 471), **Shipwreck Beach** (p. 473), and **Kaunolū Village** (p. 468).

Juggling fire at a luau on Maui.

o **Restore the Land:** Join the regenerative tourism movement and connect with ancient Hawaiian stewardship practices by helping restore its native forests. Healthy dryland forests not only support native birds, but also help keep the coral reefs below them free from damaging runoff. On Maui, volunteer with **Kīpuka Olowalu** in Olowalu Valley (p. 352) or **Maui Cultural Lands** in Honokōwai Valley (p. 352). On Hawai'i Island, tend native plants in the **Waikōloa Dry Forest** (p. 194); plant a koa seedling or collect 'a'ali'i seeds on a UTV tour on the slopes of Hualālai with **Uluha'o O Hualālai** (p. 216); on Kaua'i, volunteer to care for the rare native plants in the **National Tropical Botanical**

Volunteers planting seeds with Kīpuka Olowalu on Maui.

Garden in Limahuli Valley (p. 516), or volunteer for a community workday in the otherwise inaccessible but spectacular setting of **Alekoko (Menehune) Fishpond** (p. 504).

THE best OUTDOOR ADVENTURES

o **Surfing on O'ahu:** Whether you're learning to surf or you're a pro, O'ahu has waves for everyone. Few experiences are more exhilarating than standing on your first wave, and Waikīkī offers lessons, board rentals, and gentle surf. During the winter, the North Shore gets big and rough, so stay out of the water if you're not an experienced surfer. But even the view from the beach, watching the daredevils take off on waves twice their height, is thrilling. See p. 116.

o **Witness the Whales:** From late December through mid-March, humpback whales cruise Hawaiian waters in significant numbers. You can see these gentle giants from almost any shore; simply scan the horizon for a spout. Hear them, too, by ducking your head below the surface and listening for their otherworldly music. Boats on every island offer whale-watching cruises, but Maui is your best bet for seeing the massive marine mammals up close. Try **Trilogy** (p. 344) for a first-class catamaran ride, **Redline Rafting** (p. 351) for a zippy excursion on a 35-foot canopied raft or, if you're adventurous, climb into an outrigger canoe with **Hawaiian Paddle Sports** (p. 350).

o **Visit Volcanoes:** The entire island chain is made of volcanoes; don't miss the opportunity to explore them. On O'ahu, the whole family can hike to the top of extinct, world-famous **Diamond Head Crater** (p. 117). At **Hawai'i Volcanoes National Park** (p. 209) on Hawai'i Island, where Kīlauea's Halema'uma'u Crater and Mauna Loa's summit erupted simultaneously in late 2022, hills of black cinders and billowing sulfurous steam give hints of Pele's presence even when red-hot lava isn't visible. On Maui, **Haleakalā National Park** (p. 395) provides a bird's-eye view into a long-dormant volcanic crater.

o **Get Misted by Waterfalls:** Waterfalls thundering down into sparkling pools are some of the most beautiful natural wonders in Hawai'i. If you're on Hawai'i Island, head to the spectacular 442-foot **'Akaka Falls** (p. 197), north of Hilo. On Maui, the Road to Hāna offers numerous viewing opportunities. Kaua'i is laced with waterfalls, especially along the North Shore and in the Wailua area, where you can drive right up to the 151-foot **'Ōpaeka'a Falls** (p. 508) and the 80-foot **Wailua Falls** (p. 509). On Moloka'i, the 250-foot **Mo'oula Falls** (p. 433) can be visited only via a guided hike through breathtaking Hālawa Valley, but that, too, is a very special experience.

o **Peer into Waimea Canyon** (Kaua'i): It may not share the vast dimensions of Arizona's Grand Canyon, but this colorful gorge on Kaua'i—a mile wide, 3,600 feet deep, and 14 miles long—has a grandeur all its own, easily viewed from several overlooks just off Kōke'e Road. Hike to **Waipo'o Falls** (p. 550) to experience its red parapets up close or take one of the helicopter rides that swoop between its walls like the white-tailed tropicbird. See p. 521.

o **Explore the Nāpali Coast** (Kaua'i): With the exception of the **Kalalau Valley,** which has its own overlook (p. 513), the fluted ridges and deep, primeval valleys of the island's northwest portion can't be viewed by car. You must hike the 11-mile **Kalalau Trail** (p. 549), kayak (p. 535), take a snorkel cruise (p. 538), or book a helicopter ride (p. 551) to experience its wild, stunning beauty.

o **Four-Wheel It on Lāna'i** (Lāna'i): Off-roading is a way of life on barely paved Lāna'i. Rugged trails lead to deserted beaches, abandoned villages, sacred sites, and valleys filled with wild game. Afraid to drive yourself? **Rabaca's Limousine Service and Island Tours** (p. 465) will take you to remote areas in comfortable vehicles with friendly guides.

THE welcoming LEI

A lei is aloha turned tangible, communicating "hello," "goodbye," "congratulations," and "I love you" in a single strand of fragrant flowers. Leis are the perfect symbol for the islands: Their fragrance and beauty are enjoyed in the moment, but the aloha they represent lasts long after they've faded.

Hawaiians make leis out of flowers, shells, ferns, feathers, leaves, nuts, and even seaweed. Some are twisted, some braided, and some strung, worn to commemorate special occasions, honor a loved one, or complement a hula. Leis are available at most of the islands' airports, florists, supermarkets, and drugstores. You can find wonderful, inexpensive leis at the half-dozen lei shops on **Maunakea Street** in Honolulu's Chinatown. On Moloka'i, sew your own at **Molokai Plumerias** (p. 435).

THE best HOTELS

- **Halekulani** (O'ahu): When money is no object, this is really the only place to stay. A place of zen amid the buzz, this recently renovated beach hotel is the finest Waikīkī has to offer. Even if you don't stay here, pop by for a sunset mai tai at **House Without a Key** (p. 166) to watch live Hawaiian music accompanied by a lovely hula dancer. See p. 129.

- **Royal Hawaiian** (O'ahu): This pink oasis, hidden away among blooming gardens within the concrete jungle of Waikīkī, is a stunner. It's vibrant and exotic, from the Spanish-Moorish arches in the common areas to the pink-and-gold pineapple wallpaper in the Historic Wing's guest rooms. See p. 131.

Villas at the Fairmont Kea Lani, Maui.

o **Kahala Hotel & Resort** (O'ahu): In one of the most prestigious residential areas of O'ahu, the Kahala provides the peace and serenity of a neighbor-island vacation, but with the conveniences of Waikīkī just a 10-minute drive away. The lush, tropical grounds include an 800-foot, crescent-shaped beach and a 26,000-square-foot lagoon (home to two bottlenose dolphins, sea turtles, and tropical fish). See p. 135.

o **Four Seasons Resort Hualālai** (Hawai'i Island): The seven pools alone will put you in seventh heaven at this exclusive yet environmentally conscious oasis of understated luxury, which also offers a private, 18-hole golf course, an award-winning spa, exquisite dining (including shellfish and sea salt harvested on-site), and impeccable service—with no resort fee. Follow its shoreline north to its lower-key but still ultra-luxurious neighbor, **Kona Village, a Rosewood Resort** (p. 260), where the lodgings are sustainably designed, thatched-roof bungalows and the seclusion is exquisite. See p. 259.

o **Westin Hapuna Beach Resort** (Hawai'i Island): This hidden gem on the Kohala Coast boasts spacious rooms, an enormous beach, a large family pool with separate adult infinity-edge pool, a huge open-air, ocean-facing lobby, and several high-quality dining outlets, including a new sake brewery with sushi restaurant overlooking the championship golf course. Also consider its gorgeous but pricier sister hotel, the **Mauna Kea Beach Hotel** (p. 263), part of Marriott's Autograph Collection but independently owned, with a spectacular golf course and beach visited nightly by manta rays. See p. 266.

o **Mauna Lani, Auberge Resorts Collection** (Hawai'i Island): This luxurious oceanfront oasis in the *piko* (navel) of the island is rich with lush vegetation and subtle Hawaiian-themed art and handsome woods that complement the extensive menu of cultural activities. Near historic fishponds and beaches favored by turtles lie a serene adults pool, matching family pool, and top-notch restaurants, including dinner-only CanoeHouse and island-casual HaLani. See p. 264.

o **Fairmont Kea Lani** (Maui): This Wailea resort offers a quiet beach-front locale, beautifully renovated (and huge) suite-style rooms and residential-sized villas, a plethora of pools, an expert spa with thoughtful wellness program, and excellent dining, from the fresh poke bowls in the marketplace to the gourmet take on plantation fare at **Kō** (p. 409). Learn about the cultural roots of Wailea and Maui in the impressive new cultural center at the center of the lobby. See p. 384.

o **Hotel Wailea** (Maui): This luxurious hillside, adults-only compound in Wailea, has residential-sized, beach-chic suites set among tropical gardens with beautiful views of Kaho'olawe, Molokini, and West Maui, plus a free shuttle to shops, restaurants, and the beach. Lingering by the pool and sampling cocktails under the soaring wooden ceiling of the Birdcage lobby bar are also memorable. See p. 386.

o **Ritz-Carlton Maui, Kapalua** (Maui): A $100-million renovation that wrapped up in late 2022 has burnished this elegant resort's already deep commitment to showcasing Hawaiian culture and its reputation for attention to creature comforts. The impressive views of Honokahua Bay from the kapa-lined lobby lanai are mirrored in many rooms, all with private outdoor areas and some with firepits. Dining, spa, cultural activities, and ocean explorations (through Jean-Jacques Cousteau's Ambassadors of the Environment program) rate among the very best in Hawai'i. See p. 375.

o **Four Seasons Resort Lāna'i** (Lāna'i): This gracious resort on Lāna'i's south coast overlooks Hulopoe Beach—one of the finest stretches of sand in the state. Guest rooms are palatial, outfitted with museum-quality art and automated everything—from temperature, lighting, and sound system to bidet toilets. The suites have deep soaking Japanese cedar tubs, and views that stretch for an eternity. The restaurants and service throughout the resort are impeccable. See p. 480.

o **Grand Hyatt Kauai Resort & Spa** (Kaua'i): At this sprawling, family-embracing resort in Po'ipū, the elaborate, multi-tiered fantasy pool and saltwater lagoon more than compensate for the rough waters of Keoneloa (Shipwrecks) Beach. Don't fret: Calmer Po'ipū Beach is just a short drive away. Anara Spa and Poipu Bay Golf Course offer excellent adult diversions, too. See p. 566.

Lazy river at the Grand Hyatt Kauai Resort & Spa.

o **Kōloa Landing Resort at Po'ipū** (Kaua'i): Families come here in droves, thanks to spacious, apartment-style villas with washer-dryers and high-end kitchen appliances, large lawns for games, firepits with s'mores service, and three pools, including a sprawling, multi-level main pool with lava-tube slide. But couples can hide away here too, enjoying the tranquil, adults-only pool, in-house spa, and innovative island dining at poolside Holoholo Grill. See p. 568.

o **1 Hotel Hanalei Bay** (Kaua'i): The former Princeville Hotel, completely renovated and rebranded, now has a sustainability and wellness ethos reflected in the natural fibers, stone, and wood of its luxurious new rooms; the locally sourced and mostly organic ingredients on the menus in its multiple dining outlets; and thoughtful activities that include how to protect endangered seabirds and sea turtles. See p. 564.

THE best RESTAURANTS

o **Sushi Izakaya Gaku** (O'ahu): The city has plenty of *izakayas,* Japanese pubs serving small plates made for sharing, but this gem is the best of them all. You'll discover life beyond *maguro* and *hamachi nigiri* with seasonal, uncommon seafood, such as sea bass sashimi and grilled ray. Thanks to the large population of Japanese nationals living in Honolulu, the Japanese food here is some of the best outside of Japan. But it's not just straight-from-Tokyo fare at Gaku; the chefs scour fish markets daily for the best local fish. See p. 152.

o **The Pig and the Lady** (O'ahu): This casual restaurant, with its traditional Vietnamese noodle soups and playful interpretations of Southeast Asian food, is both soulful and surprising. The soulful: the pho of the day, drawing on recipes from Chef Andrew Le's mother. The surprising: hand-cut pasta with pork and *liliko'i* (passion fruit). The best

Dining on the terrace of Merriman's in Kapalua, Maui.

of both worlds: a pho French dip banh mi, with slices of tender brisket and a cup of pho broth for dipping. See p. 149.

o **Mala Ocean Tavern** (Maui): A miraculous survivor of the devastating fire in Lahaina, this oceanfront bistro in a century-old building at the northern end of Front St. reopened in early 2024, to the delight of residents and visitors alike. Savor American and Mediterranean classics with island-style ingredients, along with views of Māla Wharf and Lāna'i. See p. 399.

o **Mama's Fish House** (Maui): Overlooking Kū'au Cove on Maui's North Shore, this restaurant is a South Pacific fantasy. Every nook is decorated with some fanciful artifact of salt-kissed adventure. The menu lists the anglers who reeled in the day's catch; you can order ono "caught by Keith Nakamura along the 40-fathom ledge near Hana" or deep-water ahi seared with coconut and lime. The Tahitian Pearl dessert is almost too stunning to eat. See p. 417.

o **Merriman's** (O'ahu, Hawai'i Island, Maui): Chef Peter Merriman, one of the founders of Hawai'i Regional Cuisine, oversees a locally inspired culinary empire that also includes **Merriman's Fish House** on Kaua'i (p. 586), **Monkeypod Kitchen** on O'ahu (p. 158) and Maui (p. 411), as well as the **Beach House** on Kaua'i (p. 584), famed for sunset photo ops. His original Waimea restaurant, opened in 1988, still merits the drive upcountry from the coast (p. 283), while the menu at his Kapalua, Maui, outpost (p. 405) almost matches the breathtaking views.

o **Umekes Fish Market Bar and Grill** (Hawai'i Island): The island specialty of diced raw, marinated seafood poke—pronounced *po-kay*—comes in many varieties and is available for carry-out or dine-in at this handsome indoor/outdoor restaurant in Kailua-Kona. (p. 276).

o **Binchotan** (Hawai'i Island): Named for the prized white charcoal used to grill robatayaki skewers, this restaurant at the Fairmont Orchid makes for a wonderful group meal with a wide variety of dishes to share, from Wagyu beef that you sizzle yourself on hot rocks to sweet shrimp, lobster, and crab in tempura and fritter form. Happy hour at the bar brings true bargains, too. See p. 282.

o **Ama** and **Bar Acuda** (Hanalei, Kaua'i): When the sun goes down, the surfing set freshens up for a night on the town at **Bar Acuda,** a stylish tapas bar (p. 578). Created by Jim Moffat, a former star of San Francisco's culinary scene, Bar Acuda's fare is centered around fresh seafood and seasonal pairings inspired by Mediterranean cuisine. The Asian-style noodles and mountain views at Moffat's open-air **Ama** (p. 580), in the same quaint shopping center, are also impressive.

o **Red Salt** (Kaua'i): Hidden inside the jewel box of boutique hotel Ko'a Kea is this equally brilliant dining room, where local seafood and produce shine under executive chef Noelani Planas, who trained with Joël Robuchon and Michael Mina. See p. 586.

o **Eating House 1849** (Kaua'i): Hawai'i Regional Cuisine co-founder Roy Yamaguchi closed the long-lived Garden Island outpost of his signature Roy's brand to open this more casual, plantation-themed restaurant in the open-air Shops at Kukui'ula. Returning to his island roots with hearty small plates and family-style dishes made it an instant success, now replicated at two O'ahu locations. See p. 584.

o **Nobu Lāna'i** (Lāna'i): Celebrity chef Nobu Matsuhisa now has *two* restaurants on the tiny island of Lāna'i—compared with just one in Manhattan, Milan, Malibu, and Mexico City, among other urban settings. But since his **Sensei by Nobu** is generally restricted only to guests at the all-inclusive, ultra-pricey **Sensei Lāna'i, A Four Seasons Resort** (p. 481), it's easier, cheaper, and frankly more fun to indulge in classic Nobu dishes such as miso cod and yellowtail tuna sashimi with jalapeño at Nobu Lāna'i, inside the oceanfront **Four Seasons Resort Lāna'i** (p. 480). Each dish is as delicious as it is artful. See p. 483.

THE best OF HAWAI'I FOR KIDS

o **Aulani, a Disney Resort & Spa, Ko Olina, Hawai'i** (O'ahu): Disney built this high-rise hotel and spa (with timeshare condos) on 21 acres on the beach, about an hour's drive from Waikīkī. It's a great destination for families, with a full children's program, plus areas and activities for teens and tweens. Mickey, Minnie, and other Disney characters walk the resort and stop to take photos with kids. See p. 137.

o **Explore Polynesian Culture** (O'ahu): Experience the songs, dance, and costumes of six Pacific Island nations and archipelagos at this Disney-esque vision of Polynesia. Engaging activities range from spear-throwing competitions and Maori games that test hand-eye coordination, to a family-friendly evening show and luau. See p. 99.

o **Walk Under Water** (Maui): No need to wait for a rainy day to visit the **Maui Ocean Center**—it's well worth your time no matter the weather. The displays will enthrall all ages, from the brilliant garden of living coral, to the 3D dome theater surrounding you with images of humpback whales. You can ogle sharks, rays, and reef fish from the safety of an acrylic tunnel through a 750,000-gallon tank. The Center also highlights Hawaiians' cultural connections to the marine world. See p. 315.

o **Snorkel in Kealakekua Bay** (Hawai'i Island): Everyone can enjoy the dazzling display of marine life here on a **Fair Wind** cruise, which offers inner tubes and underwater viewing boxes for little ones (or

The Waikolohe Pool at Disney Aulani Resort, O'ahu.

A river cruise at the Polynesian Cultural Center.

older ones) who don't want to get their faces wet. Two water slides and a spacious boat with a friendly crew add to the fun. See p. 231.

o **Play at Lydgate Park** (Kaua'i): If kids tire of snorkeling in the protected swimming area of Lydgate Beach, a giant wooden fantasy play structure and bridge to the dunes await, along with grassy fields and several miles of biking trails. See p. 508.

o **Ride a Sugarcane Train** (Kaua'i): At **Kilohana Plantation,** families can enjoy an inexpensive, narrated train ride through fields, forest, and orchards, and stop to feed goats and wild pigs. See p. 506.

2

SUGGESTED HAWAI'I ITINERARIES

F or most people, the fetching dollops of land in the middle of the Pacific Ocean are a dream destination—but getting to this remote region can seem daunting. So once you finally arrive, you'll want to make the most of your time. In this chapter we've built six 1-week itineraries for O'ahu, Hawai'i Island, Maui, Moloka'i, Lāna'i, and Kaua'i, each designed to hit the highlights and provide a revealing window into the real Hawai'i—one whose people and culture are as compellingly vibrant as the landscape.

You can follow these itineraries to the letter or use them to build your own personalized trip. Whatever you do, *don't max out your days.* This is Hawai'i, after all—save time to smell the perfume of plumeria, listen to wind rustling through a bamboo forest, and feel the caress of the Pacific. Take advantage of opportunities to learn more about this unique ecosystem from its traditional stewards and enjoy the serendipity of local festivals and food trucks highlighting the islands' modern diversity. By not rushing from one place to the next, you'll fall more easily into the rhythm of the islands.

A WEEK ON O'AHU

O'ahu is so stunning that the *ali'i,* the kings of Hawai'i, made it the capital of the island nation. Below, we presume that you'll be staying in Honolulu, which makes a good base for the rest of the island. Plus, it has the best dining options and a cosmopolitan liveliness unavailable anywhere else in the islands. If you prefer quieter nights, though, opt for a vacation rental in Kailua or on the North Shore and factor into the following itinerary extra time for traveling.

DAY 1: arrive & hit Waikīkī Beach ★★★

Unwind from your plane ride with a little sun and sand. Take a dip in the ocean at the most famous beach in the world: **Waikīkī Beach** (p. 106). Catch the sunset with a mai tai, Hawaiian music, and some of the loveliest hula you'll ever see at **House Without a Key** (p. 166).

DAY 2: surf in Waikīkī & visit Pearl Harbor ★★★

Thanks to jet lag, you'll be up early, so take advantage with an early morning surf session, aka dawn patrol, when the waves are smooth

Palm trees on Waikīkī Beach.

and glassy. Waikīkī has great waves for learning, and a surf lesson (p. 116) will have you riding the waves in no time. The poke at **Ono Seafood** (p. 146) makes a great post-surf meal, and then you'll want to refresh yourself with a lychee-mango-pineapple shave ice drizzled with *lilikoʻi* cream at **Waiola Shave Ice** (p. 145). In the afternoon, head to the **USS *Arizona* Memorial at Pearl Harbor** (p. 82), site of the infamous 1941 attack. For dinner, go local and dine at **Highway Inn** (p. 147) for *kalua* pig, *laulau, pipikaula,* and *poi.*

DAY 3: explore the North Shore ★★★

Grab a fried *malasada* (holeless doughnut) dipped in sugar at **Leonard's Bakery** (p. 145) before heading to the **North Shore** (see "Central Oʻahu & the North Shore," on p. 101). Stop in the quaint town of **Haleʻiwa** for a pineapple-*lilikoʻi*-mango treat at **Matsumoto Shave Ice** (p. 158) and grab a picnic lunch from **Beet Box Café** (p. 157). Pick one of the gorgeous North Shore beaches for a day of swimming and sunbathing. **Waimea Beach Park** (p. 111) is a favorite, no matter the season. In winter, if the waves are pumping and conditions are right, head to **Pipeline** (p. 104) and watch pro surfers ride this tube-like wave over a razor-sharp reef. Still daylight? Take the longer coastal road back into Honolulu.

DAY 4: snorkel in Hanauma Bay ★★ & hike the Makapuʻu Lighthouse Trail ★★

Get up early and grab some freshly baked morning pastries or a local-style breakfast at **Diamond Head Market & Grill** (p. 154) before heading to **Hanauma Bay** (p. 108) for snorkeling. If you're a strong

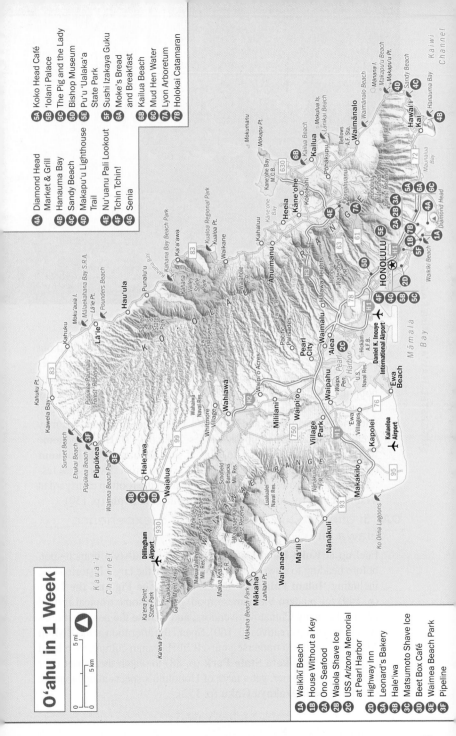

O'ahu in 1 Week

4A Diamond Head Market & Grill
4B Hanauma Bay
4C Sandy Beach
4D Makapu'u Lighthouse Trail
4E Nu'uanu Pali Lookout
4F Tchin Tchin!
4G Senia

5A Koko Head Café
5B 'Iolani Palace
5C The Pig and the Lady
5D Bishop Museum
5E Pu'u 'Ualaka'a State Park
5F Sushi Izakaya Guku
6A Moke's Bread and Breakfast
6B Kailua Beach
6C Mud Hen Water
7A Lyon Arboretum
7B Holokai Catamaran

1A Waikīkī Beach
1B House Without a Key
2A Ono Seafood
2B Waiola Shave Ice
2C USS Arizona Memorial at Pearl Harbor
2D Highway Inn
3A Leonard's Bakery
3B Hale'iwa
3C Matsumoto Shave Ice
3D Beet Box Café
3E Waimea Beach Park
3F Pipeline

19

Exploring the botanical wonders at the Lyon Arboretum.

swimmer and the water is calm (check with the lifeguard), head out past the reef and away from the crowds, where the water's clearer and you'll see more fish and the occasional turtle. Continue beach-hopping down the coastline—watch bodysurfing daredevils at **Sandy Beach** (p. 109). Hike the easy **Makapu'u Lighthouse Trail** (p. 119), with views to Moloka'i and Lāna'i on a clear day. In winter, you may even see migrating humpback whales. Take the Pali Highway home to Honolulu—and be sure to stop at the **Nu'uanu Pali Lookout** (p. 87). For a night out, head to Chinatown, where a slew of new restaurants have opened: Start with a cocktail in the rooftop courtyard at **Tchin Tchin!** (p. 166) and move on to dinner at **Senia** (p. 150).

DAY 5: glimpse historic Honolulu & experience Hawaiian culture

Fuel up at **Koko Head Café** (p. 154), an island-style brunch spot, before heading to downtown Honolulu to see the city's historic sites, including **'Iolani Palace** (p. 80). Lunch at **The Pig and the Lady** (p. 149) for modern Vietnamese food, pick up some tropical fruit at one of the many Chinatown vendors, and browse the new boutiques started by young creatives (p. 160). Spend the afternoon at the **Bishop Museum** (p. 78) to immerse yourself in Hawaiian culture, then head up to **Pu'u 'Ualaka'a State Park** (p. 88) to watch the sunset over Honolulu. For dinner, get a taste of Honolulu's spectacular Japanese cuisine at **Sushi Izakaya Gaku** (p. 152).

DAY 6: relax at Kailua Beach ★★★

On your last full day on O'ahu, travel over the Pali Highway to the windward side of the island. Dig into a stack of *liliko'i* (passion fruit) pancakes at **Moke's Bread and Breakfast** (p. 155) and then spend the rest of the day at **Kailua Beach** (p. 110). It's the perfect beach to kayak or stand-up paddle to the Mokulua Islands (or, as the locals call it, "the Mokes") or simply relax. For your last dinner, dig into a feast of small plates at **Mud Hen Water** (p. 153), which features a creative menu of uniquely Hawai'i flavors in modern, clever ways.

DAY 7: stroll through Lyon Arboretum ★★★

Head to the University of Hawai'i's **Lyon Arboretum** (p. 86) in the back of lush Mānoa Valley for a magical day of exploring this park-like botanical garden's tropical groves laden with exotic, fiery blooms. Don't forget to make reservations as far in advance as possible! Then, take one last look at Diamond Head and Waikīkī . . . from the ocean, aboard the **Holokai Catamaran** (p. 112).

A WEEK ON HAWAI'I ISLAND

Because of the distances involved, a week is barely enough time to see Hawai'i Island, justly nicknamed the Big Island; it's best to plan for 2 weeks—or even better, a return visit. Here's how to see the highlights, changing hotels as you go.

DAY 1: arrive & amble through Kailua-Kona & coffee country ★★★

Since most flights arrive at lunchtime or later, check into your Kona Coast lodgings and go for a stroll through historic **Kailua-Kona** by **Hulihe'e Palace** (p. 184) and **Mokuaikaua Church** (p. 187). Wear sandals so you can dip your feet in one of the pocket coves, such as Kamakahonu Bay, within sight of **Kamehameha's historic compound.** Or perk yourself up by touring a **Kona coffee farm** (p. 184) and sampling the wares. Enjoy a sunset dinner at an oceanview restaurant, but don't unpack—you'll be on the road early the next day.

DAY 2: take a morning sail & afternoon drive ★★★

The day starts with a morning snorkel tour (including breakfast and lunch) aboard the *Fair Wind II* (p. 231), sailing to the historic preserve of **Kealakekua Bay.** After returning to Keauhou Bay, head to **Pu'uhonua O Hōnaunau National Historical Park** (p. 189) for a brisk walk around the historic seaside compound before continuing on to **Hawai'i Volcanoes National Park** (p. 209). Suggested pit stops en route: **Ka'ū Coffee Mill** (p. 214) in Pāhala or **Ka Lae Coffee** in Nā'ālehu (p. 292) for a pick-me-up coffee or pastry, and nearby

Punalu'u Beach Park (p. 227) for a black-sand photo op, possibly with basking turtles. Check into lodgings in **Volcano Village** (p. 271) or **Volcano House** (p. 273), where you may dine overlooking Kīlauea's often-erupting Halema'uma'u Crater.

DAY 3: explore an active volcano ★★★

Stop at the national park's **Kīlauea Visitor Center** to learn about current lava flows (if any), the day's free ranger-led walks, and the transformation of the park after the upheaval of thousands of small earthquakes during the 2018 eruption. Walk to the still-puffing **steam vents** and the yellowy, sour-smelling **sulfur banks.** Bicycle or drive **Crater Rim Road** past **Halema'uma'u Crater** (p. 210) to **Nāhuku (Thurston Lava Tube;** p. 211) and **Devastation Trail** (p. 249), before heading down **Chain of Craters Road,** leading to a vast petroglyph field, sea arch and repeated lava flows that smothered parts of the coastal road.

DAY 4: tour Old Hawai'i ★★★

It's just a 45-minute drive from Volcano to **Hilo** (p. 175), so after breakfast go to **'Imiloa: Astronomy Center of Hawai'i** (p. 205), opening at 9am. Then explore **Banyan Drive** (p. 202), **Lili'uokalani Gardens** (p. 202), and one of Hilo's small but intriguing museums, such as the free **Mokupāpapa Discovery Center,** focused on the

Spot waterfalls and hidden coves from the Waipi'o Valley Lookout.

Hawai'i Island in 1 Week

0	10 mi
0	10 km

4E	Waimea
5A	Pu'ukoholā Heiau National Historic Site
5B	Lapakahi State Historical Park
5C	King Kamehameha Statue
5D	Pololū Valley Lookout
5E	Puakō Petroglyph Archaeological Preserve
6A	Kohala Coast Beaches
6B	Mauna Kea
6C	Waikōloa Dry Forest
7A	Kekaha Kai State Park
7B	Kaloko-Honokōhau National Historic Site
7C	Spa Without Walls

1A	Kailua-Kona
1B	Kona coffee farms
2A	Kealakekua Bay
2B	Pu'uhonua O Hōnaunau National Historical Park
2C	Ka Lae Coffee
2D	Ka'ū Coffee Mill
2E	Punalu'u Beach Park
3	Hawai'i Volcanoes National Park
4A	Hilo
4B	'Akaka Falls
4C	Hāmākua Coast
4D	Waipi'o Valley Lookout

natural and cultural history of the remote Northwest Hawaiian Islands (p. 204). Stroll through the **Hawai'i Tropical Botanical Garden** (p. 198) before driving along the pastoral **Hāmākua Coast** (p. 197), stopping in Honomū for a short walk to breathtaking **'Akaka Falls** (p. 197) and the similarly stunning **Waipi'o Valley Lookout** (p. 200). Dine on farm-fresh cuisine in **Waimea** (p. 282) before checking into a Kohala Coast hotel (p. 267).

DAY 5: explore the Historic Kohala Coast ★★★

Start by visiting **Pu'ukoholā Heiau National Historic Site** (p. 193), the massive temple Kamehameha built to the war god, Kū; it also

23

Halema'uma'u Crater is home to Pele, the volcano goddess.

looks impressive aboard a Hawaiian sailing canoe while on a snorkeling tour with **Hawaiian Sails** (p. 233). Continue north on Hwy. 270 to **Lapakahi State Historical Park** (p. 191) to see the outlines of a 14th-century Hawaiian village and have lunch in Hāwī or Kapa'au; the latter is home of the original **King Kamehameha Statue** (p. 190). The final northbound stop is the picturesque **Pololū Valley Lookout** (p. 191). Heading south in the late afternoon, make the short hike to the **Puakō Petroglyph Archaeological Preserve** (p. 193). To learn more Hawaiian lore, book one of Kohala's evening **luaus** (p. 298).

DAY 6: soak up the sand, sea & stars ★★★

You've earned a morning at the beach, and Hawai'i Island's prettiest beaches are on the Kohala Coast: **'Anaeho'omalu Bay (A-Bay), Hāpuna,** and **Kauna'oa** (see "Beaches," p. 217). Skip the scuba, though, because—if circumstances allow—in the afternoon you're heading up 13,796-foot **Mauna Kea** (p. 194). Let expert tour guides with four-wheel-drive, cold-weather gear, and stargazing telescopes take you there; **Mauna Kea Summit Adventures** (p. 196) or **Hawai'i Forest & Trail** (p. 217) are recommended. If the timing is right, you can book a Hawai'i Forest & Trail tour that includes a stop at the **Waikōloa Dry Forest** (p. 194), where you'll help nurture its rare native plants. The forest, home to ancient wiliwili trees, also offers free monthly guided hikes that conclude with a magnificent view of sunset over the ocean and twice-monthly morning volunteer sessions.

2

A Week on Hawai'i Island

SUGGESTED HAWAI'I ITINERARIES

DAY 7: plant a tree & pamper yourself ★★★

On your last full day, give back to the island by planting a koa tree with **Uluha'o o Hualālai** (p. 216); you'll enjoy terrific views from Hualālai, respectively, while learning about Hawaiian culture, too. Afterward, visit one of North Kona's gorgeous beaches hidden behind lava fields, such as **Kekaha Kai State Park** (p. 220) or the tranquil cove at **Kaloko-Honokōhau National Historical Park** (p. 185), then relax with a spa treatment at the Fairmont Orchid's **Spa Without Walls** or **Asaya Spa** at Kona Village, a Rosewood Resort (p. 260).

A WEEK ON MAUI

Even with most of Lahaina tragically off-limits, you'll need at least a week to savor the Valley Isle. Stay in South or West Maui, home to hot and sunny beaches, then cool off with excursions to a mountaintop and rejuvenating rainforest, with a last night closer to the airport in Central Maui. We've designed this itinerary assuming you'll stay in West Maui for the first 4 nights, but it works almost as well if you stay in Wailea or Kīhei. To minimize driving, move your headquarters to lush East Maui midweek.

DAY 1: arrive & explore West Maui ★★★

After picking up your rental car, fuel up at **Leoda's Kitchen & Pie Shop** in Olowalu (p. 400) en route to Kā'anapali and beyond. Revive with a dip at one of West Maui's prime beaches after check-in (p. 364).

DAY 2: sail to Lāna'i or snorkel off Maui ★★★

You'll likely wake up early on your first morning here, so book an early-morning trip with **Trilogy** (p. 344), the best sailing/snorkeling operation in Hawai'i. You'll spend the day (breakfast and lunch included) sailing to Lāna'i, snorkeling, and enjoying beach time before returning. You'll have the afternoon free to shop or nap. Or book a **Zodiac or catamaran snorkel tour** that arrives at Molokini Crater early, then visits one of South Maui's "turtle towns"; suggestions begin on p. 348.

DAY 3: sunbathe in South Maui ★★★

Take a drive out to **Mākena State Park** (p. 338) and soak in the raw beauty of its sprawling beach. On the way, pay a visit to the sharks and sea turtles at the **Maui Ocean Center** in Mā'alaea (p. 315). Linger in South Maui to enjoy the sunset and feast at one of the area's terrific restaurants (recommendations start on p. 406).

Dancers at the Old Lāhainā Lū'au.

DAY 4: put down roots & celebrate culture ★★★

Spend a morning volunteering to restore the habitat or plant taro in a hidden valley with **Kīpuka Olowalu** (p. 352) and learn about the biology and Native Hawaiian lore associated with this special place from friendly experts. At family-friendly **Old Lāhainā Lū'au** (p. 427), a miraculous survivor of the 2023 fires, you can immerse yourself in Hawaiian culture as the sun drops into the sea.

DAY 5: ascend a 10,000-foot volcano ★★★

Venture up to the 10,023-foot summit of **Haleakalā,** the island's dormant volcano. Book a permit well in advance to witness sunrise, which can be phenomenal but also very cold. Go later to hike in **Haleakalā National Park** (p. 395), an awe-inspiring experience any time of day. On your way down, stop and tour **Upcountry Maui** (p. 317), particularly the communities of **Kula** and **Makawao,** then visit seaside **Pā'ia** (p. 325). Reserve early for a memorable sunset dinner in Kū'au at the **Inn at Mama's Fish House** (p. 390).

DAY 6: explore heavenly Hāna ★★★

Forgo the anxiety of looking for legal places to park on the crowded, if scenic **Hāna Highway,** and book an all-day, small-group or private **tour** (suggestions begin on p. 324); and let someone else worry about sweating the hairpin turns and one-lane bridges. Longer tours allow for time to ogle waterfalls, hike through bamboo forest, and perhaps dip into the pools of **'Ohe'o Gulch** in the Kīpahulu District of

Maui in 1 Week

MOLOKA'I

Pailolo Channel

PACIFIC OCEAN

LĀNA'I

'Au'au Channel

Alalākeiki Channel

'Alenuihāhā Channel

KANAIO COAST

WEST MAUI

WEST MAUI MOUNTAINS

CENTRAL MAUI

SOUTH MAUI

UPCOUNTRY MAUI

EAST MAUI

HALEAKALĀ NATIONAL PARK

Kapalua Beach
Kapalua
Nāpili
Kahana
Māhinahina
Honokōwai
Kā'anapali
Kā'anapali Beach
Wahikuli Wayside
Lahaina
Launiupoko Beach Park
Olowalu
West Maui Natural Area Reserve
West Maui Forest Reserve
Papawai Pt.
Waihe'e
Waiehu
Wailuku
Waikapū
'Īao Valley
Mā'alaea
Mā'alaea Bay
Kealia Pond
Keālia Pond
Pu'unēnē
Kahului
Kahului Bay
Kahului Airport
H.A. Baldwin Beach Park
Ho'okipa Beach
Ku'au
Pā'ia
Ha'ikū
Pa'uwela
Hāli'imaile
Makawao
Pukalani
Ke'anae
Ke'anae Valley
Nāhiku
Huelo
Hāna Hwy.
Hāna Airport
Kaeleku
Hāna
Wai'ānapanapa State Park
Hāmoa Beach
Kīpahulu
Kīpahulu Valley
Kaupō
Kōʻolau Forest Reserve
Makawao Forest Reserve
Ko'olau Forest Reserve
Hāna Forest Reserve
Kahikinui Forest Reserve
Kīpahulu Forest Reserve
Hanakauhi
Kaupō
Kipuka
Kula
Keōkea
Kula Forest Reserve
Polipoli Spring State Rec. Area
Kanaio Natural Area Reserve
'Ulupalakua
Pu'u Ula'ula
'Āhihi-Kinau Natural Area Reserve
La Perouse Bay
Oneloa (Big) Beach
Mākena
Mākena State Park
Maluaka Beach
Wailea
Wailea Beach
Ulua/Mōkapu Beach
Kama'ole Beach
Kama'ole III Beach
Kihei
Molokini I.

Kapalua West Maui Airport
Lāhaināpali Hwy.
Honoapi'ilani Hwy.
Kahului Hwy.
Hāna Hwy.
Haleakalā Hwy.
Pi'ilani Hwy.
Kula Hwy.
Pi'ilani Hwy.

340, 30, 36, 380, 31, 311, 37, 360, 377, 378

1 Leoda's Kitchen & Pie Shop
2A Lāna'i Sail
2B Molokini Snorkel
3A Maui Ocean Center
3B Mākena State Park
4A Kipuka Olowalu
4B Old Lāhainā Luau
5A Haleakalā National Park
5B Upcountry Maui
5C Pā'ia
5D Mama's Fish House
6A Hāna Highway
6B Hāna
6C Hāmoa Beach
6D 'Ohe'o Gulch
7A 'Īao Valley
7B Wailuku

0 — 5 mi
0 — 5 km

27

Wai'ānapanapa State Park on Maui.

Haleakalā National Park, 12 miles west of Hāna (p. 329); some include admission to **Wai'ānapanapa State Park** (p. 341), where reservations are required to revel in the views from its black sand beach and trails. Or take the even more scenic, 15-minute flight into Hāna from Kahului and stay overnight at the **Hāna-Maui Resort** (p. 392), which will shuttle you to gorgeous **Hāmoa Beach** (p. 340); it's easy to explore the tiny town of **Hāna** (p. 328) on foot (p. 330).

DAY 7: hit the beach & boutiques ★★★

On your final full day, admire the green "needle" and bubbling streams at historic **'Īao Valley** (p. 313), where admission and parking are by reservation only, and browse the funky boutiques of **Wailuku** (p. 420). Then return to the west or south Maui beach of your choice for one last memorable sunset.

A WEEK ON MOLOKA'I

Some visitors would quail at the thought of spending 7 whole days on Hawaii's most low-key island, which at first glance seems to offer the fewest activities and attractions. The island's residents are also keen to keep it that way, rejecting any moves to increase tourism. But if you're committed to exploring here, you'll need to plan your vacation carefully—including the season and days of the week—to be able to experience everything on this itinerary. Our itinerary is based on a Monday arrival (weekday arrival strongly recommended). If you're staying on the

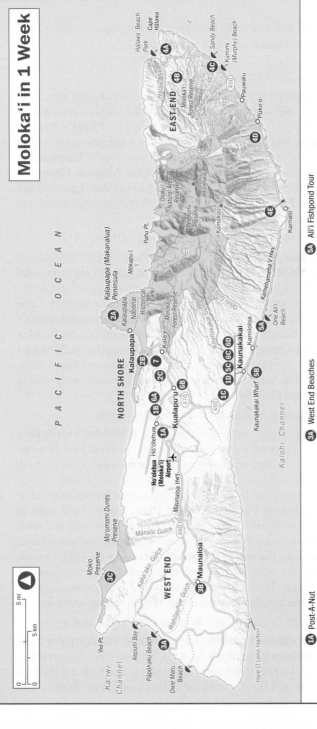

Moloka'i in 1 Week

1A Post-A-Nut
1B Purdy's Natural Macadamia Nut Farm
1C Molokai Plumerias
1D Hiro's 'Ohana Grill
2A Kalaupapa National Historical Park
2B Pālā'au State Park
2C Moloka'i Museum

3A West End Beaches
3B Maunaloa
3C Mokio Preserve
4A Hālawa Beach Park
4B Hālawa Valley Tours
4C East End Beaches
4D Our Lady of Seven Sorrows
4E St. Joseph Church

5A Ali'i Fishpond Tour
5B South Shore Ocean Excursions
5C Paddlers Restaurant
6A Ho'olehua Saturday Market
6B Aka'ula Cat Garden
6C Kamoi Snack-N-Go
6D Hot Bread Run
7 Ironwood Hills Golf Course

West End or East End, where the most desirable lodgings are, allow plenty of time to drive to Central Moloka'i attractions.

DAY 1: arrive & "go nuts" ★★

After you pick up your rental car (a must), drive just a few minutes to the tiny Ho'olehua post office to **Post-a-Nut** (p. 437)—decorating a coconut that you can mail home—and swing by **Purdy's Natural Macadamia Nut Farm** (p. 437) nearby for a free informative, tasty tour. If you're staying in a condo, pick up groceries in **Kaunakakai** (p. 457), enjoying en route the views of the **Molokai Plumerias** orchard (p. 435), typically in bloom March to October. Treat yourself to dinner at **Hiro's 'Ohana Grill** (p. 455) for gorgeous sunset and Lāna'i views over the fringing reef.

DAY 2: immerse in Kalaupapa's history ★★

Visiting **Kalaupapa National Historical Park** (p. 438) may still not be possible in 2025. If it's not available, you can still enjoy an aerial view and learn more about this beautiful, remote peninsula where two Catholic saints, Father Damien and Mother Marianne Cope (p. 439), famously helped care for those exiled here due to leprosy (now called Hansen's disease). After visiting the modern **St. Damien of Moloka'i Church** in Kaunakakai (p. 439), stop by the **Moloka'i Museum** (p. 436) to browse its Kalaupapa exhibits and short videos, en route to **Pālā'au State Park** (p. 440) and the breathtaking vista at its **Kalaupapa Overlook.**

DAY 3: savor the West End beaches ★★★

Pack a picnic, drinks, and beach gear—stop at **Molokai Fish & Dive** (p. 458)—and spend a day exploring glorious **West End beaches** (p. 444). If it's winter, don't plan on going in the water; instead, enjoy the sightings of whales (at their peak Jan–Mar) or intrepid surfers. Note that the only public restroom facilities are at the northern end of nearly 3-mile-long **Pāpōhaku Beach Park,** where you'll want to stay for sunset. Break up the day with a visit to the nearby tiny town of **Maunaloa,** home to a general store and the whimsically eclectic **Big Wind Kite Factory and Plantation Gallery** (p. 458). You can also spend the morning restoring native habitat on the dunes of Moloka'i Land Trust's **Mokio Preserve** (p. 436), overlooking the West End beaches, then unwind on the sand in the late afternoon.

DAY 4: hike to a waterfall & into the past ★★★

Anyone can take the incredibly scenic, sinuous, shore-hugging drive to pretty **Hālawa Beach Park** (p. 433), but you'll need reservations (book several weeks in advance) and a picnic lunch for the **Hālawa Valley tours** (p. 441) offered by the Solatorio and Pruet families. The

Solatorios use traditional Hawaiian protocol to welcome visitors and introduce the ancient enclave's history before hiking to the gorgeous, 250-foot Mo'oula Falls, where a dip is possible in calm conditions. Kalani Pruet's tour includes his lush flower farm and refreshing fruit smoothies after the hike. Since you have your swim gear, stop at the East End's **Sandy** and **Kūmimi** beaches (p. 443) on the drive home. Make a photo stop at St. Damien's picturesque churches on the eastern half of King Kamehameha V Highway—**St. Joseph** and **Our Lady of Seven Sorrows** (p. 439).

DAY 5: visit a fishpond & explore the South Shore's reef ★★★

Start your day with a 45-minute tour of **Ali'i Fishpond,** an example of ancient Hawaii's impressive aquaculture (p. 438). Then explore the teeming marine life and tranquil waters sheltered by the South Shore's enormous fringing reef, which is Moloka'i at its finest. Depending on your ability, book a **stand-up paddle** or **kayak tour** with **Molokai Outdoors** (p. 446), or a **snorkel/dive trip** with **Molokai Fish & Dive** (p. 445). The reef typically keeps the water calm even in winter, with **whale-watching excursions** (p. 442) at their peak in January through March. Your boat may be the only one visible for miles around. Enjoy a delicious dinner at **Paddlers Restaurant** (p. 455) with live (and lively) music several nights a week.

DAY 6: savor unique shops & local treats ★★

In the morning, browse the **Ho'olehua Saturday Market** (p. 458) for locally made jewelry, apparel, pottery, and baked goods, as well as fresh produce, flowers, and honey. Cat lovers should make an appointment to visit **Aka'ula Cat Garden** in Kualapu'u (p. 435) and shop at **Desi's Island Gifts** (p. 458) next door for souvenirs whose sales support the shelter, then head to Kaunakakai, where food trucks and mom-and-pop restaurants offer plenty of casual dining options. Don't miss an ice cream cone from **Kamoi Snack-and-Go** (p. 456) on a hot afternoon but skip dessert at dinner: You'll want to make the late-night **"hot bread run"** (p. 455) at Kanemitsu Bakery in Kaunakakai to pick up a loaf of sweet bread stuffed with cream cheese and jam, which you can also enjoy Sunday morning when most restaurants are closed.

DAY 7: enjoy the peacefulness ★★

If this is Sunday, then there's little to do on Moloka'i—besides going to one of the many churches—and that's the way local folks like it. Now's a good day to revisit a favorite beach or drive up to rustic **Ironwood Hills Golf Course** (p. 448).

A WEEK ON LĀNA'I

The smallest among the Hawaiian Islands that are open to visitors, this former pineapple plantation is now home to a posh resort, a luxurious wellness retreat, a rich and colorful history, and a postage-stamp-size town with some of the friendliest people you'll ever meet. The island has enough activities to keep you busy, but you'll probably be happiest skipping a few and slowing down to Lāna'i speed.

DAY 1: arrive & dive into Hulopo'e Bay ★★★

After settling into your lodgings, head for the best stretch of sand on the island: **Hulopo'e Beach** (p. 472). It's generally safe for swimming, and snorkeling within this marine preserve is excellent. The fish are so friendly you practically have to shoo them away; dolphins are frequent visitors. Hike up to the lookout at **Pu'u Pehe** (Sweetheart Rock, p. 478). Dine like a celebrity at **Nobu** (p. 483).

DAY 2: stroll around Lāna'i City & traverse the island ★★★

Head into quaint Lāna'i City to browse the boutiques (p. 486) and, if reopened, get a colorful history lesson at the **Lāna'i Culture & Heritage Center** (p. 468). Buckle up for a 3½-hour tour with **Rabaca's Limousine Service.** Let your driver navigate the rough road down to **Polihua Beach** (p. 473), Lanai's largest white-sand beach. On the way back, linger at **Keahiakawelo,** nicknamed the **"Garden of the Gods"** (p. 469) to snap photos of the otherworldly landscape at sunset. Finish your day at the **Lāna'i City Bar & Grill,** perhaps listening to live music and dining by the fire pits out back (p. 484).

DAY 3: enjoy a day on the water ★★★

If you're a guest of one of the two Four Seasons resorts here, you can go out with **Lāna'i Ocean Sports** (p. 474) on a snorkel, sail, or scuba adventure along the island's west coast or at **Cathedrals,** one of Hawaii's most ethereal dive sites. At night, savor hand-mixed cocktails and shoot some pool at the **Break** in the **Four Seasons Resort Lāna'i** (p. 480).

DAY 4: four-wheel it to the East Side ★★★

Lāna'i is a fantastic place to go four-wheeling. If it hasn't been raining, splurge on an ATV or four-wheel-drive vehicle and head out to the East Side. Get a picnic lunch from **Lāna'i Service Station** (p. 485) and download the Lāna'i Guide app for GPS-enabled directions, historic photos, and haunting Hawaiian chants. Find the petroglyphs at **Kaiolohia ("Shipwreck") Beach** (p. 473) and forge onward to **Keōmoku Village** and **Lōpā Beach** (p. 472).

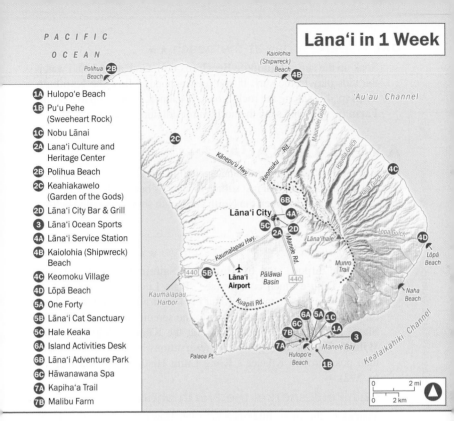

1A Hulopo'e Beach
1B Pu'u Pehe (Sweeheart Rock)
1C Nobu Lānai
2A Lana'i Culture and Heritage Center
2B Polihua Beach
2C Keahiakawelo (Garden of the Gods)
2D Lāna'i City Bar & Grill
3 Lāna'i Ocean Sports
4A Lāna'i Service Station
4B Kaiolohia (Shipwreck) Beach
4C Keomoku Village
4D Lōpā Beach
5A One Forty
5B Lāna'i Cat Sanctuary
5C Hale Keaka
6A Island Activities Desk
6B Lāna'i Adventure Park
6C Hāwanawana Spa
7A Kapiha'a Trail
7B Malibu Farm

DAY 5: brunch like royalty & frolic with felines ★★★

Fill your belly with a lavish island-style breakfast at **One Forty** (p. 483). Then drive past the airport (or take a $10 cab ride) to the endearing **Lanai Cat Sanctuary** (p. 470), an open-air compound that welcomes visitors to pet and play with some of their hundreds of friendly felines, brought here to protect the island's endangered birds. Return your ATV or car in town and catch a movie at **Hale Keaka** (p. 488).

DAY 6: choose your adventure & hit the spa ★★★

Visit the Island Activities desk in the Four Seasons Resort Lāna'i to book a **horseback ride** (p. 478) through upland Lāna'i or to try your hand at the **clay shooting** and **archery ranges** (p. 476). Or head to **Lāna'i Adventure Park** (p. 479) for exhilarating ziplines and rope courses, where you can also reserve a guided tour by electric bike. Cap your adventure with a soothing treatment at the **Hāwanawana Spa** (p. 480) at the Four Seasons Resort Lāna'i.

DAY 7: spend a day at the beach ★★

Soak up the sun at **Hulopo'e Beach** (p. 472). Grab a book and watch the kids play in the surf. If you feel inclined, follow the **Kapiha'a Trail** (p. 477) along the rocky coast. For lunch, wander up to **Malibu Farm** (p. 484) and scan the horizon for dolphins or whales.

A WEEK ON KAUA'I

Because much of the Garden Island, including the Nāpali Coast, is inaccessible to cars, a week will *just* suffice to view its beauty. To save driving time, split your stay between the North and South shores (detailed below) or stay on the East Side.

DAY 1: arrive & take a scenic drive ★★★

From the airport, stop by **Hamura's Saimin Stand** (p. 577) or another **Līhu'e** lunch counter (see "Plate Lunch, Bento & Poke," p. 578) for a classic taste of Kaua'i before driving through the bustling Coconut Coast on your way to the serenity of the rural **North Shore** (p. 495). Soak in the views at the **Kīlauea Point National Wildlife Refuge & Lighthouse** (reservations required, p. 511), and then poke around Kīlauea's **Kong Lung Historic Market Center** (p. 592).

DAY 2: hike & snorkel the North Shore ★★★

Thanks to the time difference between Hawai'i and the mainland, you'll likely wake up early—the perfect time to explore the attractions of **Hā'ena State Park** (p. 510), for which you now must reserve a parking permit or shuttle pass. Nine one-lane bridges await on the way to popular **Kē'ē Beach** (p. 497). If conditions permit, hike at least a half-hour out on the challenging **Kalalau Trail** (p. 549) for glimpses of the stunning **Nāpali Coast** or tackle the first 2 miles to **Hanakāpi'ai Beach,** 3 to 4 hours round-trip. After (or instead of) hiking, snorkel at **Kē'ē** and equally gorgeous **Mākua ("Tunnels") Beach** (p. 529), accessed from **Hā'ena Beach Park** (p. 511). Spend time in the jewel-box setting of **Limahuli Garden and Preserve** (p. 512) before returning to Hanalei to explore shops and galleries; after dinner, enjoy live Hawaiian music at the venerable **Tahiti Nui** (p. 597).

DAY 3: adventures in Hanalei & Kīlauea ★★★

The day begins on **Hanalei Bay, kayaking, surfing,** or **snorkeling** (see "Watersports," p. 532) or just frolicking at one of the three different beach parks (p. 523). If the waves are too rough, head instead to lagoonlike **'Anini Beach** (p. 526). Later, those who book in advance can tour delightful **Na 'Āina Kai Botanical Gardens** (p. 512) or take

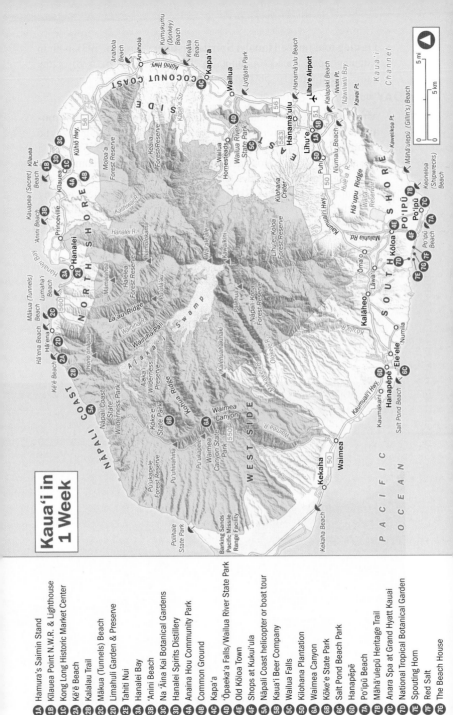

Kaua'i in 1 Week

- **1A** Hamura's Saimin Stand
- **1B** Kīlauea Point N.W.R. & Lighthouse
- **1C** Kong Long Historic Market Center
- **2A** Kē'ē Beach
- **2B** Kalalau Trail
- **2C** Mākua (Tunnels) Beach
- **2D** Limahuli Garden & Preserve
- **2E** Tahiti Nui
- **3A** Hanalei Bay
- **3B** 'Anini Beach
- **3C** Na 'Āina Kai Botanical Gardens
- **3D** Hanalei Spirits Distillery
- **4A** Anaina Hou Community Park
- **4B** Common Ground
- **4C** Kapa'a
- **4D** 'Ōpaeka'a Falls/Wailua River State Park
- **4E** Old Kōloa Town
- **4F** Shops at Kukui'ula
- **5A** Nāpali Coast helicopter or boat tour
- **5B** Kaua'i Beer Company
- **5C** Wailua Falls
- **5D** Kilohana Plantation
- **6A** Waimea Canyon
- **6B** Kōke'e State Park
- **6C** Salt Pond Beach Park
- **6D** Hanapēpē
- **7A** Po'ipū Beach
- **7B** Māhā'ulepū Heritage Trail
- **7C** Anara Spa at Grand Hyatt Kauai
- **7D** National Tropical Botanical Garden
- **7E** Spouting Horn
- **7F** Red Salt
- **7G** The Beach House

a tasting tour on the **Hanalei Spirits Distillery** farm (p. 593), both in Kīlauea. Book ahead for dinner at the **Bar Acuda** (p. 578) or the more casual **Ama** (p. 580) in Hanalei.

DAY 4: nature & culture en route to Po'ipū ★★

After breakfast, head south. Visit Kīlauea's **Anaina Hou Community Park** (p. 509) for mini-golf in a botanical garden or tour the **Common Ground** "agroforest" farm complex (p. 509). Stop for a bite at a funky cafe or gourmet burger joint in **Kapa'a** (recommendations begin on p. 574), then drive to **'Ōpaeka'a Falls** and see the cultural sites of **Wailua River State Park** (p. 508). After crossing through busy Lihue, admire the scenery on the way to **Old Kōloa Town** (p. 593), where you can browse the quaint shops before checking into your Po'ipū lodgings. Pick a dinner spot from the excellent choices in the **Shops at Kukui'ula.**

DAY 5: Nāpali by boat or helicopter ★★★

Splurge on a **snorkel boat** or **Zodiac raft tour** (p. 533) to the **Nāpali Coast** or take a **helicopter tour** (p. 551) for amazing views of Nāpali, Waimea Canyon, waterfalls, and more. For helicopter tours, most of which depart from Līhu'e, book a late-morning tour (after rush hour). Then have lunch in Līhu'e at **Kauai Beer Company** (p. 574) and

Kayaking at Mākua Beach.

Helicopter view of Nāpali Coast, Kaua'i.

drive to **Wailua Falls** (p. 509) before perusing the shops, tasting rum, or riding the train at **Kilohana Plantation** (p. 506).

DAY 6: Waimea Canyon & Kōke'e State Park ★★★

Start your drive early to "the Grand Canyon of the Pacific," **Waimea Canyon** (p. 521). Stay on the road through forested **Kōke'e State Park** (p. 519) to the **Kalalau Valley Overlook** (p. 513) and wait for mists to part for a magnificent view. Stop by the **Kōke'e Museum** (p. 520) to obtain trail information for a hike after lunch at **Kōke'e Lodge** (p. 588). Or head back down to hit the waves at **Salt Pond Beach** or stroll through rustic **Hanapēpē** (p. 500), home to a **Friday night festival** (p. 598).

DAY 7: beach & spa time in Po'ipū ★★★

Spend the morning at glorious **Po'ipū Beach** (p. 530) and then head over to **Keoneloa ("Shipwrecks") Beach** (p. 529) to hike along the coastal **Māhā'ulepū Heritage Trail** (p. 549). Later, indulge in a spa treatment at **Anara Spa** at the **Grand Hyatt Kauai** (p. 566) or take a tour (booked in advance) at the **National Tropical Botanical Garden** (p. 516), which offers a wealth of tropical plants from all over the world, rare native plants, formal gardens, a waterfall, historic cottage, and even a luau. Check out the flume of **Spouting Horn** (p. 518) before dinner at **Red Salt** (p. 586) or **The Beach House** (p. 584).

HAWAI'I IN CONTEXT

by Jeanne Cooper

3

Since the Polynesians navigated their way across the Pacific to the Hawaiian Islands a millennium ago, this chain of floating emeralds has dazzled travelers from around the globe. Now the multiethnic residents of these islands are trying to chart a new course, turning away from mass tourism yet welcoming those who will care for their unique ecosystem and culture.

The Hawaiian Islands bask in the warm waters of the Pacific, where they are blessed by a tropical sun and cooled by gentle trade winds—creating what might be the most ideal climate imaginable. Mother Nature has carved out verdant valleys, hung brilliant rainbows in the sky, and trimmed the islands with sandy beaches in a spectrum of colors. The Native Hawaiian culture, now asserting itself more forcefully in political, business, and environmental issues, still embodies "aloha spirit," an easygoing generosity that takes the shape of flower leis freely given, monumental feasts shared with friends and family, and hypnotic melodies played late into the balmy night. The polyglot cultures that arrived in Hawai'i during the plantation era have adopted this spirit as theirs, too, and adapted the feasts to include a panoply of ethnic cuisines found nowhere else.

Visitors are drawn to Hawai'i not only for its incredible beauty, but also for its opportunities for adventure. Go on, gaze into that immense volcanic crater, swim in a sea of rainbow-colored fish, hike through a rainforest to hidden waterfalls, and paddle in deep ocean waters, where whales leap out of the water for reasons still mysterious. But don't miss the opportunity to learn more about the Native Hawaiian culture that has sustained and celebrated this environment for generations. Plant a native tree or volunteer for a beach cleanup to experience a shared sense of stewardship. Learn a Hawaiian chant to start a paddle, enter a forest, or greet the day with a cultural advisor—many resort hotels offer free experiences, even to non-guests.

Above all, allow yourself time to go slow, "talk story" and share aloha with all you meet. You don't have to spend a fortune to enjoy a wonderful time in these islands, but if you give a little of yourself, your memories may truly be priceless.

THE FIRST HAWAIIANS

Throughout the Middle Ages, while Western sailors clung to the edges of continents for fear of falling off the earth's edge, Polynesian voyagers

FACING PAGE: "Hula is the language of the heart and, therefore, the heartbeat of the Hawaiian people." —King David Kalakaua.

crisscrossed the planet's largest ocean. The first people to inhabit Hawai'i were unsurpassed navigators. Using the stars, birds, currents, and wind as guides, they sailed double-hulled canoes across thousands of miles, zeroing in on tiny islands in the center of the vast Pacific. They packed their vessels with food, plants, medicine, tools, and animals: everything necessary for building a new life on a distant shore. Over a span of an estimated 800 years, the great Polynesian migration connected a vast triangle of islands stretching from Aotearoa (New Zealand) to Hawai'i to Rapa Nui (Easter Island) and encompassing the many diverse archipelagos in between. Historians surmise that the first wave of settlers in Hawai'i came via the Marquesas Islands as early as A.D. 500, though archaeological records better document the second wave of settlers from Tahiti and other Society Islands, beginning around A.D. 1000.

Over the centuries, a distinctly Hawaiian culture arose. The voyagers became farmers and fishermen, as skilled on land as they had been at sea; they built highly productive fishponds, aqueducts to irrigate terraced *kalo lo'i* (taro patches), and 3-acre *heiau* (temples) with 50-foot-high rock walls. Farmers cultivated more than 400 varieties of *kalo,* or taro, their staple food; 300 types of sweet potato; and 40 different bananas. Each variety served a different need—some were drought resistant, others medicinal, and others good for babies. Hawaiian women pounded the bark of mulberry trees to fine layers, then inked it with bamboo stamps to create intricately patterned *kapa* cloth—some of the finest in all of Polynesia. Each of the Hawaiian Islands was its own kingdom, governed by *ali'i* (high-ranking chiefs) who drew their authority from an established caste system and *kapu* (taboos). Those who broke the *kapu* could be killed.

The ancient Hawaiian creation chant, the *Kumulipo,* depicts a universe that began when heat and light emerged out of darkness, followed by the first life form: a coral polyp. The 2,000-line epic poem is a grand genealogy, describing how all species are interrelated, from gently waving seaweeds to mighty human warriors. It is the basis for the Hawaiian concept of *kuleana,* a word that simultaneously refers to privilege and responsibility. To this day, Native Hawaiians view the care of their natural resources as a familial duty and honor—and now actively encourage visitors to feel the same way.

WESTERN CONTACT
Cook's Ill-Fated Voyage

In the dawn hours of January 18, 1778, Captain James Cook of the HMS *Resolution* spotted an unfamiliar set of islands, which he later named for his benefactor, the Earl of Sandwich. The 50-year-old sea captain was already famous in Britain for "discovering" much of the South Pacific. Now on his third voyage of exploration, Cook had set sail from Tahiti northward across uncharted waters. He was searching for the mythical Northwest Passage that was said to link the Pacific and Atlantic oceans.

The royal compound at Kamakahonu Bay, former home to King Kamehameha I on Hawaiʻi Island.

On his way, he stumbled upon Hawaiʻi (which came to be known to the Western world as the Sandwich Isles) quite by chance.

With the arrival of the *Resolution,* Stone Age Hawaiʻi entered the age of iron. Sailors swapped nails and munitions for fresh water, pigs, and the affections of Hawaiian women. Tragically, the foreigners brought with them a terrible cargo: syphilis, measles, and other diseases that decimated the Hawaiian people. Captain Cook estimated the native population at 400,000 in 1778. (Later historians claim it could have been as high as 900,000.) By the time Christian missionaries arrived 42 years later, the number of Native Hawaiians had plummeted to just 150,000.

In a skirmish over a stolen boat, Cook was killed by a blow to the head. His British countrymen sailed home, leaving Hawaiʻi forever altered. The islands were now on the sea charts, and traders on the fur route between Canada and China stopped here to get fresh water. More trade—and more disastrous liaisons—ensued.

Two more sea captains left indelible marks on the islands. The first was American John Kendrick, who in 1791 filled his ship with fragrant Hawaiian sandalwood and sailed to China. By 1825, the sandalwood groves were gone, and many of those who had been forced to harvest them were dead from their labors. The second was Englishman George Vancouver, who in 1793 left behind cows and sheep, which ventured out to graze in the islands' native forest and hastened the spread of invasive species. King Kamehameha I sent for cowboys from Mexico and Spain to round up the wild livestock, thus beginning the islands' *paniolo* (cowboy) tradition, the Hawaiian word for the language these cattle experts spoke, *español.*

King Kamehameha I was an ambitious *aliʻi* who used Western guns to unite the islands under single rule. After his death in 1819, the tightly woven Hawaiian society began to unravel. One of his widows, Queen

Kaahumanu, abolished the *kapu* system, opening the door for religion of another form.

Staying to Do Well

In April 1820, missionaries bent on converting Hawaiians arrived from New England. The newcomers convinced the natives to wear clothes and abandon other traditions, eventually banning them from dancing hula—a sacred medium for celebrating both gods and humans. The churchgoers tried to keep sailors and whalers out of the bawdy houses, where whiskey flowed and the virtue of native women was never safe. To their credit, the missionaries created a 12-letter alphabet for the Hawaiian language (now 13, including the glottal stop, or *'okina*). They also taught reading and writing, started a printing press, and began recording the islands' history, which until that time had been preserved solely in memorized chants, or *oli*. Hawaiians quickly added Western-style singing (*mele*) and musical composition to their creative repertoire.

Children of some missionaries became business leaders and politicians, often marrying Hawaiians and receiving royal grants of land, causing one wag to remark that the missionaries "came to do good and stayed to do well." In 1848, King Kamehameha III enacted the Great Mahele (division). Intended to guarantee Native Hawaiians rights to their land, it ultimately enabled foreigners to take ownership of vast tracts of land. Within two generations, more than 80% of all private land was in *haole* (foreign) hands. Businessmen planted acre after acre of sugarcane and enticed waves of immigrants to work the fields: Chinese starting in 1852, Japanese in 1868, and Portuguese in 1878, among other nationalities.

King David Kalakaua was elected to the throne in 1874. This popular "Merrie Monarch" built Iolani Palace in 1882, threw extravagant parties, and lifted the prohibitions on hula and other native arts. For this, he was much loved. He proclaimed, "Hula is the language of the heart and, therefore, the heartbeat of the Hawaiian people." He also gave Pearl Harbor to the United States; it became the westernmost bastion of the U.S. Navy. While visiting chilly San Francisco

Statue of Queen Lili'uokalani at the Hawai'i State Capitol Building.

WHO IS hawaiian IN HAWAI'I?

Only *Kanaka Maoli* (Native Hawaiians) are truly Hawaiian. The sugar and pineapple plantations brought so many different people to Hawai'i that the state is now a remarkable potpourri of ethnic groups: Native Hawaiians were joined by **white U.S. citizens, Japanese, Chinese, Filipinos, Koreans, Portuguese** (largely from Madeira and the Azores), **Puerto Ricans, Samoans, Tongans, Tahitians,** and other **Asian and Pacific Islanders.** Add to that a sprinkling of **Vietnamese, Canadians, African Americans, Native Americans, South Americans,** and **Europeans** of every stripe. Many people retained the traditions of their homeland and many more blended their cultures into something new. That is the genesis of Hawaiian Pidgin, local cuisine, and holidays and celebrations unique to these Islands.

in 1891, King Kalakaua caught a cold and died in the royal suite of the Palace Hotel. His sister, Queen Lili'uokalani, assumed the throne.

The Overthrow

For years, a group of American sugar plantation owners and missionary descendants had been machinating against the monarchy, motivated by both greed and racial bias. On January 17, 1893, with the support of the U.S. minister to Hawai'i and the Marines, the conspirators imprisoned Queen Lili'uokalani in her own palace. To avoid bloodshed, she abdicated the throne, trusting that the United States government would right the wrong. As the Queen waited in vain, she penned the sorrowful lyric "Aloha 'Oe," the iconic song of farewell.

U.S. President Grover Cleveland's attempt to restore the monarchy was thwarted by Congress. Sanford Dole, a powerful sugar plantation owner, appointed himself president of the newly declared Republic of Hawaii (note the English spelling, without *'okina*). His fellow sugarcane planters, known as the Big Five, controlled banking, shipping, hardware, and every other facet of economic life in the Islands. In 1898, through annexation, Hawai'i became an American territory ruled by Dole.

O'ahu's central 'Ewa Plain soon filled with row crops. The Dole family planted pineapple on its sprawling acreage. Planters imported more contract laborers from Puerto Rico (1900), Korea (1903), and the Philippines (1907–31). Many of the new immigrants stayed on to establish families and become a part of the islands. Meanwhile, Native Hawaiians became a landless minority. Their language was banned in schools and their cultural practices devalued.

For nearly a century in Hawai'i, sugar was king, generously subsidized by the U.S. government. Sugar is a thirsty crop, and plantation owners oversaw the construction of flumes and aqueducts that channeled mountain streams down to parched plains, where waving fields of cane soon grew. The waters that once fed taro patches dried up. The sugar planters dominated the territory's economy, shaped its social fabric, and

43

kept the islands in a colonial plantation era with bosses and field hands. But the workers eventually went on strike for higher wages and improved working conditions, and the planters found themselves unable to compete with cheap labor costs in other countries.

Tourism Takes Hold

Tourism in Hawai'i began in the 1860s. Kīlauea volcano was one of the world's prime attractions for adventure travelers. In 1865, a grass structure known as Volcano House was built on the rim of Halema'uma'u Crater to shelter visitors; it was the first hotel in Hawai'i. The visitor industry blossomed as the plantation era peaked and waned.

In 1901, W. C. Peacock built the elegant Beaux Arts–style Moana Hotel on Waikīkī Beach, and W. C. Weedon convinced Honolulu businessmen to bankroll his plan to advertise Hawai'i in San Francisco. Armed with a stereopticon and tinted photos of Waikīkī, Weedon sailed off in 1902 for 6 months of lecture tours to introduce "those remarkable people and the beautiful lands of Hawaii." He drew packed houses. A

SPEAKING hawaiian

Nearly everyone in Hawai'i speaks English, though many people also speak 'ōlelo Hawai'i, the native language of these islands. Most roads, towns, and beaches possess vowel-heavy Hawaiian names, so it will serve you well to practice pronunciation before venturing out to 'Aiea ("eye-eh-uh") or Nu'uanu ("noo-ooh-ah-noo").

The Hawaiian alphabet has only 12 traditional letters: 7 consonants (h, k, l, m, n, p, and w, the latter sometimes pronounced like v) and 5 vowels (a, e, i, o, and u)—but those vowels are liberally used! Usually they are "short," pronounced: ah, eh, ee, oh, and oo. For example, wahine (woman) is wah-hee-nay or vah-hee-nay. Combinations of vowels typically produce diphthongs: ei is pronounced like ay in May, ai and ae something like eye, au and ao something like the ow in how, iu like you, and so on.

When two vowels appear consecutively, they're often separated by an 'okina, a diacritical mark shaped like a single open quotation mark that represents a glottal stop, or slight pause.

Appearing only before or between vowels, it's considered a consonant and recognized as a 13th letter. You'll also see a kahakō, or macron (line) over a vowel indicating stress. Observing these rules, you can tell that Pā'ia, a popular surf town on Maui's North Shore, should be pronounced PAH-ee-ah and Wai'anae on O'ahu's Leeward Side is Why-ah-nigh.

Incorporate aloha (hello, goodbye, love) and mahalo (thank you) into your vocabulary. If you've just arrived, you're a malihini (newcomer). Someone who's been here a long time is a kama'āina (child of the land). When you finish a job or your meal, you are pau (finished). On Friday, it's pau hana, work finished. You eat pūpū (appetizers) when you go pau hana. Any day of the week, visitors should act pono (rightly), as you will no doubt hear from travel and activity providers.

Note: Some businesses, publications and road signs and many websites do not use Hawaiian diacritical marks, in part due to typographical reasons. The edition tries to reflect their preferences.

USS *Arizona* Memorial at Pearl Harbor.

tourism bureau was formed in 1903, and about 2,000 visitors came to Hawai'i that year.

The steamship was tourism's lifeline. It took 4½ days to sail from San Francisco to Honolulu. Streamers, leis, and pomp welcomed each Matson liner at downtown's Aloha Tower. Well-heeled visitors brought trunks, servants, and Rolls-Royces and stayed for months. The population amused visitors with personal tours, floral parades, and hula shows. Beginning in 1935 and running for the next 40 years, Webley Edwards's weekly live radio show, "Hawaii Calls," planted the sounds of Waikīkī—surf, sliding steel guitar, sweet Hawaiian harmonies, drumbeats—in the hearts of millions of listeners in the United States, Australia, and Canada.

By 1936, visitors could fly to Honolulu from San Francisco on the *Hawaii Clipper,* a seven-passenger Pan American Martin M-130 flying boat, for $360 one-way. The flight took 21 hours, 33 minutes. Modern tourism was born, with five flying boats providing daily service. The 1941 visitor count was a brisk 31,846 through December 6.

World War II & Statehood

On December 7, 1941, Japanese Zeros came out of the rising sun to bomb American warships at Pearl Harbor and airfields across O'ahu. This was the "day of infamy" that plunged the United States into World War II. The attack brought immediate changes to the islands. Martial law was declared, stripping the Big Five cartel of its absolute power in a single day. Prominent Japanese Americans (or those deemed otherwise "suspect") were interned, along with German nationals. Hawai'i was "blacked out" at night, Waikīkī Beach was strung with barbed wire, and Aloha Tower was painted in camouflage. Only young men bound for the Pacific came to

45

Hawai'i during the war years; many came back to graves in a cemetery called Punchbowl. Young Japanese American men eventually formed one of the war's most decorated battalions.

The postwar years saw the beginnings of faux Hawaiian culture. The authentic traditions had long been suppressed, and into the void flowed a consumable brand of aloha. Harry Yee invented the Blue Hawaii cocktail and dropped in a tiny Japanese parasol. Vic Bergeron created the mai tai, a drink made of rum and fresh lime juice, and opened Trader Vic's, America's first themed restaurant that featured the art, decor, and food of Polynesia. Arthur Godfrey picked up a ukulele and began singing *hapa haole* tunes on early TV shows. In 1955, Henry J. Kaiser built the Hilton Hawaiian Village at the edge of Waikīkī, and the 11-story high-rise Princess Kaiulani Hotel opened not far away, where the real princess once played. Hawai'i greeted 109,000 visitors that year.

In 1959, the Territory of Hawaii became the 50th state of the United States. That year also saw the arrival of the first jet airliners, which brought 250,000 tourists to the state. By the 1980s, its annual visitor count surpassed 6 million. Fantasy megaresorts bloomed on the neighbor islands like giant artificial flowers, swelling the luxury market with ever-swankier accommodations—and sowing seeds of discontent among those who traditionally fished, harvested seaweed, or simply played along their shores, even while providing legions of jobs that helped offset the end of the plantation era. The tourist industry—the bastion of the state's economy—has survived worldwide recessions, airline-industry hiccups, increased competition from overseas, and a global pandemic. Year after year, the Hawaiian Islands continue to be ranked among the top visitor destinations in the world.

MODERN HAWAI'I
A Cultural Renaissance

Despite the ever-increasing influx of foreign people and customs, Native Hawaiian culture is experiencing a rebirth. It began in earnest in 1976, when members of the Polynesian Voyaging Society launched *Hōkūle'a,* a double-hulled canoe of the sort that hadn't been seen on these shores in centuries. In their craft—named for ancient Hawaiians' guiding star, "Star of Gladness" (Arcturus to Westerners)—the daring crew sailed 2,500 miles to Tahiti without using modern instruments, relying instead on ancient navigational techniques. Most historians at that time discounted Polynesian wayfinding methods as rudimentary; the prevailing theory was that Pacific Islanders had discovered Hawai'i by accident, not intention. The success of modern voyagers sparked a fire in the hearts of indigenous islanders across the Pacific, who reclaimed their identity as a sophisticated people with unique wisdom to offer the world.

The Hawaiian language found new life, too. In 1984, a group of educators and parents recognized that, with fewer than 50 children fluent in

Graceful hula dancers.

Hawaiian, the language was dangerously close to extinction. They started a preschool where *keiki* (children) learned lessons purely in Hawaiian. They overcame numerous bureaucratic and colonial obstacles (including a law still on the books forbidding instruction in Hawaiian) to establish Hawaiian-language-immersion programs across the state that run from preschool through post-graduate education.

Hula—which never fully disappeared despite the missionaries' best efforts—is thriving. At Hilo's annual Merrie Monarch Festival commemorating King Kalākaua, founded in 1963, hula troupes from Hawai'i and occasionally beyond gather to demonstrate their skill and artistry. Hula also played a key role in the more than 5 months' long sit-in in 2019 by demonstrators protesting the construction of a new observatory near the summit of Mauna Kea, which Hawaiian tradition holds sacred. While the protest prevented nearly everyone from ascending the mountain, visitors were welcome to watch the daily series of chants and hula at the protest site and to take cultural and natural history classes held on-site. At press time, the fate of the Thirty Meter Telescope (TMT) had not yet been determined, but the Protect Mauna Kea movement has reinvigorated Hawaiian cultural identity across the islands.

Pandemic Pain & Inspiration

In 2019, Hawai'i registered a record 10.6 million visitors, prompting loud outcries about overtourism and its effects on natural areas, traffic, and even housing, since illegal vacation rentals had taken many modest homes and in-law units off the market. The state started to limit access to some of

47

the most popular parks through increased fees and permit requirements. Then the COVID-19 pandemic struck, and from mid-March to mid-October 2020, the islands were effectively closed to tourism: Only those willing to undergo a 14-day quarantine on their own dime could fly to Hawai'i, and all cruise travel stopped.

While the economic fallout was devastating, with nearly 40% unemployment in some areas, the environmental and social impact was eye-opening. The sheen of sunscreen oils disappeared from Hanauma Bay, tropical fish and sea turtles returned to reefs around the islands, and residents (especially those on outer islands) experienced tranquil beaches and trails for the first time in 6 decades. On social media, the relatively few quarantine scofflaws became unintentional stand-ins for visitors in general, perceived as people who only care about themselves.

After tourism officially resumed in fall 2020, initially with proof of COVID-19 testing and later, vaccination, the numbers of visitors started to approach those of 2019 within a few months. With the testing and vaccination requirement dropped in spring 2022, most islands saw numbers completely rebound, even with elevated prices at hotels and restaurants that continued into 2023 and more beach parks charging entry fees for nonresidents. In the meantime, the Hawai'i Tourism Authority officially abandoned its "come one, come all" approach for a "regenerative tourism" model, one that offers opportunities for travelers to give back—and encourages residents not to give up on tourism just yet.

This approach took on greater urgency after August 8, 2023, when wildfires on Maui destroyed historic Lahaina and cut a swath through upcountry Kula. The loss of Lahaina—the former capital of the Hawaiian Kingdom, the contemporary center of island nightlife and ocean activities and the source of affordable housing and jobs for generations of Native Hawaiians, Filipino Americans, and other families—led to controversy over the reopening of West Maui to tourism just a few months after the blaze. Serious questions remain about where displaced residents can find permanent accommodations, given so many homes and condos have become high-priced vacation rentals. Visitors may well find their jaws dropping at the price of lodgings on Maui, where a simple chain hotel by the airport can charge rates rivaling those of top luxury hotels elsewhere.

In general, the Hawaiian value of hospitality still exists; however, guests who are on their best behavior will find the best reception. Or to use a local expression, "Aloha is a two-way street"—one that you'll be all the better for traveling.

DINING IN HAWAI'I

The Gang of 12

In the early days of tourism in Hawai'i, the food wasn't anything to write home about. Continental cuisine ruled fine-dining kitchens. Meat and produce arrived much the same way visitors did: jet-lagged after a long journey from a far-off land. In 1991, 12 chefs staged a revolt. They partnered with local farmers, ditched the dictatorship of imported foods, and brought sun-ripened mango, crisp organic greens, and freshly caught *uku* (snapper) to the table. Coining the name Hawai'i Regional Cuisine (HRC), they gave the world a taste of what happens when passionate, classically trained cooks have their way with ripe Pacific flavors. More than 3 decades later, the movement to unite local farms and kitchens has only grown more vibrant.

The remaining HRC heavyweights and their now established protégés continue to fill their tables, but they aren't, by any means, the sole source of good eats in Hawai'i. Shops selling fresh steaming noodles abound in O'ahu's Chinatown. You'll be hard-pressed to discover more authentic Japanese fare than can be had in the restaurants dotting Honolulu or Hilo's side streets. Humble plantation-era cuisine and local seafood inspire many a menu item at high-end resort restaurants.

Plate Lunches, Shave Ice & Food Trucks

Haute cuisine is alive and well in Hawai'i, but equally important in the culinary pageant are good-value plate lunches, shave ice, and food trucks.

The **plate lunch,** like Hawaiian Pidgin, is a result of the plantation era. You will find plate lunches of various kinds served in to-go eateries across the state. They usually consist of some protein—fried mahi-mahi, say, or teriyaki beef, shoyu chicken, or chicken or pork cutlets served katsu-style: breaded, fried, and slathered in tangy sauce—accompanied by "two scoops rice," macaroni salad, and a few leaves of green, typically julienned cabbage. Chili water and soy sauce are the condiments of

Shave ice at Ululani's, which has multiple locations throughout Maui.

49

choice. Like *saimin*—the local version of noodles in broth topped with scrambled eggs, green onions, and sometimes pork—the plate lunch is the comfort food of Hawai'i.

Because this is Hawai'i, at least a few fingerfuls of **poi**—steamed, pounded taro (the traditional Hawaiian staple crop)—are a must. Mix it with salty *kalua* pork (pork cooked in a Polynesian underground oven known as an *imu*) or *lomi* salmon (salted salmon with tomatoes and green onions). Other tasty Hawaiian foods include **poke** (pronounced *poh*-kay), a popular appetizer made of cubed raw fish seasoned with onions, seaweed, and chopped, roasted *kukui* nuts; *laulau,* pork,

Food trucks often serve Hawaiian plate lunches.

chicken, or fish steamed in *ti* leaves; **squid *lū'au,*** cooked in coconut milk and taro tops (such a popular dish that its name became synonymous with a feast); and **haupia,** a creamy coconut pudding.

For a sweet snack, the prevailing choice is **shave ice.** Particularly on hot, humid days, long lines of shave-ice lovers gather for heaps of finely shaved ice topped with sweet tropical syrups. Sweet-sour *li hing mui* is a favorite, and gourmet flavors include calamansi lime and red velvet cupcake. Aficionados order shave ice with ice cream and sweetened adzuki beans on the bottom or sweetened condensed milk on top.

Food trucks serve not only shave ice and plate lunches, but everything from tacos and Thai food to *huli huli* (barbecued) chicken and tropical fruit smoothies. Many local restaurateurs these days get their start in these mobile kitchens, so don't be shy about trying their wares—just be prepared to bring cash and a bit of patience.

WHEN TO GO

Many visitors come to Hawai'i when the weather is lousy elsewhere, but it is also a popular destination year-round, with not much of a low season; in Hawai'i, there's high and higher season.

Thus, the **peak seasons**—when prices are up and resorts are often booked to capacity—is generally from mid-December through April, and the family travel season of early June through late August. In particular, the last 2 weeks of December and first week of January are prime time for travel to Hawai'i. Spring break (typically the weeks before or after Easter) and the mid-February week including Presidents Day are also jam-packed with families taking advantage of school holidays.

on location **IN HAWAI'I**

Iconic Hawaiian landscapes serve as a backdrop for numerous films and TV shows, including **NCIS: Hawaii** and recent reboots of **Magnum P.I.** and **Hawaii Five-O.** On the big screen, **Jurassic World: Fallen Kingdom** followed the series' tradition of filming in the Aloha State, on O'ahu's North Shore and Kualoa Ranch; both also appeared in episodes of **Lost.** O'ahu's Waimea Valley appears in both the original **Jumanji** and its 2019 sequel. Johnny Depp leaps into Kīlauea Falls on Kaua'i in **Pirates of the Caribbean: On Stranger Tides.**

The Descendants, Alexander Payne's 2011 film about a dysfunctional Hawai'i *kama'aina* (long-time resident) family, features a wealth of island scenery and music. George Clooney (as Matt King) and the cast spent 11 weeks shooting on O'ahu and Kaua'i. Whether or not you're a film buff, you should definitely stream **The Descendants soundtrack.** This goldmine of modern and classic Hawaiian music features the very best island voices and slack-key guitarists. You won't find a better soundtrack for your Hawaiian vacation. More recently, the first season of HBO's critically acclaimed satirical drama **The White Lotus** was filmed at the Four Seasons Resort Maui at Wailea. For poignant accounts of Hawaiian history, watch 2009's **Princess Ka'iulani,** which includes the turbulent overthrow of the monarchy in 1893, and 2022's **The Wind and the Reckoning,** starring Jason Scott Lee as a Native Hawaiian man who escapes exile to the infamous "leper colony" of Kalaupapa.

If you're planning a trip during peak season, make hotel and rental car reservations early, expect crowds, and prepare to pay top dollar. The winter months tend to be a little rainier and cooler. But there's a perk to traveling during this time: Migratory humpback whales are here, too.

The **off-peak season,** when the best rates are available and the islands are somewhat less crowded, is late spring (May to early June) and fall (Sept to mid-Dec, except for the week in Nov that includes the Thanksgiving holiday). Areas that are the most popular with Canadian snowbirds, such as Kīhei on Maui and the West End of Molokaʻi, also offer cheaper rates in summer.

Special events drive up prices, such as with the Ironman World Championship in mid-October on Hawaiʻi Island's Kona side and the Honolulu Marathon in early December.

Climate

Because Hawaiʻi lies at the edge of the tropical zone, it technically has only two seasons, both of them warm. The dry season corresponds to **summer** (Apr–Oct) and the rainy season is **winter** (Nov–Mar). It rains every day somewhere in the islands at any time of the year, but the rainy season can bring enough gray weather to spoil your sunbathing opportunities. Fortunately, it seldom rains in one spot for more than 3 days straight.

The **year-round temperature** doesn't vary much. At the beach, the average daytime high in summer is 85°F (29°C), while the average daytime high in winter is 78°F (26°C); nighttime lows are usually about 10° cooler. But how warm it is on any given day really depends on *where* you are on the islands.

Each island has a **leeward** side (the side sheltered from the wind) and a **windward** side (the side that gets the wind's full force). The leeward sides (the west and south) are usually hot and dry, while the windward sides (east and north) are generally cooler and moist. When you want arid, sunbaked, desertlike weather, go leeward. When you want lush, wet, rainforest weather, go windward.

Hawaiʻi also has a wide range of **microclimates,** thanks to interior valleys, coastal plains, and mountain peaks. The remote summit of Mount Waiʻaleʻale on Kauaʻi may be one of the wettest spots on earth, yet Waimea Canyon, just a few miles away, is almost a desert. On Hawaiʻi Island, Hilo ranks among the rainiest cities in the nation, with 180 inches of rainfall a year. At Puakō, only 60 miles away, it rains less than 6 inches a year. The summits of Mauna Kea and Mauna Loa on Hawaiʻi Island and Haleakalā on Maui often see snow in winter—even when the sun is blazing down at the beach. The locals say if you don't like the weather, just drive a few miles down the road—it's sure to be different!

> ### Hey, No Smoking in Hawaiʻi
>
> Well, not *totally* no smoking, but Hawaiʻi has one of the toughest laws against smoking in the U.S. The Hawaiʻi Smoke-Free Law prohibits smoking and vaping in public buildings, including airports, shopping malls, grocery stores, retail shops, buses, movie theaters, banks, convention facilities, and all government buildings and facilities. There is no smoking in restaurants, bars, or nightclubs. All lodgings prohibit smoking indoors, and most hotels and resorts are completely smoke-free, even in public areas. Also, there is no smoking within 20 feet of a doorway, window, or ventilation intake. Most public beaches and parks also have no-smoking policies.

Average Temperature & Number of Rainy Days in Waikīkī

	JAN	FEB	MAR	APR	MAY	JUNE	JULY	AUG	SEPT	OCT	NOV	DEC
HIGH (°F/°C)	80/27	80/27	81/27	82/28	84/29	86/30	87/31	88/31	88/31	86/30	84/29	81/27
LOW (°F/°C)	70/21	66/19	66/19	69/21	70/21	72/22	73/23	74/23	74/23	72/22	70/21	67/19
RAINY DAYS	10	9	9	9	7	6	7	6	7	9	9	10

Average Temperature & Number of Rainy Days in Hanalei, Kaua'i

	JAN	FEB	MAR	APR	MAY	JUNE	JULY	AUG	SEPT	OCT	NOV	DEC
HIGH (°F/°C)	79/26	80/27	80/27	82/28	84/29	86/30	88/31	88/31	87/31	86/30	83/28	80/27
LOW (°F/°C)	61/16	61/16	62/17	63/17	65/18	66/19	66/19	67/19	68/20	67/19	65/18	62/17
RAINY DAYS	8	5	6	3	3	2	8	2	3	3	4	7

Holidays

On holidays (especially those over a long weekend), travel between the islands increases, inter-island airline seats are fully booked, rental cars are at a premium, and hotels and restaurants are busier.

Federal, state, and county government offices are typically closed on all federal holidays. Federal holidays in 2025 include New Year's Day (Jan 1); Martin Luther King, Jr., Day (Jan 20); Presidents' Day (Feb 17); Memorial Day (May 26); Juneteenth (June 19, not observed by state and county offices); Independence Day (July 4); Labor Day (Sept 1); Columbus Day (Oct 13), known here as Discoverers' Day but not observed at the state or

King Kamehameha I Day Parade for the state holiday June 11.

local level; Veterans Day (Nov 11); Thanksgiving (Nov 27); and Christmas (Dec 25).

State and county offices are also closed on local holidays, typically including Prince Kūhiō Day (Mar 26), celebrating the birthday of the first delegate from Hawai'i to the U.S. Congress; Good Friday (Apr 18); King Kamehameha I Day (June 11), commemorating Kamehameha the Great, who united the islands and ruled from 1795 to 1819; and Statehood Day (Aug 15), in remembrance of the admittance of Hawai'i as the 50th state on August 21, 1959. In 2025, General Election Day (Nov 4) is also a state holiday.

Lunar New Year celebrations in Honolulu.

Hawai'i Calendar of Events

Please note the following information is subject to change. Confirm details before planning a trip tied to any event.

JANUARY

PGA Tournament of Champions, Kapalua Resort, Maui. Top PGA golfers compete for a $15 million purse. Go to www.pga tour.com/schedule or call ✆ **808/665-9160.** Early January.

Narcissus Festival, Honolulu, O'ahu. Tied to the Lunar New Year (Jan 29 in 2025) but lasting through spring, this Chinese American festival includes a queen pageant, cooking demonstrations, and a cultural fair. Visit www.chinesechamber. com/events or call ✆ **808/533-3181.** January to March.

Ka Moloka'i Makahiki, Mitchell Pauole Center, Kaunakakai, Moloka'i. *Makahiki,* a traditional time of peace in ancient Hawai'i, is re-created with performances by Hawaiian music groups and *hālau* (hula schools), sporting competitions, crafts, and food. It's a wonderful chance to experience ancient Hawai'i. Search "Ka Molokai Makahiki" on Facebook or email kamolokaimakahikiboard@gmail.com. Late January.

FEBRUARY

Lunar New Year, most islands. Lion dancers wind their way around the state for Lunar New Year, also known as Chinese New Year. On O'ahu, Honolulu's Chinatown rolls out the red carpet for this fiery celebration with a parade, pageants, and street festivals. Visit www.chinese chamber.com/events or call ✆ **808/533-3181.** Late January or early February.

Waimea Cherry Blossom Heritage Festival, Waimea, Hawai'i Island. Ideally timed to coincide with the gorgeous pink blooms of cherry trees in the upcountry town's Church Row Park, the multicultural festival offers live music, dance performances, demonstrations, and numerous vendors across several venues. Call ✆ **808/961-8706.** Early February.

Maui Whale Festival, Kalama Park, Kihei, Maui. A monthlong celebration of winter's massive marine visitors, with a film festival, benefit gala, harbor party, whale-watches with experts, and the "great whale count," sponsored by the Pacific Whale Foundation. Go to www.pacificwhale.org or call ☎ **808/249-8811.** Throughout February.

Waimea Town Celebration, Waimea, Kaua'i. This annual 8-day party on Kaua'i's westside celebrates the Hawaiian and multiethnic history of the town where Captain Cook first landed. This is the island's biggest event, drawing some 10,000 people. Top Hawaiian entertainers, sporting events, rodeo, and lei contests are just a few of the draws. Get details at www.waimeatowncelebration.com. Mid-February.

Punahou School Carnival, Punahou School, Honolulu, O'ahu. This 2-day event has everything you can imagine in an enormous school carnival, from high-speed rides to homemade jellies. All proceeds go to scholarship funds for one of the state's most prestigious private high schools. Go to www.punahou.edu or call ☎ **808/944-5711.** Early to mid-February.

Buffalo's Big Board Surfing Classic, Makaha Beach, O'ahu. Now in its 5th decade, this thrilling contest features classic Hawaiian-style surfing, with longboard, tandem, and canoe surfing heats over several days. Go to www.hoomaa.org. Mid-February or early March.

MARCH

Kona Brewers Festival, King Kamehameha's Kona Beach Hotel, Kailua-Kona, Hawai'i Island. This annual event features microbreweries from around the world, with beer tastings, food, and entertainment. Proceeds benefit local nonprofits. Visit www.konabrewersfestival.com. Mid-March.

St. Patrick's Day Parade, Waikīkī (Fort DeRussy to Kapi'olani Park), O'ahu. Bagpipers, bands, clowns, and marching groups parade through the heart of Waikīkī, with lots of Irish-style celebrating all day. Visit www.friendsofstpatrickhawaii.com/parade or call ☎ **808/285-0874.** March 17.

Prince Kūhiō Day Celebrations, all islands. On this state holiday, various events throughout Hawai'i celebrate the birth of Jonah Kūhiō Kalaniana'ole, who was born on March 26, 1871, and elected to Congress in 1902. Visit https://gohawaii.com/trip-planning/events-festivals for calendars for each island. Week of March 26.

APRIL

Celebration of the Arts, Ritz-Carlton, Kapalua Resort, Maui. Contemporary and traditional Hawaiian artists give free hands-on lessons during this 2-day festival, which also features song contests and rousing debates on what it means to be Hawaiian. Go to www.kapaluacelebrationofthearts.com or call ☎ **808/669-6200.** Easter weekend (late Mar to mid-Apr).

Easter Sunrise Service, National Memorial Cemetery of the Pacific, Punchbowl Crater, Honolulu, O'ahu. For a century, people have gathered at this famous cemetery for Easter sunrise services. Go to www.cem.va.gov/cems/nchp/nmcp.asp or call ☎ **808/532-3720.**

Merrie Monarch Hula Festival, Hilo, Hawai'i Island. The world's biggest, most prestigious hula festival features a week of modern ('*auana*) and ancient (*kahiko*) dance competition in honor of King Kalākaua, the "Merrie Monarch" who revived the dance. Tickets sell out by January, so book early. Go to www.merriemonarch.com or call ☎ **808/935-9168.** Typically the week after Easter (late Mar to mid-Apr).

Kaua'i Ukulele Festival, Līhu'e, Kaua'i. Local musicians of varying renown celebrate the art and culture of the uke with free performances. Visit www.hawaiiukulelefestival.com or call ☎ **808/223-6040.**

Waikīkī Spam Jam, Waikīkī, O'ahu. Several blocks of busy Kalakaua Avenue close to cars from 4 to 10pm for this popular celebration of the beloved canned meat product, featuring food booths, arts and crafts vendors, and live entertainment. It's a benefit for the Hawai'i Food Bank, with donations of cans of Spam welcomed. Go to www.spamjamhawaii.com.

East Maui Taro Festival, Hāna, Maui. Taro, a Hawaiian staple food, is celebrated through music, hula, arts, crafts, and, of course, taro-inspired feasts on a Saturday. Go to www.tarofestival. org. Late April.

Big Island Chocolate Festival, Kohala Coast, Hawai'i Island. This 2-day celebration of chocolate (cacao) grown and produced in Hawai'i features symposiums, candy-making workshops, a silent auction and gala tasting event at the Waikoloa Beach Marriott Resort or similarly upscale hotel. Go to www.bigislandchocolate festival.com. Late April.

"I Love Kailua" Town Party, Kailua, O'ahu. This 27-year-old neighborhood party fills Kailua Road with local crafts and specialty food booths, live music, bouncy castles, and free health screenings. It's a fundraiser for the local Outdoor Circle chapter, which uses the proceeds to preserve trees and natural spaces in Kailua and Lanikai. Visit www. lkoc.org/town-party. Last Sunday in April.

MAY

Outrigger Canoe Season, all islands. From May to September, canoe paddlers across the state participate in outrigger canoe races nearly every weekend. Go to https://ohcra.com/race_schedule.aspx for this year's schedule of events.

Lei Day Celebrations, Waikīkī, O'ahu. May Day (May 1) is Lei Day in Hawai'i, celebrated with lei-making contests, pageantry, arts, and crafts. On O'ahu, enjoy the festivities from 9am to 5:30pm at the Queen Kapi'olani Regional Park Bandstand. Go to www.honolulu.gov/ parks and search "Lei Day" or call *(C)* **808/768-3041.** May 1.

World Fire-Knife Dance Championships & Samoa Festival, Polynesian Cultural Center, Lā'ie, O'ahu. Junior and adult fire-knife dancers from around the world converge on the center for 4 nights of the most amazing performances you'll ever see. Authentic Samoan food and cultural festivities on a Saturday before the final evening of competition round out the fun. Go to www.worldfireknife. com or call *(C)* **808/293-3333.** Early to mid-May.

Four Seasons Maui Food & Wine Classic, Wailea, Maui. Renowned chefs such as Wolfgang Puck and Michael Mina, international vintners, and top sommeliers present master classes and elegant wine dinners. Go to www.fourseasons.com/ maui or call *(C)* **808/874-8000.**

Lantern Floating Hawai'i, Magic Island at Ala Moana Beach Park, Honolulu, O'ahu. Some 40,000 people gather at Shinnyo-en Temple's annual Memorial Day ceremony, a beautiful appeal for peace and harmony including live music and dance. At sunset, thousands of glowing lanterns bearing names of deceased loved ones are set adrift; arrive early to write a name on one. Go to www.lanternfloatinghawaii. com or call *(C)* **808/942-1848.** Last Monday in May.

Memorial Day, National Memorial Cemetery of the Pacific, Punchbowl Crater, Honolulu, O'ahu. The armed forces hold a ceremony recognizing those who died for their country, beginning at 10am. Go to www.cem.va.gov/cems/nchp/nmcp. asp or call *(C)* **808/532-3720.** Last Monday in May.

Maui County Ag Fest, Waikapu, Maui. Maui celebrates its farmers and their fresh bounty at this well-attended event. Kids enjoy barnyard games while parents duck into the Grand Taste tent to sample top chefs' collaborations with local farmers. Go to https://mauicountyfarmbureau.org/maui-agfest-4h-livestock-fair. Late May to early June.

Kau Coffee Festival, Pahala, Hawai'i Island. The Big Island's up-and-coming southern coffee typically showcases its farms and products over 10 days with tours, tastings, and a festival with live music and food. Go to https://kaucoffee festival.com. Mid-May to early June.

Moloka'i Ka Hula Piko Festival, Mitchell Pauole Center, Kaunakakai, Moloka'i. This 3-day hula celebration occurs on the island where the Hawaiian dance was born and features performances by hula schools, musicians, and singers from across Hawai'i, as well as local food and Hawaiian crafts: quilting, woodworking, and featherwork. Go to www.facebook.com/kahulapiko. Early June.

Festival of Pacific Art and Culture Festival, Kapiolani Park, O'ahu. This fest features more than 75 artists and crafters as well as entertainment, food, and demonstrations. The 2025 theme is "Regenerating Oceania." Free admission. Check www.festpachawaii.org. Mid-June.

Obon Season, all islands. This colorful Buddhist ceremony honoring the souls of the dead kicks off in June. Synchronized dancers (you can join in) circle a tower where taiko drummers play, and food booths sell Japanese treats late into the night. Each weekend a different Buddhist temple hosts the bon dance. Check local newspaper websites for schedules.

Kapalua Wine & Food Festival, Kapalua, Maui. Elite oenophiles and food experts gather at the Ritz-Carlton, Kapalua, for 4 days of formal tastings, panel discussions, and samplings of new releases. The seafood finale ranks among the state's best feasts. Go to https://kapaluawineandfoodfestival.com. Early June.

King Kamehameha Celebration, all islands. This state holiday (officially June 11, but may be celebrated on different dates on each island) inspires floral parades, ho'olaulea (parties), and much more. The largest are on O'ahu and the king's home island of Hawai'i. Go to https://sfca.hawaii.gov/resources/king-kamehameha-celebration-commission.

JULY

Ala Moana Fourth of July Fireworks Spectacular, Ala Moana Beach Park, Honolulu, O'ahu. The 15-minute fireworks display over the ocean near Waikīkī is among the largest in the country. People gather in the park and, for the best view, on the 'Ewa parking deck of the adjacent Ala Moana Shopping Center, typically beginning at 4pm. A concert at 5pm is followed by fireworks at 8:30pm. Go to www.alamoanacenter.com/events. July 4.

Makawao Stampede & Rodeo, Makawao, Maui. This 3-day affair, including a parade, has been a highlight of this upcountry cowboy town for more than 60 years.

Ticket sales begin in May, most recently on https://etix.com. On or around July 4.

Parker Ranch Rodeo, Waimea, Hawai'i Island. Head to the heart of cowboy country for a hot competition between local *paniolo* (cowboys). The arena accommodates 2,000 people and professional caterers supply food. Go to https://parkerranch.com or call 📞 **808/885-7311.** July 4.

Prince Lot Hula Festival, Honolulu, O'ahu. A longtime event at Moanalua Gardens, where Prince Lot Kapuāiwa once lived, this free, daylong festival of dance performances now takes place on the grounds of 'Iolani Palace, where the prince reigned as King Kamehameha V (1863–72). Go to https://moanaluagardensfoundation.org. Third weekend in July.

Queen Lili'uokalani Keiki Hula Competition, Blaisdell Center, Honolulu, O'ahu. More than 500 *keiki* (children) representing nearly 20 hula schools compete as soloists and in groups in ancient and modern dance forms. Go to www.keikihula.org. Mid- to late July.

Kōloa Plantation Days, Kōloa, Kaua'i. The home of the first sugar plantation in Hawai'i, founded in 1835, celebrates its multiethnic heritage with a parade, rodeo, children's and cultural activities, fun runs, live music, and food vendors at events over 10 days. Go to https://koloaplantationdays.com.

Moloka'i 2 O'ahu Paddleboard World Championships, starts on Moloka'i and finishes on O'ahu. Some 200 international participants journey to Moloka'i to compete in this 32-mile race, considered to be the world championship of long-distance paddle boarding. The race begins at Kaluako'i Beach on Moloka'i at 7:30am and finishes at Maunalua Bay on O'ahu around 12:30pm. Go to www.molokai2oahu.com. Late July.

Hawai'i International Billfish Tournament, Kailua-Kona, Hawai'i Island. Founded in 1959, this prestigious 10-day tournament for individual anglers and teams sees record-setting catches of marlin and other fish weighing as much as 1,000 pounds. Go to www.hibtfishing.com. Late July to early August.

Pu'ukoholā Heiau National Historic Site Anniversary Celebration, Kawaihae, Hawai'i Island. This homage to authentic Hawaiian culture takes place at Pu'ukoholā Heiau, a rugged, beautiful site where attendees make leis, weave *lauhala* mats, pound *poi,* and dance ancient hula. Bring refreshments and sunscreen. Go to www.nps.gov/puhe or call ✆ **808/882-7218.** Mid-August.

Duke Kahanamoku Ocean Festival, Waikīkī, O'ahu. Nine days of water-oriented competitions and festivities celebrate the life of Duke Kahanamoku. Events include longboard surfing, paddleboard racing, swimming, tandem surfing, surf polo, beach volleyball, stand-up paddling, and a luau. Go to www.dukekahanamokuoceanfestival.org. Mid- to late August.

Kaua'i Farm Bureau Fair, Vidinha Stadium, Līhu'e, Kaua'i. The Garden Isle's largest community event includes livestock and produce exhibits, but the real draws of the 4-day affair appear to be the carnival rides, games, concerts, and, of course, tasty food. Go to https://kauai countyfarmbureau.org or call ✆ **808/855-5429.** Late August.

Maui Film Festival, Wailea Resort, Maui. This major film festival screens movies under the stars at a posh Wailea golf course, accompanied by celebrity awards and lavish parties over 5 days. Go to www.mauifilmfestival.com or call ✆ **808/579-9244.** Late Aug or Labor Day weekend.

SEPTEMBER

Aloha Festivals, various locations on all islands. Parades and other events celebrate Hawaiian culture and traditions throughout the state. The parades with flower-decked horses are particularly eye-catching. Go to www.festivalsof aloha.com/events.html. September through November.

Okinawan Festival, Hawai'i Convention Center, Honolulu, O'ahu. The state's largest ethnic festival is a lively, 3-day tribute to the unique cuisine, music, and culture of this subset of earlier immigrants from Japan. Go to www.okinawan festival.com or call ✆ **808/676-5400.** Labor Day weekend (early Sept).

Waikīkī Roughwater Swim, Waikīkī, O'ahu. This popular 2.35-mile, open-ocean swim starts at Kaimana (Sans Souci) Beach between the Natatorium and Kaimana Beach Hotel and ends near Hilton Hawaiian Village in Waikīkī. Early registration is encouraged, but last-minute entries on race day are allowed. Go to www.wrswim.com. Saturday, Labor Day weekend.

Queen Lili'uokalani Canoe Races, Kailua-Kona to Honaunau, Hawai'i Island. Thousands of paddlers of all ages—men, women, solos, and teams—compete in the world's largest long-distance canoe race and other events. Go to www.ql canoerace.com. Labor Day weekend.

Kapalua Open Tennis Championships, Kapalua, Maui. This USTA–sanctioned event features the largest tennis purse for a tournament in the state. Registration includes a tennis tourney, dinner, raffle, and T-shirt. Call ✆ **808/662-7730.** Labor Day weekend.

Na Wahine O Ke Kai, Hale O Lono Harbor, Moloka'i, to Waikīkī, O'ahu. The finale to the outrigger canoe season, this exciting race starts at sunrise on the South Shore of Moloka'i and travels 40 miles across the channel to end in triumphant festivities at the Hilton Hawaiian Village. Go to www.nawahineokekai.com. Late September.

OCTOBER

Maui County Fair, War Memorial Complex, Wailuku, Maui. Canceled in recent years due to the pandemic and Lahaina fire, but planning to return in late 2024, the oldest county fair in Hawai'i has a century of history. It features a parade, amusement rides, live entertainment, and exhibits over 4 days. Go to www.mauifair. com. Early October.

Moanikeala Hula Festival, Polynesian Cultural Center, Laie, O'ahu. Cultural workshops, concerts, and dance performances in the Hawaiian Village of this North Shore attraction honor the memory of Sally Moanikeala Wood, the center's longtime *kumu hula*. Go to www.polynesia.com or call ☎ **800/367-7060.** Early October.

Ironman Triathlon World Championship, Kailua-Kona, Hawai'i Island. Now alternating between genders each year (men in 2024, women in 2025), this event has some 2,500 world-class athletes swim 2.4 miles, bike 112 miles, and run a marathon (26.2 miles) on the Kona-Kohala Coast. Spectators watch the action along the route for free. The best place to see the 6:55am start is along the Ali'i Drive seawall, facing Kailua Bay; arrive by 5:30am to get a seat. (Ali'i Drive closes to traffic; park on a side street and walk down.) To watch finishers come in, line up along Ali'i Drive from Hualalai Street to the seawall. The first finisher can arrive as early as 2:45pm. Go to www.ironmanworld championship.com or call ☎ **808/329-0063.** Mid-October.

Honolulu Pride Parade & Celebration, Waikīkī, O'ahu. This annual rainbow-splashed parade features a gay military color guard, roller derby, and high-energy floats, while Kapi'olani Park hosts daylong festivities. Related parties and special events take place throughout the month. Go to www.honolulupride.com or call ☎ **808/369-2000.** Late October.

Hawai'i Food & Wine Festival, multiple locations on O'ahu, Hawai'i Island, and Maui. Co-founded by Alan Wong and Roy Yamaguchi (two of the state's most celebrated chefs) and Roy's spouse Denise Yamaguchi, this gourmet bonanza includes wine and spirit tastings, cooking demos, field trips, and glitzy galas over 3 weekends. Proceeds benefit agricultural education, sustainability, and cultural programs. See www.hawaiifoodandwine festival.com or call ☎ **808/738-6245.** Mid-October through early November.

NOVEMBER

Emalani Festival, Kōke'e State Park, Kaua'i. This culturally rich festival honors Queen Emma, an avid gardener and philanthropic queen, who made an adventurous trek to Kōke'e with a retinue of 100 in 1871. Go to https://kauai festivals.com or call ☎ **808/651-5744.** Early November.

Kona Coffee Cultural Festival, Kailua-Kona, Hawai'i Island. Founded in 1970, this 10-day celebration of the coffee harvest features a lantern parade (Nov 1), art exhibits, farm tours and tastings, live music, dance, and the Miss Kona Coffee Pageant (Nov 2). Go to https://konac offeefest.com or call ☎ **808/326-7820.** Nov. 1–10.

Hawai'i International Film Festival, multiple islands. Founded in Honolulu in 1980, this weeks-long festival with a cross-cultural spin features filmmakers from Asia, the Pacific Islands, and the United States. Go to www.hiff.org or call ☎ **808/792-1577.** Mid-October to early November.

Allstate Maui Invitational Basketball Tournament, Lahaina Civic Center, Lahaina. Elite college teams battle for the ball in this intimate annual preseason tournament, which also includes hoops clinics and a fun run. Go to www.maui invitational.com. Thanksgiving weekend.

Invitational Wreath Exhibit, Volcano Art Center, Hawai'i Volcanoes National Park, Hawai'i Island. Thirty-plus artists, including painters, sculptors, glass artists, fiber artists, and potters, produce both whimsical and traditional "wreaths" for this exhibit. Park entrance fees apply. Go to www.volcanoartcenter.org or call ☎ **808/967-7565.** Late November to December 31.

Vans Triple Crown of Surfing, North Shore, O'ahu. The world's top professional surfers compete in thrilling surf events for more than $1 million in prize money. Go to https://triplecrown.vans. com. Held between mid-November and late December, depending on the surf.

DECEMBER

Festival of Lights, all islands. On O'ahu, the mayor throws the switch to light up the 40-foot-tall Norfolk pine and other

Daylight Saving Time

Most of the United States observes daylight saving time, which lasts from 2am on the second Sunday in March to 2am on the first Sunday in November. **Hawai'i does *not* observe daylight saving time.** So when daylight saving time is in effect in most of the U.S., Hawai'i is 3 hours behind the West Coast and 6 hours behind the East Coast. When the U.S. reverts to standard time in November, Hawai'i is 2 hours behind the West Coast and 5 hours behind the East Coast.

trees in front of Honolulu Hale, while Moloka'i celebrates with a host of activities in Kaunakakai; on Kaua'i, the lighting ceremony takes place in front of the former county building on Rice Street in Līhu'e. Go to www.honolulucitylights.org for O'ahu and see https://kauaifestival oflights.com for Kaua'i; for other islands, check the listings on https://gohawaii. com. Early through late December.

Honolulu Marathon, Honolulu, O'ahu. More than 30,000 racers compete in this oceanfront marathon, one of the largest in the world, and receive medals and fresh *malasadas* (hole-less doughnuts) as a reward. Non-runners should be aware streets are closed all day, as there's no time limit for competitors. See www. honolulumarathon.org or call ℂ **808/ 734-7200.** Second Sunday of December.

Hawai'i Bowl, Ching Athletics Complex, University of Hawai'i, Honolulu, O'ahu. Although alliances and conferences may have shifted, currently a Pac-12 team plays a Big 12 team in this nationally televised collegiate football classic. Go to www.thehawaiibowl.com or call ℂ **808/ 523-3688.** On or near December 24.

4

O'AHU

by Natalie Schack

P art tropical-island getaway, part urban-cosmopolitan powerhouse: O'ahu remains unique even among the Hawaiian Islands for its tantalizing mix of just about everything. While serene, rainforested coastlines pepper the northeastern shores, Honolulu's bustling east-meets-west lifestyle scene pulls visitors to the south for cultural and culinary exploration. You can tackle a dramatic mountain ridgeline hike in the morning, hit the (almost) always sunny beaches by noon, and be sipping mai tais on Waikīkī's citified shore by sunset. Add in some of the country's most significant historical landmarks, surf spots worth traveling halfway across the globe for, and a unique local culture influenced by a dynamic blend of ethnic groups, and you've got a destination that is as multifaceted as it is magical.

ESSENTIALS

Arriving

Even though more and more transpacific flights are going directly to the neighbor islands these days, chances are still good that you'll touch down on O'ahu first and Honolulu will be your gateway to the Hawaiian Islands. The **Daniel K. Inouye International Airport** sits on the South Shore of O'ahu, west of downtown Honolulu and Waikīkī near Pearl Harbor. Many major American and international carriers fly to Honolulu from the Mainland; for a list of airlines, see chapter 10, "Planning Your Trip to Hawai'i."

LANDING AT DANIEL K. INOUYE INTERNATIONAL AIRPORT

You can walk or, depending on your gate, take the free airport shuttle from your arrival gate to the main terminal and baggage claim on the ground level. Unless you're connecting to an interisland flight immediately, you'll exit and cross the street to the median for a taxi or to the designated rideshare pick-up location, or head to one of the stops for **TheBus** (www.thebus.org; see "By Bus," below). For Waikīkī shuttles and rental-car vans, cross to the median and wait at the designated stop.

GETTING TO & FROM THE AIRPORT

BY RENTAL CAR All major car-rental companies have vehicles available at the airport. The new Consolidated Rental Car Facility is located directly

PREVIOUS PAGE: Fire dancer at the Polynesian Cultural Center.

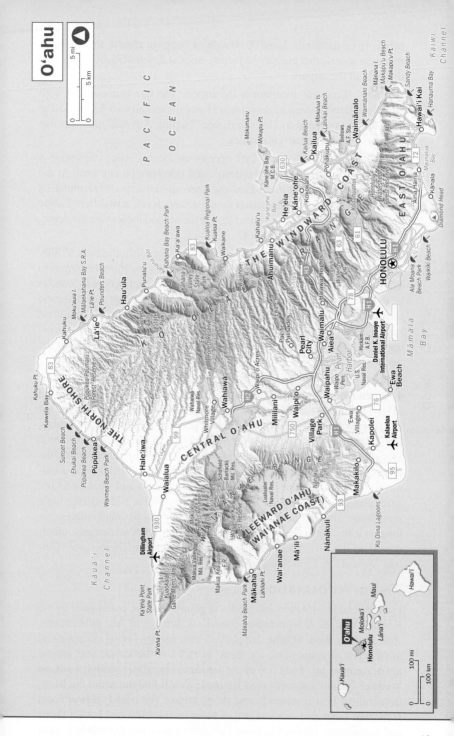

across from terminals 2 and 3, outside of baggage claims 26 and 31. A rental car shuttle that goes to the facility stops at designated pick-up points throughout the airport.

BY TAXI   Taxis are abundant at the airport. The fare is about $30 from Honolulu International to downtown Honolulu and around $35 to $50 to Waikīkī. If you need to call a taxi, see "Getting Around," p. 71 in this chapter, for a list of cab companies.

BY RIDESHARE   Uber and Lyft operate on O'ahu. After requesting a driver, wait for your ride at the designated rideshare pickup area. At the time of publication, for interisland and international arrivals (Terminal 1), pick up is at the second median on the departures level, across from Lobby 2. For domestic arrivals (Terminal 2), use the second median on the departures level, across from Lobby 8.

BY AIRPORT SHUTTLE   **SpeediShuttle** (www.speedishuttle.com; ✆ **808/242-7777**) offers transportation in air-conditioned vans from the airport to Waikīkī hotels; a trip from the airport is around $22 per person to Waikīkī or to the Ko'olina resort area on the island's western side. All domestic arrivals will meet a SpeediShuttle greeter at baggage claim. International arrivals will meet greeters at the streetside Information Counter after customs. Tips are welcome. For advance purchase of group tickets, call the number above or book online.

BY BUS   **TheBus** (www.thebus.org; ✆ **808/848-5555**) is a good option if you aren't carrying a lot of luggage. TheBus no. 20 (Waikīkī Beach and hotels) runs from the airport to downtown Honolulu and Waikīkī. The first bus from Waikīkī to the airport leaves at 4:58am Monday through Friday; the last bus departs the airport for Waikīkī at 1:21am; buses arrive about every 25 minutes. Bus stops are on the second-level roadway along the center median and marked by signs. The travel time to Waikīkī is approximately 1 hour. The one-way fare, for riders ages 6 and over, is $3.00; exact change only. One child, age 5 and under, is free if not occupying a seat. *Note:* You can board TheBus with a carry-on or small suitcase, as long as it fits under the seat and doesn't disrupt other passengers; otherwise, you'll have to take a shuttle or taxi. For more on TheBus, see "Getting Around," p. 71 in this chapter.

Visitor Information

Find general information and guides at **gohawaii.com**, maintained by the Hawai'i Visitors & Convention Bureau. A number of free publications, such as *This Week O'ahu,* are packed with money-saving coupons and good regional maps; look for them on racks at the airport and around town. *Another tip:* Snag one of the Japanese magazines scattered around Waikīkī. Even if you can't read Japanese, you'll find out about the latest, trendiest, or best restaurants and shops around the island. *Hawai'i* and *Honolulu* magazine, are also full of news on the latest and hottest shops and restaurants. *Hawai'i* is geared toward visitors and *Honolulu* toward

Surf boards lined up on Waikīkī Beach.

locals. Both can be found at grocery stores and Barnes & Noble in Ala Moana Center, 1450 Ala Moana Blvd.

The Island in Brief

HONOLULU

Hawai'i's largest city looks like any other big metropolitan center with tall buildings. In fact, some cynics refer to it as "Los Angeles West." But within Honolulu's boundaries, you'll find rainforests, deep canyons, valleys, waterfalls, a nearly mile-high mountain range, and gold-sand beaches. The city proper—where most of Honolulu's residents live—is approximately 12 miles wide and 26 miles long, running east-west roughly between **Diamond Head** and **Pearl Harbor.** Within the city are seven hills laced by seven streams that run to Mamala Bay.

A plethora of neighborhoods surrounds the central area. These areas are generally quieter and more residential than Waikīkī. They're worth venturing into for unique boutiques and some of the island's best restaurants.

Finding Your Way Around, O'ahu-Style

Mainlanders sometimes find the directions given by locals a bit confusing. Seldom will you hear the terms *east, west, north,* and *south;* instead, islanders refer to directions as either *makai* (ma-kae), meaning toward the sea, or *mauka* (mow-kah), toward the mountains. In Honolulu, people use **Diamond Head** as a direction meaning to the east (in the direction of the world-famous crater called Diamond Head), and **'Ewa** as a direction meaning to the west (toward the town called 'Ewa Beach, on the other side of Pearl Harbor).

So if you ask a local for directions, this is what you're likely to hear: "Drive 2 blocks *makai* (toward the sea), and then turn Diamond Head (east) at the stoplight. Go 1 block and turn *mauka* (toward the mountains). It's on the 'Ewa (western) side of the street."

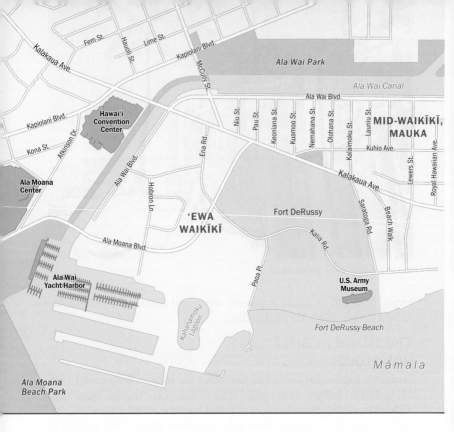

WAIKĪKĪ ★★ Waikīkī is changing almost daily. There's now a Ritz-Carlton, and the formerly bazaar-like International Marketplace has become an upscale mall. It's a sign of Waikīkī's transformation: faded Polynesian kitsch giving way to luxury retailers and residences. Still, Waikīkī tenaciously hangs on to its character: Explore just 1 block *mauka* of Kalākaua Ave. and you'll find hip boutique hotels, hidden hole-in-the-wall eateries, and walk-up apartments and nondescript condos where locals still live.

COVID-19 and the resulting standstill in travel continues to shake up the islands' typical tourism flow. But before all that, Oʻahu was seeing 5 million tourists every year—with 9 out of 10 of them staying in Waikīkī. This urban beach is where all the action is—over 150 high-rise hotels with more than 33,000 guest rooms and hundreds of bars and restaurants are all in a 1½-square-mile beach zone. The Waikīkī crowd is honeymooners and sun seekers, bikinis and bare buns, an around-the-clock beach party every day of the year. Staying in Waikīkī puts you in the heart of it all but be aware that this is far from a quiet island retreat—it's almost always crowded.

ALA MOANA ★★ A great beach as well as Hawaiʻi's largest shopping mall share the Ala Moana name, and this slice of the Honolulu shoreline is the retail and transportation heart of the city, a place where you can

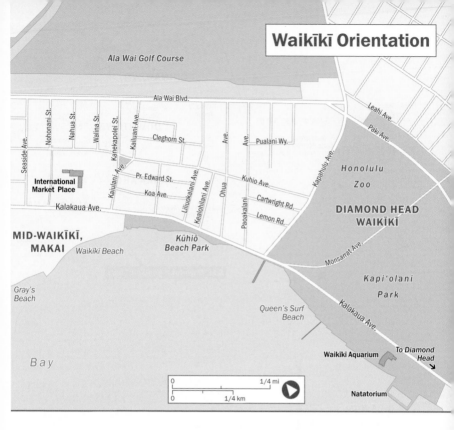

Ala Wai Golf Course

Ala Wai Blvd.

Nohonani St.

Nahua St.

Walina St.

Kanekapolei St.

Kailuani Ave.

Cleghorn St.

Seaside Ave.

Kaiulani Ave.

Pr. Edward St.

Koa Ave.

Liliuokalani Ave.

Kealohilani Ave.

Ohua

Paoakalani

Ave.

Ave.

Pualani Wy.

Kuhio Ave.

Cartwright Rd.

Lemon Rd.

Kapahulu Ave.

Leahi Ave.

Paki Ave.

Honolulu

Zoo

DIAMOND HEAD WAIKĪKĪ

International Market Place

Kalakaua Ave.

MID-WAIKĪKĪ, MAKAI   Waikīkī Beach

Kūhiō Beach Park

Monsarrat Ave.

Kapi'olani

Park

Gray's
Beach

Queen's Surf
Beach

Kalakaua Ave.

Bay

Waikīkī Aquarium

To Diamond
Head

Natatorium

| 0 | | 1/4 mi |
| 0 | 1/4 km | |

shop and suntan in the same hour. All bus routes lead to the open-air **Ala Moana Center,** across the street from **Ala Moana Beach Park ★★.** The shopping center is one of Hawai'i's most-visited destinations for its collection of luxury brands, department stores, and Hawai'i-based shops.

KAKA'AKO ★   This is Honolulu's most rapidly developing neighborhood—a former industrial area giving way to new condo buildings, from workforce housing to the island's most expensive penthouses. Sprouting up among the new construction are lively hubs of boutiques and restaurants, including a revamped **Ward Village** and **Salt.**

DOWNTOWN & CHINATOWN ★★   Here, you'll find historic Honolulu, including 'Iolani Palace, the official residence of Hawai'i's kings and queens. Downtown also has its business center in high rises, as well as the Capitol District, all jammed in about 1 square mile. On the waterfront stands the iconic 1926 **Aloha Tower.**

On the edge of downtown is the **Chinatown Historic District,** one of the oldest Chinatowns in America and still one of Honolulu's liveliest neighborhoods. It's a nonstop pageant of people, sights, sounds, smells, and tastes, though not all Chinese. Southeast Asians, including many Vietnamese, share the old storefronts, as do some of the city's hippest clubs

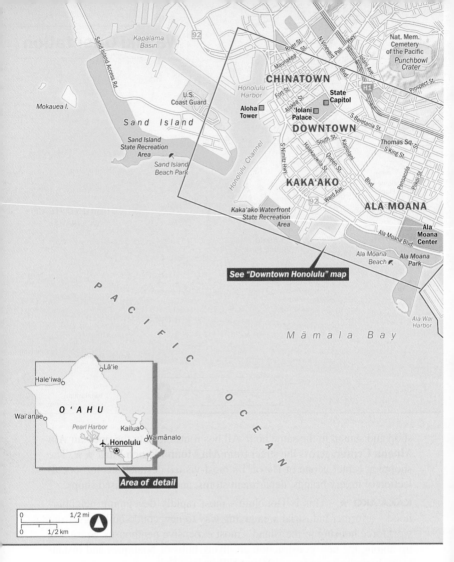

and chicest boutiques, plus Honolulu's self-proclaimed oldest bar (the dive-y **Smith's Union Bar**). Visit this neighborhood in the morning, when everyone shops for fresh goods such as mangoes (when in season), live fish (sometimes of the same varieties you saw while snorkeling), fresh tofu, and hogs' heads.

MĀNOA VALLEY ★　This verdant valley above Waikīkī, blessed by frequent rain showers, was the site of the first sugar and coffee plantations in Hawai'i. It still has vintage *kama'āina* (native-born) homes, one of Hawai'i's premier botanical gardens (**Lyon Arboretum ★**), the ever-gushing **Mānoa Falls,** and the **University of Hawai'i** campus, where 20,000 students hit the books when they're not on the beach.

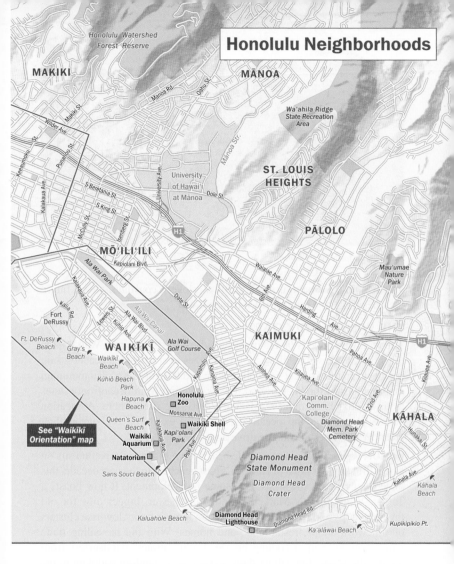

TO THE EAST: KĀHALA Except for the estates of millionaires, some stretches of coastline, and the luxurious **Kāhala Hotel & Resort ★★★**, there's little out this way that's of interest to visitors.

EAST O'AHU

Beyond Kāhala lies East Honolulu and suburban bedroom communities such as 'Āina Haina, Niu Valley, and Hawaii Kai, among others, all linked by the Kalaniana'ole Highway and loaded with homes, condos, fast-food joints, and strip malls. It looks like Southern California on a good day. You'll drive through here if you take the longer, scenic route to Kailua. Some reasons to stop along the way: to snorkel at **Hanauma Bay ★★** or watch daredevil body surfers and boogie boarders at **Sandy Beach ★**; or

Shopping for fresh fruit in Chinatown.

to just enjoy the natural splendor of the lovely coastline, which might include a hike to **Makapu'u Lighthouse ★★**.

THE WINDWARD COAST

The windward side is on the opposite side of the island from Waikīkī. On this coast, trade winds blow cooling breezes over gorgeous beaches; rain squalls keep the tropical vegetation lush; and the fluted Ko'olau mountain range preens in the background. B&Bs, ranging from oceanfront estates to tiny cottages on quiet residential streets, are everywhere. A vacation here is spent enjoying ocean activities and exploring the surrounding areas. Waikīkī is a 20-minute drive away.

KAILUA ★★★ The biggest little beach town in Hawai'i, Kailua sits on a beautiful bay with two of Hawai'i's best beaches. In the past decade, this once-sleepy beach town has seen some redevelopment. It now boasts a Target, Whole Foods Market, condos, and newer, bigger digs for old favorite shops and restaurants. In between remain funky low-rise clusters of timeworn shops, restaurants, and homes. With the prevailing trade winds whipping up a cooling breeze, Kailua attracts windsurfers from around the world. On calmer days, kayaking or stand-up paddling to the Mokulua Islands off the coast is a favorite adventure.

KĀNE'OHE BAY ★ Helter-skelter suburbia sprawls around the edges of Kāne'ohe, one of the most scenic bays in the Pacific. After you clear the traffic-heavy maze of town, O'ahu returns to its more natural state. This great bay beckons you to get out on the water; you can depart from He'eia Boat Harbor on snorkel or fishing charters. From here, you'll have a panoramic view of the Ko'olau Range.

KUALOA/LĀ'IE ★ The upper-northeast shore is one of O'ahu's most sacred places, an early Hawaiian landing spot where kings dipped their sails and ghosts still march in the night. Sheer cliffs stab the reef-fringed seacoast, while old fishponds are tucked along the two-lane coast road that winds past empty gold-sand beaches around Kahana Bay. Thousands "explore" the South Pacific at the **Polynesian Cultural Center,** an educational and entertainment destination in Lā'ie, a Mormon settlement with a temple and university.

THE NORTH SHORE ★★★   For locals, O'ahu is often divided into "town" and "country"—town being urban Honolulu, and country referring to the North Shore. This coast yields expansive, beautiful beaches for swimming and snorkeling in the summer and world-class waves for surfing in the winter. **Hale'iwa ★★** is the social hub of the North Shore, with its casual restaurants, surf shops, and clothing boutiques. Vacation rentals are common accommodations, but there's also the first-class **Turtle Bay Resort ★★.** Be forewarned: It's a long trip—nearly an hour's drive—to Honolulu and Waikīkī, and even longer during the surf season, when tourists and wave-seekers can jam up the roads in gridlock.

CENTRAL O'AHU

Flanked by the Ko'olau and Wai'anae mountain ranges, the 1,000-foot-high Leilehua Plateau runs up and down the center of O'ahu. Once covered with sandalwood forests (hacked down for the China trade) and later the sugarcane and pineapple backbone of Hawai'i, Central O'ahu is now trying to find a middle ground between farms and suburbia, from diversified agriculture in Kunia to the planned community in Mililani. Let your eye wander west to the Wai'anae Range and Mount Ka'ala, the highest summit on O'ahu at 4,020 feet; up there in the misty rainforest, native birds thrive in the hummocky bog. In 1914, the U.S. Army pitched a tent camp on the plain; author James Jones would later call **Schofield Barracks** "the most beautiful army post in the world." Hollywood filmed Jones's *From Here to Eternity* here.

LEEWARD O'AHU: THE WAI'ANAE COAST

The west coast of O'ahu is a hot and dry place of dramatic beauty: white-sand beaches bordering the deep-blue ocean, steep verdant green cliffs, and miles of Mother Nature's wildness. Tourist services are concentrated in **Ko Olina Resort,** which has a Disney hotel and a Four Seasons, pricey resort restaurants, a golf course, a marina, and a wedding chapel, should you want to get hitched. This side of O'ahu is less visited, except by surfers bound for **Mākaha Beach ★★** and those coming to see needle-nose **Ka'ena Point ★** (the island's westernmost outpost), which has a coastal wildlife reserve. That vibe could change, though, as Ko Olina lures more and more visitors from Waikīkī.

GETTING AROUND

BY CAR   O'ahu residents own more than 900,000 registered vehicles, but they have only 1,500 miles of mostly two-lane roads to use. That's 600 cars for every mile—a fact that becomes abundantly clear during morning

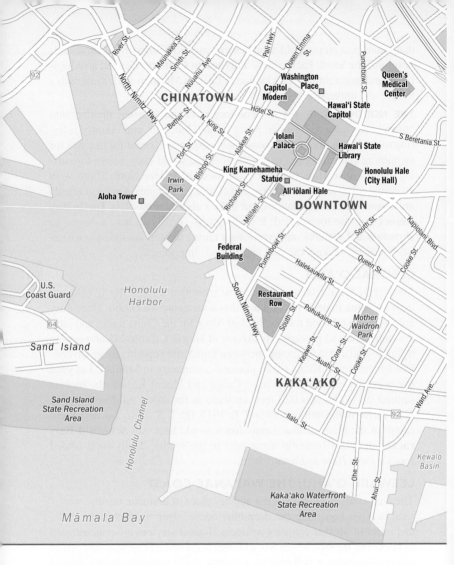

and evening rush hours. You can (mostly) avoid the gridlock by driving between 9am and 2pm or after 7pm.

All of the major car-rental firms have agencies on O'ahu at the airport and in Waikīkī. For listings, see chapter 10. For tips on insurance and driving rules in Hawai'i, see "Getting Around Hawai'i" (p. 603).

BY BUS One of the best deals anywhere, **TheBus** will take you around the whole island for $3 (one child under 5 years old is free when riding with a fare-paying adult)—if you have the time. To get to the North Shore and back takes 4 hours, twice as long as if you travelled by car. But for shorter distances, TheBus is great, and it goes almost everywhere, almost all the

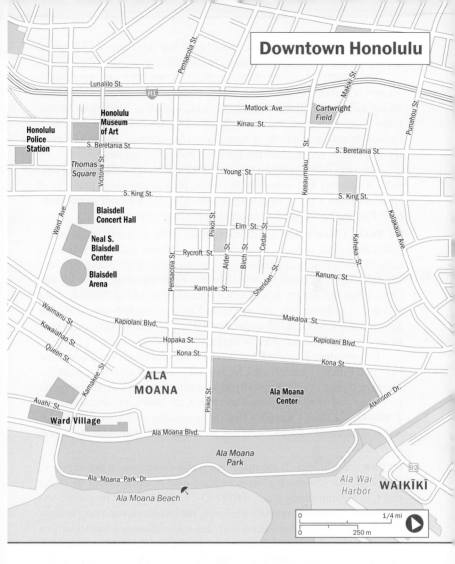

Downtown Honolulu

time. If you're planning on sticking to the Waikīkī–Ala Moana–Downtown region, TheBus will save you a lot of car hassle and expense. You can pay with cash or grab a reloadable HOLO card for $2 at 7-Eleven, Foodland, Times Supermarket, and ABC stores. The card is great if you plan to transfer a lot: After two-and-a-half bus fares purchased, you automatically get qualified for a "day pass" and aren't charged for the rest of the day.

A popular route is **no. 8,** which arrives every 10 minutes or so to shuttle people between Waikīkī and Ala Moana Center (the ride takes 15–20 min.). **No. 20** (Airport/Waikīkī Beach Hotels) and **no. 42** (Waipahu/ Ala Moana) cover the same stretch. Waikīkī service begins daily at around

6am and runs until after 10pm; most buses run about every 15 minutes during the day and every 30 minutes in the evening.

The Circle Island–North Shore route is **no. 88A** (Express North Shore via Kahekili/Ala Moana), but you can also use a combination of routes such as the 60, 65, 52, and 51, which arrive at Ala Moana Center every 30 minutes to an hour and take about 4½ hours to circle the island. Express buses are available to some areas (for example, **Route C Country Express** to Kapolei and the Ko Olina hotels and lagoons).

For more information on routes and schedules, **www.thebus.org** provides timetables and maps for all routes, plus directions to many local attractions and a list of upcoming events. You can also call ℭ **808/848-555.** Taking TheBus is often easier than parking your car.

BY TAXI O'ahu's major **cab companies** offer 24-hour, island wide, radio-dispatched service, with multilingual drivers and air-conditioned cars, limos, and vans, including vehicles equipped with wheelchair lifts (though there's a charge for wheelchairs). Fares are standard for all taxi firms. From the airport, expect to pay about $35 to $50 to Waikīkī, about $25 to $35 to downtown, $65 and up to Kailua, about $65-plus to Hawaii Kai, and about $95 to $125 to the North Shore (plus tip). Plus, there may be an around $5 fee per piece of luggage.

Use rideshare services **Uber** and **Lyft** on your phone to summon and pay for a ride in a private vehicle. Just keep in mind that the airport has designated pick-up and drop-off spots for rideshares (p. 64). If you prefer to go the old-fashioned route, try **The Cab** (www.thecabhawaii.com; ℭ **808/422-2222**) or **Charley's Taxi** (https://charleystaxi.com; ℭ **808/233-3333**), which offers flat rate specials, including a $35 fare from the airport to Waikīkī.

BY CAR You'll find all the major car rental companies at the airport in Honolulu, but car *sharing* services have also reached O'ahu in recent years. In the immediate wake of COVID-19, with the state reopening and restrictions around the country lessening, the islands saw an unexpectedly massive surge in tourism. Along with that came shortages, particularly in the car rental industry, which made car-sharing options even more appealing. **Turo** (www.turo.com) is a popular Mainland-based company that lets locals put their own vehicle up for short-term (often cheaper) rentals. You'll find everything from trucks to Teslas, from $50 a day to $200 and more. Local company **Hui** (www.drivehui.com) has their own dedicated fleet of vehicles at stations throughout Honolulu (including the airport) that can be rented by the hour for some pretty reasonable rates, which increase depending on the type of available vehicle you choose (Toyota Tacomas are on the higher end, while Priuses are on the low end). Plus, there's no arduous check-in process. You just download the app, input your information, and unlock the car via your phone. You can even extend your reservation on a whim from the app, pending availability.

[Fast FACTS] O'AHU

Dentists If you need dental attention while on O'ahu, find a dentist near you through the website of the **Hawaii Dental Association** (www.hawaiidental association.net).

Doctors Straub Clinic & Hospital's **Doctors on Call** (https://hawaiipacifichealth. org; **℃ 808/971-6000**) can dispatch a van if you need help getting to the main clinic or its clinics at the Hilton Hawaiian Village and the Sheraton Waikīkī.

Emergencies Call **℃ 911** for police, fire, or ambulance. If you need to call the **Poison Control Center** (**℃ 800/222-1222**), you will be directed automatically to the Poison Control Center for the area code of the phone you are calling from; all are available 24/7 and very helpful.

Hospitals Hospitals offering 24-hour emergency care include **Queen's Medical Center**, 1301 Punchbowl St. (**℃ 808/691-1000**); **Kuakini Medical Center**, 347 N. Kuakini St. (**℃ 808/536-2236**); **Straub Clinic & Hospital**, 888 S. King St. (**℃ 808/522-4000**); **Kaiser Permanente Medical Center**, 3288 Moanalua Rd. (**℃ 808/833-3333**; note that the emergency room is open to Kaiser members only); **Kapi'olani Medical Center for Women & Children**, 1319 Punahou St. (**℃ 808/983-6000**); and **Kapi'olani Medical Center at Pali Momi**, 98-1079 Moanalua Rd. (**℃ 808/486-6000**). On the windward side is **Castle Medical Center**, 640 Ulukahiki St., Kailua (**℃ 808/263-5500**).

Internet Access Outside of your hotel, Starbucks is your best bet for Internet access. The Royal Hawaiian Center shopping mall and International Marketplace also have free Wi-Fi.

Newspapers The daily paper is the *Honolulu Star Advertiser* (https://star advertiser.com). Online, *Honolulu Civil Beat* is a locally run, non-profit newsroom that covers important island stories and investigative pieces (https://civilbeat.org).

Post Office The downtown location is in the old U.S. Post Office, Customs, and Court House Building (referred to as the Old Federal Building) at 335 Merchant St., across from 'Iolani Palace and next to the Kamehameha Statue (bus: 1, 2, 3, 4, 20, 40). Other branch offices can be found in Waikīkī at 330 Saratoga Ave. (Diamond Head side of Fort DeRussy; bus: 20, 42 or E) and at Ala Moana Center (bus: 23, 42, 60, 65, 88A and E).

Safety Be aware of car break-ins in touristed areas and beach parks; make sure to keep valuables out of sight.

ATTRACTIONS IN & AROUND HONOLULU & WAIKĪKĪ

Historic Honolulu

The Waikīkī you see today bears no resemblance to the Waikīkī of yesteryear. This was once a place of vast taro fields extending from the ocean to deep into Mānoa Valley, dotted with numerous fishponds and gardens tended by thousands of people. You can recapture this picture of old Waikīkī by following the **Waikīkī Historic Trail ★** (www.waikikihistorictrail. org), a winding 2-mile walk with 20 bronze surfboard markers (at 6 ft., 5 in. tall—you can't miss 'em), complete with descriptions and archival photos of the historic sites. The markers note everything from Waikīkī's ancient fishponds to the history of the Ala Wai Canal. The trail begins at Kūhiō Beach and ends at the King Kalākaua statue at the intersection of Kūhiō and Kalākaua avenues.

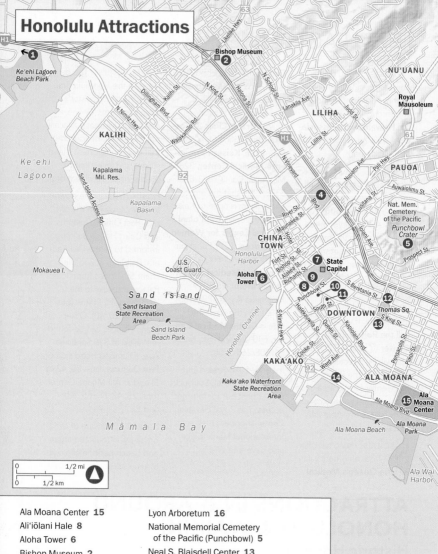

Honolulu Attractions

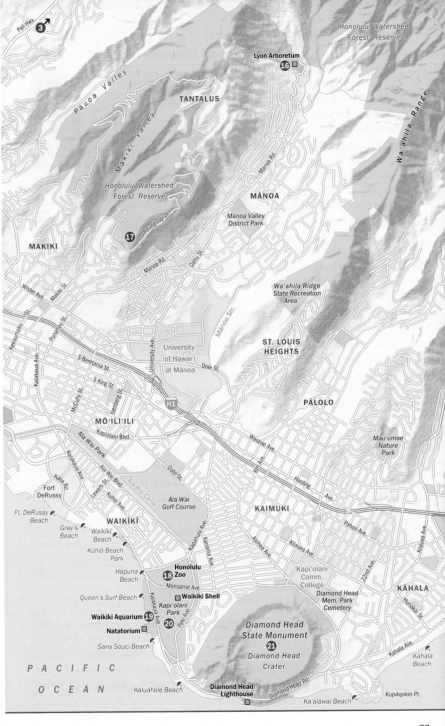

Bishop Museum ★★★ MUSEUM   This is a museum for adults and kids alike. For the adults: the original **Hawaiian Hall,** built in 1889 to house the collection of Hawaiian artifacts and royal family heirlooms of Princess Bernice Pauahi Bishop, the last descendant of King Kamehameha I. Today, the exhibits, spread out over three floors, give the most complete sense of how ancient native Hawaiians lived. On display are carvings representing Hawaiian gods and the personal effects of Hawaiian royalty, including a feathered cape worn by Kamehameha himself.

For the kids, there's the 50-foot sperm whale skeleton and the **Richard T. Mamiya Science Adventure Center,** featuring interactive exhibits on how volcanoes, wind, and waves in this remote volcanic archipelago work. Don't miss the shows at the **J. Watamull Plane-**

Inside the Hawaiian Hall at the Bishop Museum.

tarium, to explore the current evening sky and learn about ancient Polynesian navigators. The planetarium staff also hold night shows on the first Saturday of every month and are worth checking out for information on both seasonal night sky changes over the islands, as well as interesting tidbits about Hawaiian myth and the cultural significance of constellations. Native Hawaiians, after all, were skilled navigators who utilized the stars as essential tools for wayfinding between island chains. Modern revival Native Hawaiian navigators look to many of the same constellations on their journeys across the Pacific today.

Hungry? Check out the museum cafe by Highway Inn, which serves light lunch fare and snacks, including local specialties kalua pork, lomi salmon, and house-made kalo (taro) chips.

1525 Bernice St., just off Kalihi St./Likelike Hwy. www.bishopmuseum.org. ⓒ **808/ 847-3511.** $33.95 adults, $30.95 seniors, $25.95 children ages 4–12. Daily 9am–1pm. Planetarium tickets are $3 and can be purchased on site. Parking is $5. Bus: 2.

Hawaiian Mission Houses Historic Site and Archives ★ HISTORIC SITE   Centered on the first mission houses built in the 1800s, the former Mission Houses Museum has undergone a rebranding. Possibly It's because recent years have seen an interrogation of the role and impact missionary culture played in the oppression and exploitation of native Hawaiians and native Hawaiian culture. Now, instead of depicting early missionary life exclusively, the expanded focus includes collaborations

ESPECIALLY FOR kids

Checking out the Honolulu Museum of Art on Family Sunday (p. 80) Every third Sunday of the month, the Museum offers a variety of art activities and movies for the kids. Past programs have included sessions making pirate sock puppets, themes around events such as Lunar New Year, and screenings of animated shorts from around the world.

Visiting the Honolulu Zoo (p. 86) Visit Africa in Hawai'i at the zoo, where the lions, giraffes, zebras, and elephants delight youngsters and parents alike. Try one of the Twilight Tours, every Saturday evening September through March, to see the animals in, quite literally, a different light! It's a golden opportunity to spot some of the nocturnal species being friskier and more active than they would be in the daytime.

Peeking Under the Sea at the Waikīkī Aquarium (p. 87) The aquarium is pretty small, but it has a fascinating collection of alien-like jellyfish and allows for up-close encounters with the endangered Hawaiian monk seal, dragon-like eels, and festively colored crustaceans. Check the aquarium website for family-friendly activities, including arts and crafts, and virtual resources such as online lectures, marine drawing lessons and live webcams.

Snorkeling at Hanauma Bay (p. 108) Checked out the sea life at the aquarium? Now It's time to swim with some of them! The inside of sheltered Hanauma Bay is usually very calm, and well-equipped with lifeguard stations and safety information, making it the best spot for first-time snorkelers. Even from the shore, the bay itself is something to behold, a former volcanic crater that time and erosion has carved into an ideal nook for a vibrant ecosystem of marine creatures to flourish. Look for brilliant coral species, shy octopi, and the always-charming Hawaiian sea turtles, which all live, swim, and play among the brightly colored reef fish.

Eating Shave Ice (p. 145) No visit to Hawai'i is complete without shave ice—pillows of ice drenched in tropically flavored fruit syrups with options like creamy ice cream centers, sweet azuki (black bean) filling, condensed milk drizzles or sprinkles of chewy, fluffy mochi balls.

Beating Drums in a Tongan Village (p. 99) The **Polynesian Cultural Center** introduces kids to Polynesian activities, which include canoe paddling and ancient Hawaiian lawn games, every day from 12:30 to 5:30pm. As of summer 2024, check out the newly returned daily canoe pageant, a delightful spectacle that showcases the skills and talents of canoe-borne dancers and entertainers hailing from each of the Polynesian islands, at 2:30pm. Or sign up for a canoe tour on the tropical lagoon, which will take you through winding waterways of the beautiful, landscaped center and its villages.

between Hawaiians and missionaries, and the successes that were borne from that relationship, such as the printed Hawaiian language and widespread literacy (by the 1860s, Hawai'i had the highest literacy rate of any nation). Through a series of programs, including tours focusing on architecture, and Native Hawaiian perspectives, the plan is to encourage "a deeper understanding and appreciation of Hawai'i's complex history."

553 S. King St. (at Kawaiahao St.). https://missionhouses.org. © **808/447-3910.** $20, $15 military personnel and seniors, $10 students. Tours Tues–Fri 11am–2pm. Bus: 3 or 13.

Honolulu Museum of Art ★ MUSEUM   The Honolulu Museum of Art boasts a renown Asian collection that includes a significant number of items from Japan, China, and Korea, as well as modern paintings and even an Islamic art wing. But It's not just a repository—It's also a curation of exhibitions of Hawai'i's contemporary artists and their collaborations.

The Honolulu Museum of Art is also where tours of **Shangri La Museum of Islamic Art, Culture, and Design** ★★★ start. The tobacco heiress Doris Duke's private palace on a 5-acre sanctuary in Black Point is absolutely stunning, packed with Islamic art and intricate tilework from Iran, Turkey, and Syria; textiles from Egypt and India; and custom-painted ceilings by Moroccan artisans. Outside's not so bad either, with ocean views all the way to Diamond Head. Tours depart from the Honolulu Museum of Art building Thursday to Saturday at 9am, 11am, 1pm, and 3pm. Tickets sell out fast, so reserve in advance.

900 S. Beretania St. www.honolulumuseum.org and www.shangrilahawaii.org. ⓒ **808/ 532-3853.** Honolulu Museum of Art: $25 adults, free for children 18 and under. Shangri La: $25, which includes shuttle ride.

'Iolani Palace ★★ HISTORIC BUILDING   If you want to really understand Hawai'i's royal history, this 60-minute tour is worth your time. The 'Iolani Palace was built by King David Kalākaua, who spared no expense. The 4-year project, completed in 1882, cost $360,000—and nearly bankrupted the Hawaiian kingdom. This four-story Italian Renaissance palace was the first electrified building in Honolulu (it had

The grand 'Iolani Palace was completed in 1882.

electricity before the White House and Buckingham Palace). Royals lived here for 11 years, until Queen Lili'uokalani was deposed, and the Hawaiian monarchy fell forever in a palace coup led by U.S. Marines on January 17, 1893, at the demand of sugar planters and missionary descendants.

Cherished by latter-day royalists, the 10-room palace stands as an architectural statement of the monarchy period. 'Iolani attracts 60,000 visitors a year in small groups; everyone must don booties to scoot across the royal floors. Visitors take either a comprehensive **guided tour ★**, which offers a tour of the interior, or a self-led **audio tour.** Finish by exploring the Basement Gallery on your own, where you'll find crown jewels, ancient feathered cloaks, the royal china, and more.

364 S. King St. (at Richards St.). www.iolanipalace.org. © **808/522-0822.** Guided tours Wed 9am–12:30pm; Thurs 9am–2:30pm. Reservations required; book online or visit the ticket office in the 'Iolani Barracks on the Palace Grounds. Audio tour $26.95 adults, $21.95 teens, $11.95 children 5–12. Tues–Sat 9am–4pm.

Kawaiaha'o Church ★ CHURCH In 1842, Kawaiaha'o Church stood complete at last. Designed by Rev. Hiram Bingham and supervised by Kamehameha III, who ordered his people to help build it, the project took 5 years to complete. Workers quarried 14,000 coral blocks weighing 1,000 pounds each from the offshore reefs and cut timber in the forests for the beams. This proud stone church, with bell tower and colonial colonnade, was the first permanent Western house of worship in the islands. It became the church of the Hawaiian royalty and remains in use today. Take advantage of the historic walking tour by using your smartphone to scan the QR codes placed throughout the campus and downloading the audio files of descriptions of notable sites.

957 Punchbowl St. (at King St.). © **808/469-3000.** Free admission (donations appreciated). Sunday services 9:30am, but you can view the exterior of the building and grounds the rest of the week. Bus: 3, 9, 13.

Queen Emma Summer Palace ★ PALACE Hānaiakamalama, the name of the country estate of Kamehameha IV and Queen Emma, was once in the secluded uplands of Nu'uanu Valley. These days It's adjacent to a six-lane highway full of speeding cars. This simple, seven-room New England–style house, built in 1848 and restored by the Daughters of Hawai'i, is worth an hour of your time to see the interesting blend of Victorian furniture and hallmarks of Hawaiian royalty, including feather cloaks and *kahili*, the feathered standards that mark the presence of *ali'i* (royalty). Other royal treasures include a canoe-shaped cradle for Queen Emma's baby, Prince Albert, who died at the age of 4. (Kaua'i's ritzy Princeville Resort is named for the little prince.) Self-guided and docent tours are available by reservation on Tuesdays and Thursdays to Saturdays from 10am to 3pm. Otherwise, tours are self-guided.

2913 Pali Hwy. (at Old Pali Rd.). https://daughtersofhawaii.org. © **808/595-3167.** Self-guided tours $14 adults, $5 children ages 5–12, $1 children 4 and under. Fri and Sat 10am–3:30pm. Docent tours: $20 adults, $12 children ages 5–12, $3 children 4 and under.

Wartime Honolulu

National Memorial Cemetery of the Pacific ★★ CEMETERY
The National Memorial Cemetery of the Pacific (aka Punchbowl) is an ash-and-lava tuff cone that exploded about 150,000 years ago—like Diamond Head, only smaller. Early Hawaiians called it Puowaina, or "hill of sacrifice." The old crater is a burial ground for veterans as well as the 35,000 casualties of three American wars in Asia and the Pacific: World War II, Korea, and Vietnam. You'll find many unmarked graves with the date December 7, 1941. Some names will be unknown forever; others are famous, like that of war correspondent Ernie Pyle, killed by a Japanese sniper in April 1945 on Okinawa; still others buried here are remembered only by family and surviving buddies. The white stone tablets known as the Courts of the Missing bear the names of 28,788 Americans missing in action in World War II.

Punchbowl Crater, 2177 Puowaina Dr. (at the end of the road). Free admission. Daily 8am–6pm. Bus: 9.

Pearl Harbor Aviation Museum ★ MUSEUM
The Pearl Harbor Aviation Museum is the flashiest of the Pearl Harbor exhibits. There are two hangars: Hangar 37 includes planes involved in the 1942 attack, but the best is Hangar 79, the doors still riddled with bullet holes from the Pearl Harbor strafing. It houses military aircraft, old and new; you can even climb into the cockpit of some of them. In the Restoration Shop, you can see vintage aircraft awaiting restoration. For an additional $10.50, sit in a Combat Flight Simulator, like an immersive video game in which you fly a plane and shoot down the enemy.

Hangar 39, 319 Lexington Blvd., Ford Island (next to the red-and-white control tower). www.pearlharboraviationmuseum.org. © **808/441-1000.** $25.99 adults, $14.99 children ages 4–12; free audio tours. Daily 9am–5pm. See USS *Arizona* Memorial, above, for driving, bus, and shuttle directions.

USS *Arizona* Memorial at Pearl Harbor ★★★ HISTORIC SITE
On December 7, 1941, the USS *Arizona,* while moored here in Pearl Harbor, was bombed in a Japanese air raid. The 608-foot battleship sank in 9 minutes without firing a shot, taking 1,177 sailors and Marines to their deaths—and catapulting the United States into World War II.

Nobody who visits the memorial will ever forget it. The deck of the ship lies 6 feet below the surface—oil still oozes slowly up from the *Arizona*'s engine room and stains the harbor's calm, blue water; some say the ship still weeps for its lost crew. The memorial, designed by Alfred Preis, a German architect interned on Sand Island during the war, is a stark-white, 184-foot rectangular bridge that spans the sunken hull of the ship. It contains the ship's bell, recovered from the wreckage, and a shrine room with the names of the dead carved in stone.

Today, free U.S. Navy launches take visitors to the *Arizona.* You can make an **advance reservation** to visit the memorial at the website **www. recreation.gov** (get to the specific USS *Arizona* Memorial page from

The USS *Arizona* Memorial juts out over the submerged ship.

https://nps.gov/perl/uss-arizona-memorial-programs.htm) for an additional $1.00 per-ticket convenience fee. This is highly recommended; if you try to get walk-up tickets directly at the visitor center, you may have to wait a few hours before the tour. While you're waiting for the free shuttle to take you out to the ship, get the **audio tour ★★★**, which will make the trip even more meaningful. The tour (on an MP3 player) is about 2½ hours long, costs $11 for adults and $7 for children, and is worth every nickel. It's like having your own personal park ranger as your guide. It's narrated by actress Jamie Lee Curtis and features stories told by actual Pearl Harbor survivors—both American and Japanese. Plus, while you're waiting for the launch, the tour will take you step by step through the museum's personal mementos, photographs, and historic documents. You can pause the tour for the moving 20-minute film that precedes your trip to the ship. The tour continues on the launch, describing the shoreline and letting you know what's in store at the memorial itself. At the memorial, the tour gives you a mental picture of that fateful day, and the narration continues on your boat ride back. Allow a total of at least 4 hours.

Note that boat rides to the *Arizona* are sometimes suspended because of high winds. Due to increased security measures, visitors cannot carry purses, handbags, fanny packs, backpacks, camera bags (though you can carry your camera, cellphone, or video camera with you), diaper bags, or other items that offer concealment on the boat. However, there is a storage facility where you can stash carry-on-size items (no bigger than 30×30×18 in.) for a fee. *A reminder to parents:* Baby strollers, baby carriages, and baby backpacks are not allowed inside the theater, on the boat, or on the USS *Arizona* Memorial. All babies must be carried. *One last note:* Most unfortunately, the USS *Arizona* Memorial is a high-theft area—so leave your valuables at the hotel.

Pearl Harbor. www.nps.gov/usar. © **808/422-3399.** Free admission. $11 for the audio guide. **Highly recommended:** Make an advance reservation to visit the memorial at www.recreation.gov. Daily 7am–5pm (programs 8am–3:30pm). Drive west on H-1 past the airport; take the USS *Arizona* Memorial exit and follow the green-and-white signs; there's ample free parking. Bus: 42.

USS *Bowfin* Submarine Museum & Park ★ HISTORIC SITE   Ever wonder what life is like on a submarine? Then go inside the USS *Bowfin*, aka the Pearl Harbor Avenger, to experience the claustrophobic quarters where soldiers lived and launched torpedoes. The *Bowfin* Museum details wartime submarine history and gives a sense of the impressive technical challenges that must be overcome for submarines to even exist. Tours are self-guided and include free audio guides in seven languages.

11 Arizona Memorial Dr. (next to the USS *Arizona* Memorial Visitor Center). www. bowfin.org. © **808/423-1341.** $21.99 adults, $16.99 active-duty military personnel, $12.99 children ages 4–12 (children ages 3 and under not permitted for safety reasons). Daily 7am–5pm (last admission 4:30pm). See USS *Arizona* Memorial, above, for driving, bus, and shuttle directions.

USS *Missouri* Memorial ★ HISTORIC SITE   On the deck of this 58,000-ton battleship (the last one the navy launched), World War II came to an end with the signing of the Japanese surrender on September 2, 1945. The *Missouri* was part of the force that carried out bombing raids over Tokyo and provided firepower in the battles of Iwo Jima and Okinawa. In 1955, the navy decommissioned the ship and mothballed it at the Puget Sound Naval Shipyard in Washington State. But the *Missouri* was modernized and called back into action in 1986, eventually being deployed in the Persian Gulf War, before retiring once again in 1992. Here it sat until another battle ensued, this time over who would get the right to keep this living legend. Hawai'i won that battle and brought the ship to Pearl Harbor in 1998. The 887-foot ship is now open to visitors as a museum memorial.

You're free to explore on your own or take a guided tour. Highlights of this massive (more than 200-ft. tall) battleship include the forecastle (or "fo'c's'le," in navy talk), where the 30,000-pound anchors are dropped on 1,080 feet of anchor chain; the 16-inch guns (each 65 ft. long and weighing 116 tons), which can accurately fire a 2,700-pound shell some 23 miles in 50 seconds; and the spot where the Instrument of

> ### Pearl Harbor Visitor Center: Getting Tickets
>
> The **USS *Arizona* Memorial, USS *Bowfin* and Submarine Museum, USS *Missouri* Memorial,** and **Pacific Aviation Museum** are all accessed via the Pearl Harbor Visitor Center. Park here and purchase tickets for all the exhibits. (Entry to the USS *Arizona* Memorial is free, but you still must get a ticket. Better yet, for the USS *Arizona*, reserve your spot at **www.recreation.gov** to avoid a long wait.) Shuttle buses will deliver you to the sites within Pearl Harbor.

Surrender was signed as Douglas MacArthur, Chester Nimitz, and "Bull" Halsey looked on.

Battleship Row, Pearl Harbor. www.ussmissouri.org. ( ) **808/455-1600.** $34.99 adults, $17.49 children ages 4–12. Daily 8am–4pm. Check in at the USS *Bowfin* Submarine Museum, next to the USS *Arizona* Memorial Visitor Center. See USS *Arizona* Memorial above for driving, bus, and shuttle directions.

Just Beyond Pearl Harbor

Hawaiian Railway ★ TRAIN   It's like a Disneyland ride . . . through Honolulu's suburbia. It's also a quirky way to see the less-traveled leeward side of Oʻahu. Between 1890 and 1947, the chief mode of transportation for Oʻahu's sugar mills was the Oʻahu Railway and Land Co.'s narrow-gauge trains. The line carried not only equipment, raw sugar, and supplies, but also passengers from one side of the island to the other. About 6 miles of restored train tracks start in ʻEwa and end along the coast at Kahe Point. Don't expect ocean views all the way—you're passing through the heart of suburban Honolulu (yup, that's a Costco and a power plant) before you reach the ocean. Still, the 1½-hour narrated ride is pretty amusing. Book the 3pm rides, and the train stops at Ko Olina resort for guests to purchase ice cream.

91-1001 Renton Rd., ʻEwa. www.hawaiianrailway.com. ( ) **808/681-5461.** $18 adults, $13 seniors and children ages 2–12. Parlor Car 64 $35. Departures Sat noon and 3pm, Sun 1pm and 3pm, and Wed 1pm. Take H-1 west to Exit 5A; take Hwy. 76 south for 2½ miles to Tesoro Gas; turn right on Renton Rd. and drive 1½ miles to end of paved section. The station is on the left. Bus: 41, 44.

Hawaii's Plantation Village ★ HISTORIC SITE   The hour-long tour of this restored 50-acre village offers a glimpse back in time to when sugar planters shaped the land, economy, and culture of Hawaii. From 1852, when the first contract laborers arrived from China, to 1947, when the plantation era ended, more than 400,000 men, women, and children from China, Japan, Portugal, Puerto Rico, the Philippines, and Korea came to work the cane fields. The "talk story" tour brings the old village alive with 30 faithfully restored camp houses, Chinese and Japanese temples, the Plantation Store, and even a sumo-wrestling ring.

94-695 Waipahu St. (at Waipahu Depot Rd.), Waipahu. www.hawaiiplantationvillage. org. ( ) **808/677-0110.** $17 adults, $11 seniors and military personnel, $8 children ages 4–17. Mon–Sat 9am–2pm. Guided tours (10am and noon) may be requested, but only in advance by calling 808/677-0110 or emailing waipahu.hpv@gmail.com. Take H-1 west to Waikele-Waipahu exit (Exit 7); get in the left lane of the exit and turn left on Paiwa St.; at the 5th light, turn right onto Waipahu St.; after the 2nd light, turn left. Bus: 43.

Gardens, Aquariums & Zoos

Foster Botanical Garden ★ GARDEN   You could spend days in this unique historic garden, a leafy oasis amid the high-rises of downtown Honolulu. Combine a tour of the garden with a trip to Chinatown (just across the street) to maximize your time and double your pleasure. The giant trees that tower over the garden's main terrace were planted in the 1850s by William

Hillebrand, a German physician and botanist, on royal land leased from Queen Emma. Today this 14-acre public garden is a living museum of plants, some rare and endangered, collected from the tropical regions of the world. Of special interest are 26 "Exceptional Trees" protected by state law, a large palm collection, a primitive cycad garden, and a hybrid orchid collection.

180 N. Vineyard Blvd. (at Nu'uanu Ave.). ℂ **808/768-7135.** $5 adults, $1 children ages 6–12. Daily 9am–4pm; Bus: 3, A.

A distinctive orchid among the collections at the Foster Botanical Garden.

Honolulu Zoo ★ ZOO Nobody comes to Hawai'i to see an Indian elephant or African lions and zebras, right? Wrong. This 42-acre municipal zoo in Waikīkī attracts visitors in droves. If you've got kids, allot at least half a day. The highlight is the African Savanna, a 10-acre exhibit with more than 40 African critters, including antelope and giraffes. The zoo also has a rare Hawaiian nēnē goose, one of Hawai'i's critically endangered native animals. The playground has a domed jungle-like climbing area for kids to let off a little steam, with lots of shade making it an ideal spot to have a picnic lunch. (The zoo allows you to bring your own snacks and drinks—even your own cooler, provided it doesn't contain alcohol.)

151 Kapahulu Ave. (btw. Paki and Kalākaua aves.), at entrance to Kapi'olani Park. www.honoluluzoo.org. ℂ **808/971-7171.** $21 adults, $13 children ages 3–12. Daily 10am–3:00pm. Zoo parking (entrance on Kapahulu Ave.) $1.50 per hr. Bus: 2.

Lyon Arboretum ★ GARDEN The Lyon Arboretum dates from 1918, when the Hawaiian Sugar Planters Association wanted to demonstrate the value of watershed for reforestation. In 1953, it became part of the University of Hawai'i, where they continued to expand the extensive collection of tropical plants. Six-story-tall breadfruit trees, yellow orchids no bigger than a nickel, ferns with fuzzy buds as big as a human head—these are just a few of the botanical wonders you'll find at the 194-acre arboretum. A whole different world opens up to you along the self-guided, 20-minute hike through the arboretum to Inspiration Point. You'll pass more than 5,000 exotic tropical plants full of singing birds in this cultivated rainforest at the head of Mānoa Valley. Take the beautiful, lush trail all the way to the back of the valley and you'll end up at a picturesque waterfall—but not before passing quite a few beautiful tree-shaded and flower-adorned scenes ideal for sitting, gazing, picnicking or lounging.

3860 Mānoa Rd. (near the top of the road). www.manoa.hawaii.edu/lyon. ℂ **808/988-0456.** Suggested donation $10. Limited admission by reservation only. Reservations are made online and open on a weekly basis. Bus: 5, with a long walk.

Exploring the underwater world at the Waikīkī Aquarium.

Waikīkī Aquarium ★ AQUARIUM   Half of Hawaiʻi's beauty is under-water, and at the Waikīkī Aquarium you get an up-close-and-personal peek at some brilliant little pockets of the watery worlds that surround these shores. Think giant clams and herds of seahorses, seadragons, and pipefishes, plus a brilliant garden of magnificent coral and a big tank just for "hunters" (sharks, groupers, and jacks). This small aquarium, located on a live coral reef habitat, has plenty of other creatures to see, including eels and a touch tank. Check out the guided Hawaiian plants tour of the aquarium's gardens every first and third Thursday of the month. The rotat-ing jellyfish exhibit is otherworldly—It's like watching alien life. You'll probably need only an hour or less to see everything. Note that the Hawai-ian monk seal exhibit is temporarily closed, as the resident seal spends time at a monk seal behavioral research program in California.

2777 Kalākaua Ave. (across from Kapiʻolani Park). www.waikikiaquarium.org. © **808/ 923-9741.** $12 adults, $8 active military, $5 seniors and children ages 4–12. Daily 9am–4:30pm. Bus: 20 or 14.

Other Natural Wonders & Spectacular Views

In addition to the attractions listed below, check out the hike to **Diamond Head Crater** ★★★ (p. 117); almost everybody can handle it, and the 360-degree views from the top are fabulous.

Nuʻuanu Pali Lookout ★ NATURAL ATTRACTION   Gale-force winds sometimes howl through the mountain pass at this 1,186-foot-high perch guarded by 3,000-foot peaks, so hold on to your hat—and small children. But if you walk up from the parking lot to the precipice, you'll be rewarded with a view that'll blow you away. At the edge, the dizzying panorama of Oʻahu's windward side is breathtaking: Clouds low enough to pinch scoot by on trade winds; pinnacles of the pali (cliffs), green with ferns, often disappear in the mist. From on high, the tropical palette of green and blue runs down to the sea. Combine this 10-minute stop with a trip over the pali to the windward side.

Near the summit of Pali Hwy. (Hwy. 61); take the Nu'uanu Pali Lookout turnoff. Parking lot $7 per vehicle. Daily 6am–6pm.

Pu'u 'Ualaka'a State Wayside ★★★ STATE PARK/NATURAL ATTRACTION   The best **sunset view** of Honolulu is from a 1,048-foot-high hill named for sweet potatoes. Actually, the poetic Hawaiian name means "rolling sweet potato hill," for the way early planters used gravity to harvest their crop. The panorama is sweeping and majestic. On a clear day—which is often—you can see from Diamond Head to the Wai'anae Range, almost the length of O'ahu. At night, several scenic overlooks provide romantic spots high above the city lights.

2762 Round Top Dr. Free admission. Daily 7am–7:45pm. From Waikīkī, take Ala Wai Blvd. to McCully St., turn right, and drive *mauka* (inland) beyond the H-1 on-ramps to Wilder St.; turn left and go to Makiki St.; turn right, and continue onward and upward about 3 miles.

WALKING TOUR: **HISTORIC HONOLULU**

GETTING THERE:	**From Waikīkī, take Ala Moana Boulevard in the 'Ewa direction.Ala Moana Boulevard ends at Nimitz Highway. Turn right on the next street on your right (Alakea St.). Park in the garage across from St. Andrew's Church after you cross Beretania Street. Bus: 1L, 2L, 11, 20 40.**
START & FINISH:	**St. Andrew's Church, Beretania, and Alakea streets.**
TIME:	**2 to 3 hours, depending on how long you linger in museums.**
BEST TIMES:	**Monday through Saturday, daytime, when 'Iolani Palace is open.**

The 1800s were a turbulent time in Hawai'i. By the end of the 1790s, Kamehameha the Great had united all the islands. Foreigners then began arriving by ship—first explorers, then merchants, and then, in 1820, missionaries. By 1840, it was clear that the capital had shifted from Lahaina, where the Kingdom of Hawai'i was actually centered, to Honolulu, where the majority of commerce and trade was taking place. In 1848, the Great Mahele (division) enabled commoners and, eventually, foreigners to own crown land, and in two generations, more than 80% of all private lands had shifted to foreign ownership. With the introduction of sugar as a crop, the foreigners prospered, and in time they put more and more pressures on the government.

By 1872, the monarchy had run through the Kamehameha line and, in 1873, David Kalākaua was elected to the throne. Known as the "Merrie Monarch," Kalākaua redefined the monarchy by going on a world tour, building 'Iolani Palace, having a European-style coronation, and throwing extravagant parties. By the end of the 1800s, however, the foreign sugar growers and merchants had become extremely powerful in Hawai'i. With

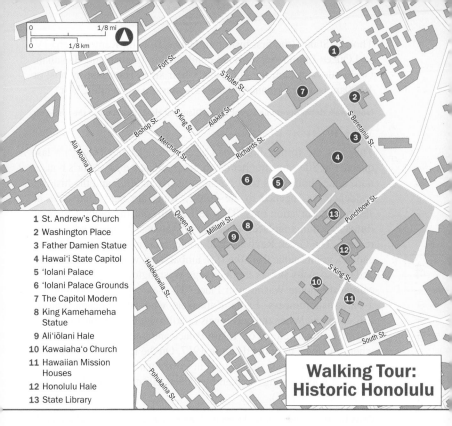

**Walking Tour:
Historic Honolulu**

1 St. Andrew's Church
2 Washington Place
3 Father Damien Statue
4 Hawaiʻi State Capitol
5 ʻIolani Palace
6 ʻIolani Palace Grounds
7 The Capitol Modern
8 King Kamehameha Statue
9 Aliʻiōlani Hale
10 Kawaiahaʻo Church
11 Hawaiian Mission Houses
12 Honolulu Hale
13 State Library

the assistance of the U.S. Marines, they orchestrated the overthrow of Queen Liliʻuokalani, Hawaiʻi's last reigning monarch, in 1893. The United States declared Hawaiʻi a territory in 1898.

You can witness the remnants of these turbulent years in just a few short blocks.

Cross the street from the garage and venture back to 1858 when you enter:

1 St. Andrew's Church

The Hawaiian monarchs were greatly influenced by the royals in Europe. When King Kamehameha IV saw the grandeur of the Church of England, he decided to build his own cathedral. He and Queen Emma founded the Anglican Church of Hawaiʻi in 1858. The king didn't live to see the church completed, however; he died on St. Andrew's Day, 4 years before King Kamehameha V oversaw the laying of the cornerstone in 1867. The church was named St. Andrew's in honor of King Kamehameha IV's death. This French-Gothic structure was shipped in pieces from England. Even if you aren't fond of visiting churches, you have to see the floor-to-eaves, hand-blown stained-glass window that faces the setting sun. In the glass is a mural of Rev.

Thomas Staley (the first bishop in Hawai'i), King Kamehameha IV, and Queen Emma. Services are conducted in English and Hawaiian. On Sundays at 8am the Hawaiian Choir sings Hawaiian hymns; at 10:00am is a performance by the 150-year-old Cathedral Choir.

Next, walk down Beretania Street in the Diamond Head direction to the gates of:

2 Washington Place

This was the former home of Queen Lili'uokalani, Hawai'i's last queen. For 80 years after her death, it served as the governor's house, until a new home was built on the property in 2002 and the historic residence was opened to the public. Tours are held Thursdays at 10am by reservation only. They're free; fill out the request form at (https://washingtonplacefoundation.org) at least 2 days in advance to reserve. The Greek Revival–style home, built in 1842 by a U.S. sea captain, got its name from the U.S. ambassador who once stayed here and told so many stories about George Washington that people started calling the home Washington Place. The sea captain's son married a Hawaiian princess, Lydia Kapaakea, who later became Queen Lili'uokalani. When the queen was overthrown by U.S. businessmen in 1893, she moved out of 'Iolani Palace and into Washington Place, where she lived until her death in 1917. On the left side of the building, near the sidewalk, is a plaque inscribed with the words to one of the most popular songs written by Queen Lili'uokalani, "Aloha Oe" ("Farewell to Thee").

Cross the street and walk to the front of the Hawai'i State Capitol, where you'll find the:

3 Father Damien Statue

The people of Hawai'i have never forgotten the sacrifice this Belgian priest made to help the sufferers of Hansen's disease (formerly known as leprosy) when he volunteered to work with them in exile on the Kalaupapa Peninsula on the island of Moloka'i. After 16 years of service, Father Damien himself died of the disease, at the age of 49. The statue is frequently draped in leis in recognition of Father Damien's humanitarian work.

Behind the Father Damien Statue is the:

4 Hawai'i State Capitol

Here's where Hawai'i's state legislators work from mid-January to the end of April every year. The building's unusual design has palm tree-shaped pillars, two cone-shaped chambers (representing volcanoes) for the legislative bodies, and an inner courtyard with a 600,000-tile mosaic of the sea (Aquarius) created by Tadashi Sato, a Hawai'i-born and world-renowned artist. A reflecting pool (representing the sea) surrounds the entire structure. Visitors are free to go into the rotunda and see the woven hangings and murals at the entrance or get a self-guided-tour brochure at the Legislative Reference Bureau website (https://lrb.hawaii.gov/par/at-the-capitol).

Walk down Richards Street toward the ocean and stop at:

5 'Iolani Palace

Hawai'i is the only state in the U.S. to have not one but two royal palaces: one in Kona, where the royals went during the summer, and 'Iolani Palace (*'Iolani* means "royal hawk").

Stained-glass windows inside St. Andrew's Church on Queen Emma Square.

Don't miss the opportunity to see this grande dame of historic buildings. Guided tours are $32.95 adults, $29.95 teens, $14.95 for children ages 5–12; self-guided audio tours are $26.95 adults, $21.95 teens, $11.95 children ages 5–12. Open Tuesday to Saturday 9am to 4pm; call ✆ **808/522-0832** or book online (www.iolanipalace.org) to reserve in advance.

In ancient times, a *heiau* (temple) stood in this area. When it became clear to King Kamehameha III that the capital should transfer from Lahaina to Honolulu, he moved to a modest building here in 1845. Construction on the palace was begun in 1879 by King David Kalākaua and was finished 3 years later at a cost of $350,000. He spared no expense, and the palace had all the modern conveniences for its time. Electric lights were installed 4 years before the White House had them, and every bedroom had its own bathroom with hot and cold running water, copper-lined tub, flush toilet, and bidet. The king had a telephone line from the palace to his boathouse a year after Alexander Graham Bell introduced it to the world.

It was also in this palace that Queen Lili'uokalani was overthrown and placed under house arrest for 9 months. Later, the territorial and then the state government used the palace until it outgrew it. When the legislature left in 1968, the palace was in shambles. It has since undergone a $7-million overhaul to restore it to its former glory.

After you visit the palace, spend some time on the:

6 'Iolani Palace Grounds

You can wander around the grounds at no charge. The ticket window to the palace and the gift shop are in the former barracks of the Royal Household Guards. The domed pavilion was originally built as a Coronation Stand by King Kalākaua (9 years after he took the throne, the king decided to have a formal European-style coronation ceremony where he crowned himself and his queen, Kapiʻolani). Later he used it as a **Royal Bandstand** for concerts (King Kalākaua, along with Henri Berger, the first Royal Hawaiian Bandmaster, wrote "Hawaiʻi Ponoʻī," the state anthem). Today, the Royal Hawaiian Band, founded in 1836 by King Kamehameha III, plays at the Royal Bandstand every Friday from noon to 1pm.

From the palace grounds, turn in the ʻEwa direction, cross Richards Street, and walk to the corner of Richards and Hotel streets to the:

A Royal Hawaiian Band performance on the grounds of ʻIolani Palace.

7 The Capitol Modern

Opened in 2002, the Hawaii State Art Museum is housed in the original Royal Hawaiian hotel, 250 South Hotel St. (on the second floor), built in 1872 during the reign of King Kamehameha V. In 2023, the museum got its new name: Capitol Modern (www.capitolmodern. org; free admission; Mon–Sat 10am–4pm). Local artists created most of the art in the 300-piece collection. The pieces were purchased by the state, thanks to a 1967 law that says that 1% of the cost of state buildings will be used to acquire works of art. Nearly 5 decades later, the state has amassed almost 6,000 pieces.

Walk *makai* down Richards Street and turn left (toward Diamond Head) on South King Street to the:

8 King Kamehameha Statue

At the juncture of King, Merchant, and Mililani streets stands a replica of the man who united the Hawaiian Islands. The striking black-and-gold bronze statue is magnificent. Try to see the statue on June 11 (King Kamehameha Day), when it is covered with leis in honor of Hawaiʻi's favorite son.

Thomas Gould cast the statue of Kamehameha I in 1880 in Paris. However, it was lost at sea somewhere near the Falkland Islands. Subsequently, the insurance money was used to pay for a second statue, but later, the original statue was recovered. The original was eventually sent to the town of Kapaʻau on Hawaiʻi Island, the birthplace of Kamehameha, and the second statue was placed in Honolulu in 1883, as part of King David Kalākaua's coronation ceremony.

9 Ali'iōlani Hale

The name translates to "House of Heavenly Kings." This distinctive building, with a clock tower, now houses the Supreme Court of Hawai'i and the Judiciary History Center. King Kamehameha V originally wanted to build a palace here and commissioned Australian architect Thomas Rowe in 1872. Kamehameha V didn't live to see it completed, and King David Kalākaua dedicated the building in 1874. Ironically, less than 20 years later, on January 17, 1893, Stanford Dole, backed by other prominent sugar planters, stood on the steps to this building and proclaimed the overthrow of the Hawaiian monarchy and the establishment of a provisional government.

Walk toward Diamond Head on King Street; at the corner of King and Punchbowl, stop in at the:

10 Kawaiaha'o Church

4

O'AHU | Walking Tour: Historic Honolulu

When the missionaries came to Hawai'i, the first thing they did was build churches. Four thatched-grass churches (one seats 300 people on lauhala mats; the last thatched church held 4,500 people) had been built on this site through 1837, before Rev. Hiram Bingham began building what he considered a "real" church: a New England–style congregational structure with Gothic influences. Between 1837 and 1842, the construction of the church required some 14,000 giant coral slabs (some weighing more than 1,000 lb.). Hawaiian divers ravaged the reefs, digging out huge chunks of coral and causing irreparable environmental damage.

Kawaiaha'o is Hawai'i's oldest church and has been the site of numerous historic events, such as a speech made by King Kamehameha III in 1843, an excerpt from which became Hawai'i's state motto (*Ua mau ke ea o ka aina i ka pono,* which translates as "The life of the land is preserved in righteousness").

The church is open Monday through Saturday 8am to 4pm. Don't sit in the back pews marked with feathered kahili staffs; they are still reserved for the descendants of royalty. Sunday service (in English and Hawaiian) is at 9:30am.

Cross the street, and you'll see the:

11 Hawaiian Mission Houses

On the corner of King and Kawaiaha'o streets stand the original buildings of the Sandwich Islands Mission Headquarters: the **Frame House** (built in 1821), the **Chamberlain House** (1831), and the **Printing Office** (1841). The complex is open Tuesday to Thursday and Saturday ($20 adults; $15 seniors and military personnel; $10 students and children ages 6 to college, with college identification), with advanced reservations strongly suggested. For information, go to www.missionhouses.org.

Believe it or not, the missionaries brought their own prefab house along with them when they came around Cape Horn from Boston in 1819. The Frame House was designed for New England winters and had small windows (it must have been stiflingly hot inside). Finished in 1821 (the interior frame was left behind and didn't arrive until Christmas 1820), it is Hawai'i's oldest wooden structure. Missionaries used Chamberlain House, built in 1831, as a storehouse.

The missionaries believed that the best way to spread the Lord's message to the Hawaiians was to learn their language, and then to print literature for them to read. So, it was the missionaries who gave the Hawaiians a written language. The Printing House on the grounds was where the lead-type Ramage press (brought from New England, of course) was used to print the Hawaiian Bible.

Cross King Street and walk in the 'Ewa direction to the corner of Punchbowl and King to:

12 Honolulu Hale

The **Honolulu City Hall,** built in 1927, was designed by Honolulu's most famous architect, C. W. Dickey. His Spanish Mission–style building has an open-air courtyard, which is used for art exhibits and concerts.

Cross Punchbowl Street and walk *mauka* to the:

13 State Library

Anything you want to know about Hawai'i and the Pacific can be found here, at the main branch of the state's library system. Located in a restored historic building, the cool air conditioning and open garden courtyard make it great for stopping for a rest on your walk.

Head down Beretania in the 'Ewa direction to Alakea back to the parking garage.

BEYOND HONOLULU: EXPLORING THE ISLAND BY CAR

Urban Honolulu, with its history, cuisine, and shopping, can captivate travelers for days. But the rest of the island draws them out with its promise of wild coastlines and unique adventures.

O'ahu's Southeast Coast

From the high-rises of Waikīkī, venture down Kalākaua Avenue through tree-lined **Kapi'olani Park** and beyond to take a look at a different side of O'ahu: the arid southeast shore. The landscape here is more moonscape, with cacti onshore and, in winter, spouting whales cavorting in the water.

To get to this coast, follow Kalākaua Avenue past the multi-tier Dill-ingham Fountain and around the bend in the road, which now becomes Poni Moi Road. Make a right on Diamond Head Road and begin the climb up the side of the old crater. Diamond Head State Monument now requires reservations through the State Parks Website. At the top are several look-out points, so if the official Diamond Head Lookout is jammed with cars, try one of the other lookouts just down the road. The view of the rolling waves and surfers is spectacular; take the time to pull over. This is also a wonderful place to begin your day early and watch the sun rise.

Diamond Head Road rolls downhill into the ritzy community of **Kahala.** At the fork in the road at the triangular Fort Ruger Park, veer to your right and continue on the palm tree-lined Kahala Avenue. Make a left on Hunakai Street, and then take a right on Kilauea Avenue and look for the sign, "H-1 west." Turn right at the sign, although you won't get on the H-1 freeway; instead, get on Kalaniana'ole Highway, a four-lane highway interrupted every few blocks by a stoplight. This is the suburban bedroom community to Honolulu, marked by malls on the left and beach parks on the right.

Drive far enough to leave the residential areas behind and you'll get to **Hanauma Bay** ★★ (p. 108); you'll see the turnoff on the right when you're about half an hour from Waikīkī. This marine preserve is one of the island's best places to snorkel; you'll find the friendliest fish on the island here. Reservations can be made online ahead of time, but they sell out quickly. *A reminder:* The bay is closed every Monday and Tuesday (no entry after 1:30pm).

Around mile marker 11, the jagged lava coast itself spouts sea foam at the **Halona Blowhole.** Look out to sea from Halona over Sandy Beach and across the 26-mile gulf to neighboring Moloka'i and the faint triangu-lar shadow of Lāna'i on the far horizon. **Sandy Beach** ★ (p. 109) is one of O'ahu's most dangerous beaches, with thundering shorebreak. Body-boarders just love it.

The coast looks raw and empty along this stretch as the road weaves past old Hawaiian fishponds and the famous formation known as **Pele's Chair,** just off Kalaniana'ole Highway (Hwy. 72) above Queen's Beach. From a distance, the lava-rock outcropping looks like a mighty throne; It's believed to be the fire goddess's last resting place on O'ahu before she flew off to continue her work on other islands.

Ahead lies 647-foot-high **Makapu'u Point,** with a lighthouse that once signaled safe passage for steamship passengers arriving from San Francisco. The automated light now brightens O'ahu's south coast for passing tankers, fishing boats, and sailors. You can take a short hike up the **Makapu'u Lighthouse Trail** ★★ (p. 119) for a spectacular vista.

Turn the corner at Makapu'u and you're on O'ahu's windward side, where trade winds propel windsurfers across turquoise bays; the waves at **Makapu'u Beach Park** ★ (p. 109) are perfect for bodysurfing.

Ahead, the coastal vista is a profusion of fluted green mountains and strange peaks, edged by golden beaches and the ever-blue Pacific. The 3,000-foot-high, sheer, green Koʻolau mountains plunge almost straight down, presenting an irresistible jumping-off spot for paragliders. Most likely, you'll spot their colorful chutes in the sky, looking like balloons released into the wind.

Winding up the coast, Kalanianaʻole Highway (Hwy. 72) leads through rural **Waimānalo,** a country beach town of plant nurseries and stables. Nearly 4 miles long, **Waimānalo Beach ★★** (p. 111) is Oʻahu's longest beach and popular with local families on weekends. Take a swim here or head on to **Lanikai Beach ★★★** (p. 109), one of Hawaiʻi's best.

The Windward Coast

From the **Nuʻuanu Pali Lookout ★**, near the summit of the Pali Highway (Hwy. 61), you get the first hint of the other side of Oʻahu, a region so green and lovely that it could be an island sibling of Tahiti. With its many beaches and bays, the scenic 30-mile Windward Coast parallels the corduroy-ridged, nearly perpendicular cliffs of the Koʻolau Range, which separates the windward side of the island from Honolulu and the rest of Oʻahu. As you descend on the serpentine Pali Highway beneath often-gushing waterfalls, you'll see the nearly 1,000-foot spike of **Olomana,** a bold pinnacle that beckons intrepid hikers, and, beyond, the town of **Waimānalo,** where many of Native Hawaiian descent live.

From the Pali Highway to the right is Kailua, Hawaiʻi's biggest beach town, with more than 50,000 residents and two special beaches, **Kailua Beach ★★★** (p. 110) and **Lanikai Beach ★★★** (p. 109). You can easily spend an entire day in Kailua, which I absolutely recommend, whether to laze on the sand or stand-up paddle to the Mokuloa Islands. But Kailua isn't all beach: Chic boutiques line the streets, and you can grab a shave ice at **Island Snow.**

After whiling away a day in Kailua, allocate another day for exploring the rest of the Windward coast. Take Highway 830N, which goes through Kāneʻohe and then follows the coast to Heʻeia State Park. Here, you'll find **Heʻeia Fish Pond,** which ancient Hawaiians built by enclosing natural bays with rocks to trap fish on the incoming tide. The 88-acre fish pond, which is made of lava rock and had four watchtowers to observe fish movement and several sluice gates along the 5,000-foot-long wall, is now in the process of being restored.

Drive onto **Heʻeia Pier,** which juts onto Kāneʻohe Bay. You can take a snorkel cruise here or sail out to a sandbar in the middle of the bay for an incredible view of Oʻahu that most people, even those who live here, never see. Incredibly scenic Kāneʻohe Bay is spiked with islets and lined with gold-sand beach parks like **Kualoa Regional Park ★** (p. 111), a favorite picnic spot. The bay has a barrier reef and four tiny islets, one of which is known as Moku o loe, or Coconut Island. Don't be surprised if it looks familiar—it appeared in *Gilligan's Island.*

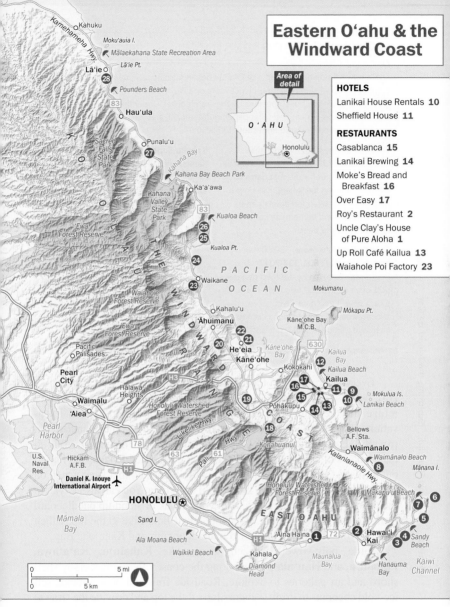

Eastern Oʻahu & the Windward Coast

Kamehameha Hwy.
Kahuku
Mokuʻauia I.
Mālaekahana State Recreation Area
Lāʻie Pt.
Lāʻie **28**
Pounders Beach
Hauʻula
Punaluʻu **27**
Kahana Bay
Kahana Bay Beach Park
Kaʻaʻawa
Kahana Valley State Park
Kualoa Beach
Kualoa Pt.
26
25
24
Waikane **23**

Sacred Falls State Park
ʻEwa Forest Reserve
Waiahole Forest Reserve
ʻEwa Forest Reserve
Pacific Palisades

PACIFIC OCEAN
Mokumanu
Mōkapu Pt.
Kāneʻohe Bay M.C.B.

Kahaluʻu
ʻĀhuimanu
22
He‘eia **21**
20
Kāneʻohe
Kāneʻohe Bay
Kokokahi
630
Kailua Bay
Kailua Beach
12
17
16
Kailua
11
9
15
Pōhākupu
14
13
10
Mokulua Is.
Lanikai Beach
Mokumanu

Pearl City
Waimalu
ʻAiea
Hālawa Heights
Honolulu Watershed Forest Reserve
H3
19
Likelike Hwy.

Pearl Harbor
U.S. Naval Res.
Hickam A.F.B.
Daniel K. Inouye International Airport
78
63
61
Pali Hwy.
18
Konahuanui
Hwy. 61
Bellows A.F. Sta.
Waimānalo
Waimānalo Beach
8
Mānana I.
Kalanianaole Hwy.

HONOLULU
Sand I.
Māmala Bay
Ala Moana Beach
Waīkīkī Beach
Kahala
Diamond Head
ʻAina Haina
1
72
2
Hawaiʻi Kai
3
4
Sandy Beach
Maunalua Bay
Hanauma Bay
Kaīwi Channel
5
7
6
Makapuʻu Beach
EAST OʻAHU

Honolulu Watershed Forest Reserve

0 ___ 5 mi
0 ___ 5 km

Area of detail
OʻAHU
Honolulu

HOTELS
Lanikai House Rentals **10**
Sheffield House **11**

RESTAURANTS
Casablanca **15**
Lanikai Brewing **14**
Moke's Bread and
  Breakfast **16**
Over Easy **17**
Roy's Restaurant **2**
Uncle Clay's House
  of Pure Aloha **1**
Up Roll Café Kailua **13**
Waiahole Poi Factory **23**

ATTRACTIONS

Ching's Punaluu Store **27**
Halona Blowhole **3**
Heeia Fish Pond **21**
Heeia Pier **22**
Hoomaluhia Botanical Gardens **19**
Kailua Beach **12**

Kualoa Ranch **26**
Kualoa Regional Park **25**
Lanikai Beach **9**
Makapuʻu Beach Park **7**
Makapuʻu Point **6**
Nuʻuanu Pali Lookout **18**

Pele's Chair **5**
Polynesian Cultural Center **28**
Sandy Beach **4**
Valley of the Temples **20**
Waikane Store **24**
Waimānalo Beach **8**

HAWAI'I'S general stores

The windward side harbors some of O'ahu's best remaining general stores—Hawai'i's mom-and-pop version of a convenience store or a New York bodega. Here, nostalgia is sold alongside the boiled peanuts by the cash register. Under the same roof, you might find smoked meat and toilet paper, butter mochi, and fishing supplies. Here are three of our favorites (listed from south to north):

Waikane Store, 48-377 Kamehameha Hwy. (© **808/239-8522**): Locals pop into this little lime-green store that dates back to 1898. Nothing fancy here, just simple maki sushi rolls wrapped in wax paper, fried chicken, and homemade cookies—all perfect for the beach.

Ching's Punalu'u Store, 53-360 Kamehameha Hwy. (© **808/237-7017**): This bright-red store, run by the third generation, offers all the local favorites—from chili to soft serve. Don't miss the butter mochi—a local sweet treat made with glutinous rice flour. It's pure, chewy comfort.

Kahuku Superette ★★★, 56-505 Kamehameha Hwy. (© **808/293-9878**): Kahuku's shrimp trucks may entice with their potent, garlicky smells, but absolutely don't miss the poke (seasoned raw fish) from Kahuku Superette. If you're not afraid of kimchi, get the special poke: fresh ahi tuna with a housemade, fermented, gingery paste that's sure to waken your taste buds. Want something milder? Try the shoyu poke. This nondescript store is a must-stop for many of Honolulu's notable chefs.

Everyone calls the other distinctively shaped island **Chinaman's Hat,** but It's really named **Mokoli'i.** It's a sacred *puu honua,* or place of refuge, like the restored Pu'uhonua O Hōnaunau on Hawai'i Island. Excavations have unearthed evidence that this area was the home of ancient *alii* (royalty). Early Hawaiians believed that Mokoli'i (Fin of the Lizard) is all that remains of a *mo'o,* or lizard, slain by Pele's sister, Hiiaka, and hurled out to sea. At low tide you can swim out to the island, but keep watch on the changing tide, which can sweep you out to sea. You can also kayak to the island; park your car and launch your kayak or stand-up paddleboard from Kualoa Regional Park. It's about a half-hour hike to the top, which rewards you with views of the Ko'olau mountains and Kāne'ohe Bay.

Little poly-voweled beach towns like **Kahalu'u, Ka'a'awa, Punalu'u,** and **Hau'ula** pop up along the coast, offering passersby shell shops and art galleries to explore. Roadside fruit and flower stands sell ice-cold coconuts to drink (vendors lop off the top and provide the straws) and tree-ripened mangoes, papayas, and apple bananas (short bananas with a tart apple aftertaste).

Sugar, once the sole industry of this region, is gone. But **Kahuku,** the former sugar-plantation town, has found new life as a small aquaculture community with shrimp farms. Not all of the shrimp trucks use local shrimp, however—**Romy's** is one of the few, while the perpetually popular Giovanni's cooks up imported, frozen shrimp. Definitely stop for a poke bowl at **Kahuku Superette** (see above).

From here, continue along Kamehameha Highway (Hwy. 83) to the North Shore.

Attractions Along the Windward Coast

The attractions below are arranged geographically as you drive up the coast from south to north.

Hoomaluhia Botanical Garden ★ GARDEN   This 400-acre botanical garden at the foot of the steepled Ko'olau Range is the perfect place for a picnic. Its name means "a peaceful refuge," and that's exactly what the Army Corps of Engineers created when they installed a flood-control project here, which resulted in a 32-acre freshwater lake and garden. Just unfold a beach mat, lie back, and watch the clouds race across the rippled cliffs of the majestic Ko'olau Mountains. This is one of the few public places on O'ahu that provides a close-up view of the steepled cliffs. The park has hiking trails and a lovely, quiet campground (p. 138). If you like hiking and nature, plan to spend a half-day here. *Note:* Be prepared for rain, mud, and mosquitoes.

45-680 Luluku Rd., Kāne'ohe. ✆ **808/233-7323.** Free admission. Daily 9am–4pm. Take H-1 to the Pali Hwy. (Hwy. 61); turn left on Kamehameha Hwy. (Hwy. 83); at the 4th light, turn left onto Luluku Rd. Bus: 60 will stop on Kamehameha Hwy.; It's a 2-mile walk to the visitor center.

Kualoa Ranch ★★ ACTIVITY PARK   In recent years, Kualoa Ranch has been going back to its roots. It has revived its cattle operations and is now a working ranch. In addition to raising livestock on the land, it developed an aquaculture program in an ancient Hawaiian fishpond, dating back between 800 to 1,000 years ago. You'll find Kualoa Ranch shrimp and oysters on menus all over Honolulu. On the Taste of Kualoa Farm Tour, you can visit the fishpond and learn more about native Hawaiian practices of fish farming. In more modern times, Kualoa Ranch and its 4,000 lush acres and dramatic valleys have also been the backdrop for many movies. Adventure packages include ATV rides through the locations where movies like *Jurassic Park* and *Godzilla* were filmed. You can also take horseback rides or get your adrenaline going while flying through the treetops on the zipline.

49-560 Kamehameha Hwy., Ka'a'awa. www.kualoa.com. ✆ **800/237-7321.** Reservations recommended. Various packages available; single activities $50–$250. Daily 7:30am–6:00pm. Take H-1 to the Likelike Hwy. (Hwy. 63), turn left at Kahekili Hwy. (Hwy. 83), and continue to Ka'a'awa. Bus: 60.

Polynesian Cultural Center ★ THEME PARK   This is the Disneyland version of Polynesia, operated by the Mormon Church. It's a great show for families, informative and fun (the droll Samoan presentation amuses both adults and children). Here you can see the lifestyles, songs, dance, costumes, and architecture of six Pacific islands or archipelagos—Fiji, New Zealand, Samoa, Tahiti, Tonga, and Hawai'i—in the re-created villages scattered throughout the 42-acre park. You won't be able to see it all in a day, but a day is enough for a great experience.

Native students from Polynesia who attend Hawai'i's Brigham Young University are the "inhabitants" of each village. They engage the audience with spear-throwing competitions, coconut tree-climbing presentations, and invitations to pound Tongan drums. Don't miss the recently returned canoe pageant, daily at 2:30pm; each island puts on a representation of their dance, music, and costume atop canoes in the lagoon.

Ha: Breath of Life is a coming-of-age story told through different Polynesian dances, some full of grace, some fierce, and all thrilling. It's one of O'ahu's better shows and another must-see experience here.

The Polynesian Cultural Center.

Just beyond the center is the **Hawaii Temple of the Church of Jesus Christ of Latter-day Saints,** built of volcanic rock and concrete in the form of a Greek cross; it includes reflecting pools, formal gardens, and royal palms. Completed in 1919, it was the first Mormon temple built outside the continental United States. An optional tour of the Temple Visitors Center, as well as neighboring Brigham Young University Hawaii, is included in the package admission price.

55-370 Kamehameha Hwy., La'ie. www.polynesia.com. ✆ **800/367-7060** or 808/293-3333. Packages available for $89.95–$289.95 adults and $71.96–$231.96 children ages 4–11. Mon–Tues and Thurs–Sat 12:30am–9pm. Take H-1 to Pali Hwy. (Hwy. 61) and turn left on Kamehameha Hwy. (Hwy. 83). Bus: 60.

Valley of the Temples ★ HISTORIC SITE   This famous cemetery is in a cleft of the pali. Wild peacocks stroll among the nearly 700 curious daily visitors, who pay to see the 9-foot meditation Buddha, acres of ponds full of more than 10,000 Japanese koi carp, and a replica of Japan's 900-year-old Byodo-In Temple of Equality. The original, made of wood, stands in Uji, on the outskirts of Kyoto; the Hawai'i version, made of concrete, was erected in 1968 to commemorate the 100th anniversary of the arrival of the first Japanese immigrants to Hawai'i. It's not the same as seeing the original, but It's worth a detour.

47-200 Kahekili Hwy. (across the street from Ko'olau Center), Kāne'ohe. www.byodo-in.com. ✆ **808/239-8811.** $5 adults, $4 seniors, $2 children ages 2–12. No cash. Daily 8:30am–4:30pm. Take the H-1 to the Likelike Hwy. (Hwy. 63); after the Wilson Tunnel, get in the right lane and take the Kahekili Hwy. (Hwy. 63); at the 6th traffic light is the entrance to the cemetery (on the left). Bus: 65.

Central O'ahu & the North Shore

If you can afford the splurge, rent a convertible—the perfect car for O'ahu to enjoy the sun and soaring views—and head for the North Shore and Hawai'i's surf city: **Hale'iwa ★★★**, a former sugar-plantation town and a designated historic site. Although in recent years, Hale'iwa has been spruced up—even the half-century old, formerly dusty **Matsumoto Shave Ice** (p. 158) has new digs now—it still maintains a surfer/hippie vibe around the edges. For more, see "Surf City: Hale'iwa," below.

Getting there is half the fun. You have two choices: The first is to meander north along the lush Windward Coast, following the coastline lined with roadside stands selling mangoes, bright tropical pareu, fresh corn, and pond-raised prawns. The previous section describes the attractions along this route.

The second choice is to cruise up the H-2 through O'ahu's broad and fertile central valley, past Pearl Harbor and the Schofield Barracks of *From Here to Eternity* fame, and on through the red-earthed heart of the island, where pineapple and sugarcane fields stretch from the Ko'olau to the Wai'anae mountains, until the sea reappears on the horizon.

Once you're on H-1, stay to the right side; the freeway divides abruptly. Keep following the signs for the H-1 (it separates off to Hwy. 78 at the airport and reunites later on; either way will get you there), and then the H-1/H-2. Leave the H-1 where the two highways divide; take the H-2 up the middle of the island, toward the town of Wahiawā. That's what the sign will say—not North Shore or Hale'iwa, but Wahiawā.

The H-2 runs out and becomes a two-lane country road about 18 miles outside downtown Honolulu, near Schofield Barracks. The highway becomes Kamehameha Highway (Hwy. 99 and later Hwy. 83) at Wahiawā. Just past Wahiawā, about a half-hour out of Honolulu, the **Dole Plantation,** 64-1550 Kamehameha Hwy. (www.doleplantation.com; *©* **808/621-8408;** daily 9:30am–5:30pm; bus: 52), offers a rest stop, with pineapples, pineapple history, pineapple trinkets, pineapple juice, and Dole Whip, a pineapple soft serve. This agricultural exhibit/retail area features a train ride and maze that kids will love to wander through; It's open daily from 9:30am to 5:30pm (activities start at $8 adults, $7.25 children 4–12).

"Kam" Highway, as everyone calls it, will be your road for most of the rest of the trip to Hale'iwa, on the North Shore.

CENTRAL O'AHU ATTRACTIONS

On the central plains of O'ahu, tract homes and malls with factory-outlet stores are now spreading across former sugarcane fields. Hawaiian chiefs once sent commoners into thick sandalwood forests to cut down trees, which were then sold to China traders for small fortunes.

Kūkaniloko Birthing Stones ★ HISTORIC SITE   This is the most sacred site in central O'ahu. Two rows of 18 lava rocks once flanked a central birthing stone, where women of ancient Hawai'i gave birth to

Surfing can be a family affair.

potential *ali'i* (royalty). The rocks, according to Hawaiian belief, held the power to ease the labor pains of childbirth. Birth rituals involved 48 chiefs who pounded drums to announce the arrival of newborns likely to become chiefs. Used by O'ahu's *ali'i* for generations of births, the *pōhaku* (rocks), many in bowl-like shapes, now lie strewn in a grove of trees that stands in a pineapple field here. Some think the site may also have served ancient astronomers—like a Hawaiian Stonehenge. Petroglyphs of human forms and circles appear on some stones.

Off Kamehameha Hwy., btw. Wahiawā and Hale'iwa, on Plantation Rd., opposite the road to Whitmore Village.

NORTH SHORE ATTRACTIONS

Pu'u o Mahuka Heiau ★ HISTORIC SITE   Go around sundown to feel the *mana* (sacred spirit) of this Hawaiian place. The largest sacrificial temple on O'ahu, It's associated with the great Kaopulupulu, who sought peace between O'ahu and Kaua'i. This prescient *kahuna* predicted that the island would be overrun by strangers from a distant land. In 1794, three of Capt. Vancouver's men of the *Daedalus* were sacrificed here. In 1819, the year before missionaries landed in Hawai'i, King Kamehameha II ordered all idols here to be destroyed.

A national historic landmark, this 18th-century *heiau,* known as the "hill of escape," sits on a 300-foot bluff overlooking Waimea Bay and 25 miles of O'ahu's wave-lashed north coast—all the way to Kaena Point, where the Wai'anae Range ends in a spirit leap to the other world. The *heiau* appears as a huge rectangle of rocks twice as big as a football field, with an altar often covered by the flower and fruit offerings left by native Hawaiians.

1 mile past Waimea Bay. Take Pupukea Rd. *mauka* (inland) off Kamehameha Hwy. at Foodland, and drive 1 mile up a switchback road. Bus: 60, then walk up Pupukea Rd.

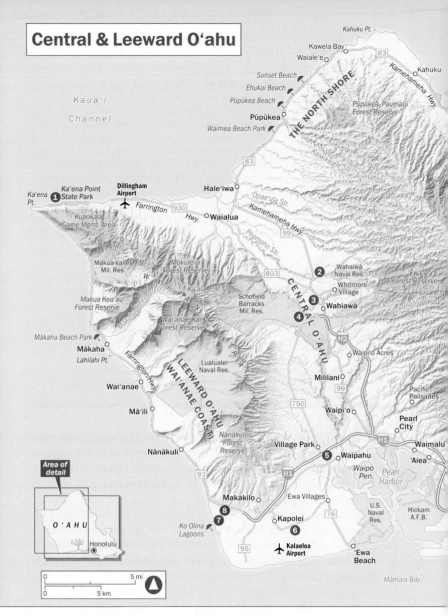

Central & Leeward Oʻahu

Kauaʻi Channel

Kahuku Pt.

Kawela Bay
Waialeʻe
83
Kamehameha Hwy.
Kahuku

THE NORTH SHORE

Sunset Beach
Ehukai Beach
Pūpūkea Beach
Pūpūkea
Waimea Beach Park

Pūpūkea-Paumalū
Forest Reserve

Kaiwikoʻele Str.

Kauaʻi
Channel

83

Kaʻena Point
State Park **1**
Kaʻena
Pt.

Kuaokalā
Game Mgmt. Area

**Dillingham
Airport**
✈
Farrington

Haleʻiwa

ʻŌpaeʻula Str.

930

Kamehameha Hwy.

Hwy. **Waialua**

Poʻomoho Str.

99

Mākua Valley
Mil. Res.

Mokuleʻia
Forest Reserve

803

Wahiawā
Naval Res.
2

ʻEwa
Forest Reserve

Kaʻala

Whitmore
Village

Makua Keaʻau
Forest Reserve

Waiʻanae Kai
Forest Reserve

Schofield
Barracks
Mil. Res.

3 **Wahiawā**

Kaukonahua Str.

Mākaha Beach Park

4

H2

Mākaha
Lahilahi Pt.

Waiʻanae

Lualualei
Naval Res.

Waipiʻo Acres

Mililani

99

Pacific
Palisades

Farrington Hwy.

Māʻili

750

Waipiʻo

**Pearl
City**

WAIʻANAE COAST

LEEWARD OʻAHU

WAIʻANAE RANGE

CENTRAL OʻAHU

H1

Waimalu

Nānākuli
Forest
Reserve

Village Park

5 **Waipahu**

ʻAiea

Nānākuli

93

H1

Waipo
Pen.

Waipahu

Pearl
Harbor

Makakilo

ʻEwa Villages

U.S.
Naval
Res.

Hickam
A.F.B.

8

Kapolei

76

Ko Olina
Lagoons

7

6

95

✈ **Kalaeloa
Airport**

ʻEwa
Beach

Māmala Bay

**Area of
detail**

OʻAHU

Honolulu ⊛

0 ——————— 5 mi
0 ——————— 5 km

ATTRACTIONS

Dole Plantation **2**
Hawaii's Plantation Village **5**
Hawaiian Railway **6**
Kaʻena Point State Park **1**
Kūkaniloko Birthing Stones **3**
Schofield Barracks **4**

HOTELS

Aulani, a Disney Resort & Spa,
Ko Olina Hawaiʻi **7**

RESTAURANTS

Monkeypod Kitchen **8**

103

SURF CITY: Hale'iwa

Only 28 miles from Waikīkī, **Hale'iwa ★★★**, is a funky, former sugar-plantation town that's now the world capital of big-wave surfing. Hale'iwa comes alive in winter, when the waves rise and surfers the world over come here to see and be seen. Officially designated a historic cultural and scenic district, this beach town was founded by sugar baron Benjamin Dillingham, who built a 30-mile railroad to link his Honolulu and North Shore plantations in 1899. He opened a Victorian hotel overlooking Kaiaka Bay and named it Hale'iwa, or "house of the 'iwa," the tropical seabird often seen here. The hotel and railroad are gone, but the town of Hale'iwa, which was rediscovered in the late 1960s by hippies, manages to hold onto some of its rustic charm. Of course, like other places on O'ahu, that is changing; some of the older wooden storefronts are being redeveloped and local chains such as T&C Surf are moving in. Arts and crafts, boutiques, and burger joints line both sides of the town. There's also a busy fishing harbor full of charter boats and captains who hunt for tuna, mahi-mahi, and marlin.

Just down the road are the fabled shrines of surfing—**Waimea Beach, Banzai Pipeline, Sunset Beach**—where some of the world's largest waves, reaching 20 feet and higher, rise up between November and January. November to December is the holding period for **Vans Triple Crown of Surfing** (https://vanstriplecrownofsurfing.com), one of the world's premier surf competition series, when professional surfers from around the world descend on the 7-mile miracle of waves. Hang around Hale'iwa and the North Shore and you're bound to run into a few of the pros. Battle the traffic to come up on competition days (when it seems like everyone ditches work and heads north): It's one of O'ahu's best shows. For details on North Shore beaches, see p. 111.

Waimea Valley ★★ NATURAL ATTRACTION For nearly 3 decades, this 1,875-acre park has lured visitors with activities from cliff diving and hula performances to kayaking and ATV tours. The Office of Hawaiian Affairs formed a nonprofit corporation, Hi'ipaka, to run the park, with an emphasis on perpetuating and sharing the "living Hawaiian culture." Think of it as the antidote to the heavily commercialized Polynesian Cultural Center. A visit here offers a lush walk into the past. The valley is packed with archaeological sites, including the 600-year-old Hale O Lono, a *heiau* dedicated to the Hawaiian god Lono, the god of peace, fertility, and agriculture. The botanical collection has 35 different gardens, including super-rare Hawaiian species such as the endangered *Kokia cookei* hibiscus. The valley is also home to fauna such as the endangered *'alae 'ula,* or Hawaiian moorhen; look for a black bird with a red face cruising in the ponds. The 150-acre Arboretum and Botanical Garden contains more than 5,000 species of tropical plants. Included with admission are guided tours in which you can learn more about plants here and daily sessions like at the Hawaiian games site, where you can participate in *'ulu maika* and *moa pahe'e* (games of skill), *konane* (a game of strategy), and *'o'o 'ihe* (a game of strength). Check the website for potential

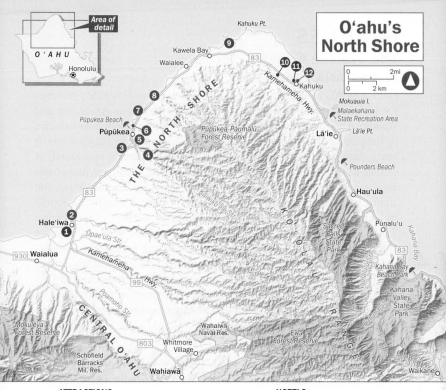

O'ahu's North Shore

ATTRACTIONS

Banzai Pipeline (Ehukai Beach Park) **7**
Hale'iwa Beach Park **2**
Kahuku Superette **12**
Pu'u o Mahuka Heiau **5**
Shark's Cove, Pupukea Beach Park **6**
Sunset Beach **8**
Waimea Beach Park **3**
Waimea Valley **4**

HOTELS

Turtle Bay Resort **9**

RESTAURANTS

Beet Box Café **1**
Hale'iwa Beach House **1**
Hale'iwa Joes **1**
Island Vintage Coffee **1**
Kahuku Farms **10**
Matsumoto Shave Ice **1**
Shrimp trucks **11**

closings due to weather. Journey all the way into the back of the valley, and you'll find one of the area's highlights: a beautiful, easily accessible waterfall with clear, fresh waters and a picturesque pool that makes for an attractive swimming hole. Lifeguards are always on duty, and life jackets are required, so this is a swimming experience ideal for newbie swimmers or those wary about the Pacific Ocean's often unpredictable waves. Waterfall access is dependent on daily conditions—lifeguards make a safety call every day at around 9am.

59-864 Kamehameha Hwy. www.waimeavalley.net. ✆ **808/638-7766.** $25 adults, $20 seniors, $15 children ages 4–12. Daily 9am–4pm. Bus: 60.

BEACHES
The Waikīkī Coast

ALA MOANA BEACH PARK ★★

Gold-sand Ala Moana (meaning "path to the sea" in Hawaiian) stretches for more than a mile along Honolulu's coast between downtown and Waikīkī. This 76-acre midtown beach park, with spreading lawns shaded by banyans and palms, is one of the island's most popular playgrounds. It has a manmade beach, created in the 1930s by filling in marshland, as well as its own lagoon, yacht harbor, tennis courts, music pavilion, bathhouses, picnic tables, and wide-open green spaces. The water is calm almost year-round, protected by a reef just offshore. It's easily accessible by a large parking lot, making this the beach for locals who like to leave Waikīkī to the tourists. There's also lots of space to spread out, whether you're part of a family with small children looking to do some close-to-shore wading, or a more serious lap swimmer venturing slightly farther out to traverse the buoy courses that also attract paddleboarders and kayakers. Just beyond the reef is a popular surf break, so you're likely to come across surfers paddling through the gaggles of water-goers, on their way through to catch some waves.

WAIKĪKĪ BEACH ★★

It's hard to think of a beach as widely known or universally sought after as this narrow, 1½-mile-long crescent of sand (artificially deposited there from offshore sites) at the foot of a string of high-rise hotels. Waikīkī attracts nearly 5 million visitors a year from every corner of the planet, and unfortunately, It's beginning to show in terms of crowds. Definitely

Waikīkī Beach is one of the island's most popular.

Beaches & Outdoor Activities on O'ahu

BEACHES

Ala Moana Beach Park 1
Banzai Pipeline 24
Hanauma Bay 7
Kailua Beach 13
Kualoa Regional Park 18
Lanikai Beach 12
Mākaha Beach Park 28
Makapu'u Beach Park 10
Sandy Beach 8
Sunset Beach 23
Waikīkī Beach 2
Waimānalo Beach 11
Waimea Beach Park 25
Yokohama Bay 27

HIKES

Diamond Head Crater 4
Ka'ena Point 26
Koko Crater Railway Trail 6
Kuli'ou'ou Ridge Trail 5
Makapu'u Lighthouse Trail 9
Mānoa Falls Trail 15
Pali (Maunawili) Trail 16

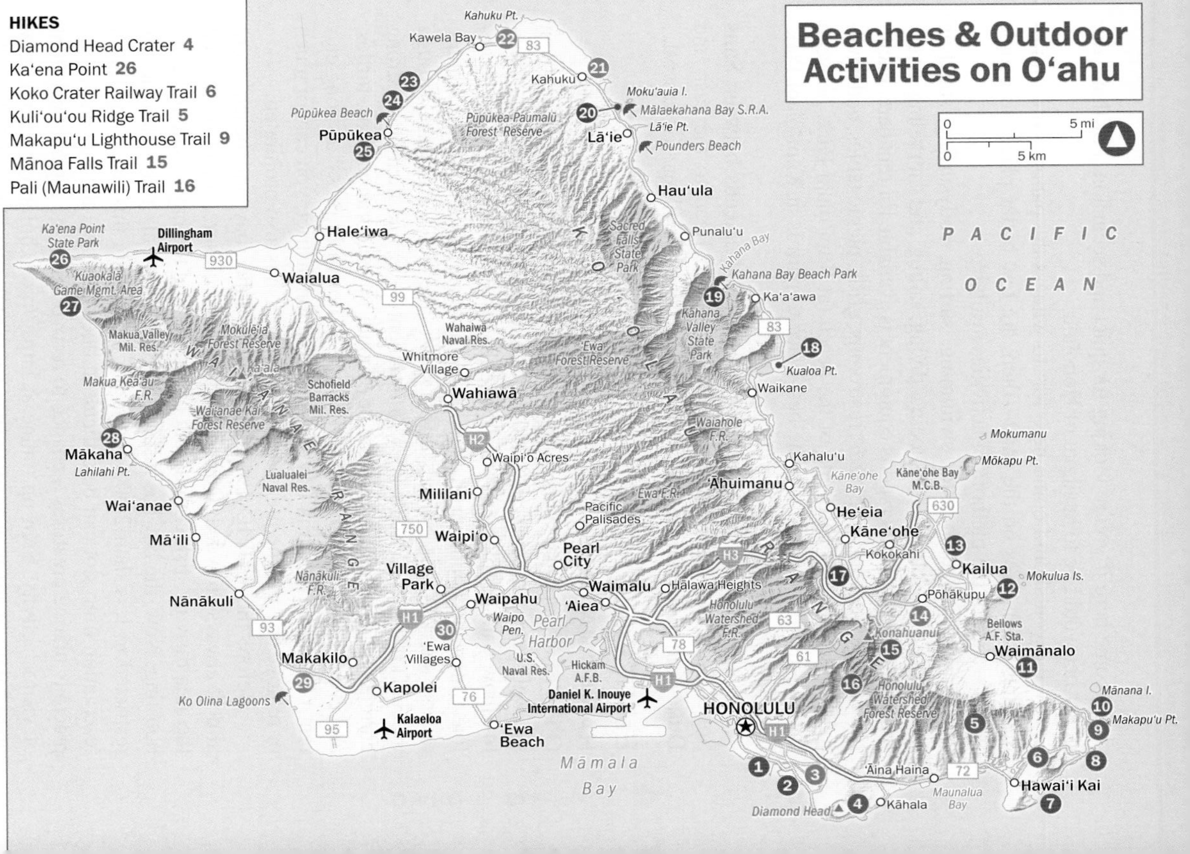

CABINS & CAMPGROUNDS

Hoomaluhia Botanical
Garden 17
Kahana Bay Beach Park 19
Mālaekahana Bay State
Recreation Area 20

GOLF COURSES

Ala Wai Municipal Golf
Course 3
Kahuku Golf Course 21
Ko 'Olina Golf Club 29
Royal Hawaiian Golf Club 14
Turtle Bay Resort 22
West Loch Municipal
Golf Course 30

107

don't come here if you're looking for quiet and seclusion. For that, your better bet would be to head out of Honolulu.

What you should come here for: to witness the panoply of cultures sunning themselves on the sand—there are few better places to people watch—and for the plethora of activities available.

Waikīkī is fabulous for swimming, surfing, bodysurfing, stand-up paddle boarding, outrigger canoeing, diving, sailing, and snorkeling. Every imaginable type of watersports equipment is available for rent here. Facilities include showers, lifeguards, restrooms, grills, picnic tables, and pavilions at the **Queen's Surf** end of the beach (at Kapiʻolani Park, between the zoo and the aquarium). The best place to park is at Kapiʻolani Park, near Sans Souci.

Waikīkī is actually a string of beaches that extends between **Sans Souci State Recreational Area,** near Diamond Head to the east, and **Duke Kahanamoku Beach,** at the Hilton Hawaiian Village to the west.

East Oʻahu

HANAUMA BAY ★★

Oʻahu's most popular snorkeling spot is this volcanic crater with a broken sea wall; its small, curved, 2,000-foot gold-sand beach is packed elbow-to-elbow with people year-round. The inner bay's shallow (10-ft.) shoreline water and abundant marine life is the main attraction as a vibrant, diverse snorkel spot. Serious divers shoot "the slot" (a passage through the reef) to get to Witch's Brew, a turbulent cove, and then brave strong currents in 70-foot depths at the bay mouth to see coral gardens, turtles, and even sharks. (*Divers:* Beware of the Molokaʻi Express, a strong current.) Because Hanauma Bay is a conservation district, you cannot touch or remove any marine life here. Feeding the fish is also prohibited.

Before the COVID-19 pandemic, the inner bay and beach, were almost always crowded. During the pandemic closure, scientists noticed the area thriving, fish coming out of hiding, and the bay's general health boosting. Now, the bay has instated a reservation-only policy, and access restricted to less than 2,000 guests per day. While this means getting a reservation time slot can be difficult, it does also give the bay and all its precious marine creatures a chance to recover from the typical onslaught of visitor activity. Sign up online at https://pros6.hnl.info/hanauma-bay up to 2 days in advance or try to snag some of the very limited daily walk-in slots at 6:45am each morning.

Facilities include parking, restrooms, a pavilion, a grass volleyball court, lifeguards, barbecues, picnic tables, and food concessions. Alcohol is prohibited in the park; there is no smoking past the visitor center. Expect to pay $3 per vehicle to park (with no in-out privileges) plus an entrance fee of $25 per person (free for children 12 and under, military I.D. holders, and Hawaiʻi residents).

If you're driving, take Kalanianaʻole Highway to Koko Head Regional Park. Avoid the crowds by going early, before the gate opens at

6:45am; once the parking lot's full, you're out of luck. Alternatively, take TheBus to escape the parking problem: The 1L runs from Lunalilo Home Road and Kalaniana'ole Highway, which is about a 23-minute (uphill!) walk from the parking lot entrance to the bay. For information, call © **808/ 768-6861** or visit https://hanaumabaystatepark.com. Hanauma Bay is closed every Monday and Tuesday so that the fish can have a day off, but It's open all other days from 6:45am to 4pm. No entry after 1:30pm, guests need to clear the beach by 3:15pm.

SANDY BEACH ★

Sandy Beach is one of the best bodysurfing beaches on O'ahu; It's also one of the most dangerous. It's better to just stand and watch the daredevils literally risk their necks at this 1,200-foot-long gold-sand beach, which is pounded by wild waves and haunted by a dangerous shore break and strong backwash. Weak swimmers, or those who don't have experience in rough ocean conditions or among treacherous shore breaks, and children, should definitely stay out of the water here.

Facilities include restrooms and parking. Go weekdays to avoid the crowds or weekends to catch the bodysurfers in action. From Waikīkī, drive east on the H-1, which becomes Kalaniana'ole Highway; proceed past Hawaii Kai, up the hill to Hanauma Bay, past the Halona Blowhole, and along the coast. The next big gold beach on the right is Sandy Beach. TheBus no. 23 will bring you here.

MAKAPU'U BEACH PARK ★

Makapu'u Beach is a beautiful 1,000-foot-long gold-sand beach cupped by the stark Ko'olau cliffs on O'ahu's easternmost point. Even if you never venture into the water, It's worth a visit just to enjoy the great natural beauty of this classic Hawaiian beach. (You've probably already seen it in countless TV shows, from *Hawaii Five-O* to *Magnum, P.I.*) In summer, the ocean here is as gentle as a Jacuzzi, and swimming and diving are perfect; come winter, however, and Makapu'u is a hit with expert bodysurfers, who come for the big, pounding waves that are too dangerous for most regular swimmers.

Facilities include restrooms, lifeguards, barbecue grills, picnic tables, and parking. To get here, follow Kalaniana'ole Highway toward Waimānalo, or take TheBus no. 23.

The Windward Coast

LANIKAI BEACH ★★★

One of Hawai'i's best spots for swimming, gold-sand Lanikai's crystalclear lagoon is like a giant saltwater swimming pool that you're lucky enough to be able to share with the resident tropical fish and sea turtles. Almost too gorgeous to be real, this is one of Hawai'i's postcard-perfect beaches: It's a mile long and thin in places, but the sand's as soft as talcum powder. Kayakers or stand-up paddlers often head out to the two tiny offshore Mokulua Islands, which are seabird sanctuaries. Unfortunately, Lanikai is no longer a secret—the residential community that lives along the beach has fought against the tourist hordes and erected strict parking rules. So, the bad news is that parking is now limited, but the good news is that means less people on the sand. Get here early to try to grab a spot. Another reason to come in the morning: The Koʻolau Range tends to block the afternoon sun. Or for a rare, magical moment, come to watch the full moon rise over the water.

There are no facilities here. From Waikīkī, take the H-1 to the Pali Highway (Hwy. 61) through the Nuʻuanu Pali Tunnel to Kailua, where the Pali Highway becomes Kailua Road as it proceeds through town. At Kalaheo Avenue, turn right and follow the coast about 2 miles to Kailua Beach Park; just past it, turn left at the T intersection and drive uphill on Aalapapa Drive, a one-way street that loops back as Mokulua Drive. Make sure to read the signs carefully for where and when you can park, and walk down any of the eight public-access lanes to the shore. Or take TheBus no. 671 (Kailua).

KAILUA BEACH ★★★

Windward Oʻahu's premier beach is a wide, 2-mile-long golden strand with dunes, palm trees, panoramic views, and offshore islets that are home to seabirds. The swimming is excellent, and the azure waters are usually decorated with bright sails—this is Oʻahu's premier windsurfing and kite-surfing beach. It's also a favorite spot to bodysurf the gentle waves or paddle a kayak. Water conditions are quite safe, especially at the mouth of Kaelepulu Stream, where toddlers play in the freshwater shallows in the middle of the beach park. The water is usually about 78°F (26°C), the views are spectacular, and the setting, at the foot of the sheer green Koʻolau Range, is idyllic. It's gotten so crowded over the years that the city council banned all commercial activity on the beach, which has led to a decrease in kayak traffic jams both on the beach and in the water. These days you can usually find a less-occupied stretch of sand the farther you are from the beach park.

Facilities at the beach park include picnic tables, barbecues, restrooms, a volleyball court, a public boat ramp, and free parking. To get here, take Pali Highway (Hwy. 61) to Kailua, drive through town, turn right on Kalaheo Avenue, and go a mile until you see the beach on your left. Or take TheBus no. 67.

Kailua Beach is Oʻahu's premier kitesurfing beach.

WAIMĀNALO BEACH ★★★

At almost 6 miles long, this is O'ahu's longest beach and a favorite among locals. The water can be a little rougher than at Kailua, making it fun for bodysurfing and boogie boarding. The wide, sandy beach is backed by shady ironwood trees should you tire of the sun. On weekdays, it will feel like you have the whole place to yourself; on weekends, locals bring out the grills and pop-up tents. *Note:* Make sure your valuables are hidden in your car; break-ins have occurred in the parking lot.

Facilities include restrooms, picnic tables, outdoor showers, and parking. Waimānalo Beach has a few points of entry—my pick would be the Waimānalo Bay Recreation Area. To get there, follow Kalaniana'ole Highway toward Waimānalo and turn right at the Waimānalo Bay sign, or take TheBus no. 67.

KUALOA REGIONAL PARK ★

This 150-acre coco-palm-fringed peninsula is located on Kāne'ohe Bay's north shore at the foot of the spiky Ko'olau Ridge. The park has a broad, grassy lawn and a long, narrow, white-sand beach ideal for swimming, walking, beachcombing, kite-flying, or just enjoying the natural beauty of this once-sacred Hawaiian shore, listed on the National Register of Historic Places. The waters are shallow and safe for swimming year-round. Offshore is Mokoli'i, the picturesque islet otherwise known as Chinaman's Hat. You can swim or wade out to the island (during low tide only) or kayak/stand-up paddle when the tide is higher. A small sandy beach can be found on the backside, and it takes less than half an hour to reach the top of this tiny island.

Facilities at both sites include restrooms, outdoor showers, picnic tables, and drinking fountains. To get to the park, take the Likelike Highway (Hwy. 63); after the Wilson Tunnel, get in the right lane and turn off on Kahekili Highway (Hwy. 83). Or take TheBus no. 60.

The North Shore

WAIMEA BEACH PARK ★★★

This deep, sandy bowl has gentle summer waves that are excellent for swimming, snorkeling, and bodysurfing. To one side of the bay is a huge rock that local kids like to climb and dive from. It's a placid scene in the summer, but what a difference a season makes: Winter waves pound the narrow bay, sometimes rising to 50 feet high. When the surf's really up, very strong currents and shorebreaks sweep the bay, and everyone except highly experienced and professional ocean athletes stay far out of the water. It also seems like everyone on O'ahu drives out to Waimea to check out the monster waves and those rare few with the skills to ride them. From December to the end of February, if the waves are big enough, big-wave surfers from around the world compete to ride mountainous waves in the Eddie Aikau Big Wave Invitational.

Facilities include lifeguards, restrooms, showers, parking, and nearby restaurants and shops in Hale'iwa town. The beach is located on Kamehameha Highway (Hwy. 83); from Waikīkī, take TheBus no. 60.

Leeward O'ahu: The Wai'anae Coast

MĀKAHA BEACH PARK ★★★

When the surf's up here, It's spectacular: Monstrous waves pound the beach. Nearly a mile long, this half-moon, gold-sand beach is tucked between 231-foot Lahilahi Point, which locals call Black Rock, and Kepuhi Point, a toe of the Wai'anae mountain range. Summer is the best time to hit this beach—the waves are small and the water safe for swimming. Children hug the shore on the north side of the beach, near the lifeguard stand, while divers seek an offshore channel full of big fish.

Facilities include restrooms, lifeguards, and parking. To get here, take the H-1 freeway to the end, where it becomes Farrington Highway (Hwy. 93), and follow it to the beach; or take TheBus no. 40 or C.

YOKOHAMA BAY ★★★

Where Farrington Highway (Hwy. 93) ends, the wilderness of **Ka'ena Point State Park** begins. It's a remote 853-acre coastline park of empty beaches, dunes, cliffs, and deep-blue water. This is the last sandy stretch on the northwest coast. Sometimes It's known as Keawaula Beach, but everybody here calls it Yokohama, after the Japanese immigrants who came to work the cane fields and fished along this shoreline. When the surf's calm—mainly in summer—this is a good area for snorkeling, diving, swimming, fishing, and picnicking. Lifeguards and a restroom are only at the park entrance. Unfortunately, there's no bus service.

WATERSPORTS

Boating

One of the best things about Hawai'i? The ocean. There are a million ways to enjoy it, but to get far from the shore and see the incredible beauty of the sea, hop on a boat.

Holokai Catamaran ★★   One of the most fun and effortless ways to get in the water is a sail off of Waikīkī. Holokai Catamaran is a popular "booze cruise." The 1½-hour **Sunset Cruise** is the most popular and festive, with an open bar, while the 1½-hour **Tradewind Sail,** which pushes off in the afternoon, is more mellow. Or, for a bit of an adventure, try the 2½-hour Turtle Canyon Snorkel Sail, which aims to get you face to face with some of Waikīkī's magnificent marine creatures, from the Hawaiian green sea turtle to the *tako* (octopus) to *wana* (sea urchin).

Check in at The Outrigger Reef Waikīkī Beach at 2169 Lewers St. www.sailholokai.com. ✆ **808/922-2210.** Tours and cruises $50–$95. Arrive 30 min. ahead. Bus: E or 20.

A great place to learn bodyboarding is Waikīkī Beach.

Wild Side Specialty Tours ★★ Picture this: You're floating in the calm waters off the Wai'anae coast, where your catamaran has just dropped you off. Below, in the reef, are turtles, and suddenly in the distance, you see spinner dolphins. This happens almost every day on the 3½-hour tours (check-in 7am or 11:15am) operated by the Cullins family, who have swum in these waters for decades. In winter, you may spot humpback whales on the morning cruise, which includes lunch, snorkel gear, instruction, and snacks. The other thing that sets this company apart is its small group sizes, limited to six on the tour.

Wai'anae Boat Harbor, 85-371 Farrington Hwy., Wai'anae. www.sailhawaii.com. ✆ **808/306-7273.** Best of the West $205 for ages 10 and up (not recommended for younger children). Bus no. 40 or C.

Bodyboarding (Boogie Boarding) & Bodysurfing

Good places to learn to bodyboard are in the small waves of **Waikīkī Beach ★★★**, **Kailua Beach ★★★**, **Waimānalo Beach ★★** (all reviewed under "Beaches," earlier in this chapter), and **Bellows Field Beach Park,** off Kalaniana'ole Highway (Hwy. 72) in Waimānalo, which is open to the public on weekends (from Fri noon to Sun 8pm and holidays). To get here, turn toward the ocean on Hughes Road, and then right on Tinker Road, which takes you to the park.

Ocean Kayaking/Stand-Up Paddling

Revel in amazing views both above and below the water on the Windward Coast with **Kama'aina Kids Kayak and Snorkel Eco Adventures ★**, 46-465 Kamehameha Hwy., Kāne'ohe, at He'eia State Park (www. kamaainakidskayaking.org; ✆ **808/781-4773**). Go at your own pace on these self-guided kayak adventures, which give you half-day (4 hr.) or

113

full-day (8 hr.) options. You'll see the majestic Koʻolau Range from your kayak. Then, as you head to Coconut Island (aka Gilligan's Island), stop to snorkel and admire the fish and turtles in the almost-always calm Kāneʻohe Bay. Then, head toward the not-to-miss disappearing "island," the sandbar Ahu o Laka, a favorite spot for frolicking in shallow water in what feels, incredibly, like the middle of the bay. What's even better? Proceeds go to Kamaʻaina Kids (which runs environmental education programs for children) and improving Heʻeia State Park.

For a wonderful adventure, rent a kayak or a stand-up paddleboard (SUP), arrive at Lanikai Beach just as the sun is appearing. Paddle across the channel to the pyramid-shaped islands called Mokulua, or the Mokes, as locals call them—It's an unforgettable experience, but be prepared for a solid paddle! The trip can take 30 minutes to an hour. **Kailua Beach Adventures,** 130 Kailua Rd., is a block from Kailua Beach Park (www. kailuabeachadventures.com; ℂ **808/262-2555**) and offers single kayaks and SUP boards at $69 for a half-day and double kayaks are $85 for a half-day. *Note:* Paddling to the islands is not allowed on Sundays.

If you're staying on the North Shore, go to **Surf-N-Sea,** 62-595 Kamehameha Hwy., Haleʻiwa (www.surfnsea.com; ℂ **808/637-3483**), where kayak rentals start at $20 per hour and go to $100 for a full day, and paddleboards at $20 an hour and $60 for a full day. During the summer, you can make a semi-ambitious trip from Haleʻiwa to Waimea Bay. For a more relaxing, but absolutely beautiful SUP experience, start in the bay right behind the shop (you rent the boards a mere few feet from the water), then head into Anahulu Stream, which takes you under the iconic Rainbow Bridge and on a journey along placid, calm waters, past jungle-y views, lush, draping trees, and, more likely than not, a few sea turtles.

Scuba Diving

Oʻahu is a wonderful place to scuba dive, especially for those interested in wreck diving. One of the more famous wrecks in Hawaiʻi is the *Mahi,* a 185-foot former minesweeper easily accessible just south of Waiʻanae. Abundant marine life makes this a great place to shoot photos—schools of lemon butterfly fish and taape (blue-lined snapper) are so comfortable with divers and photographers that they practically pose. Eagle rays, green sea turtles, manta rays, and white-tipped sharks occasionally cruise by as well, and eels peer out from the wreck.

For non-wreck diving, one of the best dive spots in summer is **Kahuna Canyon.** In Hawaiian, *kahuna* means priest, wise man, or sorcerer; this massive amphitheater, located near Mokuleia, is a perfect example of something a sorcerer might conjure up. Walls rising from the ocean floor create the illusion of an underwater Grand Canyon. Inside the amphitheater, crabs, octopuses, slippers, and spiny lobsters abound (be aware that taking them in summer is illegal), and giant trevally, parrotfish, and unicorn fish congregate as well. Outside the amphitheater, you're likely to see an occasional shark in the distance.

EXPERIENCING jaws: SWIM WITH THE SHARKS

Ocean Ramsey and her crew at **One Ocean Diving** ★★★ (www.oneoceandiving. com; ✆ **808/649-0018**) are on a first-name basis with some of the sharks they swim with. That's right, *swim with*, cage free. And you can, too, with little more than a snorkel, mask, and fins on your feet (this is a snorkeling trip, not scuba diving). As you ride the boat out, a few miles offshore from Hale'iwa, where sharks are known to congregate, the crew educates you about shark behavior. For one, they're really not that interested in humans. Two, most of the sharks you'll see are sandbar and Galapagos sharks, which are not considered dangerous. And three, if you should see a potentially more threatening shark, such as a tiger shark, they teach you how to conjure your alpha shark: Stay at the top of ocean, and don't turn your back on them. Your guides are always alert and nearby; only three people are allowed in the water at a time. Once I got used to the sight of the sharks around me, I began to admire their beauty and grace. One Ocean Diving hopes to change misconceptions about sharks and bring awareness to their plight as their numbers dwindle. A trip with them is as educational as it is exciting. Rates are $150 a person, and a snorkel mask and fins are provided; must be 4 feet or taller to enter the water.

Because O'ahu's greatest dives are offshore, your best bet is to book a two-tank dive from a dive boat. **Honolulu Scuba Company** ★, 670 Auahi St. (www.honoluluscubacompany.com; ✆ **808/201-4711**), offers dives for both first-time and certified divers. Charter options include wreck and reef dives and dusk/night dives and range from $89 to $249.

Snorkeling

Some of the best snorkeling in O'ahu is at **Hanauma Bay** ★★. It's crowded—sometimes it seems there are more people than fish—but

Hanauma has clear, warm, protected waters and an abundance of friendly reef fish, including Moorish idols, scores of butterfly fish, damselfish, and wrasses. Hanauma Bay has two reefs, an inner and an outer—the first for novices, the other for experts. The inner reef is calm and shallow (less than 10 ft.); in some places, you can just wade and put your face in the water. Reserve early: Time slots can sell out within 5 minutes of becoming available (which happens 2 days before, online). And It's **closed on Mondays and Tuesdays.** For details, see p. 108.

On the North Shore, head to **Shark's Cove ★★**, just off Kamehameha Highway, between Hale'iwa and Pupukea. In the summer, this big, lava-edged pool is one of O'ahu's best snorkel spots. Waves splash over the natural lava grotto and cascade like waterfalls into the pool full of tropical fish. To the right of the cove are deep-sea caves and underwater tunnels to explore.

If you want to rent snorkel equipment, check out **Snorkel Bob's** on the way to Hanauma Bay at 700 Kapahulu Ave. (at Date St.), Honolulu (www.snorkelbob.com; © **808/735-7944**).

Sport Fishing

Kewalo Basin, located between the Honolulu International Airport and Waikīkī, is the main location for charter fishing boats on O'ahu. From Waikīkī, take Kalākaua Avenue 'Ewa (west) beyond Ala Moana Center; Kewalo Basin is on the left, across from Ward Centers. Look for charter boats lined up in their slips; the captains display the catch of the day in the afternoon. You can also take TheBus no. 40 or 42.

Sport-fishing booking desk **Sportfish Hawaii ★** (www.sportfish hawaii.com; © **877/388-1376** or 808/295-8355) books boats on all the islands. These fishing vessels have been inspected and must meet rigorous criteria to guarantee that you will have a great time. Prices range from $1,250 to $2,600 for exclusive charters that range from 4-hour to 8-hour blocks. An array of boat types with capacities for 6 or 12 are available.

Surfing

In summer, when the water's warm and a soft breeze floats in the air, the south swell comes up. It's surf season in Waikīkī, the best place on O'ahu to learn how to surf. For lessons, find **Hans Hedemann Surf School** (www.hhsurf.com; © **808/924-7778**) at the Queen Kapi'olani Hotel (and, if you're on the North Shore, an outpost is at Turtle Bay Resort), founded by Hedemann, a champion surfer for more than 30 years. Lessons begin at $95 for a 2-hour group lesson. Surfboards are also available for rent on the North Shore at **Surf-N-Sea,** 62-595 Kamehameha Hwy., Hale'iwa (www.surfnsea.com; © **800/899-7873**), for $6 to $9 an hour. Lessons start at $85 for 2 to 3 hours.

More experienced surfers should drop into any surf shop around O'ahu or call the **Surf News Network Surfline** (© **808/596-SURF [7873]**) to get the latest surf conditions. The breaks at the base of Diamond Head are popular among intermediate-to-expert surfers.

If you're in Hawai'i in winter and want to see the serious surfers catch the really big waves, bring your binoculars and grab a front-row seat on the beach at **Waimea Bay, Sunset Beach,** or **Pipeline.**

HIKING

People are often surprised to discover that the great outdoors is often minutes from downtown Honolulu. The island's major hiking trails traverse razor-thin ridgebacks, deep waterfall valleys, and more. The best source of hiking information on O'ahu is the state's **Na Ala Hele (Trails to Go On) Program** (https://hawaiitrails.ehawaii.gov/trails/#/).

Honolulu-Area Hikes

DIAMOND HEAD CRATER ★★★

This is a moderate but steep walk to the summit of Hawai'i's most famous landmark. Kids love to look out from the top of the 760-foot volcanic cone, where they have 360-degree views of O'ahu up the leeward coast from Waikīkī. The 1.5-mile round-trip takes about 1½ hours, and the entry fee is $25 per car; if you walk in, It's $5 per person.

A volcanic explosion about half a million years ago created Diamond Head. The Hawaiians called the crater Leahi ("the brow of the ahi," or tuna, referring to the shape of the crater). Diamond Head was considered a sacred spot; some historians believe King Kamehameha offered human sacrifices at a *heiau* (temple) on the western slope. It wasn't until the 19th century that Mount Leahi got its current name, when a group of sailors found what they thought were diamonds in the crater; they turned out to be just worthless crystals, but the name stuck.

Before you begin your journey to the top of the crater, put on some comfortable shoes and don't forget water (very important), sunscreen, a hat to protect you from the sun, and a camera. You might want to put all your gear in a pack to leave your hands free for the climb.

Go early, preferably just after the 6am opening (the trail closes at 4pm), before the midday sun starts

Mānoa Falls is an excellent hiking option for families.

beating down. The hike to the summit starts at Monsarrat and 18th avenues on the crater's inland (or *mauka*) side. To get here, take TheBus nos. 23, 9 or 2, or drive to the intersection of Diamond Head Road and 18th Avenue. Follow the road through the tunnel (daily 6am–6pm) and park in the lot. From the trailhead in the parking lot, you'll proceed along a paved walkway (with handrails) as you climb up the slope. You'll pass World War I and World War II pillbox fortifications, gun emplacements, and tunnels built as part of the Pacific defense network. Several steps take you up to the top observation post on Point Leahi. The views are wonderful.

MĀNOA FALLS TRAIL ★★

This easy .75-mile (one-way) hike is terrific for families; it takes less than an hour to reach idyllic Mānoa Falls. The trailhead, marked by a footbridge, is at the end of Mānoa Road, past Lyon Arboretum. The staff at the arboretum prefers that hikers not park in their lot, so the best place to park is in the residential area below Paradise Park; you can also get to the arboretum via TheBus no. 5. The often-muddy trail follows Waihi Stream and meanders through the forest reserve past guavas, mountain apples, and wild ginger. The forest is moist and humid and inhabited by giant bloodthirsty mosquitoes, so bring repellent. If it has rained recently, stay on the trail and step carefully because it can be very slippery (and It's a long way down if you slide off the side).

East O'ahu Hikes

KOKO CRATER RAILWAY TRAIL ★★

If you're looking for quiet, you'll want to find another trail. This is less a hike than a strenuous workout, and It's popular among fitness buffs who climb it daily, people trying to stick to New Year's resolutions to be more active, and triathletes in training. But first-timers and tourists also tackle the 1,048 stairs along the railway track—once part of a World War II–era tram system—for the panoramic views from the Windward Coast to Waikīkī. It's a tough hike, but you'll have lots of friendly company along the way, and the view from the top is worth it. As they say, no pain, no gain. It's unshaded the whole way, so try to go early in the morning or in the late afternoon to catch the sunset and bring plenty of water.

To get to the trailhead from Waikīkī take Kalaniana'ole Highway (Hwy. 72) to Hawaii Kai, turn left at Lunalilo Home Road, and follow Anapalau Street to the trailhead parking lot; you can also take TheBus no. 23.

KULI'OU'OU RIDGE TRAIL ★★

One of Honolulu's best ridge trails, this moderate 2.5-mile hike (each way) starts in the middle of a residential neighborhood, then ascends through ironwood and pine trees, and drops you in the middle of a native Hawaiian forest. Here, *'ōhi'a lehua,* with its distinctive red pom-pom–like flowers would grow, but in recent years they've gotten rarer. Hawaiian legend has it that 'ōhi'a and Lehua were lovers. Pele fell in love with 'ōhi'a, but when he rejected her advances, she turned him into a tree. The gods took pity on the heartbroken Lehua and turned her into a flower on the tree. According to the story, if you pick a flower from the 'ōhi'a lehua, it will rain, representing the separated lovers' tears. If you're lucky enough to see a flower, leave it intact, if only to assure clear views at the top of the summit—on a good day, you can see all the way to Waimānalo.

To get there from Waikīkī, take Kalaniana'ole Highway (Hwy. 72) and turn left on Kuli'ou'ou Road. Turn right on Kalaau Place and look for street parking. You'll find the trailhead at the end of the road. No bus service.

MAKAPU'U LIGHTHOUSE TRAIL ★★

You've seen this famous old lighthouse on episodes of *Magnum, P.I.* and *Hawaii Five-O*. No longer staffed by the Coast Guard (It's fully automated now), the lighthouse sits at the end of a precipitous cliff trail on an airy perch over the Windward Coast, Manana (Rabbit) Island, and the azure Pacific. It's about a 45-minute, 1-mile hike from Kalaniana'ole Highway (Hwy. 72), along a paved road that begins across from Hawaii Kai Executive Golf Course and winds around the 646-foot-high sea bluff to the lighthouse lookout.

The view of the ocean all the way to Moloka'i and Lāna'i is often so clear that, from November to March, if you're lucky, you'll see migrating humpback whales.

To get to the trailhead from Waikīkī, take Kalaniana'ole Highway (Hwy. 72) past Hanauma Bay and Sandy Beach to Makapu'u Head, the southeastern tip of the island; you can also take TheBus no. 23.

Windward Coast Hikes

PALI (MAUNAWILI) TRAIL ★

For a million-dollar view of the Windward Coast, take this 11-mile (one-way) foothill trail. The trailhead is about 6 miles from downtown Honolulu, on the windward side of the Nu'uanu Pali Tunnel, at the scenic lookout just beyond the hairpin turn of the Pali Highway (Hwy. 61). Just as you begin the turn, look for the scenic overlook sign, slow down, and pull off the highway into the parking lot (sorry, no bus service available).

The mostly flat, well-marked, easy-to-moderate trail goes through the forest on the lower slopes of the 3,000-foot Ko'olau mountain range and ends up in the backyard of the coastal Hawaiian village of Waimānalo. Go halfway to get the view and then return to your car or have someone meet you in 'Nalo.

To Land's End: A Leeward O'ahu Hike

KA'ENA POINT ★

At the very western tip of O'ahu lie the dry, barren lands of **Ka'ena Point State Park,** 853 acres of jagged sea cliffs, deep gulches, sand dunes, endangered plant life, and a remote, wild, wind- and surf-battered coastline.

Kaʻena means "red hot" or "glowing" in Hawaiian; the name refers to the brilliant sunsets visible from the point.

Kaʻena is steeped in numerous legends. A popular one concerns the demigod Maui: Maui had a famous hook that he used to raise islands from the sea. He decided that he wanted to bring the islands of Oʻahu and Kauaʻi closer together, so one day he threw his hook across the Kauaʻi Channel and snagged Kauaʻi (which is actually visible from Kaʻena Point on clear days). Using all his might, Maui was able to pull loose a huge boulder, which fell into the waters very close to the present lighthouse at Kaʻena. The rock is still called Pōhaku o Kauaʻi (the Rock from Kauaʻi). Like Black Rock in Kaʻanapali on Maui, Kaʻena is thought of as the point on Oʻahu from which souls depart.

To hike out to this departing place, take the clearly marked trail from the parking lot of Kaʻena Point State Park. The moderate 5-mile round-trip hike to the point will take a couple of hours. The trail along the cliff passes tide pools abundant in marine life and rugged protrusions of lava reaching out to the turbulent sea; seabirds circle overhead. Do *not* go off the trail; you might step on buried birds' eggs. There are no sandy beaches, and the water is nearly always turbulent here. In winter, when a big north swell is running, the waves at Kaʻena are the biggest in the state, averaging heights of 30 to 40 feet. Even when the water appears calm, offshore currents are powerful, so don't plan on taking a swim. Go early in the morning to see the schools of porpoises that frequent the area.

To get to the trailhead from Honolulu or Waikīkī, take the H-1 west to its end; continue on Hwy. 93 past Mākaha and follow Hwy. 930 to the end of the road. There is no bus service.

OTHER OUTDOOR ACTIVITIES
Biking

Oʻahu as a whole is not particularly bike-friendly, as drivers still need to learn to share the road. But that has been slowly changing with the installation of new bike lanes and the introduction of **Biki** (www.gobiki.org), Honolulu's bikeshare program, which placed over 1,300 bikes at 130 docking stations throughout metro Honolulu. Modeled after other systems in cities such as Paris and New York, you can purchase single ride passes ($4.50 for 30 min.) or passes ($30 for a prepaid bank of 300 min. to use over 1 year). Biki makes short trips, such as from your hotel to the beach a breeze.

For a bike-and-hike adventure, contact **Bike Hawaii** ★ (www.bike hawaii.com; ✆ **808/734-4214**), which has a variety of group tours, such as their Honolulu e-bike rainforest tour. This guided tour features electric-assist bicycles, which will help getting you up to all those scenic spots, with an elevation gain of 1,600 feet! You'll ride on paved roads past Honolulu's bordering tropical rainforests, and be treated to views of Waikīkī, Mānoa Valley and Diamond Head. The 10-mile trip of around 3 hours of stop-and-go riding, includes van transportation from your hotel, a bike, helmet, snacks, water bottle, and guide; It's $134 per person. Prefer a more downhill ride? Their downhill option is family friendly, using conventional bikes—and you'll still get some sweet views and rainforest vibes (3 hr.; $91 adults, $62 kids ages 5–14).

Golf

Oʻahu has nearly 3 dozen golf courses, ranging from bare-bones municipal courses to exclusive country-club courses with membership fees running to six figures a year. Below are the best of a great bunch.

As you get to know Oʻahu's courses, you'll see that the windward courses play much differently than the leeward ones. On the windward side, the prevailing winds blow from the ocean to shore, and the grain direction of the greens tends to run the same way—from the ocean to the mountains. Leeward golf courses have the opposite tendency: The winds usually blow from the mountains to the ocean, with the grain direction of the greens corresponding.

Tips on beating the crowds and saving money: Oʻahu's golf courses tend to be crowded, less-so in midweek. Also, most courses have twilight rates that offer deep discounts if you're willing to tee off in the afternoon; these are included in the listings below, where applicable.

Transportation note: TheBus does not allow golf-club bags onboard, so if you want to use TheBus to get to a course, you're going to have to rent clubs there.

WAIKĪKĪ

Ala Wai Municipal Golf Course ★　This is Oʻahu's most popular municipal course. Translation: It gets really crowded; some 500 rounds a

The golf course at Turtle Bay Resort.

day are played on this 18-hole course. But It's the closest course, and within walking distance, to Waikīkī's hotels. It's something of a challenge to get a tee time at this busy par-70, 6,020-yard course, with only limited day-of reservations, stand-bys, and walk-ins, but keep trying. Ala Wai has a flat layout bordered by the Ala Wai Canal on one side and the Mānoa-Palolo Stream on the other. It's less windy than most O'ahu courses, but pay attention to the 372-yard, par-4 1st hole, which demands a straight and long shot to the very tiny green. If you miss, you can make it up on the 478-yard, par-5 10th hole—the green is reachable in two, so with a two-putt, a birdie is within reach.

404 Kapahulu Ave., Waikīkī. www8.honolulu.gov/des/ala-wai-golf-course/. ✆ **808/207-6856.** Greens fees $86. From Waikīkī, turn left on Kapahulu Ave.; the course is on the *mauka* side of Ala Wai Canal. Bus: 13, 20.

THE WINDWARD COAST

Royal Hawaiian Golf Club ★★   Here's another gorgeous course, often referred to as the Jurassic Park of golf courses, so named for both the breathtaking scenery and because It's not for the faint-hearted. Designed by Perry and Pete Dye, the club has been redeveloped by hall-of-fame golfer Greg Norman. Switchback trails lead you up to wide vistas that take the sting out of losing so many balls. Facilities include a pro shop, driving range, putting and chipping greens, and a snack bar.

770 Auloa Rd., Kailua. www.royalhawaiiangc.com. ✆ **808/262-2139.** Greens fees $165. Take H-1 to the Pali Hwy. (Hwy. 61); turn right onto Auloa Rd.

THE NORTH SHORE

Kahuku Golf Course ★   This 9-hole budget golf course is a bit funky. Don't expect a clubhouse: There's only a dilapidated shack where you check in and minimal facilities consisting of golf club rentals, a few pull carts, and some vending machines. But a round at this scenic oceanside course amid the tranquility of the North Shore is quite an experience nonetheless. Duffers will love the ease of this recreational course, and walkers will be happy with its gently sloping greens. Don't forget to bring your camera for the view. With plenty of retirees happy to sit and wait, the competition is fierce for early tee times. Book online for the best results or call for same day reservations.

56-501 Kamehameha Hwy., Kahuku. ✆ **808/207-7076.** Greens fees $60. Take H-1 west to H-2; follow H-2 through Wahiawā to Kamehameha Hwy. (Hwy. 99, then Hwy. 83); follow it to Kahuku. Bus: 60.

Turtle Bay Resort ★★★   This North Shore resort is home to two of Hawai'i's top golf courses. The challenging 18-hole **Arnold Palmer Course** (formerly the Links at Kuilima) was designed by Arnold Palmer and Ed Seay. Now that the casuarina (ironwood) trees have matured, It's not as windy as it used to be. The front 9, with rolling terrain, only a few trees, and plenty of wind, play like a British Isles course. The back 9 have narrower tree-lined fairways and water. The course circles Punaho'olapa Marsh, a protected wetland for endangered Hawaiian waterfowl.

Also on site is the par-71, 6,200-yard **George Fazio Course**—the only Fazio course in Hawai'i. It's temporarily closed at the time of writing, but has plans to open again in the future.

Facilities include a pro shop, driving range, putting and chipping greens, and snack bar. Weekdays are best for tee times.

57-049 Kamehameha Hwy., Kahuku. www.turtlebayresort.com. © **808/293-8574.** Greens fees: Arnold Palmer Course $229; twilight rates (after 1pm) starting at $159. Take H-1 west past Pearl City; when the freeway splits, take H-2 and follow the signs to Hale'iwa; at Hale'iwa, take Hwy. 83 to Turtle Bay Resort. Bus: 60.

LEEWARD O'AHU

Ko 'Olina Golf Club ★★★ This Ted Robinson–designed course has rolling fairways and elevated tee and water features. *Golf Digest* once named it one of "America's Top 75 Resort Courses." The signature hole—the 12th, a par-3—has an elevated tee that sits on a rock garden with a cascading waterfall. At the 18th hole, you'll see and hear water all around you—seven pools begin on the right side of the fairway and slope down to a lake. A waterfall is on your left off the elevated green. You'll have no choice but to play the left and approach the green over the water. Book in advance; this course is crowded all the time. Facilities include a driving range, locker rooms, a Jacuzzi, steam rooms, a restaurant, and bar. Lessons are available.

92-1220 Aliinui Dr., Kapolei. www.koolinagolf.com. © **808/676-5300.** Greens fees $255 ($225 for guests staying at any Ko Olina resorts); twilight rates (after 1pm) $190. Ask about transportation from Waikīkī hotels. Collared shirts for men and women. Take H-1 west until it becomes Hwy. 93 (Farrington Hwy.); turn off at the Ko Olina exit; take the exit road (Aliinui Dr.) into Ko Olina Resort; turn left to the clubhouse. No bus service.

West Loch Municipal Golf Course ★ This par-72, 6,615-yard course located just 30 minutes from Waikīkī, in 'Ewa Beach, offers golfers a challenge at bargain rates. The difficulties on this unusual municipal course, designed by Robin Nelson and Rodney Wright, are water (lots of hazards), constant trade winds, and narrow fairways. To help you out, the course features a "water" driving range (with a lake) to practice your drives. In addition to the driving range, West Loch has practice greens, a pro shop, and a restaurant. Call for same day reservations.

91-1126 Okupe St., 'Ewa Beach. © **808/675-6076.** Greens fees $86. Take H-1 west to the Hwy. 76 exit; stay in the left lane and turn left at West Loch Estates, just opposite St. Francis Medical Center. To park, take 2 immediate right turns. Bus: 42.

Horseback Riding

You can gallop on the beach at the **Turtle Bay Resort** ★★, 57-091 Kamehameha Hwy., Kahuku (www.turtlebayresort.com; © **866/475-2567**), where 45-minute rides through the tranquil North Shore trails cost $115. For children 6 and under, check out the adorable Pony Experience, a hands-on opportunity for the little ones to groom, feed, and ride a pony. Romantic sunset rides are $175 per person and happen just at the perfect golden hour, when the North Shore sun does its stunning, mood-setting show. For more advanced riders, book a private ride for 1 hour, which lets you have a little more freedom to walk, trot, and canter about, at $350 per person. **Kualoa Ranch ★★**, 49-560 Kamehameha Hwy., Ka'a'awa (www.kualoa.com; ✆ **800/231-7321** or 808/237-7321) also offers 2-hour horseback tours (starting at $145) into the verdant Ka'a'awa Valley, against the backdrop of the Kualoa mountains.

ORGANIZED TOURS
Guided Sightseeing Tours

If your time is limited, you might want to consider a guided tour. These tours are informative, can give you a good overview of Honolulu or O'ahu in a limited amount of time, and are surprisingly entertaining.

E Noa Tours, 1141 Waimanu St., Suite 105, Honolulu (www.enoa. com; ✆ **808/591-2561**), offers a couple of narrated tours: an island loop and explorations of Pearl Harbor—on air-conditioned, 27-passenger minibuses. The Majestic Circle Island Tour (from $163 for adults, $125 for children) stops at Diamond Head Crater, Byodo-In Temple, Waimea Valley (admission included), and various beach sites along the way. Dress comfortably and bring swimwear and towel, as drivers will stop for swimming, weather permitting. Pearl Harbor offerings include a city tour option. It takes you into other areas in Honolulu relevant to the Pearl Harbor story, such as 'Iolani Palace and the King Kamehameha Statue.

Waikīkī Trolley Tours ★, 1141 Waimanu St., Suite 105, Honolulu (www.waikikitrolley.com; ✆ **808/591-2561**), offers tours of sightseeing, entertainment, dining, and shopping that give you the lay of the land. You can get on and off the trolley as needed (trolleys come along every 2–20 min.). All day passes for adults start at $5.50 for the Pink Line, to $31.50 for the Red and Blue lines; a 4-day pass is $68.25.

---

bird's-eye VIEW: AIR TOURS

To understand why O'ahu was the island of kings, you need to see it from the air. **Paradise Helicopters ★★★** (www.paradisecopters.com; ✆ **866/876-7422** or 808/969-7392) offers a circle-island tour that's doors off, making the experience ever more thrilling (make sure to bring a jacket—it gets chilly and windy up in the air!).

The approximately 75-minute tour ($535 per person) gives you aerial views of Waikīkī Beach, Diamond Head Crater, and Hanauma Bay, all the way up to the North Shore and down the less-visited Wai'anae Coast. You'll glimpse Kaliuwaa, or Sacred Falls, an 1,100-foot waterfall that's inaccessible by land, in all its majestic glory, as it streams down the mountains. To make this over-the-top, breathtaking experience even more extra, opt for an additional landing spot (an extra $100 per person) above Ka'a'awa Valley for a unique panorama all the way to Chinaman's Hat.

Kō Hana rum is made of heritage sugarcane on Oʻahu.

Specialty Tours

Below is a sampling of specialty tours found on Oʻahu.

CHOCOLATE FACTORY TOUR

Hawaiʻi is the only state in the U.S. to grow cacao commercially, and at bean-to-bar maker **Mānoa Chocolate ★★**, 333 Uluniu St. (www.manoa chocolate.com; ℂ **808/263-6292**), you can find out more about Hawaiʻi's burgeoning chocolate scene and see what it takes to turn cacao beans into smooth chocolate bars. For $25 a person (reservations required) you get to tour the factory, taste fresh cacao fruit when in season, attend a chocolate tea service and taste the Mānoa Chocolate creations alongside their Chocolate Sommelier team. Compare this 60- to 90-minute tour to a winery or distillery tour.

KŌ HANA RUM TOUR

Discover how rum is made, from grass to glass at **Kō Hana ★★★**, 92-1770 Kunia Rd. #227 (www.kohanarum.com; ℂ **808/649-0830**). This is not just any rum—this is Hawaiian agricole rum, distilled from pure cane juice, fresh-pressed from heirloom varieties of Hawaiian sugarcane. Most rum starts from molasses, whereas at Kō Hana, it begins with sugarcane, and each bottle is labeled with the varietal it was distilled from. The tour in Kunia, in the heart of Oʻahu's farmland, will give you sweeping views all the way to Diamond Head, and take you through the cane gardens, the distillery, and the tasting room to sample white rums alongside barrel-aged ones. The estate tour takes you deeper into the fields with the company's Farm Manager and concludes with a tasting of four different rums. Tours are $35 to $50 for adults.

WHERE TO STAY ON O'AHU

Before you book a place to stay, consider when you'll be visiting. The high season, when hotels are full and rates are at their peak, is typically mid-December to March. The secondary high season, when rates are high, but rooms are somewhat easier to come by, is typically June to September. The low seasons—when you can expect fewer tourists and better deals—are typically April to June and September to mid-December. Since the COVID-19 pandemic, however, tourism has had some topsy-turvy changes. There are a host of other factors you'll want to consider when picking the perfect time, too. While Hawai'i, for the most part, does have balmy weather year-round, seasonal changes could have a big effect on the activities you'll want to take in during your stay. Huge winter swells on the North Shore, for example, make it prime time for big wave surfing and surf competition, events that attract massive, wave-watching crowds. South Shore summer swells, on the other hand, mean great, accessible surfing close to town for the less advanced. If crowds are on your mind, school breaks, like Christmas, will see hotels fill up with folks escaping their own wintery weather or families with kids on vacation.

For a description of each neighborhood, see "The Island in Brief" (p. 65). It can help you decide where you'd like to base yourself.

Remember that hotel and room taxes of about 18% will be added to your bill (O'ahu has a 3% additional tax that the other islands do not have). And don't forget about parking charges—at $40 or more per day in Waikīkī, they can add up quickly.

Note that more and more hotels charge a mandatory daily "resort fee" or "amenity fee," usually somewhere between $40 and $60, which can increase the room rates by 20%. Hotels say these charges cover amenities, some of which you may not need (such as movie rentals, a color photograph of you on the property—drinking that welcome drink, perhaps?) and some of which are awfully handy (such as Internet access and parking).

VACATION RENTALS   O'ahu has few true bed-and-breakfast inns. Instead, if you're looking for a non-hotel experience, your best bet is a vacation rental. You can rent direct from owners via **VRBO.com** (Vacation Rentals by Owner) and **Airbnb.com**. On these sites, you'll find a range of offerings, from $80-a-night studios to unique, off-the-beaten-path lodgings, like a Portlock cottage near Hanauma Bay on the water (listed on VRBO.com) or a North Shore treehouse (listed on Airbnb.com). Read the reviews before booking so you have a general idea of what you're getting into. Note that some vacation rentals will require your stay to be a minimum of 30 days. This is due to a resort area law which only allows for short-term stays in specific, designated areas on the island.

Waikīkī

'EWA WAIKĪKĪ

All the hotels listed below are located between the ocean and Kalākaua Avenue, and between Ala Wai Terrace in the 'Ewa (western) direction and

Waikīkī Hotels

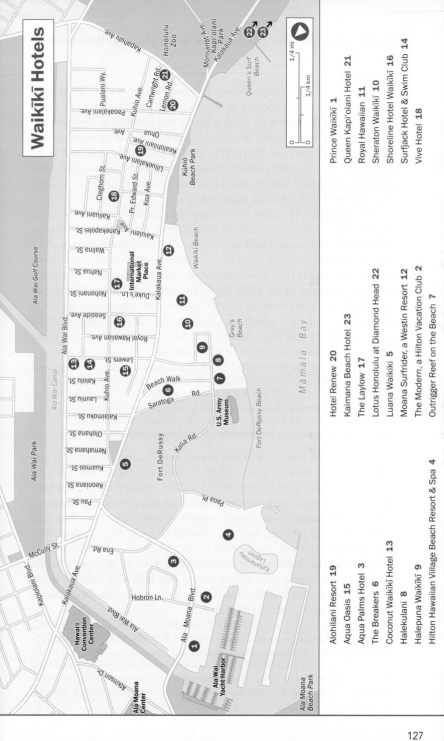

Alohilani Resort **19**
Aqua Oasis **15**
Aqua Palms Hotel **3**
The Breakers **6**
Coconut Waikīkī Hotel **13**
Halekulani **8**
Halepuna Waikīkī **9**
Hilton Hawaiian Village Beach Resort & Spa **4**

Hotel Renew **20**
Kaimana Beach Hotel **23**
The Laylow **17**
Lotus Honolulu at Diamond Head **22**
Luana Waikiki **5**
Moana Surfrider, a Westin Resort **12**
The Modern, a Hilton Vacation Club **2**
Outrigger Reef on the Beach **7**

Prince Waikīkī **1**
Queen Kapiʻolani Hotel **21**
Royal Hawaiian **11**
Sheraton Waikīkī **10**
Shoreline Hotel Waikīkī **16**
Surfjack Hotel & Swim Club **14**
Vive Hotel **18**

Olohana Street and Fort DeRussy Park in the Diamond Head (eastern) direction.

Expensive

Hilton Hawaiian Village Beach Resort & Spa ★★   This sprawling resort is like a microcosm of Waikīkī—on good days it feels like a lively little beach town with hidden nooks and crannies to discover and great bars in which to make new friends; on bad days It's just an endless traffic jam, with lines into the parking garage, at the front desk, and in the restaurants. Need an oasis in the middle of it all? Choose the Aliʻi Tower; it has its own lobby lounge, reception, and concierge, and even its own pool and bar; It's like a hotel within a hotel.

But the Hilton Hawaiian does have something for everyone—families takeover the pool, winter breakers sashay from Tapa Tower (the largest tower) to hit the bars, and well-heeled (literally) tourists return to the Aliʻi Tower with their shopping bags. Room views can range from a straight-on view of the tower in front to oceanfront, so close to the water you can hear the waves. Cheaper rooms are in the Kalia, Tapa, and Diamond Head towers (which are farther from the beach), and the more expensive ones are in the Rainbow and Aliʻi, which are closest to the water. Rooms in all the towers tend to be spacious, clean, and comfy, so ultimately it may come down to how close you want to be to the beach.

2005 Kalia Rd. (at Ala Moana Blvd.), Honolulu. www.hiltonhawaiianvillage.com. ✆ **808/949-4321.** 2,860 units. $192–$330 double; from $560 suite. $50 resort fee includes Internet access and beach rental discounts. Children 17 and under stay free in parent's room. Valet parking about $78; self-parking about $68. Bus: 20, 42 or 13. **Amenities:** 12+ bars and restaurants; kids' activities such as fish feeding, hula lessons, and more; concierge; fitness center; pools; room service; Wi-Fi.

Prince Waikīkī ★★   These two towers look like they're from *The Jetsons*, especially with the glass-walled elevators zipping up and down the exterior. The hotel's extensive remodel in 2017 installed more restaurants and an infinity pool; most eye-catching are the 800 pieces of shimmering copper, reminiscent of fish scales, suspended from the lobby ceiling. The rooms were also updated, but you'll probably spend most of your time looking outward; every room, even on the lower floors, boasts a yacht harbor view. This hotel is on the quiet side of Waikīkī. Without a beach, It's about a 10-minute walk to Ala Moana Beach Park, a more local and less-busy beach than Waikīkī. The hotel's **Katsumidori Sushi** restaurant offers quality sushi at reasonable prices.

100 Holomoana St. (just across Ala Wai Canal Bridge, on the ocean side of Ala Moana Blvd.), Honolulu. www.princewaikiki.com. ✆ **808/956-1111.** 563 units. $225–$335 double; from $544 suite. $42 resort fee includes reduced admission to the Honolulu Museum of Art, Internet access, newspaper and magazines, spa and golf discounts, and more. Bus: E, 42 or 65. **Amenities:** 2 restaurants; outdoor bar; concierge; 27-hole golf club a 40-min. drive away in ʻEwa Beach (reached by hotel shuttle); fitness room; pool; room service; small day spa; Wi-Fi.

Moderate

The Modern, a Hilton Vacation Club ★   Step into a hip and modern Waikīkī—you won't find rattan furniture anywhere nor any slack key music. Instead, you get sleek, all white with blond-wood-accented rooms and electronic funk a la Ibiza played in the common areas. Come here to see and be seen, at the breezy poolside bar, and lounge on some expansive daybeds. The pool has its own sand—a blend culled from all the islands—to pretend the hotel has beach access (it doesn't).

1775 Ala Moana Blvd. (at Hobron Lane), Honolulu. www.themodernhonolulu.com. ℂ **808/943-5800.** 353 units. $180–$445 double. Parking $35. Bus: E or 20. **Amenities:** Restaurant; nightclub; 4 lounges; concierge; fitness center; pool; 24-hr. room service; spa; free Wi-Fi.

MID-WAIKĪKĪ

All the hotels listed below are between Fort DeRussy in the 'Ewa (western) direction and Kaiulani Street in the Diamond Head (eastern) direction.

Expensive

Halekulani ★★★   This is one of Waikīkī's most luxurious hotels; its name means "house befitting heaven." The history of the Halekulani tracks that of Waikīkī itself: At its inception at the turn of the 20th century, it was just a beachfront house and a few bungalows, and Waikīkī was an undeveloped stretch of sand and drained marshland. By the 1980s, Waikīkī was a different place, and so was the Halekulani, which was relaunched as an oasis of mostly oceanfront hotel rooms and beautifully landscaped courtyards—and so it remains. It's all very understated—it actually doesn't

---

AFFORDABLE parking IN WAIKĪKĪ

It *is* possible to find affordable parking in Waikīkī if you know where to look. I've divided up the parking into free or metered parking and carry-a-big-wallet parking.

FREE OR METERED PARKING:

o All side streets in Waikīkī. Some have time limits, make sure to check the posted signs.

o Ala Wai Boulevard along the Ala Wai Canal

o Kalākaua Avenue along Kapi'olani Park

o Alongside Waikīkī Zoo

BEST OF THE NOT-SO-AFFORDABLE PARKING:

o International Marketplace, 2330 Kalākaua Ave. Parking entrance at Kūhiō

Ave. and Walina St. First hour free with validation (a purchase of $25 from the Marketplace gets you validation), $2 per hour for the next 2 hours.

o Royal Hawaiian Shopping Center, 2201 Kalākaua Ave. First hour free with validation (also a purchase of $25 or more), then $2 per hour for the next 2 hours.

o Waikīkī Shopping Plaza, 2270 Kalākaua Ave. $3 per half hour, $15 flat rate up, with a $50 daily maximum.

look like much from the outside. But what it lacks in splashy grandeur, a la Royal Hawaiian, it makes up with a quiet elegance.

The large rooms are done in what the Halekulani calls its signature "seven shades of white." Generously sized tile-and-marble bathrooms and louver shutter doors separating the lanais contribute to the spare yet luxe feel. Of all the hotels in Waikīkī, this one feels the most peaceful, abetted by lovely, personable service. It's a true escape.

2199 Kalia Rd. (at the ocean end of Lewers St.), Honolulu. www.halekulani.com. © **808/923-2311.** 453 units. $640–$750 double. 1 child 17 and under stays free in parent's room using existing bedding. Bus: 23 or 20. **Amenities:** 3 restaurants; 3 bars; 24-hr. concierge; gym; pool; room service; spa.

Moana Surfrider, a Westin Resort ★★ This is Waikīkī's oldest hotel, built in 1901. Even after more than 100 years, multiple renovations, and the construction of two towers in the '50s and '60s, the hotel has managed to retain its original and still grand Beaux Arts main building. It's so picturesque you're likely to encounter many a wedding couple posing for a shot along the staircase and in the lobby. I prefer the rooms in the Banyan Wing for their nostalgic character, but these tend to be small in size. Larger rooms with lanais are in the Tower Wing, and although they are as well appointed as any you'll find at other Westin properties, with granite bathrooms and signature Heavenly beds, they don't feel very Hawai'i. Of course, to change that, get a room with a view of Diamond Head, or just step out under the giant banyan tree in the courtyard and enjoy the nightly live Hawaiian music and a mai tai.

2365 Kalākaua Ave. (ocean side of the street, across from Kaiulani St.), Honolulu. www.moana-surfrider.com. © **808/922-3111.** 793 units. $247–$550 double. Valet parking $65. Resort fee $49.55. Bus: E or 4. **Amenities:** 3 restaurants; bar; concierge; nearby fitness room; pool; room service; Wi-Fi.

Outrigger Reef on the Beach ★★ You may arrive by car, but the Outrigger reminds you—with the 100-year-old koa wood canoe suspended in the longhouse entryway—that long ago, the Polynesians came to Hawai'i by boat, navigating their way only by the stars. The Hawai'i-based Outrigger chain has a handful of hotels on O'ahu, and this one is its most striking, with lovely Hawaiian cultural touches. You'll find the outrigger theme throughout the hotel, such as in the collection of Polynesian canoe art by Herb Kane, who some call the "father of the Hawaiian Renaissance." (Most notably, he built the double-hulled voyaging canoe the *Hokulea* in 1975, which revived ancient celestial navigation methods—see p. 46.) But don't worry: At Outrigger Reef, you can have your historical culture and modern amenities, too, such as a large pool and two restaurants, plus modern Hawaiian decor and spacious rooms.

Note that **Outrigger Waikīkī on the Beach** (www.outriggerwaikiki hotel.com) has a similar feel and price point to Outrigger Reef on the Beach, but its location in the center of Waikīkī and its resident bar—Duke's

Waikīkī, the area's most happening bar—means It's a little more bustling and noisy.

2169 Kalia Rd. (at Saratoga Rd.), Honolulu. www.outriggerreef.com. ℂ **808/923-3111.** 639 units. $259–$498 double. $45 resort fee includes Wi-Fi, in-room coffee and tea, spa access, discounts to the museum and aquarium, and more. Valet parking only, $50. Bus: 20. **Amenities:** 2 restaurants, fitness center; spa; pools and hot tub; Wi-Fi.

Royal Hawaiian ★★★   Every time I step into the "Pink Palace of the Pacific," it takes my breath away. I love its vibrant exoticism—the Spanish-

Pretty in pink, the Royal Hawaiian Hotel overlooks Waikīkī Beach.

Moorish architecture manifested in graceful stucco arches, the patterned floor tiles, the ornate lamps. Who knew that pink could look so good against Hawai'i's blue skies and seas? The historic rooms are my favorite, with the pink and gold-embossed wallpaper and dark-wood furniture. Rooms in the Mailani Tower wing are larger, the colors more muted (don't worry, there are still pink accents) and the bathrooms have fancy Toto toilets. Here, even your *'okole* (rear end) is pampered.

2259 Kalākaua Ave. (at Royal Hawaiian Ave., on the ocean side of the Royal Hawaiian Shopping Center), Honolulu. www.royal-hawaiian.com. ℂ **808/923-7311.** 528 units. $335–$615 double. $49.55 resort fee includes Wi-Fi, welcome bag, morning yoga, cultural activities, stand-up paddleboard demonstration, and a 1-day GoPro rental. Valet parking $65. Bus: E. **Amenities:** 4 restaurants; iconic bar; concierge; preferred tee times at area golf courses; pool; room service; spa; Wi-Fi.

Sheraton Waikīkī ★   At 30 stories tall, the Sheraton towers over its neighbors. Looking for a peaceful getaway? Look elsewhere because this Sheraton has almost 2,000 rooms smack in the middle of the busiest section of Waikīkī. What you do get: views of the ocean from most rooms, the Helumoa Playground pool for kids, and a gorgeous infinity pool for adults. Expect crowds, though. Drinks at **Rumfire** are fun, with great views to match; the **Kai Market** breakfast spot offers morning classics like waffles, French toast, and omelets. Dining is expensive (as in most Waikīkī hotels); for cheap, grab-and-go meals, I like to go to **Lawson Station,** something of a Japanese version of 7-Eleven but with much better food, such as bento boxes, oden, and tasty desserts made by local companies.

2255 Kalākaua Ave. (at Royal Hawaiian Ave., on the ocean side of the Royal Hawaiian Shopping Center and west of the Royal Hawaiian), Honolulu. www.sheraton-waikiki. com. ⓒ **808/922-4422.** 1,852 units. $312–$559 double; from $705 suite. $45 resort fee includes Internet, cultural activities, local and long-distance calls, and a 1-day GoPro rental. Valet parking $65, self-parking $55. Bus: E. **Amenities:** 2 restaurants; bar; nightclub; concierge; fitness center; 2 large pools, including an infinity pool; room service; Wi-Fi.

Moderate

Halepuna Waikīkī ★ Unveiled in 2019, this is the Halekulani's younger, more relaxed sister, located across the street. It has a similar understated palette with teak finishes and airy lobby, but the real draw is the eighth-floor pool deck with ocean views (and, of course, its budget-friendly price).

2233 Helumoa Rd. (at Lewers St.), Honolulu. www.halepuna.com. ⓒ **808/921-7272.** 288 units. From $400 double. Parking $50. Bus: E. **Amenities:** Restaurant; bakery, concierge; fitness center; 8th-floor pool deck; room service; free Wi-Fi.

The Laylow ★★ The Laylow opened in 2017 for the Instagram jet-set crowd. It's part of the Marriott Autograph Collection, but with under 200 rooms and a lovely midcentury Hawai'i aesthetic, it feels like a boutique hotel. Despite its location right next to the International Marketplace and in the middle of Waikīkī, the second floor **Hideout** restaurant and lounge creates an oasis edged with tropical foliage, low-slung banquettes, wicker chairs, and fire pits. There are even sandy areas to dig your toes into. The rooms capture the same vibe, with minimalist 1960s furniture, warmed up with teal-and-pink palm wallpaper.

2299 Kūhiō Ave., Honolulu. www.laylowwaikiki.com. ⓒ **808/922-6600.** 186 units. $231–$330 double. $35 resort fee includes welcome basket, live music nightly, mocktails and shave ice, activities, bicycles, pool towels, and more. Valet parking $60. Bus: 2 or 20. **Amenities:** 2 restaurants; pool; room service; Wi-Fi.

Surfjack Hotel & Swim Club ★★★ Step back into the golden ages of Waikīkī when Don Ho crooned in lounges and low-slung buildings and bungalows dotted the beachfront. The Surfjack was remade from a 1960s budget hotel. Its founders enlisted a considerable amount of local talent, from young designers to established artists, to create a space that screams midcentury beach-house cool, from the "Wish You Were Here" mosaic on the swimming pool floor to the pretty blue and white tiling in the bathrooms to the vintage headboard upholstery by Tori Richard. It's not close to the beach, and the views are mostly of buildings, and yet, there's a charm to this soulful enclave, where you can get excellent cocktails by the pool or a cup of coffee while you browse the on-site boutique, **The Surfjack Shop.**

412 Lewers St., Honolulu. www.surfjack.com. ⓒ **808/923-8882.** 112 units. $186–$506 double; from $217 suite. Free parking off-site for the first car. Dog-friendly. Bus: 2 or 8. **Amenities:** Restaurant; pool; free Wi-Fi.

AFFORDABLE waikīkī

Inexpensive accommodations are few and far between on Oʻahu, and especially in Waikīkī… at least places you'd actually *want* to stay in. But hidden among the big and luxurious resorts are satisfactory, inexpensive-to-moderately priced properties (from just over $100 a night) that are sometimes downright charming. These small hotels vary in quality (with furnishings ranging from dated tropical to bright and modern). Here are some clean, well maintained and regularly updated options to consider.

The **Aqua Oasis,** 320 Lewers St. (✆ **808/923-2300**), is just that: a cheery property with a lush courtyard and lounge area as well as clean rooms with city views and plumeria accents. Rates start at $170. Rooms in the **Luana Waikīkī,** 2045 Kalākaua Ave. (✆ **808/955-6000**), start at $150 with kitchenette and full kitchen offerings, a pool, and suites. Another mid-range choice is the **Aqua Palms,** 1850 Ala Moana Blvd. (✆ **808/947-7256**), located right at the gateway to Waikīkī, making it just as easy to walk to Ala Moana Center as it is to the beach, starting at $190 a night.

Inexpensive

The Breakers ★   In the 1950s and '60s, thanks to statehood and the jet age, Waikīkī's low-rise skyline gave way to larger and taller hotels. A lot of the more modest hotels are long gone, except for The Breakers. The two-story building, built in 1954, has managed to hold on to its family feel and prime real estate (just a few minutes' walk to the beach and the center of Waikīkī). It's like a Hawaiʻi-style motel, built around a pool, with charming touches such as double-pitched roofs, shoji doors to the Lānaʻi, and tropical landscaping. All of the rooms come with a kitchenette, though the appliances look like they're from the '70s. Sure, the decor is dated and worn, but It's clean.

250 Beach Walk (btw. Kalākaua Ave. and Kalia Rd.), Honolulu. www.breakers-hawaii.com. ✆ **808/923-3181.** 64 units, all with shower only. From $150 double; $300 garden suite. Limited free parking (just 6 stalls). Bus: 20, E. **Amenities:** Restaurant; grill; pool; free Wi-Fi (in lobby).

Coconut Waikīkī Hotel ★   Rooms at this family-friendly hotel are spacious and immaculate and come with a small lanai and wet bar. The tiny pool is kind of wedged between the hotel and a fence—better to grab the free beach-towel rental and head to the ocean.

450 Lewers St. (at Ala Wai Blvd.), Honolulu. https://coconutwaikikihotel.com. ✆ **808/923-8828.** 81 units. From $130 double; from $249 suite. Bus: 2, 8, 13, 20. **Amenities:** Tiny pool w/sun deck; free Wi-Fi.

Shoreline Hotel Waikīkī ★   While the rest of the Waikīkī hotels went for makeovers with a soft, nostalgic vibe, Shoreline went for Nature Meets Neon, electrifying the lobby and rooms with color. You can't miss it at night: glowing like a Las Vegas club. Rooms can be a bit small and noisy, but who'll notice those things in your Instagram post? Check out

Heavenly, inside the Shoreline, with its surfer-chic decor and delicious brunch fare, including the French toast and loco moco.

342 Seaside Ave., Honolulu. https://shorelinehotelwaikiki.com. © **808/931-2444.** 125 units. From $138 double; from $249 suite. Resort fee $30. Valet parking only, $45. Bus: 2, 8, 13 or 20. **Amenities:** Pool; Wi-Fi.

Vive Hotel ★ The good: a stylish lobby, clean rooms, free continental breakfast, and no resort fee (when you book online). The bad: small, bordering on cramped quarters. But you can take advantage of the free beach mats, chairs, and umbrellas to escape to the beach just minutes away. The hotel also offers beach toys, board games, coloring sheets, crayons and a welcome balloon on arrival for kids. With a generous and friendly staff, this is a great value option.

2426 Kūhiō Ave., Honolulu. https://vivehotelwaikiki.com. © **808/687-2000.** 119 units. $136–$390 double. $34 resort fee waived when booked directly through the hotel. Valet parking $40. Bus: 2, 8, 13 and 20. **Amenities:** Free Wi-Fi.

DIAMOND HEAD WAIKĪKĪ

You'll find all these hotels between Ala Wai Boulevard and the ocean, and between Kaiulani Street and world-famous Diamond Head itself.

Moderate

Alohilani Resort ★★★ The Alohilani is one of the most impressively renovated and rebranded city hotels. The lobby opens up to ultra-high ceilings and a cocktail bar next to a two-story, 280,000-gallon aquarium. On the fifth floor is an infinity pool with an urban-meets-tropical vibe and ocean views (believe it or not, this used to be a parking lot in the old hotel). Rooms are fresh and light, in hues of white and natural wood, and the top floor oceanfront rooms feel like you're floating in the sky. Crowning the uber-cool, modern vibe are two restaurants by celebrity chef Morimoto—the upscale **Morimoto Asia Waikīkī** and the noodle-focused **Masaharu Momosan.**

2490 Kalākaua Ave., Honolulu. www.alohilaniresort.com. © **808/922-1233.** 839 units. $237–$383 double; from $1,500 suite. Resort fee $48. Valet parking $48–$55, self-parking $50. Bus: 2 or 20. **Amenities:** 10 eateries; pool; concierge; Wi-Fi.

Hotel Renew ★★ This is a stylish boutique hotel just a block from the beach. Like its lobby bar, rooms at Hotel Renew are small but well edited and well designed. You get a minimalist, Japanese aesthetic, mood lighting, and plush beds with a down featherbed and down comforter. The crowd that stays here are 20- and 30-somethings who don't need hibiscus and tropical prints to tell them they're vacationing in Hawai'i.

129 Paoakalani Ave., Honolulu. www.hotelrenew.com. © **808/687-7700.** 72 units. $166–$330 double. Resort fee $33. Valet parking $49. Bus: E, 2, 8, 13 or 20. **Amenities:** Lounge; concierge; Wi-Fi.

Kaimana Beach Hotel ★ It's almost a different world here, with Kapi'olani Park providing a buffer from the frenzy of Waikīkī. The hotel's best feature is its location right on Kaimana Beach, where the crowds are thinner and the water cleaner. The rooms can be a bit tight, but the pricier ones face the ocean straight on, with no obstructions, and have a lanai where you can lose yourself to the aquamarine blues stretching all the way to the horizon. Start your day with brunch at **Hau Tree** restaurant, now a bright, hip, tropical space that looks directly out onto Kaimana Beach. Or, have some cocktails under the canopy of the age-old tree, steps from the water, as you watch the sun set over the ocean.

2863 Kalākaua Ave. (ocean side of the street just before Diamond Head and just past the Waikīkī Aquarium, across from Kapiʻolani Park), Waikīkī. www.kaimana.com. ℂ **808/923-1555.** 124 units. $204–$293 double. Resort fee $25. Valet parking $40. Bus: 20 or 14. **Amenities:** Restaurants; beach bar, coffee shop; concierge; room service; Wi-Fi.

Lotus Honolulu at Diamond Head ★★

Here on the quiet side of Waikīkī, between Kapiʻolani Park and Diamond Head, you can sleep with the windows open. A former W Hotel property, the Lotus was updated with dark hardwood floors, platform beds, granite-tiled bathrooms, and—in the corner units—a lanai and window that frame Diamond Head beautifully.

2885 Kalākaua Ave., Waikīkī. www.lotushonolulu.com. ℂ **808/922-1700.** 51 units. $328–$350 double. $38 resort fee includes beach cruiser bikes, beach towels, beach chairs, complimentary wine hour, and more. Parking $40. Bus: 14 or 20. **Amenities:** Restaurant; concierge; Wi-Fi.

Queen Kapiʻolani Hotel ★★

The Queen Kapiʻolani hotel was built in the 1960s, during Waikīkī's Golden Age, and now, during Waikīkī's renaissance, It's gotten the refresh it deserves. Everything from the open-air lobby to the third-floor restaurant and bar, oriented so that Diamond Head fills your view, oozes soothing, beachy comfort. Not too hip, not too fussy, but just right.

150 Kapahulu Ave., Honolulu. www.queenkapiolani.com. ℂ **808/922-1941.** 315 units. $161–$340 double. Resort fee $50. Valet parking $50. Bus: 2 or 20. **Amenities:** Restaurant; pool; concierge; Wi-Fi.

HONOLULU BEYOND WAIKĪKĪ

To the East: Kahala

Kahala Hotel & Resort ★★★ Hotel magnate Conrad Hilton opened the Kahala in 1964 as a secluded and exclusive retreat away from Waikīkī. Fifty years and a different owner later, the hotel retains that feeling of peacefulness and exclusivity. Its rooms convey a unique island luxury, aka "Kahala chic." On the property, you have access to a small beach with a private feel (in Hawaiʻi, all beaches are public, but few people come here). The resort offers Dolphin Quest, which allows you to get up close and personal with the dolphins in the lagoon. The hotel's restaurants range from beachfront brunch buffet, to afternoon tea on the veranda, and an upscale Pacific Rim dinner, all of which make the Kahala a worthy escape from the bustle of Waikīkī.

5000 Kahala Ave. (next to the Waialae Country Club), Honolulu. www.kahalaresort. com. ℂ **808/739-8888.** $520–$740 double. Parking $50. **Amenities:** 5 restaurants; 4 bars; concierge; nearby golf course; fitness center; pool; room service; free Wi-Fi.

A Signature Suite at Kahala Hotel & Resort.

THE WINDWARD COAST

For the Windward side, your best bet is VRBO.com and Airbnb.com (mentioned earlier in "Vacation Rentals"), where beachy bungalows start at around $150 (plus cleaning fees) a night. *Note:* Windward Coast accommodations are located on the "Eastern Oʻahu & the Windward Coast" map (p. 97).

Kailua

Lanikai House Rentals ★　Lanikai clings tenaciously to its laidback, beachy vibe, even in the face of a growing number of visitors. Spend the night in an old-style, homey, and comfortable Lanikai house just across the street from the beach to feel a part of the neighborhood. Lanikai House Rentals offers a range of units, from a garden studio decorated in Hawaiiana print and rattan furniture, to the beachfront house once the residence of John Walker, who built the Bishop Museum and Honolulu Hale. The properties have washing machines, cooking utensils, and beach equipment—all you need to make it home.

1277 Mokulua Dr. (btw. Onekea and Aala drives in Lanikai), Kailua. www.lanikaibeach rentals.com. ✆ **808/476-7195.** From $315 for a studio to over $2,900 for a sprawling estate that sleeps nine. Some minimum night stays apply. Bus: 671. **Amenities:** Free Wi-Fi.

Sheffield House ★　Kailua is a small beach town, with restaurants, shops, and a business center. Staying with long-time Kailua residents Paul and Rachel Sheffield (they live in a separate, adjacent house on the property) puts you right in the middle of everything—It's just a few minutes' walk to the beach but also a short stroll to Whole Foods, the Sunday farmer's market, and "town" for groceries and entertainment. (Convenience does have its drawbacks, though—the house is on one of Kailua's busy streets, which means traffic sounds.) The two vacation rentals—a one-bedroom and a studio—each have their own private entry and kitchenette.

131 Kuulei Rd. (at Kalaheo Dr.), Kailua. www.hawaiisheffieldhouse.com. © **808/262-0721.** $239–$289 studio double; $259–$614 suite. Rates include 1st day's continental breakfast. Free parking. Bus: 66. **Amenities:** Free Wi-Fi.

THE NORTH SHORE

The North Shore has few tourist accommodations—some say that's its charm. VRBO.com and Airbnb.com (mentioned earlier in "Vacation Rentals") offer a good range of places to stay, with options like a Turtle Bay loft, a surfer-chic townhouse in Hale'iwa, and even a glamping-style bell tent on a Hale'iwa farm.

Note: North Shore accommodations are located on the "O'ahu's North Shore" map (p. 105).

Expensive

Turtle Bay Resort ★★★ The North Shore's only resort possesses a beachy, laidback, but luxurious style befitting the less-developed, unhurried area. The lobby and gym open up with ocean views, the restaurants' menus highlight locally grown ingredients, and rooms have ocean views, calming, neutral palettes and walk-in stone showers. Turtle Bay has also embraced its role as a surf-scene hub, especially in the wintertime, when the surfing season is in full swing. The resort really feels like a part of the North Shore landscape. Of all the resorts outside of Waikīkī (including Kahala and Aulani), this would be my pick, for the vibe, the value, and the surroundings.

57-091 Kamehameha Hwy. (Hwy. 83), Kahuku. www.turtlebayresort.com. © **808/293-6000.** $540–$770 double; from $566 suite or villa. $50 resort fee includes lei making, hula lessons, other activities, use of cruiser bikes, boogie boards, beach chairs and beach umbrellas, and more. Parking $40. Bus: 60. **Amenities:** 7 restaurants; 2 bars; concierge; golf course; horseback riding; 2 heated pools (with water slide); room service; spa; gym; tennis courts; watersports rentals; Wi-Fi.

LEEWARD O'AHU: THE WAI'ANAE COAST

Ko 'Olina is growing as the luxury hotel hub of the Leeward coast with Aulani and the Four Seasons.

Aulani, a Disney Resort & Spa, Ko Olina, Hawai'i ★★★ Aulani offers plenty of fun from Mickey and friends to entertain the kids, such as a character breakfast with photo ops, but It's also a celebration of Hawaiian culture. Disney's "Imagineers" worked with locals to get many of the details just right, from murals and woodcarvings throughout the property that tell the story of Hawai'i. At the **'Olelo Room Bar and Lounge,** common objects are labeled with their Hawaiian names (everyone learns a new language better when they're drinking, right?) and there's live Hawaiian music every night. A 900-foot-long lazy river threads through the resort, which—along with children's programs like storytelling nights under the stars, Hawaiian crafts classes, and Disney movies on the lawn—makes the Aulani, perhaps unsurprisingly, one of the best lodging choices for families. Even as a cynical adult, I am always delighted when I set foot on this property.

92-1185 Aliinui Dr., Kapolei. www.disneyaulani.com. © **866/443-4763.** 359 units. From $470 double. Parking $40. No bus. Take H-1 west toward Pearl City/Ewa Beach; stay on H-1 until it becomes Hwy. 93 (Farrington Hwy.); look for the exit sign for Ko Olina Resort; turn left on Aliinui Dr. **Amenities:** 8 restaurants; 4 bars; championship 18-hole golf course; numerous pools and water features; room service; spa; watersports rentals; free Wi-Fi.

Camping & Wilderness Cabins

If you plan to camp, you'll need to bring your own gear; there aren't places on the island to rent equipment.

The best places to camp on Oʻahu are listed below. TheBus can get you to or near all these sites but remember: You're allowed only one bag onboard, which has to fit under the seat. If you have more gear, you're going to have to drive or take a cab.

THE WINDWARD COAST

Hoomaluhia Botanical Garden ★

This little-known windward campground outside Kāneʻohe is a real treasure. It's hard to believe that It's just half an hour from downtown Honolulu. The name Hoomaluhia, or "peace and tranquility," accurately describes this 400-acre botanical garden at the foot of the jagged Koʻolau Range. In this lush setting, gardens are devoted to plants specific to tropical America, native Hawaiʻi, Polynesia, India, Sri Lanka, and Africa. A 32-acre lake sits in the middle of the scenic park (no swimming or boating allowed), and numerous hiking trails offer further exploring. The visitor center hosts events throughout the year at this and other public botanical gardens, such as garden meditation, crafts, and nature journaling.

Facilities for this tent-camp area include restrooms, cold showers, dishwashing stations, picnic tables, and water. Shopping and gas are available in Kāneʻohe, 2 miles away. Stays can be either 3 nights at $32.75, or 5 nights at $53.32. Reserve a campsite up to 2 weeks in advance at **https:// camping.honolulu.gov**. To get here from Waikīkī, take H-1 to the Pali Highway (Hwy. 61); turn left on Kamehameha Highway (Hwy. 83); and at the fourth light, turn left on Luluku Road. TheBus no. 60 stops nearby on Kamehameha Highway; from here, you'll have to walk 2 miles to the visitor center.

Kahana Bay Beach Park ★

Lying under Tahiti-like cliffs, with a beautiful gold-sand crescent beach framed by pine-needle casuarina trees, Kahana Bay Beach Park is a place of serene beauty. You can swim, bodysurf, fish, hike, and picnic or just sit and listen to the trade winds whistle through the beach pines (and sometimes, cars—the campsite is along Kamehameha Hwy.).

Facilities include restrooms, outdoor showers, picnic tables, and drinking water. *Note:* The restrooms are at the north end of the beach, far away from the camping area.

Permits can be obtained at **https://camping.ehawaii.gov** for $30 a night. Camping is only allowed Friday through Wednesday.

Kahana Bay Beach Park is located in the 52-222 block of Kamehameha Highway (Hwy. 83) in Kahana. From Waikīkī, take the H-1 west to the Likelike Highway (Hwy. 63). Continue north on the Likelike, through the Wilson Tunnel, turning left on Hwy. 83; Kahana Bay is 13 miles down the road on the right. You can also get here via TheBus no. 60.

THE NORTH SHORE
Malaekahana Bay State Recreation Area ★★

This is one of the state's most beautiful beach-camping areas, with a mile-long, gold-sand beach on Oʻahu's North Shore. At low tide, you can wade/swim out to Goat Island, a sanctuary for seabirds and turtles. There are two areas for tent camping. Facilities include picnic tables, restrooms, showers, sinks, and drinking water. For your safety, the park gate is closed between 6:45pm (7:45pm in the summer) and 7am; vehicles cannot enter or exit during those hours. An overnight parking permit is required. Groceries and gas are in Laʻie and Kahuku, each less than a mile away.

Permits are $30 a night and available at **https://camping.ehawaii.gov**. Camping is limited to Friday through Wednesday. Check-in time is 3pm.

The recreation area is located on Kamehameha Highway (Hwy. 83) between Laʻie and Kahuku. Take the H-2 to Hwy. 99 to Hwy. 83 (both roads are called Kamehameha Hwy.); continue on Hwy. 83, just past Kahuku. You can also get here via TheBus no. 60.

WHERE TO EAT ON OʻAHU

Hawaiʻi offers food experiences that exist nowhere else in the world. You'll feast on a mighty variety, from foods eaten by ancient Native Hawaiians to plate lunches in which you can taste the multi-ethnic history of modern Hawaiʻi. Dining ranges from postwar-era holes-in-the-wall (where the only thing that's changed is the prices) to fancy dining rooms that spawned the birth of Hawaiʻi Regional Cuisine. Asian food dominates, thanks to the state's demographics (2023 census data show "Asian" as the largest race demographic category, at 37.1% of the total population). On Oʻahu, the most promising places to eat are often in the most unexpected places. For the adventurous, eating here is like a treasure hunt.

Honolulu: Waikīkī

Dining out in Waikīkī is not just about the food. It's also about the extensive beverage lists, charming-to-grandiose ambience, and some of Honolulu's most luxurious dining room views.

La Mer ★★ NEOCLASSICAL FRENCH La Belle Époque meets Pacific teak and rattan against heart-achingly romantic views of the ocean and Diamond Head. Sometimes It's all a little over the top, like when a red rose the size of your fist is perched on your cocktail, but those into haute French cuisine with a touch of the theatrical will love La Mer. Choose from three- or four-course tasting menus or the *menu dégustation,* seven courses featuring luxe ingredients such as foie gras tiled with shiitake mushrooms, abalone *meunière,* lobster tail bathed in butter and lobster consommé, and a filet of beef with truffle. La Mer is one of the few restaurants that requires men to wear a jacket or long-sleeved shirt. Luxe indeed. At the Halekulani, 2199 Kalia Rd., Waikīkī, Honolulu. www.halekulani.com. © **808/ 923-2311.** Reservations recommended. Jackets or long-sleeved shirts required for men. From $255 tasting menu, $295 *menu dégustation;* $175 for wine pairing. Tues– Sat 5:30–8:30pm.

La Vie ★ MODERN FRENCH La Vie's elegant dining room is an open-air lanai up on the eighth floor of the sleek Ritz-Carlton Residences, fitted with eye-catching green tile, clean wood accents, and modern design touches that feel both upscale and understated. Watch the sun set over Waikīkī as you dine but you might be distracted from the views by the parade of playful dishes from the kitchen. La Vie offers a prix fixe dining affair, with a range of offerings that in the past have included luxurious go-to's such as oysters with smoked potato, chive and roe or a foie gras brûle with poached grape, baby fennel, and almond crème. Truffle squab or dry-aged yellow-tail are entree-sized options you may encounter but their delectable desserts steal the show: an airy cake with flavors of raspberry and *liliko'i,* or a truffled cheese tarte, for instance. A word to the

dining out **AT THE HALEKULANI**

Sure, dining in Waikīkī's high-end hotels is often an overpriced affair, but sometimes the occasion warrants everything that comes with it—including ocean views and upscale service. My pick for special events is the **Halekulani ★★★** (p. 129). Here are my favorite ways to soak up some rarefied restaurant experiences:

○ The **Sunday brunch buffet** at **Orchids** is a must—It's the best in Hawai'i, with everything from a roast-suckling-pig carving station to a sashimi and poke bar. Leave room for the Halekulani's signature fluffy coconut cake, and lots of dainty desserts. (**Note:** Reserve a spot weeks in advance.) Love afternoon tea? Orchids also serves my favorite **afternoon tea** service on the island, with an array of sandwiches and sweets, as well as an excellent selection of premium teas.

○ Come sunset, head to **House Without a Key** for a mai tai and the lovely hula of former Miss Hawaiis.

○ If the occasion calls for something more romantic and intimate, I go to **L'Aperitif,** the bar inside La Mer, 19th-century French cocktail culture inspires the drinks.

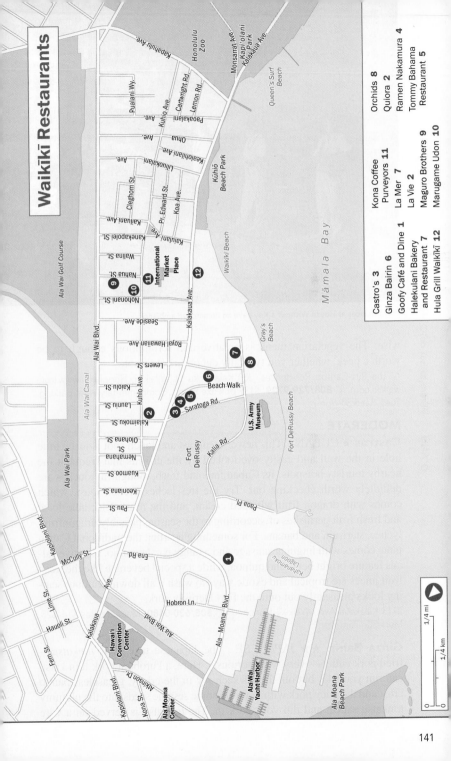

Waikīkī Restaurants

Castro's **3**
Ginza Bairin **6**
Goofy Café and Dine **1**
Halekulani Bakery and Restaurant **7**
Hula Grill Waikīkī **12**

Kona Coffee Purveyors **11**
La Mer **7**
La Vie **2**
Maguro Brothers **9**
Marugame Udon **10**

Orchids **8**
Quiora **2**
Ramen Nakamura **4**
Tommy Bahama Restaurant **5**

Performances at House Without a Key have an unmatched ambiance.

wise: The vegetarian menu is creative and scrumptious enough to be worth a peek, whether you typically cut out meat or not.

At the Ritz-Carlton Residences, 383 Kalaimoku St., Waikīkī, Honolulu. www.lavie waikiki.com. © **808/729-9729.** $139 prix fixe menu. Complimentary valet parking. Tues–Sat 5:30–9pm.

MODERATE

Castros ★ CUBAN   This newer breakfast and lunch spot is just a little hole in the wall and easily overlooked by the crowds that frequent the nearby touristy hotspots. Its Cuban fare and fresh, thoughtful touches are definitely worth checking out. Try the tres leches French toast, which comes with dragon fruit whipped cream, and the most delectable local and fresh fruit garnishes of, according to the season, possibly dragonfruit, lychee, starfruit, and banana. For something heartier, the traditional Cuban plate comes with linguica sausage and a tangy parsley mojo. Creative salads feature bright beets and quinoa, while a special beverage like the fresh fruit juices are tropical and exotic ways to wash it all down. Outdoor seating looks pleasantly out onto the Fort Derussy park.

2113 Kalākaua Ave., Waikīkī, Honolulu. © **808/630-0480.** Main courses $14–$25. Mon–Sun 7am–1pm.

Ginza Bairin ★★ JAPANESE   The Japanese take their *tonkatsu*— fried pork cutlets—very, very seriously. Here, a kurobota pork loin katsu can run you $43, but oh, there's such joy in the crispy, greaseless panko crust and the juicy pork within. Grind some sesame seeds into the plummy tonkatsu sauce, and dip your pork in. The tonkatsu is served on a wire pedestal (to keep the bottom from steaming and going soggy) and a bottomless chiffonade of cabbage salad.

255 Beach Walk, Waikīkī, Honolulu. www.ginzabairin.com. © **808/926-8082.** Main courses $12–$36. Daily 11am–2:30pm; dinner 4–9:15pm.

Goofy Café and Dine ★ HEALTHY   Named not after the Disney character but the right-foot-forward surfing stance, this charming spot has a cozy, beachy vibe, lined with reclaimed wood and decorated with surfboards that, from the looks of it, are waxed and ready to go. (The popular locals' surfing spot, Bowls, is nearby.) Goofy's breakfast menu is a hot commodity: Look for eggs Benedict, French toast drizzled with creamy Hawai'i Island honey, green smoothies poured over chia seeds, and huge açai bowls mounded over with fresh fruit.

1831 Ala Moana Blvd., Suite 201., Waikīkī, Honolulu. www.goofy-honolulu.com. © **808/943-0077.** Breakfast $13–$27. Daily 7am–2pm; dinner 5–9pm.

Hula Grill Waikīkī ★ AMERICAN   The night before, you might be slamming back tiki drinks and making new friends at the ever popular and rowdy Duke's (p. 166) down below. For the morning after, head to Hula Grill (owned by the same group as Duke's), where the ocean views, banana-and-macnut pancakes. and chewy strawberry mochi waffle will smooth out any hangover. Breakfast and brunch are the most reasonably priced meals.

At the Outrigger Waikiki on the Beach, 2335 Kalākaua Ave., Waikīkī, Honolulu. www.hulagrillwaikiki.com. © **808/923-HULA** [4852]. Reservations recommended for dinner. Breakfast $15–$23. Daily 7am–10:30pm.

Kona Coffee Purveyors ★ CAFE/BAKERY   One of Hawai'i's best coffee companies teamed up with one of San Francisco's best pastry chefs, Belinda Leong, and the result is a perfect cup of coffee paired with perfect baked goods. Don't miss the *kouign-amann,* flaky croissant dough crusted with caramelized sugar and layered with flavors such as black sesame, chocolate or *li hing* (a sweet, salty, sour plum flavor that's big with locals) with *liliko'i* and mango. The coffee and lattes are excellent, made with 100% Kona coffee thoughtfully sourced from Hawai'i Island of Hawai'i. The ambience—with its French-style bistro chairs and tiled European cafe interior—is perfect for morning sipping. But be warned: This coffee shop has gotten *wildly* popular in recent years, thanks to the top-tier quality and chic ambience. Be prepared to wait in line if you're going at prime morning coffee hour or wait until things die down around late morning.

At International Marketplace, 2330 Kalākaua Ave, Waikīkī, Honolulu. www.konacoffeepurveyors.com. © **808/450-2364.** Pastries $4–$15. Daily 7am–4pm.

Quiora ★★ ITALIAN   Also perched up on the Ritz-Carlton Residences' eight floor among some winding, scenic vistas, this newer, upscale spot scores big points for dishing out top-tier Italian fare that doesn't stray too far from the tried-and-true classics. Simply great ingredients get fantastic results with dishes like the delectably succulent Calabrian garlic shrimp, made with Kauaʻi prawns, or an easy array of housemade spreads that include cannellini bean spread, citrus ricotta, and smoked ahi dip. Hearty pasta dishes like the porcini pappardelle or spaghetti carbonara hit the pasta spot, while non-pasta entrees include Wagyu ribeye and wood grilled fish. Try this spot for a breezy, sunshine-filled rooftop wine lunch, or as a romantic Friday night dinner (you'll get the perfect view of the Fri night fireworks).

At The Ritz-Carlton Residences, 383 Kalaimoku St., Waikīkī, Honolulu. www.quiora waikiki.com. © 808/729-9757. Reservations recommended for dinner. Main courses $20–$32 lunch; $37–$78 dinner. Daily 11:30am–3:30pm; dinner 5:30–9pm.

Tommy Bahama Restaurant ★ AMERICAN/PACIFIC RIM   I know, It's weird, a restaurant in a clothing store? But there are many reasons to eat here: the relaxing rooftop bar with sand and firepits (your new aloha shirt would fit right in here, but so would shorts and a T-shirt), a menu that sounds cliche (aka coconut shrimp and macadamia nut-crusted fish) but is actually pretty tasty, and great cocktails, including martinis with blue cheese-stuffed olives for when you tire of tropical drinks.

298 Beachwalk Drive, Waikīkī, Honolulu. www.tommybahama.com. © 808/923-8785. Main courses $29–$56. Daily 2–9pm.

INEXPENSIVE

Halekulani Bakery and Restaurant ★ BAKERY   Walk into this beautiful little bakery on the quiet, back end of Helumoa Road, and you'll be treated to the most beautiful rows of gleaming, picture-perfect breads and (generously sized) pastries. The glazed cinnamon roll, creamy melon pan, and rich chocolate croissant are all winners.

2233 Helumoa Rd., Waikīkī, Honolulu. www.halekulani.com. © 808/921-7272. Bakery items $4–$20. Daily 6:30am–11:30am.

Maguro Brothers ★★★ SEAFOOD   Poke bowls have swept the continental U.S., but the best one you'll ever have is in Hawaiʻi at this little takeout window. You'll find pristine ahi (tuna) in a variety of poke seasonings, from the classic shoyu (soy sauce and sesame oil) to the bright ume shiso (an herby, pickled-plum concoction). If you need a break from poke, don't miss the chirashi donburi featuring a variety of super-fresh sashimi. Better yet, get both. (There's also a Chinatown location inside Kekaulike Market, open for lunch.)

415 Nahua St., Waikīkī, Honolulu. © 808/230-3470. Bowls $16.50–$25.50. Mon–Sat 5pm–8pm.

Marugame Udon ★★ JAPANESE/UDON   There's always a massive line out the door at this cafeteria-style noodle joint, but it moves quickly. Pass the time by watching the cooks roll out and cut the dough for udon right in front of you. Bowls of udon, hot or cold, with toppings such as a soft poached egg or Japanese curry, are all under $12 before tempura add-ons.

2310 Kūhiō Ave., Waikīkī, Honolulu. © 808/931-6000. Noodles $6–$12. Daily 10am–10pm.

going local: UNIQUELY HAWAIIAN EATS

Talk to locals who move away from Hawai'i, and these are the foods they miss. Everyone's got their own go-to place and go-to dishes—people here could spend hours arguing over the best. Here are some of my favorites:

Poke Ruby-red cubes of fresh 'ahi (tuna), tossed with limu (seaweed), kukui nut, and Hawaiian chili pepper: Ahi poke (pronounced "po-kay") doesn't get better than the Hawaiian-style version at **Ono Seafood** ★★ (p. 146) or any variety at **Maguro Bros** ★★★ (p. 144).

Saimin An only-in-Hawai'i mashup of Chinese-style noodles in a Japanese dashi broth. Join the regulars at the communal table at **Palace Saimin,** 1256 N. King St. (© 808/841-9983), where the interior is as simple as this bowl of noodles. Palace Saimin has been around since 1946, and it looks like it. (I mean that in the nicest way possible.)

Loco moco Two sunny side up eggs over a hamburger patty and rice, all doused in brown gravy. I love it at **Liliha Bakery** ★ (p. 151).

Spam musubi Ah yes, Spam. Hawai'i eats more Spam per capita than any other state. A dubious distinction to some, but don't knock it before you try it. Spam *musubi* (think of it as a giant piece of sushi topped with Spam) is so ubiquitous you can find it at 7-Elevens and convenience stores (where It's pretty good). But for an even finer product, **Musubi Café Iyasume,** Ala Moana Center (© 808/304-8558), is great for grabbing a bit for the beach and has some

odd-yet-delectable combinations, such as takuan (pickled radish—so good!), ume (pickled plum), shiso, and avocado spam musubis.

Hawaiian plate *Laulau* (pork wrapped in taro leaves), kalua pig (shredded, roasted pork), poi (milled taro), and haupia (like coconut Jell-O): It's Hawaiian lū'au food, based on what native Hawaiians used to eat. Find it at **Helena's Hawaiian Food** ★★★ (p. 151) and **Highway Inn** ★ (p. 147).

Malasadas Hole-less doughnuts, rolled in sugar, by way of Portugal. **Leonard's Bakery,** 933 Kapahulu Ave. (© 808/737-5591), opened in 1946 by the descendants of Portuguese contract laborers brought to work in Hawai'i's sugarcane fields. I love Leonard's *malasadas* dusted with *li hing mui* powder (made from dried, sweet-tart plums).

Shave ice Nothing cools better on a hot day than powdery-soft ice drenched in tropical fruit syrups. **Matsumoto** (p. 158) is the classic, but I go to **Waiola Shave Ice,** 2135 Waiola St., for the nostalgia factor. Since you'll probably need more than one shave ice while you're in town, also hit up **Uncle Clay's House of Pure Aloha,** 820 W. Hind Dr., No. 116 (© 808/520-5898), which offers a variety of homemade syrups from real fruit (a rarity).

Ramen Nakamura ★ JAPANESE/RAMEN Squeeze into this narrow ramen bar, grab a seat at the U-shaped counter, and get ready to slurp some noodles. It's famous for its oxtail ramen (think of oxtail like ribs—meaty chunks eaten off the bone—but from the tail), served with a side of fresh grated ginger and soy sauce for dipping. The spicy ramen is also a winner.

2141 Kalākaua Ave., Waikīkī, Honolulu. © **808/922-7960.** Noodles $14–$25. Daily 11am–11:30pm.

Honolulu Beyond Waikīkī

KAPAHULU

Moderate

Side Street Inn on Da Strip ★ LOCAL   This comfort food locale is a local favorite, but don't expect a lot of health food! We're talking hearty, flavorful dishes heavy on the frying and starches, similar to other Asian-cuisine-heavy bar-food menus you'll find around town. The original location near Ala Moana had a divey, locals-only atmosphere, but you'll find the same menu of fried pork chops and kimchi fried rice with bacon, Portuguese sausage, and *lup cheong* (a sweet-ish Chinese sausage) at this bigger, newer spot. Portion sizes are as huge as ever.

614 Kapahulu Ave., Honolulu. www.sidestreetinn.com. ℘ **808/739-3939.** Starters $11–$22; main courses $20–$31. Mon–Fri 4–8:30pm; Sat–Sun 11am–8:30pm.

Inexpensive

Ono Seafood ★★ LOCAL   This little seafood counter serves some of Honolulu's freshest and best poke—cubes of ruby-red ahi (tuna) seasoned to order with soy sauce and onions for the shoyu poke or *limu* (seaweed) and Hawaiian salt for Hawaiian-style poke.

747 Kapahulu Ave., Apt. 4, Honolulu. ℘ **808/732-4806.** Poke bowls start at $17. Tues–Sat 9am–4pm.

ALA MOANA & KAKA'AKO

Expensive

53 by the Sea ★ FUSION FINE DINING   From the industrial park setting outside, you wouldn't believe this ultra-elegant spot existed. Step through the doors, though, and you find a palatial interior, complete with grand staircase. The real reason to stop by: a jaw-dropping view through the expansive picture windows of the Waikīkī coastline all the way to Diamond Head. Stop in at the bar for an elegant or romantic cocktail, enjoy a killer sunset view, or take advantage of their delectable brunch (with mimosa or breakfast cocktail, options!) on Sunday from 10am to 1pm.

53 Ahui St., Honolulu. www.53bythesea.com. ℘ **808/536-5353.** Main courses $32–$100. Wed–Sun 5pm–9pm; Sun brunch 10am–1pm.

MW Restaurant ★★ HAWAI'I REGIONAL CUISINE   Michelle Karr-Ueoka and Wade Ueoka, the wife-and-husband team in the kitchen, are Alan Wong alums, and here they give their own take on Hawai'i Regional Cuisine. What that means at MW is local comfort food re-envisioned for fine dining. An ahi poke dish turns the familiar staple into something unexpected, with spicy tuna, ikura, 'ahi, and uni topped with crispy rice crackers. Oxtail soup becomes oxtail, deboned and stuffed with more meat, and set on beef-stew risotto. Desserts outshine the entrees, though, such as a chocolate banana cream pie layered into a jar or a lemon meringue brûlée, full of custard, chewy jellies, and lemon sorbet, and sealed with a torched sugar crust. You've never had anything like it.

888 Kapi'olani Blvd., #201, Honolulu. www.mwrestaurant.com. ✆ **808/955-6505.** Reservations recommended. Main courses $26–$79 dinner; desserts $14–$16. Tues–Fri lunch to-go only 11am–2pm; dinner 5–9pm.

Moderate

Highway Inn ★ HAWAIIAN/LOCAL   The original Highway Inn in Waipahu opened in 1947, serving Hawaiian food such as *laulau* (pork wrapped in taro leaves and steamed), *kalua pig* (smoky, roasted pork), and *poi* (mashed taro). Also on the menu: classic American fare, such as beef stew and hamburgers, recipes that founder Seiichi Toguchi picked up in internment-camp mess halls during World War II. For decades, Highway Inn remained a snapshot of food in post-war Hawai'i. The Honolulu location opened in 2012 and introduced a few twists. The old favorites still remain, though, in the newer plantation-era-inspired restaurant.

680 Ala Moana Blvd., Honolulu. www.myhighwayinn.com. ✆ **808/954-4955.** Plates $16–$31. Mon–Thurs 9:30am–8pm; Fri until 8:30pm; Sat 9–8:30pm; Sun 9:30am–3pm.

Moku Kitchen ★ MODERN AMERICAN/HAWAI'I REGIONAL CUISINE   Fun cocktails, cold beers, plates made for sharing, burgers, and live music make Moku Kitchen a lively place to refuel. This is the latest concept from Chef Peter Merriman, one of the original Hawai'i Regional Cuisine founders, and It's a crowd pleaser.

660 Ala Moana Blvd., Honolulu. www.mokukitchen.com. ✆ **808/591-6658.** Plates $17–$37. Sun–Wed 11am–9pm; Thurs–Sat until 10pm; daily happy hour 2–5:30pm.

Inexpensive

Aloha Beer Co. ★ BREWERY   Drinking in carports, like the poor man's lanai, is a Hawai'i thing. You can approximate it at this craft brewery's warehouse digs, where the atmosphere is casual and the tables communal. Choose from a wide range of beers, some seasonal and experimental, which range from light session beers to extra-hoppy IPAs. Pair them with any of the hearty pizzas, pretzels or salads.

700 Queen St., Honolulu. www.alohabeer.com. ✆ **808/544-1605.** Pizzas and small plates $12–$32. Mon–Fri 11am–10pm; Sat 10am–11pm; Sun 10am–10pm.

DOWNTOWN/CHINATOWN

Expensive

Fête ★ MODERN AMERICAN   In a space that's come to define the new modern Chinatown aesthetic—lofty ceilings and redbrick walls—Chef Robynne Maii (who won a James Beard Award in 2022, making her the first female chef from Hawai'i to win!) serves the food she craves. What that means: polished comfort food with no boundaries. You'll find housemade pasta, fresh and lively salads that utilize local and seasonal produce (like sunchokes) to gorgeous effect, an absolutely perfect Korean chicken sandwich, and to-die-for rocky road ice cream made in house.

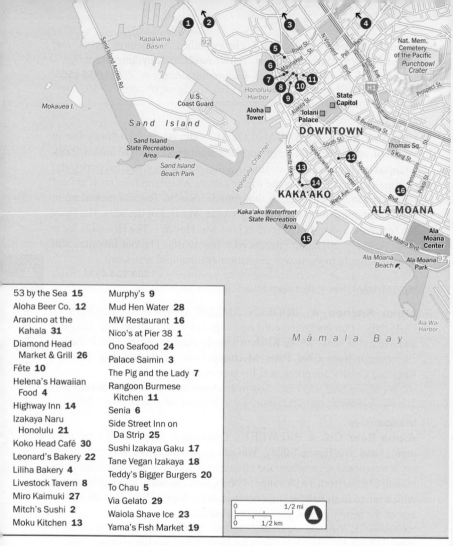

53 by the Sea **15**	Murphy's **9**
Aloha Beer Co. **12**	Mud Hen Water **28**
Arancino at the Kahala **31**	MW Restaurant **16**
Diamond Head Market & Grill **26**	Nico's at Pier 38 **1**
	Ono Seafood **24**
Fête **10**	Palace Saimin **3**
Helena's Hawaiian Food **4**	The Pig and the Lady **7**
Highway Inn **14**	Rangoon Burmese Kitchen **11**
Izakaya Naru Honolulu **21**	Senia **6**
Koko Head Café **30**	Side Street Inn on Da Strip **25**
Leonard's Bakery **22**	Sushi Izakaya Gaku **17**
Liliha Bakery **4**	Tane Vegan Izakaya **18**
Livestock Tavern **8**	Teddy's Bigger Burgers **20**
Miro Kaimuki **27**	To Chau **5**
Mitch's Sushi **2**	Via Gelato **29**
Moku Kitchen **13**	Waiola Shave Ice **23**
	Yama's Fish Market **19**

This is also a great spot just for grabbing a cocktail, with a well-stocked bar that serves up excellent classics with subtle, creative twists.

2 N. Hotel St., Honolulu. www.fetehawaii.com. © **808/369-1390.** Main courses $18–$55. Mon–Sat 11am–9pm.

Moderate

Livestock Tavern ★★ AMERICAN For the past 2 decades, restaurateurs and artists have been trying to revitalize Chinatown, which, in the second half of the 20th century, became better known as a red-light district than a place to eat and hang out. Restauranteurs have helped make Chinatown a destination with eateries like Livestock Tavern. It serves modern American food at its finest, with an excellent cocktail menu to boot. The menu changes throughout the year, but always has a range of

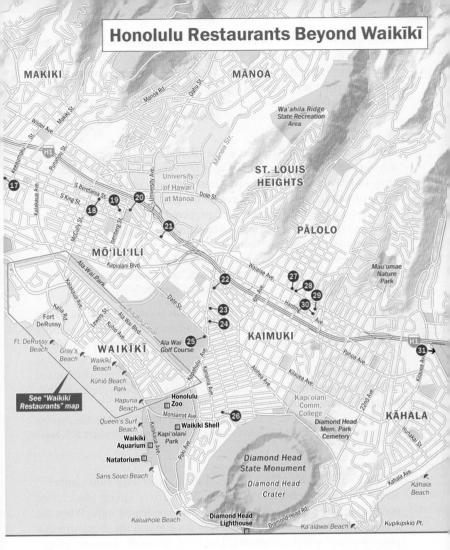

small-to-large and light-to-heavy elevated comfort foods. Think lobster rolls and ultra-savory oxtail mac and cheese, smoked octopus with sausage and crab-crusted salmon. Their hamburger is one of Honolulu's best. 49 N. Hotel St., Honolulu. www.livestocktavern.com. ☏ **808/537-2577.** Reservations recommended. Main courses $16–$45. Daily 5–10pm; Sat–Sun brunch 10am–2pm.

The Pig and the Lady ★★★ MODERN VIETNAMESE   This is one of Chinatown's liveliest dining rooms, with brick walls, long communal tables hewed from single slabs of mango wood, benches reupholstered with burlap rice bags, and a rotating display of fun, bright prints by local, young artists. The Pig and the Lady introduces you to a world of Vietnamese noodle soups beyond pho—such as one with oxtail, another with crab and tomato. But Chef Andrew Le also applies creative twists to Southeast

Asian food for unique eats like a pho French dip banh mi—an absolute must with its melting slices of braised brisket, smeared with a bright Thai basil chimichurri and served with a side of pho broth for dipping. Everything is on point here, from the cocktails to the dessert.

83 N. King St., Honolulu. www.thepigandthelady.com. ℗ **808/585-8255.** Reservations recommended. Main courses $24–$45. Tues–Sat lunch 11:30am–2:30pm; dinner 5:30–9:30pm.

Rangoon Burmese Kitchen ★★★ BURMESE   Come for the stews, stay for the salads at this gem of spot just off of Hotel Street. The vast array of heavily spiced southeast Asian dishes on offer means a diverse menu of unusual and new flavors and textures to explore and discover. Options range from the tea leaf salad peppered with crunchy garlic chips, beans and seeds, and an ultra-tangy tamarind dressing, to the wok-tossed pork belly and pickled mustard greens, to the whole fish marinated with herbs and aromatics and wrapped in banana leaves.

1131 Nu'uanu Ave., Honolulu. ℗ **808/367-0645.** Reservations recommended. Main courses $15–$25 dinner. Mon–Sat lunch 11am–2pm; dinner 5–10pm.

Senia ★★★ MODERN AMERICAN   This is one of Honolulu's most exciting restaurants, where something as ordinary as cabbage can surprise and delight. Senia, deriving from "xenia," the Greek word for hospitality, is a rare mesh of the fine dining and comfort food worlds. The food is fancy—bone marrow custard, foie gras terrine, and pretty presentations of smoked salmon with date and cauliflower—but the flavors are accessible, the setting leans casual, and the prices are moderate.

75 N. King St., Honolulu. www.restaurantsenia.com. ℗ **808/200-5412.** Reservations recommended. Small plates $12–$40; shareable large-format dishes from $88. Tues–Sat 5:30–9:30pm.

Inexpensive

To Chau ★ VIETNAMESE PHO   Walk in, order a medium number 9, meat outside, and iced coffee with milk. What arrives: strong, black coffee percolating into a mug and a cup of ice and condensed milk. When the coffee is finished brewing, dump it into the cup and stir. Next arrives a plate mounded with bean sprouts, Thai basil, sawtooth coriander, jalapeños, and lemon wedges. Soon after comes the bowl, with flank, tendon, and tripe, as well as slices of rare steak to dip into the hot broth like fondue. You can get your pho with all the meat in and just steak if you want. Getting the pho and Vietnamese coffee are easy choices. What's more difficult is choosing from over a dozen possible combinations of toppings.

1007 River St., Honolulu. ℗ **808/533-4549.** Reservations not accepted. Main courses $13–$17. Cash only. Daily 8:30am–2:30pm.

KALIHI/LILIHA/SAND ISLAND

Moderate

Mitch's Sushi ★★ SUSHI   The family that owns Mitch's Sushi also owns a seafood import business, which is why Mitch's has some of the freshest fish around. It's one of Honolulu's most expensive sushi bars, as well as its most casual, a place where slippers (local lingo for flip-flops) and T-shirts are the norm, along with a cooler of beer (Mitch's is BYOB). Here you'll find New Zealand salmon, as luxurious as fatty tuna belly, and Mitch's famous lobster sashimi, which you inspect as It's brought to your table, alive and kicking, and then sample in the form of sashimi and lobster miso soup.

524 Ohohia St., Honolulu. www.mitchssushi.com. © **808/837-7774.** Reservations recommended. Sushi $4–$95. Daily 11:30am–8pm.

Inexpensive

Helena's Hawaiian Food ★★★ HAWAIIAN   When first-generation-Chinese Helen Chock started Helena's in 1946 (she added an "a" at the end to make it sound more "Hawaiian"), she served Chinese and Hawaiian food. Eventually, she pared down the menu to the most popular items—Hawaiian food such as *laulau*, kalua pig, and poi. Sixty years later, her grandson runs the place, and It's as popular as ever. What makes Helena's stand out among other Hawaiian food restaurants? The *pipikaula:* marinated, bone-in short ribs hung above the stove to dry and fried right before they land on your table.

1240 N. School St., Honolulu. www.helenashawaiianfood.com. © **808/845-8044.** Most individual items under $10; plates $16–40. Tues–Fri 10am–7:30pm.

Liliha Bakery ★ AMERICAN/LOCAL   It's a bakery, well known for its Coco Puffs (similar to cream puffs), but It's also one of O'ahu's favorite old-school diners, beloved by young and old alike. Sit at the counter and watch the ladies at the flattop and grill deftly turning out light and fluffy pancakes, crispy, buttery waffles, loaded country-style omelets, and satisfying burgers and hamburger steaks. A newer location is on Nimitz, but the original's quaint diner counter ambience is hard to beat.

515 N. Kuakini St., Honolulu. www.lilihabakeryhawaii.com. © **808/531-1651.** Plates $14–27. Daily 6am–10pm.

Nico's at Pier 38 ★ FRESH FISH   Nico's has expanded from a hole-in-the-wall to a gleaming, open-air restaurant almost four times its original size. The food isn't quite as good as it used to be, but It's still one of the best places around to get fresh fish plates for under $20. I also love its setting along the industrial waterfront, where Hawai'i's commercial fishing fleet resides—this isn't a fake fisherman's wharf but the real deal. Popular dishes here are the furikake pan-seared ahi and the catch-of-the-day special—perhaps opah sauced with tomato beurre blanc or swordfish topped with crab bisque. They also have a fish market next door where you can take fresh poke and smoked swordfish to eat on the tables outside. Renting a place with a kitchen? Pick up fresh fish filets to take home and cook. (There's also a new location in Kailua.)

Pier 38, 1129 N. Nimitz Hwy., Honolulu. www.nicospier38.com. © **808/540-1377.** Main courses $8–$15 lunch; $14–$38 dinner. Mon–Sat 6:30am–9pm; Sun 10am–9pm.

MĀNOA VALLEY/MŌʻILIʻILI/MAKIKI

Expensive

Sushi Izakaya Gaku ★★★ JAPANESE   There is life beyond maguro and hamachi nigiri, and the best place to experience it is at Izakaya Gaku. The Izakaya restaurants embrace small plates as the best way to eat and drink with friends; although Honolulu offers many of them, Izakaya Gaku is the best. Here you can get uncommon seasonal sushi and seafood, such as wild yellowtail and grilled ray. One of the best dishes here is a hamachi tartare, with hamachi scraped off the bones and topped with tobiko and raw quail egg, served with sheets of crisp nori. You're not likely to be disappointed with any dish here.

1329 S. King St., Honolulu. ℂ **808/589-1329.** Reservations highly recommended. Main courses $5–$50. Mon–Sat 5–9:30pm.

Tane Vegan Izakaya ★ VEGAN SUSHI   The tasteful interior of this modern Japanese restaurant, a sister to San Francisco's popular Shizen sushi bar, looks just like any other sushi joint at first glance. It's got cool stone detailing and a glass-faced counter where sushi chefs busily carve out rolls. A closer look will show you that instead of salmon and ahi filets, however, the knives are at work on chunks of smoked beet and tempura eggplant, or sweet potato and pickled mango. In fact, the restaurant is fully plant-based, which makes the depth and richness of their satisfying sushi all the more impressive—for vegetarians or non-vegetarians alike.

2065 S. Beretania St., www.tanevegan.com. ℂ **808/888-7678.** Reservations highly recommended. Sushi and small plates $7–$18. Tues–Sat 4:30pm–10pm.

Moderate

Izakaya Naru Honolulu ★★ OKINAWAN/JAPANESE   What this little spot lacks in size, it makes up for in lively style. A festive, izakaya ambience prevails over a handful of tables and some counter seating. The playful menu merges more delicate Japanese delicacies with quintessential bar and comfort foods, making it a lot of fun for dinner. By playful menu, I mean both the types of dishes tucked in here and there (like that gyoza pizza), but also the hand-written specials and stripped-down feel. If It's available on special, try the yuzukosho (a tangy, ultra-flavorful condiment made from the Japanese citrus fruit, yuzu) on anything. This place gets packed quick, so make reservations.

2700 King St., Honolulu. www.naru-honolulu.com. ℂ **808/951-0510.** Reservations recommended. Plates $7–$50. Mon–Sat 5:30pm–2am, Sun until 1am.

Inexpensive

Teddy's Bigger Burgers ★ BURGERS   The first Teddy's Bigger Burgers opened over 2 decades ago at the foot of Diamond Head. Since then, It's become a bit of an island staple, expanding locations all across the state. It's still a great place to go to indulgently satiate a burger-n-shake mood, and you'll be able to spot some uniquely Hawaiian flavors among their lineup of options, like teri burgers and Kilauea Fire bbq sauce. The shakes are as thick and ice-creamy as a shake ought to be, and the umami fries—doused in furikake and garlic butter—are a must.

2424 S. Beretania St., Honolulu. www.teddysbb.com. ✆ **808/949-0050.** Main courses $8–$20. Daily 10am–9pm.

Yama's Fish Market ★ LOCAL   While Helena's and Ono's get a lot of attention for great Hawaiian food, Yama's seems to fall under the radar. Locals know, though, that this unassuming spot in a decidedly non-touristy area of Honolulu, is the place to go for an island-style plate lunch. You'll find Hawaiian lū'au classics like laulau, lomi salmon, and kalua pig. Other local comfort food favorites that have a bit more Western-influence include beef stew, Hawai'i-style (which means extra tomato-y), and chicken long rice, featuring savory chicken broth and glass noodles. You can also get all the fun sides here, from poi to poke to kimchi cucumber to pipikaula, and local desserts like broken glass Jell-O (condensed milk Jell-O with rainbow Jell-O cubes mixed in), cheesecake squares, and kulolo.

2332 Young St., Honolulu. www.yamasfishmarket.com. ✆ **808/941-9994.** Plates and bowls $10–$25. Wed–Sun 9am–5pm.

KAIMUKI
Moderate
Miro Kaimuki ★ CONTEMPORARY FRENCH/JAPANESE   Miro Kaimuki (which is a partnership between well-known Honolulu chef Chris Kajioka and San Francisco's Mourad Lahlou, of Aziza fame), describes its creations as part of "a French-inspired menu punctuated with Japanese flavors and techniques." For a diner, it feels like a parade of little works of art, with Asian and Western touches sprinkled throughout, but always coming together into something very beautiful, very modern, and very delicious. The prix fixe menu changes regularly, so you're sure to find something fresh and inspiring when you visit.

3446 Waialae Ave., Honolulu. www.mirokaimuki.com. ✆ **808/379-0214.** Reservations highly recommended for dinner. From $100 prix fixe, with $50 wine pairings and optional add-ons. Wed–Mon 5–9pm. Sunday brunch 9:30am–12:30pm.

Mud Hen Water ★ MODERN HAWAIIAN   Mud Hen Water's hip, inventive menu draws inspiration from all the cultures influencing Hawai'i. What that translates into: mapo tofu gravy and biscuits, croquettes stuffed with chicken long rice and doughnuts made with 'uala, or Hawaiian sweet potato. You won't find dishes like this anywhere else, and the cocktails and casual-artsy bar atmosphere make this spot worth hitting up just for happy hour. It's also one of my favorite spots for brunch, thanks to top-tier options on both the savory (pork *sisig,* an incredible Filipino pig head dish) and sweet (sourdough pancakes) ends of the spectrum. Most dinner plates are small and made for sharing.

3452 Waialae Ave. (at 9th St.), Honolulu. www.mudhenwater.com. ✆ **808/737-6000.** Reservations highly recommended for dinner. Small plates $8–$30. Tues–Thurs 11am–9pm; Fri–Sat until 9:30pm; Sun 9:30am–2pm.

Inexpensive

Koko Head Café ★ BREAKFAST/BRUNCH   This "island-style brunch house" offers inspired takes on breakfast classics. There's the cornflake French toast, crunchy on the outside and custardy on the inside, crowned with frosted flake gelato, and the Don Buri Chen, a rice bowl for carnivores, with miso-smoked pork, five-spice pork belly, and eggs.

1120 12th Ave., Honolulu. www.kokoheadcafe.com. © **808/732-8920.** Main courses $9–$30. Wed–Sun 7am–2pm.

Via Gelato ★ DESSERT   When you've had your fill of shave ice, come here for gelato churned daily in island-inspired flavors such as guava, lychee, strawberry, and *ume* (salted plum). It's a tough decision, though, choosing between those and other favorites such as green tea Oreo and black sesame. The flavors change daily. Be sure to get here early on weekend nights before they run out.

1142 12th Ave., Honolulu. www.viagelatohawaii.com. © **808/732-2800.** Scoops starting around $5. Daily 11am–10pm.

TO THE EAST: DIAMOND HEAD & KAHALA

Expensive

Arancino at the Kahala ★★ MODERN ITALIAN   This, Arancino's third location (the other two are in Waikīkī), isn't a casual trattoria; It's meant to be a fine-dining destination with a dress code (pants and shoes required for men). Menu standouts in the past have included a *bagna cauda*, with the vegetables planted in a pot of cremini mushroom "dirt"; grilled calamari, shrimp, and seafood over housemade squid-ink chitarra; and a decadent uni spaghetti. For a town surprisingly short on alfresco dining, especially outside of Waikīkī, Arancino at the Kahala is a breath of fresh air (even if it is facing the Kahala Resort's valet).

At the Kahala Hotel Resort, 5000 Kahala Ave., Honolulu. www.kahalaresort.com. © **808/380-4400.** Reservations recommended. Collared shirts and long pants required for men. Main courses $18–$100 and up. Daily 5pm–9pm.

Inexpensive

Diamond Head Market & Grill ★ AMERICAN/LOCAL   Here you'll find some of our favorite plate lunches, near the base of Diamond Head. Lunch and dinner offerings have just the right balance of not-too-heavy comfort food on-the-go, with tasty offerings that include ahi steaks and kalbi (Korean-marinated short ribs), plus a pretty killer portobello mushroom burger and miso ginger salmon. Don't miss dessert: The lemon crunch cake is the stuff of dreams, and the perfect capper to a Diamond Head hike—or really, any activity.

3158 Monsarrat Ave., Honolulu. www.diamondheadmarket.com. © **808/732-0077.** Plates $9–$27. Daily 7:30am–8pm.

East O'ahu

EXPENSIVE

Roy's Restaurant ★ HAWAI'I REGIONAL CUISINE   This is the original Roy's, the one that launched more than 30 Roy's restaurants around the world (six of them in Hawai'i). One of Hawai'i Regional Cuisine's most famous founders, Roy Yamaguchi started fusing local flavors and ingredients with European techniques some 20 years ago. The original menu items are still here, such as blackened island ahi with spicy soy mustard and Roy's famous melting-hot chocolate soufflé. Sit on the lanai to watch the sunset over Maunalua Bay.

6600 Kalaniana'ole Hwy., Hawaii Kai. www.royyamaguchi.com/roys-hawaiikai. © **808/ 396-7697.** Reservations recommended. Main courses $16–$70; $76 3-course prix fixe. Sun–Thurs 4:30–9pm; Fri–Sat until 9:30pm.

The Windward Coast

Note: The following restaurants are located on the "Eastern O'ahu & the Windward Coast" map (p. 97).

MODERATE

Casablanca ★ MOROCCAN   Walk into this 20-year-old family-owned restaurant, and don't be surprised if you suddenly feel worlds away from Honolulu. The exterior is the same brilliant shade of blue as Marrakech's Jardin Majorelle, and onion dome silhouette cutouts welcome you as walk in. The interior is decked out: Moroccan-style rugs hang above richly upholstered couches, low tables with beautiful inlaid patterns are dotted here and there, and leather ottomans abound. The menu is a multi-course affair, beginning with an orange blossom-scented hand-washing ritual. Next is typically a luscious mezze dip appetizer spread, and various options for entrees that include Moroccan classics like couscous or tagine. Even better? This place is BYOB (we suggest bringing a bottle that pairs well with lamb).

19 Hoolai St., Kailua. © **808/262-8196.** Main courses $55–$60. Reservations recommended. Tues–Sat 6–8:30pm.

INEXPENSIVE

Lanikai Brewing ★ BREWERY   As with the rest of the country, craft brewery is booming in Hawai'i and there is no shortage of places to drink locally brewed beer. Come to this tasting room for a pint of the Moku Imperial IPA, with a whisper of pīkake flowers, tropical and sweet, or the Pillbox Porter, made with Hawai'i-grown vanilla. The experimental and seasonal brews are also worth checking out, particularly those made with wild Hawai'i yeast. They're now serving in-house brick-fired pizza and sandwiches as well.

167 Hamakua Dr., Kailua. www.lanikaibrewing.com. No phone. Beers start at $3.25 for 4 oz., $8 for 12 oz. Pizzas $15–$21. Daily noon to 10pm.

Moke's Bread and Breakfast ★ BREAKFAST/BRUNCH   Of all the pancake joints in Kailua, Moke's is my pick—their *liliko'i* pancakes are unmatched. A light passion fruit cream sauce cascades over fluffy pancakes—a perfect blend of tart and sweet, simple and sinful. Other staples, such as the loco moco and omelets, are also spot-on.

27 Hoolai St., Kailua. https://mokeshawaii.com. ℂ **808/261-5565.** Main courses $12–$22. Wed–Fri 7am–1pm; Sat–Sun until 2pm.

Over Easy ★ BREAKFAST/BRUNCH   The Kailua brunch scene has stiff competition, so when Over Easy opened up the brunch crowd wondered: Do we really need another breakfast spot? Judging from the lines, yes, we do. There's a lot of care put into the short menu, from the light, crisp-edged pancakes to the kalua pig hash, brightened with a green goddess dressing.

418 Kuulei Rd. Kailua. www.overeasyhi.com. ℂ **808/260-1732.** Main courses $11–$20. Wed–Fri 7am–1pm; Sat–Sun until 1:30pm.

Up Roll Café Kailua ★ MODERN SUSHI   It's sushi in a way you don't see every day. Up Roll's lunch counter concept takes any fussiness out of sushi culture, with a check-list style menu that lets you opt for bowl or roll (the fillings stuffed between rice like a sushi-rice burrito), proteins like seasoned creamy crab, fresh ahi in a ginger marinade, or vegan inari simmered in shiitake broth. To finish it off, order as many toppings as your heart desires: pickled daikon, avocado, sprouts, tofu, crunchy garlic chips. Your bowl or roll can get as out-of-control as you please. This spot is especially appealing as a grab-and-go option, when you don't have the time to spend waiting in lines or for your food to get cooked.

573 Kailua Rd., Kailua. www.uprollcafe.com. ℂ **808/262-7002.** Rolls and bowls start at $11. All sauces and toppings add a small additional charge. Daily 11am–3pm.

Waiahole Poi Factory ★ LOCAL   On your way up the beautiful Windward coast, stop by this ramshackle, roadside spot. More than likely you'll notice the lines of hungry patrons before you notice the structure itself, which is just a little shed you'd find alongside a farmhouse. All those folks are waiting for a bite of Waiahole's classic Hawaiian plate lunch, with smoky kalua pig, succulent laulau, and fresh poi made on-site. Linger over the *kulolo* (a sticky dessert made with taro and coconut), served warm and topped with a scoop of coconut ice cream. Parking on the side of a busy, high-speed highway, especially with the types of crowds this joint attracts, can be treacherous. Speeding on this highway is practically to be expected, so be particularly careful backing out into or off of the road, and always be vigilant crossing streets to get to the factory.

48-140 Kamehameha Hwy., Waiahole. www.waiaholepoifactory.com. ℂ **808/239-2222.** Plates $13–$20. Mon–Fri 10am–6pm; Sat–Sun until 5pm.

The North Shore

Note: The following are on the "O'ahu's North Shore" map (p. 105).

MODERATE

Hale'iwa Beach House ★ AMERICAN/LOCAL   When you tire of the North Shore food trucks, come here. This beachy restaurant opens up to a fabulous view of Hale'iwa beach park; come during *pau hana* (happy hour) when you can watch the sun set. Menu highlights include whole fried fish, kalua pig grilled cheese, and Beach House fries—thick, spiral-cut fries tossed with garlic and furikake.

62-540 Kamehameha Hwy., Hale'iwa. www.haleiwabeachhouse.com. © **808/637-3435.** Main courses $16–$25 lunch; $25–$55 dinner. Mon–Thurs 11am–3pm; Fri–Sun until 8pm.

Hale'iwa Joes ★ AMERICAN/LOCAL   There are some solid stand-outs here, like the crispy, fried coconut shrimp that comes with a delightful pair of plum and honey mustard dipping sauces, with a fresh and crunchy green papaya salad on the side. The collection is a very hearty, classic American-meets-local-palates affair, with staples like pork chops and fried fish, but also poke and kalbi. The dining area has a pleasant, family-friendly plantation house/surf cottage vibe, with a porch that looks just out onto the harbor. Take a detour to the left just as you enter, and you'll find yourself in the decidedly less pastoral bar area. The pupu (appetizer) menu at Hale'iwa Joe's is incidentally also perfect bar food (sizzling mushroom and ahi spring rolls, for example), so grab a brew and set up shop there to watch the latest surf competition on TV or opt for a leisurely glass of wine over a full dinner overlooking the lawn.

66-011 Kamehameha Hwy., Hale'iwa. www.haleiwajoes.com. © **808/637-8005.** Main courses $14–$34. Mon–Sat 11am–2pm and 5–11pm; Sun 9am–3pm.

INEXPENSIVE

Beet Box Café ★ VEGETARIAN   For me, a perfect day on the North Shore involves waves and a stop at Beet Box. Warm wood paneling (upcycled, of course) welcomes you into the space. Veggie-forward fare comes in the form of satisfying sandwiches with Portobello and feta or avocado and local greens. The vegetarian burger is incredible, the local kombucha is a nice addition, and those vegan desserts are irresistible. There's a new location in Kailua as well.

66-437 Kamehameha Hwy., Hale'iwa. www.thebeetboxcafe.com. © **808/637-3000.** Sandwiches $13–$17. Daily 9am–3pm.

Island Vintage Coffee ★ COFFEE & LUNCH COUNTER   Island Vintage has locations across the islands, but this one is always a great spot for a casual, quick breakfast or lunch, thanks to a gets-the-job-done menu of açai bowls, bagel sandwiches, and poke bowls (what more could you want?) and a bright, pleasant aesthetic. Plus, the crowds at the North Shore space are usually at least slightly less maddening than the serpentine lines that materialize at the Waikīkī location. Get a fun coffee with flavors like macadamia nut, and a one of their unusual açai bowls. Along with the typical piles of fruit, you can get one with house-made *liliko'i* honey, frozen haupia (a coconut pudding or mousse) or local cacao nibs.

66-111 Kamehameha Hwy., Hale'iwa. www.islandvintagecoffee.com. © **808/637-5662.** Lunch items $10–$25. Daily 7am–5pm.

Shrimp farming took hold in Kahuku in the '90s and, before long, the first shrimp truck set up, serving fresh shrimp from a lunch wagon window. Now you can smell the garlic cooking before you see all the trucks and shrimp shacks. **Giovanni's Original White Shrimp Truck,** 56-505 Kamehameha Hwy. (© **808/293-1839**), is the most popular—so popular that a makeshift food court with picnic tables, shade, and a handful of other businesses has sprung up around the beat-up old white truck scrawled with tourists' signatures. Scampi style is a favorite—shell-on shrimp coated in lots of butter and garlic. A plate comes with a dozen, plus two scoops of rice. Head north from Giovanni's about a mile, and you'll hit **Romy's,** 56-781 Kamehameha Hwy. (© **808/232-2202**), a shrimp shack instead of a truck. Expect some stand-out sauce—tons of sauteed and fried garlic over a half-pound of head-on shrimp, plus a container of spicy soy sauce for dipping.

Kahuku Farms ★ SANDWICHES & SNACKS   Not a fan of shrimp? Then stop by Kahuku Farms' Farm Café, where you can get a simple grilled veggie panini made with veggies all grown right here on the farm, and a smoothie with papaya and banana, also grown here. Try the grilled banana bread topped with caramel and haupia (coconut) sauce and a scoop of ice cream. So decadent and so good.

56-800 Kamehameha Hwy., Kahuku. www.kahukufarms.com. © **808/628-0639.** $6–$15 lunch items. Thurs–Mon 11am–4pm.

Matsumoto Shave Ice ★ DESSERT COUNTER   This island classic has everything you need for the quintessential shave ice experience: a rainbow of flavors, from tropical fruits to classics like root beer and vanilla; creamy ice cream to nest in the center; sweet adzuki beans; and toppings like condensed milk (affectionately called a snowcap) and mochi balls to finish it all off. There's a reason Matsumoto's has been an island staple for generations. Hit it up after a long, hot day on the beach and you'll see why. Just be ready for a wait—the line isn't anything to sneer at.

66-111 Kamehameha Hwy., Hale'iwa. www.matsumotoshaveice.com. © **808/637-4827.** Dishes $4–$10. Daily 10am–6pm.

Leeward O'ahu: The Wai'anae Coast
MODERATE

Monkeypod Kitchen ★ AMERICAN   This is the best dining option at Ko 'Olina Station, a strip mall of casual eateries. One of the latest ventures from Peter Merriman, who pioneered farm-to-table fine dining on Hawai'i Island in the '80s, Monkeypod is a larger, more casual restaurant (with another location on Maui). The vibe in this two-story space is welcoming and friendly, with live music on the lanai and a long bar of beer taps to choose from. Expect fresh salads and entrees like fish and chips and burgers. To drink: the bracingly zingy housemade ginger beer. *Tip:* For a cozier bar experience, head upstairs, where the bartenders spend a little more time making your cocktails, which include fresh takes on the mai tai (topped with a honey *liliko'i* foam) and the Makawao Ave, made with rye and that terrific ginger beer.

At Ko 'Olina Station, 92-1048 Olani St., Kapolei. www.monkeypodkitchen.com. © **808/ 380-4086.** Reservations recommended. Main courses $18–$58. Daily 11am–10pm.

O'AHU SHOPPING

Honolulu shopping leans heavily on luxury brands and tends to cater to Japanese (and increasingly, Chinese) tourists. For example, International Marketplace, open-air marketplace had become mostly a maze of kitschy junk, closed after a 56-year run. The high-end **International Marketplace mall** opened in 2016 in its place. Many people still feel sentimental about losing the market.

You can find plenty of luxury goods at the new **Ala Moana Center.** But just as the luxury market is growing, so is Honolulu's boutique culture and local crafts scene, as artisans endeavor to capture what makes Hawai'i so unique. You'll find the best boutique shopping in Chinatown and Hale'iwa, but you'll find gems even at the malls.

Shopping in & Around Honolulu & Waikīkī

CLOTHING

The **aloha shirt** is alive and well, thanks to a revival of vintage aloha wear and the modern take, which features more subdued prints and slimmer silhouettes.

Vintage 1930s to 1950s Hawaiian wear is still beautiful and can be found in collectibles shops, such as the packed-to-the-rafters **Bailey's**

---

lū'au!

The sun is setting, the tiki torches are lit, the pig is taken from the *imu* (an oven in the earth), the *pu* (conch) sounds—It's lū'au time! In ancient times, the lū'au was called *aha 'aina* (*aha* means "gathering" and *'aina*, "land"); these were celebrations with family and friends to mark important occasions, such as a victory at war or a baby's first birthday. Lū'au are still a part of life in Hawai'i; in particular, the tradition of baby's first lū'au lives on.

For visitors, lū'au are a way to experience a feast of food and entertainment, Hawaiian style. The lū'au at the **Royal Hawaiian,** 2259 Kalākaua Ave. (www.royal-hawaiianluau.com; © **808/921-4600**), is the only beachfront one in Waikīkī and offers the best food and quality entertainment. It takes place every Monday and Thursday and starts at $240 for adults.

About an hour outside of Waikīkī on the Leeward coast, **Paradise Cove**

Lū'au, 92-1089 Alii Nui Dr., Kapolei (www.paradisecove.com; © **808/842-5911**), is a popular option. It has a lovely setting, perfect for sunset photos, and the evening starts with arts and crafts and activities for kids. Waikīkī bus pickup and return is available for $35. Paradise Cove's lū'au is nightly at 5pm and costs $150 to $240 for adults, $125 to $210 for youth ages 13 to 20, and $110 to $185 for children ages 4 to 12.

Antiques and Aloha Shirts, 517 Kapahulu Ave. (© **808/734-7628**). The following three boutiques are all in the Ala Moana Center. Of the contemporary aloha-wear designers, one of the best based in O'ahu is **Tori Richard** (www.toririchard.com; © **808/949-5858**), who creates tasteful tropical prints in the form of linen and silk shirts for men and flowy dresses for women. **Reyn Spooner** (www.reynspooner.com; © **808/949-5929;** with three other O'ahu locations) is another source of attractive aloha shirts in traditional and contemporary styles; the festive patterns and sleek cuts appeal to younger tastes, while keeping their offerings featuring Reyn Spooner's classic prints feeling fresh and of-the-times. Also check out **Kahala** (www.kahala.com; © **808/941-4010;** with four other O'ahu locations in Kaka'ako, Waikīkī, and Hale'iwa), which has been designing aloha shirts since 1936 and remains an island favorite.

The hippest guys and gals go to **Roberta Oaks,** 1152 Nu'uanu Ave. (www.robertaoaks.com; © **808/526-1111**), in Chinatown, where a slew of trendy boutiques has opened in recent years. Roberta Oaks ditches the too-big aloha shirt for a more stylish, fitted look, but keeps the vintage designs. Plus, she even has super-cute, tailored aloha shirts for women. Newer to Chinatown, but a fixture in Hilo on Hawai'i Island and in politicians' closets are Sig Zane aloha shirts. At the Honolulu outpost, **Sig on Smith,** 1020 Smith St. (www.sigzanedesigns.com) you'll find Zane's designs inspired by native Hawaiian culture, such as plants significant to hula and patterns based on Hawaiian legends. The Chinatown location

SHOPPING IN chinatown

In the 1840s, Honolulu's Chinatown began to take shape as many Chinese brought in to work on the sugar plantations opted not to renew their contracts and instead moved to Chinatown to open businesses. Fronting Honolulu harbor, Chinatown catered to whalers and sailors. It reached its zenith in the 1920s, with restaurants and markets flourishing by day, and sex workers and opium dens doing brisk business at night. As its reputation as a red-light district began to eclipse everything else, the neighborhood slowly declined. That is, until recent decades. Fresh boutiques and restaurants are filling in previously abandoned storefronts—which retain much of their original architectural details from the 1900s—as Chinatown once again attracts the entrepreneurial.

At the original location of **Fighting Eel,** 1133 Bethel St. (www.fightingeel. com; © **808/738-9300;** multiple locations on O'ahu), you'll find bright, easy-to-wear dresses and shirts with island prints that are in every local fashionista's closet—perfect for Honolulu weather, but chic enough to wear back home. Go treasure-hunting at **Tin Can Mailman** (p. 162) and the funky **Hound & Quail,** 1156 Nu'uanu Ave. (www.houndandquail.

com), where a collection of antiques and curiosities, from a taxidermied ostrich to old medical texts, make for a fascinating perusal. At **Ginger13,** 22 S. Pauahi St. (www.ginger13.com; © **808/531-5311**), local jewelry designer Cindy Yokoyama offers a refreshing change from the delicate jewelry found all over Hawai'i by creating asymmetrical styles with chunky stones such as agate and opal.

also features limited-release capsule collections: Visit the shop's Instagram (www.instagram.com/sigonsmith) to see the latest.

Just 2 years after its launch, **Manaola,** Ala Moana Center (www.manaolahawaii.com; *©* **808/943-6262**), debuted to an international audience with its own runway show at New York Fashion Week. Now they're rocking two locations on Oʻahu, with the second one out west at Pearlridge Center. Native Hawaiian designer Manaola Yap creates clothing for both men and women, with prints that rely on repetition and symmetry to convey Hawaiʻi's natural beauty and oral stories, in an elegant, modern package that is both tasteful and eclectic.

FLOWERS & LEIS

The best place to shop for leis is in Chinatown, where lei vendors line Beretania and Maunakea streets and the fragrances of their wares mix with the earthy scents of incense and ethnic foods. Try **Nita's Leis,** 59 N. Beretania St. (*©* **808/521-9065**), which has fresh *puakenikeni,* gardenias that last, and a supply of fresh and reasonable leis; **Lin's Lei Shop,** 1017-A

Maunakea St. (*©* **808/537-4112**), with creatively fashioned, unusual leis; and **Cindy's Lei Shoppe,** 1034 Maunakea St. (*©* **808/536-6538**), with terrific sources for unusual leis such as feather dendrobiums and firecracker combinations, as well as everyday favorites like ginger, tuberose, orchid, and *pīkake.*

HAWAIIANA & GIFT ITEMS

Visit the **Museum Shop** at the Honolulu Museum of Art, 900 S. Beretania St. (*©* **808/532-8701**), for crafts, jewelry, prints, and stationery featuring some of the iconic pieces you'll see in the museum (p. 80), like The Lei Maker, a beautiful and serene painting of a young Hawaiian girl crafting lei, created by Theodore

Shop for plumeria leis in Chinatown.

Wores. You'll find gifts to bring home, such as some gorgeously crafted ceramics and stunning coffee table books with vivid images of Asian and Pacific art.

Na Mea Hawaiʻi ★ A one-stop shop and resource for all things local and Hawaiian, you'll find cultural items such as hula stones and *ipu* (gourds); Niʻihau shell lei; prints, crafts, and jewelry from local artists; local jams and coffee; and shelves of Hawaiian history and culture books. At the Ward Village Shops, 1200 Ala Moana Blvd. www.nameahawaii.com. *©* **808/596-8885.**

farmer's MARKETS

Farmer's markets have proliferated on O'ahu—there's now one for every neighborhood for every day of the week. Unfortunately, the number of farmers has not kept up. In fact, some of the markets have vendors that sell repackaged Mainland produce. The best farmer's markets are those run by the **Hawai'i Farm Bureau Federation** (**HFBF**; www.hfbf.org) and **FarmLovers** (www.farmloversmarkets.com), which mandate locally grown meats, fruits, and veggies. Check their websites for detailed information. Here are some favorites:

○ **Kapi'olani Community College:** The original and still one of the biggest and best. Unfortunately, you'll have to deal with crowds—busloads of tourists get dropped off here. But you'll find items unavailable at any other market—endless varieties of bananas and mangoes, tropical fruit you've never seen before, persimmons, and local duck eggs. Pick up cut, chilled pineapple or jackfruit to snack on, local yogurt, and perhaps some grilled abalone from Kona, and corn from Kahuku. And with a healthy dose of prepared-food vendors serving everything from fresh tomato pizzas to raw, vegan snacks, you won't go hungry. 4303 Diamond Head Rd.; **②** **808/848-2074;** Sat 7:30–11am; TheBus: 2 or 3.

○ **Kaka'ako Farmer's Market:** One could say this market has a hipper vibe than the market at Kapi'olani Community College. While it has expanded in recent years and gained more of a following, you'll still see some smaller farms and businesses, and a lot of real locals shopping for their weekly groceries. Find a variety of island grown and caught meats, including venison and fresh fish from the vendor Forage, fresh, sustainably caught fish from Local 'Ia, lots of leafy greens and locally grown fruits, and some really delightful ready-to-eat treats, from honey slushies to crepes to mango ricotta toast. 919 Ala Moana Blvd.; **②** **808/388-9696;** Sat 8am–noon; TheBus: 20, 42, E.

Nohea Gallery ★ Since its inception in 1990 Nohea Gallery has carried the work of hundreds of artists, almost all local. Here you'll find incredible woodwork, including beautiful bowls, calabashes, and even elegant urns and furniture, made of mango wood and the coveted koa wood. You'll find ceramics of all types, from the functional to the decorative, porcelain to stoneware and, of course, paintings and prints. The gallery's collection shows the myriad ways the Hawaiian Islands can inspire, with soft scenic mountain landscapes as well as traditional gyotaku, the Japanese art of fish printing. At Kahala Mall, 4211 Waialae Ave. www.nohea gallery.com. **②** **808/762-7407.**

Tin Can Mailman ★ What, not looking for a 1950s oil hula lamp? Check out this shop anyway. It's packed with vintage Hawaiiana to emulate old-school general stores. The emphasis is on ephemera, such as pinups, postcards, old sheet music, and advertisements, and the elusive Betty Boop hula girl bobblehead. 1026 Nuuanu Ave. www.tincanmailman.net. **②** **808/524-3009.**

HAWAIIAN & JAPANESE SNACKS

Choco le'a ★   This cute little chocolate shop is tucked away on a charming side street of lush Mānoa valley. Peek inside and choose from the assortment of gleaming, gem-like truffles (look for flavors like affogato, *liliko'i,* birthday cake, and many, many more), as well as other delectable like the unique and oh-so-toothsome dark-chocolate-dipped jabong (it also comes in pineapple and mango). Seasonal flavors get especially interesting here: At Lunar New Year, look for gau-filled truffles and strawberry pistachio for spring. 2909 Lowrey Ave. www.chocolea.com. ✆ **808/371-2234.**

Fujiya Hawai'i ★   Another old-school bakery and confectionary shop, Fujiya has been selling locals snacks and sweets since 1953. Today, look for creative, modern takes on mochi favorites, with twists such as almond float mochi and POG mochi specials, alongside favorites such as fresh strawberry-stuffed mochi. 930 Hauoli St. www.fujiyahawaii.com. ✆ **808/845-2921.**

Nisshodo Candy Store ★   Mochi (Japanese rice cake) is so essential to locals' lives that even the drugstores sell it. But for the freshest and widest variety, go straight to the source: Nisshodo, an almost century-old business. Choose among pink-and-white *chichi dango* (or milk mochi), mochi filled with smooth azuki bean, *monaka* (delicate rice wafers sandwiching sweetened lima-bean paste), and much more. 1095 Dillingham Blvd. www.nisshodomochicandy.com. ✆ **808/847-1244.**

Whole Foods Market ★   Okay, hear us out here. Whole Foods does a seriously great job of sourcing local, both in top-tier tropical produce and in specialty items such as honey, jams, hot sauces, coffee, and chocolate. Even local cheese, beers, and wines are on selection here. Plus, It's also got one of the best selections of locally made soaps, great for gifts to take home. 4211 Waialae Ave at Kahala Mall. ✆ **808/738-0820.** Two other locations on O'ahu at Ward and Kailua.

SHOPPING CENTERS

Ala Moana Center ★★   Hawai'i's largest mall includes luxury brands and mainstream chains. But it also offers a selection of local stores. Make sure to browse **Manaola** and stop by **Tori Richard** and **Reyn Spooner** (see "Clothing," above, for all three); for surf-and-skate wear, check out **Hawaiian Island Creations** or **T&C Surf Designs.** For presents to bring home, stop in **Blue Hawaii Lifestyle,** which offers locally made food gifts such as chocolate and honey, as well as Hawai'i-made soaps and beauty products. Pick up beautifully packaged, chocolate-dipped mac nut shortbread at **Big Island Candies** and only-in-Hawai'i treats such as *manju* (resembling a filled cookie) and ume-shiso chocolates. Hungry? You've got plenty of options: **The Lanai** is the newer of the mall's food courts, with fresh poke bowls at **'Ahi and Vegetable,** ultra-snackable, Japanese-style rice balls called musubi at **Musubi Cafe Iyasume,** and soft rolls and mochi bread at the Japanese **Brug Bakery.** Head downstairs to **Foodland Farms** to hit up that expansive Foodland poke bar, and raid the bakery section, full of local treats like guava chiffon cake. Treat yourself to a slice of light-as-air sponge cake or green tea roll cake, and a plantation iced-tea jelly at the Japanese/French patisserie **Palme D'Or.** The center is open daily 10am to 8pm. 1450 Ala Moana Blvd. www.alamoanacenter. com. *©* **808/955-9517.** Bus: 20, 60, or 53. Various shuttles also stop here. For Waikīkī Trolley information, see "Getting Around" (p. 71).

Salt at Kaka'ako ★   There are grand plans for Kaka'ako, the neighborhood between Waikīkī and downtown. Mostly, It's a lot of new, hi-rise luxury condos, but developers are also trying to create an interesting mix of restaurants and retailers. Here, you'll find **Milo,** a hip surf shop that also carries home accessories; elegant urban-meets-beachy resortwear and accessories at dreamy boutique **Here.;** and **Treehouse,** a must for any photography lover, especially those with a penchant for vintage and film. Sample local chocolate at **Lonohana Estate Chocolate Tasting Bar,** a company that grows its own cacao and turns it into smooth bars, from milk chocolate to extra dark. 691 Auahi St. www.saltatkakaako.com.

Ward Village Shops ★   You'll find a lot of young Hawai'i fashion designers at the **South Shore Market,** the building that houses the vibrant designs of **Jana Lam** and cute, local products for kids and babies at **Hopscotch. Mori by Art + Flea** is a charming gifts and art shop housing a collection of creations from local artists and makers, from stationery to clothing. 1200 Ala Moana Blvd. www.wardvillage.com. *©* **808/591-8411.**

Shopping in Kailua

Befitting O'ahu's favorite beach town, many of the boutiques in Kailua offer plenty of swimsuits, breezy styles for men and women, and T-shirts from homegrown brands. In addition to the shops below, also make sure to stop by Mānoa Chocolate (see "Specialty Tours," p. 125).

Island Bungalow ★   Come here to furnish the beachy bohemian house of your dreams. Don't have one? Pretend you do while browsing block printed pillowcases, boho crochet hammocks, and breezy, resort-appropriate maxi dresses and caftans. 131 Hekili St., Kailua. www.islandbungalow hawaii.com. *©* **808/536-4543.**

The Lauren Roth Art Gallery ★   The boutique of painter-illustrator Lauren Roth matches her cheery, bright color palette. Here, she offers her own original paintings and prints, tropical jungle-scapes that conjure bohemian and psychedelic vibes. Look for prints, cards (with art by Roth and other local artists), as well as other goodies like cute bags and accessories. 131 Hekili St., Kailua. www.mynameislauren.com. *©* **808/439-1993.**

Oliver Men's Shop ★   This tiny, quirky shop for stylish men sells understated aloha shirts, minimalist ceramic mugs, and earthy, urban-meets-explorer-meets-surfer men's clothing and accessories. Next door,

Olive is for women, offering beach gear, über-stylish swimsuits (to match Oliver's über-stylish man), plus casual-chic homewares, beauty products, candles, and well-made dresses and apparel. 49 Kihapai St., Kailua. www. oliverhawaii.com. © **808/261-6587.**

Shopping on the North Shore

The newly developed **Hale'iwa Store Lots,** 66-087 Kamehameha Hwy. (www.haleiwastorelots.com), replaces some of the old, dusty buildings (some would say charming) in Hale'iwa with an open-air, plantation-style shopping center. You'll also find the **Clark Little Gallery,** showcasing the photographer's shorebreak photos, which capture the fluidity, beauty, and power of a wave just as It's about to hit the shoreline. Don't miss **Polu Gallery** featuring local artists' work, including Punky Aloha's bold and bright retro-style art and Pegge Hopper's iconic, serene images of island women among tropical botanicals. **Guava Shop** is Hale'iwa's quintessential clothing boutique. Its beachy, bohemian styles of swimwear and airy coverups and clothing, have a mix of playful-meets-sexy appeal, with fun, festive, bohemian touches that really capture the aesthetic of a North Shore surfer girl.

Farther south into Hale'iwa is **Coffee Gallery,** 66-250 Kamehameha Hwy., Suite C106 (© **808/824-0368**), the best cafe in town, with a great selection of locally grown coffee beans to take home. **Tini Manini,** 66-250 Kamehameha Hwy. (www.tinimanini.com; © **808/637-8464**), is an adorable children's shop with everything from bathing suits to baby blankets for your little one.

Over in Waialua, a collection of surfboard shapers and small businesses have turned the **Waialua Sugar Mill,** which stopped producing sugar in 1996, into a low-key retail and industrial space. Stop at **North Shore Soap Factory,** 67-106 Kealohanui St. (www.northshoresoapfactory.com; © **808/ 637-8400**), to watch all-natural and fragrant soaps being made. You can even stamp your bar of soap with a shaka or the silhouette of the sugar mill. The factory also has a line of bath and body care, with scrubs, lotions, and moisturizing kukui-nut oil. Then, head over to the warehouse-like **Island X Hawaii** (www.islandxhawaii.com; © **808/637-2624**) for local gifts galore, from Hawai'i-produced cigars to coffee to salts to honey. They've also got a pretty appealing selection of frozen treats, perfect for a snack after hitting the sundrenched beach all day. Try their all-natural shave ice using real fruit, coffee, and coconut milk toppings, or Ono Pops, popsicles handmade in Hawai'i that feature fun local flavors such as chocolate apple banana, salted watermelon cream (a nod to the islands' crackseed snack history), butter mochi (a quintessentially local baked good), guava tamarind, and pineapple *li hing*.

O'AHU NIGHTLIFE

Nightlife in Hawai'i begins at sunset, when all eyes turn westward to see how the day will end. Sunset viewers always seem to bond in the mutual enjoyment of a natural spectacle, and you'll often spot small music-filled gatherings or even practicing fire-dancers congregating on the sand as the light fades.

The Bar Scene

ON THE BEACH Waikīkī's beachfront bars offer many possibilities. Options include the **Mai Tai Bar** (© 808/923-7311) at the Royal Hawaiian (p. 131), a few feet from the sand; the **Beach Bar** (© 808/922-3111), under the banyan tree at the Moana Surfrider (p. 130); and the unfailingly enchanting **House Without a Key** (© 808/923-2311), at the Halekulani (p. 129), where a lovely hula dancer sways to live Hawaiian music with the sunset and ocean glowing behind her—a romantic, evocative, nostalgic scene. (It doesn't hurt, either, that the Halekulani happens to make an excellent mai tai.)

Another great bar for watching the sun sink into the Pacific is **Duke's Waikīkī** (www.dukeswaikiki.com; © 808/922-2268), in the Outrigger Waikīkī Beach Resort. The outside Barefoot Bar is perfect for sipping a tropical drink with a backdrop of waves, sunset, and live Hawaiian music. It can get crowded, so get here early.

DOWNTOWN/CHINATOWN Chinatown's typically bustling nightlife scene, has started to pick up again post-pandemic, with queues going out the doors of bars, and dancing crowds once more. The activity is concentrated on Hotel Street, on the block between Smith and Nuuanu. That's where you'll find **Tchin Tchin!,** 39 No. Hotel St., a classy upstairs lounge and wine bar that's also got a great eats menu, and **The Manifest,** 32 N. Hotel St., with a stellar selection of whiskeys and gins. The bartenders here are happy to whip up complex whiskey drinks or simple, classic cocktails. On weekend evenings, DJs and live music make the laidback bar clubbier. Across the street is **Bar 35,** 35 N. Hotel St., which boasts an outdoor patio in the back, complete with its own bar.

Hanks Cafe, around the corner on Nu'uanu Avenue between Hotel and King streets, is a tiny, kitschy, friendly pub with an artsy upstairs bar space called **The Dragon Upstairs.** You'll find live music, DJs, and special events that attract great talent and an eclectic crowd. At the *makai* end of Nu'unau, toward the pier, **Murphy's Bar and Grill ★** (© 808/531-0422) is a popular and homey, downtown alehouse.

Hawaiian Music

O'ahu has a few key spots for Hawaiian music. **House Without a Key** (see "The Bar Scene," above) is one of my favorite places to listen to Hawaiian music, both for the quality and the ambience. You'll find Hawaiian artists singing their melodies in the evenings at many of the other hotel bars as well, especially beachside ones like **Tropics Bar and Grill** (© 808/949-4321), at the Hilton Hawaiian Village.

Kana ka pila means to make music, so it makes sense then that the **Kana Ka Pila Grille** (© 808/924-4994), at the Outrigger Reef Waikīkī

Beach, stays true to its musical namesake and offers nightly Hawaiian live shows for bargoers. **Chart House Waikīkī,** 1765 Ala Moana Blvd., on the outskirts of the hotel and resort scene (✆ **808/941-6669**), is a classic, old-school neighborhood icon that still has a Hawai'i-of-yesteryear vibe. Here, you'll find a line-up of different musicians for every day of the week, from around 6pm to 9pm.

Live Blues, R&B, Jazz & Pop

Blue Note Hawaii, inside the Outrigger Waikīkī Beach Resort, 2335 Kalākaua Ave. (www.bluenotehawaii.com; ✆ **808/777-4890**), from the owner of the Blue Note jazz club in New York City, is the city's go-to venue for jazz, blues, and favorite local entertainers. It has a great, old-school jazzy vibe, and the restaurant offers hearty plates like seared ahi and braised short ribs. Past performers have included Dee Dee Bridgewater and 'ukulele virtuoso Jake Shimabukuro.

Tops in taste and ambience is the perennially alluring **Lewers Lounge** in the Halekulani, 2199 Kalia Rd. (www.halekulani.com; ✆ **808/923-2311**). Comfy intimate seating around the pillars makes this a great spot for contemporary jazz. You can find artists performing Tuesday through Saturday 8:30pm to midnight.

Outside Waikīkī, **The Veranda,** at the Kahala Hotel & Resort, 5000 Kahala Ave. (www.kahalaresort.com; ✆ **808/739-8760**), is a popular spot for the over-40 crowd, with live music Thursday through Saturday and a gorgeous view of the ocean as the sun sets.

The Performing Arts

Audiences have grooved to the beat of the Hawaii International Jazz Festival, the American Repertory Dance Company, barbershop quartets, and John Kaimikaua's *halau*—all at the **Hawaii Theatre,** 1130 Bethel St., Downtown (www.hawaiitheatre.com; ✆ **808/528-0506**). The theater is basking in its renaissance as a leading multipurpose center for the performing arts. The neoclassical Beaux Arts landmark features a dome from 1922, 1,400 plush seats, a hydraulically elevated organ, breathtaking murals, and gilt galore.

In 2011, a new symphony orchestra was reborn from the disbanded century-old **Hawai'i Symphony Orchestra** (https://myhso.org; ✆ **808/380-7724**). Catch them at a variety of venues around town, including the beautiful, outdoor Waikīkī Shell, an amphitheater smack in the middle of Kapi'olani Park, which also hosts other traveling acts and shows, from comedians to popular musical acts to local bands.

Meanwhile, the **Hawaii Opera Theatre** (www.hawaiiopera.org; ✆ **808/596-7858**), celebrating more than 50 seasons, still draws fans to the **Neal S. Blaisdell Center** (www.blaisdellcenter.com; ✆ **808/591-2211**), as does **Ballet Hawaii** (www.ballethawaii.org). Contemporary performances by **Iona** (www.iona360.com), a strikingly creative group whose dance evolved out of Butoh (a contemporary dance form that originated in Japan), are worth tracking down if you love the avant-garde.

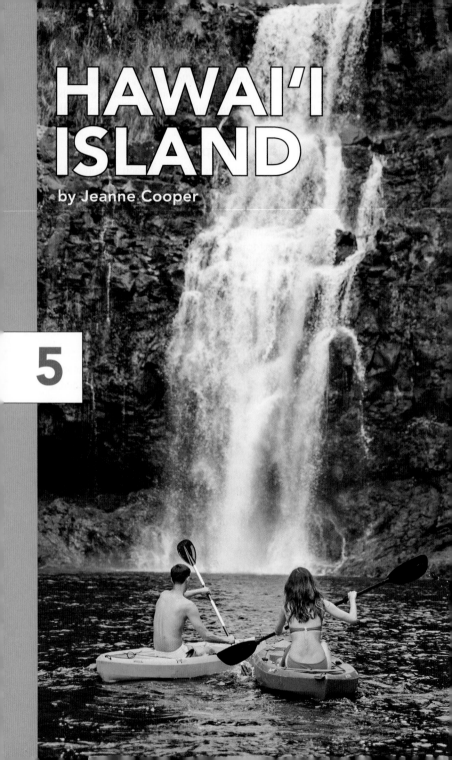

HAWAI'I ISLAND

by Jeanne Cooper

5

Larger than all the other Hawaiian Islands combined, Hawai'i Island truly deserves its nickname. Its 4,029 square miles—a figure that has grown recently, thanks to one of its three active volcanoes—contain 10 of the world's 13 climate zones. In less than a day, a visitor can easily traverse tropical rainforest, lava desert, verdant pastures, misty uplands, and chilly tundra, the last near the summit of Mauna Kea, almost 14,000 feet above sea level. The shoreline also boasts diversity, from golden beaches to enchanting coves of black sand with flecks of white coral. Equally diverse are the people themselves—in the 2020 Census, 30% of Hawai'i Island residents listed themselves as being of two or more ethnic backgrounds. More than a third of Hawai'i Island residents reported some or all Native Hawaiian or other Pacific Islander ancestry, with more than 40% describing their ethnic heritage as all or part Asian. Japanese Americans, in particular, have contributed much to this island's modern culture and cuisine.

This island shares its name with the entire state for good reason. The dramatic landscape—including the home of Pele, the volcano demi-goddess—has inspired numerous chants and hula, celebrated in the weeklong Merrie Monarch Festival in Hilo. This is the birthplace of King Kamehameha, who, after his bloody conquests, united all the islands and enacted laws that protected the rights of commoners; horseback parades around the island still honor his birthday each June. In recent years, demonstrations against further development atop Mauna Kea, the highest mountain in the islands, have united senior cultural practitioners and young activists across the state. Although not everyone shares their views on observatory construction, their passion for their majestic island is unmistakable—and infectious.

ESSENTIALS

Arriving

Hawai'i Island has two major airports for interisland and trans-Pacific jet traffic: Kona and Hilo.

FACING PAGE: Kayaking off Hawai'i Island takes you to dramatic waterfalls and hidden coves.

Most people arrive at **Kona International Airport** (**KOA;** https://hawaii.gov/koa) in Keāhole, the island's westernmost point, and can be forgiven for wondering if there's really a runway among all the crinkly black lava and golden fountain grass. Leaving the airport, the ritzy Kohala Coast is to the left (north) and the town of Kailua-Kona—often just called "Kona," as is the airport—is to the right (south). *Warning:* Don't be tempted to speed on the slow road between the terminals and the highway; police are often monitoring your velocity.

U.S. carriers offering nonstop service to Kona, in alphabetical order, are: **Alaska Airlines** (www.alaskaair.com; ✆ **800/252-7522**), with flights from the Pacific Northwest hubs of Seattle, Portland, and Anchorage and from San Diego and San Jose; **American Airlines** (www.aa.com; ✆ **800/433-7300**), departing from Los Angeles and Phoenix; **Delta Air Lines** (www.delta.com; ✆ **800/221-1212**), flying from Los Angeles and Seattle; **Hawaiian Airlines** (www.hawaiianairlines.com; ✆ **800/367-5320**), departing from Los Angeles (and Tokyo's Haneda airport); **Southwest Airlines** (www.southwest.com; ✆ **800/435-9792**), from San Jose, Los Angeles, Oakland, Las Vegas, and seasonally from Phoenix; and **United Airlines** (www.united.com; ✆ **800/864-8331**), with flights from Los Angeles, San Francisco, Denver, and Chicago.

Air Canada (www.aircanada.com; ✆ **888/247-2267**) and **WestJet** (www.westjet.com; ✆ **888/937-8358**) also offer nonstop service to Kona, with frequency changing seasonally, from Vancouver, while WestJet also flies from Calgary.

Although most international and domestic travelers arrive in Kona, **Hilo International Airport** (**ITO;** https://hawaii.gov/ito) in the past has had nonstop service to and from Los Angeles on United (see above) and on **Japan Airlines** (www.jal.co.jp/jp/en; ✆ **800/525-3663**); check current schedules to see if service has resumed.

For connecting flights or island-hopping, Hawaiian and Southwest (see above) are the only carriers offering inter-island jet service. Hawaiian flies several times a day from Honolulu and Kahului, Maui, to both Kona and Hilo airports; it also flies daily nonstop between Kaua'i and Kona. Southwest operates Hilo-Honolulu, Kona-Honolulu, and Kona-Kahului routes (low, refundable fares and two free bags, including surfboards, make these flights very attractive).

Mokulele Airlines (www.mokuleleairlines.com; ✆ **866/260-4040**) flies nine-passenger, single-engine turboprops to Kona, Waimea (Kamuela) and Hilo from Kahului, Maui. *Note:* Mokulele asks passengers their weight and weighs their carry-ons to determine seats; those totaling 350 pounds or more must contact the airline in advance.

Visitor Information

The **Island of Hawai'i Visitors Bureau** (www.gohawaii.com/big-island; ✆ **800/648-2441**) has an office on the Kohala Coast in the Shops at

Bodyboarding on the Kohala Coast.

Mauna Lani, 68-1330 Mauna Lani Dr., Suite 109B, Mauna Lani Resort (© **808/885-1655**).

This Week (www.thisweek hawaii.com/big-island) and *101 Things to Do: Big Island* (www. 101thingstodo.com/big-island) are free publications that offer good, useful information amid the advertisements, as well as discount coupons for a variety of island adventures. Copies are easy to find all around the island.

Konaweb.com has an extensive event calendar and handy links to sites and services around the island, not just the Kona side. Those fascinated by the island's active volcanoes—including Mauna Loa, which erupted at its remote summit in late 2022, and more accessible Kīlauea, which had a lava lake at the summit in early 2023—should check out the updates, maps, photos, videos, and webcams on the U.S. Geological Survey's **Hawaiian Volcano Observatory** website (www.usgs.gov/observatories/hvo), which also tracks the island's frequent but usually minor earthquake activity.

The Island in Brief

THE KONA COAST

Kona means "leeward side" in Hawaiian—and that means hot, dry weather virtually every day of the year on the 70-mile stretch of black lava shoreline encompassing the North and South Kona districts.

NORTH KONA With the exception of the sumptuous but serenely low-key **Four Seasons Resort Hualālai ★★★** and **Kona Village ★★★** north of the airport, most of what everyone just calls "Kona" is a relatively affordable vacation spot. An ample selection of mid-priced condo units, timeshares, and several recently upgraded hotels lies between the bustling commercial district of **Kailua-Kona ★★★**, a one-time fishing village and royal compound now renowned as the start and finish of the Ironman World Championship, and Keauhou, an equally historic area about 6 miles south that boasts upscale condominiums, a shopping center, and golf-course homes.

The rightly named Aliʻi ("Royalty") Drive begins in Kailua-Kona near King Kamehameha's royal compound at **Kamakahonu Bay,** which includes the off-limits temple complex of **Ahuʻena Heiau,** and continues past **Huliheʻe Palace ★★★**, an elegant retreat for later royals that sits across from the oldest church in the islands. Heading south, the road

Luau grounds of the Kona Brewers Festival.

passes by the snorkelers' haven of **Kahalu'u Beach** ★, as well as sacred and royal sites on the former Keauhou Beach Resort, before the intersection with King Kamehameha III Road, which leads to that monarch's birthplace by Keauhou Bay. Several kayak excursions and snorkel boats leave from Keauhou, but **Kailua Pier** (the start of the Ironman championship) sees the most traffic—from cruise-ship tenders to fishing and dive boats, dinner cruises, and other sightseeing excursions.

Beaches between Kailua-Kona and Keauhou tend to be pocket coves but heading north toward South Kohala (which begins near the entrance to the Waikoloa Beach Resort), beautiful, mostly uncrowded sands lie out of sight from the highway, often reached by unpaved roads across vast lava fields. Among the steep coffee fields in North Kona's cooler upcountry, you'll find the rustic, artsy village of **Hōlualoa.**

SOUTH KONA   Numerous bays cut into the rural, serrated coastline here, from **Kealakekua,** a marine life and cultural preserve that's the island's best diving spot, down to **Hōnaunau,** where a national historical park recalls the days of old Hawai'i. This is a great place to stay, if you want to get away from crowds but still be within driving distance of beaches and Kailua-Kona—you may hear the all-night cheeping of coqui frogs, though. The higher, cooler elevation of the main road means you'll pass many coffee, macadamia nut, and tropical fruit farms, some with tours or roadside stands.

THE KOHALA COAST

Also on the island's "Kona side," sunny and dry Kohala is divided into two distinctively different districts, although the resorts are more glamorous and the rural area that much less developed.

SOUTH KOHALA   Pleasure domes rise along the sandy beaches carved into the craggy shores here, from the more moderately priced **Waikoloa Beach Resort** at 'Anaeho'omalu Bay to the posher **Mauna Lani** and **Mauna Kea** resorts to the north. Mauna Kea is where Laurance Rockefeller opened the area's first resort in 1965, a mirage of opulence and tropical greenery rising from bleak, black lava fields, framed by the white sands of Kauna'oa Beach and views of the mountain. But you don't have to be a billionaire to enjoy South Kohala's fabulous beaches and historic sites (such as petroglyph fields); all are open to the public, with parking and other facilities (including restaurants and shopping) provided by the resorts. Parking may be in short supply during peak periods, though.

Several of the region's attractions are also located off the resorts, including the white sands of 'Ōhai'ula Beach at **Spencer Park** ★★; the massive **Pu'ukoholā Heiau** ★★★, a lava rock temple commissioned by King Kamehameha the Great; and the handful of restaurants and shops in **Kawaihae,** the commercial harbor just after the turnoff for upcountry Waimea. *Note:* The golf course community of **Waikoloa Village** is not in the Waikoloa Beach Resort, but instead lies 5½ miles uphill from the coastal highway. Besides the golf course and two small shopping centers with dining options, its main attraction to visitors is the **Waikoloa Dry Forest ★★★**.

WAIMEA (KAMUELA) & MAUNA KEA   Officially part of South Kohala, the old upcountry cow town of Waimea on the northern road between the coasts is a world unto itself, with rolling green pastures, wide-open spaces dotted by *pu'u* (cinder cone hills, pronounced *"pooh-ooh"*) and real cowpokes who work mammoth **Parker Ranch,** the state's largest working

Keck Observatory on Mauna Kea.

ranch. The postal service gave it the name Kamuela, after ranch founder Samuel (Kamuela) Parker, to distinguish it from another cowboy town, Waimea, Kaua'i. It's split between a "dry side" (closer to the Kohala Coast) and a "wet side" (closer to the Hāmākua Coast), but both sides can be cooler than sea level. It's also headquarters for the **Keck Observatory,** whose twin telescopes atop the nearly 14,000-foot **Mauna Kea ★★★,** some 35 miles away, are the largest and most powerful in the world. Those opposing the building of more observatories often stage peaceful protests in Waimea, including along its historic Church Row, a popular spot for local food vendors and site of the annual Cherry Blossom Festival. Waimea is home to several shopping centers and affordable lodgings, while **Merriman's ★★★** remains a popular foodie outpost at Opelo Plaza.

NORTH KOHALA   Locals may remember when sugar was king here, but for visitors, little-developed North Kohala is most famous for another king, Kamehameha the Great. His birthplace is a short walk from one of the Hawaiian Islands' largest and most important temples, **Mo'okini Heiau ★,** which dates to A.D. 480; you'll want a four-wheel-drive (4WD) for the rugged road there or plan for a long, hot hike. Much easier to find (and photograph): the yellow-cloaked bronze statue of the warrior-king in front of the community center in **Kapa'au,** a small plantation-era town. The road ends at the breathtaking **Pololū Valley Overlook ★★★.**

Once the center of Hawai'i Island's sugarcane industry, **Hāwī** remains a regional hub, with a 3-block-long strip of sun-faded, false-fronted buildings holding a few shops and restaurants of interest to visitors. Eight miles south, **Lapakahi State Historical Park ★** merits a stop to explore how less-exalted Hawaiians than Kamehameha lived in a simple village by the sea. Beaches are less appealing here, with the northernmost coves subject to strong winds blowing across the 'Alenuihāhā ("Great billows smashing") Channel from Maui, 26 miles away and visible on most days.

THE HĀMĀKUA COAST

This emerald coast, a 52-mile stretch from Honoka'a to Hilo on the island's windward northeast side, was once planted with sugarcane; it now blooms with macadamia nuts, papayas, vanilla orchids, and mushrooms. Resort-free and virtually without beaches, the Hāmākua Coast includes the districts of Hāmākua and North Hilo, with two unmissable destinations. Picture-perfect **Waipi'o Valley,** only viewable from the **Waipi'o Valley Overlook ★★★** unless you're going down with a permitted shuttle or tour company, has impossibly steep sides, taro patches, a green riot of wild plants, and a winding stream leading to a broad, black-sand beach, while **'Akaka Falls State Park ★★★** offers views of two lovely waterfalls amid lush foliage. Also worth checking out: **Laupāhoehoe Point ★,** with its mournful memorial to young victims of a 1946 tsunami, and the quirky assortment of antique shops, stylish Hawaiian-style boutiques, and homespun restaurants in the plantation town of **Honoka'a.**

HILO

The largest metropolis in Hawai'i after Honolulu is a quaint, misty, flower-filled city of Victorian and plantation-style houses overlooking a half-moon bay, a historic downtown and a clear view of Mauna Kea, often snowcapped in winter. It rains a lot in Hilo—about 128 inches a year—which tends to dampen visitors' enthusiasm for longer stays. It's ideal for growing ferns, orchids, and anthuriums, but not for catching constant rays.

Yet there's a lot to see and do in Hilo and the surrounding South Hilo district, including indoor attractions such as the **'Imiloa Astronomy Center ★★★**, **Lyman Museum and Mission House ★★**, **Mokupāpapa Discovery Center ★★**, and the **Pacific Tsunami Museum ★**. Outdoors, you'll want to see **Hilo Bay ★★**, the bayfront **Lili'uokalani Gardens ★★**, and **Rainbow Falls (Wai'anueanue) ★★★**—so grab your umbrella. The rain is warm (the temperature seldom dips below 70°F/21°C), and a rainbow usually follows afterward.

The town also holds the island's best bargains for budget travelers, with plenty of hotel rooms—most of the year, that is. Hilo's magic moment comes in spring, the week after Easter, when hula *halau* (schools) arrive for the annual **Merrie Monarch Festival ★★★** hula competition (www.merriemonarch.com). Although the numerous arts and craft fairs, cultural workshops, popup clothing boutiques, and daytime hula performances and concerts are free, plan ahead for lodging and seeing the competition in person: Tickets are sold out by the first week in January, and hotels within 30 miles are usually booked solid. Hilo is also the gateway to **Hawai'i Volcanoes National Park ★★★**, where hula troupes have traditionally performed chants and dances before the Merrie Monarch festival; the park is 30 miles away, or about an hour's drive up-slope.

Wai'anueanue (Rainbow Falls), the legendary home of Hina, the mother of demigod Maui.

PUNA DISTRICT

PĀHOA & KALAPANA   Between Hilo and Hawai'i Volcanoes National Park lies the "Wild Wild East," which gained international fame in 2018 with the onset of devastating, dramatic lava flows that lasted 4 months. Although no lives were lost (scientific monitoring allows for early warning, and lava doesn't move that fast here), the flows claimed some 700 homes—including oceanfront vacation rentals, an isolated suburban subdivision, and farmsteads—and filled all of Kapoho Bay with molten rock up to 900 feet deep. The Lower Puna eruption also caused the crater-top Green Lake to evaporate, and buried the volcanically heated waters of 'Ahalanui Park, and Wai'opae tidepools, all beloved and unique ecosystems. However, not all was lost: The ghostly hollowed trunks of **Lava Tree State Monument ★★** remain standing, while a new black-sand beach, a lagoon, and small thermal ponds formed at Pohoiki Harbor in **Isaac Hale Beach Park ★★**. A lively night market still takes place in **Kalapana** on the acres of lava that rolled through the hamlet in 1986. The part-Hawaiian, part-hippie and increasingly suburban plantation town of **Pāhoa** was threatened by a lava flow in 2014 that consumed miles of forest before stopping just short of the village and Hwy. 130, its lifeline to the rest of the island.

HAWAI'I VOLCANOES NATIONAL PARK ★★★   This is America's most exciting national park, where a live volcano called Kīlauea put on many memorable displays long before Mark Twain recorded its scenery and sulfurous odors in 1866. It continuously erupted from 1983 to 2018, the final year bringing months of sporadic but massive, steam-driven eruptions of ash at the summit. The 2018 eruption not only drained the famous lava lake at Halema'uma'u Crater inside Kīlauea's caldera, but also quadrupled the size of the caldera, which expanded more than a square mile. The crater floor dropped from 280 feet to as much as 1,500 feet in places. A bubbling lava lake on the crater floor that appeared in 2021 dazzled nighttime onlookers into 2023 before drying up. Visitors should ideally plan to spend 3 days at the park exploring its spectacular landscape, including a lava tube, cinder mounds, lush rainforest, stark-hued shoreline, and cultural sites. Even if you have only a day, it's worth the trip. Bring your sweats or jacket (honest!); it's cool and often misty up here.

VOLCANO VILLAGE   If you're not camping or staying at the historic, 33-room **Volcano House ★★** inside the park, you'll want to overnight in this quiet hamlet, just outside the national park entrance. Several cozy inns and vacation rentals, some with fireplaces, reside under tree ferns in this cool mountain hideaway. The tiny highland community (elevation 4,000 ft.), first settled by Japanese immigrants, is now home to artists, soul-searchers, and others who like the crisp high-country air.

KA'Ū DISTRICT

Pronounced *"kah-oo"* (and sometimes spelled Kā'ū), this windswept, often barren district between Puna and South Kona is one that visitors are

Rock art at the Kalapana lava flow.

most likely to just drive through on their way to and from the national park. Nevertheless, it contains several noteworthy sites.

KA LAE (SOUTH POINT)　This is the Plymouth Rock of Hawai'i. The first Polynesians are thought to have arrived in seagoing canoes, most likely from the Marquesas Islands, as early as A.D. 124 at this rocky promontory 500 feet above the sea. To the west is the old fishing village of Waiahukini, populated from A.D. 750 until the 1860s; ancient canoe moorings, shelter caves, and *heiau* (temples) poke through windblown pili grass today. The east coast curves inland to reveal **Papakōlea (Green Sand) Beach ★★**, a world-famous anomaly that's best accessed on foot to prevent environmental damage, although the numerous trails have also led to erosion and community concerns over overtourism. Along the point, the southernmost spot in the 50 states, trees grow sideways due to the relentless gusts that also power wind turbines in the area. It's a slow, nearly 12-mile drive from the highway to the tip of Ka Lae, so many visitors simply stop at the marked overlook on Highway 11, west of South Point Road.

NĀ'ĀLEHU, WAI'ŌHINU & PĀHALA　Nearly every business in Nā'ālehu and Wai'ōhinu, the two wide spots on the main road near South Point, claims to be the southernmost this or that. But except for delicious *malasadas* (doughnut holes) from the **Punalu'u Bake Shop ★**, coffee from **Ka Lae ★★** or a hearty meal from **Hana Hou Restaurant ★**, there's no reason to linger before heading to **Punalu'u Beach ★★★**, between Nā'ālehu and Pāhala. Protected green sea turtles bask on the fine black-sand beach—usually behind small rock walls created by lifeguards to remind you to keep 20 feet away—when they're not bobbing in the clear waters, chilly from fresh springs bubbling from the ocean floor. Pāhala is the center of the burgeoning Ka'ū coffee-growing scene ("industry" might

177

be overstated), so caffeine fans should allot at least 45 minutes to visit **Ka'ū Coffee Mill ★**. The tiny, bright-hued **Wood Valley Temple ★**, visited twice by the Dalai Lama, is also worth the scenic detour past the coffee mill.

GETTING AROUND

The Hawaiian directions of *makai* (toward the ocean) and *mauka* (toward the mountains) come in handy when looking for unfamiliar sites, especially since numbered address signs may be invisible or nonexistent. They're used with addresses below as needed.

BY TAXI & RIDESHARE   Ride-sharing platforms Uber and Lyft operate on the island, although coverage is spotty outside of Kailua-Kona and Hilo. A similar Hawai'i-based rideshare app, Holoholo (www.ride holoholo.com), launched in 2021 and allows you to make reservations, too. Kona airport pickups are allowed at the median between Terminal 1 and 2; in Hilo, find your ride-share curbside, near the helicopter tours. Licensed taxis with professional, knowledgeable drivers are readily available at both Kona and Hilo airports, although renting a car (see below) is a more likely option. Rates set by the county start at $3, plus $3.20 each additional mile—about $25 to $30 from the Kona airport to Kailua-Kona and $50 to $60 to the Waikoloa Beach Resort. On the Kona side, call **Kona Taxicab** (https://konataxicab.com; ✆ **808/324-4444**), which can also be booked in advance for airport pickups; drivers will check on your flight's arrival. On the Hilo side, call **Kwiki Taxi** (https://kwikitaxi. wordpress.com; ✆ **808/498-0308**).

BY CAR   You'll want a rental car on Hawai'i Island for at least a few days—or your entire trip, if you're not staying in Kailua-Kona or a Kohala resort with easy access to services, beaches, and excursions. All major car-rental agencies have airport pickups in Kona and Hilo; some even offer cars at Kohala and Kona resorts. (If using Turo.com, be aware that using the airport parking lot for pickups and drop-offs is illegal and can incur fines.) For tips on insurance and driving rules, see "Getting Around Hawai'i" (p. 603).

Hawai'i Island has more than 480 miles of paved road. The highway that circles the island is called the **Hawai'i Belt Road.** From North Kona to South Kohala and Waimea, you have two driving choices: the scenic "upper" road, **Māmalahoa Highway** (Hwy. 190), or the speedier "lower" road, **Queen Ka'ahumanu Highway** (Hwy. 19). South of Kailua-Kona, the Hawai'i Belt Road continues on Māmalahoa Highway (Hwy. 11) all the way to downtown Hilo, where it becomes Highway 19 again and follows the Hāmākua Coast before heading up to Waimea.

North Kohala also has upper and lower highways. From Kawaihae, you can follow **Kawaihae Road** (Hwy. 19) uphill to the left turn onto the often-misty **Kohala Mountain Road** (Hwy. 250), which eventually drops down into Hāwī. *Tip:* The view is better when starting in Hāwī and heading toward Waimea—majestic Mauna Kea and Mauna Loa suddenly rise from ranchlands and you're on the best side for ocean panoramas, too, as long as the area's signature mists are at bay. The **'Akoni Pule Highway** (Hwy. 270) hugs the coast from Kawaihae to pavement's end at the Pololū Valley Lookout.

Note: **Saddle Road** (Hwy. 2000) snakes between Mauna Kea and Mauna Loa en route from Hilo to Māmalahoa Highway (Hwy. 190). Once considered quite dicey, it now offers 45¾ miles of relatively easy driving and some stunning views. Just be careful not to speed, especially close to Hilo or the U.S. Army's Pōhakuloa Training Area, and be prepared for rain, mists, and temperatures that drop sharply as the elevation rises. This route has no services, other than restrooms at the Gilbert Kahele State Recreation Area and the **Kaulana Manu Nature Trail.**

BY BUS & SHUTTLE **SpeediShuttle** (www.speedishuttle.com; ✆ **808/ 329-5433**) and **Roberts Hawaii** (www.robertshawaii.com; ✆ **866/570-2536** or 808/954-8640) offer door-to-door airport transfers to hotels and other lodgings. Sample round-trip, shared-ride rates from the Kona airport are $34 per person to Kailua-Kona, and $63 per person to the Mauna Lani Resort; Roberts agents meet you outside security and provide porter service in baggage claim, but be aware there may be up to five stops before your destination.

The island-wide bus system, the **Hele-On Bus** (www.heleonbus. org; ✆ **808/961-8744**), is free for all riders. Most routes have limited value for all but the most adventurous visitors, other than the Intra-Kona line between Kailua-Kona's big-box stores (Walmart, Costco) and the Keauhou Shopping Center, which also stops at the Old Kona Airport Beach. For a live, mobile-friendly map of bus routes and arrival times, go to www.myheleonbus.org.

Travelers staying in Kailua-Kona and the Keauhou Resort can pay $2 to hop on the open-air, 44-seat **Kona Resort Trolley** (www.robertshawaii. com/transportation/kona-trolley; ✆ **808/539-9400**), running daily from 7am to 8pm (except for Ironman race day in Oct) along Ali'i Drive.

The **Waikoloa Beach Resort trolley** runs daily from noon to 8pm from Hilton Waikoloa Village and the Waikoloa Beach Marriott to the Kings' Shops and Queens' Marketplace; it costs $3 adults, $2 ages 5 to 11 (kids 10 and under are free). Guests at Kings' Land by Hilton Grand Vacations can catch a free shuttle to Hilton Waikoloa Village and pick up the trolley from there. Hilton Waikoloa Village also runs golf shuttles for guests.

BY BIKE Due to elevation changes, narrow shoulders (with the notable exception of the Queen Ka'ahumanu Hwy. between Kailua-Kona and Kawaihae), and high traffic speeds, point-to-point bike travel without a tour guide isn't recommended. However, several areas are ideal for recreational cycling and sightseeing. See "Biking" under "Other Outdoor Activities" for rental shops and routes.

BY MOTORCYCLE & SCOOTER The sunny Kohala and Kona coasts are ideal for tooling around on a motorcycle, while those sticking to one resort or Kailua-Kona can easily get around by scooter. **Big Island Mopeds** (www.konamopedrentals.com; © **808/443-6625**) will deliver mopeds to your door for $55 a day ($365 weekly; note prices rise to $125 daily/$625 weekly during Ironman week in mid-Oct). Based in the Kings' Shops on the Waikoloa Beach Resort, **Big Island Motorcycle Company** (www.bigislandmotorcyclecompany.com; © **808/886-2011**) rents Harley-Davidsons starting at $172 a day to ages 21 and older.

BY ELECTRIC CART If you're staying on the Waikoloa Beach or Mauna Lani resorts, you can also rent electric golf carts and Mokes (open-air Jeeplike carts) to ride to shops, restaurants, and beaches on those resorts, but not beyond, since they only go up to 25mph and venturing farther afield would mean accessing the highway. **Big Island Motorcycle Company** (www.bigislandmotorcyclecompany.com; © **808/886-2011**), in the Kings' Shops on the Waikoloa Beach Resort, rents Mokes that seat four starting at $150 a day. For those staying in condos at the Mauna Lani Resort, **Resort Carts** (www.resortcarts.com) offers electric golf cart rentals from $595 for up to 7 days, with custom rates for longer stays. *Note:* Hotel guests are not allowed to rent these, due to lack of the 110-volt outlets required for recharging these carts, near the hotel parking lots.

[FastFACTS] HAWAI'I ISLAND

Air Quality Although air quality has been excellent since Kīlauea's 35-year eruption ceased in 2018, you can find daily **air-quality reports,** based on sulfur dioxide and particulates measured at eight different sites, at https://air.doh. hawaii.gov/home/text/118.

ATMs/Banks ATMs are located everywhere on Hawai'i Island, at banks, supermarkets, Longs Drugs, and at some shopping malls. The major banks on Hawai'i Island are First Hawaiian, Bank of Hawaii, American Savings, and Central Pacific, all with branches in both Kona and Hilo.

Business Hours Most independent businesses on the island are open Monday to Saturday from 8 or 9am to 5 or 6pm. Stores in resort shopping areas are open daily.

Dentists If staying on the Kohala Coast, in Waimea or North Kohala, call **Dr. David Doi** or **Dr. Trevor Hartwell** of Hawaiian Holistic Dentistry, 64-5191 Kinohou St. (www.hawaiianholistic dentistry.com; © **808/885-7144**). In Kailua-Kona, call **Dr. Christopher Bays** at **Kona Coast Dental Care,** 75-5591 Palani Rd., above the KBXtreme Bowling Center (www.konacoastdental. com; © **808/329-8067**). In

Hilo, **Island Ohana Dental,** 519 E. Lanikaula St. (www. islandohanadental.com; © **808/935-4800**), is open Monday through Saturday, with three siblings—**Drs. Germaine, Garrett,** and **Jill Uehara**—on staff.

Doctors For drop-in visits in Kona, head to **Urgent Care of Kona,** 77-311 Sunset Dr., Kailua-Kona (www.urgentcareof kona.com; © **808/327-4357;** Mon–Fri 8am–5pm and Sat 9am–3pm). On the Kohala Coast, book a general clinic visit or IV rehydration at **Kohala Coast Urgent Care** (www.kohala coasturgentcare.com; © **808/880-3321**), inside the Westin Hapuna Beach Resort, 62-100 Kauna'oa Dr. It's open Monday to Friday 9am to 5pm, Saturdays 9am to 2pm, and Sunday by appointment. Dr. Ka'ohimanu Dang Akiona leads the friendly, caring medical team. **Hilo Urgent Care Center** at 670 Kekuanaoa St., Hilo (www.hilourgentcare.com; ☏ **808/969-3051**) is affiliated with Kaiser Permanente; its sister branch, **Kea'au Urgent Care Center** (☏ **808/966-7942**), is closer to Volcano Village at 16-612 Old Volcano Rd., Kea'au. Both are open Monday to Friday 9am to 7pm and Saturday and Sunday 8:30am to 4pm.

Emergencies For ambulance, fire, or rescue services, dial ☏ **911.**

Hospitals Hospitals offering 24-hour, urgent-care facilities include three designed as Level III trauma centers, able to perform emergency surgeries among other critical care: **Kona Community Hospital,** 79-1019 Haukapila St., off Highway 11, Kealakekua (www.kch.hhsc.org; ☏ **808/322-9311**); **Hilo Medical Center,** 1190 Wai'anuenue Ave., Hilo

(www.hilomedicalcenter.org; ☏ **808/932-3000**); and **Queen's North Hawai'i Community Hospital,** 67-1125 Māmalahoa Hwy., Waimea (www.queens.org/locations/hospitals/north-hawaii; ☏ **808/885-4444**). Two smaller rural hospitals will stabilize patients needing emergency care before transferring them to larger facilities: **Kohala Hospital,** 54-383 Hospital Rd., Kapa'au (https://kohala.hhsc.org; ☏ **808/889-6211**) and **Ka'ū Hospital,** 1 Kamani St., Pāhala (www.kauhospital.org; ☏ **808/932-4200**).

Internet Access Pretty much every lodging on the island has Wi-Fi; resorts typically include it in their exorbitant resort fees. All **Starbucks** and **McDonald's** locations, plus numerous local coffee shops also offer free Wi-Fi. The state has also created 33 Wi-Fi hotspots with 1-hr. free use from remote Nā'ālehu and Pāhala to more populous Hilo, Kailua-Kona, and Waimea; for the full list, see https://cca.hawaii.gov/broadband/dcca-designated-wifi-hotspots.

Pharmacies The only 24-hour pharmacy is in Hilo

at **Longs Drugs,** 555 Kīlauea Ave., one of 12 around the island (www.cvs.com; ☏ **808/935-9075**). The rest open Monday through Saturday as early as 7am and close as late as 9pm; some are closed Sunday. Kona and Hilo's national chain stores such as **Kmart, Safeway, Target, Walmart,** and **Costco** (Kailua-Kona only) also have pharmacies with varying hours.

Police Dial ☏ **911** in case of emergency; otherwise, call the **Hawai'i Police Department** at ☏ **808/935-3311** island-wide.

Post Office The **U.S. Postal Service** (www.usps.com; ☏ **800/275-8777**) has 28 branches around the island, including in Kailua-Kona at 74-5577 Palani Rd., in Waimea (Kamuela) at 67-1197 Māmalahoa Hwy., and in Hilo at 1299 Kekuanaoa St. All are open Monday to Friday, with widely varying hours, but generally open by 9am and closed by noon, with larger ones open as late as 4:30pm. Some are also open Saturday morning, typically 9am to noon; all are closed Sun.

Volcanic Activity Before you visit **Hawai'i Volcanoes National Park,** learn if lava is flowing and check for any closures at www.nps.gov/havo/planyourvisit/index.htm.

EXPLORING HAWAI'I ISLAND
Attractions & Points of Interest

Although parks are open year-round, some of the other attractions below may be closed on major holidays such as Christmas, New Year's, or Thanksgiving Day (fourth Thurs in Nov). Admission is often reduced for Hawai'i residents with state ID.

A Hawaiian ceremony at Kaloko-Honōkohau National Historical Park.

NORTH KONA

Hawai'i Ocean Science and Technology Park (HOST) ★★ AQUA-CULTURE/NATURAL ATTRACTION   Formerly known as the Natural Energy Laboratory of Hawai'i (NELHA), this 870-acre, craggy oceanfront complex in Kailua-Kona, just south of the airport, hosts a variety of attractions that rely on its access to cold, pure water pumped from the ocean depths, or solar power, or both. **Kona Sea Salt** ★★, 73-907 Makako Bay Dr. (www.konaseasalt.com; © **808/326-9301**), harvests delicately crunchy salt from the water, the product of Greenland glacial melt that takes 900 years to wend its way via a major current to Keāhole Point, the western-most tip of the island. Daily 45-minute farm tours ($25 adults; $15 ages 14 and under) cover the salt-making process and the cultural significance of the site and salt (*pa'akai*) in Hawai'i, and end with a tasting of a variety of pure and flavored sea salts. Book the sunset tour if you can. If you don't have time for a tour, you can still drop by the store daily 9am to 4pm.

HOST is also where imported lobsters from Maine stay cool, where succulent Kona kampachi fish are sustainably raised, and **Big Island Abalone** ★★, 73-357 Makako Bay Dr. (www.bigislandabalone.com; © **808/327-9585**), tends its delicious, rare shellfish. The latter's 45-minute **farm tour** ($25 adults, $12 ages 8 and under), offered Monday through Saturday, includes learning about abalone's history and life cycle, a hands-on experience with it and other shoreline marine life such as sea urchins and sea stars, and a tasting of grilled abalone. You can also buy abalone and other ingredients, with complimentary loan of BBQ utensils, for a barbecue picnic at nearby **Wawaloli Beach Park**, 73-188 Makako Bay (daily sunrise to half-hour after sunset). Other marine life attractions at

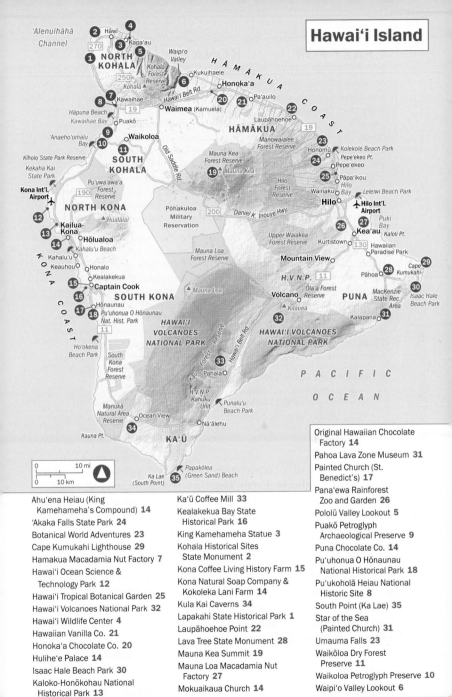

Hawai'i Island

CRAZY FOR (real) KONA coffee

More than 600 farms grow coffee in the Kona Coffee Belt on the slopes of Hualālai, from Kailua-Kona and Hōlualoa in North Kona to Captain Cook and Hōnaunau in South Kona. The prettiest time to visit is between January and May, when the rainy season brings white blossoms known as "Kona snow." Harvesting is by hand—one reason Kona coffee is so costly—from July through January. Several farms offer regular **tours with tastings,** and many more provide samples. **Note:** Buying directly from the farm, and only buying coffee labeled 100% Kona, is the best way to avoid being ripped off by bogus beans with inferior taste. In recent years, several small Kona coffee farmers won settlements from Costco, Marshalls, Safeway and other larger retailers after filing lawsuits that accused the vendors of deceiving consumers through sales of fake "Kona coffee" and highly adulterated blends.

To find the real thing, you can make impromptu stops along Māmalahoa Highway (Hwy. 11 and Hwy. 180) or find more obscure farms and those requiring reservations via the **Kona Coffee Farmers Association** (www.konacoffee farmers.org). Some highlights, heading north to south (these farms are highlighted on the map "Beaches & Outdoor Activities on Hawai'i Island," p. 219):

○ **Holualoa Kona Coffee Company,** 77-6261 Māmalahoa Hwy. (Hwy. 180), Hōlualoa (© **800/334-0348** or 808/322-9937): Owned by Desmond and Lisen Twigg-Smith, this organic farm and mill sells its own and others' premium Kona coffee. Take a free guided tour that showcases the roasting and packaging processes while learning about the orchards (mowed and fertilized by a flock of about 50 geese, but off limits due to a new coffee pest); it's offered Monday through Thursday 8am to 3pm, with a free 4-ounce cup of coffee afterwards.

○ **Kona Joe Coffee,** 79-7346 Māmalahoa Hwy. (Hwy. 11 btw. mile

HOST have more of a conservation focus. I no longer recommend the **Ocean Rider Seahorse Farm Tour** (www.seahorse.com; © **808/329-6840**) due to its expense ($73–$76 ages 11 and older; $63–$66 ages 5–10), rapid-fire narration, and overcrowding on its 1-hour tours; still, many have enjoyed the brief thrill of having a seahorse wrap its tiny tail around their finger, and some portion of proceeds benefit species preservation. A hospital for the highly endangered Hawaiian monk seal (see "Spotting Rare Monk Seals," p. 188), **Ke Kai Ola,** 73-731 Makako Bay Dr. (www.marinemammalcenter.org/monkseals; © **808/326-7325**), does not let you into its wards, but usually has interpretive signs and videos about its work in a small area outside its facility, so it's an easy stop to add to the salt or abalone farm tours.

73-4660 Hwy. 19, Kailua-Kona. https://nelha.hawaii.gov. © **808/327-9585.** Daily 5am–8pm.

Hulihe'e Palace ★★★ HISTORIC SITE   John Adams Kuakini, royal governor of the island, built this stately, two-story New England–style mansion overlooking Kailua Bay in 1838. It later became a summer home markers 113 and 114), Kainaliu (www. konajoe.com; ℭ **808/322-2100**): The home of the world's first trellised coffee farm offers a free, self-guided tour of the 20-acre estate, with 5-minute video, daily from 8am to 3pm. Book an hourlong guided tour ($30 adults, free for kids 12 and under) and receive a mug, coffee, and chocolate; tours run at 9am, 11am, and 1pm. True coffee lovers (ages 16 and older only) should book the $125 roasting tour, which sends them home with a 10-ounce bag they roasted themselves.

○ **Greenwell Farms,** 81-6581 Māmalahoa Hwy. (*makai* side of Hwy. 11, south of mile marker 112), Kealakekua (www.greenwellfarms. com; ℭ **808/323-9616**): If any farm can claim to be the granddaddy of Kona coffee, this would be it. Englishman Henry Nicholas Greenwell began growing coffee in the region in 1850. Now operated by

his great-grandson and agricultural innovator Tom Greenwell, the farm offers free, 45-minute guided tours daily, starting at 9am and then on the half-hour from 10am to 3pm. Private tours and tastings cost $40, available Monday to Friday 9:30am and 1:30pm.

○ **Kona Coffee Living History Farm,** 82-6199 Māmalahoa Hwy., *makai* side, Captain Cook (www.kona historical.org/kona-coffee-living-history-farm; ℭ **808/323-3222**): Take a self-guided tour among the coffee trees on the Uchida family homestead, representative of the strong Japanese American role in developing Kona coffee, including milling and roasting. You can peek in the 20th century farmhouse, learn about coffee production and meet a "Kona nightingale," Shizu the donkey. It's open Tuesday and Friday 10am and 2pm; $20 adults, $10 ages 7 to 17 (kids 16 and under are free).

for King Kalākaua and Queen Kapiʻolani and, like Queen Emma's Summer Palace and ʻIolani Palace on Oʻahu, is now lovingly maintained by the Daughters of Hawaiʻi as a showcase for royal furnishings and Native Hawaiian artifacts, from hat boxes to koa furniture and a 22-foot spear. You can view its six spacious rooms and learn more of the monarchs' history and cultural context on guided or self-guided tours, but reservations are recommended in either case. Limited to 15 people, the guided tours take place by reservation Wednesday through Friday at 11:30am and 2:30pm. Expect to remove your shoes before entering, with free booties provided upon request.

75-5718 Aliʻi Dr., Kailua-Kona. https://daughtersofhawaii.org. ℭ **808/329-1877.** Docent-led tours by reservation Wed–Fri 11:30am and 2pm: $22 adults, $16 seniors 62 and older, $14 children ages 5–12, $3 ages 4 and under. Self-guided tours Wed–Thurs and Sat 10am–3pm and Fri 10am–2pm: $16 adults, $10 seniors and children 5–12, $1 ages 4 and under.

Kaloko-Honōkohau National Historical Park ★★★ HISTORIC SITE/NATURAL ATTRACTION   With no volcano, tikis, or massive temples, this 1,160-acre oceanfront site just north of Honōkohau Harbor

tends to get overlooked by visitors in favor of its showier siblings in the national park system. That's a shame for several reasons, among them: It's a microcosm of ancient Hawai'i, from fishponds (one with an 800-ft.-long rock wall), house platforms, petroglyphs, and trails through barren lava to marshlands with native waterfowl, reefs teeming with fish, and a tranquil beach where green sea turtles bask in the shadow of Pu'u Oina Heiau. Plus, it's rarely crowded, and admission is free. Stop by the visitor center to ask about ocean conditions (if you're planning to snorkel), and then backtrack to Honōkohau Harbor, a half-mile south, to park closer to the beach.

Ocean side of Hwy. 19, 3 miles south of Kona airport. www.nps.gov/kaho. © **808/ 326-9057.** Daily dawn to dusk. Visitor center and parking lot ½-mile north of Honōkohau Harbor daily 8:30am–4pm (closed 1 Sat in Oct for Ironman). Kaloko Rd. gate daily 8am–5pm. No time restrictions on parking at Honōkohau Harbor; from Hwy.19, take Kealakehe Pkwy. west into harbor, then take 1st right, and follow to parking lot near Kona Sailing Club, a short walk to beach.

Kona Natural Soap Company & Kokoleka Lani Farm ★★★   To visit Kokoleka Lani ("Heavenly Chocolate") Farm, an award-winning bean-to-bar producer, you have to book its once-a-week, 2½- to 3-hr. tour ($25). The 5-acre sustainable farm on the site of a former hillside quarry is the source of meltingly delicious chocolate bars in 50% and 70% cacao varieties and also expertly roasted Kona coffee. On the tour, affable co-owner **Greg Colden** discusses the farm's flora and fauna (including wild chickens and pet dogs and cats) and how he and co-owner **Marty Corrigan** produce their coffee and chocolate (samples included). In his workshop for **Kona Natural Soap Company,** he explains how he makes his exquisite, chemical-free soaps, some using farm-grown coffee and cacao chaff, and Hawai'i's traditional skincare remedy of *kukui* (candlenut) oil. If you can't make the Thursday morning tour, Colden can often be found at Kona

Natural Soap Company's booth at Ali'i Gardens Marketplace in Kailua-Kona (see "Hawai'i Island Shopping," p. 292). *Note:* Open for tours by reservation, the farm is conveniently next to **Hawaii Island Humane Society,** which has a well-stocked pet boutique and allows visitors to take its rescued dogs on outings (see "Field Trips with Fido," p. 186).

78-6749 Māmalahoa Hwy., *mauka* side, Hōlualoa. www.konanaturalsoap.com. ⓒ **808/987-3131.** Tours by reservation only Thurs 9am. $40.

Mokuaikaua Church ★ RELIGIOUS/HISTORIC SITE In 1820, the first missionaries to land in Hawai'i arrived on the brig *Thaddeus* and received the royals' permission to preach. Within a few years, a thatched-roof structure had risen on this site, on land donated by Gov. Kuakini, owner of Hulihe'e Palace across the road. But after several fires, Rev. Asa Thurston had this massive, New England–style structure erected, using

lava rocks from a nearby *heiau* (temple) held together by coral mortar, with gleaming koa for the lofty interior. The 112-foot steeple is still the tallest structure in Kailua-Kona. Once ongoing renovations are complete, visitors will be welcome again to view the sanctuary and a rear room with a small collection of artifacts, including a model of the *Thaddeus,* a rope star chart used by Pacific Islanders, and a poignant plaque commemorating Henry 'Ōpūkaha'ia. As a teenager, the Hawai'i Island native (known then as "Obookiah") boarded a ship to New England in 1807, converted to Christianity, and helped plan the first mission to the islands, but he died of a fever in 1818, the year

A snorkeler exploring Kealakekua Bay.

before the *Thaddeus* sailed. (In 1993, his remains were reinterred at Kahikolu Congregational Church, 16 miles south of Mokuaikaua in Captain Cook.)

75-5713 Ali'i Dr., Kailua-Kona, across from Hulihe'e Palace (parking behind the church off Kuakini Hwy.). www.mokuaikaua.org. ⓒ **808/329-0655.** Open during and after 9am Sunday worship; check website for additional hours.

SOUTH KONA

Kealakekua Bay State Historical Park ★★ NATURAL ATTRACTION The island's largest natural sheltered bay, a marine life conservation district, is not only one of the best places to snorkel on Hawai'i Island, it is also an area of deep cultural and historical significance. On the southern Nāpo'opo'o (*"nah-poh-oh-poh-oh"*) side stands the large stacked-rock platform of **Hikiau Heiau,** a temple once used for human sacrifice and still considered sacred. A boulder-strewn beach park here includes picnic tables, barbecues, and restrooms. On the north side, a steep but relatively broad 2-mile trail leads down to Ka'awaloa, where *ali'i* (royalty) once lived; when they died, their bodies were taken to **Puhina O Lono Heiau** on the slope above, prepared for burial, and hidden in caves on the 600-foot-cliff above the central bay. The **Captain Cook Monument** is an obelisk on Ka'awaloa Flat, near where the British explorer was slain in 1779, after misunderstandings between Hawaiians and Cook's crew led to armed conflict. The Hawaiians then showed respect by taking Cook's body to Puhina O Lono before returning some of his remains to his crew. Please do not tread on the reef or cultural sites; to protect the area, only hikers and three guided kayak tour companies have access to Ka'awaloa Flat (see "Kayaking," on p. 234).

https://dlnr.hawaii.gov/dsp/parks/hawaii. From Hwy. 11 in Captain Cook heading south, take right fork onto Nāpo'opo'o Rd. (Hwy. 160). Ka'awaloa trailhead is about 500 ft. on right. By car, continue on Nāpo'opo'o Rd. 4¼-mile to left on Puuhonua Rd.; go ⅕-mile to right on Manini Beach Rd. Free admission. Daily dawn to dusk.

The Painted Church (St. Benedict's) ★★ RELIGIOUS SITE Beginning in 1899, Father John Berchman Velghe (a member of the same order as St. Damien of Moloka'i) painted biblical scenes and images of saints inside quaint St. Benedict's Catholic Church, founded in 1842 and restored in 2002. As with stained-glass windows of yore, his pictures, created with simple house paint, were a way of sharing stories with illiterate parishioners. It's a wonderfully trippy experience to look up at arching palm fronds and shiny stars on the ceiling. Health issues forced the priest to return to Belgium in 1904 before finishing all the pictures. The ocean-view church is open for visitors Tuesday through Friday 9:30am to 3:30pm; please dress respectfully. It's an active parish, with Mass celebrated

SPOTTING RARE monk seals

The endangered Hawaiian monk seal is so rare—about 1,300 in the remote Northwestern Hawaiian Islands and 100 in the main islands—that reporting any sightings can help scientists learn how to protect them. If you see one lying on the sand or swimming near you, first ensure you are at least 50 feet away, then note your location and any details about the monk seal's appearance. Then call ℂ **808/987-0765,** the hotline of Ke Kai Ola, the Hawaiian monk seal hospital, to describe what you've seen. (If you spot one on another island, call ℂ **888/256-9840.**) On the grounds of the Hawai'i Ocean Science and Technology Park (https://nelha.hawaii.gov), a vast research and business compound near the airport, the hospital treats ill and injured seals from throughout the archipelago. Above all, don't be like the tourists in a viral video from 2021 who touched a snoozing monk seal, earning them substantial fines as well as notoriety. It's considered a felony under state and federal law, due to the monk seals' endangered status.

The very vibrant Painted Church.

Tuesday, Thursday, and Friday at 7am; Saturday at 4pm; and Sunday at 7 and 10am.

84-5140 Painted Church Rd., Captain Cook. https://thepaintedchurchhawaii.org. © **808/328-2227.** From Kailua-Kona, take Hwy. 11 south 20 miles to a right on Rte. 160. Go 1 mile to the 1st turnoff on the right, opposite a King Kamehameha sign. Follow the narrow, winding road about ¼-mile to church sign and turn right. Free admission.

Pu'uhonua O Hōnaunau National Historical Park ★★★ HISTORIC SITE

With its fierce, haunting carved idols known as *ki'i*—the Hawaiian word for tiki—this sacred, 420-acre site on the black-lava Kona Coast certainly looks forbidding. To ancient Hawaiians, it served as a 16th-century place of refuge (*pu'uhonua*), providing sanctuary for defeated warriors and *kapu* (taboo) violators. A great rock wall—1,000 feet long, 10 feet high, and 17 feet thick—defines the refuge. On the wall's north end is **Hale O Keawe Heiau,** which holds the bones of 23 Hawaiian chiefs. Other finds include a royal compound, burial sites, old trails, and a portion of the ancient village of Ki'ileae (a 2-mile hike). You can learn about thatched huts, canoes, and idols on a self-guided tour. Check the schedule online for free ranger talks in an amphitheater, as well as cultural craft demonstrations. *Note:* The park only sells bottled water, but picnic tables are on the sandy stretch of the south side to enjoy refreshments you bring with you.

Hwy. 160, Hōnaunau. www.nps.gov/puho. © **808/328-2288.** From Kailua-Kona, take Hwy. 11 south 20 miles to a right on Hwy. 160. Head 3½ miles and turn left at park sign. $20 per vehicle; $15 per motorcycle; $10 per person on foot or bicycle; good for 7 days. Visitor center daily 8:30am–4:30pm; park daily 8:15am–sunset.

NORTH KOHALA

It takes some effort to reach the **Kohala Historical Sites State Monument ★**, but for those with 4WD vehicles or the ability to hike 3 miles round-trip, visiting the windswept, culturally important site on the island's northern tip can be worth it. It includes a memorial at the birthplace of King Kamehameha and the 1,500-year-old **Moʻokini Heiau,** once used by kings to pray and offer human sacrifices. This is among the oldest, largest (the size of a football field), and most significant shrines in Hawaiʻi. It's off a

Puʻuhonua O Hōnaunau National Historical Park.

coastal dirt road, 1½ miles southwest of ʻUpolu Airport (https://dlnr. hawaii.gov/dsp/parks/hawaii; free admission; daily 7am–6:45pm).

Hawaiʻi Wildlife Center ★★ AVIAN HOSPITAL/EDUCATIONAL ATTRACTION   While visitors can't go into the actual clinic that treats injured and diseased native and migratory birds (and the occasional native Hawaiian bat), you can take a virtual tour and watch these special patients via video monitor. You can also learn more about their unique ecosystem and its challenges in the engaging Hoʻopūlama Science and Discovery Center, a covered outdoor pavilion with kid-friendly interactive exhibits and a native plant garden. The gift shop (closed during lunchtime) has delightful bat- and bird-themed items whose sales help support the critical work done here.

53-324 Lighthouse Rd., Kapaʻau. www.hawaiiwildlifecenter.org. ℂ **808/884-5000.** Free admission. Tues–Sat 10am–3pm.

King Kamehameha Statue ★★ MONUMENT   Here stands King Kamehameha the Great, right arm outstretched, left arm holding a spear, as if guarding the seniors who have turned a century-old, New England–style courthouse into an airy civic center. There's one just like it in Honolulu, across the street from ʻIolani Palace, and another in the U.S. Capitol, but this is the original: an 8-foot 6-inch bronze by Thomas R. Gould, a Boston sculptor. Cast in Europe in 1880, it was lost at sea on its way to Hawaiʻi. After a sea captain recovered the statue, it was placed here, near Kamehameha's Kohala birthplace, in 1912. The unifier of the islands, Kamehameha is believed to have been born in 1758 under Halley's Comet and became ruler of Hawaiʻi in 1810. He died in Kailua-Kona in 1819, but his burial site remains a mystery.

North Kohala Civic Center, 54-3900 Hwy. 270, *mauka* side, Kapaʻau, just north of Kapaʻau Rd.

Lapakahi State Historical Park ★★ HISTORIC SITE This 14th-century fishing village on a hot, dry, dusty stretch of coast offers a glimpse into the lifestyle of the ancients. Lapakahi is the best-preserved fishing village in Hawai'i. Take the self-guided, 1-mile loop trail past stone platforms, fish shrines, rock shelters, salt pans, and restored *hale* (houses) to a coral-sand beach and the deep-blue sea of Koai'e Cove, a marine life conservation district. Wear good walking shoes and a hat, go early in the morning or late in the afternoon to beat the heat, and bring your own water. Facilities include portable toilets and picnic tables. ***Note:*** The parking lot gate is locked promptly at 4pm, with no recourse for getting your car out until the next morning, and no cell service, so plan visits accordingly. Makai side of Hwy. 270, Mahukona, 12½ miles north of Kawaihae. https://dlnr.hawaii.gov/dsp/parks/hawaii. ✆ **808/327-4958.** Free admission. Daily 8am–4pm (last entry 3:30pm).

Pololū Valley Lookout ★★★ NATURAL ATTRACTION At this end-of-the-road scenic lookout, you can gaze at the vertical dark-green cliffs of the Hāmākua Coast and two islets offshore or peer back into the

---

SWEET ON chocolate

Tucked between coffee orchards in the uplands of Keauhou, the **Original Hawaiian Chocolate Factory,** 78-6772 Makenawai St., Kailua-Kona (www.ohcf.us; ✆ **888/447-2626** and 808/322-2626), began growing cacao in 1993. It was the first in the islands to produce 100% Hawaiian chocolate. The 1-hour walking tour ($25 adults, $10 kids 6–12, free kids 5 and under) includes the orchard, small factory, and chocolate sampling, plus the option to buy the expensive but delectable chocolate bars and pieces shaped like plumeria flowers. Tours are Wednesday and Friday at 9 and 11am by reservation only; book well in advance. The factory store is open Tuesday through Friday 10am to 3pm.

Despite its name, the **Puna Chocolate Co.** (www.punachocolate.com; ✆ **808/489-9899**) has a cacao farm in Kona, at 78-6537 1 Road, Hōlualoa. The 90-minute strolling and tasting tour of the farm, which also grows coffee, macadamia nuts, and tropical fruits, takes place Sunday, Monday, Wednesday, and Friday at 9am, noon, and 2:30pm, by reservation only; it's $30 for adults, $26 ages 10 to 16, and $25 for ages 9 and under. A longer, hiking version of the tour, which includes walking uphill for 300 yards (274m), is Sunday and Wednesday at 9am; lasting 1 hour, 45 minutes, it's $20 for ages 3 to 11, $25 ages 12 to 16, and $30 for adults.

Chocolate lovers can taste samples of an intriguing variety of velvety-smooth chocolate bars, including several award-winning versions made with 100% Hawaiian grown cacao, goat milk, or coconut milk, at the **Honoka'a Chocolate Co.** store 45-3587 Māmane Hwy. (Main St.), Honoka'a (www.honokaachocolateco.com; ✆ **808/494-2129**). Or take a deeper dive on a 2-hour tour of its 2.5-acre cacao farm outside of town Tuesday through Thursday at 2pm, an adult-oriented experience that concludes with a visit to the shop to see the chocolate-making machinery at work. It's $80 for ages 10 and older ($65 for ages 5–10, who may find it a bit too deep on the cacao details). Directions are emailed to you once you've reserved your spot.

The postcard-perfect view from Pololū Valley.

often-misty uplands. The view may look familiar once you get here—it often appears on travel posters. In good conditions, adventurous travelers with sturdy shoes should take the switchback trail (a good 30-min. hike) to a secluded black-sand beach at the mouth of a wild valley once planted in taro. Bring water and bug spray, avoid the surf (subject to strong currents), and refrain from creating new stacks of rocks, which disrupt the beach ecology. (*Note:* Camping is not permitted in the valley, despite the tents you might spot.) Parking near the lookout has become tight in recent years; the county has also hired local ambassadors to help advise visitors on safety and cultural issues. Look for their frequent updates on trail and weather conditions on the Protect Pololū Facebook page.

At the northern end of Hwy. 270, 5½ miles east of Kapa'au.

SOUTH KOHALA

Hamakua Macadamia Nut Factory ★ FACTORY TOUR   The self-guided tour of shelling, roasting, and other processing that results in flavored macadamia nuts and confections is not that compelling if production has stopped for the day, so go before 3pm or plan to watch a video to get caught up. But who are we kidding—it's really all about the free tastings here: generous samples of big, fresh nuts in island flavors such as chili "peppah," Spam, and Kona-coffee glazed. Outside the hilltop factory warehouse are picnic tables with an ocean view.

61-3251 Maluokalani St., Kawaihae. www.hawnnut.com. ℂ **888/643-6688** or 808/882-1690. Free admission. Daily 9am–4:30pm. From Kawaihae Harbor, take Hwy. 270 north ¾-mile, turn right on Maluokalani St., factory is on right.

Kohala Petroglyph Fields ★★★ ROCK CARVINGS   Hawaiian petroglyphs are an enigma of the Pacific—no one knows who made them or why. They appear at 135 different sites on six inhabited islands, but most are found on Hawai'i Island, and include images of dancers and paddlers, fishermen and chiefs, and tools of daily life such as fishhooks and canoes. The most common depictions are family groups, while some petroglyphs depict post-European contact objects such as ships, anchors, horses, and guns. Simple circles with dots were used to mark the *puka,* or holes, where parents would place their child's umbilical cord (*piko*).

The largest concentration of these stone symbols in the Pacific lies in the 233-acre **Puakō Petroglyph Archaeological Preserve** next to the Fairmont Orchid, Hawai'i, at the Mauna Lani Resort. Some 3,000 designs have been identified. The 1.5-mile **Mālama Trail,** which passes through a kiawe forest on the way to the large, reddish lava field of petroglyphs, starts north of the hotel, *makai* side, with parking at Holoholokai Beach Park. Go in the early morning or late afternoon when it's cooler; bring water, wear shoes with sturdy soles (to avoid kiawe thorns), and stay on the trail.

The fascinating **Waikoloa Petroglyph Preserve** is a short stroll from the parking lot near the Kings' Shops gas station in the Waikoloa Beach Resort. Follow the signs to the trail (.5 mile/.8km round-trip) through the petroglyph field, but be aware that the trail is exposed, uneven, and rough; wear closed-toe shoes, a hat, and sunscreen. Look for the post-Western contact etched image of a person on horseback.

Note: Some of the petroglyphs are thousands of years old and easily destroyed. Do not walk on them or take rubbings (the Puakō preserve has a replica petroglyph you may use instead). The best way to capture a petroglyph is with a photo in the late afternoon, when shadows are long.

Puakō Petroglyph Archaeological Preserve: At end of 1.5-mile Mālama Trail on Mauna Lani Resort. From Hwy. 19, take Mauna Lani Rd. to traffic circle and first right on North Kanikū Drive, which ends at the Holoholokai Beach Park parking lot; a sign marks the trailhead on your right. The beach park is open daily 6:30am to 6:30pm.

Waikoloa Petroglyph Preserve: On Kings' Trail in Waikoloa Beach Resort, ¼ mile north of Shell gas station, 69-250 Waikoloa Beach Dr., Waikoloa. Daily sunrise to sunset.

Pu'ukoholā Heiau National Historic Site ★★★ HISTORIC SITE

This seacoast temple, called "the hill of the whale," is the single most imposing and dramatic structure of the early Hawaiians, built by Kamehameha I from 1790 to 1791. The *heiau* stands 224 feet long by 100 feet wide, with three narrow terraces on the seaside and an amphitheater to view canoes. Kamehameha built this temple to Ku, the war god, after a prophet told him he would conquer and unite the islands if he did so. He also slayed his cousin on the site, and 4 years later fulfilled his kingly goal. The site includes a small visitor center with intriguing displays and a thoughtful gift shop; a smaller *heiau*-turned-fort; the homestead of John Young (a British seaman who became a trusted advisor of Kamehameha); and, offshore, the submerged ruins of what is believed to be **Hale O Kapuni,** a shrine dedicated to the shark gods or guardian spirits called *'aumakua.* (You can't see the temple, but shark fins are often spotted slicing through the waters.) Paved trails lead around the complex, with restricted access to the *heiau.*

62-3601 Kawaihae Rd. (Hwy. 270, *makai* side, south of Kawaihae Harbor). www.nps. gov/puhe. ℭ **808/882-7218.** Free admission. Daily 7:30am–5pm (parking lot closes promptly at 4:30pm).

Waikōloa Dry Forest Preserve ★★ NATURAL AREA Some of Hawai'i's rarest and oldest endemic trees, the *wiliwili,* grow amid other native plants in this hot, dry, windswept preserve about 5 miles uphill from the Waikoloa Beach Resort. The best season to see the trees, some thought to be 300 years old, is spring and summer, when they lose their dark green leaves and showy blossoms in a variety of hues (orange, white, yellow) appear. Still, the **sunset** *huaka'i* (journeys), led the first Friday of the month, and occasionally at other times by staff and volunteers, are worth experiencing year-round. The free, informative tours start at the front gate, traverse an old lava flow and *kīpuka* (a mini forest oasis), and end about 90 minutes later at the Hana Hou Hale open-air pavilion, in time for sunset and refreshments (donations appreciated). Sign up online to **volunteer** on the second and fourth Saturday morning of each month, where you'll learn how to collect seeds from various plants, tend seedlings or help with other easy tasks in the beautiful setting, with refreshments and potluck lunch included.

Off Quarry Rd., a right turn off Waikoloa Rd., 4¾ miles east of Hwy. 19, Waikoloa (see website for more detailed directions). www.waikoloadryforest.org. ℭ **808/494-2208.** Free tours first Fri of the month at 5pm (Nov–Jan 4:30pm) and possibly other dates; volunteer sessions 2nd and 4th Sat of the month 8am to noon. Reserve online. Donations accepted. **Note:** Wear sturdy shoes and sun protection and bring water.

WAIMEA & MAUNA KEA

Mauna Kea ★★★ NATURAL ATTRACTION The 13,796-foot Mauna Kea ("white mountain") is sometimes spelled Maunakea, a contraction of *Mauna a Wākea,* or "the mountain of Wākea," referring to the sky father and ancestor of all Hawaiians. According to some traditions, all of creation began here, while the mountain's frequent mantle of snow and mists are attributed to the goddesses Poli'ahu and Lilinoe. This helps explain why some Hawaiians hold it sacred even today—and at press time were still fighting the construction of the proposed Thirty Meter Telescope. The observatory would be the latest in a series to take advantage of the summit's pollution-free skies, pitch-black nights,

On the way to Mauna Kea on horseback.

and a tropical location. In 2019, protesters known as *kia'i* (protectors) closed the access road to the summit for nearly half a year by camping on-site, chanting, dancing hula and teaching classes on Native Hawaiian culture. At press time, the road had reopened, but no resolution on the fate of the TMT had been reached.

SAFETY TIPS Before heading out, make sure you have four-wheel drive and a full gas tank, and check current weather and road conditions (http://mkwc.ifa.hawaii.edu/current/road-conditions; 🕿 **808/935-6268**). The drive via Saddle Road (Hwy. 2000) to the visitor center takes about an hour from Hilo and 90 minutes from Kailua-Kona; take at least 30 to 45 minutes to acclimate before ascending to the summit, a half-hour further on a steep, largely unpaved road. Dress warmly: It's chilly and windy by day, and after dark, temperatures drop into the 30s (from 3°C to 1°C). To avoid the bends, don't go within 24 hours of scuba diving. Pregnant women and those with heart or lung conditions should also skip this trip, while children 12 and under are not allowed at the summit. At night, bring a flashlight, with a red filter to reduce glare.

Note: Many rental-car agencies ban driving to the summit, so a private tour, while pricey, is probably the safest and easiest bet (see "Seeing Stars While Others Drive," below).

VISITOR CENTER Named for Ellison Onizuka, the Hawai'i Island-born astronaut aboard the ill-fated *Challenger* space shuttle, the **Onizuka Center for International Astronomy Visitor Information Station** (https://hilo.hawaii.edu/maunakea/visitor-information; 🕿 **808/934-4550**) is 6¼ miles up Summit Road and at 9,200 feet elevation. It's open daily 9am to 9pm, with exhibits, 24-hour restrooms, and a bookstore with gloves and other cold-weather gear for sale. While waiting to acclimate, day visitors can peer through a solar telescope and take a short hike to see *'āhinahina,* rare silversword plants whose blooms burst from a tall shoot growing from a low cluster of spiky silver fingers.

AT THE SUMMIT It's another steep 6 miles, most of them unpaved, to the summit from the visitor center. If you're driving, make sure your 4WD vehicle has plenty of gas and is in good condition before continuing on. Up here, 11 nations have set up a dozen infrared telescopes to look into deep space, making this the world's largest astronomical observatory. From the summit parking lot, you have an unparalleled view of other peaks, such as Mauna Loa and Haleakalā, and the bright Pacific.

Despite calling it a "temporary" closure due to COVID-19 concerns, the **W. M. Keck Observatory** still has yet to reopen its summit visitor gallery, which has informational panels, restrooms, and a viewing area of the eight-story-high telescope and dome. Check www.keckobservatory. org for any updates.

Another sacred site is **Lake Waiau,** which, at 13,020 feet above sea level, is one of the highest in the world. Although it shrinks drastically in time of drought, it has never dried up. It's named for one of the sisters of

seeing stars WHILE OTHERS DRIVE

Two excellent companies offer Mauna Kea tour packages that provide cold-weather gear, dinner, hot drinks, guided stargazing, and, best of all, someone else to worry about maneuvering the narrow, unpaved road to the summit. All tours are offered weather permitting, but most nights are clear—that's why the observatories are here, after all. Pickups are available from several locations. Read the fine print on health and age restrictions before booking, and don't forget to tip your guide (suggested $20 per person).

○ **Hawai'i Forest & Trail** (www.hawaii-forest.com; ℂ **800/464-1993** or 808/331-8505), the island's premier outfitter, operates the daily **Maunakea Summit & Stars Adventure,** which leaves Kona in time for a late-afternoon picnic dinner on the mountain, sunset at the summit, and stargazing at the visitor center, for $295. The company uses two customized off-road buses (14 passengers max each) for the 7- to 8-hour tour. The **"Give Back"** version of this trip ($309) departs 75 minutes earlier and includes a 1-hour stop at the **Waikōloa Dry Forest** (p. 194), a grove of rare wiliwili trees and other tropical plants that can grow in hot, rocky, windy conditions. You'll tour the forest and help with seed collection or another volunteer task before continuing on to Mauna Kea. Like all Hawai'i Forest & Trail's tours, these are exceptional, with well-informed guides.

○ **Monty "Pat" Wright** was the first to run a Mauna Kea stargazing tour when he launched **Mauna Kea Summit Adventures** (www.maunakea.com; ℂ **888/322-2366** or 808/322-2366) in 1983. Guests now ride in a large-windowed, four-wheel-drive (4WD) van instead of a Land Cruiser and don parkas instead of old sweaters; otherwise, it's much the same, with veggie lasagna for dinner at the visitor center before a spectacular sunset and stargazing. The 7½- to 8-hour tour costs $282 ($273 without dinner), open to ages 13 and older.

Stargazing at Mauna Kea.

The Keck Observatory at Mauna Kea.

Poliʻa hu, the snow goddess said to make her home atop Mauna Kea. To see it, take a brief hike: At Park 3, the first intersection on the road to the summit above the visitor center, follow the trail to the south for .5 mile, then take the branch to the right that leads to the top of a crater and the small, shallow, greenish lake. *Note:* Please respect cultural traditions by not drinking or entering the water and leave all rocks undisturbed.

THE HĀMĀKUA COAST

Don't forget bug spray when exploring this warm, moist region, beloved by mosquitoes, and be ready for passing showers—you're in rainbow territory here. *Note:* Some sights below are in the North Hilo district, just south of the official Hāmākua district, which shares its rural character.

ʻAkaka Falls State Park ★★★ NATURAL ATTRACTION   See one of the most scenic waterfalls in Hawaiʻi via a relatively easy .4-mile paved loop through a rainforest, past bamboo and flowering ginger, and down to an observation point. You'll have a perfect view of 442-foot ʻAkaka Falls, plunging down a horseshoe-shaped green cliff, and nearby Kahuna Falls, a mere 100-footer. Keep your eyes peeled for rainbows; your ears are likely to pick up the two-note chirp of coqui frogs (see below). Facilities include restrooms and drinking water.

End of ʻAkaka Falls Rd. (Hwy. 220), Honomū. https://dlnr.hawaii.gov/dsp/parks/hawaii. From Hilo, drive north 8 miles on Hwy. 19 to left at ʻAkaka Falls Rd. Follow 3½ miles to parking lot. $5 per person. $10 parking (if inside gates). No cash. Daily 8am–5pm.

Botanical World Adventures ★ WATERFALL/GARDEN   Just north of Hilo is one of the largest botanical gardens in Hawaiʻi, with some 5,000 species, plus a huge children's maze (second in size only to Dole Plantation's on Oʻahu), a tropical fruit arboretum, ethnobotanical and

An easy walk brings you to 'Akaka Falls.

wellness gardens, and flower-lined walks. Book online in advance for zipline and Segway tours but ignore the "no online availability" message to book self-guided walking tours ($10). You can just drop in to see the gardens and waterfalls, including 100-foot **Kamae'e Falls** and the shorter, bubbling cascades in **Hanapueo Stream;** call ahead to book the 90-minute Segway tour ($137), open to ages 14 and older. All tours include admission to the gardens for 1 week.

31-240 Old Māmalahoa Hwy., Hakalau. www.botanicalworld.com. ⓒ **888/947-4753** or 808/963-5427. Daily 8am–4pm. Zipline tours: Mon–Sat hourly 9–11am and 1–3pm; $197 adults, $167 ages 4–12. Segway tours: by reservation for ages 14 and older; $137. Self-guided walking tours: $10 adults, $5 ages 6 to 12, free for kids 5 and under.

Hawai'i Tropical Botanical Garden ★★ GARDEN   More than 2,000 species of tropical plants thrive in this little-known Eden by the sea. The 40-acre valley garden, nestled between the crashing surf and a thundering waterfall, includes torch gingers (which tower on 12-ft. stalks), a banyan canyon, an orchid garden, a banana grove, a bromeliad hill, and a golden bamboo grove, which rattles like a jungle drum in the trade winds. Some endangered Hawaiian specimens, such as the rare *Gardenia remyi,* flourish here. The self-guided tour takes about 90 minutes, but you're welcome to linger. Borrow an umbrella at the visitor center so that passing showers don't curtail your visit. *Note:* You enter and exit the garden via a 500-foot-long boardwalk that descends along a verdant ravine.

27-717 Old Māmalahoa Hwy. (4-Mile Scenic Route), Pāpa'ikou. www.htbg.com. ⓒ **808/964-5233.** $30 adults, $22 children 6–16, free for children 5 and under. Daily 9am–5pm (last entry 4pm).

Laupāhoehoe Point ★ HISTORIC SITE/NATURAL ATTRACTION
This idyllic place holds a grim reminder of nature's fury. On April 1, 1946, a tsunami swept away the schoolhouse that once stood on this peninsula and claimed the lives of 24 students, teachers, and residents. Their names are engraved on a stone memorial in a pretty beach park, and a display holds newspaper stories on the tragedy. The land here ends in black sea stacks that resemble tombstones; when high surf crashes on them, it's positively spooky (and dangerous if you stand too close). The rough shoreline is not a place to swim, but the views are spectacular. Services in **Laupāhoehoe Beach Park** include restrooms, picnic tables, and drinking water; see "Camping," p. 274, for details on obtaining camping permits.

Laupāhoehoe. From Hilo, take Hwy. 19 north 25 miles to Laupāhoehoe Point exit, *makai* side; the exit is 31 miles south of Waimea.

Umauma Falls ★★ WATERFALL/GARDEN   The triple-tiered, cascading pools of Umauma Falls are the exclusive province of the Umauma Experience, which offers an array of ziplining, swimming, kayaking,

---

Co-key, Co-key: What Is That Noise?

That loud, chirping noise you hear after dark in Hilo, Puna, the Hāmākua Coast, South Kona, and increasingly elsewhere on the island, is the cry of the male coqui frog looking for a mate. A native of Puerto Rico, where the frogs are kept in check by snakes, coqui came to Hawai'i in some plant material, found no natural enemies, and spread quickly across Hawai'i Island. (A handful have made it to O'ahu, Maui, and Kaua'i, where they've been swiftly captured by state agriculture teams devoted to eradicating the invasive species.) A few frogs will sound like singing birds; a chorus of thousands can be deafening—and they can reach densities of up to 10,000 an acre. Cooler elevations have fewer coqui, but anywhere else that's lush and rural is likely to have large populations. Pack earplugs if you're a light sleeper.

NOTHING PLAIN ABOUT THIS vanilla

When the Hamakua Sugar Company—Hawai'i Island's last sugar plantation—closed in 1996, it left a huge void in the local economy, transforming already shrinking villages into near ghost towns. But some residents turned to specialty crops that are now sought after by chefs throughout the islands. Hidden in the tall eucalyptus trees outside the old plantation community of Pa'auilo, the **Hawaiian Vanilla Company** ★★ (www.hawaiianvanilla.com; © **808/776-1771**) is the first U.S. farm to grow vanilla. Before you even enter the huge Vanilla Gallery, the heavenly scent of vanilla will embrace you. The farm hosts one of the most sensuous experiences on the island, the 2-hour, four-course **Hawaiian Vanilla Luncheon** ($75 for ages 12 and up; $50 for kids 4–12), served Monday to Friday at 12:30pm and including a farm tour afterward. The hour-long **Farm Tour** ($35 all ages), including dessert and tastings, takes place Monday to Friday at 1:15pm. Or just skip all the farm talk and indulge instead in vanilla-scented teas, pastries, finger sandwiches, soup, salad, and sorbet at the **Upcountry Afternoon Tea** ($60 ages 14 and older), Sundays at 1pm. Reservations are required for tours, luncheon, and tea. The gallery and gift shop are open Monday through Saturday 10am to 3pm.

> **Tip:** Staying in Kona and short on time? Book an hourlong tour at Guy and Jeannie Cellier's petite farm **Kona Vanillerie,** 73-4301 Laui St., Kailua-Kona (www.thevanillerie.com; © **808/331-8535**). Tours ($20 adults, $10 ages 14 and under) are Tuesday through Friday at 10am and noon and end with a tasty scoop of vanilla ice cream.

horseback riding (see Wailea Horseback Adventure, p. 250), and ATV excursions on its lush 90 acres. The new waterfall rappel tour combines hiking, rappelling, floating, and swimming to navigate among five waterfalls along the Umauma River. The less adventurous can also just pay $12 to drive the paved road to the waterfall lookout, and then take a self-guided garden hike with several more overlooks—it's worth it. Pick up a map at the visitor center, which also sells snacks and drinks, and enjoy your repast at the river walk's observation area, under guava trees (feel free to sample their fruit when ripe), or on the visitor center's back lanai, which overlooks the river and the last line on the zip course (see "Ziplining," on p. 252). *Note:* Book online for best rates. Also, the swim in a waterfall pool allows a peek at one of the only petroglyphs on the island's east side. 31-313 Old Māmalahoa Hwy., Hakalau. https://umaumaexperience.com. © **808/ 930-9477.** $12 adults, free for children 11 and under; includes waterfall viewing, garden, and river walk. Mon–Sat 8am–5pm. ATV tours from $217 for driver only to $552 for driver and up to 3 passengers; kayak/swim/picnic $85 adults, $75 ages 4–10; zipline tour $229 adults, $219 ages 4–10 (with kayak/swim/picnic, $314 adults, $294 ages 4–10); horseback tour with swim $145 ages 8 and older; waterfall rappel tour, $399 ages 10 and older.

Waipi'o Valley Lookout ★★★ NATURAL ATTRACTION/HISTORIC SITE   The breathtakingly beautiful valley below this lookout has long been a source of fascination, inspiring song and story. From the black-sand bay at its mouth, Waipiʻo ("curving water") sweeps 6 miles between sheer, cathedral-like walls some 2,000 feet high. The tallest waterfall in Hawaiʻi, Hiʻilawe, tumbles 1,300 feet from its rear cliffs. Called "the valley of kings" for the royal burial caves dotting forbiddingly steep walls, this was Kamehameha's boyhood residence; up to 10,000 Hawaiians are thought to have lived here before Westerners arrived. Chinese immigrants later joined them, and a modest town arose, but it was destroyed in 1946 by the same tsunami that devastated Hilo and Laupāhoehoe, though luckily without fatalities. The town was never rebuilt; only about 50 people live here today, most with no electricity or phones, although others come down on weekends to tend taro patches, camp, and fish.

In recent years, though, their quiet lifestyle has been overrun—sometimes literally—by hordes of visitors driving down into the privately owned valley and across wetland farms, destroying crops, polluting streams and de-fouling the black-sand beach, which has no bathroom facilities but is close to unmarked burial sites. Concerns about overtourism as much as dangerous driving conditions—the steep road has a grade of nearly 40% in places and is narrow and potholed—led Hawaiʻi County in 2022 to limit access only to valley residents. The move has upset many on the island who were used to surfing and fishing there, too. So now Hawaiʻi Island residents with ID and a 4WD vehicle can also drive down, but not visitors. *Note:* There's generally someone on hand to check that's what you're driving; even so, rental-car agencies ban their vehicles from it, to avoid pricey tow jobs. Pedestrians are also prohibited; hiking down the 900-foot-road is hard on the knees going down and the lungs coming up and requires dodging cars in both directions. Residents may also be confrontational of those who flout the rules.

However, you *can* still book a ride on the **Waipiʻo Valley Shuttle ★★** (www.waipiovalleyshuttle.com; ✆ **808/775-7121**) for a 90- to 120-minute guided tour that begins with an exciting (and bumpy) drive down in an open-door van. Once on the valley floor, you'll be rewarded with breathtaking views of Hiʻilawe, plus a narrated tour of the taro patches (*loʻi*) and ruins from the 1946 tsunami. The tour is Monday through Saturday at 9am, 11am, 1pm, and 3pm; tickets are $72 for adults ($67 if booked online) and $37 for kids 10 and under (minimum two adult fares); reservations recommended. Check in 20 minutes in advance at **Waipiʻo Valley Artworks,** 48-5416 Kukuihaele Rd., Honokaʻa (www.waipiovalleyartworks.com; ✆ **808/775-0958**), about a mile from the lookout.

Waipiʻo Valley Lookout, 48-5446 Waipiʻo Valley Rd. (end of Hwy. 240), Honokaʻa. Free admission for residents.

HILO

Pick up the map to a self-guided walking tour of Hilo, which focuses on 21 historic sites dating from the 1870s to the present, at the information kiosk of the **Downtown Hilo Improvement Association** (www.downtownhilo.org; ✆ **808/935-8850**) in the Moʻoheau Park Bus Terminal, 329

Kamehameha Ave.—the first stop on the tour. You can also find the map online at www.downtownhilo.org/home/walking-tour.

Hilo Bay ★★★ NATURAL ATTRACTION   Old banyan trees shade **Banyan Drive** ★, the lane that curves along the waterfront from Kamehameha Avenue (Hwy. 19) to the Hilo Bay hotels. Most of the trees were planted in the mid-1930s by visitors like Cecil B. DeMille (here in 1933 filming *Four Frightened People*), Babe Ruth (his tree is in front of the Hilo Hawaiian Hotel), King George V, Amelia Earhart, and celebs whose fleeting fame didn't last as long as the trees themselves. The now-overgrown trees look unkempt by day and spooky by night.

It's worth a stop along Banyan Drive—especially if the coast is clear and the summit of Mauna Kea is free of clouds—to make the short walk across the concrete-arch bridge to **Moku Ola (Coconut Island)** ★, for a panoramic sense of Hilo Bay and its surroundings.

Continuing on Banyan Drive, just south of Coconut Island, are **Liliʻuokalani Gardens** ★★, the largest formal Japanese garden this side of Tokyo. The 30-acre park was named for the last monarch of Hawaiʻi, Queen Liliʻuokalani and dedicated in 1917 to the islands' first Japanese immigrants. Stone lanterns, koi ponds, pagodas, rock gardens, bonsai, and a moon-gate bridge make the gardens particularly picturesque. Admission is free; it's open 24 hours.

Kaūmana Caves Park ★★ NATURAL ATTRACTION   Pick up an inexpensive flashlight or headlight ($5–$15) at Walmart in Hilo or Kona before visiting this wilder, longer sibling to the more famous Nāhuku (Thurston) lava tube (p. 211) in Hawaiʻi Volcanoes National Park. As the sign warns, there are "no lights, no walkway" in this eerily fascinating set of caves formed by an 1881 lava flow that threatened downtown Hilo. Princess Ruth Keʻelikōlani is credited with saving the town by praying to Pele to halt the lava. You can thank the county for maintaining the steep concrete stairs leading into the lava tube's fern-lined "skylight," where the larger right entrance offers a short loop trail and the left entrance leads to a more challenging (that is, watch your head) out-and-back path. Your flashlight will help you spot the lava that cooled fast enough to keep its red color, and help you avoid stumbling over protruding roots. Wear long sleeves,

Petroglyph on Hawaiʻi Island.

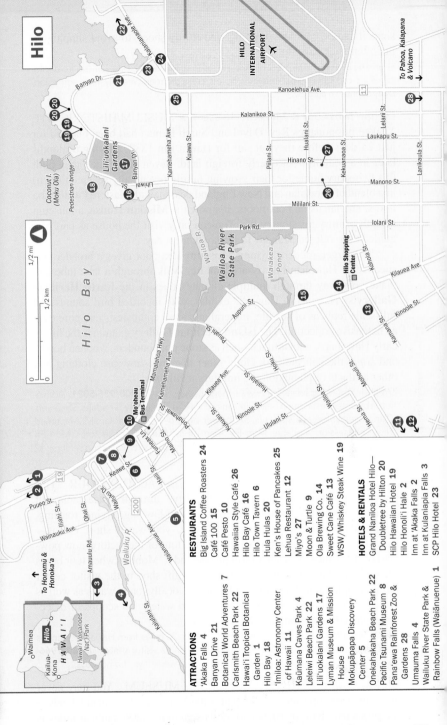

Hilo

Hilo Bay

HILO INTERNATIONAL AIRPORT

To Pahoa, Kalapana & Volcano →

Lili'uokalani Gardens

Coconut I. (Moku Ola)
Pedestrian bridge

Wailoa River State Park

Waiakea Pond

Hilo Shopping Center

Mo'oheau Bus Terminal

To Honomū & Honoka'a ←

Hawai'i Volcanoes Nat'l Park

ATTRACTIONS

'Akaka Falls **4**
Banyan Drive **21**
Botanical World Adventures **7**
Carlsmith Beach Park **22**
Hawai'i Tropical Botanical Garden **1**
Hilo Bay **18**
'Imiloa: Astronomy Center of Hawaii **11**
Kaūmana Caves Park **4**
Leleiwi Beach Park **22**
Lili'uokalani Gardens **17**
Lyman Museum & Mission House **5**
Mokupāpapa Discovery Center **5**
Onekahakaha Beach Park **22**
Pacific Tsunami Museum **8**
Pana'ewa Rainforest Zoo & Gardens **28**
Umauma Falls **4**
Wailuku River State Park & Rainbow Falls (Waiānuenue) **1**

RESTAURANTS

Big Island Coffee Roasters **24**
Café 100 **15**
Café Pesto **10**
Hawaiian Style Café **26**
Hilo Bay Café **16**
Hilo Town Tavern **6**
Hula Hulas **20**
Ken's House of Pancakes **25**
Lehua Restaurant **12**
Miyo's **27**
Moon & Turtle **9**
Ola Brewing Co. **14**
Sweet Cane Café **13**
WSW/Whiskey Steak Wine **19**

HOTELS & RENTALS

Grand Naniloa Hotel Hilo—Doubletree by Hilton **20**
Hilo Hawaiian Hotel **19**
Hilo Honoli'i Hale **2**
Inn at 'Akaka Falls **2**
Inn at Kulaniapia Falls **3**
SCP Hilo Hotel **23**

since it can be cool and dripping, and sturdy shoes, to avoid slipping on the often-slick cave floor.

Kaūmana Dr. (Hwy. 200), west of 'Ākala Road (4-mile marker), Hilo. Driving from Hilo, caves are on right and parking lot is on left; cross the road carefully. Free admission. Daily sunrise to sunset.

Lyman Museum & Mission House ★★ MUSEUM/HISTORIC SITE Yankee missionaries Rev. David and Sarah Lyman had been married for just 24 days before they set sail for Hawai'i in 1832, arriving 6 months later in a beautiful but utterly foreign land. Seven years later, they built this two-story home for their growing family (eventually seven children) in a blend of Hawaiian and New England design, with plastered walls, koa floors, and lanais on both floors. It's now the **Mission House,** a museum of 19th-century missionary life. You can only visit the house as part of a guided tour, offered Monday to Friday twice a day.

The larger, modern **Lyman Museum** next door gives a broader perspective of Hawaiian history and culture. Walk through a lava tube and make your way through multiple climate zones in the **Earth Heritage Gallery**'s "Habitats of Hawai'i" exhibit, with recorded bird sounds and full-scale replicas of sea life; mineral and shell enthusiasts can pore over an extensive collection. The **Island Heritage Gallery** examines the life of early Hawaiians, with artifacts such as stone poi pounders, wooden bowls, and *kapa,* the delicate bark cloth; other displays showcase clothing and other artifacts of plantation-era immigrant cultures.

276 Haili St. (at Kapiolani St.). www.lymanmuseum.org. © **808/935-5021.** Admission is by timed reservation only, with limited walk-in availability. $7 adults, $5 seniors 60 and over, $5 college students, $2 children ages 6–17; $21 per family. 2-hr. timed admission session available Mon–Fri 10am–3pm. Guided house tours Mon–Fri 10:05am, 12:25pm, and 2:35pm, by reservation only; $3 adults (including seniors), $2 college students, $1 children ages 6–17.

Mauna Loa Macadamia Nut Factory ★ FACTORY TOUR This popular attraction lies after a 3-mile drive through macadamia nut orchards. Visit on a weekday, when the actual husking, drying, roasting, and candy-making takes place; otherwise, you watch short videos—sometimes on the fritz—on the self-guided tour of the factory, now powered by a 1.2-megawatt solar farm just behind it. Mobbed when tour buses are in the parking lot, the newly renovated gift shop in the visitor center offers samples and showcases high-quality, locally made wares as well as various macadamia nut confections, bottled water, and scoops of delectable, dairy-free macadamia nut ice cream.

16-701 Macadamia Rd., Kea'au (5 miles from Hilo, 20 miles from Hawai'i Volcanoes National Park). www.maunaloa.com/pages/maunaloa-visitor-center. © **808/966-8614.** Visitor center open Mon–Sat (factory closed weekdays and holidays).

Mokupāpapa Discovery Center ★★ MUSEUM You may never get to the vast coral-reef system that is the Northwest Hawaiian Islands—the protected chain of islets and atolls spanning 1,200 nautical miles is

IMILOA: EXPLORING THE unknown

The star attraction, literally and figuratively, of Hilo is **'Imiloa: Astronomy Center of Hawai'i ★★★**. The 300 exhibits in the 12,000-square-foot gallery make the connection between the Hawaiian culture and its explorers, who "discovered" the Hawaiian Islands, and the astronomers who explore the heavens from the observatories atop Mauna Kea. *'Imiloa* means "explorer" or "seeker of profound truth," the perfect name for this architecturally stunning center overlooking Hilo Bay on the University of Hawai'i at Hilo Science and Technology Park campus, 600 'Imiloa Pl. (www.imiloahawaii.org; ℂ **808/969-9700**). Plan to spend at least a couple of hours here to browse the excellent, family-friendly interactive exhibits on astronomy and Hawaiian culture, and to take in a planetarium show with its state-of-the-art digital projection system. You'll also want to stroll through the native plant garden and make a lunch reservation (11am–3pm) or dinner (5–9pm) in the newly refined and renamed **Lehua Restaurant (ℂ 808/969-9753)**. The center is open Tuesday through Sunday from 9am to 4:30pm; admission is $19 for adults, $17 for seniors, $12 for children 5 to 12, and free for kids 4 and under. Prices include one planetarium show.

Imiloa Astronomy Center of Hawaii
University of Hawai'i at Hilo

remote (stretching from Nihoa, 155 miles northwest of Kaua'i, to Kure Atoll, 56 miles west of Midway), and visitation is severely limited. But if you're in downtown Hilo, you can explore the wonders of the region that President George W. Bush protected as **Papahānaumokuākea Marine National Monument** in 2008 (and President Barack Obama expanded in 2016). Inside a handsomely renovated, century-old building, the Mokupāpapa Discovery Center reveals the beauties and mysteries of the World Heritage Site's ecosystem and its relationship with Hawaiian culture. Exhibits include a 3,500-gallon saltwater aquarium with brilliant coral and reef fish; the sounds of Hawaiian chants and seabirds; interactive displays on each of the islets; a life-size Hawaiian monk seal exhibit, and life-size models of giant fish, sharks, and the manta ray. Both the content and the cost of admission—free—are great for families.

76 Kamehameha Ave. (at the corner of Waiānuenue Ave.). www.papahanau mokuakea.gov/education/center.html. ☎ **808/498-4709.** Free admission. Tues– Sat 9am–4pm.

Pacific Tsunami Museum ★ MUSEUM This compact museum features poignant exhibits on Japan's 2011 tsunami, which also caused significant property damage on Hawai'i Island) and the 2004 Indian Ocean catastrophe, with displays explaining the science of the deadly phenomenon. Stories and artifacts related to Hilo's two most recent calamitous tsunamis are impressive, including a parking meter nearly

Peaceful sea turtle and seal at Papahānaumokuākea Marine National Monument, a series of remote islands.

bent in two by the force of the 1960 killer waves, and accounts from survivors of the 1946 tsunami that washed away the school at Laupāhoehoe. Many of the volunteers have hair-raising stories of their own to share—but you'll feel better after reading about the warning systems now in place.

130 Kamehameha Ave. (at the corner of Kalākaua Ave.). www.tsunami.org. ☎ **808/935-0926.** $15 adults, $10 seniors, $5 children 6–17, free for children 5 and under. Daily 10am-4pm.

Pana'ewa Rainforest Zoo & Gardens ★ ZOO/GARDEN This 12-acre zoo, in the heart of the Pana'ewa Forest Reserve south of Hilo, is the only outdoor rainforest zoo in the U.S. Some 80 species of animals from rainforests around the globe call Pana'ewa home, including tigers Tzatziki and Sriracha, as do a couple of "Kona nightingales"—donkeys that escaped decades ago from coffee farms. (Though highway signs still warn of them, virtually all were relocated to California in 2011 during a prolonged drought.) The Pana'ewa residents enjoy fairly natural, sometimes overgrown settings. Look for cute pygmy goats, capuchin monkeys, sloths, and giant anteaters, among other critters. A new aviary is dedicated to the rare Hawaiian crow, once thought extinct. This free attraction includes a large, covered playground popular with local families and a gift shop that includes snacks and beverages.

800 Stainback Hwy., Kea'au (off Hwy. 11, 5 miles south of its intersection with Hwy. 19 in downtown Hilo). www.hilozoo.org. ☎ **808/959-9233.** Free admission. Daily 10am–4pm; petting zoo Sat 1:30–2:30pm.

Wailuku River State Park ★ WATERFALLS Go in the morning, around 9 or 10am, just as the sun comes over the mango trees, to see **Rainbow Falls** ★★, or Waiānuenue, at its best. Part of the 16-acre

Wailuku River State Park, the 80-foot falls (which can be slender in times of drought) spill into a big round natural pool surrounded by wild ginger. If you're lucky, you'll catch a rainbow created in the falls' mist. According to legend, Hina, the mother of demigod Maui, once lived in the cave behind the falls. Swimming in the pool is not allowed, but you can follow a trail left through the trees to the top of the falls (watch your step). Swimming in **Boiling Pots** ★★ (*Pe'epe'e* in Hawaiian), a series of cascading pools 1½ miles west, is extremely risky due to flash floods, but the view from an overlook near the parking lot is impressive.

Rainbow Falls area: Rainbow Dr., just past the intersection of Waiānuenue Ave. (Hwy. 200) and Pu'uhina St. Boiling Pots area: end of Pe'epe'e Falls Dr., off Waiānuenue Ave. https://dlnr.hawaii.gov/dsp/parks/hawaii. Free admission. Daily dawn to dusk.

PUNA

Most visitors understandably want to head straight to **Hawai'i Volcanoes National Park** ★★★ (p. 209) when exploring this region, where Pele has consumed the land while creating even more. But the celebrated national park is far from the only place where you can experience Puna's geothermal wonders or see the destruction Kīlauea and Mauna Loa have wrought—provided it's safe and legal to do so.

Start in Pāhoa with a 5-minute detour from the plantation town's center to its transfer station (i.e., landfill and recycling center) on Cemetery Road. There you'll see the ominous edge of the thick but slow-moving lava flow in 2014–2015 that halted only after many in its predicted path had relocated. In 2018, residents of isolated Pāhoa suburbs Leilani Estates and Lanipuna Gardens were not so lucky; many lost their homes and farms to rivers of lava that eventually spewed from fissures that slowly started to appear in the Lower East Rift Zone—a known hazard at the time the county approved those subdivisions. (Please respect their privacy as some try to rebuild.) Also in Pāhoa, watch exclusive, enthralling video of the 2018 eruption, and see exhibit props from the former Jaggar Museum at **Hawai'i Volcanoes National Park** (p. 209), at the **Lava Zone Museum** ★, 15-2959 Pāhoa Village Rd. (https://pahoalavazonemuseum.com; ✆ **808/937-4146**), next to **Kaleo's** (p. 291). The free museum is generally open daily 11am to 4:30pm, but since it's volunteer-run, call to confirm.

Many in the area still have memories of the 1990 eruption that covered the town of **Kalapana,** 9 miles from Pāhoa along Highway 130. Steam came out of cracks in the road during the 2018 eruption, prompting the county to put steel plates over them, but luckily the highway survived.

Just before Highway 130 meets Highway 137 in Kalapana, you'll see **Star of the Sea Painted Church** ★ on your left. Built in 1930, the quaint, pale-green wooden church features an elaborately painted interior similar to St. Benedict's in Captain Cook (p. 188). It was moved from Kalapana to a site near here in advance of the 1990 lava flow, and then again in 1996. It's generally open daily at 9am, with Mass held the first Friday of the month at 4pm.

The 1990 lava flow also entombed the town of Kaimū and its beautiful beach under acres of rock, while leaving behind a new **black-sand beach.** Safe only when admired from the bluffs, New Kaimū (or Kalapana) Beach lies at the end of a .25-mile red-cinder trail from the parking area in Kalapana. Amid fascinating fissures and dramatically craggy rocks, 'ōh'ia lehua and recently planted coconut palms are growing rapidly. Such trees are used to rugged conditions, as are the people of Puna, who gather in great numbers at the open-air **Uncle Robert's Awa Club** (p. 299) for its two weekly evening events: the vibrant Wednesday-night food and crafts market and Hawaiian music on Fridays. The rest of the week, the club sells snacks and drinks during the day "by donation" for permit purposes (be aware the staff will let you know *exactly* how much to donate).

Adventurers (or exhibitionists) may want to make the tricky hike down to unmarked **Kehena Black Sand Beach ★**, off Highway 137 about 3½ miles east of Kalapana. Here the law against public nudity is widely ignored, although the view of the ocean is usually more entrancing. (Clothed or not, avoid going into the water—currents are dangerous.) Thanks to the 2018 lava flow, Highway 137, also known as the "Red Road" (for the rosy-hued cinders that once paved it), currently dead-ends about 9 miles northeast of Kalapana, at the spooky, ironwood-shaded cliffs in **MacKenzie State Recreation Area ★**, which has picnic and restroom facilities. The surf crashes fiercely against the rocks here; stay away from the edge and watch your footing.

A new, well-paved access road crosses over the buried highway from MacKenzie to **Isaac Hale Beach Park ★★** in Pohoiki, which emerged from the 2018 eruption minus its harbor access, popular surf breaks, children's playground, and water fountains, among other facilities. On the plus side: The park has four new thermal ponds and a lagoon created by a black-sand beach that blocked the harbor when sizzling lava fragmented in the cool ocean water. The state plans to restore the harbor eventually, so visit sooner rather than later. *Note:* Bring your own drinking water and stay out of the warm ponds if you have any cuts or open wounds. There's a lifeguard station but leave the ocean to the area's intrepid surfers; lifeguards report frequent rescues here.

The same immense lava flow, which covered almost 14 square miles of Lower Puna and add 875 acres of new land, unfortunately destroyed the main road and almost every attraction east of Pohoiki, filling Kapoho Bay with lava and evaporating Green Lake, a former natural reservoir inside Kapoho Crater. South of Pāhoa, at the end of the 4WD-only road that begins where newly restored Highway 132 ends, one surviving landmark stands as a literal beacon of hope and resilience. Marking the island's easternmost point, **Cape Kumukahi Lighthouse ★** miraculously survived the 1960 lava flow that destroyed the original village of Kapoho and then remained untouched again in 2018. Who cares if its modern steel frame isn't all that quaint? The fact that it's standing at all is impressive—in

Vog & Other Volcanic Vocabulary

Hawaiian volcanoes have their own unique vocabulary. The lava that resembles ropy swirls of brownie batter is called **pāhoehoe** (pah-hoy-hoy); it results from a fast-moving flow that ripples as it moves. The chunky, craggy lava with spiky formations is **'a'ā** (ah-ah); it's caused by lava that moves slowly, breaking apart as it cools, and then overruns itself. **Vog** is smog made of volcanic gases and smoke, which can sting your eyes and over long exposure can cause respiratory issues. Present whenever there's an active eruption, vog drifts toward Kona (and even as far as Maui or beyond) during prevailing trade winds. During eruptions, the state **Department of Health** (https://air.doh.hawaii.gov/home/text/118) typically lists current air-quality advisories based on sulfur dioxide levels.

1960, the molten lava parted in two and flowed around it—while its bright-white trusses provide a striking contrast to the black lava.

Lava Tree State Monument ★★ (see below), 2¾ miles southeast of Pāhoa off Highway 132, is an equally fitting if eerie reminder of nature's power in Puna. In 1790, a fast-moving lava flow raced through a grove of 'ōhi'a lehua trees here, cooling quickly and so creating rock molds of their trunks. Today the ghostly sentinels punctuate a well-shaded, paved .7-mile loop trail through the rich foliage of the 17-acre park. Facilities include restrooms and a few spots for picnicking (or ducking out of the rain during one of the area's frequent showers). Some areas with deep fissures are fenced off but do keep to the trail regardless for safe footing. It's open daily during daylight hours; see the state parks site, https://dlnr.hawaii.gov/dsp/parks/hawaii, for details.

HAWAI'I VOLCANOES NATIONAL PARK ★★★

Historically, the islands' singular attraction for visitors wasn't the beach, but rather the volcano. From the world over, curious spectators gathered on the rim of Kīlauea's Halema'uma'u crater to see one of the greatest wonders of the globe. More than a century after it was named a national park in 1916, **Hawai'i Volcanoes National Park** (www.nps.gov/havo; ⓒ **808/985-6000**) remains the state's premier natural attraction, home to two active volcanoes and one of only two World Heritage Sites in the islands.

In May 2018, earthquakes rattled Halema'uma'u and its lava lake started to drain. At the same time lava started coursing through fissures in Puna, the crater began expelling ash and rocks in a manner not seen since 1924, when boulders landed a half-mile away due to steam explosions caused by magma sinking into the water table. Forced to close for safety reasons, the park reopened in September 2018, but not before the seismic upheaval had caused the crater to quadruple in volume. While some repairs to roads and facilities were continuing at press time, it has been easy to walk to overlooks of Halema'uma'u to see the eruptions since then.

A ranger guides a tour of Hawai'i Volcanoes National Park.

Sadly, after driving about 100 miles from Kailua-Kona or 29 miles from Hilo, many visitors pause only briefly by the highlights along **Crater Rim Drive ★★★** before heading back to their hotels. To allow the majesty and *mana* (spiritual energy) of this special place to sink in, you should really take at least 2 or 3 days—and certainly 1 night—to explore the park, including its miles of trails.

Fortunately, the admission fee ($30 per vehicle, $15 per bicyclist or hiker) is good for 7 days. Be prepared for rain and bring a jacket, especially in winter, when it can be downright chilly at night, in the 40s or 50s (single digits to mid-teens Celsius). *Note:* For details on hiking and camping in the park, see "Hiking" (p. 246) and "Camping" (p. 274).

Crater Rim Drive Tour

Stop by the **Kīlauea Visitor Center** (daily 9am–5pm) to get the latest updates on any lava flows and to join the day's free ranger-led tours. Just beyond the center lies vast **Kīlauea Caldera ★★★**, a circular depression now nearly 2 miles by 3 miles and 1,600 feet deep. It's easy to imagine Mark Twain marveling over the sights here in 1866, when a wide, molten lava lake bubbled in the caldera's **Halema'uma'u Crater ★★★**, the legendary home of volcano goddess Pele.

Though different today, the caldera's panorama is still compelling, especially when viewed while enjoying drinks or dinner in **Volcano House ★★** (p. 273), the only public lodge and restaurant in the park. The 2018 eruption that drained the lava lake at Halema'uma'u and snuffed out its decade-old plume of ash also caused wall collapses that dramatically widened and deepened the crater. A 1.3-mile hike from Volcano House along **Halema'uma'u Trail** that leads to **Uēaloha (Byron Ledge)** offers peek-a-boo views of Kīlauea caldera.

The unrelenting seismic activity in 2018 also cracked pavement and damaged the Jaggar Museum along Crater Rim Drive, half of which has been closed since 2008 due to potentially toxic fumes. The museum will never reopen on its former clifftop perch at Uēkahuna, but many of its exhibit props are on display at the **Pahoa Lava Zone Museum ★** (p. 207). You can also hike the half-mile portion of **Crater Rim Trail ★★** from the Kīlauea Overlook to the Uēkahuna bluff, another potential lava lake viewpoint.

Less than a mile from the visitor center, you'll want to check out the several **steam vents ★★★** that line the rim of the caldera, puffing out moist warm air. Across the road, a boardwalk leads through the stinky, smoking **Ha'akulamanu (Sulphur Banks) ★★★**, home to 'ōh'ia lehua trees and unfazed native birds. (As with all trails here, stay on the path to avoid possible serious injury, or worse.)

Heading southeast from the visitor center, Crater Rim Drive passes by the smaller but still impressive **Kīlauea Iki Crater ★★**, which in 1959 was a roiling lava lake flinging lava 1,900 feet into the air. From here, it's a half-mile walk or drive to **Nāhuku (Thurston Lava Tube) ★★★**, a 500-year-old lava cave in a pit of giant tree ferns and partly illuminated

Please Brake for Nēnē

Nēnē, the endangered native Hawaiian goose and state bird, are making a comeback in Hawai'i Volcanoes National Park where they feast on the cranberry-like 'ōhelo berries that grow at upper elevations. Unfortunately, the park's uplands are often misty, and the birds' feathers blend easily with the pavement, making it hard for inattentive drivers to see them. Drive carefully, and to discourage nēnē from approaching cars, don't feed them. (Leave 'ōhelo berries to the birds, too.) **Note:** Increasingly, you may also spot nēnē around lower-altitude golf courses, resort landscaping, and beach parks.

(8am–8pm) for easier traversing of its damp, uneven floor. Take a flashlight and wear sturdy shoes so you can explore the unlit area for another half-mile or so. The lava tube is less crowded before 9am and after 4pm.

Continuing on Crater Rim Drive leads to the **Pu'u Pua'i Overlook ★** of Kīlauea Iki, where you find the upper trailhead of the aptly named half-mile **Devastation Trail ★★**, an easy walk through a cinder field. Be aware both the overlook and upper trailhead may close to protect breeding nēnē. However, you can always pick up the lower trailhead where Crater Rim Drive meets **Chain of Craters Road ★★★**.

Only pedestrians and cyclists can continue on Crater Rim Drive for the next ¾ mile of road, closed to vehicular traffic since the 2008 eruption and now sporting a few deep cracks from 2018. After passing through forest, this pavement leads to **Keanakāko'i Crater ★★**, scene of several eruptions in the 19th and 20th centuries, and continues on to dazzling perspectives of expanded Kīlauea Caldera, with a closed part of Crater Rim Drive that fell 500 feet visible in the distance. In late 2021, it became one of the best spots to view the then-active lava lake at night. But even if it's not closest to any evening action, it's still worth a daytime hike. Turn your gaze north for an impressive view of Mauna Loa and Mauna Kea, the world's two highest mountains when measured from the sea floor.

Chain of Craters Road ★★★

It's natural to drive slowly down the 19-mile **Chain of Craters Road,** which descends 3,700 feet to the sea and ends in a thick black mass of rock from a 2003 lava flow. You feel like you're driving on the moon, if the

---

THE BRUTE FORCE OF THE volcano

Volcanologists refer to Hawaiian volcanic eruptions as "quiet" eruptions because gases escape slowly instead of building up and violently exploding all at once. Hawai'i Island's eruptions produce slow-moving, oozing lava that generally provide excellent, safe viewing when they're not in remote areas. Even so, **Kīlauea** has still caused its share of destruction. Between 1983 and 2018, lava covered more than 60 square miles of lowland and rainforest, ruining 1,000 homes and businesses, wiping out the pretty, black-sand beach of Kaimū, filling in beautiful Kapoho Bay and its adjacent thermal ponds and tidepools, and burying other landmarks. Kīlauea has also added some 1,375 acres of new land on its southeastern shore. (Such land occasionally collapses under its own weight into the ocean—26 recently formed oceanfront acres slowly gave way on New Year's Eve 2016.) Now drained of lava, the most prominent vent of the 2018 eruption was Pu'u 'Ō'ō, a 760-foot-high cinder-and-spatter cone 10 miles east of Kīlauea's summit, which sent forth fiery torrents from several fissures in its flank. The most dramatic was Fissure 8, which started to erupt in the middle of the remote Leilani Estates community and eventually grew to a 60-foot cinder cone. In late 2022, **Mauna Loa** erupted for several weeks for the first time since 1984, sending lava in a fiery ribbon from the summit crater through an uninhabited area, stopping almost 2 miles short of Saddle Road. Scientists are also keeping an eye on **Hualālai,** which hovers above Kailua-Kona and last erupted in 1801.

lunar horizon were a brilliant blue sea. Pack food and water for the journey, since there are officially no concessions after you pass the Volcano House; the nearest fuel lies outside the park, in Volcano Village, and the limited snack stand at the end may not be open when you arrive.

Two miles down, before the road really starts twisting, the one-lane, 9-mile **Hilina Pali Road** ★★ veers off to the west, crossing windy scrublands and old lava flows. After 5 miles, you reach Kulanokuaiki Campground, where you currently have to leave your car and start hiking or biking. The payoff is at the end, where you stand nearly 2,300 feet above the coast along the rugged 12-mile *pali* (cliff). Some of the most challenging trails in the park, across the Ka'ū Desert and down to the coast, start here.

Back on Chain of Craters Road, 10 miles below the Crater Rim Drive junction, the picnic shelter at **Kealakomo** ★ provides a sweeping coastal vista. At mile marker 16.5, you'll see the parking lot for **Pu'u Loa** ★★★ , an enormous field of some 23,000 petroglyphs—the largest in the islands. A gently rolling lava trail leads to a boardwalk where you can view the stone carvings, 85% of which are *puka,* or holes; Hawaiians often placed their infants' umbilical cords in them. At the end of the paved Chain of Craters Road, a lookout allows a glimpse of 90-foot **Hōlei Sea Arch** ★★. Stop by the ranger station before treading across "some of the youngest land on Earth," as the park calls it, or heading out on foot or mountain bike across the gravel emergency road, which follows the coast for several miles before being blocked by lava flow. Take lots of water with you, and bear in mind it's a slow drive back up in the dark.

KA'Ū

At the end of 11 miles of bad road that peters out at Kaulana Bay, in the lee of a jagged, black-lava point, is Ka Lae ("The Point")—the tail end of the United States, often called South Point. From the tip, the nearest continental landfall is Antarctica, 7,500 miles away. It's a rugged 2-mile hike down a cliff from Ka Lae to the anomaly known as **Papakōlea (Green Sand) Beach** ★★ (p. 227). In May, the 10-day **Ka'ū Coffee Festival** (www.kau coffeefestival.com) in Pāhala includes hikes, music, hula, and farm tours.

Kahuku Unit, Hawai'i Volcanoes National Park ★ NATURAL ATTRACTION   Few visitors are familiar with this 116,000-acre portion of the national park, some 24 miles from the Kīlauea Visitor Center. You can hike through forest and fields that include a cinder cone, tree molds from an 1866 lava flow, a native forest refuge in a massive pit crater, and ranch-era relics. Check online for ranger orientation talks and free 90-minute guided hikes. *Note:* There are restrooms but no drinking water. The modest visitor center also has a small gift shop and exhibitions featuring local artists and wares.

Mauka side of Hwy. 11, btw mile markers 70 and 71, Pāhala. www.nps.gov/havo/plan yourvisit/kahuku.htm. ✆ **808/985-6000.** Free admission. Thurs–Sun 8am–4pm.

The lunar landscape of the Chain of Craters Road.

Ka'ū Coffee Mill ★★ FACTORY TOUR   In the former sugarcane fields on the slopes of Mauna Loa, a number of small farmers grow coffee beans whose quality equals—some say surpasses—Kona's. More and more tasting competitions seem to agree; in any case, this farm and mill in tiny Pāhala provides an excellent excuse to break up the long drive to the main entrance of Hawai'i Volcanoes National Park, 23 miles northeast. Free 20-minute "seed to cup" tours are offered weekdays at 11am and 1pm; enjoy tastings of coffee and macadamia nuts throughout the day in the pleasant visitor center and gift shop, which also has smoothies and iced coffee drinks for sale.

96-2694 Wood Valley Rd., Pāhala. https://kaucoffeemill.com. 𝄐 **808/928-0550.** Free admission. Mon–Fri 9am–4:30pm. Tours at 11am and 1pm, weather permitting. From Kailua-Kona, take Hwy. 11 71 miles to a left on Kamani St., take 3rd right at Pīkake St., which becomes Wood Valley Rd., and follow uphill 2½ miles to farm on left.

Kula Kai Caverns ★★ NATURAL ATTRACTION   Ric Elhard and Rose Herrera have mapped out the labyrinth of lava tubes and caves, carved out over the past 1,000 years or so, that crisscross their property near Ka Lae. Their "expeditions" range from the Lighted Trail tour, an easy, hourlong walk suitable for families, to longer, more adventurous caving trips, where you crawl through tunnels and wind through mazelike passages (some only for ages kids 8 and up). Wear sturdy shoes.

92-8864 Lauhala Dr., Ocean View (46 miles south of Kailua-Kona). www.kulakai caverns.com. 𝄐 **808/929-9725.** Lighted Trail tour $28 adults, $18 children 6–12, free for children 5 and under; longer tours $95 adults ($65 children 8–12). By reservation only; gate security code provided at booking.

Organized Tours

Farms, gardens, and historic houses that may be open only to guided tours are listed under "Attractions & Points of Interest" on p. 181. For boat, kayak, bicycle, and similar tours, see listings under "Outdoor Activities."

HELICOPTER TOURS ★★

Don't believe the brochures with pictures of fountains of lava and "liquid hot magma," as Dr. Evil would say in the *Austin Powers* movies. There are no guarantees you'll see red-hot lava, and for safety reasons, you wouldn't fly all that close to it. Still, a helicopter ride offers a unique perspective on the island's thousands of acres of hardened black lava, Kīlauea's enormous caldera, and the remote, now eerily drained Puʻu ʻŌʻō vent. If you're pressed for time, a helicopter ride beats driving to the volcano and back from Kohala and Kona resorts.

Blue Hawaiian Helicopters ★★★ (www.bluehawaiian.com; ⓒ **800/ 745-2583** or 808/886-1768) is a local company with comfortable, top-of-the-line copters that are quieter than most (noise is an issue for residents and wildlife in some areas) and pilots who are all instrument-rated (meaning they can fly even if visibility is poor). Its pilots are also certified guides, knowledgeable about everything from volcanology to Hawaiʻi lore. Two of its tours depart from its Kohala Coast heliport, on the *mauka* side of Highway 19 and Waikoloa Road. The 2-hour **Big Island Spectacular ★★** stars the volcano, tropical valleys, Hāmākua Coast waterfalls, and the Kohala Mountains, and costs $699 per person; an optional 20-minute landing at 1,200-foot Punalulu waterfall at remote Laupāhoehoe Nui brings the total to $874. If time is money for you, and you've got all that money, it's an impressive trip. If you just want to admire waterfalls, green mountains, and the deep valleys, including Waipiʻo, of North Kohala and the Hāmākua Coast, the 50-minute **Kohala Coast Adventure ★**, at $399, is a less exorbitant but reliably picturesque outing. Both tours use the somewhat quieter Eco-Star helicopters with panoramic views from the large cockpit.

Blue Hawaiian also operates out of the Hilo heliport at 2450 Kekuanaoa St. (ⓒ **808/961-5600**), flying the 55-minute **Pele's Creation ★★** tour ($439), showcasing the Kīlauea Iki and Halemaʻumaʻu craters and, if weather permits, the remnants of the November 2022 eruption on Mauna Loa. The 50-minute **Circle of Fire** tour also focuses on Kīlauea and Hawaiʻi Volcanoes National Park ($399). *Note:* If you drive to Hilo, you really should continue on to the national park to see it closer up.

The similarly professional **Sunshine Helicopters ★★** (www. sunshinehelicopters.com; ⓒ **866/501-7738** or 808/270-3999) offers a **Volcano Deluxe Tour ★**, a 105-minute ride out of the Hāpuna heliport, which includes Kohala Mountains/Hāmākua waterfalls. It's also pricey: $639 for open seating, $714 for reserved seating next to the pilot on the six-passenger Whisper Star choppers. Less of a splurge—and less dependent on the ooh factor of oozing lava—is Sunshine's 40- to 45-minute **Kohala/Hāmākua Coast Tour ★★**, which hovers above waterfall-lined sea cliffs and the Pololū, Waimanu, and Waipiʻo valleys, for $324 ($399 reserved seating).

Paradise Helicopters ★★ (https://paradisecopters.com; ⓒ **866/876-7422**) may be the most eco-friendly operator, thanks to a carbon-offset

PLANTING A legacy tree

Some of the most inspiring and memorable experiences I've had in Hawai'i have involved planting native trees—a fascinating way to reduce your vacation's carbon footprint while also learning about Hawai'i's unique ecosystem and culture. Planting a tree protects reefs from runoff, provides native birds shelter and sustenance, and also permits you to visit otherwise inaccessible, magical areas.

Hawaiian Legacy Tours ★★★ (www.hawaiianlegacytours.com; (✆ 808/509-8733) offers the 1- to 2-hour Hiker's Tour, starting in the hamlet of 'Umikoa, on the misty upper eastern slopes of Mauna Kea. After snacking on some warm, fresh-baked scones, you'll walk or hike at a leisurely pace while learning about King Kamehameha's private grove and other lore. Then you'll plant a koa seedling, which you can dedicate to a loved one and receive a commemorative certificate with GPS coordinates to monitor its growth via Google Earth. It costs $175 for the tour and one koa seedling, and an additional $120 per seedling to plant more than one. Children ages 5 to 12 may accompany adults for $55 (but cost does not include a seedling).

Uluhao O Hualalai ★★★ (www.uluhao.com; ✆ 808/896-5034) offers a more homespun, but no less intriguing outing above Kailua-Kona. Led by Kimo

Duarte, whose family has helped reforest this *wahi pana* (sacred site) for generations, the 5-hour Hualalai Crater Experience ($200, maximum four participants) includes learning the legends and history of this active volcano, stopping at Duarte's cabin with sweeping views of the Kona coastline, hiking 2 miles near the 8,000-foot summit, and planting a baby koa tree. The drive up to the end of Kaloko Road, where you'll meet Duarte and transfer to a Polaris 4×4, is a scenic adventure all of its own.

Don't have time but still want to plant a tree? The **Waikōloa Dry Forest Initiative** will plant a wiliwili tree at its reserve (p. 194) on your behalf for $50; you receive GPS coordinates to track its process. **Hawaiian Legacy Reforestation Initiative** (https://legacyforest.org/plant-a-tree) will do the same with a koa ($120) planted on Hawai'i Island, or a milo or kou tree (also native plants) on O'ahu.

---

program that plants native trees on the island. It may also be the most exciting for adventure seekers, with six doors-off excursions among its many tours departing from either Hilo or Waimea and several that include landings and short hikes in remote areas with further awe-inspiring views. My favorites include the 1-hour **Kohala Coast & Waterfalls** tour ($420), which can be combined with a guided half-mile hike through a guava forest on the island's northeastern tip that leads to a breathtaking vista high above the rugged shoreline and Mokupuku islet ($499); it departs from the tiny Waimea airport and is free to upgrade to the doors-off option. The 40-minute **Lava & Rainforests Adventure** ($399) departs from the Hilo airport, soaring over the vast lava fields and black-sand beaches formed by the 2018 eruption, plus the lush Puna rainforest and Mauna Loa; the doors-off option costs $449. Paradise also flies other intriguing routes from Kona, Hilo, and Waimea.

Note: Book online for best rates; ask about AAA discounts if booking in person. On all rides, your weight may determine where you sit in the helicopter. Wear dark shades to prevent glare, and dress in light layers.

VAN & BUS TOURS

Many of the outdoor-oriented, but not especially physically taxing, excursions of **Hawai'i Forest & Trail ★★★** (www.hawaii-forest.com; ✆ **800/464-1993** or 808/331-8505) include a significant time in comfy vans heading to and from remote areas, with guides providing narration along the way. Thus, they're ideal for seeing a large chunk of the island without having to drive yourself. The island's premier outfitter, this eco-friendly company has exclusive access to many sites, including the falls on its **Kohala Waterfalls Adventure** ($229 adults, $204 children 12 and under). Most of its tours depart daily from several locations on the Kona side. **Bird-watchers** can take exceptional all-day tours, offered one to four times a month, that include 2 to 4 miles of hiking over 4 hours and access to the otherwise restricted Hakalau wildlife refuge ($260 ages 8 and older only; maximum nine guests) in luxurious 4WD Mercedes Sprinters. *Note:* Mauna Kea tours (see "Seeing Stars While Others Drive," p. 196) are restricted to ages 16 and up, due to high elevation.

Note: Tipping your tour guide/driver $20–$25 per person (roughly 10%) is customary and appreciated.

BEACHES

Too young geologically to have many great beaches, Hawai'i Island instead has more colorful ones: brand-new black-sand beaches, salt-and-pepper beaches, and even a green-sand beach. If you know where to look, you'll also find some gorgeous pockets of golden sand off the main roads, plus a few longer stretches, often hidden from view by high-end resorts. Thankfully, by law all beaches are public, so even the toniest hotels must provide access (including free—if limited—parking) to the sands they front. *Tip:* Never leave valuables in your trunk, particularly in remote areas, and respect the privacy of residents with homes on the beach.

For details on shoreline access around the island, go to **www.planning.hawaiicounty.gov/resources/shoreline-public-access**. For more info on state beaches, visit **https://dlnr.hawaii.gov/dsp/parks/hawaii**. Hawai'i County closes a few of its beach parks once a month for maintenance; look for the current schedule, water-quality advisories, and camping info at **https://hawaiicounty.gov/parks-and-recreation**. To avoid disappointment or danger, it's always wise to check on current wind and surf conditions first; **https://safebeachday.com/county/big-island** posts daily updates for 11 Hawai'i Island beaches with lifeguards.

Note: You'll find relevant sites on the "Hawai'i Island" map on p. 183. Unless otherwise stated, admission is free.

KAHALU'U BEACH PARK ★

The most popular beach on the Kona Coast has reef-protected lagoons and county park facilities that draw more than 400,000 people a year—one reason I can't recommend it as much these days. Coconut trees line a narrow strand that gently slopes to turquoise pools, home to schools of brilliantly colored tropical fish. This is an ideal spot for children and beginning snorkelers in summer. The water is so shallow you can just stand up if you feel uncomfortable—but please, not on the living coral, which can take years to recover. Too many people make this mistake every year, degrading reef life in the process. Coral bleaching events caused by high temperatures have also occurred in 2015 and 2019. In winter, the high surf rolls in, bringing a rip current along; look for any lifeguard warnings. Kahalu'u isn't the biggest beach on the island, but it's one of the best equipped, with parking ($12 for nonresidents, good for 4 hr.), a pavilion, restrooms, barbecue pits, and a food concession. Be sure to talk to volunteers from the **Kahalu'u Bay Education Center** (https://kohalacenter. org/kbec) if you have any questions about protecting the reef, including using only mineral-based sunscreen. If you have to park on Ali'i Drive, be sure to peek over the fence around tiny, blue-roofed **St. Peter's by the Sea,** a Catholic chapel next to an old lava rock *heiau* where surfers once prayed for waves. *Note:* The park is closed until 10am the first Thursday of each month for maintenance. It also closes once a year for 5 days during coral spawning, with dates predicted by lunar cycles and other natural elements. It's off Ali'i Drive at Makolea Street, 5 miles south of Kailua Pier. The parking lot is open daily 7am to 7pm.

An ancient fish pond at Kīholo Bay.

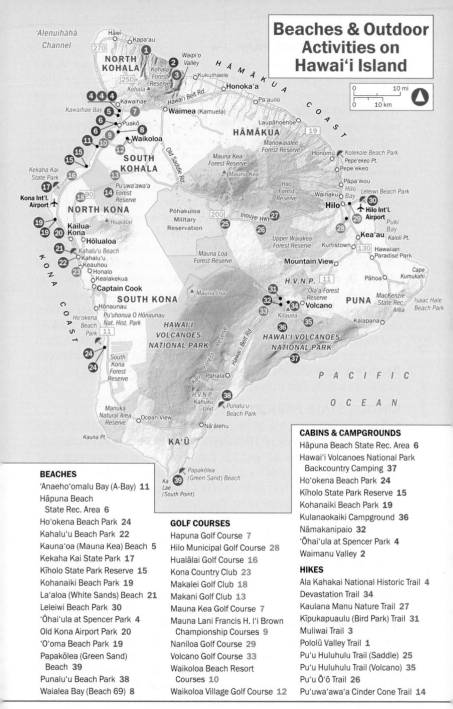

Beaches & Outdoor Activities on Hawai'i Island

'Alenuihāhā Channel

NORTH KOHALA
Kohala Forest Reserve
Kawaihae Bay
SOUTH KOHALA
Kekaha Kai State Park
Kona Int'l. Airport
NORTH KONA
Kailua-Kona
Hōlualoa
Kahalu'u Beach
Kahalu'u
Keauhou
Honalo
Kealakekua
Captain Cook
SOUTH KONA
Hōnaunau
Pu'uhonua O Hōnaunau Nat. Hist. Park
Ho'okena Beach Park
South Kona Forest Reserve
Manukā Natural Area Reserve
Ocean View
Nā'ālehu
KA'Ū
Kauna Pt.
Ka Lae (South Point)
Papakōlea (Green Sand) Beach

HĀMĀKUA COAST
Hāwī
Kapa'au
Waipi'o Valley
Kukuihaele
Honoka'a
Pa'auilo
Waimea (Kamuela)
Laupāhoehoe
HĀMĀKUA
Manowaialee Forest Reserve
Mauna Kea Forest Reserve
Mauna Kea
Honomū
Kolekole Beach Park
Pepe'ekeo Pt.
Pepe'ekeo
Pāpa'ikou
Hilo Forest Reserve
Wainaku
Leleiwi Beach Park
Hilo Bay
Hilo
Hilo Int'l. Airport
Puki Bay
Kea'au
Kaloli Pt.
Hawaiian Paradise Park
Kurtistown
Mountain View
Pōhakuloa Military Reservation
Upper Waiakea Forest Reserve
Mauna Loa Forest Reserve
H.V.N.P.
'Ōla'a Forest Reserve
Volcano
PUNA
Pāhoa
Cape Kumukahi
MacKenzie State Rec. Area
Isaac Hale Beach Park
Kalapana
Kīlauea
HAWAI'I VOLCANOES NATIONAL PARK
PACIFIC OCEAN
Pahala
H.V.N.P. Kahuku Unit
Punalu'u Beach Park

Old Saddle Rd.
Hawai'i Belt Rd.
Inouye Hwy.
Ka'ū Forest Reserve
Hawai'i Belt Rd.
Hualālai
Mauna Loa

0   10 mi
0   10 km

KEKAHA KAI STATE PARK ★★

Brilliant white sand offsets even more brilliant turquoise water at this beach park with several sandy bays and coves well hidden from the highway. About 4½ miles north of the airport off Highway 19 (across from West Hawai'i Veterans Cemetery) is the turnoff for Manini'ōwali Beach, better known as **Kua Bay ★★**. A (thankfully) paved road crosses acres of craggy lava, leading to the parking lot and a short, paved walkway to an even shorter, sandy scramble down a few rocks to the beach. It has restrooms and showers, but absolutely no shade or drinking water. Locals flock here to sunbathe, swim, bodyboard, and bodysurf, especially on weekends, so go during the week, and in mornings, when it's cooler; exercise caution since serious injuries have occurred in the strong shore break. County officials are lobbying the state to provide lifeguards here. If you have 4WD, you can take the marked turnoff 2½ miles north of the airport off Highway 19 and drive 1½ bumpy miles over a rough lava road to the parking area for sandy **Mahai'ula Beach ★**, reached by another short trail. Sloping more steeply than Kua Bay, this sandy beach has stronger currents too, although if you're fit you can still swim or snorkel in calm conditions. The only facilities here are picnic tables. Laze in the shade— you're likely to see a snoozing green sea turtle or two—or hike the rugged 1-mile path north through the lava to the sandy coves of **Makalawena Beach ★★** (no facilities); please don't try to drive to Makalawena. The park is open daily 8am to 6:45pm.

KĪHOLO STATE PARK RESERVE ★★★

To give yourself a preview of why you want to visit here, pull over at the marked Scenic Overlook on Highway 19 north of Kekaha Kai State Park, between mile markers 82 and 83. You'll see a shimmering pale blue lagoon, created by the remains of an ancient fishpond, and the bright cerulean **Kīholo Bay,** jewels in a crown of black lava. Now take the unmarked lava-gravel road (much smoother than Kekaha Kai's road to Mahai'ula Beach) about ¼ mile south of the overlook and drive carefully to the even bumpier day-lot parking area. An unpaved road to the left leads to the campground parking lot; both lots have portable toilets (but no potable water) and are a short walk to the shore. The "beach" here is black sand, lava pebbles, and coral, but it's fine for sunbathing or spotting dolphins and seasonal humpback whales. Keep your sturdy-soled shoes on, though, because you'll want to keep walking north to **Keanalele** (also called "Queen's Bath"), a collapsed lava tube found amid kiawe trees with steps leading into its freshwater pool, great for a cooling dip (no soap or sunscreen, please). Continue on past several mansions to the turquoise waters of the former fishpond, cut off by a lava flow, and the darker bay, clouded by freshwater springs. Green sea turtles love this area—as do scampering wild goats. The reserve land was a gift to The Nature Conservancy from the son of the late hair product tycoon Paul Mitchell, who had a home here. The reserve is co-managed by the conservancy, the state, and a community group, Hui Aloha Kīholo, which holds monthly workdays to help restore its fishpond and other treasures; see www.nature.org/en-us/get-involved/how-to-help/places-we-protect/kiholo-preserve for details. The park is open daily at 7am, with the access gate off the highway locked promptly at 6:45pm. See "Camping" (p. 274) for details on reserving campsites, open Friday to Sunday.

Note: You'll see cars pulled over at two sites north of the Scenic Overlook next to a lava field with rough foot trails leading closer to the Kiholo lagoon. Be aware the hike is hot and rugged, and car break-ins are not uncommon.

KOHANAIKI BEACH PARK (PINE TREES) ★★

Hidden behind the Kohanaiki golf community 2 miles north of the main entrance to Kaloko-Honōkohau National Historical Park off Highway 19, the 1½ miles of shoreline here include anchialine ponds, white-sand beaches, and a reef- and rock-lined bay that's home to a popular surf break called Pine Trees. Paddlers, snorkelers, and fishermen also flock to the rugged coastline, where a county park offers parking, restrooms, showers, a water fountain, campsites, and a pavilion; there's also a well-marked petroglyph. From the Kohanaiki entrance on Highway 19 (at Hulikoa Dr.), turn right at the first fork and follow nearly 1 mile to the first parking lot for beach access; facilities and more parking are farther south along the 1-lane paved road; you can also explore the shore to the north. It's open daily from 5:30am to 9pm; no camping Tuesday and Wednesday.

LA'ALOA BEACH PARK (WHITE SANDS/MAGIC SANDS) ★★

Don't blink as you cruise Ali'i Drive, or you'll miss La'aloa, often called White Sands, Magic Sands, or Disappearing Beach. That's because the sand at this small pocket beach, about 4½ miles south of Kailua-Kona's historic center, does occasionally vanish, especially at high tide or during storms. On calm summer days, you can swim here, next to bodyboarders and bodysurfers taking advantage of the gentle shore break; you can also snorkel in a little rocky cove just to the south. In winter, though, a dangerous rip develops and waves swell, attracting expert surfers and eager spectators; stay out of the water then, but enjoy the gawking. The palm-tree-lined county beach park includes restrooms, showers, a lifeguard station, and a small parking lot off Ali'i Drive.

OLD KONA AIRPORT PARK ★

Yes, this used to be the airport for the Kona side of the island—hence the copious parking on the former runway at the end of Kuakini Highway about a half-mile north of Palani Road in Kailua-Kona. Now it's a park jointly managed by the county and state, which in 1992 designated its waters a marine life conservation district. It's easy to get distracted by all the other free amenities: two Olympic-size pools in the **Kona Community Aquatic Center** (℗ **808/327-3500**), a gym, pickleball and tennis courts, and ball fields. Yet there's a mile of sandy beach here, fronting tide pools perfect for families with small children, and Pawai Bay, whose reefs draw turtles and rays, and thus snorkelers and divers. The beach area also has covered picnic tables and grills, restrooms, and showers.

'O'OMA BEACH PARK ★★

Like Kohanaiki Beach Park, which lies immediately to the south, this half-mile of shoreline includes anchialine ponds, tidepools, and white sand along a rocky bay. In calm conditions, you can enjoy good snorkeling, with the best entrance to the water from the middle of the beach. Shade trees also make it a nice place for just lounging on shore. From the Kohanaiki entrance on Highway 19 (at Hulikoa Dr.), turn right at the first fork and follow nearly 1 mile to the first parking lot for beach access. Park there and follow the dirt road north to the beach, which has portable toilets (head to Kohanaiki Beach for more facilities). It's open daily 6am to 9pm.

South Kona

HO'OKENA BEACH PARK ★★

At this secluded, taupe-colored sandy beach, visitors can rent kayaks and snorkel gear to explore Kauhako Bay's populous reefs (avoid during high surf) or camping gear to enjoy the view—sometimes including wild spinner dolphins—from the shore. You'll see traditional Hawaiian fishing canoes at work in search of *'opelu* (mackerel scad), too. Reservations for gear and campgrounds offered by the community-based **Friends of Hookena** (www.hookena.org) can be made online; the nonprofit's welcome concession stand at this remote spot even accepts credit cards. Facilities include showers, restrooms, water fountains, picnic tables, pavilions, and parking. From Kailua-Kona, take Highway 11 south 22 miles to the Ho'okena Beach Road exit (just past Ho'okena Elementary School), between mile markers 101 and 102. Follow it downhill 2 miles to the end and turn left on the one-lane road to the parking area. The parking lot is open daily 6:30am to 8:45pm.

The Kohala Coast

'ANAEHO'OMALU BAY ★★★

Hawai'i Island makes up for its dearth of beaches with a few spectacular ones, like 'Anaeho'omalu, or A-Bay, as many call it (but do try saying *Ah-nigh-hoe-oh-mah-loo,* which means "restricted mullet"). This popular gold-sand beach, fringed by a grove of palms and backed by royal fishponds still full of mullet, is one of the most beautiful in Hawai'i. It fronts Marriott's Waikoloa Beach complex, whose guests enjoy it alongside locals. The beach slopes gently from shallow to deep water; swimming, snorkeling, diving, kayaking, and windsurfing are all popular here. At the northern edge of the bay (the best spot for water clarity), snorkelers and divers can watch endangered green sea turtles line up and wait their turn to have small fish clean them. Equipment rental and snorkeling, scuba, and windsurfing instruction are available at the north end of the beach.

'Anaeho'omalu Bay.

Tip: Follow the shoreline trail at the southern end 1 mile to the usually deserted sands of **Kapalaoa Beach;** there are no facilities or shade, but it can be heavenly in calm weather. 'Anaeho'omalu's facilities include restrooms, showers, picnic tables, and plenty of parking; look for the shoreline access sign off Waikoloa Beach Road, about 1 mile west of the Queen Ka'ahumanu Highway (Hwy. 19). No lifeguards.

HĀPUNA BEACH STATE RECREATION AREA ★★★

Just below the bluffs of the Westin Hapuna Beach Resort lies this vast trove of gold sand—a half-mile long and up to 200 feet wide. In summer, when the beach is widest, the ocean calmest, and the crowds biggest, this is a terrific place for swimming, bodysurfing, and snorkeling. But beware of Hāpuna in winter or stormy weather when its thundering waves and strong rip currents should only be plied by local experts. Facilities include A-frame cabins (for camping by permit), picnic tables, restrooms, showers, a snack bar (temporarily closed at press time), and beach rentals kiosk (daily 10am–4pm), water fountains, lifeguard stations, and parking. You can also pick up the coastal **Ala Kahakai National Historic Trail** (p. 247) here to the Mauna Kea resort's beaches to the north and Mauna Lani resort's beaches to the south, respectively. From Queen Ka'ahumanu Highway (Hwy. 19) near mile marker 69, follow signs to Hāpuna Beach Road and the large parking lot ($10 per vehicle for nonresidents). Admission is $5 for nonresidents (as with parking, payable by credit card only). The beach park is open daily 7am to 7:30pm; gates close by 8pm.

KAUNA'OA BEACH (MAUNA KEA BEACH) ★★★

Nearly everyone refers to this beach of off-white sand at the foot of Mauna Kea Beach Hotel by its hotel nickname, but its real name is Hawaiian for

Playing in the soft sand of Kauna'oa Beach (Mauna Kea) Beach.

"native dodder," a lacy, yellow-orange vine that once thrived on the shore. A coconut grove sweeps around this golden arc, where the water is calm and protected by two black-lava points. The sandy bottom slopes gently into the bay, which often fills with tropical fish, sea turtles, and manta rays, especially at night, when lights shine down from a viewing promontory. Swimming is excellent year-round, except in rare winter storms. Facilities include restrooms, showers, lifeguards, and limited public access parking; staff at the resort's security gate on the *makai* side of Highway 19, 30 miles north of the airport, will let you know if space is available in the paved lot for Kauna'oa Beach. You can also request parking (off an unpaved road) for **Mau'umae Beach ★★**, an undeveloped, sandy beach on the north side of the golf course, or reach it via a 15-minute hike from the southern end of Spencer Park. *Tip:* If spaces are full, use valet parking and pay half the current parking rates with restaurant validation.

SPENCER PARK (ŌHAI'ULA BEACH) ★★

Virtually in the shadow of the massive Pu'ukoholā Heiau (p. 193) to the north, this is a great place to stop when heading to or from the scenic and historic sites in North Kohala. The gently sloping, white-yellow sand beach is **'Ōhai'ula,** though most just call it "Spencer," since it's part of **Samuel M. Spencer County Park.** Protected by a long reef and Kawai-hae Harbor, the beach has relatively safe swimming year-round; steps from the pavilion at its southern end lead straight into a popular snorkeling area. The same pavilion is also next to the trailhead for Ala Kahakai National Historic Trail (www.nps.gov/alka), which leads to a shell cove and, after about a 15-minute hike, undeveloped **Mauʻumae Beach** ★★, heading south to the Mauna Kea Beach Hotel. Parking is plentiful, but it may fill up on weekends and holidays. From the intersection of highways 19 and 270, take Highway 270 a half-mile north to a left turn at the sign for the park, next to **Puʻukoholā Heiau National Historic Site** (p. 193), and follow this to either of two parking areas. Facilities include picnic tables, restrooms, showers, lawns, and shade trees; lifeguards are on duty weekends and holidays. Campsites at either end of the beach sometimes serve the area's homeless population. (It's safe during daylight hours, but I'd avoid walking through the tents section.) *Note:* The park is typically closed the second Wednesday and Thursday of each month September through May.

WAIALEA BAY (BEACH 69) ★★

Once a hidden oasis, this coral-strewn beach in Puakō, between the Mauna Lani and Mauna Kea resorts, earned its nickname from the number on a former telephone pole off Old Puakō Road, which signaled one of the public-access points. Tucked behind private homes, it's now part of Hapuna Beach State Recreation Area with a parking lot, a trail to the beach, restrooms, and water fountains—but no lifeguards. The bay is generally calm in summer, good for swimming and snorkeling; waves get big in winter, when surfers and bodyboarders tend to show up. From Kailua-Kona, take Highway 19 north to a left on Puakō Road, and then a right on Old Puakō Road; the road to the parking area is on your left, near telephone pole No. 71 (the nickname has not caught up with the times). It's open daily 7am to 6:45pm. Now officially part of **Hapuna Beach State Recreation Area** (p. 223), it now charges nonresidents $10 per vehicle to park and $5 per person for admission, assuming the kiosk is staffed.

Hāmākua Coast

This lush area of steep cliffs and plunging valleys makes up in waterfalls what it lacks in sandy beaches, but a few shoreline areas are worth visiting, even if only for a photo. The strong currents and typically crashing surf on the rocks at **Laupāhoehoe Beach Park** ★ should dissuade you from entering the water, although on calm days you'll see people swimming close to the protective boat dock. Instead, enjoy the slow, mile-long descent from Hwy. 11 past modest plantation-era homes to **Laupāhoehoe Point** (p. 199). Check out the monument to the victims of the 1946 tsunami victims, marvel at the massive banyan tree by the cemetery, and picnic with beautiful coastal views; camping is also available by county permit here (see "Camping," p. 274). It's open daily 6:30am to 8pm. Just north of Honomū, home to ʻAkaka Falls (p. 197), **Kolekole Beach Park** ★★ also requires a steep, winding downhill ride from Hwy. 11. Reopened in early 2024 after nearly 3 years of repairs to the aging bridge above it and renovations to park facilities, the 5.5-acre park is a verdant oasis lined by Kolekole Stream; you may see kids splashing under a small waterfall, or expert surfers navigating the waves near where the stream enters the ocean. The brand-new pavilions, picnic tables, and restrooms make this a welcome pit stop; it's open daily 7am to 8pm.

Hilo

LELEIWI BEACH PARK ★★

This string of palm-fringed, black-lava tide pools fed by freshwater springs and rippled by gentle waves is a photographer's delight—and the perfect place to take a plunge. In winter, big waves can splash these ponds, but the shallow pools are generally free of currents and ideal for families with children, especially in the protected inlets at the center of the park. Leleiwi often attracts endangered sea turtles, making this one of the island's most popular snorkeling spots. Open daily 7am to 7pm, the beach park is 4 miles east of town on Kalaniana'ole Avenue. Facilities include a lifeguard station (staffed weekends, holidays, and summer), picnic tables, pavilions, and parking. A second section of the park, known as **Richardson's Ocean Park,** includes showers, restrooms, daily lifeguards, and exhibits at Richardson Ocean Center.

Tip: If the area is crowded, check out the tide pools and/or small sandy coves in the five other beach parks along Kalaniana'ole Avenue between Banyan Drive and Leleiwi, especially the protected white-sand lagoon of **Carlsmith Beach Park ★**, just a 2-minute drive west. It has lifeguard service in summer and on weekends and holidays, as does the rocky but kid-friendly **Onekahakaha Beach Park ★**, at the end of Onekahakaha Road off Kalaniana'ole Avenue, just under a mile west from Carlsmith.

Richardson's Ocean Park in Hilo.

Puna District

Most of the shoreline in this volcanically active area is craggy, with rough waters and dangerous currents. Pounding waves have reclaimed much of the black-sand beach near **Kalapana ★**, born in the 1990 lava flow that buried Kaimū Beach and sometimes called New Kaimū. It's best viewed from the cliff above, since rogue waves may suddenly break high on the beach.

To see the new lagoon and black-sand beach created by the 2018 eruption at **Isaac Hale Beach Park ★★** off Highway 137 in Pohoiki, you'll need to drive slowly over the new access road across lava, starting from MacKenzie State Recreation Area. The county has placed portable restrooms and a second lifeguard station here, but at press time had not restored potable water. Swim in the lagoon but avoid the ocean's dangerous surf. The park and access road are open daily 9am to 6pm, with security officers on site from 6pm to 5am.

Note: Although nudism is common at secluded, unmarked **Kehena Beach** (p. 270), also off Highway 137, it is illegal.

Ka'ū District

PAPAKŌLEA (GREEN SAND) BEACH ★★

The island's famous green-sand beach is located at the base of Pu'u o Mahana, an old cinder cone spilling into the sea. It's difficult to reach; the open bay is often rough; there are no facilities, fresh water, or shade; and howling winds scour the point. Nevertheless, each year the unusual olive-brown sands—made of crushed olivine, a semiprecious green mineral found in eruptive rocks and meteorites—attract thousands of beachgoers, which unfortunately damages the delicate area. Although driving to the top of the cinder cone is no longer permitted by the Department of Hawaiian Homelands, enterprising residents now offer a round-trip shuttle for $10 to $20 (cash only). This is one of those places it's best to admire from afar, but if you feel you must go, you'll cause less environmental damage by undertaking the windy, challenging hike along the 2½ miles from the parking lot, which crosses unshaded dirt roads and lava rock (wear closed-toe shoes, sunglasses, and a hat, and bring lots of water). In either case, you'll still need to clamber carefully down the steep eroded cinder cone to the sand. If the surf's up, check out the beach from the cliff's edge; if the water's calm, you can go closer, but keep an eye on the ocean at all times (rip currents are strong here). From Highway 11, between mile markers 69 and 70, take South Point Road about 8 miles south to a left fork for the Papakōlea parking lot; be aware much of it is one lane.

PUNALU'U BEACH PARK ★★★

Green sea turtles love to bask on this remote, black-sand beach, beautifully framed by palm trees and easily photographed from the bluff above. The deep-blue waters can be choppy; swim only in very calm conditions (and only when lifeguards are present, daily 8:30am–5pm). You're welcome to

The enticing Papakōlea (Green Sand) beach is best accessed with local guides or admired from afar.

admire the turtles, but at a respectful distance, keeping behind low rock barriers erected for their protection; the law against touching or harassing them is enforced here (if not by authorities, then by residents who also like to congregate in the park). Park facilities include camping, restrooms, showers, picnic tables, pavilions, water fountains, a concession stand, and parking. Two roads access the beach from Highway 11, at 7¾ and 8 miles northeast of Nā'ālehu. The first, Nīnole Loop Road, leads past the rather unkempt Sea Mountain golf course to a turnoff for a paved parking lot by the bluff. The second access from Highway 11, Punalu'u Road, has a turn-off for a smaller, unpaved parking area.

WATERSPORTS

Boat, Raft & Submarine Tours

The relatively calm waters of the Kona and Kohala coasts are home to inquisitive reef fish, frolicking spinner dolphins, tranquil sea turtles, spiraling manta rays, and spouting whales and their calves in season (at their peak Jan–Mar). A wide variety of vessels offer sightseeing and snorkel/dive tours (gear provided), while cocktail and dinner cruises take advantage of the region's predictably eye-popping sunsets.

Note: Prices below reflect discounts for online bookings, where applicable; book well in advance whenever possible. For fishing charters, see p. 238.

KONA COAST

Atlantis Submarines ★   If you have what it takes (namely, no claustrophobia), head 100 feet below the sea in a 65-foot **submarine,** with a large porthole for each of the 48 passengers. During the 45 minutes underwater, the sub glides slowly through an 18,000-year-old, 25-acre coral reef in **Kailua Bay,** teeming with fish (including, unfortunately, invasive goatfish and *ta'ape*) and two shipwrecks encrusted in coral. You'll take a 5-minute boat shuttle from Kailua Pier, across from the ticket office, to the air-conditioned submarine. *Note:* Children are allowed, but all passengers must be at least 3 feet tall.

75-5669 Ali'i Dr. (across the street from Kailua Pier), Kailua-Kona. www.atlantis adventures.com/kona. ⓒ **800/381-0237.** Tours daily at 10:15am, 11:30am, 12:45pm, and 2pm (check-in 30 min. beforehand). $148 ages 13 and older, $66 under 13. $10 for 4-hr. parking at Courtyard Marriott King Kamehameha Kona Beach Hotel with validation.

Body Glove Cruises ★★   Body Glove's *Kanoa II,* a 65-foot, solar-powered catamaran carrying up to 100 passengers, runs an eco-friendly, 4½-hour **Snorkel & Dolphin Adventure** morning cruise, along with shorter dinner excursions and seasonal whale-watching trips; all depart from Kailua Pier. In the morning, you'll be greeted with coffee, fruit, and breakfast pastries before heading north to **Pawai Bay,** a marine preserve where you can snorkel, scuba dive, swim, or just hang out on deck. (Spinner dolphin sightings are guaranteed, but for their health and your safety, you do not swim with them.) Before chowing down on the lunch buffet, take the plunge off the boat's 20-foot water slide or 15-foot-high diving board. The only thing you need to bring is a towel; all gear is provided, along with mineral sunscreen. *Note:* If you crave a zippier ride, Body Glove's 41-foot Super-Raft offers the speed of a raft with the amenities of a catamaran (such as bathroom, shade, and cushioned seats). The

Too Many Manta Boats

Watching the mysterious gentle giants known as manta rays somersault toward you in the ocean as they sweep up microscopic plankton and krill has long been one of Hawai'i Island's unique thrills. Unfortunately, too many boats have now launched night snorkel/dive tours focused on manta rays, generally with the help of artificial lights that attract plankton. Since mantas are reliably spotted in only a few areas, the increased traffic has radically diminished the wonder of the experience and raised concern for the mantas. In Makako Bay, humans may outnumber the serene sea creatures 250 to 1 on a given night, with the ratio not much better in Keauhou. While legislation to limit operators is being debated, I can only recommend the small-group, **swim-in experience**

on the Kohala Coast led by two of the world's experts on manta rays, James and Martina Wing (www.mantaray advocates.com; ⓒ 808/987-5580). Instead of taking a diesel-powered boat out to an area crowded with other boats, where you enter the water en masse and try not to jostle each other or the mantas, the Wings will lead your small group (typically six to eight people) from the beach directly into the water, wading and then swimming a short distance to the area where mantas congregate. It's more intimate and more eco- and manta-friendly. This experience is $145 for ages 10 and up (and an additional $35 if you need a lesson to brush up on your snorkel skills); book online, call or e-mail info@mantarayshawaii.com for location and reservations.

Super-Raft's 4-hour morning snorkeling cruises include drinks and snacks and cost $130 for adults, $110 for children ages 6 to 17. For health and safety reasons, younger children, pregnant women, and those with back and neck problems are not allowed on Super-Raft excursions. Options include a sunset dinner cruise, winter whale watching, and the "Offshore Adventure," a combination snorkeling/wildlife-watching cruise. Dinner cruises on the catamaran feature a historian who points out significant sites on the 12-mile trip from Kailua Pier to Kealakekua Bay, where passengers feast on a buffet and enjoy live Hawaiian music. All cruises are free for children 5 and under, and the boat, including restrooms, is wheelchair accessible.

Kailua Pier, Kailua-Kona. www.bodyglovehawaii.com. © **800/551-8911** or 808/326-7122. **Catamaran cruises:** Snorkeling (daily 8am) $169 adults, $99 children 6–17; sunset dinner (Tues–Sun 4pm) $169 adults, $99 children 6–17; whale-watching (Dec–Mar only; daily 1pm) $110 adults, $99 children 6–17. **Super-Raft cruises (ages 6 and older):** Snorkeling (Thurs–Tues 8:30am) $130 adults, $110 children 6–17; sunset dinner (Mon, Wed, and Fri 4:30pm) $119 adults, $99 children 6–17; Offshore Adventure (Mon and Fri 1pm) $120 adults, $100 ages 6–17; whale-watching (Dec–Mar only; daily 1:30pm) $120 adults, $100 ages 6–17.

Captain Dan McSweeney's Whale Watch Learning Adventures ★★★

The islands' most impressive visitors—45-foot humpback whales—return each winter to warm Hawaiian waters. Capt. Dan McSweeney, who founded the Wild Whale Research Foundation in 1979, has no problem finding them. During his 3½-hour **whale-watching tours,** he drops a hydrophone (an underwater microphone) into the water so you can listen to their songs, and sometimes uses an underwater video camera to show you what's going on. Cruises are aboard the 40-foot *Lady Ann,* which has restrooms and a choice of sunny or shaded decks; cold drinks, snacks, and cooling face towels are provided. Trips depart from Honōkohau Harbor, where parking is ample and free.

Honōkohau Harbor, 74-380 Kealakehe Pkwy. (off Hwy. 19), Kailua-Kona. www.ilovewhales.com. © **888/942-5376.** Tours Mon–Tues and Thurs–Fri Jan–Mar 31 7 and 11am. $135 adults, $125 children 11 and under who also weigh under 90 lb.

Captain Zodiac ★

It's a wild, 14-mile ride to Kealakekua Bay aboard one of Captain Zodiac's 16-passenger, 24-foot **rigid-hull inflatable rafts,** or Zodiacs. There you'll spend about an hour snorkeling in the bay, perhaps with spinner dolphins, and enjoy snacks and beverages at the site. The small size of the craft means no restrooms, but it also means you can explore sea caves on this craggy coast. Four-hour **snorkel trips** are twice daily, while the 5-hour midday tour ingeniously arrives at Kealakekua when most other boats have left, leaving extra time for a second snorkel site, seasonal **whale-watching,** or other experiences at the captain's discretion, plus a deli lunch. Be prepared to get wet regardless (that includes your camera). Captain Zodiac also offers a twice-weekly, 4- to 5-hour **Pelagic Wildlife Excursion** with a trained naturalist. You'll be on the lookout for some of the 17 species of whales and dolphins found in these waters, plus turtles, Hawaiian monk seals, sharks, and sea birds.

In Gentry's Kona Marina, Honōkōhau Harbor, 74-425 Kealakehe Pkwy. (off Hwy. 19), Kailua-Kona. www.captainzodiac.com. © **808/329-3199.** 4-hr. snorkel cruise (Sun, Tues, Thurs, and Sat 8am and 12:45pm) $140 adults, $105 children 4–12; 5-hr. snorkel cruise (Mon–Tues and Thurs–Fri 10am), $155 adults, $120 children 4–12. Pelagic Wildlife Excursion (Sat 9am), $140 adults, $105 children 7–12. Whale-watching (Jan–Mar only; Thurs–Tues 8 and 11:45am) $115 adults, $90 children 5–12.

Fair Wind Snorkeling & Diving Adventures ★★★   I love Fair Wind for several reasons, starting with the environmental pledge it requires of guests, who also receive free reef-friendly sunscreen and reusable soda cups on tours. Another is its home port in **Keauhou Bay,** 8 miles south of Kailua Pier and that much closer to **Kealakekua Bay,** where its two very different but impressively equipped boats head for **snorkel/dive tours:**

FAIR WIND II   When traveling with kids, I book a cruise on the *Fair Wind II,* a 60-foot catamaran that includes two 15-foot water slides, a high-dive jump, playpens, and child-friendly flotation devices with viewfinders, so even toddlers can peek at Kealakua's glorious sea life. Year-round, the *Fair Wind II* offers a 4½-hour morning snorkel cruise that includes a breakfast and barbecue lunch, most of the year it also sails a 3½-hour afternoon snorkel cruise that provides snacks, which in summer becomes a deluxe 4½-hour excursion with barbecue dinner. Swimmers ages 8 and up can also try **SNUBA**—kind of a beginner's version of scuba—for an optional $69, with an in-water guide. The gourmet plant-based menu—including hearty, savory substitutes that most carnivores relish—is another plus.

Snorkeling off Hawai'i Island.

HULA KAI When traveling with teens or adults, I prefer the *Hula Kai,* the Fair Wind's 55-foot foil-assist catamaran, open only to ages 7 and up. The boat provides a plusher experience (such as comfy seating with headrests) and, on its 5-hour morning snorkel cruise, a faster, smoother ride to two uncrowded Kona Coast snorkeling sites (usually neither is Kealakekua Bay), based on conditions. Guests have the option to try **stand-up paddleboarding,** SNUBA (see above), or the propulsive **"Sea Rocket"** ($25 per half-hour) to cover even more ground underwater.

Keauhou Bay Pier, 78-7130 Kaleiopapa St., Kailua-Kona. www.fair-wind.com. ✆ **808/ 322-2788.** *Fair Wind II* morning snorkel cruise (4–7 days a week, 8:30am) $159 ages 13 and older, $99 children 4–12, $39 children 3 and under. Afternoon snorkel cruise (daily 1:30pm) $115 adults, $70 ages 4–12, $25 for ages 3 and under. *Hula Kai* morning snorkel/dive cruise (3–5 days a week, 9am) $173 ages 7 and up only. Park on opposite side of Keauhou Bay, at end of King Kamehameha III Rd.

KOHALA COAST

If you're staying on or near the Waikoloa Beach Resort, **Hawai'i Ocean Sports** (www.hawaiioceansports.com; ✆ **808/886-6666**) conveniently offers a multitude of excursions from 'Anaeho'omalu Bay, where it also operates glass-bottom boat cruises (see "High & Dry," below). A tender takes you from the beach to a comfortable sailing catamaran for snorkeling trips from A-Bay on Monday and Wednesday, while a similar catamaran departs Kawaihae Harbor to the north on Friday and Saturday ($180 adults, $90 ages 6–12, free for kids 5 and under). Sunset sails also depart Monday and Wednesday from 'Anaeho'omalu and Friday and Saturday from Kawaihae (adults $160, children $80); between December 15 and March 31, the sunset sails become whale-watching excursions (adults $115, children $58). *Note:* Kawaihae Harbor is about a 25-minute drive north of 'Anaeho'omalu Bay.

Even if you're not staying there, it's worth the drive to the **Mauna Kea Beach Hotel** (p. 263) to experience the traditional sailing canoe of **Hawaiian Sails** (see "Sail Like Ancient Voyagers," p. 233), which cruises

---

High & Dry: Glass-Bottom Boats

If you're not a swimmer, no need to forgo seeing the multihued marine life for which the Kona and Kohala coasts are justly famous. Tours with **Kailua Bay Charters** ★ on the 36-foot *Marian,* which has comfy benches and shade, are well suited to families. The trip is just an hour long, with a naturalist on board to explain what you're seeing. Tours leave Kailua Pier at 9am, 10am, 12:15pm, and 1:30pm Monday, Thursday, and Saturday (www.konaglassbottomboat.com; ✆ **808/324-1749;** $58 adults, $28 children ages 3–12, $5 ages 2 and under; reservations required). You can see the underwater sights of 'Anaeho'omalu Bay on a 26-foot glass-bottom boat with **Hawai'i Ocean Sports** ★★; it too has benches, shade, and a naturalist. Half-hour tours depart from the beach multiple times daily from 8:45am in winter and 9:15am in summer (www.hawaii oceansports.com; ✆ **808/886-6666;** $49 adults, $20 children 4–11, and free for children 3 and under). *Tip:* Earlier trips tend to have the best visibility.

SAIL LIKE ancient voyagers

In ancient times, fearless Polynesians found new homes across the Pacific by sailing in double-hulled canoes, *wa'akaulua*, with only the stars, winds, waves, and seabirds to guide them. The revival of celestial wayfinding and building these ocean-going canoes began in the 1970s, but only recently have visitors had a chance to experience this tradition for themselves. Expect to see a whale or two in winter.

Sailing from Kauna'oa Beach at Mauna Kea Beach Hotel, Koko and Mahea Gionson of **Hawaiian Sails** (www.hawaiiansails.com; ✆ **808/640-6340**) and a crew of their teenagers offer 2-hour snorkeling tours ($165) for up to six people aboard the 35-foot replica sailing canoe *Hahalualele* ("Flying Manta Ray"). The $165 cost per person includes drinks, snacks, and use of towels. The double-hulled canoe sails Monday to Saturday at 8am, 10am, noon, and 2pm (with minimum of four guests).

Capt. Kiko Johnston-Kitazawa's **Waakaulua Sailing Excursions** (www.waakaulua.com; ✆ **808/895-3743**) charters 3-hour sailing trips out of Hilo's Wailoa Harbor for $125 per person for up to six people (minimum of four per trip). A longtime boat builder, Capt. Kiko shares Hawaiian lore and natural history on his cruises, while also teaching passengers paddling techniques.

near Puakō or Kawaihae, depending on the conditions, up to four times a day Monday through Saturday. The 2-hour tours for up to six passengers cost $165 per person (www.hawaiiansails.com; ✆ **808/640-6340**).

The South Kawaihae Small Boat Harbor, a short detour off 'Akoni Pule Highway (Hwy. 270) just north of Pu'ukoholā Heiau (p. 193), is the departure point for whisper-quiet cruises aboard the *Dolce Vita,* the solar- and wind-powered electric sailing catamaran of **Kohala Blue Sail Hawai'i ★★★** (www.kohalablue.net; ✆ **808/556-7649**). You can book a private, 3-hour morning, afternoon, or sunset sail along the Kohala Coast for up to six passengers ($1,295 total) or see if a shared charter ($235 per person, minimum four guests) is available. Snorkeling gear, drinks, and snacks are provided. Captain Suelang Watson is a marine naturalist who sometimes takes the role of deckhand so she can guide your snorkeling; fellow captain Damon Little capably take the wheel in that case. *Note:* This the island's best area for whale-watching (Dec–Mar); this boat doesn't disturb underwater life with noise or diesel pollution.

HILO

Hilo Ocean Adventures (www.hilooceanadventures.com; ✆ **808/934-8344**) offers the uniquely informative Cliffs of Hawai'i Onomea Waterfall cruise ($159), departing Monday through Friday at 9:30am; the 2-hour excursions aboard a 28-foot motorboat also serve as whale-watching trips in winter. From December to April, the 90-minute **Royal Humpback Whale Experience** ($139) cruises specifically in search of cetaceans at 8:30am, 10:30am, and 12:30pm several days a week. Hilo Ocean

Adventure also offers frequent snorkel boat and beach trips ($119–$159, gear and refreshments included) in and around Hilo Bay.

Bodyboarding (Boogie Boarding) & Bodysurfing

As with other watersports, it's important to stay out of rough surf in winter or during storms that bring big surf. In normal conditions, the best beaches for bodyboarding and bodysurfing on the Kona side of the island are **Hāpuna Beach ★★★** on the Kohala Coast, **La'aloa Beach (White Sand/ Magic Sands Beach) ★★** in Kailua-Kona, and **Kua Bay (Manini'ōwali Beach) ★★** in **Kekaha Kai State Park,** north of the airport. Experienced bodysurfers may want to check out South Kona's **Ho'okena Beach Park ★★**; on the Hilo side, try **Leleiwi Beach Park ★★**. See "Beaches" (p. 217) for details.

Beach concessions and most surf shops (see "Surfing," on p. 239) rent bodyboards, but you can also find inexpensive rentals at **Snorkel Bob's** in the parking lot of Huggo's restaurant, 75-5831 Kahakai St. at Ali'i Drive, Kailua-Kona (www.snorkelbob.com; ✆ 808/329-0770), and on the Kohala Coast in the Shops at Mauna Lani, 68-1330 Mauna Lani Dr. (✆ **808/885-9499**). Both stores are open daily 8am to 5pm.

Kayaking

Imagine sitting at sea level, eye to eye with a turtle, a dolphin, even a whale—it's possible in an ocean kayak. Although you're not to approach them, these creatures may approach you! After a few minutes of instruction and a little practice in a calm area (like **Kamakahonu Cove** in front of the Courtyard King Kamehameha Kona Beach Hotel), you'll be ready to explore. Beginners can practice their skills in **Kailua Bay,** intermediate kayakers might try paddling from **Honōkohau Harbor** to **Kekaha Kai State Park,** and the more advanced can tackle the 5 miles from **Keauhou Bay** to **Kealakekua Bay** or the scenic but challenging **Hāmākua Coast.**

You'll find rentals at nearly every beachfront Kona and Kohala resort; hourly rates typically start at $30 to $40. Departing from the Grand Naniloa Hotel Hilo (p. 269), **Kapohokine Adventures** (https://kapohokine.com; ✆ **808/964-1000**) leads 2-hour tours of historic **Hilo Bay** and area waterfalls for kayakers and stand-up paddlers ($153); hardy types can opt for a 3-hour version ($329).

KEALAKEKUA BAY GUIDED TOURS & RENTALS Although technically you can rent kayaks for exploring Kealakekua Bay on your own, it's best to go with a guided tour. Only three kayak companies are allowed to offer guided tours that land at the Cook monument (Ka'awaloa), all launching from Nāpo'opo'o Wharf. Due to concerns over frequent cancellations with refunds by one company, I now only recommend the two companies named below. These tours include equipment, snorkeling gear, snacks or lunch, and drinks, and they should be booked in advance, due to the

12-guest limit per tour. Note that Nāpoʻopoʻo is a residential area, where parking can be difficult if you're not on a tour.

Kona Boys ★★ (www.konaboys.com; © **808/328-1234**) was the first to offer kayak rentals in Kona and is still widely regarded as the best. Its 3½-hour Kealakekua Bay kayak snorkel tours (Mon–Sat by reservation) meet at the shop at 79-7539 Māmalahoa Hwy. (Hwy. 11), Kealakekua, at 7am; tours cost $224 for adults, $199 for ages 18 and under. You can rent gear from Kona Boys' **beach shack** at Kamakahonu Bay (© **808/329-2345**); it's the only site that offers kayaks by the hour, not just by the day or week. Rentals include kayak, paddles, backrests, cooler, life jackets, dry bag, and a soft rack to carry kayaks on top of your car (including convertibles). Daily rates are $69 single kayak, $99 double (weekly $199/$299).

The environmentally conscious **Adventures in Paradise** ★★ (www.bigislandkayak.com; © **808/447-0080**) has a small office at 82-6020 Māmalahoa Hwy. (Hwy. 11) in Captain Cook, but generally meets clients at Nāpoʻopoʻo for its 3½-hour Kealakekua tours ($120 for ages 10–60), departing Monday, Wednesday, and Friday at 8:30am and noon. *Tip:* Book the early tour for the least crowded snorkeling.

Parasailing

Get a bird's-eye view of Hawaiʻi Island's pristine waters with **UFO Parasail** (www.ufoparasail.net; © **800/359-4836** or 808/325-5836), which offers parasail rides daily between 8am and 5:30pm from Kailua Pier. The cost is $136 for 10 minutes in the air at 1,200 feet ($116 for 6 min. at 800 ft.). You can go up alone or with a friend (or two) ages 5 and older; single riders must weigh at least 160 pounds, and groups no more than 450 pounds. The boat may carry up to eight passengers (those only observing pay $79), and the total time in the boat, around an hour, varies on the rides they've booked. *Tip:* Save nearly 30% by booking online.

Scuba Diving

Hawaiʻi Island's leeward coast offers some of the best diving and snorkeling in the world; the water is calm, warm, and clear. Want to swim with fast-moving game fish? Try **Ulua Cave,** at the north end of the Kohala Coast, from 25 to 90 feet deep; dolphins, rays, and the occasional Hawaiian monk seal swim by. More than 2 dozen dive operators on island offer everything from scuba-certification courses to guided dives to snorkeling cruises.

Founded in 1984, **Kohala Divers** ★★★ (www.kohaladivers.com; © **808/882-7774**) offers one-tank ($159) and two-tank dives ($209) to spectacular sites off North and South Kohala, including a 30-foot-high lava dome covered in plate and knob coral that attracts huge schools of fish, and several spots off Puakō frequented by green sea turtles. This is a great outfit for beginners as well as experienced divers, with friendly, well-versed guides. Snorkelers (gear included) pay $145 to join a one-tank dive (offered afternoons only, typically once a week) and $175 for the two-tank dives, which depart daily at 7:30am; ride-alongs (people not going in the water) pay $110 on either dive. The well-equipped 42-foot dive boat, which includes two heated freshwater showers, books just 15 spots of its 24-passenger capacity. You can also rent scuba and snorkel gear at its well-stocked shop in Kawaihae Harbor Shopping Center, 61-3665 'Akoni Pule Hwy. (Hwy. 270), about a mile north of its intersection with Highway 19. It's open daily 8am to 5pm.

Farther south, **Kona Diving Company ★★**, 74-5467 Luhia St. (at Eho St.), Kailua-Kona (www.konadivingcompany.com; ✆ **808/331-1858**), prides itself on heading to uncommon dive sites in a 34-foot catamaran complete with showers, TV, and restrooms. Two-tank morning dives cost $195 and depart daily at 7:45am, one-tank night reef dives cost $170, offered by request and departing a half-hour before sunset.

One of Kona's oldest and most eco-friendly dive shops, **Jack's Diving Locker ★★**, in the Coconut Marketplace, 75-5813 Ali'i Dr., Kailua-Kona (www.jacksdivinglocker.com; ✆ **800/345-4807** or 808/329-7585), boasts an 8,000-square-foot dive center with swimming pool classrooms, full-service rentals, and sports-diving and technical-diving facilities. It offers a two-tank dive for $200 (same for snorkelers, minimum of two), departing daily at 8:30am; Jack's roomy boats take 10 to 18 divers (split into groups of six). **Pelagic Magic,** a one-tank descent that reveals iridescent jellies and evanescent zooplankton ($230), starts at the shop Tuesday and Thursday at 5:30pm.

On the island's east side, Hilo's **Puhi Bay** and the waters of **Leleiwi Point** teem with turtles, octopus, goatfish and other sights for divers. **Hilo Ocean Adventures ★★**, 1717 Kamehameha Ave., at Banyan Drive (www.hilooceanadventures.com; ✆ **808/934-8344**), offers introductory morning beach dives ($325) Monday to Saturday at 9am and also night beach dives for certified divers ($189) Monday and Wednesday at 7pm.

Snorkeling

If you come to Hawai'i and don't snorkel, you'll miss half the sights. The clear waters along the dry Kona and Kohala coasts, in particular, are home to spectacular marine life, including spinner and spotted dolphins. Please remember not to touch or stand on live coral, which can take decades to grow back, and either apply reef-safe sunscreen a half-hour before entering the ocean, or just use protective clothing such as rash guards to avoid harming the reefs. *Tip:* Go in the mornings, before afternoon clouds and winds lessen visibility.

Spinner dolphins leap near kayakers and snorkelers.

GEAR RENTALS   If you're staying at a Kona or Kohala resort, the hotel concession should have basic gear for hourly rental. If you're thinking of exploring more than the beach outside your room, an inexpensive place to get basic rental equipment ($12 per week) is **Snorkel Bob's,** in the parking lot of Huggo's restaurant, 75-5831 Kahakai St. at Ali'i Drive, Kailua-Kona (www.snorkelbob.com; ✆ **808/329-0770**), and on the Kohala Coast in the Shops at Mauna Lani, 68-1330 Mauna Lani Dr., facing the road on the Mauna Lani Resort (✆ **808/885-9499**). Higher-quality gear costs $68 a week for adults, $30 for children; prescription masks are also available. Both stores are open daily 8am to 5pm.

You can also rent high-quality gear from **Jack's Diving Locker,** Coconut Grove Shopping Center (next to Outback Steakhouse), 75-5813 Ali'i Dr., Kailua-Kona (www.jacksdivinglocker.com; ✆ **800/345-4807** or 808/329-7585), open daily 8am to 4pm. Snorkel sets cost $15 a day. On the Kohala Coast, visit **Kohala Divers** (www.kohaladivers.com; ✆ **808/882-7774**) in the Kawaihae Shopping Center, 61-3665 'Akoni Pule Hwy. (Hwy. 270), in Kawaihae, a mile north of the intersection with Highway 19. It's open daily 8am to 5pm, with snorkel sets starting at $10 a day.

Hilo Ocean Adventures, 1717 Kamehameha Ave., at Banyan Drive (www.hilooceanadventures.com; ✆ **808/934-8344**), has twice-daily beach snorkel tours for $159. Snorkel sets are $15 a day, $75 per week.

TOP SNORKEL SITES   If you've never snorkeled before, **Kahalu'u Beach** ★★ (p. 218) is the best place to start, as long as the crowds don't throw you off. Just carefully wade in on one of the small, sandy paths through the lava-rock tide pools and you'll see colorful fish; be sure to not touch or stand on the coral reef. Even better, swim out to the center of the shallow, well-protected bay to see schools of surgeonfish, Moorish idols, butterflyfish, and even green sea turtles. The friendly and knowledgeable volunteers of the **Kahalu'u Bay Education Center** (https://kohalacenter.org/kbec; ✆ **808/887-6411**) are on-site daily from 8:30am to 3pm to explain reef etiquette—essentially: "Look, but don't touch"—and answer questions about its marine life.

Kealakekua Bay ★★★ may offer the island's best overall snorkeling (coral heads, lava tubes, calm waters, underwater caves, and more), but because it's a marine life conservation district and state historical park (p. 187), access is restricted to preserve its treasures. The best way to snorkel here is via permitted **boat tours** (p. 228), generally departing from Kailua Pier or Keauhou Bay, or **kayak tours** (p. 234) with permits to launch from Nāpo'opo'o Wharf and land near the Captain Cook Monument. You can paddle a rental kayak, canoe, or stand-up paddleboard from Nāpo'opo'o on your own if the company has acquired a special permit; otherwise, it's about a 10-mile round-trip paddle from Keauhou. Carrying your snorkel gear down and up the steep 5-mile trail from the highway is possible but not recommended. Watch out for spiny urchins as well as fragile coral when entering the water from lava rocks along the shore.

Much more easily accessible snorkeling, with a terrific display of aquatic diversity, can be found at **Hōnaunau Bay,** nicknamed "Two Step" for the easy entry off flat lava rocks into the clear waters just before **Puʻuhonua O Hōnaunau National Historical Park** (p. 189). Snorkeling is not permitted in the park (and using bathrooms for changing in and out of swimsuits is discouraged), but you can pay the entrance fee to use the parking lot and walk to the bay if the 25 or so spaces on the waterfront road (look for the coastal access sign off Hwy. 160) are taken.

Beyond the beaches of the Kohala resorts, the well-protected waters of Ōhaiʻula Beach at **Spencer Park** (p. 224) are a great site for families to snorkel, with convenient facilities (such as restrooms, showers, and picnic tables), not to mention a lifeguard on weekends and holidays, and a reputation for attracting green sea turtles (let them come to you, but don't touch or approach them). It can get windy, so mornings are your best bet here; be careful not to brush up against one of the spiny urchins clinging to the rocks near the pavilion. Puakō's **Waialea Bay** (p. 225), home to coral colonies, reef fish, and turtles, provides good snorkeling in calm waters, typically in summer.

Sport Fishing: The Hunt for Granders ★★

Big-game fish, including gigantic blue marlin and other Pacific billfish, tuna, sailfish, swordfish, ono (wahoo), and giant trevallies (*ulua*), roam the waters of the Kona Coast, known as the marlin capital of the world. When anglers catch marlin weighing 1,000 pounds or more, they call them "granders"; there's even a "wall of fame" in Kailua-Kona's Waterfront Row shopping mall honoring those who've nailed more than 20 tons of fighting fish. Nearby photos show celebrities such as Sylvester Stallone posing with their slightly less impressive catches. The celebrities of the fishing world descend on Kailua-Kona in August for the 5-day **Hawaiian International Billfish Tournament** (www.hibtfishing.com), founded in 1959. Note that it's not all carnage out there: Teams that tag and release marlin under 300 pounds get bonus points.

Nearly 100 charter boats with professional captains and crew offer fishing charters out of **Keauhou, Kawaihae, Honōkohau,** and **Kailua Bay** harbors. Prices typically range from $950 to $3,000 or so for a full-day exclusive charter (you and up to five friends have an entire boat to yourselves) or $850 to $1,000 for a half-day. One or two people may be able to book a "share" on boats that hold four to eight anglers, who take turns fishing—generally for smaller catch—to increase everyone's chances of hooking something. Shares generally start at $150 to $250 per person for half-day trips, $350 for a full day. You can comparison-shop among 29 Kailua-Kona charters on https://fishingbooker.com.

Note: Most big-game charter boats carry six passengers max, and the boats supply all equipment, bait, tackle, and lures. No license is required. Many captains now tag and release marlins; other fish caught belong to the boat, not to you—that's island style. If you want to eat your catch or have your trophy mounted, arrange it with the captain before you go.

Stand-Up Paddleboarding (SUP)

Anywhere the water is calm is a fine place to learn stand-up paddleboarding (SUP), which takes much less finesse than traditional surfing but offers a fun alternative to kayaking for exploration. Numerous hotel concessions offer rentals and lessons, as do traditional surf shops.

Kona Boys ★★ (www.konaboys.com; ℂ **808/328-1234**) has the best location in Kailua-Kona to try your hand at SUP: **Kamakahonu Cove,** next to Kailua Pier and King Kamehameha's royal (and sacred) compound. The spring water in the well-protected cove is a little too cool and murky for snorkeling, but just right for getting your bearings. The 90-minute lessons cost $129 in a group setting, $169 private; once you've got the hang of it, you can also reserve one of Kona Boys' 90-minute tours ($129 group/$169 private) or just pick up a rental ($29 hourly, $89 daily). It also offers lessons and rentals at its Kealakekua location, 79-7539 Māmalahoa Hwy. (Hwy. 11), 1¼ miles south of its intersection with Highway 180. Both sites are open daily until 5pm; the Kamakahonu beach shack opens at 8am, Kealakekua at 9am.

Another good option in North Kona is at Keauhou Bay, where **Ocean Safaris** (www.oceansafariskayaks.com; ℂ **808/326-4699**) offers 2-hour SUP tours ($89), typically spring through fall, daily at 9 and 11am, for ages 5 and older.

On the Kohala Coast, the smooth swells of **'Anaeho'omalu Bay** and **Puakō Bay** are well suited to exploring via SUP. **Ocean Sports** (www. hawaiioceansports.com) rents boards for $50 an hour from its kiosk on the sand at the Waikoloa Beach Marriott, open daily 8am to 2pm. **Hulakai** rents stand-up paddleboards from its outlet in the Kings' Shops (https:// hulakai.com; ℂ **808/731-7945**). Open daily 10am to 8pm, it offers 90-minute "adventures" ($115 semiprivate, $175 solo) that include a lesson and guided tour, plus premium rentals for $84 a day, $298 a week. Hulakai's Hilo store, 284 Kamehameha Ave. (ℂ **808/933-4852**), also offers SUP rentals for the same rates.

Departing from the Grand Naniloa Hotel Hilo (p. 269), **Kapohokine Adventures** (https://kapohokine.com; ℂ **808/964-1000**) leads 2-hour tours of historic **Hilo Bay** and area waterfalls for kayakers and stand-up paddlers ($153).

Surfing

Most surfing off Hawai'i Island is for the experienced only, thanks to rocks, reefs, and rip currents at many of the reliable breaks. As a rule, the beaches on the North and West Shores of the island get northern swells in winter, while those on the South and East shores get southern swells in summer. You will need to radiate courtesy and expertise in the lineup with local surfers; they're territorial about their challenging breaks.

In Kailua-Kona, experienced surfers should check out the two breaks in **Hōlualoa Bay** off Aliʻi Drive between downtown Kailua-Kona and Keauhou: **Banyans** near the northern point and **Lyman's** near the southern point, once home to a surfers' temple. If you don't have the chops, don't go in the water; just enjoy the show. Another surfing shrine, its black-lava rock walls still visible today, stands near **Kahaluʻu Beach ★** (p. 218), where the waves are manageable most of the year and there's also a lifeguard. Less-experienced surfers can also try **Pine Trees,** north of town at **Kohanaiki Beach ★★** (p. 221); best to avoid the busy weekends.

Surf breaks on the island's east side are also generally best left to skilled or local surfers. They include **Honoliʻi Point,** north of Hilo; **Richardson's Point** at **Leleiwi Beach Park** (p. 226); and **Hilo Bay Front Park.**

PRIVATE & GROUP LESSONS   You can have a grand time taking a surf lesson, especially with instructors who know where the breaks are best for beginners and who genuinely enjoy being out in the waves with you. The Native Hawaiian–owned **Hawaiʻi Lifeguard Surf Instructors** (HLSI; www.surflessonshawaii.com; ✆ **808/324-0442**), which gives lessons at Kahaluʻu Beach, has a knack with kids and teens. For $175, adults and children as young as 5 can take a 90-minute private lesson (little ones under 55 lb. ride on the same board as their lifeguard/teacher). Lessons for ages 11 and up cost $115 per person for small groups (no more than four students per instructor), or $275 for a class with just two people (who split the cost). On days when the waves are tame, HLSI offers the same lessons with stand-up paddleboards. Classes are daily up to three times a day.

BOARD RENTALS   You're never going to rent a board as good as your own, but you'll enjoy the local vibe at the appropriately named **Pacific Vibrations,** 76-5663 Palani Rd., Kailua-Kona (✆ **808/329-4140**), founded in 1978 by the McMichaels, a Native Hawaiian family with deep ties to surfing and the Ironman triathlon. Surfboards rent for $25 to $45 a day, and bodyboards for just $8; be sure to browse the surf-themed T-shirt selection, too. The staff is happy to steer you to waves to match your skills.

In the Kings' Shops at Waikoloa Beach Resort, surfboard shaper **Hulakai** (www.hulakai.com; ✆ **808/731-7945**) rents soft-top surfboards for $50 a day ($175 a week); soft racks for transporting them cost $10 a

---

WALKING ON WATER via hydrofoil

Well-heeled surfers who want to expand their repertoire can try **hydrofoil surfing**—surfing on a board raised above the water by a long fin known as a hydrofoil—or its electrically powered version, **efoil surfing.** Collectively known as foiling, this sport makes it looks like you're walking on water at breakneck speed. Based in Keauhou, **Hawaiian Foils** (www.hawaiianfoils.com; ✆ **808/990-9590**) introduces efoiling through 90-minute private classes, offered Monday through Saturday at 8am, 11am, and 5pm ($300, including Fliteboard rental and all gear).

day ($25 a week). Two-hour private surfing lessons are $199 per person or $169 for two or more, respectively; call (C) **808/652-7555** to book. Hulakai's Hilo store, 284 Kamehameha Ave. ((C) **808/933-4852**), offers similar surfboard rentals.

OTHER OUTDOOR ACTIVITIES
Biking

Note: In addition to the rental fees mentioned below, expect to put down a deposit on a credit card or leave your credit card number on file.

KONA & KOHALA COASTS

When you're planning to spend a fair amount of time in Kailua-Kona, where parking can be at a premium, consider renting a bicycle for easy riding and sightseeing along flat Ali'i Drive. A cruiser can also be handy if you're staying at a Kohala Coast resort and want an easy way to reach shops, beaches, and condos without having to jump in the car. Experienced cyclists may also want to trace part of the Ironman course (112 miles round-trip) along the wide-shouldered Queen Ka'ahumanu ("Queen K") and 'Akoni Pule highways from Kailua-Kona to Hāwī or join in one of several weekly group rides of the **Hawai'i Cycling Club** (www.hawaii cyclingclub.com). A ride that leaves on Saturdays at 7am sharp from the *makai* side of Target's parking lot, 74-5455 Makala Blvd., Kailua-Kona, heads north on Hwy. 19 (the Queen K), with options for cyclists to return after 12, 18, or 24 miles—the Waikoloa Beach Resort is the last turnaround point, providing a place for riders to refresh or relieve themselves.

To rent simple cruisers, head to **Bike Works Beach & Sports** in Queens' Marketplace at Waikoloa Beach Resort (www.bikeworkshawaii. com; (C) **808/886-5000**), which rents seven-speed men's and women's models for $40 a day ($35 for 3- to 7-day rentals). It also offers hybrid city bikes for the same rates; electric bikes and elite road and triathlon bikes run $80 to $95 for 24 hours, with deep discounts for longer rentals. Its sister store, **Bike Works,** 75-5660 Kopiko St., Unit A1 (in the Kopiko Plaza area), Kailua-Kona (www.bikeworkskona.com; (C) **808/326-2453**), boasts an even bigger selection of bikes, including mountain bikes, road bikes, and triathlon bikes, starting at $75 daily. Its upcountry sibling, **Bike Works Mauka,** 64-1066 Māmalahoa Hwy., Waimea (https://bikeworks mauka.com; (C) **808/885-7943;** bikes $95 daily), is ideal for nearby **Mana Road** in Waimea.

Note: Reserve rentals well in advance for the 2 weeks in October that include the lead up to the Ironman World Championship.

HAWAI'I VOLCANOES NATIONAL PARK & PUNA

The national park has miles of paved roads and trails open to cyclists, from easy, flat rides to challenging ascents, but you'll need to watch out for cars and buses on the often winding, narrow roads, and make sure you carry plenty of water and sunscreen. Download a cycling guide on the

Riding Like (or with) a Pro

Former U.S. pro cyclist Alex Candelario's **Big Island Bike Tours ★★★** (https://bigislandbiketours.com; *©* **800/331-0159** or 808/769-1308) boasts experienced guides, elite-level mountain and road bikes, and, in several cases, exclusive access to scenery well worth the pedal. Based in a quaint shed at Waimea's picturesque **Anna Ranch Heritage Center**, 65-1480 Kawaihae Rd. (Hwy. 11; www.annaranch.org; *©* **808/885-4426**), the company offers a variety of day trips and longer tours for varying abilities. Ride a mountain bike or e-bike to otherwise off-limits waterfalls above Anna Ranch (which also offers a short interpretive trail for non-cyclists, plus gift shop). Other tours traverse rolling pastures along Waimea's unpaved Mana Road, cruise from Honoka'a to the Waipi'o Valley Overlook, or explore via e-bike Puakō Petroglyph Park and Mauna Lani resort's fish ponds and black sand beach. Most tours last 3 to 4 hours and cost $189 to $199; multiday tours can be arranged.

park's website (www.nps.gov/havo/planyourvisit/bike.htm) or pick one up at the Kīlauea Visitor Center. The closest bike-rental shops are in Hilo, including **Mid-Pacific Wheels,** 1133 Manono St. (www.midpacific wheelsllc.com; *©* **808/935-6211**), which rents Giant Mountain and road bikes for $35 a day, including a helmet; bike racks are $10 a day. It's open Monday to Saturday 10am to 4pm. Or leave the planning to **Volcano Bike Tours** (www.bikevolcano.com; *©* **888/934-9199** or 808/934-9199), which sets cyclists up with GPS-based audio tours ($119) in the national park that include some off-road biking.

HILO

Mountain bikers with good technical skills will have a blast exploring the twisting, narrow, rocky trails and forest roads of **Kūlanihāko'i Mountain Bike Park** (https://hawaiitrails.hawaii.gov), a 330-acre former eucalyptus plantation. Turn off Highway 11 at the Stainback Highway and head 1½ miles west to a left on Quarry Road. Take the second gravel road on the left to the parking lot and sign in at the check-in station. Wear bright clothing, since there are hunters in the area, and be aware dogs and hikers may also be on the trails.

Golf

Greens fees below are for visitors and include carts, unless noted; those with Hawai'i state ID may receive substantial discounts. Where noted, "dynamic pricing" means greens fees may be adjusted lower or higher than the quoted standard rates, based on demand. *Tip:* Check with **Hawaii Tee Times** (https://hawaiiteetimes.com: *©* **877/465-3170**) or **www.teeoff.com** for discounts of as much as $85 off specific tee times.

THE KONA COAST

The fabulous **Hualālai Golf Course ★★★** at the Four Seasons Resort Hualālai (p. 259) is open only to members and resort guests—for committed golfers, this Jack Nicklaus–designed championship course is reason enough to book a room and pay the greens fee of $350 ($250 after 2pm, $200 for kids 13–18, free for children 12 and under with paying guest).

Kona Country Club ★★ When William Bell designed the popular oceanfront course here in 1966, he took full advantage of the views of azure waves crashing on black lava rocks; watch for the blowhole by No. 13. Facilities include club rentals, driving range, a well-stocked pro shop, locker rooms, putting and chipping greens, and **The View** ★ restaurant (© **808/731-5033**), open for lunch and dinner (main courses $15–$29).

78-7000 Ali'i Dr., Kailua-Kona. www.konacountryclub.com. © **808/322-3431.** Greens fees $189 ($165 for Keauhou Resort guests), $125 after 1pm, $60 juniors (ages 8–17); 9 holes after 3pm $105.

Makalei Golf Club ★ This par-72, 18-hole upcountry course—some 1,800 to 2,850 feet in elevation—goes up and down through native forests, cinder cones, and lava tubes over its championship length of 7,091 yards. The signature hole is the par-3 No. 15, offering a distant view of Maui and the best chance for a hole-in-one. A local favorite, Makalei is visited by wild peacocks, pheasants, turkeys, and the occasional wild pig. Facilities include driving range, putting greens, and club rentals (drop-off and pickup available). The golf shop and **Peacock Grille** ★ restaurant, which normally offers a full bar and a menu of burgers, salads, and snacks, have been closed while a new clubhouse is under construction. It's due to open by 2025.

72-3890 Hawai'i Belt Rd. (Māmalahoa Hwy./Hwy. 190), Kailua-Kona. www.makalei. com. © **808/325-6625.** Greens fees $109 before noon, $89 noon to 2, $59 2–4pm (carts must return by 5:30pm). From the intersection of Palani Rd. and Hwy. 11 in Kailua-Kona, take Palani Rd. (which becomes Hwy. 190) east 7¼ miles, and look for green gates and a small white sign on the right.

Makani Golf Club ★★ Formerly known as the Big Island Country Club, this renovated, par-72, 18-hole course showcases sweeping views of towering Mauna Kea and the bright blue coastline from its perch 2,000 feet above sea level. Designer Perry Dye included water features around nine of the holes, including the spectacular par-3 No. 17. Waterfalls, tall palms, and other lush greenery add to the tropical feel; look for native birds such as the nēnē (Hawaiian geese), hawks, stilts, and black-crowned night herons. The wide fairways and gently rolling terrain make it appropriate for players of every level—one reason kids ages 8 to 15 only "pay their age" (for example, an 8-year-old golfer pays $8) after 1pm. Facilities include club rentals, driving range, pro shop, lounge, and snack bar.

71-1420 Māmalahoa Hwy. (Hwy. 190), Kailua-Kona. www.makanigolfclub.com. © **808/ 325-5044.** Green fees Fri–Sun $135 morning, $115 afternoon; Mon–Thurs $119 morning, $99 afternoon, $55 for 9 or 11 holes after 2pm; $30 juniors.

THE KOHALA COAST

Hapuna Golf Course ★★★ Since its opening in 1992, this 18-hole championship course has been named the most environmentally sensitive course by *Golf* magazine, as well as "Course of the Future" by the U.S. Golf Association. Designed by Arnold Palmer and Ed Seay, the links-style course extends nearly 6,900 yards from the shoreline to 700 feet above sea level, with views of the pastoral Kohala Mountains and the coastline; look for Maui across the channel from the signature 12th hole. The elevation changes on the course keep it challenging (and windier the higher you go). There are a few elevated tee boxes and only 40 bunkers. Facilities include putting and chipping greens, driving range, practice bunker, lockers, showers, a pro shop, and rental clubs. The clubhouse is also home to **Islander Sake Brewery ★★**, which offers a brewery tour with bento box lunch ($43) and serves sake-pairing dinners ($75).

At the Westin Hapuna Beach Hotel, 62-100 Kauna'oa Dr., off Hwy. 19 (*mauka* exit near mile marker 69). www.maunakearesort.com/golf/hapuna-golf-course. ℂ **808/ 880-3000.** $225; $165 after 1pm, 9 holes $100; all juniors (17 and under) $60.

Mauna Kea Golf Course ★★★ This breathtakingly beautiful, par-72, 7,114-yard championship course designed by Robert Trent Jones, Jr., and later updated by son Rees Jones, has been consistently rated one of the top golf courses in the United States. Renovations began in 2024 but are unlikely to change its signature 3rd hole. The Pacific Ocean and shoreline cliffs stand between the tee and the green, giving every golfer, from beginner to pro, a real challenge on the 175-yard hole. Book ahead; the course is very popular, especially for early weekend tee times. Facilities include a pro shop and a clubhouse. **Number 3 ★** restaurant is named for the hole that Jones, Sr., once called "the most beautiful in the world," and has tasty fish tacos, sliders, and other casual fare.

At the Mauna Kea Beach Hotel, 62-100 Mauna Kea Beach Dr., off Hwy. 19 (*makai* exit near mile marker 68). www.maunakearesort.com/golf/mauna-kea-golf-course. ℂ **808/882-5400.** Greens fees $295 ($260 resort guests); $220 after 11am ($195 resort guests), 9 holes $185 ($160 resort guests); all juniors (17 and under) $110.

Mauna Lani Francis H. I'i Brown Championship Courses ★★★ Carefully wrapped around ancient trails, fishponds, and petroglyphs, the two 18-hole courses here have won *Golf* magazine's Gold Medal Award every year since the honor's inception in 1988. The **South Course,** a 7,029-yard, par-72, has two unforgettable ocean holes: the over-the-water 15th hole and the downhill, 221-yard, par-3 No. 7, which is bordered by the sea, a salt-and-pepper sand dune, and lush kiawe trees. The **sunset golf cart tour** ($45 for two people in one cart) visits both, along with other beautiful stops. The **North Course** may not have the drama of the oceanfront holes, but because it was built on older lava flows, the more extensive indigenous vegetation gives the course a Scottish feel. The hole that's cursed the most is the 140-yard, par-3 17th: It's beautiful but plays right into the surrounding lava field. Facilities include two driving ranges, a golf shop (with teaching pros), a restaurant, and putting greens. Mauna Lani also has the island's only *keiki* (children's) course, the 9-hole

WikiWiki walking course for juniors, beginners, and families (golfers under 14 must be with an adult).

At the Mauna Lani, an Auberge Resort, Mauna Lani Dr., off Hwy. 19 (20 miles north of Kona Airport). https://aubergeresorts.com/maunalani/experiences/golf. © **808/885-6655.** $275 before 1pm; $180 after 1pm; juniors 15 and under free after 3pm (free clubs all day). WikiWiki course: $39 adults (plus $15 for 3 clubs), $29 for ages 15 and under. Dynamic pricing.

Waikoloa Beach Resort Courses ★★ Three 9-hole courses beckon here, allowing you to mix-and-match for an 18-hole round. Designer Robert Trent Jones, Jr., created the original 18-hole course that's been halved into the par-35, 3,281-yard **Beach Nine,** while Tom Weiskopf and Jay Morrish created the original 18 holes that led to today's par-36, 3,522-yard **Kings' Nine.** Carefully placed bunkers see a lot of play, courtesy of the ever-present trade winds. The **Lakes Nine,** part of the original Beach Course, incorporates the elevation changes of the lava beds in the area; it's par 35 and 3,285 yards. Facilities include a golf shop and a practice range (with free clubs and unlimited balls for just $15). *Tip:* Check online for discounts and family packages.

At the Waikoloa Beach Resort, 600 Waikoloa Beach Dr., Waikoloa. www.waikoloa beachgolf.com. © **808/886-7888.** $200 ($162 for resort guests), $139 11am–1pm, $108 1pm to sunset. $89 for 9 holes after 11am. $75 juniors (ages 6–17).

Waikoloa Village Golf Course ★ This semiprivate 18-hole course, with a par-72 for each of the three sets of tees, is hidden in the town of Waikoloa, next to the Paniolo Greens resort, 6½ miles uphill from Hwy. 19. Overshadowed by the resort courses of the Kohala Coast, it's nevertheless a beautiful course with some terrific views. The wind plays havoc with your game here (like most Hawai'i courses). Robert Trent Jones, Jr., in designing this challenging course, inserted his trademark sand traps, slick greens, and great fairways. The par-5, 490-yard 18th hole is a thriller: It doglegs to the left, and the last 75 yards up to the green are water, water, water. Enjoy the views of Mauna Kea and Mauna Loa, and—on a clear day—Maui's Haleakala. **Johnny's Restaurant** ★ provides hearty options for refueling after a round; it's open Monday to Saturday 9am to 8pm and Sunday 8am to 8pm.

In Waikoloa Village, 68-1793 Melia St., Waikoloa. www.thevillagecourse.com. © **808/883-9621.** $135 before 2pm; $110 after 2pm; $65 children ages 7–17.

HILO

Hilo Municipal Golf Course ★ This 146-acre course is great for the casual golfer: It's flat, scenic, and often fun. Just don't go after heavy rain (especially in winter); the fairways can get really soggy and play can slow way down. The rain does keep the 18-hole course green and beautiful, though. Wonderful trees (monkeypods, coconuts, eucalyptus, and banyans) dot the grounds, and the views—of Mauna Kea on one side and Hilo Bay on the other—are breathtaking. There are four sets of tees, with a par-71 from all; the back tees give you 6,325 yards of play. It's the only municipal course on the island, so getting a tee time can be a challenge; it's open daily 7am to 6pm, but weekdays are the best bet. Facilities include a driving range, pro shop, club rentals, the excellent value-priced **Fairway Grill** ★★ restaurant, and snack bar.

340 Haihai St. (btw. Kino'ole and 'Iwalani sts.), Hilo. www.parks.hawaiicounty.gov/facilities-parks/hilo-municipal-golf-course. ℂ **808/959-7711.** $42 Mon–Fri, $50 Sat–Sun (closed Dec 25 and Jan 1); carts $24 for 2 riders, $15 for 1, for 18 holes; carts $15/$8 for 9 holes.

Naniloa Golf Course ★   At first glance, this semiprivate 9-hole course just off Hilo Bay looks pretty flat and short, but once you get beyond the 1st hole—a wide, straightforward 330-yard par-4—things get challenging. The tree-lined fairways require straight drives, and the huge lake on the 2nd and 5th holes is sure to haunt you. It's somewhat neglected, so only bargain hunters should seek it out. Facilities include a driving range, putting green, pro shop, and club rentals. *Note:* At night, the driving range becomes **Cosmic Drive** ★ (https://cosmicdrivehi.com; ℂ 808/427-3996), a fun challenge with whimsical glowing targets that make noise when you hit them; you get 75 glowing balls per 1-hr session ($40–$44).

120 Banyan Dr. (at the intersection of Hwy. 11 and Hwy. 19), Hilo. ℂ **808/935-3000.** $14 adults, $9 seniors 62 and over, $5 kids 16 and under. Carts $12.

VOLCANO VILLAGE

Volcano Golf Course ★★   The island's first and oldest golf course, opened in 1921 with just three holes in a pasture, is now an 18-hole beauty in the cool rainforest at 4,000 feet of elevation on the slope of the active Kīlauea volcano. Framed by views of the often snow-topped, dormant Mauna Kea and the active Mauna Loa volcanoes, its mostly flat, manicured greens with elevated tees are visited by nēnē (the native goose) and kalij pheasant, a colorful crested bird with distinctive red patch around the eyes, introduced in 1962 as a gamebird. You'll need to keep your eyes on the Norfolk pines marking the dogleg turn on the 4th hole, the toughest on the par-72, 6,547-yard course, currently managed by a subsidiary of Troon, the leading golf management company. It's owned by Kamehameha Schools, whose plans to replace a clubhouse that burnt down in 2019 were delayed by the pandemic and are still in process; a temporary, portable pro shop and snack shop are on site for now.

99-1621 Pi'i Mauna Dr., Volcano. www.volcanogc.com. ℂ **808/319-4745.** Mon–Thurs 18 holes $60 before 2pm, 9 holes $52 after 2pm; Fri–Sun 18 holes $56 before 2pm, 9 holes $46 after 2pm. Carts $15 for 9 holes for single rider ($24 for 2), $20 for 18 holes for single rider ($30 for 2); pushcarts $5. Driving range $3. Rental clubs $25.

Hiking

Trails on Hawai'i Island wind through fields of coastal lava rock, deserts, rainforests, and mountain tundra, sometimes covered with snow. It's important to wear sturdy shoes, sunscreen, and a hat, and take plenty of water; for longer, more remote hikes, it may be essential to bring food, a flashlight, and a trail map—not one that requires a cellphone signal to access (coverage may be nonexistent). Hunting may be permitted in rural, upcountry, or remote areas, so stay on the trails and wear bright clothing. Please, leave no trace and do not stack rocks, no matter how many piles you see—stacking disturbs beach and lava ecosystems, disrespects local cultural traditions, and in some cases can disorient hikers using official cairns.

The island has 26 hiking trails and access roads in the state's **Nā Ala Hele Trail & Access System** (https://hawaiitrails.hawaii.gov; ✆ **808/974-4382**), highlights of which are included below; see the website for more information. For detailed descriptions of some 60 trails on a variety of public lands, see **www.bigislandhikes.com**.

NORTH KONA

The **Puʻuwaʻawaʻa Cinder Cone Trail** is a 3.2-mile trail with 2,000 feet of elevation winding through native dryland forest to the top of the island's largest cinder cone, where Hawaiians once quarried for pumice and obsidian. This distinctively furrowed "jelly mold," just off the Māmalahoa Highway (Hwy. 190) between Kailua-Kona and Waimea, is the result of a 110,000-year-old eruption on the slopes of Hualālai. Visible from much of North Kona and South Kohala, the cinder cone offers spectacular views from Maui to Mauna Kea to Kona. A working cattle ranch is at its base, with sheep and goats nibbling grasses next to the paved road and lava rock trail from the parking lot, about 1½ miles to the start of the ascent to the 3,967-foot summit.

KOHALA COAST

The **Ala Kahakai National Historic Trail** (www.nps.gov/alka; ✆ **808/326-6012**, ext. 101) is part of an ancient, 175-mile series of paths through coastal lava rock, from Upolu Point in North Kohala along the island's west coast to Ka Lae (South Point) and east to Puna's Wahaʻula Heiau, an extensive temple complex. Some were created as long-distance trails, others for fishing and gathering, while a few were reserved for royal or chiefly use. There's unofficial access through the four national park sites—Puʻukoholā Heiau, Kaloko-Honōkohau, Puʻuhonua O Hōnaunau, and Hawaiʻi Volcanoes (see "Attractions & Points of Interest," on p. 181)—but it's easy, free, and fun to walk a portion of the 15½-mile stretch between Kawaihae and ʻAnaehoʻomalu Bay, part of the state's **Nā Ala Hele** trails system. Signs mark only the 8-mile portion of Ala Kahakai between Ōhaiʻula Beach at **Spencer Park** (p. 224) through Puakō to **Holoholokai Beach Park,** near the petroglyph field on the Mauna Lani Resort, but it's fairly simple to follow farther south by hugging the shoreline, past resort hotels and multimillion-dollar homes, anchialine ponds, and jagged lava formations.

SADDLE ROAD (HWY. 2000)

The state's **Nā Ala Hele** trails system (https://hawaiitrails.hawaii.gov) also includes several great choices for stretching your legs along Saddle

Road, the fastest route between Hilo and Kona. Just keep in mind that at 5,000 to 6,000 feet in elevation, this area can turn very cool and misty quickly. The **Puʻu Huluhulu Trail** is an easy, 1-mile hike that gradually loops around both crests of this forested cinder cone, with panoramic views of Mauna Kea and Mauna Loa between the trees. A parking lot is in front of the hunter check-in station at the junction of the Mauna Loa observatory access road and Saddle Road. *Note:* There's a similarly named trail, albeit spelled as one word, in Hawaiʻi Volcanoes National Park. The **Kaulana Manu Nature Trail** is a relatively flat, 1-mile hike starting near a paved parking lot at the 21-mile marker on the north side of Saddle Road. Learn about the native forest and native birds (*manu*), such as the bright red ʻapapane and the russet-hued ʻelepaio, through nine interpretive panels and 25 plant identification signs. The loop through a *kīpuka,* a natural area surrounded by lava, also offers several viewing platforms with impressive mountain views on clear days. The more strenuous but still moderate **Puʻu ʻŌʻō Trail,** at the 23-mile marker on the south side of Saddle Road, heads 3¾ miles inland over lava flows from 1855 and 1881, through several forested *kīpuka* with native flora and fauna.

THE HĀMĀKUA COAST

The 1-mile "hike" down the 25% grade road to **Waipiʻo Valley** (p. 200) is no longer permitted for safety reasons. It's a killer on the knees, and no picnic coming back up. Save your strength for the 18-mile round-trip adventure of the **Muliwai Trail,** a strenuous hike to primeval, waterfall-laced **Waimanu Valley.** This often-overgrown trail is the island's closest rival to Kauaʻi's **Kalalau Trail** (p. 549), and should only be attempted by very physically fit, environmentally conscious, and well-prepared hikers. For visitors, the journey begins by arranging with the **Waipiʻo Valley Shuttle** (p. 201) to take you down and pick you up. If you're camping overnight, you'll need a permit for one of Waimanu Valley's nine sites (see "Camping," p. 274); plan to leave your car at the shuttle pickup, **Waipiʻo Valley Artworks,** 48-5416 Kukuihaele Rd., Honokaʻa (www.waipivalley artworks.com; ℂ **808/775-0958**), for an additional $20 per night. Waipiʻo Valley, you must follow the beach to Wailoa Stream, ford it, and cross the dunes to the west side of the valley. There the zigzag Muliwai Trail officially begins, carving its way some 1,200 feet up the cliff; the reward at the third switchback is a wonderful view of Hiʻilawe Falls. Ahead lie 5 miles and a dozen tree-covered gulches to cross before your first view of pristine Waimanu Valley. The campground has two outhouses, but no drinking water. The trail is eroded in places and slippery when wet—which is often, due to frequent rains, which can also flood streams. No wonder the vast majority of those who see Waimanu Valley do so via helicopter (p. 215).

HAWAIʻI VOLCANOES NATIONAL PARK

This magnificent national treasure and Hawaiian cultural icon (p. 209) has more than 150 miles of trails, including many day hikes, most of which are well-maintained and well-marked; a few are paved or have board-walks, permitting strollers and wheelchairs. *Warning:* If you have heart or respiratory problems or if you're pregnant, don't attempt any hike in the park; the fumes may bother you. Also: Stacked rocks known as *ahu* mark trails crossing lava; please do not disturb or create your own.

Plan ahead by downloading maps and brochures on the park website (www.nps.gov/havo), which also lists areas closed due to previous or current eruptions. Always check conditions with the rangers at the Kīlauea Visitor Center, where you can pick up detailed trail guides. *Note:* All overnight backcountry hiking or camping requires a $10 permit, available only the day of or the day before your hike, from the park's **Backcountry Office** (✆ **808/985-6178**).

In addition to the sights described on the **Crater Rim Drive** tour (p. 210) and **Chain of Craters Road** tour (p. 212), here are some of the more accessible highlights for hikers, all demonstrating the power of Pele:

DEVASTATION TRAIL ★★★   Up on the rim of Kīlauea Iki Crater, you can see what an erupting volcano did to a once-flourishing 'ōh'ia forest. The scorched earth with its ghostly tree skeletons stands in sharp contrast to the rest of the lush forest. Everyone can take this 1-mile round-trip hike on a paved path across the eerie bed of black cinders. Trailheads are on Crater Rim Road at Pu'upua'i Overlook and the intersection with Chain of Craters Road.

KĪPUKAPUAULU (BIRD PARK) TRAIL ★   This easy 1.2-mile round-trip hike lets you see native Hawaiian flora and fauna in a little oasis of living nature in a field of lava, known as a *kīpuka*. For some reason, the once red-hot lava skirted this mini-forest and let it survive. Go early in the morning or in the evening (or, even better, just after a rain) to see native birds like the 'apapane (a small, bright-red bird with black wings and tail) and the 'i'iwi (larger and orange-vermilion colored, with a curved salmon-hued bill). Native trees along the trail include giant 'ōh'ia, koa, soapberry, kolea, and māmane.

PU'UHULUHULU ★★★   This moderate 3-mile round-trip to the summit of a cinder cone (which shares its name, in a slightly different spelling, with Pu'u Huluhulu on Saddle Rd., described above) crosses lava flows from the 1970s, lava tree molds, and *kīpuka*. At the top is a vista of Mauna Loa, Mauna Kea, the coastline, and the vent of Pu'u 'Ō'ō, drained of lava in 2018 but still emitting steamy wisps. The trailhead is in the Maunaulu parking area on Chain of Craters Road, 8 miles from the visitor center. Download a trail guide at www.nps.gov.havo/planyourvisit/upload/mauna_ulu_trail_guide.pdf or, if available on-site, pick up one for $2. (*Note:* Sulfur fumes may be stronger here than on other trails.)

At the end of Chain of Craters Road, a 1¼-mile stretch of pavement leads to the 8-mile **emergency access gravel road ★★** to Kalapana, overrun midway by a 2016 lava flow; the first few miles have interpretive signs. For avid trekkers, several long, steep, unshaded hikes lead to the beaches and rocky bays on the park's remote shoreline; they're all overnight backcountry hikes and require a permit. *Note:* The 19.5-mile **Mauna Loa Trail,** perhaps the most challenging hike in all of Hawai'i due to the risk of high-altitude sickness or becoming lost in snowy or foggy conditions; only the first 10.2 miles (including its two high-altitude cabins) were open at press time, due to the effects of the eruption at the volcano's summit in December 2022. Check www.nps.gov/havo for updates.

Horseback Riding

Although vast Parker Ranch, the historic center of Hawaiian ranching, no longer offers horseback tours, several other ranches in upcountry Waimea provide opportunities for riding with sweeping views of land and sea. *Note:* Most stables require riders to be at least 8 years old and weigh no more than 230 pounds; confirm before booking.

The 11,000-acre Ponoholo Ranch, whose herd of cattle (varying between 6,000 and 8,000) is second only to Parker Ranch, is the scenic home base for **Paniolo Adventures** (www.panioloadventures.com; ℂ **808/889-5354**). Most of its five rides are open-range style and include brief stretches of trotting and cantering, although the gorgeous scenery outweighs the equine excitement—all but the 4-hour Wrangler Ride ($225, for ages 12 and older) are suitable for beginners and open to ages 8 and older. The tamest option is the 1-hour City Slicker ride ($120), but the 1½-hour Sunset Ride ($135) is the most popular. Boots, light jackets, Australian dusters, chaps, helmets, hats, drinks, and even sunscreen are provided. Look for Paniolo Adventures' barn on Kohala Mountain Road (Hwy. 250), just north of mile marker 13, between Waimea and Kapa'au.

Na'alapa Stables (www.naalapastables.com; ℂ **808/889-0022**) operates rides at Kahua Ranch, which also has an entrance on Kohala Mountain Road, north of mile marker 11. Riding open-range style, you'll pass ancient Hawaiian ruins, through lush pastures with grazing sheep and cows, and along mountaintops with panoramic coastal views. The horses and various riding areas are suited to everyone from first-timers to experienced equestrians. There are several trips daily: a 2½-hour tour at 10am and 12:30pm for $150, and a 1½-hour tour at 9am and 2:30pm for $110; check-in is a half-hour earlier.

Enjoy a swim or paddle at breathtaking, triple-tiered Umauma Falls and scenic vistas of Mauna Kea and the bright Pacific from horseback on the 2½-hour **Waterfall Swim & Trail Ride** offered by **Wailea Horseback Adventure** (www.waileahorsebackadventure.com; ℂ **808/775-1007**). Rides (105 min. in the saddle, 45 min. at the falls) go out Monday to Saturday at 9am and 12:30pm with a minimum of two riders and a maximum of 10; the cost is $145 per guest, and an adult must accompany any rider younger than 18.

Tennis & Pickleball

KONA

You can play well into the balmy night at Kona's **Hōlua Racquet and Paddle** (www.holuaracquetandpaddle.com; ✆ **808/989-4611**) thanks to seven lighted tennis courts and 20 lighted pickleball courts—the largest such facility in the state. Hidden inside Hōlua at Mauna Loa Village (78-7190 Kaleiopapa St., Kailua-Kona), the private club with pro shop allows the public to rent tennis courts for $25 per hour. Nonmembers who want to drop into the daily open pickleball sessions pay $10 for one session; if you come back for an afternoon or evening after paying for the morning session, you'll pay $5 for the second round. Seven- and 10-session passes are available for $60 and $80, respectively.

You can also play for free at any Hawai'i County tennis or pickleball court (many are dual-striped). For those in Kailua-Kona, the four lighted tennis courts and four dedicated pickleball courts at **Old Kona Airport Park** (p. 221) offer the best experience.

KOHALA COAST

The **Seaside Tennis Club** (✆ 808/882-5420) at the Mauna Kea Beach Hotel (p. 263) is frequently ranked among the world's finest for good reason: Three of its nine tennis courts ($35 per person) are right on the ocean, and all enjoy beautiful landscaping; there are also eight pickleball courts ($25 per person) and a full-service pro shop. The downside: Access is for guests only.

Just as highly ranked, but luckily still open to the public, the **Hawai'i Tennis Center** (✆ 808/887-7532) at the Fairmont Orchid, Hawai'i (p. 265) offers 10 tennis courts (including one stadium court), a pro shop, rental rackets and ball machines, daily hour-long clinics at 9am, and lessons. Tennis courts are $30 per person for all-day play. Two not-so-nice pickleball courts ($15 per person, per hour) and inexpensive rental gear are also available by reservation. Also on the Mauna Lani Resort, the recently refreshed, full-service **Cliff Drysdale Tennis Garden** at the Mauna Lani Sports and Fitness Club, 68 Pauoa Rd., Kamuela (https://cliffdrysdale.com/mauna-lani-resort; ✆ **808/885-7765**), allows public access to its six tennis courts ($25 per hour) and four pickleball courts ($25 per person per hour), most of which are lighted; you just can't reserve them in advance, although guests of the Auberge-managed Mauna Lani (p. 264) and club members can. Drop-in pickleball socials typically take place Saturday to Monday and Thursday from 4 to 5:30pm.

The two lighted tennis courts at **Waimea Park,** at the intersection of Kawaihae and Lindsey roads in Waimea, are the best free options near the Kohala resorts.

Yoga

As with most resort hotels in Hawai'i, those on the Kohala Coast offer frequent classes for guests and drop-ins, typically starting at $20 to $25 an hour. In the Queens' Marketplace at Waikoloa Beach Resort, 69-201 Waikoloa Beach Dr., **Yoga Barre Hawaii** (www.yogabarrehawaii.com; ✆ **808/209-0043**) is a convenient non-hotel alternative for yoga devotees on the Kohala Coast. Its indoor and outdoor classes ($20, five-class pass $70) include Buti yoga, heated yoga, Vinyasa flow, Pilates, barre, and other techniques; there's also a shop and cafe in case you forgot your Lululemon leggings or yoga mat, or need an espresso or açai bowl as a pick-me-up afterward.

In Kailua-Kona, **Yoga Nest,** 75-159 Lunapule Rd. (www.theyoganesthi.com; ✆ **808/315-8675**), offers a full schedule of Hatha, Vinyasa, Yin, and restorative yoga and meditation classes. Drop-in rates are $25 a class, with multi-class passes starting at $55 for three classes; a 30-day pass with unlimited classes costs $140. If you forgot your mat, rentals are just $3. For more body positivity, book a massage treatment ($90 for 60 minutes) or a 1-hour reiki session ($77).

Ziplining

Ziplining gives Hawai'i Island visitors an exhilarating way to view dramatic gulches, thick forests, gushing waterfalls, and other inspiring scenery—without significantly altering the landscape. Typically, the pulley-and-harness systems have redundant safety mechanisms, with lines and gear inspected daily and multiple checks of your equipment during the tour; your biggest worry may be losing your cellphone or anything not in a zipped pocket. Most outfitters also rent GoPro video cameras that attach to your helmets, so you can relive your whizzing rides at home.

Note: For safety reasons, tours have minimum ages (listed below) and/or minimum and maximum weights; read the fine print carefully before booking. Prices reflect online booking discounts.

NORTH KOHALA The Australian eucalyptus and native kukui trees on **Kohala Zipline's Canopy Tour** ★★ (www.kohalazipline.com; ✆ **808/331-3620**) might not provide the most colorful panoramas, but this nine-line adventure ($225 adults, $200 kids 8–12) emphasizes eco-awareness and cultural history in a compelling way—and the extra-quiet ziplines and multiple suspension bridges are a hoot, too. You'll fly from platform to platform in a sylvan setting that includes ancient taro terraces believed to have been farmed by a young Kamehameha. Tours depart from the zip station on Highway 270 between Hāwī and Kapa'au daily from 8am to 2pm. For a very special splurge, take the outfitter's 8-hour **Kohala Zip & Dip** ★★★, which combines the Canopy Tour with Hawai'i Forest & Trail's fascinating Kohala Waterfalls Adventure (p. 217), including a waterfall swim and picnic overlooking Pololū Valley. The Zip & Dip tours ($299 ages 8 and up) depart from Queens' Marketplace in Waikoloa Beach Resort and Hawai'i Forest & Trail headquarters in Kailua-Kona, 74-5035 Queen Ka'ahumanu Hwy. (Hwy. 19, north of Kealakehe Pkwy).

HILO & THE HĀMĀKUA COAST **Hawai'i Zipline Tours** ★★ (zipline tourshawaii.com; ℂ **808/963-6353**) zips past the nearly 250-foot-tall **Kolekole Falls** in Honomū, 12 miles north of Hilo. The seven-line course builds in length and speed, while the well-informed guides share insights on local flora and fauna—including apple banana, taro, and wild pigs—and the area's history as a sugar plantation. Open to ages 10 and older, the 2½-hour tour costs $199. Want to see the falls without zipping? The company has added a **waterfall hiking tour** ($125, all ages) that showcases several otherwise-inaccessible waterfalls, including Kolekole; the educational, 2½-hour tour takes place Tuesday, Thursday, and Saturday at 8:30am.

The **Umauma Falls Zipline Tour** ★★★ (www.ziplinehawaii.com; ℂ **808/930-9477**) lives up to its name, where you see the captivating, three-tiered falls (p. 199) and 13 other smaller cascades as you zip along its 2-mile, nine-line course ($229 adults, $219 ages 4–10) in Hakalau, about 16 miles north of Hilo. The **Zip & Dip** option ($314 adults, $294 ages 4–10) includes an hour of kayaking and swimming under a waterfall, next to the region's only known petroglyph.

WHERE TO STAY ON HAWAI'I ISLAND

In addition to the lodgings below, you'll find numerous listings of condos and houses on sites such as VRBO.com and Airbnb.com. *Note:* While county legislation limiting such rentals in non-resort areas has started to reduce the number of vacation rentals, local resentment over unpermitted rentals remains high. To help you compare legally permitted units and complexes, as well as guarantee rapid assistance should issues arise during your stay, consider booking rentals that have professional management, or go through an island-based company, such as those listed for specific regions below.

Note: Rates do not include the state and county's combined 13.25% transient accommodations tax plus another 4.712% in general excise taxes. All rooms listed below have a private bathroom and free parking unless otherwise noted; all pools are outdoors. For vacation rentals, cleaning fees and damage protection waivers (an unfortunate new fee) are one-time charges, while any listed resort and parking fees are charged daily; all fees also incur general excise taxes and, unbelievably, some hotels are charging the transient accommodations tax on fees, too.

Tip: Due to the limited number of resort hotels on the Kohala Coast, the anonymous, deeply discounted deals on booking websites and apps such as Priceline and Hotwire will usually not disappoint when the name of your hotel is revealed post-booking. See the box "Internet or Apps for Hawai'i Hotel Discounts" on p. 602.

The Kona Coast

Many of the lodgings in Kailua-Kona and Keauhou are timeshares or privately owned condos; rates, decor, and amenities may vary widely by unit. For a broad selection of well-managed condos and a smaller selection of homes (most with pools), contact **Kona Vacation Rentals** (www.konarentals.com; ✆ **808/334-1199**) or **Knutson & Associates** (www.konahawaiirentals.com; ✆ **808/329-1010**). I especially appreciate that Knutson & Associates' website includes a page noting which complexes may be undergoing noise-causing renovations, and when, so you can avoid those dates or those properties when booking.

Note: Prices and minimum-stay rules may be considerably higher during the weeks around the Ironman World Championship (usually the second Sat in Oct), and during holidays.

CENTRAL KAILUA-KONA

In addition to the lodgings below, consider booking a condo at the **Royal Sea Cliff ★★**, on the ocean side of Ali'i Drive about 2 miles south of the Kailua Pier. There's no beach, but it has two oceanfront pools, often the site of free entertainment, and a tennis court. **Outrigger Hotels & Resorts** (www.outrigger.com; ✆ **800/688-7444** or 808/329-8021) manages a number of its 148 large, well-appointed air-conditioned units, ranging from studios (650 sq. ft., starting at $200 per night) up to two-bedroom, two-bathroom units (1,100–1,300 sq. ft., starting at $369), all with full kitchens and washer/dryers. Outrigger requires a 2-night minimum, and also charges cleaning fees of $214 to $314 and a $59 damage protection waiver. A new, moderately priced design hotel option, **Pacific 19 Kona ★★**, 76-5646 Palani Rd. (www.pacific19.com/kona; ✆ **808/334-8050**), sits just above the bay and busy Kailua Pier. A luxurious transformation of one wing of the former budget Kona Seaside Hotel, it offers custom wood furnishings, island photography, "macro bars" with locally sourced snacks, and quality linens in its 122 rooms, all with private lanais (from $103). Unusual for the island, it's also allows dogs. The $25 daily amenity fee includes two welcome drinks, daily poolside yoga, loaner bicycles and beach gear, and a discount at nearby **Cheeky Tiki** (see "Where to Eat," p. 275).

Expensive

Courtyard King Kamehameha's Kona Beach Hotel ★★★   This Courtyard Marriott–managed hotel lives up to its premium setting in front of King Kamehameha's royal compound on Kailua Bay—and it commands kingly prices now, too. A mural inspired by the blue ocean and rocky coastline adds color to the earth tones of the dark wood furniture and tropical prints in the decent-size rooms (330 sq. ft.). All have flatscreen TVs, updated bathrooms, a choice of two queen beds or king bed with sofa sleeper, and balconies. The high-ceilinged, bright lobby is home to a gallery of royal portraits and Hawaiian cultural scenes by the late Herb Kawainui Kāne. The hotel also hosts two championship tennis courts and

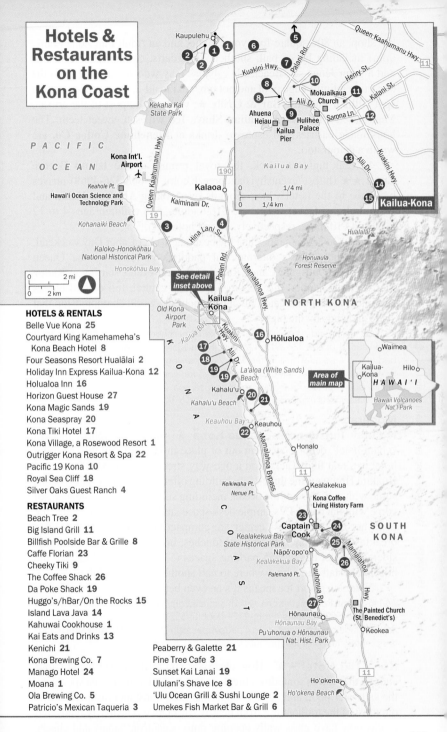

Hotels & Restaurants on the Kona Coast

Map labels

Kaupulehu

Queen Kaahumanu Hwy.

11

Kuakini Hwy.

Palani Rd.

Palani Rd.

Henry St.

Kalani St.

Mokuaikaua Church

Alii Dr.

Sarona Ln.

Ahuena Heiau

Hulihee Palace

Kailua Pier

Kailua Bay

Kuakini Hwy.

Alii Dr.

Kailua-Kona

0   1/4 mi
0   1/4 km

PACIFIC OCEAN

Kona Int'l. Airport

Keahole Pt.

Hawai'i Ocean Science and Technology Park

190

Kalaoa

Kohanaiki Beach

Kaiminani Dr.

Hina Lani St.

Kaloko-Honokōhau National Historical Park

Honokōhau Bay

Hualālai

Honuaula Forest Reserve

See detail inset above

Kailua-Kona

Old Kona Airport Park

Kailua Bay

Palani Rd.

Mamalahoa Hwy.

NORTH KONA

0   2 mi
0   2 km

K   O   N   A   C   O   A   S   T

Kuakini Hwy.

Alii Dr.

La'aloa (White Sands) Beach

Hōlualoa

Area of main map

Waimea

Kailua-Kona

Hilo

HAWAI'I

Hawaii Volcanoes Nat'l Park

Kahalu'u

Kahalu'u Beach

Keauhou Bay

Keauhou

Mamalahoa Bypass

Honalo

11

Keikiwaha Pt.

Nenue Pt.

Kealakekua

Kona Coffee Living History Farm

Caffe Florian

Captain Cook

SOUTH KONA

Kealakekua Bay State Historical Park

Nāpo'opo'o

Kealakekua Bay

Palemanō Pt.

Puʻuhonua Rd.

Mamalahoa Hwy.

The Painted Church (St. Benedict's)

Keokea

Hōnaunau

Hōnaunau Bay

Pu'uhonua o Hōnaunau Nat. Hist. Park

11

Ho'okena

Ho'okena Beach

HOTELS & RENTALS

Belle Vue Kona **25**
Courtyard King Kamehameha's Kona Beach Hotel **8**
Four Seasons Resort Hualālai **2**
Holiday Inn Express Kailua-Kona **12**
Holualoa Inn **16**
Horizon Guest House **27**
Kona Magic Sands **19**
Kona Seaspray **20**
Kona Tiki Hotel **17**
Kona Village, a Rosewood Resort **1**
Outrigger Kona Resort & Spa **22**
Pacific 19 Kona **10**
Royal Sea Cliff **18**
Silver Oaks Guest Ranch **4**

RESTAURANTS

Beach Tree **2**
Big Island Grill **11**
Billfish Poolside Bar & Grille **8**
Caffe Florian **23**
Cheeky Tiki **9**
The Coffee Shack **26**
Da Poke Shack **19**
Huggo's/hBar/On the Rocks **15**
Island Lava Java **14**
Kahuwai Cookhouse **1**
Kai Eats and Drinks **13**
Kenichi **21**
Kona Brewing Co. **7**
Manago Hotel **24**
Moana **1**
Ola Brewing Co. **5**
Patricio's Mexican Taqueria **3**
Peaberry & Galette **21**
Pine Tree Cafe **3**
Sunset Kai Lanai **19**
Ululani's Shave Ice **8**
'Ulu Ocean Grill & Sushi Lounge **2**
Umekes Fish Market Bar & Grill **6**

pro shop, an 800-square-foot yoga studio, and an Adult Fun Zone (9am–9pm) including bocce ball, shuffleboards, darts, cornhole, table tennis, and a giant Jenga set. Beachside cabanas may woo some away from the attractive infinity-edge pool and hot tub, next to all-day, oceanview dining spot **Billfish Poolside Bar & Grille ★**; while an outpost of the artisan, Maui-based **Ululani's Hawaiian Shave Ice** will sate sweet teeth. The housemade pastries and espresso drinks at **Menehune Coffee Co.** are worth a detour, too.

Several nights a week, the royal retinue of the **Island Breeze Luau ★★** (https://eventsbyislandbreeze.com; ✆ **808/326-4969**) arrives by canoe to the hotel's luau grounds overlooking **Ahuʻena Heiau** and **Kamakahonu Cove;** tickets are $169 adults, $85 children ages 4 to 12 ($20 and $10 more, respectively, during holidays).

Note: Outrigger canoes line the beach here over Labor Day weekend, when the hotel hosts international paddlers in town for the Queen Liliʻuokalani Outrigger Canoe Race, a series of events starting at Kailua Pier. In mid-October, this becomes Ironman central, full of buff bodies and international triathletes, all abuzz about the world championship that starts and ends by the pier.

75-5660 Palani Rd., Kailua-Kona. www.konabeachhotel.com. ✆ **888/236-2427** (reservations) or 808/329-2911. 452 units. From $354 for 2 queens or king with sofa bed (up to 4 people). Resort fee $22. Valet parking $45; parking $35. **Amenities:** Restaurant; bar; coffee shop; convenience store; coin laundry; fitness center; luau; infinity pool; hot tub; rental cars; room service; spa; 2 lighted tennis courts and pro shop; watersports equipment rentals; yoga studio; Wi-Fi.

Moderate

Holiday Inn Express Kailua-Kona ★ Its neutral-toned, modern "chain hotel" decor may seem out of place in Hawaiʻi, but this 75-room hotel is a real find. Tucked on a one-way street between Aliʻi Drive and Kuakini Highway, the three-story building offers surprisingly quiet rooms, some with a glimpse of the ocean, including suites with a sofa sleeper. All come with flat panel TVs, ample desk space, and gleaming bathrooms; the pool, hot tub, and fitness center are compact but also immaculate. The breakfast buffet may lack tropical touches, but it's free. The one downside: The hotel has just 55 parking spaces ($10) in a shared lot, but the hospitable staff can advise where to nab another spot if it's full.

Note: No resort fee means it's an even better value.

77-146 Sarona Rd., Kailua-Kona. www.hiexpress.com/kailua-kona. ✆ **855/373-5450** or 808/329-2599. 75 units. From $317 double; $321 suite; $334 oceanview suite. Rates include breakfast and up to 4 people per room. Parking $10. **Amenities:** Business center; fitness center; hot tub; laundry; pool; free Wi-Fi.

Kona Tiki Hotel ★★ How close are you to the ocean here? Close enough that waves sometimes break on the seawall, sending sea spray into the saltwater pool, and close enough that their constant crashing drowns out most of the traffic noise from nearby Aliʻi Drive. The newly renovated rooms now have glass walls opening onto oceanfront lanais and cheery

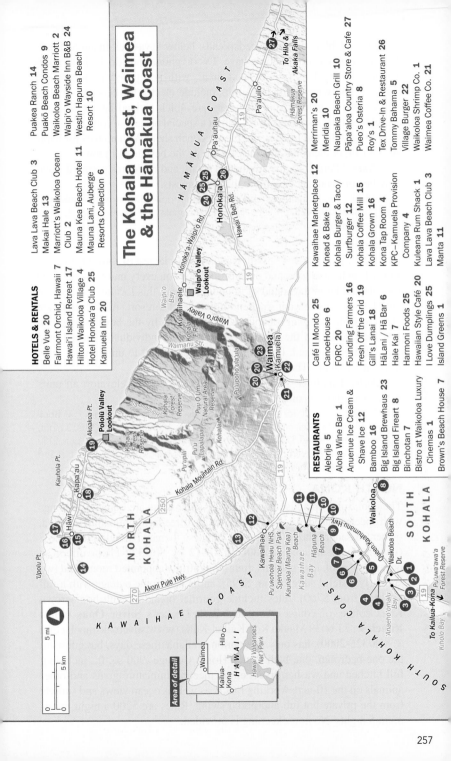

The Kohala Coast, Waimea & the Hāmākua Coast

yellow and blue tiki-print bedspreads below lava-rock-inspired head-boards. The 16 rooms don't have TV or phone, but do include mini-fridges, ceiling fans (you'll need them, with no air-conditioning), and kitchenettes (which in deluxe units include electric skillets and kitchen sinks). Warm, helpful staff members are quick to lend beach gear and travel tips; they also make every sunset a special occasion, enlisting guests to help light the tiki torches and blow a conch shell. With no fees for parking, Wi-Fi, or cleaning, this may be one of the best deals in town.

Note: "Petite" rooms are indeed small, and no rooms permit a rollaway bed or occupancy by more than two guests.

75-5968 Ali'i Dr., Kailua-Kona (about a mile from downtown). www.konatikihotel.com. ℂ **808/329-1425.** 16 units. From $289 double. 3-night minimum. Deposit required. **Amenities:** Pool; free Wi-Fi.

Inexpensive

Kona Magic Sands ★   With Kailua-Kona's largest (if somewhat fickle) sandy beach next door, and oceanfront lanais on every unit to soak in the sunsets and let in the sound of pounding waves, this location is ideal for couples who don't want to spend a bundle at a resort. All the units are studios, with the living/sleeping area bracketed by the lanai on one end and the kitchen on the other. Because they're individually owned, and individually managed, furnishings vary greatly unit to unit; corner units have larger lanais. The pool is also right on the ocean.

Note: This three-story building does not have an elevator; all units have small showers only.

77-6452 Ali'i Dr. (next to La'aloa/Magic Sands Beach Park), Kailua-Kona. Book through VRBO (13 units) or Airbnb (7 units). 37 units. VRBO rates from $180 a night, plus $160 host fee and $92 service fee. Airbnb rates from $200 a night, plus $130 cleaning fee and $160 Airbnb fee. **Amenities:** Pool; Magic's Grill restaurant, bar, and beach shack; free Wi-Fi.

NORTH KONA

The cool, rural uplands above central Kailua-Kona are home to lodgings with spectacular views. Part of a 30-acre coffee farm in quaint Hōlualoa, owner Cassandra Hazen's gorgeous, Balinese-themed **Holualoa Inn** ★★★ (www.holualoainn.com; ℂ **800/392-1812** or 808/324-1121) offers an oceanview pool, lush gardens, four thoughtfully appointed rooms and two similarly tasteful suites (from $595), and a handsome cottage with a full kitchen (from $760); rates include gourmet breakfast with homegrown Kona coffee, of course. Amy and Rick Decker's **Silver Oaks Guest Ranch** ★, 73-6039 Mauka Rd., Kailua-Kona (www.silveroaksranch.com; ℂ **808/325-2000**), has only one option available these days, but guests in the one-bedroom, one-bath Ranch House Cottage (900 sq. ft., including full kitchen and washer/dryer) enjoy meeting miniature goats and other animals on the 10-acre working ranch, as well as ocean views and sunsets from the private hot tub and porch swing. Rates are $200 a night, minimum 5 nights. No housekeeping is provided.

Very Expensive

Four Seasons Resort Hualālai ★★★ Sometimes you do get what you pay for—and that's just about anything you could desire at this serenely welcoming resort, only a 15-minute drive from the airport but worlds away from anything resembling hustle and bustle. The newly renovated rooms in the small clusters of two-story guestroom buildings and villa start at 635 square feet, with private lanais and large bathrooms outfitted with glass-walled showers and deep soaking tubs; ask for one with an outdoor lava-rock shower. All have ocean views or one of eight swimming pools; the adults-only Palm Grove Pool offers a swim-up bar and daybeds, but snorkeling in the protected Kings' Pond amid rays and tropical fish remains a top draw, especially with a new infinity pool and lounging area above. Dinner at **'Ulu Ocean Grill** ★★★ (p. 277) or the casual **Beach Tree** ★★ is consistently excellent, if costly; it can be hard to tear yourself away in search of cheaper options nearly a half-hour away. The resort's wine dinners and annual Chef Fest in November are also worth seeking out. Kudos to the Four Seasons for bucking the resort-fee trend, for not charging for its children's or cultural programs, and for numerous environmental measures.

Note: The 18-hole Jack Nicklaus signature golf course with virtual training options in its golf *hale* (hangout), excellent indoor/outdoor spa with water garden, and huge fitness center (including an Olympic-size pool) are open only to hotel guests and members.

72-100 Ka'ūpulehū Dr., Kailua-Kona. www.fourseasons.com/hualalai. © **888/340-5662** or 808/468-2050. 243 units. From $1,300 double; from $2,290 suite. Children 18 and under stay free in parent's room (maximum 3 guests per room). Valet parking $30; self-parking is free. **Amenities:** 5 restaurants; 2 bars; babysitting; kid's program; concierge; cultural center; fitness center; 18-hole golf course; 8 pools; 5 hot tubs; room service; spa; tennis and pickleball courts; watersports rentals; free Wi-Fi.

Presidential Villa at the Four Seasons Hualālai.

Kona Village, a Rosewood Resort ★★★   The original Kona Village debuted in 1965 as a collection of thatched-roof bungalows on a field of black lava next to a sandy crescent beach and tranquil Kahuwai Bay. It closed for more than a decade and reopened in 2023 after extensive rebuilding and renovation. Today's resort has an ultra-luxurious ambiance (reflected in very high rates that only include breakfast) and, in keeping with the original resort character, still no TVs. At the lowest price point are the 600-square-foot, garden- or mountain-view *hale* (bungalows) with outdoor shower, starting at $1,376 a night; similarly sized oceanview *hale* start at $1,567 (both with either king bed or two queens, rustic-chic furnishings, and locally made Hawaiian-themed artwork). At the higher end, and closer to the ocean, you'll find one- and two-bedroom *kauhale* bungalows (1,000 and 1,600 sq. ft., respectively), starting at $2,622. Is it worth mentioning the four-bedroom oceanfront residences with private pools that start at $13,500 a night? There's a dizzying array of options in between, too. Dining is generally exquisite and equally expensive at the signature, open-air **Moana ★★** restaurant and the more casual **Kahuwai Cookhouse ★★** (which accept non-guests by reservation only and depending on staffing and hotel occupancy). Two spacious infinity-edge pools, a lap pool, and *keiki* (children's) pool offer plenty of lounge chairs and room to splash; depending on where your bungalow is, you may want to take advantage of cart service or a loaner bicycle to make your way across the winding crushed-stone pathways. The best innovation of the new Kona Village, typically open to non-guests, may be **Asaya Spa ★★★** (*℮* **808/865-2530**), a state-of-the-art wellness oasis whose open-air treatment rooms appear to float in a sea of black lava with dreamy views of Hualālai.

72-300 Maheawalu Dr., Kailua-Kona. www.rosewoodhotels.com/kona-village. *℮* **808/865-0100.** 150 stand-alone units. From $1,376 double; from $2,622 suite (*kauhale*), including breakfast. Children 12 and under stay free in parent's room ($200 for third person 13 years and older). Valet parking $40; self-parking is free. **Amenities:** 2 restaurants, 3 bars; kid's program; concierge; cultural center; fitness center; gift shop; 4 pools; 3 hot tubs; market; room service; spa; tennis and pickleball courts; watersports rentals; free Wi-Fi.

KEAUHOU
Expensive
Outrigger Kona Resort & Spa ★★   The name and look have changed several times over the years, but the resort's oceanfront fantasy pool (one of two pools) and its views of manta rays in Keauhou Bay remain its prime draws. At press time, Outrigger was still planning a major renovation of rooms and public areas (including the currently closed **Rays on the Bay** restaurant). Families will appreciate the sandy-bottomed pool, water slide, and kid-pleasing fountain play area by the ocean. The majority of rooms have lanais, most with full or partial ocean views—all the better to ogle the manta rays that frequent this area, and humpback whales in season (Dec–Mar). Learn more about the former at

kona village THEN & NOW

Kona Village dates back to 1965, when it was opened "in the middle of nowhere," before the modern highway and airport were built. Several generations of guests socialized with each other during buffets and meals in the bungalow-style restaurants or over cocktails at the Shipwreck Bar (reclaimed from a sunken boat towed here) or the Talk Story Bar. In later years, its discreet location and no-phone, no-TV policy also attracted celebrities and business tycoons, including Apple founder Steve Jobs. But its bungalows were starting to look a little frayed, and its all-inclusive model was falling out of favor, by the time a tsunami destroyed most of its structures and ravaged the natural areas in 2011. (This was the same tsunami that devastated northeastern Japan and also inundated other low-lying parts of Kona.) This history helps explain the tightrope the redevelopers (including Laurene Powell Jobs, widow of Steve Jobs) and Rosewood management have walked trying to please former guests and attract new ones to the reimagined resort. Without constant lobbying by Kona Village's legion of devotees, including philanthropist Powell Jobs, the resort might never have returned.

the Manta Center and explore Hawaiian cultural activities at the Aloha Center, which also offers a guided walking tour of nearby historical sites. Book a club-level room to enjoy complimentary breakfast and afternoon drinks and hors d'oeuvres in the Voyager 47 Club Lounge.

78-128 'Ehukai St., Kailua-Kona. www.outrigger.com/kona. © **888/488-3535** or 808/930-4900. 509 units. From $463 double; from $710 suite. Resort fee $35. Valet parking $35; self-parking $25. Extra person or rollaway $65. Children 18 and under stay free in adult's room using existing bedding. **Amenities:** Restaurant; 2 bars; babysitting; rental cars and bikes; club lounge; concierge; fitness center; family center; twice-weekly luau; multilevel pool w/water slide; room service; spa; 2 tennis courts, basketball and volleyball courts; whirlpool; Wi-Fi.

Moderate

Kona Seaspray ★   Pay close attention to the details when booking a unit at this small condo complex across Ali'i Drive from bustling Kahalu'u Beach. The complex includes a three-story main building with eight, spacious two-bedroom/two-bathroom units and two one-bedroom units in an adjacent two-story building. In the main building, all offer ocean views (best from the top two floors), full kitchens, and washer/dryers, but some have been remodeled with granite counters in the kitchen and slate tiles on the lanai, while others look worn and dated. Optional air conditioning (a necessity during the day) may cost $10 extra per day, depending on your rental platform (including Hotels.com, Airbnb, and VRBO). A pretty, blue-tiled wall provides privacy for the ground-floor pool, with lounges and a hammock next to a grill and dining area. Brian and Gay Lena manage three of the more luxurious two-bedroom units (from $325 per night, plus $250 cleaning fee); view and book at www.bihiadventures.com or call © **931/200-2370** for more information.

78-6671 Ali'i Dr., Kailua-Kona. 10 units. Rates vary widely by rental platform. **Amenities:** Barbecue; pool; whirlpool spa; free Wi-Fi.

SOUTH KONA

This rural region of steeply sloping hills, often dotted with coffee and macadamia nut farms, may appeal to travelers who don't mind being far from the beach.

At the higher end, in every sense, **Horizon Guest House** ★★ (www.horizonguesthouse.com; ✆ 808/938-7822) offers four handsome suites ($325–$425, minimum 2- or 3-night stay) with private entrances and lanais on a 40-acre property, including a spacious infinity-edge pool and whirlpool spa, at 1,100 feet of elevation in Hōnaunau, 21 miles south of Kailua-Kona. Rates include a gourmet breakfast by hosts Clem and Angus, who also share great Kona tips on their website's blog. *Note:* Children 13 and under are not allowed

For much lower rates closer to town, but still great views, consider one of the two suites in **Belle Vue Kona** ★ (www.kona-bed-breakfast.com; ✆ 808/328-9898). The Orchid Suite has a living room with queen sofa bed, a bedroom with queen bed, breakfast room (microwave, fridge, toaster, coffeemaker, plus table and seating for four), and covered lanai; the Rose Garden Suite is similarly equipped, except the bedroom and living area are one room, with a king bed and queen sofa bed. Rates are $95 to $165 double occupancy; $25 per extra person. Like its companion Belle Vue in Waimea (p. 268), the furniture is dated but the price and location may be right for you.

The Kohala Coast

SOUTH KOHALA

There's no way around it: The three resort areas here are very costly, but the beaches, weather, amenities, and services are among the best in the state. Although you'll miss out on fabulous pools and other hotel perks, you can shave costs (and save money on dining) by booking a vacation rental. For some of the most affordable, rent one of the 38 **Puakō Beach Condos** ★★ in Puakō, a one-road, oceanfront town hidden between the Mauna Lani and Mauna Kea resorts. **Island Beach Rentals** (www.vacationbigisland.com; ✆ 808/882-7000) has some of the best units, including prime corner unit No. 101, offering three bedrooms, two remodeled baths, a well-stocked kitchen, two lanais, air-conditioning, and fun Hawaiian/tiki decor; its rates start at $209 (minimum 7 nights), plus $200 cleaning fee, but check for specials. The **Puakō General Store** is conveniently next door. Down the road is Bailey and Baki Wharton's spacious, ground-floor one-bedroom **Puakō Beach rental** ★ (www.vrbo.com/821534) with a large, screened porch; the rental is below their second-story home and runs $290 a night plus $200 cleaning fee and VRBO service fee (starting at $247 for 5 nights, the minimum rental stay).

South Kohala Management boasts 100-plus listings of condos and homes in the Mauna Lani, Mauna Kea, and Waikoloa Beach resorts (www.southkohala.com; © **800/822-4252** or 808/883-8500). **Outrigger Hotels & Resorts** also manages well-maintained condos and townhomes in six attractive complexes in the Mauna Lani and Waikoloa Beach resorts (www.outrigger.com; © **866/956-4262**). Be sure to factor in cleaning fees and additional-person charges when comparing rates. Some of my favorite units on the Mauna Lani resort are available through **Kona Coast Vacations** (www.konacoastvacations.com; © **808/329-2140**), which manages 32 properties out of 250 spread along the Kona and Kohala coasts. They include Mauna Lani Point's **Unit F106 ★★**, a ground-floor, 2 bedroom, 2½ bathroom, nearly 1,600-square-foot corner unit with a large lanai and ocean views (the shoreline lies 150 yards across a golf fairway). Handsomely renovated in 2022 with tropical hardwood cabinets, ceramic tile floors, and high-end appliances, it starts at $611 a night (a good deal for two couples traveling together), with a 5- to 10-night minimum. Rates include free covered parking and access to a private beach club, swimming pool, and hot tub, among other amenities.

The lively **Lava Lava Beach Club** restaurant and bar (www.lavalavabeachclub.com/bigisland/stay-play; © **808/769-5282**) also offers four luxurious, light-filled, and light-hearted **beach cottages ★★★** (from $565) on the sand at 'Anaeho'omalu Bay. They include kitchenettes, king beds, day beds, large lanais, air-conditioning, and whimsical decor, including a concert-size koa ukulele. Wrap yourself in your complimentary sarong ("lava lava") after an outdoor shower in a private garden. The bar stays open nightly until 10pm, with live music on a small lawn stage until 9pm; it's not too loud and the scene is all part of the fun of staying here. You'll enjoy the calm waters just outside your door; in the morning, take advantage of one of the stand-up paddleboards.

Very Expensive

Mauna Kea Beach Hotel ★★★   Old-money travelers have long flocked to Hawai'i's first golf-course resort, which began as a twinkle in Laurance Rockefeller's eye and in 1965 became the first hotel development on the rugged lava fields of the Kohala Coast. Known for exuding upscale tranquility with an uncluttered, Asian-inspired aesthetic, and its exclusive perch above lovely **Kauna'oa Beach ★★★** (p. 223), the resort recently embarked on the first major makeover in 15 years, adding a stand-alone destination spa and an adults-only infinity pool, renovating the golf course, updating all the restaurants, and refreshing the guest rooms; the phased work is expected to be complete by the second quarter of 2025. An array of cultural activities include Hawaiian language lessons and sunrise beach chants, while the views from the golf course (p. 244) and tennis center (p. 251), as well as from three of its four dining outlets, are glorious. The true pearls are the gracious staff members, many of whom know several generations of guests by name.

Note: The hotel is part of Marriott's Autograph Collection, but is owned by Prince Resorts, which also owns the **Westin Hapuna Beach Resort** (p. 266) and runs a shuttle between the two.

At the Mauna Kea Resort, 62-100 Mauna Kea Beach Dr., Kamuela. https://maunakea beachhotel.com. ✆ **866/977-4589** or 808/882-7222. 252 units. From $1,000 double; connecting rooms available. Extra person $95. Parking $35. **Amenities:** 4 restaurants; 3 bars; cafe; babysitting; seasonal kids' program; concierge; 18-hole golf course (p. 244); fitness center; luau; pool; hot tub; room service; spa; 10 tennis courts; 4 pickleball courts; watersports rentals; free Wi-Fi.

Mauna Lani, Auberge Resorts Collection ★★★

After a $100-million renovation and more than a year's closure, the 30-acre oceanfront resort formerly known as Mauna Lani Bay Hotel & Bungalows debuted in early 2020. Everything still seems brand-new, especially its sophisticated blend of Hawaiian culture and subtle, modern design. A bamboo forest, wooden platforms, and Hawaiian-inspired murals help soften the formerly airy but stark lower lobby, which includes an open-air living room overlooking the new all-ages, oceanfront pool (an adults-only pool is nearby). Understated rooms feature natural fabrics in subdued tones and midcentury modern-style furnishings. The best improvements are outside. At beachfront **CanoeHouse ★★★** (p. 281), the innovative Japanese/island-inspired menu relies on local seafood and produce, while **HāLani ★★** and the poolside **Hā Bar** offer casual, island-style cuisine with nightly live music and occasional hula. The monthly free "Twilight at Kalahuipua'a" program (p. 297) and also offers frequent classes and chats from the handsome new cultural center off the upper lobby. The sandy-entry kiddie pool sits next to the **Surf Shack ★**, which has friendly water experts and beach gear to get you in the ocean, and also serves delicious if pricey casual fare like lobster rolls and tater tots and drinks.

At the Mauna Lani Resort, 68-1400 Mauna Lani Dr., Puakō. https://aubergeresorts. com/maunalani. ✆ **808/657-3293** or 855/201-3179. 334 units. From $899 double; from $1,260 suite. Resort fee $50. **Amenities:** 4 restaurants; 2 bars; deli/gift shop; concierge; cultural programs; kids' program; fitness center; off-site fitness and tennis center w/lap pool; 2 pools; 2 hot tubs; room service; spa; watersports rentals; Wi-Fi.

Turtle celebration at the Mauna Lani.

Expensive

Fairmont Orchid, Hawai'i ★★★ The serenity of burbling water-falls and lush greenery at this hotel on the northern end of the Mauna Lani Resort create the definition of oasis. The resort also has a warm energy, thanks to popup beach bars (sponsored by the likes of Veuve Clicquot or Bruno Mars's rum company), eco-friendly initiatives supporting local bees and reefs, and a reinvigorated and expanded Hawaiian cultural program. Dining is first-rate, especially at **Binchotan** ★★ (p. 282), a lively Japanese-inspired grill and sushi bar. A toes-in-the-sand lunch with *liliko'i* margarita at casual **Hale Kai** ★★ is worth putting on your agenda, too. Traditional draws include the 10,000-square-foot swimming pool, the thatched-roof huts and oceanfront cabanas in the **Spa Without Walls** ★★, and the Hui Holokai Beach Ambassadors, who make guests feel at home in the water and on shore, teaching all kinds of Hawaiiana and sharing their knowledge about the area's cultural treasures, such as the nearby **Puakō Petroglyph Archaeological Preserve** (p. 193). The generously proportioned rooms (starting at 510 sq. ft.) with lanais offer subtle island accents such as rattan and carved wood, marble bathrooms, and other luxurious fittings, but are due for updating. Spring for an upgrade to the Gold Floor for a more intimate breakfast setting and tasty treats throughout the day.

At the Mauna Lani Resort, 1 N. Kanikū Dr., Kamuela. www.fairmont.com/orchid-hawaii. ✆ **800/845-9905** or 808/885-2000. 540 units. From $531 double; $1,183 Gold Floor double; from $1,498 suite. Extra person $75. Children 17 and under stay free in parent's room. Resort fee $48, includes self-parking, photo shoot, resort shuttle, various activities, and discounts. Valet parking $35. **Amenities:** 6 restaurants; 3 bars; babysitting; bike rentals; kids' program; concierge; 2 golf courses; gym; weekly luau (p. 298); pool; room service; spa; theater; 10 tennis courts (2 striped for pickleball); watersports rentals; Wi-Fi.

Hilton Waikoloa Village ★★ It's up to you how to navigate this 62-acre oceanfront Disneyesque golf resort, laced with fantasy pools, lagoons, and a profusion of tropical plants in between three low-rise towers (one now reserved for Hilton "vacation ownership" use). If you're in a hurry, take the Swiss-made air-conditioned tram; for a more leisurely ride, mahogany boats ply frond-lined canals with tropical fish. Or just walk a half-mile or so through galleries of priceless Asian and Pacific art and artifacts on your way to the ample-sized rooms designed for families. Among the best are the 161 rooms and eight suites in the Lagoon Tower's Makai section—all oceanview, with upgraded bathrooms and high-end bedding. Kids will want to head straight to the 175-foot water slide and 1-acre pool and might pester you to pony up for the Dolphin Quest encounter. The actual beach is rough, but the 4-acre, sand-fronted swimming lagoon that's home to sea turtles and other marine life—marvelous for protected snorkeling—more than makes up for it. Take note of the times for free crafts and ukulele lessons in the spacious cultural center, which is also where you pick up fish food for the daily feeding at the south end of the canal. Couples may want to splurge on steak and seafood at oceanfront, island-sourced **KPC–Kamuela Provision Co. ★★**, but prices at the other restaurants and the morning line at the coffee bar make it worth your while to go offsite. Luckily, you can unwind on-site at **Kona Tap Room ★**, which offers **Kona Brewing Co.'s** (p. 278) full lineup on tap.

69-425 Waikoloa Beach Dr., Waikoloa. www.hiltonwaikoloavillage.com. ℂ **800/445-8667** or 808/886-1234. 1,240 units. From $322 double; $544 suite. Resort fee $48. Extra person $50. Children 18 and under stay free in parent's room. Valet parking $55; Self-parking $48. **Amenities:** 9 restaurants; 5 bars; babysitting; bike rentals; kids' program; concierge; gym; 2 golf courses; luau (p. 298); 2 pickleball courts; 3 pools; whirlpools; room service; spa; 8 tennis courts; watersports rentals; Wi-Fi.

Waikoloa Beach Marriott Resort & Spa ★★ Of all the lodgings in the Waikoloa Beach Resort, this hotel has the best location on **'Anaeho'omalu Bay ★★** (nicknamed "A-Bay"; p. 222), with many rooms offering views of the crescent beach and historic fishponds; others look across the parking lot and gardens toward Mauna Kea. The luxury Na Hale wing (closest to the water) debuted in 2018 with larger rooms and suites, plus private outdoor showers on ground-floor lanais. Besides numerous beach watersports, kids enjoy the sandy-entrance children's pool, while adults delight in the heated infinity-edge pool, the open-air espresso bar **Aka'ula Lanai,** the two-level **Mandara Spa,** and the spacious, well-equipped fitness center. The light-hued rooms are also enticing, with glass-walled balconies and plush beds with down comforters in crisp white duvets. Families should book one of the spacious corner 'Ohana rooms, with a king-size bed and a sofa bed. Despite the daily resort fee ($30, including Wi-Fi and activities), this hotel usually offers the best prices of the Kohala Coast resorts.

Note: Even better values are found at **Marriott's Waikoloa Ocean Club ★★★**, handsome one- and two-bedroom timeshare suites with king beds, living rooms with sofa beds, and kitchenettes, with starting rates of $599 with advance purchase—plus free Wi-Fi, free parking ($10 valet), and no resort fee.

69-275 Waikoloa Beach Dr., Waikoloa. www.marriott.com. ℂ **888/236-2427** or 808/886-6789. 290 hotel units. From $429 double; $510 larger 'Ohana room; Nā Hale wing from $1,045 1-bedroom, from $2,770 2-bedroom. Resort fee $30. Parking $30. Children 17 and under stay free in parent's room. Rollaway bed $45. 112 Ocean Club units: 1-bedroom from $559, 2-bedroom from $793. Valet parking $10; self-parking is free. **Amenities:** Restaurant; 2 bars; babysitting; cafe; concierge; cultural activities; fitness center; Jacuzzi; luau; 3 pools; waterslide; rental-cars; room service; spa; watersports rentals; free Wi-Fi.

Westin Hapuna Beach Resort ★★★ Flying the Westin flag since 2018, this dramatically reshaped sister property to the Mauna Kea Beach Hotel has become a polished gem above the wide sands of **Hāpuna Beach** (p. 223). Its open-air entrance now cascades directly to its large, tropically landscaped pool complex that includes a new infinity pool just for adults, lined by koi ponds and recliners. All of its cafes, bars, and restaurants have also recently been reimagined. Grab an espresso or a cocktail and enjoy the view from **Piko** ★★ ("navel"), in the heart of the new lobby, or chow down on a burgers and sip *li hing* lemonade under trellises by the pool at **Naupaka Beach Grill** ★. Sunsets pair well with a cocktail, poke, or a flatbread pizza from **Meridia** ★★★ above the pool. Although one ocean-front wing has been converted to vacation condos, the remaining, sleekly refreshed rooms still start at 600 square feet, the largest standard rooms on the Kohala Coast, all with balconies and an ocean view. The sprawling, terraced grounds also host an 18-hole Arnold Palmer championship golf course (p. 243), **Islander Sake Brewery** (p. 244), a vast fitness center, and a spa. Service is always especially friendly here, from valets to waiters. Hopefully you won't need to use the urgent care service based here (see "Fast Facts," p. 180), but it's excellent too.

At the Mauna Kea Resort, 62-100 Kauna'oa Dr., Kamuela. www.westinhapunabeach. com. ✆ **800/882-6060** or 808/880-1111. 249 units. From $599 double; from $1,699 suite. Children 17 and under stay free in parent's room using existing bedding. Resort fee $37. Parking $30. **Amenities:** 4 restaurants; 2 bars; babysitting; gift shops; kids' program; concierge; golf course (p. 243); fitness center; pool; room service; spa; watersports rentals; Wi-Fi.

NORTH KOHALA

This rural area, steeped in Hawaiian history and legend, has few overnight visitors, given its distance from swimmable beaches and other attractions. But it does include two distinctive accommodations that reflect its heritage in unique ways. At eco-friendly **Puakea Ranch** ★★★ (www.puakearanch. com; ✆ **808/315-0805**), west of Hāwī and 400 feet above the coast, three plantation-era bungalows and a former cowboy bunkhouse have been beautifully restored as vacation rentals ($359–$729; 3- to 7-night minimum; $150–$200 cleaning fee). Sizes vary, as do amenities such as soaking tubs and swimming pools, but all have access to the organic farm produce and eggs, plus fast Wi-Fi. On the ocean bluff between Hāwī and Kapaʻau, hidden from the road, the "eco-boutique" **Hawaiʻi Island Retreat** ★★ (www. hawaiiislandretreat.com; ✆ **808/889-6336**) offers 10 posh guest rooms and three bungalows with large bathrooms and balconies ($425–$500 double; 2-night minimum). Clustered near the saltwater infinity pool are seven yurts (large tentlike structures) with private bathrooms and shared indoor/outdoor showers ($225 double). Rates include a sumptuous, homegrown organic breakfast; stay 2 nights or more for 20% off the normal rate.

Near North Kohala's southern end at windy, higher-elevation Kohala Ranch, **Makai Hale** ★★ bed-and-breakfast provides panoramic ocean and Maui views. Jerry and Audrey Maluo offer one modern guest suite with queen bed, kitchenette, and bath ($275; 3-night minimum), plus an optional queen bedroom with private bath ($165), both with access to the private pool and whirlpool spa (www.makaihale.com; ✆ **808/880-1012**).

WAIMEA

Within a 15-minute drive of Spencer Park (p. 224), this cowboy town can be a good alternative to pricey resorts. Attractively remodeled with wrangler-chic touches, the 30-unit **Kamuela Inn ★★**, 65-1300 Kawaihae Rd. (www.thekamuelainn.com; © **800/555-8968** or 808/885-4243), sits in a quiet enclave off the main road, but still within walking distance of **Merriman's ★★★** (p. 283) and other dining and shopping. Room rates (from $309 double, $328 suites) include continental breakfast and organic Hawai'i-made bath products; some units include kitchenettes and pillow-top bedding for up to six, while new executive suites ($476) offer two bedrooms, two baths (one with clawfoot tub), and a full kitchen. Close to the center of town, the two-story, two-unit **Belle Vue ★** (www.hawaii-bellevue.com; © **800/772-5044** or 808/885-7732) vacation rental has a penthouse apartment with high ceilings and views from the mountains to the distant sea, and a downstairs studio ($95–$175 double; $25 per extra person). The decor is very dated, but both sleep four and include breakfast fixings in kitchenettes.

The Hāmākua Coast

Honoka'a's new restaurants, boutiques, and cultural center may make this emerald-green, virtually empty coast more of a destination than in years past. Two miles north of Honoka'a off Highway 240, the **Waipi'o Wayside Inn Bed & Breakfast ★★** (www.waipiowayside.com; © **800/833-8849** or 808/775-0275) perches on a sunny ocean bluff. The restored former plantation supervisor's residence has five antiques-decorated rooms with modern bathrooms ($140–$225 double; $30 for extra person); the innkeepers serve delicious breakfasts with island fruit and smoothies, a freshly baked item, and a hot entree promptly at 8am.

Bargain hunters will love the old-school **Hotel Honoka'a Club ★**, 45-3480 Māmane St., Honoka'a (http://alohaall.com; © **800/808-0678** or 808/775-0678). Built in 1928, the two-story building in the heart of town features second-story oceanview rooms with a queen bed (and some with an additional single bed) and private bath start at $119, while ground-floor rooms with single or full beds start at $99. Those rates also include a light continental breakfast. If you're willing to share a common bathroom with showers, you can book a private hostel room for $40 or a shared dorm room for $25, plus $10 linens charge (breakfast not included).

Note: You'll find these accommodations on "The Kohala Coast, Waimea & the Hāmākua Coast" map on p. 257.

Hilo

Be aware you may hear coqui frogs all night wherever windows are open in Hilo; air-conditioning is your friend here for several reasons.

On a hilltop, off-grid 22-acre compound boasting its own waterfall swimming pool, the **Inn at Kulaniapia Falls ★★** (www.waterfall.net; © **808/935-6789**) offers a choice of 10 Asian- or Hawaiian-themed rooms (from $259, with full breakfast), plus the private Jade Cottage (including a queen bed and a waterfall view from the lanai, from $399) and the Pagoda Guest House (from $519 for four, with kitchen stocked with breakfast supplies). The luxuriously appointed, 1,200-square-foot, one-bedroom Residence Suite with an ocean view is available for booking (adults only, from $599) when the owner is not on site. At the cheaper end of the spectrum, three oceanview and two garden-view farm cabins share bathrooms and a kitchen, and have access to the falls but no electricity other than a USB charger and light ($149 oceanview, $109 garden-view, optional $19 per person for breakfast at the inn). Kayaks, paddleboards, yoga, and farm dinners are available, as are 3- and 5-night packages with rides on Icelandic horses.

Hilo Honoli'i Hale ★ (https://hilohonoliihale.wordpress.com; ✆ **866/963-6076**) is a 700-square-foot studio overlooking Hilo's popular surf spot of Honoli'i Beach and including a full kitchen, king bed, and roomy sitting area as well as a garden dining and lounge area ($150, 3-night minimum).

Built in 1931 and recently updated with tasteful modern furnishings, the still-modest **Inn at 'Akaka Falls ★**, 8-1692 Māmalahoa Hwy., Honomū, is a pleasant budget option within a 15-minute drive of Hilo. Rooms come with private bathrooms, lanais, and air conditioning, while the communal kitchen is stocked with fruit, oatmeal and coffee for breakfast. It's booked via Airbnb for $159 per night, plus $30 cleaning and $25 service fees. Enter "Honomu, HI" in Airbnb search field and look for any listings described as "Room in boutique hotel hosted by Cody."

Note: The lodgings in this section are on the "Hilo" map on p. 203.

MODERATE

Grand Naniloa Hotel Hilo—A DoubleTree by Hilton ★★

This 12-story, thoroughly renovated oceanfront hotel with wonderful views of Hilo Bay has declared itself "the home of hula," although in 2021 it gained a new reputation as the home of reality TV's *Love Island*. Renowned photographer Kim Taylor Reese's images of hula dancers hang on virtually every wall, and video of the Merrie Monarch hula competition plays in the open-air lobby by a stylish central bar. **Hula Hulas ★★** poolside restaurant offers locally sourced dishes, live music, and hula. The refurbished rooms (most 312–330 sq. ft.) sport marble bathrooms and floors, flatscreens, and triple-sheet white bedding; some suites (660 sq. ft.) include kitchenettes, while corner rooms with wrap-around lanais offer sweeping vistas. Rent a kayak or paddleboard or book a helicopter, Mauna Kea, or volcano excursion at the KapohoKine Adventure Store, which includes a small market. The $39 resort fee includes use of snorkel gear, Wi-Fi, self or valet parking, daily golf at the quirky **Naniloa Golf Course** (p. 246), and a 20% discount on a KapohoKine volcano tour, among other amenities.

93 Banyan Dr., Hilo. www.grandnaniloahilo.com. ✆ **808/969-3333.** 407 units. From $195 double; from $399 suite w/kitchenette. Resort fee $30. **Amenities:** Activity desk; bar; fitness center; 9-hole golf course; pool; restaurant; room service; Wi-Fi.

Hilo Hawaiian Hotel ★

Now managed by Castle Resorts, this formerly dowdy hotel on Banyan Drive now boasts some upgrades, such as a lobby showcasing Hawaiian hardwood and featherwork. Although the rooms' dark wood furniture and patterned carpets still seem dated, the views of Hilo Bay are exceptional and the staff is well-versed in Hawaiian hospitality. The hotel's **Waioli Lounge** remains a pleasant place to lift a mai tai, while whiskey fans will want to check out the extensive collection at its dinner-only, bay-view **WSW / Whiskey Steak Wine ★★** restaurant.

71 Banyan Dr., Hilo. www.castleresorts.com/big-island/hilo-hawaiian-hotel. ✆ **808/935-9361** or 877/367-1912 (reservations). 286 units. From $239 double; from $339 suite. Resort fee $30. **Amenities:** Bar; fitness center; gift shop; pool; restaurant; Wi-Fi.

SCP Hilo Hotel ★★★   A thorough makeover and rebranding of the former, funky Hilo Seaside Hotel, the SCP Hilo Hotel capitalizes on its great location. The resort faces Reeds Bay with koi-filled anchialine ponds at the south end of Banyan Drive; it's also close to the Hilo airport, iconic **Ken's House of Pancakes** (p. 286), the new **Big Island Coffee Roasters** cafe and tasting room (p. 287), Hilo's best beaches (p. 226), and the highway to Hawai'i Volcanoes National Park (p. 209). Though rooms (most without water views) remain small with minimalist decor, and the rabbit-warren layout over several floors does not include elevators, this is still a find. Boutique hotel touches (locally sourced food and gifts in its marketplace, loaner bikes and stand-up paddleboards, well-equipped fitness center, bold artwork, etc.) dovetail with the sustainability and cultural initiatives that are part of the brand of SCP ("Soul, Community, Planet"), which manages nine similarly earth-friendly, moderately priced properties on the West Coast and in Costa Rica. Its unique Fair Trade Pricing allows you to adjust your rate at checkout if something wasn't up to your satisfaction, provided you gave the hotel a chance to address the problem during your stay.

During the **Merrie Monarch Festival** (p. 175), the entire block of Banyan Way and the open-air lobby become the site of a lively craft fair and free live entertainment by top Hawaiian musicians and hula dancers.

126 Banyan Way, Hilo. https://scphotel.com/hilo. ✆ **808/935-0821.** 128 units. From $157 double with 2 double beds ($168 with king bed), $194 triple (2 doubles, 1 twin, maximum 4 people). Free parking. **Amenities:** Bicycles; fitness center; gift shop and market; pool; airport/rental car shuttle by reservation ($40); standup paddleboards; free Wi-Fi.

Puna

Among other destruction, Kīlauea's 2018 eruption along its Lower East Rift Zone sadly claimed one of the island's most special areas for vacation rentals: the thermal ponds and tidepools of Kapoho. But you can find unique, licensed vacation rentals near the new thermal ponds at Isaac Hale Beach Park (p. 208) and black-sand Kehena Beach, including a bright, one-bedroom cottage on a banana farm just off the "Red Road" (Hwy. 137) in Kalapana Seaview neighborhood. **Bananarama Cottage ★★** (https://bananacottagehawaii.com or www.airbnb.com/rooms/11045386) includes a king bed, screened-in lanai, full kitchen, and whirlpool bathtub,

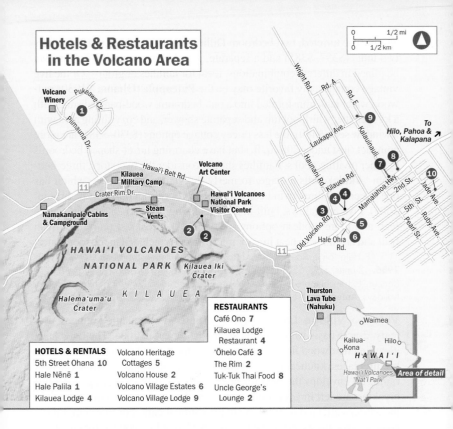

Hotels & Restaurants in the Volcano Area

Volcano Winery **1**

Pukeawe Cir.
Pliimauna Dr.
Wright Rd.
Rd. A
Rd. E
Laukapu Ave.
Kalaiinauli
9

To Hilo, Pahoa & Kalapana

Hawai'i Belt Rd.
Kilauea Military Camp
Crater Rim Dr.

Volcano Art Center

Hawai'i Volcanoes National Park Visitor Center

11

Nāmakanipaio Cabins & Campground

Steam Vents

2 **2**

Haunani Rd.
Kilauea Rd.
Mamalahoa Hwy.
2nd St.
5th St.
Jade Ave.
Ruby Ave.
Pearl St.
Old Volcano Rd.

7 **8**

10

4 **4**

3

5

Hale Ohia Rd.

6

HAWAI'I VOLCANOES
NATIONAL PARK

Kilauea Iki Crater

K I L A U E A

Halema'uma'u Crater

Thurston Lava Tube (Nahuku)

RESTAURANTS
Café Ono **7**
Kilauea Lodge Restaurant **4**
'Ōhelo Café **3**
The Rim **2**
Tuk-Tuk Thai Food **8**
Uncle George's Lounge **2**

HOTELS & RENTALS
5th Street Ohana **10**
Hale Nēnē **1**
Hale Palila **1**
Kilauea Lodge **4**
Volcano Heritage Cottages **5**
Volcano House **2**
Volcano Village Estates **6**
Volcano Village Lodge **9**

Waimea
Kailua-Kona
Hilo
H A W A I ʻ I
Hawai'i Volcanoes Nat'l Park
Area of detail

plus fresh banana bread and fruit; it's typically $149 a night, plus $85 cleaning fee and $26 nightly Airbnb service fee.

Lower Puna is notorious for noisy coquis at night, but in **Volcano Village,** the frogs are somewhat fewer, thanks to the misty, cool nights at 3,700 feet. Ask about heating options for any rentals booked for winter and be aware of neighborhood quiet hours from 9pm to 9am. **Hale Nēnē ★** (www.airbnb.com/rooms/45299189) and **Hale Palila ★** (www.airbnb.com/rooms/45299321) are darling, light-filled A-frame cottages overlooking the Volcano Golf Course, with queen beds, futon sofas, and a large shared deck with hot tub, BBQ, and dining area (each $115–$145 a night, plus $80 cleaning and $45–$47 booking fees).

Note: You'll find Hale Nēnē and Hale Palila and the following accommodations on the "Hotels & Restaurants in the Volcano Area" map (above).

VOLCANO VILLAGE

Expensive

Volcano Village Estates ★★ Recently renamed under its new owners, Emma Spencer Living, which also operates **Volcano Village Lodge ★★★** (see below), the tranquil garden compound formerly known as Hale 'ōh'ia has a fresh sheen of rustic elegance, while still brimming with "old Volcano" charm. The turreted, two-bedroom Dillingham House, built in 1931, offers two units ($357–$385) and a separate, grand living room ($770) that can be joined in different combinations, ideal for families or groups. Of the five vintage cottages, my favorite may be the **Pineapple 'Ohana,** a 1930s redwood water tank transformed into a one-bedroom, wood-paneled suite with a kitchenette, whirlpool tub and separate shower, and cozy sitting area with a window seat ($489); the less pricey cottage options ($330–$385) are more compact (just under 200 sq. ft.) but have charming turret-shaped bedrooms or other inviting nooks. Families should consider the two-story, three-bedroom **'Akaka Falls** cottage, formerly the gardener's cottage, which has one queen and three twin beds and a full kitchen (but only one bathroom; $605). Five bungalows, built in 2015 and ranging from 280 to 750 square feet, add more modern options ($379–$781). Breakfast (currently fresh fruit and an entree to heat in your microwave) is included in the room rates. 11-3968 Hale 'ōh'ia Rd., Volcano. https://volcanovillageestates.com. Ⓒ **808/967-7986.** 12 units. $275–$525 cottages; $320–$1,200 bungalows and Dillingham Residences. Extra person $30. Self-serve breakfast included. 2-night minimum during holidays. **Amenities:** Free Wi-Fi at main property.

Volcano Village Lodge ★★★   These five romantic cottages in a leafy, 2-acre oasis were built as an artists' retreat in 2004. The units have gleaming hardwood floors and paneled walls, vaulted ceilings, gas or electric fireplaces, kitchenettes, and endless walls of windows, while the lush rainforest envelops the oh-so-peaceful lodge in privacy. Fixings for a full breakfast are left in your room each night. Enjoy the communal hot tub in the gardens after a day of hiking in the national park. For true sumptuousness or extra guests, book the two-room Mauna Loa cottage (from $471), which includes a "meditation" loft under the eaves. The same proprietor, Emma Spencer Living, also manages **Volcano Village Estates** ★★ (see above) and the **5th Street Ohana** ★ vacation rental (https://5thstohana.com; $220–$330), which has two family-friendly units (one has two bedrooms, the other is a studio) available as a single home. 19-4183 Road E, Volcano. www.volcanovillagelodge.com. Ⓒ **808/985-9500.** 5 units. From $396 double (up to 4 guests); breakfast included. **Amenities:** Hot tub; DVD library; free Wi-Fi.

Moderate

Kilauea Lodge ★★   This former YMCA camp, built in 1938, has served as a gracious inn since 1986. Although the original innkeepers sold the property in 2018, the new California-based owners have kept its island style and spirit. The 10-acre campus has 12 units in two wings and one cottage; most have gas fireplaces, along with European-Hawaiian decor and thoughtful touches such as heated towel racks, and all have access to private sessions in the garden hot tub. Cozy **Kilauea Lodge Restaurant** ★★★ (p. 289) is currently open daily 9am to 8:30pm. 19-3948 Old Volcano Rd., Volcano. www.kilauealodge.com. Ⓒ **808/967-7366.** 15 units. From $259 double; $299 cottage. Extra person $20 (ages 2 and up). **Amenities:** Restaurant; gift shop; hot tub; free Wi-Fi.

Volcano Heritage Cottages ★★ Formerly part of Kilauea Lodge, these two cottages facing each other on a leafy side street in Volcano are now managed separately by the lodge's original owners, Albert and Lorna Jeyte. **Ola'a House,** a two-bedroom, one-bath, 1,700-square-foot home from 1929 features handsome, Craftsman and contemporary tropical decor, a gas fireplace, and a modern full kitchen; the twin sofa bed means the house can accommodate up to five adults. It can be combined with similarly equipped, light and bright **Tutu's Place,** a 1,000-square-foot, two-bedroom, one-bath 1929 cottage that also has bedding for five.

Volcano Village (address given upon booking). www.volcanoheritagecottages.com. 2 units. $295–$325 a night, 3-night minimum. Cleaning fee $125. **Amenities:** DVD players; free Wi-Fi.

HAWAI'I VOLCANOES NATIONAL PARK
Moderate

Volcano House ★★ This historic two-story wooden inn is fairly modest, especially compared with the grand lodges of other national parks. Still, its location on the very rim of dramatically expanded Kīlauea Caldera is nothing short of spectacular, even without the glow of a lava lake, seen as recently as 2021, or billowing ash, which ended with the 35-year eruption in 2018. Rooms are on the small and plain side and the vintage bathrooms downright tiny, so explore your surroundings during the day—perhaps using your complimentary loaner bike—and then enjoy a fresh-baked macadamia nut cookie before dinner and drinks at **The Rim** ★★ (p. 290) or **Uncle George's Lounge.** Now that the crater-view rooms have risen to $335 and higher, it's a borderline splurge, especially since 'ōhi'a lehua trees may partially block the views. Annoyingly, the hotel also won't guarantee bed configurations, so friends traveling together could find themselves sharing a king rather than two doubles. The hotel also manages 10 much less expensive refurbished cabins and 16 campsites with rental tents and "glamping" setups elsewhere in the park; see "Camping," below.

1 Crater Rim Dr., Hawai'i Volcanoes National Park. www.hawaiivolcanohouse.com. ✆ **866/536-7972** or 808/756-9625. 33 units. From $285 forest-view double, $335 crater-view double. Extra person $30. $30 park entrance fee per vehicle, valid for 7 days. Check for special rates online. **Amenities:** Restaurant; bar; bicycles; gift shops; free Wi-Fi.

Ka'ū

As with the Hāmākua Coast, few visitors overnight in this virtually undeveloped area, halfway between Kailua-Kona and Hawai'i Volcanoes National Park. One lodging does encourage guests to linger: In a tranquil setting above the road to Ka Lae (South Point), luxurious **Kalaekilohana Inn & Retreat** ★★ (www.kau-hawaii.com; ✆ **808/939-8052**) has four large guest suites ($429) in a modern plantation-style home. After 1 night in a plush sleigh bed, a rain shower in the morning with treetop views, a beautifully presented breakfast on the lanai, and true Hawaiian hospitality from hosts Kenny Joyce and Kilohano Domingo, many guests kick themselves for not having booked a second night or more. Multi-night discounts start at $75 off a 3-night stay. Kenny's delicious dinners ($35 per person) are a nightly option; snacks and self-service laundry are complimentary. *Tip:* The hosts are seeking to sell within the next few years to like-minded owners, so if this area is on your bucket list, I'd go now.

Camping

Camping is available at eight county beach parks (plus one on the slopes of Mauna Kea), six state parks and reserves, a few private campgrounds, and Hawai'i Volcanoes National Park. I don't recommend most county parks, because of security concerns (such as at remote **Punalu'u Beach Park,** p. 227), but **Kohanaiki Beach Park** (p. 221) is zealously well maintained, and **Ōhai'ula Beach at Spencer Park** (p. 224) has a night patrol. County campsites require advance-purchase permits, which cost $21 a night per person for nonresidents ($20 for ages 12 and under). For details, see https://hawaiicounty.ehawaii.gov or call ☏ **808/961-8311.**

State campsites also require permits that must be booked in advance (https://camping.ehawaii.gov; ☏ **808/961-9540**). The most desirable are at **Hāpuna Beach State Recreation Area** (p. 223), which offers six A-frame screened shelters with wooden sleeping platforms and a picnic table, plus communal restrooms and cold showers. Nonresidents pay $70 per shelter per night for permits; purchase at least a month in advance. Friday through Sunday nights, **Kīholo State Park Reserve** (p. 220) allows tent camping in a kiawe grove on a pebbly beach, with portable toilets but no water; nonresidents pay $30 per campsite per night for up to 10 people. For hardcore backpackers, camping in the state preserve of remote **Waimanu Valley** is typically the reward for tackling the extremely arduous **Muliwai Trail** (see "Hiking," p. 246, which also includes details on a shuttle to the valley and overnight parking). Permits for nonresidents are $30 per site, hosting up to 10 people.

At South Kona's **Ho'okena Beach Park** (p. 222), the privately run campground with local security is perfect for pitching a tent by the waves. Campsites for nonresidents cost $21 per person per night for ages 7 and older; reserve at least 72 hours in advance (www.hookena.org; ☏ **808/328-7321**). You can also rent tents, camping stoves, tables, and chairs for use on-site; Wi-Fi is available for $10 a day for two devices.

In **Hawai'i Volcanoes National Park** (p. 209), two campgrounds are accessible by car. The easiest to reach and best supplied is **Nāmakanipaio Campground ★★**, which offers 10 cabins and 16 campsites. The updated one-room cabins sleep four, with bed linens and towels provided, grills, and a community restroom with hot showers; the cost is $80 a night. Tent campers have restrooms but not showers; sites cost $15 a night, on a first-come, first-served basis, with a 7-night maximum stay. Both cabins and campsites are managed by **Volcano House ★★** (p. 273; www.hawaii volcanohouse.com; ☏ **866/536-7972** or 808/756-9625). Call the hotel in advance to rent a tent set up with a comfy foam mattress, linens, cooler, lantern, and two chairs for $40 a night, plus the $15 site fee. Park entrance fee of $30 per vehicle is additional. *Note:* It can be very cool and damp here, especially at night.

A 5-mile drive down Hilina Pali Road, **Kulanaokuaiki Campground** has nine campsites with picnic tables and vault toilet but no running water. It's first-come, first-served; pay the $10 nightly fee (1-week maximum stay) at the self-registration station. Backpack camping is allowed at seven remote areas in the park (some with shelters, cabins, and water catchment tanks), but first you must register for a $10 permit, good for up to 12 people and 7 nights, at the **Backcountry Office** (www.nps.gov/havo; ✆ **808/985-6178**), no more than 1 day in advance.

Unfortunately, no stores are currently renting camping gear, so you'll need to bring your own or buy it on island. **Hilo Surplus Store,** 148 Mamo St., Hilo (www.hilosurplusstore.com; ✆ **808/935-6398;** Mon–Sat 9am–4pm), has the best selection. Another way to go, literally, is with a fully equipped rooftop tent in a pickup truck from **Huakai Campers** (www.huakaicampers.com; ✆ **808/990-2238**); rentals run $139 to $159 a night with 3-night minimum and pickup in Hilo. *Note:* Vehicle camping is allowed at county parks and the two national park campgrounds with standard camping permits.

WHERE TO EAT ON HAWAI'I ISLAND

Thanks to its deep waters, green pastures, and fertile fields, Hawai'i Island provides local chefs with a cornucopia of fresh ingredients. But the challenge for visitors on the Kona side has always been finding restaurants to match their budgets. Don't be afraid to nosh at a roadside stand, food truck, or farmer's market (see "Hawai'i Island Shopping," p. 292), as residents do, but indulge at least once on an oceanfront sunset dinner for the best of all Hawai'i Island has to offer. Reservations are advised whenever possible; check OpenTable.com, Yelp.com, or the restaurant's website or Facebook page for options. Be aware that in peak periods, resort restaurants may not offer reservations to non-guests, but walk-ins may still be available.

The Kona Coast

Note: You'll find the following restaurants on the "Hotels & Restaurants on the Kona Coast" map on p. 255.

CENTRAL KAILUA-KONA

Though the island's most ambitious chefs work elsewhere, this neighborhood does have some satisfying, reasonably priced options. **Billfish Poolside Bar & Grille ★★** (✆ **808/329-2911;** daily 11am–9pm) is now the primary restaurant at the Courtyard King Kamehameha Kona Beach

Hotel (p. 254). Although its outdoor decor is bare bones, this casual family spot overlooks not only the pool but also Kailua Pier, Kamakahonu Cove, and Kailua Bay. The menu is simple but appealing, with great tropical cocktails like the *li hing mui* margarita ($10), tasty, fresh-catch fish tacos and sandwiches ($24), and local favorites like ahi poke nachos ($19) and kalbi short ribs ($26). The youngest member of the Huggo's family, **Kai Eats and Drinks ★★**, 75-5776 Ali'i Dr. (https://kaieatsanddrinks.com; ✆ **808/900-3328,** text only), serves a family- and budget-friendly menu of wood-fired pizzas, hefty burgers, and tacos ($16–$19), plus a few more expensive main courses like baby back ribs and flank steak ($36). Service has been speedy by Kona standards, and the oceanfront seating is perfect for enjoying a sunset cocktail ($14–$24). It's open Monday to Friday noon to 9pm and Saturday and Sunday from 9am (brunch until 2pm). For brunch, try the kalua pig eggs benedict on a housemade English muffin with jasmine rice ($21) or the local avocado toast with macadamia nut pesto ($16).

Big appetites should head to the **Big Island Grill ★**, 75-5702 Kuakini Hwy. (south of Henry St.), at a strip mall with parking (a rarity in Kona). American fare and local favorites here include loco moco (eggs, burger, gravy, and rice, $17) and *saimin* noodle soup ($17). It's open Tuesday to Thursday 8am to 5pm and Friday and Saturday until 2pm (www.facebook.com/BigIslandGrill; ✆ **808/326-1153**). **Cheeky Tiki ★**, 75-5669 Ali'i Dr. (https://cheekytikikona.com), opens daily at 11am and stays open late: until 10pm Sunday to Thursday and until 11pm Friday and Saturday. But you'll best enjoy the casual island/American menu when you can also see the view of Kailua Bay from its second-story, open-air perch. On offer are fish tacos, bao buns, burgers, and the like at lunch ($17–$24), with dinner plates ($24–$32) such as baby back ribs, jerk chicken, and garlic miso duck breast.

TAKE YOUR PICK OF poke

With all the fishing boats plying Kona waters, it's no wonder places selling ahi poke—the finely diced raw tuna staple of the islands—and similar dishes pride themselves on just-caught ingredients. Fisherman Albert Vasconcelles' **Da Poke Shack ★★** (https://dapokeshack.com; ✆ **808/329-POKE** [7653]; daily 10am–4pm) has built a loyal following for its to-go ahi poke bowls and lunch plates ($16–$22, priced by the pound) in a hole in the wall in the Kona Bali Kai complex, at 76-6246 Ali'i Dr., Kailua-Kona. Award-winning chef Nakoa Pabre operates out of the much more spacious **Umekes Fish Market Bar and Grill ★★★**, 74-5559 Pawai Place (www.umekesrestaurants.com; ✆ **808/238-0571**), but call for reservations to avoid disappointment. Open daily 11am to 9pm, **Umekes** ("bowls" in Hawaiian) sports a handsome wood and aqua interior and a full bar, not to mention plenty of parking and a market counter with to-go options and an outdoor picnic table. Grilled fish is good here, too, but don't miss the poke flight with 4 different poke choices—and poke bowls with quinoa or native fiddlehead fern salad as side options ($16–$24).

Expensive

Huggo's ★★★ PACIFIC RIM/SEAFOOD   The setting doesn't get any better in Kailua-Kona than this: a covered wooden deck overlooking tide pools and the sweep of Kailua Bay. The inventive small-plates menu at Huggo's chic lounge, **hBar** ★★, has been combined with some of the stellar mains from the dining room menu (like adobo-glazed lamb chops, teriyaki steak, or the fresh catch, also available as coconut-crusted tofu), available throughout the restaurant. Next door is the more casual, moderately priced **On the Rocks** ★, which serves lunch and dinner; after sunset, it's a pulsating nightclub.

75-5828 Kahakai Rd., Kailua-Kona. www.huggos.com. ✆ **808/329-1493 (text preferred).** Reservations recommended. **Huggo's** and **hBar:** Small and shared plates $9–$28, main courses $24–$49. Daily 4–9pm (full menu from 5pm). **On the Rocks:** https://huggosontherocks.com. ✆ **808/329-1493.** Main courses $19–$29. Daily noon to 9pm; happy hour 3–5pm; live music from 5pm.

Moderate

Island Lava Java ★★ AMERICAN   Founded in 1994, this former espresso bar later blossomed into a full-service restaurant for breakfast, lunch, and dinner in its oceanview location in the Coconut Grove Marketplace, which also has a large bar area. The coffee is 100% Kona, breads and desserts are made in house, and organic salads, sandwiches, and pizzas feature mostly local ingredients. Compared with the resorts' offerings, prices here are almost reasonable for the Hawai'i Island grass-fed beef burger ($16) or 10-inch pizzas ($20–$22); ordering the New York strip ($29) and "market price" fresh catch, poke, or fish and chips can add up quickly.

75-5801 Ali'i Dr., Kailua-Kona. www.islandlavajava.com. ✆ **808/327-2161.** Main courses $14–$23 breakfast; $15–$39 lunch and dinner. Daily 7am–9pm.

NORTH KONA

Picture this: You've just landed at the airport and you're starving. Unless you've booked a room at the Four Seasons (p. 259) or Kona Village (p. 260), you've got two decent choices, both in a shopping strip just off the highway 3 miles south, although their address says Kailua-Kona. **Patricio's Mexican Taqueria** ★, 73-4038 Hulikoa (www.patriciostaqueria. com; ✆ **808/334-1008**), has a huge menu of Mexican dishes, but don't skip the fish tacos on fluffy, white corn tortillas ($6 each, $3 on Taco Tuesday). For more local flavor, **Pine Tree Café** ★, 73-4040 Hulikoa (www. pinetreecafehi.com; ✆ **808/327-1234**), cranks out plate lunches with beef stew, grilled ahi, shoyu chicken, fried poke, and myriad other choices ($19–$28) with near factory-like precision and speed. Don't step up to the counter until you know what you want and be prepared for big portions.

'Ulu Ocean Grill & Sushi Lounge ★★★ ISLAND FARM/SEAFOOD

No matter which chef is at the helm, this beachfront destination restaurant remains a superb showcase for the wares of 160 local fishermen and farmers. Refined yet approachable dishes include crispy whole fresh-catch fish with black bean sauce, pineapple fried rice, and brussels sprouts, and the

TAP INTO local brews

Kona Brewing Co. ★★★ (www.konabrewinghawaii.com; ✆ **808/334-2739**) began as a father-and-son microbrewery in Kailua-Kona in 1994. More recently it became two independent companies—one in Hawai'i, one on the U.S. mainland—who share brand names and logos for popular brews such as Fire Rock Pale Ale and Longboard Lager. But all the beer brewed in Hawai'i stays here, and it's all produced in the state-of-the-art, solar-powered, eco-friendly brewery next to its original Kona brewpub, at 74-5612 Pawai Pl. Learn more about the sustainable brewery and its tasty suds on a lively, small-group tour ($25, ages 15 and older; six times a day, by reservation only) with multiple samples, the last in a private second-story bar with an ocean view. The brewpub still offers affordable island and American specials at lunch and happy hour (Mon–Fri 3–5pm), including fish caught by its own fisherman and seasonal draft brews on a palm-shaded patio; it's open daily 10am to 9pm.

Ola Brewing ★★ (www.olabrewco.com; ✆ **808/339-3599**) is the community-owned brainchild of Native Hawaiian entrepreneur Naehalani Breeland, who wanted to give the island's farmers another outlet for their produce. She and co-founder Brett Jacobson have created a delectable array of tropical ciders (try the pineapple), hard (that is, alcohol-infused) fruit juices, hard seltzers, hard teas (brewed with Kona coffee leaves and black tea), and, of course, IPA and lager beer. The original tap room in Kona (74-5598 Luhia St.) is open Monday to Thursday 11:30 to 10pm, Friday and Saturday until 11pm, and Sunday until 8pm; pair your drinks with tacos ($12) or flatbreads ($15–$22), among other good options. The Hilo tap room, 1177 Kīlauea Ave. (✆ **808/731-0917**), serves an eclectic, pan-Asian menu (main courses $18–$34; Mon–Thurs 11:30am–11pm and Sun 10:30am–8pm; Sun brunch menu 10am–2pm; the kitchen typically closes an hour before the restaurant closes).

In Waimea, **Big Island Brewhaus** ★★, 64-1066 Māmalahoa Hwy. (https://bigislandbrewhaus.com; ✆ **808/887-1717**), makes a great pit stop between the Kohala and Hāmākua coasts. Master brewer Tom Kerns' wide-ranging taps pair well with an equally diverse, locally sourced menu with burgers, Mexican, and Mediterranean fare ($8–$18). Its covered patio and smaller indoor dining area/bar are open daily 11am to 8pm. Don't forget to bring a jacket—it gets cold up here.

New York steak in a miso glaze with kiawe-smoked mashed potatoes and baby vegetables from Waimea's Kekela Farms. Jewel-like sashimi and artful sushi rolls can be ordered in the oceanview lounge (with fire pits) or the open-air dining room, behind roelike curtains of glass balls; a separate sushi counter was in the planning for 2024. *Note:* The breakfast menu is also locally sourced but is more exorbitant and less enticing. During peak holiday periods, only resort guests are can make reservations (always a good idea otherwise).

At the Four Seasons Resort Hualālai, 72-100 Ka'ūpūlehu Dr., Kailua-Kona (off Hwy. 19, 6 miles north of Kona airport). https://fourseasons.com/hualalai/dining. ✆ **808/325-8000.** Reservations recommended. Main courses $37–$47 breakfast; $57–$75 dinner. Daily 6:30–11am and 5:30–9pm (sushi until 10pm).

KEAUHOU

The most popular spot in Keauhou Shopping Center, 78-6831 Ali'i Dr., is **Kenichi ★** (www.kenichipacific.com; © **808/322-6400**), a stylish Asian fusion/sushi dinner spot ($30–$40), open Tuesday to Sunday 4:30 to 9:30pm. The bar and lounge rea offer great happy hour deals on sushi, appetizers, and drinks daily 4:30 to 6pm. For breakfast or lunch, the shopping center's long-running favorite is **Peaberry & Galette ★** (www.facebook.com/peaberryandgalette; © **808/322-6020**), a small cafe with a wide selection of savory and sweet crepes, including gluten-free options ($11–$15), plus soup, sandwiches, salads, and 100% Kona coffee; it's open Sunday to Friday 8am to 2pm and Saturday from 7:30am.

Moderate

Sunset Kai Lanai ★ ISLAND/AMERICAN The miles-long, 230-degree coastal views from this former Wendy's are spectacular. After years of ups and downs following its initial reincarnation as Sam Choy's Kai Lanai, this restaurant is once again sitting pretty. The lunch menu caters mostly to local tastes—e.g. kalua pork tacos, beef stew, chili garlic shrimp—but with familiar options such as burgers and fish and chips, too. At dinner, filet mignon, grilled salmon, and slow-roasted pork ribs have broad appeal; order the sesame-crusted fresh ahi with unagi sauce and rice or the grilled Hawaiian chicken with pineapple salsa for more island-style flavors.

Above Keauhou Shopping Center, 78-6831 Ali'i Dr., Kailua-Kona. https://sunsetkai lanai.com. © **808/333-3434.** Reservations recommended for dinner. Main courses $22–$50 (most $29–$39) dinner; $17–$26 lunch. Sun–Thurs 11am–8pm; Fri–Sat until 8:30pm; daily happy hour 3–5pm.

SOUTH KONA

To savor ocean views and 100% Kona coffee, consider two cafes on the *makai* side of Highway 11. **The Coffee Shack ★**, 83-5799 Māmalahoa Hwy. (between mile markers 108 and 109), in Captain Cook, serves tasty eggs benedict and other egg dishes ($12–$22), plump sandwiches on fresh-baked bread ($18–$20), and 8-inch pizzas on homemade crusts ($15–$18); it's open Thursday to Tuesday 7:30am to 3:30pm, with breakfast until noon (www.coffeeshack.com; © **808/328-9555**). Call ahead to be placed on the waiting list and check the website for tips on parking the area. Don't be surprised to spot a gecko or two here. Italian-themed **Caffe Florian ★** serves panini ($10–$12), quiche, salads, sandwiches, and housemade pastries. It's open Monday to Friday 6:30am to 2pm and Saturday 7am to 1:30pm at 81-6637 Māmalahoa Hwy., Kealakekua (at Nani Kupuna Place; www.caffefloriankona.com; © **808/238-0861**).

Inexpensive

Manago Hotel Restaurant ★★ AMERICAN Although the county plans to turn this former hotel, which opened in 1917, into affordable housing, the family-run dining room with Formica tabletops and vinyl-backed chairs that have changed little over the years is expected to continue. Service is friendly and swift, with three family-style sides (rice, potato salad, and fresh vegetables), plus steamed rice accompanying hearty main dishes such as pork chops with gravy and grilled onions ($17), teriyaki chicken, and sautéed mahimahi, among other choices (but none for vegetarians). Sandwiches (including mahimahi, tuna, burgers, and BLT) come with potato salad or chips.

At the Manago Hotel, 82-6151 Māmalahoa Hwy. (Hwy. 11), Captain Cook, btw. mile markers 109 and 110, *makai* side. www.managohotel.com/restaurant. ℭ **808/323-2642.** Reservations recommended for dinner. Main courses $15–$25. Wed–Sat 11am–2pm and 5–7:30pm.

The Kohala Coast

Note: You'll find the following restaurants on the "Kohala Coast, Waimea & the Hāmākua Coast" map on p. 257.

SOUTH KOHALA

In this region dominated by resorts with empty acres of lava in between, most convenient dining options for visitors lie in luxury hotels (where prices tend to be highest; see "Top Views, Top Dollars," p. 281) or in resort shopping centers.

WAIKOLOA BEACH RESORT The **Queens' Marketplace** mall holds several hidden, affordable treasures, starting with its food court, open daily 11am to 8pm. This is where **Island Greens ★** (www.islandgreenshi.com) assembles custom bowls ($14) with a base of local greens, wild rice, or pasta; proteins range from seared sesame tofu and seared ahi to Kona coffee-rubbed steak; and a rainbow of other toppings and add-ins. Across the food court, **Waikoloa Shrimp Co.** (www.waikoloashrimpco.com) has a much more streamlined menu, with five kinds of shrimp plates ($20; my favorite is tempura with dynamite sauce), garlic steak ($21), and two kinds of wings ($18); all come with an irresistible macaroni salad with bacon and potato, white rice, and a pineapple ring dusted with *li hing mui* (sweet and sour dried plum powder.) On the main plaza, **Kuleana Rum Shack ★★** (https://kuleanarum.com; ℭ **808/238-0786**) is the place to pair locally made rum and artisan cocktails ($15) with coconut veggie curry, fish tacos, a burger, or steak ($24–$38). The restaurant is open daily 3 to 9pm, with happy hour 3 to 5pm. Rum aficionados will want to book a mai tai-making class ($50) or tasting flight ($25) in the new tasting room, opened in 2024.

Also in the Queens' Marketplace, the open-air **Bistro at Waikoloa Luxury Cinemas ★** (https://hawaiicinemas.com/the-bistro) offers a broad menu—pizzas, tacos, plate lunches, burgers, baby back ribs, etc., in hearty portions—daily 11am to 8pm. You can also enjoy your selection while watching a movie, thanks to retractable trays in the theaters' plush seats. **Aloha Wine Bar ★**, inside Island Gourmet Markets, serves burgers, pizzas, and local plates ($14–$19) with good wine specials (www.

islandgourmethawaii.com; © **808/886-3500;** Mon–Thurs 3–10pm; Fri–Sun until 10:30pm); happy hour runs 3 to 5pm and 9 till closing.

Across the road at the Kings Shops, 250 Waikoloa Beach Dr., you'll find one of Hawai'i Regional Cuisine co-founder Roy Yamaguchi's many dining outlets across the state. **Roy's ★★** (www.royyamaguchi.com/roys-waikoloa; © **808/886-4321**) has maintained his high standards for steak and seafood with French, Asian, and island influences. His silky misoyaki butterfish ($57), delicate jade pesto steamed snapper ($51), and sumptuous bone-in Duroc pork chop ($46) remain diners' favorites. At these prices, the sunset, three-course prix fixe ($49) is a bargain. Roy's is open daily 4:30 to 8:30pm.

The proximity to 'Anaeho'omalu Bay, especially at sunset, never fails to please at the open-air **Lava Lava Beach Club ★★** (www.lavalava beachclub.com; © **808/769-5282**), which serves fresh American and island food daily 8am to 9pm on the beach, with happy hour appetizer and drink specials 3 to 5pm, and nightly live music. Breakfast (8–10:30am) features hearty egg dishes and skillets ($18–$26); even the piled-high avocado toast ($22) comes with potatoes or rice. At lunch (11:30am–3pm), main courses run $25 to $40 (unless you want to break the bank on a $56 fresh catch); at dinner (3–9pm), they're $26 to $56. Owned by the team behind **Huggo's** (p. 277), it's at the end of Ku'uali'i Place, past the public beach access parking lot.

TOP VIEWS, top dollars

There's no getting around sticker shock when dining at the South Kohala resort hotels, especially at breakfast and lunch. Dazzling sunsets help soften the blow at dinner when chefs show more ambition. Here's a quick guide to help you distinguish among the top oceanfront hotel restaurants, most dinner-only, and all serving excellent (for the most part) yet costly variations on farm-to-table cuisine:

○ **Mauna Lani: Brown's Beach House ★★★** at the Fairmont Orchid, Hawai'i (p. 265), offers attentive service and exquisite seafood such as king crab crusted kampachi and Kona lobster, on the lawn just a stone's throw from the water; main courses are $38 to $62. At Mauna Lani, an Auberge Resort (p. 264), similarly beachfront **CanoeHouse ★★★** serves decadent Japanese-inspired fare (Wagyu steaks, lobster miso soup) and island seafood ($46–$148).

○ **Mauna Kea:** At the Mauna Kea Beach Hotel (p. 263), **Manta ★★★** offers a sweeping ocean view and the artful cuisine of O'ahu native Bryan Nagao; main courses run $52 to $75. At Westin Hapuna Beach Resort (p. 266), the smart-casual **Meridia,** which overlooks the pool and beach, serves an impeccable island-sourced Mediterranean-inspired menu ($47–$57), accompanied by a talented pianist.

○ **Waikoloa Beach: KPC–Kamuela Provision Company, ★** at the Hilton Waikoloa Village (p. 265), has a spectacular oceanfront setting to match its expert seafood ($48–$65) and chophouse menu ($59–$76). Book an outdoor table for at least a half-hour before sunset.

MAUNA LANI RESORT   At the Fairmont Orchid (p. 265), **Binchotan Bar & Grill ★★★** (www.fairmont.com/orchid-hawaii/dining; *Ⓒ* **808/887-7320**) is a dining hot spot that takes its name from Japan's gourmet white charcoal. Although the robata-grilled items ($16–$26) are fine, go for the small or shareable plates such as macadamia nut shrimp with local honey ($27), salt and pepper lobster ($38), crab and corn croquettes with tonkatsu sauce ($23), and Wagyu beef strips that you grill yourself on a hot rock ($32). The large lanai has only peek-a-boo ocean view but sunsets are still gorgeous; it's open Friday to Tuesday 5 to 9pm (reservations recommended), with happy hour specials 5 to 6pm. I'm also a fan of the *liliko'i* margarita ($22) and crispy fish sandwich ($28), among other casual fare, at the Fairmont Orchid's oceanview (and sandy-floored) poolside restaurant **Hale Kai ★★** (www.fairmontorchid.com/dine/hale-kai; *Ⓒ* **808/885-2000**). It's open daily 11am to 9pm.

The Shops at Mauna Lani, 68-1330 Mauna Lani Dr., have two stalwarts: Upstairs, above the eponymous clothing store, **Tommy Bahama ★★** (www.tommybahama.com/restaurants/mauna-lani; *Ⓒ* **808/881-8686;** daily 11:30am–8:30pm; daily happy hour 3–5pm and live music 5–8:30pm) serves reliably prepared island and American cuisine (main courses $17–$44 lunch; $26–$46 dinner) in a bustling dining room with a large sunset-facing lanai. Downstairs, **Knead & Bake ★** (www.kneadandbake.com; *Ⓒ* **808/731-4490;** daily 11am–8pm) makes tasty, hand-tossed pizzas (12 inches, $17–$22). Be sure to order your pie in advance. Upstairs newcomer **Alebrije ★★** (www.alebrijehawaii.com) has proved a welcome addition with ceviche, tacos, and a limited but artful menu of other Mexican specialties for brunch ($18–$22; Thurs–Sun 10am–2:30pm) and dinner ($20–$60; Wed–Sun 5–8:30pm), not to mention hand-crafted margaritas ($16).

KAWAIHAE   A few minutes past the Mauna Kea Resort, this small commercial port also harbors several homespun eateries, including **Kohala Burger & Taco** and its companion **SurfBurger ★★** in the Kawaihae Shopping Center, 61-3665 'Akoni Pule Hwy. (Hwy. 270, www.kohalaburgerandtaco.com; *Ⓒ* **808/880-1923**). Their juicy burgers are made with local grass-fed beef, while buns and tortillas (used for fresh fish, chicken, and beef tacos) are housemade; burger combos with fries and soft drink start at $16. Hours, days, and menu specials vary so frequently, it's best to check their Instagram account, @kohalaburger, or just show up. You're unlikely to go away disappointed, since it's next to the hugely popular, **Anuenue Ice Cream & Shave Ice ★** stand, typically open daily 11am to 6pm (cash only). At the end of this strip is **Kawaihae Marketplace ★** (*Ⓒ* **808/731-4886**), a family-run convenience store, deli counter, and fish market, with daily hot lunch specials, espresso bar, and poke bar; it's open Monday to Friday 6am to 6pm and Saturday 7am to 5pm.

WAIMEA

Daunted by high-priced Kohala resort menus? Visit the inexpensive **Hawaiian Style Café ★**, 65-1290 Kawaihae Rd. (Hwy. 19, 1 block east of Opelo Rd.; https://hawaiianstylecafe.us; © **808/885-4925**), which serves pancakes bigger than your head (try them with warm *haupia,* a coconut pudding), kalua pork hash, and other local favorites, along with burgers and sandwiches ($9–$24). Open daily 7am to 1pm, it's very crowded on weekends; it also only accepts cash but has an ATM inside. For a lighter (but still filling) breakfast or lunch, served with excellent coffee, the cozy **Waimea Coffee Co. ★★**, 65-1279 Kawaihae Rd. (www.waimeacoffeecompany.com; © **808/885-8915**), is a find among the red barnlike buildings of Parker Square. I love their crusty tuna melt with a side of hearty tomato soup ($16). It's open daily 6:30am to 5:30pm, although the kitchen only stays open till 2pm.

Besides iconic Merriman's (see below), foodies will want to visit **FORC ★★** ("Farmer Ocean Rancher Cook"), chef Allen Hess' surprisingly upscale restaurant at homespun Waimea Country Lodge, 65-1214 Lindsey Rd. (https://forchawaii.com; © **808/731-4656**). A devotee of bacon, Allen Hess serves a seasonal menu of steak, local fish, and other rib-sticking dishes ($39–$66), with local ranchers bellying up to the bar. It's open for dinner daily 3 to 8:30pm.

Expensive

Merriman's ★★★ HAWAI'I REGIONAL   This is where it all began in 1988 for Chef Peter Merriman, one of the founders of Hawai'i Regional Cuisine and an early advocate of the farm-to-table trend. Now head of a culinary empire with various incarnations on four Hawaiian islands, the busy Merriman has entrusted others with maintaining his high standards and inventive flair while focusing on making his restaurants carbon neutral. Lunch offers the best value, such as the grilled fresh fish tacos ($24) or Hawai'i Island beef cheeseburger ($16). At dinner, Merriman's classics include wok-charred ahi with garlic jasmine rice ($51), Waipi'o taro enchiladas ($42), and Kahua Ranch lamb ($55). Cocktails show the same care in crafting; the mai tai with honey *liliko'i* foam is a must.

In Opelo Plaza, 65-1227 Opelo Rd., off Hwy. 19, Waimea. www.merrimanshawaii.com. © **808/885-6822.** Reservations strongly recommended. Main courses $14–$35 lunch; $20–$60 dinner. Mon–Sat 11:30am–2pm and 5–8:30pm; Sun brunch 10:30am–1pm.

Inexpensive

Village Burger ★★ BURGERS   This burger stand created by former Four Seasons chef Edwin Goto has a compact menu. Choose from plump burgers made with local grass-fed beef, veal, ground ahi, taro, or Hāmākua mushrooms; thick, sumptuous shakes; and hand-cut, twice-cooked fries. Other than that, there's just a grilled ahi Niçoise salad featuring island greens—but it's also delicious. Village Burger is tucked into a cowboy-themed shopping center with a drafty food court (bring a jacket).

Village Burger: In the Parker Ranch Center, 67-1185 Māmalahoa Hwy., Waimea. www.villageburgerwaimea.com. © **808/885-7319.** Burgers $12–$18. Daily 10:30am–5pm.

WAIKOLOA VILLAGE

Not to be confused with Hilton Waikoloa Village Resort, or the larger Waikoloa Beach Resort, the residential community of Waikoloa Village (6 miles uphill) has one destination restaurant, **Pueo's ★★★** (see below) and a variety of affordable, casual dining options. The best of the latter is in Waikoloa Plaza, 68-1820 Waikoloa Rd.: **Big Island Fireart ★** (www. bigislandfireart.com; ✆ **808/498-0415**) serves classic Chinese dishes such as honey walnut shrimp, kung pao chicken, and orange beef ($14–$16) and, in an unusual pairing, Cajun boiled or fried seafood baskets by the pound ($16–$56); it's open daily 10:30am to 9pm. You can reserve a table or order takeout online.

Expensive

Pueo's Osteria ★★★ ITALIAN Upcountry residents and night owls flock to this restaurant in Waikoloa Plaza, named for the native owl. The osteria's appeal goes far beyond its location and late hours. Executive chef-owner James Babian, who lined up more than 150 local food purveyors for Four Seasons Hualālai during his tenure there, still works his connections for the freshest seafood, meat, and produce, while importing only the finest of everything else (including olive oil and well-priced wines) to create a delicious Italian menu. Babian has a tender touch with fresh pasta, such as radiatori alla vodka with Hāmākua mushrooms and prosciutto ($34), but also adds zest to hearty dishes such as the Chianti-braised short ribs with kabocha pumpkin puree ($48). A bright San Marzano tomato sauce perfectly complements delicately breaded eggplant parmigiana ($29). Gluten-free bread and pasta are also available.

In Waikoloa Plaza, 68-1820 Waikoloa Rd., Waikoloa. www.pueososteria.com. ✆ **808/339-7566.** Reservations recommended. Main courses $29–$48. Daily 5–9pm; bar 5–11pm (last call 10:30pm).

NORTH KOHALA

For a light meal or snack, including locally made Tropical Dreams ice cream, stop at **Kohala Coffee Mill ★**, 55-3412 'Akoni Pule Hwy. (*mauka* side, across from Bamboo [see below]; ✆ **808/889-5577**). It's open daily 7am to 4pm, with very limited seating. A wider selection of freshly prepared, mostly organic hot and cold food and beverages, and slightly more seating, is across the street at **Kohala Grown ★★**, 55-3419 'Akoni Pule Hwy. (https://kohalagrownmarket.com; ✆ **808/937-4930**). Also a great place to shop for local produce, honey, and other foodstuffs, it's open Monday to Thursday and Saturday 9am to 6pm, Sunday until 5pm, and Friday until 8pm.

In Kapaʻau, homey **Gill's Lanai ★**, 3866 'Akoni Pule Hwy. (*mauka* side, at Kamehameha Rd.; www.gillslanai.com; ✆ **808/315-1542**), serves heaping portions of fresh fish or kalua pork tacos, poke, fish and chips, and other island staples ($14–$17), plus gourmet hot dogs (including a vegan version, $9–$11) on a small porch. It's open Tuesday to Saturday 11:30am to 7pm, with live entertainment some evenings on the upstairs deck. Close to the Pololū Valley Overlook, the solar-powered **Fresh Off the Grid food truck** ★, 52-5088 ʻAkoni Pule Hwy. (*makai* side), Kapaʻau (*⊘* **808/895-2963**), offers shave ice, smoothies, a tropical fruit stand, picnic tables, and a welcome portable toilet; it's open Friday to Tuesday 11:30am to 5pm, with additional hot dishes like *ʻulu* (breadfruit chowder) and live music on Sundays.

Moderate

Bamboo ★★ PACIFIC RIM   Dining here is a trip, literally and figuratively. A half-hour from the nearest resort, Bamboo adds an element of time travel, with vintage decor behind the screen doors of its pale-blue, plantation-era building. An art gallery and quirky gift shop provide great browsing if you have to wait for a table. The food is generally worth it, from local lunch faves like barbecued baby-back ribs to free-range grilled chicken with a kicky Thai-style coconut sauce. Be sure to sample one of the cocktails or mocktails made with *lilikoʻi* (passionfruit).

55-3415 ʻAkoni Pule Hwy. (Hwy. 270, just west of Hwy. 250/Hāwī Rd.), Hāwī. www. bamboorestauranthawaii.com. *⊘* **808/889-5555.** Main courses $17–$25. Tues–Sun 11:30am–2pm and Thurs–Fri 6–8:30pm.

The Hāmākua Coast

In increasingly vibrant Honokaʻa, Italian bistro **Café Il Mondo** ★, 45-3580 Māmane St. (*⊘* **808/775-7711**), serves tasty pizza ($16–$22), calzones ($19), pastas ($22–$30), and daily specials, but be prepared for a long wait for food. It's open Tuesday to Saturday noon to 4pm. Also requiring a wait, since it's a one-woman show, Korean-inspired **Harmoni Foods** ★, 45-3596 Māmane St. (*⊘* **808/557-7394**), has tantalizing lunch plates ($10–$20) in traditional options like bibimbap (beef or vegan) and fusion fare like grilled cheese with kimchi. Chef-owner Susie tries to source everything locally, including the Okinawan sweet potatoes available as a side. It's open Wednesday to Sunday noon to 6pm. **I Love Dumplings** ★★, 45-3625 Māmane St. (*⊘* **808/657-4044**), has attracted a loyal following for innovative dishes like the "crumpling," coconut beef

---

Get the Scoop on Founding Farmers Ice Cream

Opened in Hāwī in 2023 by Canadian transplant Mark Smith, **Founding Farmers** ★★★ (www.ourfounding farmers.com; *⊘* **808/785-7092**) would make an ice cream fan out of anyone. He and his friendly team are certainly willing to dole out as many samples as it takes to convince you. Made daily, Smith's rich ice cream and coconut milk-infused sorbets ($8 for a towering scoop in a bowl) incorporate fresh local ingredients, such as strawberries, papaya, mango, passionfruit, dragonfruit, and jaboticaba (Java plum). Chocolate chili, ginger snap, fignut, and matcha tea are also standouts. The large shop with covered lanai sits at the western entrance to town, 55-3409 ʻAkoni Pule Hwy., *makai* side, making it a perfect pit stop when coming back from Pololū Valley. It's open Tuesday to Sunday 11am to 6pm.

curry in deep-fried croissant dough, and classic gyoza, steamed buns, *saimin* (noodle soup), rice bowls, and salads ($13–$17). It's also celiac-friendly, using tamari sauce rather than soy, and offering the option of mung bean noodles instead of wheat. It's open Tuesday and Wednesday 11:30am to 3:30pm, and Thursday and Friday until 7pm, and Saturday until 2:30pm.

Closer to Highway 19, the iconic, counter-service **Tex Drive-In & Restaurant ★**, 45-690 Pakalana St. (https://texdrivein-hawaii.com; *©* **808/ 775-0598**), is worth braving possible tour-bus crowds for its *malasadas*— Portuguese doughnut holes fried to order, dusted in sugar, and available with a filling, such as Bavarian cream, tropical jellies, or chocolate, for about $2. Founded in 1969, Tex also serves breakfast, burgers, wraps, tacos, and plate lunches ($9–$16), but the *malasadas* are the real draw; open daily 6am to 6pm.

About 19 miles south, and a short detour off Hwy. 11 to tiny Pāpaʻaloa, the **Pāpaʻaloa Country Store & Cafe,** 35-2032 Old Māmalahoa Hwy. (www.papaaloacountrystore.com; *©* **808/339-7614**), offers wonderful browsing in a 1910 plantation-era store while you wait to pick up a home-style breakfast ($8–$15), plate lunch ($16), or other lunch item ($7–$16); the bakery sells delicious pastries. Each section has its own opening hours. The store is Monday to Wednesday 10am to 7pm, Thursday to Saturday until 8pm, and Sunday until 3pm. The to-go kitchen counter is Tuesday and Wednesday 10am to 2:30pm and Thursday to Saturday until 8pm; you can find seating (plus beer and wine) in the cafe and bar Tuesday to Saturday 10am to 2pm. The cafe also offers full-service dining Thursday to Saturday 4 to 8pm, with live entertainment 5:30 to 7:30pm.

Note: You'll find the five restaurants above on "The Kohala Coast, Waimea & the Hāmākua Coast" map on p. 257.

Hilo

The second largest city in the state hosts many unpretentious eateries that reflect East Hawaiʻi's plantation heritage. A prime example of the former is **Ken's House of Pancakes ★**, 1730 Kamehameha Ave., at the corner of Hwy. 19 and Hwy. 11 (www.kenshouseofpancakes.com; *©* **808/935-8711**), which serves heaping helpings of local dishes, amazingly fluffy omelets, and American fare daily 6am to 9pm ($14–$21). The **Hawaiian Style Café ★**, 681 Manono St. (www.hawaiianstylecafe.us; *©* **808/969-9265**), is an outpost of the Waimea favorite (p. 282) with the same hearty local fare, but it accepts credit cards and also serves dinner; it's open daily 7am to 2pm, Tuesday to Thursday 5 to 8:30pm, and Friday and Saturday until 9pm. Food comes on paper plates at the venerable **Café 100 ★** (www.cafe100.com; *©* **808/935-8683**), 969 Kīlauea Ave., but the price is right for more than 30 varieties of "loco moco" (meat, eggs, rice, and gravy), starting at $9, and other hearty fare. It's open Monday to Friday 9:30am to 7pm, with Saturday hours possible when staffing allows.

For slightly lighter fare, **Miyo's ★**, 564 Hīnano St. (www.miyos restaurant.com; *©* **808/935-2273**), prides itself on "homestyle" Japanese cooking, with locally sourced ingredients. At dinner, patrons can also sit in the new 23-seat bar to sample its special *izakaya* (small plates) menu with craft cocktails. Miyo's is open Monday through Saturday 11am to 2pm and 5 to 8:30pm with main courses under $20; reservations are recommended. Vegetarians and vegans will especially appreciate **Sweet Cane Café ★★**, 48 Kamana St. (www.sweetcanecafe.com; ✆ 808/934-0002). The owners got their start pressing fresh sugarcane juice that now makes delectable smoothies ($9), great for drinking with veggie burgers ($15) made from taro, breadfruit, black bean, or chickpeas, or other savory plant-based dishes such as the spicy pickled pepper sandwich with mac nut spread and avocado ($15). Those on a gluten-free diet will also find plenty to nosh. It's open daily 9am to 4pm. Known for its premium coffee, **Big Island Coffee Roasters** (https://bigislandcoffeeroasters.com/pages/hilo-cafe) has drawn a steady stream of java lovers to its corner perch at 76 Kalaniana'ole St. since opening in 2023; its food menu is small, but its locally made popovers, egg bites, and mac nut butter sandwich with *liliko'i* butter or honey provide a satisfying breakfast ($5–$8) on the go. Besides expertly made lattes and espresso drinks, the counter-service cafe also specializes in nitro cold brew coffee and *māmaki* tea. It's open daily 6:30am to 2pm.

For finer dining, besides the restaurants below, consider **Lehua Restaurant ★★**, at 'Imiloa Astronomy Center, 600 'Imiloa Place (www.lehuarestaurant.com; ✆ 808/932-8904). Owners Brandon Lee and Keoni Regidor also operate **Tuesdays** wine store in Waikoloa Village (see "Hawai'i Island Shopping," p. 292), a Berkshire pig farm in Honoka'a, and the well-regarded **Nāpua ★★** at the private Mauna Lani Beach Club on the Kohala Coast (www.napuarestaurant.com; open to the public, but reservations are very hard to nab). At Lehua, the lunch menu ($18–$36) is family-friendly, with a BLT, burger, and fish sandwich, yet also showcases local and sustainable ingredients in an elevated style. The sweeping views of Hilo and the bay are a bonus. Dinner choices (main courses $24–$48) include seared ahi with sweet potato gnocchi, black garlic braised short ribs, and an appetizer of deep-fried taro.

Inside Hilo Hawaiian Hotel (p. 269), the cavernous **WSW / Whiskey Steak Wine ★** restaurant (https://wswsteakhouse.com; ✆ 808/969-6470) also benefits from views of the bay and Mokuola (Coconut Island) just outside its walls of glass. As the name implies, dinner (daily 5–9pm) leans heavily into steak ($38–$52), but there's also fresh catch, misoyaki butterfish, and other seafood and proteins to cover the bases; the whiskey selection is more impressive than the wine menu. The restaurant also serves breakfast daily 6:30 to 10am, with housemade croissant sandwiches ($15–$17), oxtail soup (a local favorite, $20), and red velvet pancakes ($13) among the highlights. Sunday adds a Champagne brunch from 10:30am to 2pm.

Note: You'll find the following restaurants and the ones listed above on the "Hilo" map on p. 203.

MODERATE

Café Pesto ★★ PIZZA/PACIFIC RIM   The menu of this cafe features wood-fired pizzas, pastas, risottos, fresh local seafood, and artfully prepared "creative island cuisine." Set in a restored 1912 building, the airy dining room has black-and-white tile floors and huge glass windows overlooking picturesque downtown Hilo. Service is attentive and swift, especially by island standards, but don't shy away from the two counters with high-backed chairs if tables are full.

At the S. Hata Bldg., 308 Kamehameha Ave., Hilo. www.cafepesto.com. © **808/969-6640.** Reservations recommended. Pizzas $13–$19; main courses $16–$30 lunch; $20–$39 dinner. Daily 11am–8:30pm.

Hilo Bay Café ★★ PACIFIC RIM   In the running for Hilo's most eclectic and polished restaurant, this cafe overlooks Hilo Bay, next to Suisan Fishmarket and the lovely Liliʻuokalani Gardens. Fittingly, sushi and seafood dishes such as misoyaki butterfish salad are reliable pleasers, but fresh produce from the Hilo Farmer's Market also inspires several dishes. Vegetarians will appreciate thoughtful options such as the mushroom curry potpie. The drink list is similarly wide-ranging, including locally sourced kombucha, superb cocktails, and craft beer. At lunch, ask for a seat with a bay view.

123 Lihiwai St., just north of Banyan Dr., Hilo. www.hilobaycafe.com. © **808/935-4939.** Reservations recommended for dinner. Main courses $18–$29 lunch; $18–$42 dinner. Tues–Sat 11am–2:30pm and 5–8:30pm.

Moon & Turtle ★★★ ASIAN FUSION/INTERNATIONAL   Chef-owner Mark Pomaski grew up in Hilo and worked as a sushi chef for Roy's Waikiki Beach and Nobu 57 in New York City before opening Hilo's best date-night/foodie restaurant. At Moon & Turtle, in the historic downtown, he combines locally sourced ingredients in exciting new ways. His signature "Smokey Sashimi" ($17) dresses velvety ahi sashimi with kiawe (mesquite)-smoked soy sauce Hawaiian chili pepper water, and extra virgin olive oil—a savory, slippery dish with a kick. The menu changes frequently, but salting, curing, and smoking are some of his favorite techniques, inspired by hunting and fishing in his youth; you might see a smoked ahi Caesar ($16) or toast with *pipikaula* (smoked and dried beef, $16) among the small plates. Vegetarians usually have at least one large-plate option, such as a mushroom risotto with Hāmākua Aliʻi and shiitake mushrooms ($31), and pastas with veggies plus proteins like spicy Portuguese sausage ($30), can be made vegetarian. Save room for one of the rotating flavors of pot de crème ($9), and an inventive tropical cocktail created by co-owner and bartender Soni Pomaski, chef Mark's spouse.

51 Kalākaua St., Hilo. www.facebook.com/moonandturtle. © **808/961-0559.** Reservations strongly recommended. Main courses $16–$30. Tues–Sat 5:30–9pm.

Puna District

Options are more limited here, so plan meals carefully and consider stocking up on supplies in Kailua-Kona or Hilo. Two shopping centers with a mix of national fast-food chains (McDonalds, Coffee Bean & Tea Leaf, and so forth) and independent restaurants offer some relief. The **Kea'au Shopping Center** (https://keaaushoppingcenter.com), which also holds a KTA grocery store, is at 16-586 Old Volcano Rd., near the intersection of Hwys. 11 and 130 in Kea'au. The newer **Puna Kai Shopping Center,** 15-2714 Pāhoa Village Rd., Pāhoa (www.punakaishoppingcenter.com), has a **Malama Market** grocery store and inexpensive Mexican, Thai, and Hawaiian barbecue outlets as well as local cafes and national chains.

Note: You'll find the following restaurants on the "Hotels & Restaurants in the Volcano Area" map (p. 271).

VOLCANO VILLAGE

In addition to the listings below, look for the **Tuk-Tuk Thai Food ★★** truck (www.instagram.com/tuktuk_thaifoodtruck; ✆ **808/936-4864;** Wed–Sun 11am–6pm at Volcano Inn, 19-3820 Old Volcano Rd.). You can even call ahead for its hearty curries and noodle dishes ($16–$17). Tiny **'Ōhelo Café ★★**, 19-4005 Haunani Rd. (www.ohelocafe.com; ✆ **808/ 339-7865;** Thurs–Mon 11am–3:30pm and 5–8:30pm), may have a casual ambience, but it aims high. Lunch and dinner both offer custom 12-inch wood-fired pizzas ($16–$18) and wood-fired baby back ribs in a Fuji apple barbecue sauce ($35). Gourmet burgers ($19) and salads ($13–$18) dominate the rest of the lunch menu, while market-price fresh catch, lemony Kaua'i shrimp risotto ($36), and pastas ($24–$34) are standouts at dinner (reservations strongly recommended). *Note:* Portions are small by local standards, so order an appetizer if you've been hiking.

Moderate

Kilauea Lodge Restaurant ★ ISLAND/AMERICAN   Although it's no longer owned by a German chef, this airy restaurant still radiates *gemütlichkeit,* that ineffable German sense of warmth and cheer, symbolized by the "International Fireplace of Friendship" studded with stones from around the world. The restaurant focuses on locally sourced versions of omelets, French toast, and pancakes at breakfast and similarly hearty fare like burgers, sandwiches, and fresh catch at lunch. Dinner has become more ambitious recently, such as New Zealand lamb chops served Greek style with baba ghanoush, lemon zaatar vegetables, basmati rice, and garlic yogurt sauce ($41) and seafood risotto with Kaua'i shrimp, New Zealand mussels, and claims ($36).

19-3948 Old Volcano Rd., Volcano. www.kilauealodge.com. ✆ **808/967-7366.** Reservations recommended. Main courses $13–$28 breakfast and lunch; $28–$40 dinner. Daily 9am–10:45am, 11am–3pm, 5–9pm (last seating 8:30pm); happy hour 1pm–3pm; Sun brunch 9am–3pm.

Inexpensive

Café Ono ★ VEGETARIAN   When burgers and plate lunches start to pall, this cafe and tearoom hidden in Ira Ono's quirky art studio/gallery provides a delectably light alternative. The vegetarian/vegan menu is concise: Mexican casserole (corn tortillas with two types of refried beans), lasagna, crustless quiche (highly recommended), and open-faced pesto artichoke and egg salad sandwiches, served with soup side salads. Don't pass up the peanut butter and pumpkin soup ($10) if it's available and allow time to explore the lush gardens outside and colorful gallery inside. In Volcano Garden Arts, 19-3834 Old Volcano Rd., Volcano. www.cafeono.net. ℂ **808/985-8979.** Reservations recommended for groups of 3 or more. Main courses $15–$20. Thurs–Sun 11am–2pm.

HAWAI'I VOLCANOES NATIONAL PARK
Moderate

The Rim ★★ ISLAND FARM/SEAFOOD By no means is this your typical national park concession, as some hot dog–seeking visitors are discouraged to find. The Rim and the adjacent **Uncle George's Lounge** ★★ try to match their premier views of Kīlauea Caldera with a menu that's relatively artful and hyper-local. The Taste of Hawai'i lunch plate ($22) offers a choice of kalua pork, teriyaki chicken, an organic veggie/tofu stir-fry, or macadamia-nut mahimahi, while kalua pork pizza, a local grass-fed beef burger, and coconut-crusted fish and chips are also available. Dinner highlights include pan-seared Kona kampachi, and coffee-rubbed rack of lamb. The lounge serves burgers, sashimi, and most of the Rim's lunch menu ($16–$27) all day. You can also catch live music nightly 6 to

---

A TASTE OF honey . . . and wine

A sweet reason to make a short detour off Hwy. 11 between Hilo and Volcano, **Big Island Meadery** ★★★, 16-313 Shipman Rd., Kea'au (www.bigislandmeadery.com), provides an engaging introduction to the world of mead (honey wine), and the importance of honeybees in Hawai'i. Step up to the gleaming wooden bar (made from a fallen 'ōhi'a tree) to sample fruit- and spice-infused mead ($1.50–$2.50 per pour); you can also order nonalcoholic fruit slushies ($5), honey samplers ($6), and cheese and charcuterie boards ($20). Spouses Vanessa Houle and Devin Magallanes started bee-keeping in 2013, eventually starting Kilohana Honey Co. before expanding into honey wine. The gift shop sells honey, beeswax candles, traditional mead hot glasses made of horn, and other island-made wares. The meadery is open Tuesday to Saturday 10am to 6pm; check the website for yoga classes, lei-making workshops, food truck gatherings, and other special events onsite.

Although their wines are not the world's finest, **Volcano Winery** ★ (www.volcanowinery.com; ℂ **808/967-7772**) has been a unique attraction near Hawai'i Volcanoes National Park since 1993, when it began selling traditional grape wines, honey wines, and grape wines blended with tropical fruits. Marie Bothof and her late husband Del acquired the winery in 1999 and began branching into the tastier option of tea in 2006. Wine tasting flights, for ages 21 and up, are $10 and $20, tea tasting is $5. Vineyard and tea farm tours ($40 and $60, respectively) are available by advance reservation and include tastings plus a picnic area under cork and koa trees. The tasting room and store, 35 Pi'i Mauna Dr., in Volcano (just off Hwy. 11, near the 30-mile marker), are open daily 10am to 5:30pm.

8:30pm. *Note:* Diners must also pay park admission ($30 a vehicle, good for 7 days).

In Volcano House, 1 Crater Rim Dr., Volcano. www.hawaiivolcanohouse.com/dining. ℂ **808/930-6910.** Reservations recommended. Main courses $16–$27 lunch; $29–$49 dinner. Daily breakfast buffet ($24 adults, $14 children 12 and under) 7am–10:30am, lunch 11am–2:30pm, dinner 5–8:30pm. Lounge daily 11am–9:30pm.

PĀHOA

Kaleo's Bar & Grill ★★ ECLECTIC/LOCAL   The best restaurant for miles around has a broad menu, ideal for multiple visits, and a welcoming, homey atmosphere. Local staples such as chicken katsu and spicy Korean kalbi ribs won't disappoint, but look for dishes with slight twists, such as tempura ahi roll or the blackened-ahi BLT with avocado and mango mayo. Save room for the *liliko'i* cheesecake or banana spring rolls with vanilla ice cream. There's live music nightly, too. *Note:* A newer Kaleo's location lies 8 miles north in Orchidland (Kea'au), 16-110 Orchid Land (ℂ **808/333-3533**), and is open daily 11am to 9pm, with additional breakfast hours Saturday and Sunday 8 to 11am.

15-2969 Pāhoa Village Rd., Pāhoa. www.kaleoshawaii.com. ℂ **808/965-5600.** Reservations recommended. Main courses $16–$38. Thurs–Sun 4–8pm.

Ka'ū District

While driving between Kailua-Kona and Hawai'i Volcanoes National Park, it's good to know about a few places in Nā'ālehu for a quick pick-me-up. The standard option is the always-jammed, tour bus-magnet of **Punalu'u Bake Shop** ★ (www.bakeshophawaii.com; ℂ **866/366-3501** or 808/929-7343), famed for its multihued sweet Portuguese bread now seen in stores across the islands; clean restrooms, a deli with plate lunches (all under $13), outdoor seating, and a gift shop, are also part of the appeal. It's open daily 8:30am to 5pm. Across the highway, off a small lane, lies

Punalu'u Bake Shop.

Welcome to the "Southernmost Bakery in the USA!"

Hana Hou Restaurant ★, 95-1148 Nā'ālehu Spur Rd. (https://naalehu restaurant.com; ⓒ **808/929-9717**), which boasts a bakery counter with equally tempting sweets (try the macadamia nut pie or passionfruit bar) and a retro dining room serving simple but filling plate lunches ($13–$17), plus burgers, sandwiches, pizza, and quesadillas ($9–$18); it's open Sunday, Monday, and Thursday 11am to 5pm, and Friday and Saturday until 7pm. Its sister takeout restaurant, **Taco Tita ★**, offers serviceable Mexican fare like tacos and burritos ($5–$13, cash only) Thursday to Tuesday from 11am to 3pm and Wednesday 9am to 3pm. A hipper buzz, partly due to its excellent Ka'ū coffee, can be found at **Ka Lae Coffee ★★**, 95-1165 Ka'alaiki St. (https://kalaecoffee.com; ⓒ **646/257-0339**). Stop in the cheery bungalow (just off Hwy. 11) for fresh-baked galettes and other enormous pastries, taro and fruit milk shakes and smoothies

HAWAI'I ISLAND SHOPPING

This island is fertile ground, not just for coffee, tea, chocolate, macadamia nuts, honey, and other tasty souvenirs, but also for artists inspired by the volcanic cycle of destruction and creation, the boundless energy of the ocean, and the timeless beauty of native crafts. For those cooking meals or packing a picnic, see the "Food & Farmer's Market" listings.

Note: Stores are open daily unless otherwise stated. Hours are typically 10am to 6pm, with significantly shorter hours noted below; changing hours is common, though, so call ahead to confirm.

The Kona Coast

KAILUA-KONA

For bargain shopping with an island flair, bypass the T-shirt and trinket shops and head 2 miles south from Kailua Pier to **Ali'i Gardens Marketplace,** 75-6129 Ali'i Dr., a friendly, low-key combination food hall, flea market, and crafts fair, with plenty of parking and tent-covered stalls (Tues–Sun 10am–5pm). You'll find fun items both handmade in Hawai'i and manufactured in Chinese factories. Visit the **Kona Natural Soap Company** stand (www.konanaturalsoap.com) and learn about the ingredients grown on Greg Colden's Hōlualoa farm, which you can also tour Thursday at 9am ($40) if booked in advance online (see "Organized Tours," p. 214).

In Kailua-Kona's historic district, the nonprofit gift shop at **Hulihe'e Palace** (p. 184) stocks arts and crafts by local artists, including gorgeous feather leis, silk scarves, and woven lauhala hats (www.daughtersof hawaii.org; ⓒ **808/329-6558**); it's open Tuesday to Saturday 10am to 4pm. Hidden from view at the end of an arcade at 75-5725 Ali'i Dr., Jenny Hulen's **Kona Cat Café** not only sells Kona coffee and cute feline-themed merchandise, but also has an option to do yoga or just hang out with cute adoptable cats and kittens in an Instagram-ready play area; if you fall in love, they'll help you find a way to get your kitty home with you (www.konacatcafe.com; © **808/444-5744**). For surf gear and locally designed surf wear, visit family-run **Pacific Vibrations Surf Shop,** 75-5663 Palani Rd. (© **808/329-4140;** Mon–Sat 10am–3pm).

Keauhou Shopping Center, above Aliʻi Drive, at King Kamehameha III Road (www.keauhoushoppingcenter.com), has more restaurants and services than shops, but check out **Kona Stories** (www.konastories.com; © **808/324-0350**) for thousands of books, especially Hawaiiana and children's titles, plus toys, cards, and gifts. **Jams World** (www.jamsworld.com; © **808/322-9361**), founded in 1964, sells comfortable resort wear in bright prints for men and women.

HŌLUALOA

Endearingly rustic Hōlualoa, 1,400 feet and 10 minutes above Kailua-Kona at the top of Hualālai Road, is the perfect spot for visiting coffee farms (p. 184) and tasteful galleries, with a half-dozen or more within a short distance of each other on Māmalahoa Highway (Hwy. 180). Among them, **Studio 7 Fine Arts** (www.studiosevenfinearts.com; © **808/324-1335**) is a virtual Zen garden with pottery, wall hangings, and paper collages by Setsuko Morinoue, as well as paintings and prints by husband Hiroki. It's open Monday to Saturday 9am to 3:30pm. *Note:* Some galleries are closed both Sunday and Monday.

Revel in the Hawaiian art of weaving leaves (*lau*) from the pandanus tree (*hala*) at **Kimura's Lauhala Shop,** farther south on the *makai* side of Māmalahoa Hwy., at 77-996 Hualālai Rd. (© **808/324-0053**). Founded in 1914, the store brims with locally woven mats, hats, handbags, and slippers, plus Kona coffee, koa wood bowls, and feather hatbands. It's open Wednesday to Friday 10am to 4:30pm and Saturday until 4pm.

SOUTH KONA

Many stores along Highway 11, the main road, are roadside fruit and/or coffee stands, well worth pulling over for. Fabric aficionados must stop at **Kimura Fabrics,** a quaint general store and textile emporium with more than 10,000 bolts of aloha prints and other cloth, at 79-7408 Māmalahoa Hwy. (*makai* side), Kainaliu (© **808/322-3771;** closed Sun).

The Kohala Coast

SOUTH KOHALA

Three open-air shopping malls claim the bulk of stores here, hosting a few island-only boutiques amid state and national chains. Prices tend to be somewhat lower than those of shops in resort hotels, and most stores are open daily, often as late as 8pm.

The Waikoloa Beach Resort has two malls, both off its main drag, Waikoloa Beach Road. **Kings' Shops** (www.kingsshops.com) hosts luxury stores such as **Tiffany & Co.** and **Michael Kors,** and batik-print fashions at Hawaiʻi-based **Noa Noa** (www.noanoahawaii.com; © **808/886-5449**).

5

Hawaiʻi Island Shopping

Across the road, the shops at **Queens' Marketplace** (www.queensmarket place.com) include the **Hawaiian Quilt Collection** (www.hawaiian-quilts.com; ℂ **808/886-0494**), which also offers purses, placemats, and pottery with the distinctive quilt patterns of the islands; **Mahina** (https://shopmahina.com; ℂ **808/886-4000**), known for casual chic women's apparel; and other island style-setters such as **Volcom, Reyn Spooner, and Quiksilver.**

In the **Shops at Mauna Lani** (www.shopsatmaunalani.com), on the main road of the Mauna Lani Resort, **Hawaiian Island Creations** (www.hicsurf.com; ℂ **808/881-1400**) stands out for its diverse lineup of local, state, and national surfwear brands for men and women.

Less than 10 minutes north of the Mauna Kea Beach Resort, the unassuming **Kawaihae Shopping Center,** 61-3665 'Akoni Pule Hwy. (Hwy. 270), has two shops worth browsing. **Harbor Gallery** (www.harbor gallery.biz; ℂ **808/882-1510**) features the works of more than 200 Hawai'i Island artists, specializing in koa and other wood furniture, bowls, and sculpture; Sew Da Kine cork purses are an easy-to-pack item. A few doors down, **Fashion Consignment Studio** (https://fashionconsignmentstudio. com; ℂ **808/885-7923**) is a well-priced resale shop with a carefully selected assortment of international designer handbags, alohawear, casual wear, shoes, jewelry, and home decor. Head another mile north to stock up on savory souvenirs at the **Hamakua Macadamia Nut Factory** (p. 192).

NORTH KOHALA

When making the trek to the Pololū Valley Lookout, you'll pass two small clusters of gift stores and art galleries along Highway 270. Highlights in Hāwī include **As Hawi Turns,** 2 miles west of the Kohala Mountain Road (Hwy. 250), at 55-3412 'Akoni Pule Hwy., *mauka* side, which offers eclectic women's clothing, locally made jewelry and accessories, and home decor (www.instagram.com/ashawiturns; ℂ **808/889-5023**). Across the road, visit **Kohala Grown** (see "Where to Eat," p. 275) for island-made edible souvenirs and gifts (honey, jam, coffee, and so forth). In Kapaʻau, across from the King Kamehameha Statue (p. 190), **Ackerman Galleries,** 54-3897 'Akoni Pule Hwy., features Hawai'i Island arts and crafts, colorful alohawear, clothing, and gifts for adults and kids (www. ackermanhawaii.com; ℂ **808/896-7728**). Next door, in the vintage Nanbu Building, **Old Hawaii Trading Company,** 54-3885 'Akoni Pule Hwy., likes to say it has "a little bit of everything," and it's true: Ignore the kitschy factory-made souvenirs and look for a rainbow of sarongs, framed original island art and prints, and locally designed jewelry, among other gems (www.instagram.com/oldhawaiitradingcompany).

WAIMEA

The barn-red buildings of **Parker Square,** 65-1279 Kawaihae Rd. (Hwy. 19), east of Opelo Road, hold several pleasant surprises. The **Gallery of**

Great Things (www.galleryofgreatthingshawaii.com; $\mathcal{C}$ **808/885-7706**) has high-quality Hawaiian artwork, including quilts and Niʻihau shell leis, as well as pieces from throughout the Pacific. Open since 1970, **Waimea General Store** (www.waimeageneralstore.com; $\mathcal{C}$ **808/885-4479**) has more affordable gifts, including candles, aloha print oven mitts, Kona coffee, and more. Across the road, stop by **Isaacs Art Center,** 65-1274 Kawaihae Rd. (https://isaacsartcenter.hpa.edu; $\mathcal{C}$ **808/885-5884**), for museum-quality artwork and frequent exhibitions by island artisans such as wood turners and ukulele makers; it's open Monday to Friday 10am to 4pm and Saturday by appointment.

East Hawaiʻi

HĀMĀKUA COAST

Park on Māmane Street (Hwy. 240) in "downtown" **Honokaʻa** to peruse antique shops, clothing boutiques, and locally sourced gift shops. Start with **Big Island Grown,** 45-3626 Māmane St., selling local edibles such as coffee, tea, and honey, plus island-made gifts and clothing ($\mathcal{C}$ **808/775-9777;** closed Sun). **Waipiʻo Valley Artworks,** 48-5416 Kukuihaele Rd. (www.waipiovalleyartworks.com; $\mathcal{C}$ **808/775-0958**), near the overlook, offers handsome wood items, ceramics, prints, and more, plus a simple cafe; it's open Monday to Saturday 8am to 5pm.

HILO

The second-largest city in Hawaiʻi has both mom-and-pop shops and big-box stores. The **Hilo Farmer's Market** is a prime attraction (see "A Feast for the Senses," below), but you should also hit the following for *omiyage,* or edible souvenirs: **Big Island Candies,** 585 Hīnano St. (www.bigisland candies.com; $\mathcal{C}$ **808/935-5510**), and **Two Ladies Kitchen,** 274 Kīlauea Ave. (www.instagram.com/twoladieskitchen_hilo; $\mathcal{C}$ **808/961-4766**). Big Island Candies is a busy tourist attraction that cranks out addictive macadamia-nut shortbread cookies, among other sweets. A cash-only, hole-in-the-wall, Two Ladies Kitchen makes delicious mochi, a sticky rice-flour treat with a filling of sweet bean paste, peanut butter or a giant strawberry, and *manju,* a kind of mini-turnover. It's open Tuesday to Saturday 10am to 4pm.

Visit **Sig Zane Designs,** 122 Kamehameha Ave. (www.sigzane.com; $\mathcal{C}$ **808/935-7077**), for apparel, surfwear, and home items with Zane's fabric designs, inspired by native Hawaiian plants and culture, including wife Nālani Kanakaʻole's hula lineage; son Kūhaʻo Zane also contributes designs to clothing lines that often sell out quickly. It's open Monday to Saturday 10am to 4pm. **Basically Books,** 334 Kīlauea Ave. (www.basically books.com; $\mathcal{C}$ **808/961-0144**), has a wide assortment of maps and books about Hawaiʻi and the Pacific; it's open Monday to Saturday 10am to 5pm.

PUNA DISTRICT

One of the prettiest places to visit in **Volcano Village** is **Volcano Garden Arts,** 19-3834 Old Volcano Rd. (www.volcanogardenarts.com; ☏ **808/967-7261**), offering beautiful gardens with sculptures and open studios; the delicious **Café Ono** (p. 289); and an airy gallery of artworks (some by owner Ira Ono), jewelry, and home decor by local artists. Look for Hawaiian quilts and fabrics, as well as island butters and jellies, at **Kilauea Kreations,** 19-3972 Old Volcano Rd. (www.kilaueakreations.com; ☏ **808/967-8090**); it's open Tuesday to Friday 10am to 4pm, Saturday until 3pm, and Sunday until 2pm.

In Hawai'i Volcanoes National Park, the two **gift shops** at Volcano House (p. 273) stock tasteful gifts, many made on Hawai'i Island, as well as attractive jackets for chilly nights. The original 1877 Volcano House, a short walk from the Kīlauea Visitor Center, is home to the nonprofit **Volcano Art Center** (www.volcanoartcenter.org; ☏ **808/967-8222**), which sells locally made artworks, including the intricate, iconic prints of the late Dietrich Varez, who worked at the modern Volcano House in his youth.

> ### A Feast for the Senses: Hilo Farmer's Market
>
> You can't beat the **Hilo Farmer's Market,** 57 Mamo St. (www.hilofarmersmarket.com; ☏ **808/933-1000**), considered by many to be the best in the state. The market ranges from dazzling displays of tropical fruits and flowers (especially orchids) to savory prepared foods such as pad Thai and bento boxes, plus locally made crafts and baked goods. It draws a crowd Wednesday and Saturday 7am to 3pm; go early for the best selection. (Fewer stands set up the rest of the week, also 7am–3pm, but it's not quite the same experience.)

Food & Farmer's Markets

Since most visitors stay on the island's west side, the Hilo Farmer's Market isn't really an option to stock their larders. Happily for Kona-area visitors, the **Keauhou Farmer's Market** (www.keauhoufarmersmarket.com), Saturday from 8am to noon at the **Keauhou Shopping Center,** 78-6831 Ali'i Dr., can supply locally grown produce, fresh eggs, baked goods, coffee, and flowers. Pick up the rest of what you need at the center's **KTA Super Stores** (www.ktasuperstores.com; ☏ **808/323-2311**), a Hawai'i Island grocery chain founded in 1916, selling local specialties (poke, mochi) as well as national brands. Other KTA locations convenient to Kona-Kohala Coast visitors are in the Kona Coast Shopping Center, 74-5588 Palani Rd. (☏ **808/329-1677**); in Waikoloa Highlands Shopping Center, at 68-3916 Paniolo Ave., Waikoloa (☏ **808/883-1088**); and in Waimea Center, Highway 19 at Pukalani Road in Waimea (☏ **808/885-8866**).

If you don't want to leave your resort, **Foodland Farms** in the Shops at Mauna Lani (www.foodland.com; ☏ **808/887-6101**), has top-quality local produce and seafood. In the Queens' Marketplace on the Waikoloa Beach Resort, **Island Gourmet Markets** (www.islandgourmethawaii.com;

ϕ **808/886-3577**) has an impressive array of delicacies, including 200-plus kinds of cheese.

Waimea Town Market (www.waimeatownmarket.com), one of several Saturday farmers markets in Waimea, offers prepared food, crafts, and produce, plus live music, 7:30am to noon at Parker School, 65-1224 Lindsey Rd.

For wine lovers, **Kona Wine Market,** near Home Depot at 73-5613 Olowalu St., Kailua-Kona (www.konawinemarket.com; ϕ **808/329-9400**), has a large and well-priced selection. On the Kohala Coast, head uphill to either **Tuesdays** in Waikoloa Highlands Shopping Center (https://visittuesdays.com; ϕ **808/731-6343**) or **Kamuela Liquor,** 64-1010 Hawai'i Belt Road, Waimea (ϕ **808/885-4674**); both have excellent wines at reasonable prices. At Kamuela Liquor, founded in 1946, you'll also find imported cheeses and snacks as well as local macadamia nuts and seasonal white pineapple, among other treats.

HAWAI'I ISLAND NIGHTLIFE

Hawai'i Island residents tend to tuck in early, all the better to rise at daybreak, when the weather is cool and the roads (and waves) are open. But raising a glass at sunset to celebrate *pau hana* (end of work) is also a popular tradition, best observed with live Hawaiian music.

Kailua-Kona

Don's Mai Tai Bar, inside the Royal Kona Resort, 75-5882 Ali'i Dr. (www.royalkona.com/dining; ϕ **808/329-3111**), is the largest open-air, oceanfront bar in town, with excellent mai tais for sunset watching, but it really glows on Thursdays, when top Hawaiian music artists perform from 5 to 7pm. The bar is open daily 6:30am to 9pm with happy hour 4 to 6pm. **On the Rocks,** next to Huggo's restaurant (p. 277) at 75-5824 Kahakai Rd. (www.huggosontherocks.com; ϕ **808/329-8711**), has Hawaiian music and hula nightly from 5 to 8:30pm. The motto of the lively, LGBTQ+ friendly **MyBar,** 74-5606 Luhia St., a block *makai* of Highway 19 (www.mybarkona.com; ϕ **808/331-8789**), is "We accept everyone as long as you want to have fun." It has darts, pool tables, karaoke, drag nights, and $6 cocktails (Sun noon–midnight, Fri–Sat 5pm–2am).

Sharing Stories & Aloha Under the Stars

Twilight at Kalāhuipua'a, a monthly Hawaiian-style celebration, takes place on the lawn in front of the oceanside Eva Parker Woods Cottage on the Mauna Lani Resort (https://aubergeresorts.com/maunalani/experiences/twilight-live-music-storytelling; ϕ **855/267-0516**). On the Saturday closest to the full moon, revered entertainers and local elders gather to "talk story," play music, and dance hula. The 3-hour show starts at 5:30pm, but the audience starts arriving an hour earlier, with picnic fare and beach mats. Parking is free, too, at the nearby beach club or Mauna Lani Sports & Fitness Club (a 15- to 20-min. walk).

The Kohala Coast

All the resorts have at least one lounge with nightly live music, usually Hawaiian, often with hula. Enjoy creative cocktails and choice small plates with nightly music and hula at the chic **Copper Bar** at the **Mauna Kea Beach Hotel** (p. 263). Outside of the hotels, hopping **Lava Lava Beach Club** (p. 281) offers nightly music and hula on the sands of Waikoloa Beach Resort, where the **Waikoloa Luxury Cinemas** includes a restaurant, bar, and leather loveseats to watch first-run films (www.hawaiicinemas.com). In Kawaihae, about 10 minutes' drive north of the Mauna Kea Beach Resort, you can dance under the stars at **Blue Dragon Tavern & Cosmic Musiqarium,** 61-3616 Kawaihae Rd. (www.bluedragontavern.com; ✆ 808/882-7771). The supper club with craft bar features live music (Hawaiian, swing, blues, or rock) Thursday through Saturday, usually starting at 7pm (tickets $15–$20) and open-mic karaoke Sunday, starting at 6pm (no cover); doors open at 5:30pm and close at 10pm.

For a uniquely Hawai'i Island alternative to a luau, try the **Paniolo Sunset BBQ Buffet** at Kahua Ranch (https://paniolobbqdinner.com; ✆ 808/430-6113), a weekly barbecue dinner with rope tricks, live country music, and campfire sing-along with s'mores on a ranch at 3,200 feet above sea level. The 3-hour event costs $85 for adults and $43 for kids 6 to 12 (ages 5 and under free). Festivities start on Wednesdays at 5:30pm.

luaus' new taste OF OLD HAWAI'I

You may never have a truly great meal at a luau (*lū'au* in Hawaiian, which is also the name of stewed taro leaves). Still, you can have a very good one, with a highly enjoyable—and educational—show to top it off. Menus offer intriguing, tasty items such as pōhole ferns and Moloka'i sweet potatoes, while shows feature local history, from the first voyagers to *paniolo* (cowboy) days, plus spectacular fire knife and Polynesian dances. Below are my favorites, which may add additional performances during peak periods.

○ **Island Breeze Lū'au "He 'Ohana Kākou" ("We Are Family")** ★★, on the oceanfront lawn at the Courtyard Marriott King Kamehameha's Kona Beach Hotel (p. 254), is simply the best in Kailua-Kona (www.ibluau.com; ✆ 808/326-4969; $169–$199 adults, $85–$115 children 4–12; Tues, Thurs, and Sun 5:30pm).

○ **Hawai'iloa Lū'au,** at the **Fairmont Orchid, Hawai'i** ★★ (p. 265; www.fairmontorchid.com/dine/hawaiiloa-luau; ✆ 808/887-7320), has the best selection of island-style food,

including *lū'au* (Sat 5:30pm; $194–$227 adults, $100–$135 children 6–12).

○ **Legends of Hawai'i,** at Hilton **Waikoloa Village** ★★★ (p. 265; https://legendsluau.com; ✆ 808/886-1234, ext. 54), is the most family-friendly, with a delicious buffet (try the ahi poke with the fresh Waipi'o poi) and a special kids' buffet that's open as soon as the luau starts, so jetlagged little ones don't have to wait (Tues, Fri, and Sun 5pm; $206–$236 adults, $107–$137 children 5–12)

Hilo & the Hāmākua Coast

Opened in 1925, the neoclassical **Palace Theater,** 38 Haili St., Hilo (www.hilopalace.com; © **808/934-7010**), screens first-run independent movies and hosts concerts, festivals, hula, and theater to pay for its ongoing restoration. **Hilo Town Tavern,** 168 Keawe St. (www.hilotowntavern.com; © **808/935-2171**), is a Cajun restaurant and dive bar open Monday to Saturday 4pm to midnight, with live music, from hip-hop to Hawaiian. The **Grand Naniloa Hotel Hilo** (p. 269) typically offers live music nightly 6 to 8pm in either its Hula Lounge lobby bar or poolside restaurant Hula Hulas. Quaint Honoka'a boasts the island's largest theater, the restored 1930 **People's Theatre,** 45-3574 Māmane St., seating 525 for first-run movies, concerts, and other events (www.honokaapeople.com; © **808/775-0000**). **Honoka'a Public House,** 45-3490 Māmane St. (in the vintage First Bank of Hilo building), stays open Friday and Saturday till 10pm and the rest of the week until 9pm (closed Tues), offering pizza, pub grub, and frequent live music (www.honokaapub.com; © **808/775-1666**).

Puna District

Although the revered founder of **Uncle Robert's Awa Bar and Night Market** (© **808/443-6913**) passed away in 2015, the bustling Wednesday-night marketplace ($10 admission; 5–9pm) continues at Robert Keli'iho'omalu's Kalapana compound with live music from 6 to 9pm. Sample the mildly intoxicating *'awa* (the Hawaiian word for "kava") at the tiki bar or come back Friday at 6pm for more live music. In Pāhoa, **Kaleo's Bar & Grill ★** (p. 291) offers live music, including jazz and slack key, Thursday to Sunday.

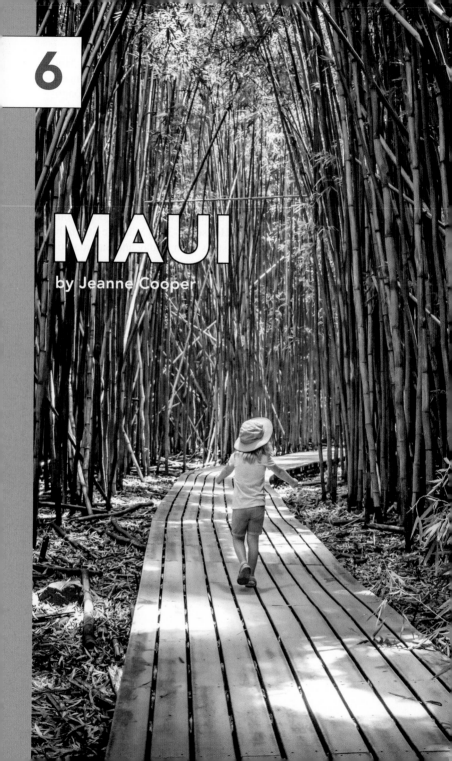

MAUI

by Jeanne Cooper

The world watched aghast in 2023 as flames engulfed Lahaina—a historic capital of the Hawaiian kingdom and the modern center of tourism in Maui. This bustling town was home to many Native Hawaiians, descendants of plantation-era immigrants, and more recent transplants. In the months just after the fire, many visitors chose to avoid Maui all together, prompting fears of a second economic catastrophe similar to that wrought by the COVID-19 pandemic. More than a year later, Maui needs travelers to come enjoy its sunny beaches, lush rainforests, teeming coral reefs, unparalleled whale watching, and towering volcano Haleakalā—the legendary "House of the Sun"—as long as they can respect the island's culture and environment, and show compassion for its people. The outpouring of aloha and donations many former visitors shared in the immediate aftermath of the fires reflects how many memorable experiences the Valley Isle has shared with the world over the years. On your visit to Maui, you'll discover that several businesses today continue to funnel their profits to relief and rebuilding efforts. Even as Maui begins the slow rebuilding of Lahaina, it remains *nō ka ʻoi*—beyond compare.

ESSENTIALS
Arriving

BY PLANE   If you think of the island of Maui as the shape of a person's head and shoulders, you'll probably arrive near its neck, at **Kahului Airport** (OGG). Many airlines offer direct flights to Maui from the mainland U.S., including **Hawaiian Airlines** (www.hawaiianair.com; © 800/367-5320), **Alaska Airlines** (www.alaskaair.com; © 800/252/7522), **United Airlines** (www.united.com; © 800/864-8331), **Delta Air Lines** (www.delta.com; © 800/221-1212), **American Airlines** (www.aa.com; © 800/443-7300), and **Southwest Airlines** (www.southwest.com; © 800/435-9792). The only international flights to Maui originate in Canada, via **Air Canada** (www.aircanada.com; © 888/247-2262), which has daily service from Vancouver, British Columbia, and Calgary, Alberta; and **West Jet**

FACING PAGE: The Pīpīwai Trail near the Kīpahulu Ranger Station in Haleakalā National Park leads to tropical waterfalls.

(www.westjet.com; © 888/937-8538), which flies daily from Vancouver with seasonal service (Dec–Apr) from Calgary and Edmonton, Alberta.

Other major carriers stop in Honolulu (HNL), where you can catch an interisland flight to Maui. **Hawaiian** offers daily nonstop flights to Kahului from Honolulu, Kaua'i (LIH) and Hawai'i Island's Kona and Hilo airports (KOA and ITO, respectively), while Southwest flies to Maui from Honolulu and Kona. A small commuter service, **Mokulele Airlines** (www.mokuleleairlines.com; © **866/260-7070**) flies from Honolulu to Kahului and Maui's two other, smaller airstrips. **Kapalua–West Maui Airport** (JHM) is only a 10- to 15-minute drive to most hotels in West Maui, as opposed to an hour or more from Kahului, while **Hāna Airport** (HNM): Flying directly here will save you a 3-hour drive. However, rental car pickup at either Kapalua or Hāna airports is limited.

Mokulele also flies between Kahului and Moloka'i, Hawai'i Island (Kona and the small airfield in Kamuela, or MUE), and Lāna'i. Check-in is a breeze: no security lines (unless leaving from Honolulu). After your bags are weighed, you'll be escorted onto the tarmac and welcomed aboard a nine-seat Cessna. The plane flies low, and the views between the islands are outstanding.

ARRIVING AT KAHULUI All of the major car rental companies have branches at Kahului. Hop aboard the delightfully plantation-era-styled "train" (light rail) across from baggage claim or walk 8 minutes to the new central rental-car garage and follow signs to your specific agency. The car-sharing platform Turo operates on Maui but note that picking up your car from the airport parking lot is illegal. For information on driving rules in Hawai'i, see "Getting Around Hawai'i" (p. 603).

If you're not renting a car, the cheapest way to exit the airport is the **Maui Bus** (www.mauicounty.gov/bus; © **808/871-4838**). For $2 (free for ages 65 and older or students 24 years old and younger, with ID), it will deposit you at any one of the island's major towns. Simply cross the street at baggage claim and wait under the awning. Unfortunately, bus stops are few and far between, so you'll end up lugging your suitcase a long way to your destination. A much more convenient option is **Roberts Hawaii Express Shuttle** (www.airportshuttlehawaii.com/shuttles/maui; © **808/439-8800**), which offers curb-to-curb service in a shared van or small bus and easy online booking. Plan to pay $52 (one-way) to Wailea and $76 to Kā'anapali. Prices drop if you book round-trip. **SpeediShuttle Maui** (www.speedishuttle.com; © **877/242-5777**). Prices (one-way, from Kahului, for a shared van) range from $54 to Wailea to $73 to Kā'anapali. You must book 24 hours in advance. ***Bonus:*** You can request a fresh flower lei greeting for an added fee.

Taxis usually cost 30% more than the shuttles—except when you're traveling with a large party, in which case they're a deal. **West Maui Taxi** (www.westmauitaxi.com; © **888/661-4545** or 808/661-1122), for example,

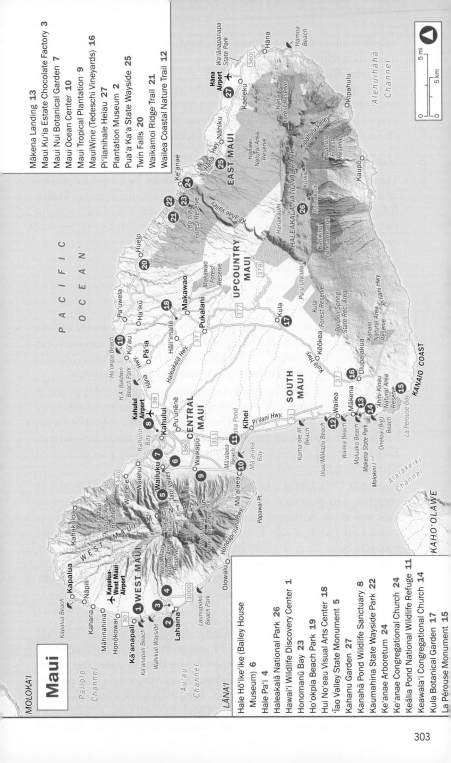

Maui

MOLOKA'I

LĀNA'I

MāKena Landing 13
Maui Ku'ia Estate Chocolate Factory 3
Maui Nui Botanical Garden 7
Maui Ocean Center 10
Maui Tropical Plantation 9
MauiWine (Tedeschi Vineyards) 16
Pi'ilanihale Heiau 27
Plantation Museum 2
Pua'a Ka'a State Wayside 25
Twin Falls 20
Waikamoi Ridge Trail 12
Wailea Coastal Nature Trail 12

Hale Hō'ike'ike (Bailey House Museum) 6
Hale Pa'i 4
Haleakalā National Park 26
Hawai'i Wildlife Discovery Center 1
Honomanū Bay 23
Ho'okipa Beach Park 19
Hui No'eau Visual Arts Center 18
'Īao Valley State Monument 5
Kahanu Garden 27
Kanahā Pond Wildlife Sanctuary 8
Kaumahina State Wayside Park 22
Ke'anae Arboretum 24
Ke'anae Congregational Church 24
Keālia Pond National Wildlife Refuge 11
Kula Botanical Garden 17
La Pérouse Monument 15

PACIFIC OCEAN

EAST MAUI

UPCOUNTRY MAUI

SOUTH MAUI

CENTRAL MAUI

WEST MAUI

WEST MAUI MOUNTAINS

HALEAKALĀ NATIONAL PARK

KANAIO COAST

KAHO'OLAWE

303

will drive up to six people from Kahului Airport to Kāʻanapali for $80, reservation required.

Note: **Ride-sharing services** Lyft and Uber are now authorized to make airport pickups and drop-offs at a designated area, but do not have as wide a network of drivers as some North American cities, and airport rides to resort areas can be costly. The new Hawaiʻi-based rideshare platform, Holoholo (www.rideholoholo.com), is starting to offer competition.

Visitor Information

The website of the **Hawaiʻi Tourism Authority** (www.gohawaii.com/maui) is chock-full of helpful facts and tips. Visit the state-run **Visitor Information Center** at the Kahului Airport baggage claim for brochures and the latest issue of *This Week Maui,* which features great regional maps.

The Island in Brief

This medium-sized island lies in the center of the Hawaiian archipelago.

CENTRAL MAUI

Maui, the Valley Isle, is so named for the large isthmus between the island's two towering volcanoes: Haleakalā and Mauna Kahālawāi, also known as the West Maui Mountains. The flat landscape in between, Central Maui, is the heart of the island's business community and local government.

KAHULUI Most Maui visitors fly over former sugarcane fields to land at Kahului Airport, just yards away from rolling surf. Your first sight out of the airport will likely be Target or Costco—hardly icons of Hawaiiana but handy first stops if you're stocking the kitchen of your rental. Beyond that, Kahului is a grid of shops and suburbs that you'll likely pass through en route to your destination.

WAILUKU Wailuku is a time capsule of faded wooden storefronts, old churches, and plantation homes. Although most people zip through on their way to see the natural beauty of **ʻĪao Valley,** this quaint little town is worth a brief visit, if only to see a real place where real people actually appear to be working at something other than a suntan. This is the county seat, so you'll see folks in suits (or at least aloha shirts and long pants). The town has some great budget restaurants, a wonderful historic B&B, and the intriguing **Hale Hōʻikeʻike.**

WEST MAUI

West Maui remains a place of beauty, though you will see sobering reminders of the tremendous loss of Lahaina. Privacy fencing around the burn zone provides a degree of respect for the disaster zone. The jagged green peaks of Mauna Kahālāwai (West Maui Mountains) hide pristine valleys above miles of sandy beaches, lined with condos and resorts yet offering inspiring sunsets and views of Molokaʻi and Lānaʻi. Vacationers on this coast can choose from several beachside neighborhoods, each with

Hale Hō'ike'ike, the former home of missionary and teacher Edward Bailey.

its own identity and microclimate. The West Side tends to be hot, humid, and sunny; as you travel north, the weather grows cooler and mistier.

A few shops and restaurants at the northern end of Lahaina escaped destruction and reopened in 2024. Moving northward, the coastal communities look like this:

KĀ'ANAPALI The first master-planned destination resort in Hawai'i opened here in 1963. Along nearly 3 miles of sun-kissed golden beach, pricey midrise hotels are linked by a landscaped parkway and a beachfront walking path. Golf greens wrap around the slope between beachfront and hillside properties. Convenience is a factor here: **Whalers Village** shopping mall and numerous restaurants are easy to reach on foot or by resort shuttle. Kā'anapali is popular with groups and families—and especially teenagers, who like all the action.

HONOKŌWAI, MĀHINAHINA & KAHANA In the building binge of the 1970s, condominiums sprouted along this gorgeous coastline like mushrooms after a rain. Today, these older oceanside units offer excellent bargains for astute travelers. The great location—within minutes of both the Kapalua and Kā'anapali resort areas, and close enough to the goings-on in the area—makes this a haven for the budget-minded, although be aware that beach erosion is an issue in some areas.

In **Honokōwai** and **Māhinahina,** you'll find mostly older, cheaper units. There's not much shopping here (mostly convenience stores), but you'll have easy access to the shops and restaurants of Kā'anapali. **Kahana** is a little more upscale than Honokōwai and Māhinahina, and most of its condos are big high-rise types, newer than those immediately to the south.

NĀPILI A quiet, tucked-away gem, this tiny neighborhood feels like a world unto itself. Wrapped around deliciously calm Nāpili Bay, Nāpili offers convenient activity desks and decent eateries and is close to the gourmet restaurants of Kapalua. Lodging is generally more expensive here—although a few hidden jewels at affordable prices can be found. Parking is difficult if you're not based here.

KAPALUA Beyond the activity of Kāʻanapali and Kahana, the road starts to climb and the vista opens up to include unfettered views of Molokaʻi across the channel. A country lane lined with Cook pines brings you to Kapalua. It's the exclusive domain of the luxurious Ritz-Carlton and Montage resorts and expensive condos and villas, set above two sandy beaches. Just north are two treasured bays: marine-life preserves and a world-class surf spot in winter. Although rain is frequent here, it doesn't dampen the enjoyment of this wilder stretch of coast.

Anyone is welcome to visit Kapalua: The Ritz-Carlton provides free public parking and beach access. The resort has swank restaurants, spas, golf courses, and hiking trails—all open to the public.

SOUTH MAUI

The hot, sunny South Maui coastline is popular with families and sun worshippers. Rain rarely falls here, and temperatures hover around 85°F (29°C) year-round. Cows once grazed and cacti grew wild on this former scrubland from Māʻalaea to Mākena, now home to four distinct areas—**Māʻalaea, Kīhei, Wailea,** and **Mākena.** Māʻalaea is off on its own, at the mouth of an active small boat harbor, Kīhei is the working-class, feeder community for well-heeled Wailea, and Mākena is a luxurious wilderness at the road's end.

MĀʻALAEA If West Maui is the island's head, Māʻalaea is just under the chin. This windy, oceanfront village centers on a small-boat harbor (with a general store and a handful of restaurants) and the **Maui Ocean Center,** an aquarium/ocean complex. Visitors should be aware that trade winds are near constant here, so a stroll on the beach often comes with a free sandblasting.

KĪHEI Less a proper town than a continuous series of condos and mini-malls lining South Kīhei Road, Kīhei is Maui's best vacation bargain. Budget travelers swarm like sun-seeking geckos over the eight sandy beaches along this scalloped, 7-mile stretch of coast. Kīhei is neither charming nor quaint; what it lacks in aesthetics, though, it more than makes up for in sunshine, affordability, and convenience. If you want the beach in the morning, shopping in the afternoon, and Hawaiʻi Regional Cuisine in the evening—all at decent prices—head to Kīhei.

WAILEA Just 4 decades ago, the road south of Kīhei was a barely paved path through a tangle of kiawe trees. Now Wailea is a manicured oasis of luxurious resorts along 2 miles of palm-fringed gold coast. Wailea has warm, clear water full of tropical fish; year-round sunshine and clear blue skies; and pleasure palaces on 1,500 acres of black-lava shore indented by five beautiful beaches, each one prettier than the last.

This is the playground of the stretch-limo set. The planned resort community has a shopping village, a plethora of award-winning restaurants, several prized golf courses, and a tennis complex. A growing number of large homes sprawl over the upper hillside; some condos offer reasonable prices when compared to the cost of multiple hotel rooms.

MĀKENA   Suddenly, the road enters raw wilderness. After Wailea's overdone density, the thorny landscape is a welcome relief. Although beautiful, this is an end-of-the-road kind of place: It's a long drive from Mākena to anywhere on Maui. If you're looking for an activity-filled vacation, stay elsewhere, or you'll spend most of your vacation in the car. But if you want a quiet, relaxing respite, where the biggest trip of the day is from your bed to the beach, Mākena is the place.

Part of Mākena State Park, Puu Ōla'i stands like Maui's Diamond Head near the southern tip of the island. The red-cinder cone shelters tropical fish and **Mākena Beach,** a vast stretch of golden sand spanked by feisty swells. Beyond Mākena, you'll discover Haleakalā's most recent lava flow; the bay famously visited by French explorer La Pérouse; and a sunbaked lava-rock trail known as the King's Highway, which threads around the southern shore through the ruins of bygone fishing villages.

UPCOUNTRY MAUI

It's hard to miss the 10,023-foot mountain towering over Maui. The leeward slopes of Haleakalā (House of the Sun) are home to cowboys, farmers, and other rural folks who might wave as you drive by. They're all up here enjoying the crisp air, emerald pastures, eucalyptus, and flower farms of this tropical Olympus.

The neighborhoods here are called "upcountry" because they're halfway up the mountain. You can see a thousand tropical sunsets reflected in the windows of houses old and new, strung along a road that runs like a

Sunrise along Mākena Beach.

loose hound from Makawao to Kula, leading up to the summit and **Haleakalā National Park.** If you head south on Kula Highway, beyond the tiny outpost of Kēōkea, the road turns feral, undulating out toward the **MauiWine Vineyards,** where cattle, elk, and grapes flourish on 'Ulupalakua Ranch. A stay upcountry is usually affordable and a nice contrast to the sizzling beaches and busy resorts below.

MAKAWAO This small, two-street town has plenty of charm. It wasn't long ago that Hawaiian *paniolo* (cowboys) tied up their horses to the hitching posts outside the storefronts here; working ranchers still stroll through to pick up coffee and packages from the post office. The eclectic shops, galleries, and restaurants have a little something for everyone—from blocked Stetsons to wind chimes. Nearby, the **Hui Noʻeau Visual Arts Center,** a premier arts collective, is definitely worth a detour. Makawao's only accommodations are a yoga-centric, beautifully repurposed historic building and reasonably priced B&Bs, ideal for those who love splendid views and don't mind slightly chilly nights.

KULA A feeling of pastoral remoteness prevails in this upcountry community of old flower farms, humble cottages, and new suburban ranch houses with million-dollar views that take in the ocean, the isthmus, the West Maui Mountains, and, at night, the lights that run along the gold coast like a string of pearls from Māʻalaea to Puʻu Ōlaʻi. Everything flourishes at a cool 3,000 feet (bring a jacket), just below the cloud line, along a winding road on the way up to Haleakalā National Park. Everyone here grows something—Maui onions, lavender, orchids, persimmons, proteas, and strawberries, to name a few—and lodgings cater to guests seeking cool tropical nights, panoramic views, and a rural upland escape. Here you'll find the true peace and quiet that only farming country can offer—yet you're still just 40 minutes away from the beach.

Upcountry Maui offers a different perspective on the island's coastline.

ON THE ROAD TO HĀNA   On Maui's North Shore, **Pāʻia** was once a busy sugar plantation town with a railroad, two movie theaters, and a double-decker mercantile. As the sugar industry began to wane, the tuned-in, dropped-out hippies of the 1970s moved in, followed shortly by a cosmopolitan collection of windsurfers. When the international wave riders discovered **Hoʻokipa Beach Park** just outside of town, their minds were blown; it's one of the best places on the planet to catch air. Today high-tech windsurf shops, trendy restaurants, bikini boutiques, and modern art galleries inhabit Pāʻia's rainbow-colored vintage buildings. The Dalai Lama himself blessed the beautiful Tibetan stupa in the center of town. The iconic dining destination, **Mama's Fish House,** is 10 minutes east of Pāʻia in the tiny community of **Kūʻau.**

Once a pineapple plantation village, complete with two canneries (both now shopping complexes), **Haʻikū** is an intriguing detour for those who want to get off the beaten path and experience the quieter side of Maui.

HĀNA   Set between an emerald rainforest and the blue Pacific is a Hawaiian village blissfully lacking in golf courses, shopping malls, and fast-food joints. Hāna is more of a sensory overload than a destination; here you'll discover the simple joys of rain-misted flowers, the sweet taste of backyard bananas and papayas, and the easy calm of old Hawaiʻi. What saved "Heavenly" Hāna from the inevitable march of progress? The 52-mile **Hāna Highway,** which winds around 600 curves and crosses more than 50 one-lane bridges on its way from Kahului. You can go to Hāna for the day—it's 3 hours (and a half-century) from Kīhei and Lahaina—but 3 days are better.

Note: Be sure to drive and park with consideration, as the highway is the lifeline for residents trying to get to work, school, and medical care, and it's not worth risking your safety or others'.

GETTING AROUND

BY CAR   The simplest way to see Maui is by rental car; public transit is still in its infancy here. All of the major car-rental firms—including Alamo, Avis, Budget, Dollar, Enterprise, Hertz, National, and Thrifty—have agencies on Maui. If you're on a budget or traveling with sports gear, you can rent an older vehicle by the week from **Aloha Rent-a-Car** (www.aloharentacar.com; ☏ **877/452-5642**); rates include two beach chairs and a cooler (if requested and based on availability).

Note: Hāna has no rental car agencies, although there are a handful of listings on the carshare platform Turo and the Hāna-Maui Resort has a few rental Jeeps for guests; if you plan to fly to Hāna and explore, plan accordingly.

Maui has only a handful of major roads, and you can expect a traffic jam or two heading into Kīhei, Kāʻanapali or Pāʻia. In general, the roads hug the coastlines; one zigzags up to Haleakalā's summit. *Note:* Residents use the names of highways, not their numbers, when giving directions.

Traffic advisory: Drivers between Kīhei and Wailea should be aware of a rare multi-lane roundabout at Piʻilani Highway (Hwy. 31) at Kūlanihākoʻi Street in Kīhei. From Dec–Apr, be alert to whale watchers on the Honoapiʻilani Highway (Hwy. 30) south of the Lahaina Bypass (Hwy. 3000). Drivers ogling whales in the channel between Maui and Lānaʻi often slam on the brakes and cause major tie-ups and accidents. This is the main road connecting the west side to the rest of the island; if an accident, rockslide, flooding, or other road hazard occurs, traffic can back up for 1 to 8 hours. Check with Maui County for road closure advisories (www.mauicounty.gov; © **808/986-1200**) before you set off. Up-to-date info is usually on its X feed (@CountyofMaui) or that of a local news agency (@MauiNow).

BY MOTORCYCLE   Feel the wind on your face and smell the salt air as you tour the island on a Harley or another motorcycle available for rent from two **Eaglerider** locations: 1975 S. Kīhei Rd., Kīhei (www.eaglerider.com/mauikihei; © **808/667-7000** or 877/351-9666). Rentals start at $179 a day ($139 for a Suzuki motor scooter).

BY TAXI   Because Maui's various destinations are so spread out, taxi service can be quite expensive and should be limited to local travel. **West Maui Taxi** (www.westmauitaxi.com; © **888/661-4545** or 808/661-1122) offers 24-hour service island-wide, while **Kihei Wailea Taxi** (www.waileataxi.com; © **808/298-1877**) serves South Maui. The metered rate is $3 per mile after the first mile, which is $6. **Ride-sharing services** Lyft, Uber, and Hawaiʻi-based Holoholo (www.rideholoholo.com) offer competitive rates, but prices vary by demand.

BY BUS   The **Maui Bus** (www.mauibus.org; © **808/871-4838**) is a public/private partnership that provides affordable public transit to various communities across the island. Expect hour waits between rides; at least you can track your bus's arrival on the website or the Maui Bus app. Air-conditioned buses service 14 routes, including several that stop at the airport. All routes operate daily, including holidays. Suitcases (one per passenger) and bikes are allowed; surfboards are not. Fares are $2 (free for ages 65 and older or students 24 years old and younger, with ID).

[FastFACTS] MAUI

Dentists   If you have dental problems, a nationwide referral service known as **1-800-DENTIST** (© **800/336-8478**) will provide the name of a nearby dentist or clinic. Emergency care is available at two locations of **Hawaii Family Dental**

(www.hawaiifamilydental.com): in Kihei Pacific Plaza, 1847 S. Kīhei Rd., Ste. 101, Kīhei (© **808/856-4625**) and in the Queen Kaʻahumanu Center, 275 W. Kaʻahumanu Ave., Ste. 188, Kahului (© **808/856-4640**).

Doctors   **Urgent Care West Maui,** located in the Fairway Shops, 2580 Kekaʻa Dr., Suite 111, Kāʻanapali (www.westmauidoctors.com; © **808/667-9721**), is open daily; no appointment necessary. In Kīhei, visit **Minit Medical,** 1325 S.

Kīhei Rd., Suite 103 (at Līpoa St., across from Times Market), Kīhei (⌀ **808/667-6161**); it's open Monday to Saturday 8am to 6pm, Sunday 8am to 4pm.

Emergencies Call ⌀ **911** for police, fire, and ambulance service. For the **Poison Control Center,** call ⌀ **800/222-1222.**

Hospitals The only acute-care hospital on the island is **Maui Memorial Medical Center,** at 221 Mahalani, Wailuku (www.mauihealth.org ⌀ **808/244-9056**). East Maui's **Hāna Community Health Center** is open Monday to Saturday at 4590 Hāna Hwy. (www.hanahealth.org; ⌀ **808/248-7515,** after-hours

doctor **808/268-0688**). In upcountry Maui, **Kula Hospital** offers urgent and limited emergency care at 100 Kēōkea Pl., Kula (www.mauihealthsystem.org/kula-hospital; ⌀ **808/878-1221**).

Internet Access The state has created thousands of free Wi-Fi hot spots on Maui, including Hasegawa General Store in Hāna, and other islands, and many businesses provide free Wi-Fi. **Starbucks** (www.starbucks.com/store-locator) provides it in its cafes across the island. If you need a computer with Wi-Fi, visit a **public library** (for locations, see www.librarieshawaii.org). A library card gets you free

access; you can purchase a 3-month visitor card for $10.

Post Office To find the nearest post office, visit www.usps.com. Most are only open weekdays from 9am to 4pm, but the branches at Lahaina Civic Center, 1760 Honoapi'ilani Hwy., Lahaina, and 1254 S. Kīhei Rd., Kīhei, closest to West and South Maui resorts, respectively, are also open 9am to 1pm Saturday.

Weather For the current weather forecast on Maui or its marine and surf conditions, check with the **National Weather Service** (⌀ **866/944-5025** or 808/944-3756) or visit www.weather.gov/hfo and click on the island of Maui.

EXPLORING MAUI
Attractions & Points of Interest

Although it's still unclear which of the many attractions of Lahaina may ever be rebuilt, Maui's bountiful wealth of cultural, historic, and natural attractions are worth including in your itinerary.

CENTRAL MAUI
Kahului
Kanahā Pond Wildlife Sanctuary ★ NATURAL ATTRACTION

Directly outside the Kahului Airport lies this unlikely nature preserve. From the parking area off the Haleakalā Highway Extension (just past Krispy Kreme), you'll find a 50-foot trail meandering along the shore to a shade shelter and lookout. A former royal fishpond, this wetland is the permanent home of the endangered black-neck Hawaiian stilt. It's also a good place to see endangered Hawaiian *koloa* (ducks), coots, and migrating shorebirds.

Off Haleakalā Highway Extension (Hwy. 36A) across from Triangle Square, btw. Hanakai and Koloa streets, Kahului. ⌀ **808/984-8100**. Free admission. Daily dawn to dusk.

Maui Nui Botanical Garden ★ GARDEN

Although occasionally scruffy, this garden is a living treasure box of native Hawaiian coastal species and plants brought here by Polynesian voyagers in their seafaring canoes. Stroll beneath the shade of the *hala* and breadfruit trees. Learn how the first Hawaiians made everything from medicine to musical instruments out of the plants they found growing in these islands. Ask to see the

The ʻĪao Needle in Wailuku.

hapai (pregnant) banana tree—a variety with fruits that grow inside the trunk. You can take a self-guided audio tour or make a reservation online for one of the excellent, hour-long docent-led tours ($10), limited to 40 guests and held at 10am and 2pm Tuesday through Friday. If the garden happens to be hosting a lei-making or kapa-dyeing workshop while you're on the island, don't miss it.

150 Kanaloa Ave., Kahului. www.mnbg.org. *C* **808/249-2798.** $10 adults, free for children 12 and under; guided tours $40 per person, by reservation, Tues–Thurs 10am. Garden Tues–Sat 8am–4pm.

Wailuku

Wailuku, the historic gateway to ʻĪao Valley, is worth a visit for a little shopping (p. 420) and a stop at the small but fascinating Hale Hōʻikeʻike.

Hale Hōʻikeʻike (Bailey House Museum) ★★ HISTORIC SITE

Since 1957, the Maui Historical Society has welcomed visitors to the charming former home of Edward Bailey, a missionary, teacher, and artist. The 1833 building—a hybrid of Hawaiian stonework and Yankee-style architecture—is a trove of Hawaiiana. Inside you'll find pre-contact artifacts: precious feather leis, *kapa* (barkcloth) samples, a wooden spear so large it defies believability, and a collection of gemlike Hawaiian tree-snail shells. Bailey's exquisite landscapes decorate the rock walls, capturing on canvas a Maui that exists only in memory. Admission includes access to a virtual tour guide mobile app.

2375-A Main St., Wailuku. www.mauimuseum.org. *C* **808/244-3326.** $10 adults, $8 seniors, $5 students with ID, $4 children ages 5–18; free for children ages 4 and under. Mon–Fri 10am–3pm.

ʻĪao Valley State Monument ★★★ NATURAL ATTRACTION/
HISTORIC SITE   Millions of people from around the world have
enjoyed the verdant nature, waterfalls, swimming holes, and two short
trails of this beautiful 6¼-acre state preserve for more than a century. To
limit overcrowding, nonresidents must reserve parking ($10) and entry
($5 per person) in advance through an online reservation system.

For many, the main draw are the views of **ʻĪao Needle,** an erosional
remnant of basalt that juts an impressive 2,250 feet above sea level. (Its
Hawaiian name, Kūkaemoku, is less lofty, meaning "broken excrement.")
A .6-mile paved trail with a fair number of steps over its 200 feet of elevation provides the closest look at the emerald pillar, with a covered lookout
point at the end. Below, a short path through ethnobotanical gardens leads
to **ʻĪao Stream,** a peaceful brook that belies its bloody history. In 1790,
King Kamehameha the Great and his men engaged in the battle of ʻĪao
Valley to gain control of Maui. When the battle ended, so many bodies
blocked ʻĪao Stream that the battle site was named Kepaniwai, or "Dam-
ming of the Waters."

Note: An architectural heritage county-owned park of Hawaiian, Japanese, Chinese, Filipino, Korean, Portuguese, and New England–style
houses (in various states of repair) lies just outside the state monument,
also along ʻĪao Stream. The **Heritage Gardens at Kepaniwai Park** ★ is
a good picnic spot, with plenty of tables and benches. You can see ferns,
banana trees, and other native plants along the stream.

End of ʻĪao Valley Rd., Wailuku. https://dlnr.hawaii.gov/dsp/parks/maui/iao-valley-
state-monument. ⓒ **808/984-8109.** Nonresidents $5 per person; $10 parking.
Reservations required from https://gostateparkspuc.hawaii.gov. Daily 7am–6pm.

Heritage architecture at Kepaniwai Park.

Waikapu

About 3 miles south of Wailuku lies the tiny village of Waikapu, close to the clefted slopes of Kahālāwai (West Maui Mountains)—a picturesque spot for two golf courses and a farm-themed attraction.

Maui Tropical Plantation ★ GARDEN This garden has plenty to do: Shop for locally made souvenirs, gawk at longhorn cattle, and zoom on a zipline over the plantation's lush landscape (see "Ziplining," p. 362). Relive Maui's past by taking a 40-minute narrated tram ride around fields of pineapple, sugarcane, and papaya at a working plantation. Tram tours start at 9am and run every hour until 4pm. The grounds are fantastically landscaped with tropical plants and sculptures made from repurposed sugarcane-harvesting equipment. The on-site organic farmers, Kumu Farms, and Maui ʻOma Coffee Roasting Company have transformed the old gift shop into the foodie-focused **Country Market,** while **Kumu Cafe & Farm Bar** offers coffee and more casual fare. **Cafe Oʻ Lei at the Mill House** restaurant offers inventive twists on local cuisine for lunch and dinner (Tues–Sun 11am–8pm), with specialty cocktails at happy hour, 3 to 6pm, and weekend brunch from 9am.

1670 Honoapiʻilani Hwy. www.mauitropicalplantation.com. Free admission. Tram tours $24 adults, $13 children 3–12. Daily 7:30am–8pm.

WEST MAUI

The destruction of Lahaina's historic buildings, museums, and other cultural treasures compounded the tragic loss of life during the 2023 fire. Please be respectful of the latter by not treating the disaster zone as an attraction. It is illegal to enter closed areas, and also against the law to stop on the bypass highway to snap photos. A few attractions remain on the relatively unscathed area on the northern edge of town, including the small but endearing **Plantation Museum** ★ in Lahaina Cannery Mall, 1221 Honoapiʻilani Hwy. (www.lahainacannerymall.com; © **808/661-5304**). The Lahaina Restoration Foundation curated the self-guided exhibits, which include artifacts from the pineapple cannery that was later transformed into this mall, and other objects and images from the late 19th and 20th centuries that reflect the daily life of West Maui's multiethnic agricultural communities. Opened in 2010 at the Wharf Center on Lahaina's Front Street, the free museum was scheduled to move in 2022 to the Old Lahaina Courthouse, which like the Wharf Center did not survive the 2023 wildfire. Fortunately, the Plantation Museum had relocated instead to the Lahaina Cannery Mall, where it remains free of charge to visit (donations welcome); it's open daily 10am to 6pm.

Hale Paʻi ★ (www.lahainarestoration.org/halepai.html) is a two-room printing museum and archive in an 1830s fieldstone cottage, at Lahainaluna High School, 980 Lahainaluna Rd. Home to a vintage press that in 1834 produced the first newspaper west of the Rockies (the Hawaiian-language weekly *Ka Lama Hawaii*), the museum reopened to the school's students in March 2024, the first time since the wildfire. At press time, Lahaina Restoration Foundation still hoped to be able to resume public tours a few days a week; check www.lahainarestoration.org or call the nonprofit at © **808/661-3132** for updates.

Maui Kuʻia Estate Chocolate Factory ★★, 78 Ulupono Rd. (https://mauichocolate.com; © **844/844-5842**), miraculously escaped the blaze that consumed buildings just across the street and its nearby 20-acre cacao farm in Lahaina's foothills reopened to tours in April 2024. The **Guided Cacao Farm Tour** takes small groups on an interactive tour of both the cacao farm and chocolate factory (the largest in the state), including sampling nine pieces of its gourmet chocolate in a treehouse-style tasting room. Don't miss the well-blended tropical fruit flavors such as calamansi lime, mango, and guava in dark and dark milk chocolate varieties. The 90-minute tour costs $85 for ages 13 and older, $75 for ages 3 to 12 (younger not allowed on farm), and takes place Monday to Friday at 9am, 11am, and 1:30pm. The 90-minute **Chocolate Factory Experience** ($125 ages 8 and older only) skips the farm but goes deep into the chocolate-making process, with samples of the intermediate steps and seven finished products. Dr. Gunars Vilkirs, the founder and CEO, often leads the tours, available Monday through Friday six times a day and including a $25 gift card to use in the factory shop or cafe; proceeds from special Sunday tours go to local nonprofits. Stocked with decadent pastries and beverages, the cafe justifies a visit even without a factory tour; it's open Monday to Friday 10am to 4pm.

Kāʻanapali

Showcasing the work of the nonprofit Hawaiʻi Wildlife Fund, the **Hawaiʻi Wildlife Discovery Center** ★★ (www.hawaiiwildlifediscoverycenter.org; © **808/900-7124**) packs a surprising amount of intriguing information and eye-catching, multimedia imagery into its 5,000 square feet on the third floor of Whalers Village, 2434 Kāʻanapali Pkwy. A mural-sized video of whales shimmers across the wall near the entrance, while other colorful exhibits highlight the importance of conservation, the plague of plastic pollution, Hawaiian culture, and the history of whaling in Lahaina (a little disconcerting when you've just bonded with the cetaceans in the entrance video). A "kids' zone" provides educational arts and crafts. It's open daily from 9am to 3pm, with admission by donation.

SOUTH MAUI

Māʻalaea

Maui Ocean Center ★★★ AQUARIUM   This 5-acre facility is one of the best aquariums in the U.S. Visitors can discover the rich marine life of the shoreline, coral reefs, and ocean waters of Hawaiʻi without needing to don a snorkel mask. Yellow tang and other colorful tropical fish dart among the undulating brain and fan corals in the 18,000-gallon Living Reef exhibit, while an underwater tunnel showcases the tiger, gray, and white-tip sharks in the 100-foot-long, 600,000-gallon Open Ocean tank. The Humpbacks of Hawaiʻi "sphere" uses 4K image and 3D glasses for a

Getting up close with marine life at Maui Ocean Center.

stunning simulation of whales swimming all around you; it screens every half-hour. Newer exhibits "Kaho'olawe: A Story of History and Healing" and "Hawaiians and the Sea" share the deep cultural connection of Native Hawaiians to both land and sea. For a real deep-dive into coral propagation, aquaculture, and Hawaiian marine life, book the 1-hour "Behind the Scenes" tour, led by a naturalist, Monday, Wednesday, Thursday, and Friday at 11:30am and 1:30pm.

At Maalaea Harbor Village, 192 Māʻalaea Rd. (the triangle btw. Honoapiʻilani Hwy. and Māʻalaea Rd.). www.mauioceancenter.com. ✆ **808/270-7000.** $50 adults, $45 seniors 65 and older, $40 children 4–12; with "Behind the Scenes" tour, $70 adults, $55 seniors and $50 children (recommended for ages 6 and up). $5 discount for booking minimum 1 day in advance. Daily 9am–5pm.

Kīhei

Keālia Pond National Wildlife Refuge ★ NATURE PRESERVE
Wedged between the highway and Sugar Beach, this 700-acre wetland reserve provides habitat for endangered Hawaiian stilts, coots, ducks, and black-crowned herons. The picturesque ponds work both as bird preserves and as sedimentation basins that protect coral reefs. If possible, stop at the visitor center, then take a self-guided tour along a boardwalk dotted with interpretive signs as it winds around ponds and sand dunes. From July to December, hawksbill turtles come ashore to lay eggs. October through March, rangers typically offer guided bird walks Tuesday at 9am and family-friendly educational presentations, guided walks, and children's crafts the third Saturday of the month from 9am to 2pm.

Entrance near mile marker 6 on Maui Veterans Hwy (Hwy. 311). www.fws.gov/refuge/kealia-pond. ✆ **808/875-1582.** Free admission. Visitor Center Mon–Fri 8am–3pm (closed during stilt nesting season Mar–Aug); refuge Mon–Fri 7:30am–4pm; boardwalk daily 6am–7pm.

Wailea

The best way to explore this golden resort coast is to head for Wailea's 1.5-mile **coastal nature trail ★**, stretching between the Fairmont Kea Lani Maui and the kiawe thicket just beyond the Wailea Beach Resort—Marriott, Maui. The serpentine path meanders past an abundance of native plants (on the *makai,* or ocean side), old Hawaiian habitats, and a billion dollars' worth of luxury hotels. You can pick up the trail at any of the resorts or from clearly marked shoreline access points along the coast. As the path crosses several bold black-lava points, it affords new vistas of islands and ocean; benches allow you to pause and contemplate the view across ʻAlalākeiki Channel, where you may spy whales in season, to rose-hued Kahoʻolawe. It's nice in the cool hours of the morning (though often clogged with joggers) and during the brilliant hues of sunset.

Mākena

A few miles south of Wailea, the manicured coast returns to wilderness; now you're in Mākena. At one time, cattle were driven down the slope from upland ranches, lashed to rafts, and sent into the water to swim to boats that waited to take them to market. Now **Mākena Landing ★** is a beach park and a great spot to launch kayaks and dive trips.

From the landing, go south on Mākena Road; on the right is **Keawalaʻi Congregational Church** (www.keawalai.org; ✆ **808/879-5557**), built in 1855, with walls 3 feet thick. Surrounded by *ti* leaves, which by Hawaiian custom provide protection, and built of lava rock with coral used as mortar, this church sits on its own cove with a gold-sand beach. It always attracts a Sunday crowd for its 7:30am and 10am Hawaiian-language services.

Farther south on the coast is **La Pérouse Monument,** a pyramid of lava rocks that marks the spot where French explorer Adm. Comte de la Pérouse set foot on Maui in 1789. He described the "burning climate" of the leeward coast, observed several fishing villages near Kīhei, and sailed on into oblivion, never to be seen again. To get here, drive south past **Mākena State Park ★★★**, home to popular beaches and Puu Ōlaʻi cinder cone, to ʻAhihi Bay, where the road turns to gravel. Just beyond this is **ʻĀhihi-Kīnaʻu Natural Reserve,** 1,238 acres of rare anchialine ponds and sunbaked lava fields from the last eruption of Haleakalā now thought to have occurred between 1480 and 1600. Continue another 2 miles past ʻĀhihi-Kīnaʻu to **La Pérouse Bay;** the monument sits amid a clearing in black lava at the end of the dirt road. If you've got plenty of water, sunblock, and sturdy shoes, you can embark on foot on the King's Highway (Hoapili Trail) a rugged path built by ancient Hawaiian royals.

UPCOUNTRY MAUI

Makawao

Makawao is Hawaiian cowboy country—yup, the islands have a longstanding tradition of ranchers and rodeo masters, and this cool, misty upcountry town is its Maui epicenter. Modern-day *paniolo* come here to fuel up

317

on cream puffs and stick donuts from **T. Komoda Store & Bakery,** 3674 Baldwin Ave. (ⓒ **808/572-7261**), a family grocery founded in 1916 that seems frozen in time. Neighboring shops offer Tibetan jewelry, shabby-chic housewares, and marvelous paintings by local artists. A handful of decent restaurants crowd the intersection of Baldwin and Makawao avenues.

Five minutes down Baldwin Avenue, the **Hui Noʻeau Visual Arts Center** ★, 2841 Baldwin Ave. (www.huinoeau.com; ⓒ **808/572-6560**), occupies a two-story, Mediterranean-style home designed in 1917 by C. W. Dickey, one of the most prominent architects in Hawaiʻi. You can take a self-guided tour of the 9-acre estate, known as **Kaluanui,** or listen to a lecture or take a class from a visiting artist. The gallery's exhibits include work by established and emerging artists, and the shop features many one-of-a-kind works, including ceramic seconds at a steal. Hours are Tuesday through Saturday 9am to 4pm.

Kula

While in the upcountry Kula region, visit one of the area's many farms (see "Maui Farms: Taste & See," p. 332).

Kula Botanical Garden ★ GARDEN   You can take a leisurely self-guided stroll through this collection of more than 700 native and exotic plants—including three unique displays of orchids, proteas, and bromeliads—at this 5-acre garden. It offers a good overview of tropical flora in one small, cool place, plus some nifty fauna in its aviary.

638 Kekaulike Ave, Kula. www.kulabotanicalgarden.com. ⓒ **808/878-1715.** $10 adults, $3 children 6–12. Daily 9am–4pm.

MauiWine (Tedeschi Vineyards) ★★ VINEYARD/WINERY   On the southern shoulder of Haleakalā is **ʻUlupalakua Ranch,** a 20,000-acre spread once owned by the legendary sea captain James Makee, celebrated in the Hawaiian song and dance "Hula O Makee." Wounded in a Honolulu brawl in 1843, Makee moved to Maui and bought ʻUlupalakua. He renamed it Rose Ranch, planted sugar as a cash crop, and grew rich. The ranch is now home to Maui's only winery, established in 1974 by Napa vintner Emil Tedeschi, who began growing California and European grapes here. The winery produces serious still and sparkling wines, plus a silly wine made of pineapple juice. Late afternoons tend to get quite busy as tour vans returning from Hāna arrive en masse. Reservations are strongly encouraged for tastings, a seated experience in the King's Cottage that includes optional food pairings and a map for self-guided property tours afterwards.

14815 Piʻilani Hwy., Kula. www.mauiwine.com. ⓒ **808/878-6058.** Free admission. Tasting flights $12–$15. Tues–Sun 11am–5pm; reservations strongly recommended.

House of the Sun: Haleakalā National Park ★★★

The summit of Haleakalā, the House of the Sun, is a spectacular natural phenomenon. More than 1.3 million people a year ascend the 10,023-foot-high mountain to peer into the world's largest dormant volcano, which has not erupted for centuries. The lunarlike volcanic landscape is a national park, home to numerous rare and endangered plants, birds, and insects. Hardy adventurers hike and camp inside the crater's wilderness (see "Hiking," p. 356, and "Camping," p. 394). Those bound for the interior should bring survival gear, for the terrain is not unlike the moon. Keep your voices down on the trails, and you'll realize that Haleakalā's interior is one of the world's quietest places.

Haleakalā National Park (www.nps.gov/hale) extends from the volcano's summit down its southeast flank to Maui's eastern coast, beyond Hāna. There are actually two separate districts within the park: **Haleakalā Summit** and **Kīpahulu** (see "Tropical Haleakalā: 'Ohe'o Gulch at Kīpahulu," p. 329). No roads link the summit and the coast; you have to approach them separately, and you need at least a day to see each.

THE DRIVE TO THE SUMMIT

Just driving up the mountain is an experience. **Haleakalā Crater Road (Hwy. 378)** is one of the fastest-ascending roads in the world. Its 33 switchbacks pass through several climate zones, passing in and out of clouds to finally deliver a view that spans more than 100 miles. The trip takes 1½ to 2 hours from Kahului. No matter where you start, follow Highway 37 (Haleakalā Hwy.) to Pukalani, where you'll pick up Highway 377 (also called Haleakalā Hwy.), which you take to Highway 378. Fill up your tank before you go—Pukalani is the last stop for gas. Along the way, expect fog, rain, and wind. Be on the lookout for bicyclists, stray cattle, and **nēnē** (*"nay-nay"*), gray-brown native Hawaiian geese.

Remember, you're entering a high-altitude wilderness area; some people get dizzy from lack of oxygen. Bring water, a jacket, and, if you go up for sunrise, every scrap of warmth you can find. There are no

Sunrise in Haleakalā National Park.

BEFORE THE sunrise

You need reservations to view sunrise from the summit. The National Park Service limits how many cars can access the summit between 3 and 7am. You must book your spot, up to 60 days in advance, at **www.recreation.gov**. A fee of $1 per vehicle (on top of the park entrance fee) applies, limited to one per customer every 3 days. You'll need to show your reservation receipt and photo I.D. to enter the park.

Watching the sun's first golden rays break through the clouds *is* spectacular. But no matter when you go, realize that weather is extreme at the summit, from blazing sun to sudden snow flurries. As you ascend the slopes, the temperature drops about 3 degrees every 1,000 feet (305m), so the top can be 30 degrees cooler than at sea level. But it's the wind that really stings. Come prepared with warm layers and rain gear, and bring a flashlight. And remember, glorious views aren't a given; the summit may be misty or overcast at any time of day. Before heading up the mountain, get current weather conditions from the park (© **808/572-4400**) or the **National Weather Service** (© **866/944-5025**, option 4), and check the park website (www.nps.gov/hale) for any current alerts.

concessions in the park—not a coffee urn in sight. If you plan to hike, bring extra water and snacks.

At the **park entrance,** you'll pay a fee of $30 per car, $25 per motor-cycle, or $15 per cyclist/pedestrian; bring a credit card. Your entry pass is good for 3 days and includes access to the Kīpahulu district on the east side of the island. Immediately after the entrance, take a left turn into **Hosmer Grove.** A small campground abuts a beautiful evergreen forest. In 1902, forester Ralph Hosmer planted experimental groves, hoping to launch a timber industry. It failed, but a few of his sweet-smelling cedars and pines remain. Birders should make a beeline here. A half-mile loop trail snakes from the parking lot through the evergreens to a picturesque gulch, where rare **Hawaiian honeycreepers** flit above native 'ohi'a and **sandalwood trees.** The charismatic birds are best spotted in the early morning.

One mile from the park entrance, at 7,000 feet, is **Haleakalā National Park Headquarters** (© **808/572-4400**), open daily from 9am to 4pm. Stop here to pick up park information and camping permits, use the rest-room, fill your water bottle, and purchase park swag. Keep an eye out for the native Hawaiian goose. With its black face, buff cheeks, and partially webbed feet, the nēnē looks like its cousin, the Canada goose, but the Hawaiian bird doesn't migrate and prefers lava beds to lakes. It once flourished throughout Hawai'i, but habitat destruction and introduced predators (rats, cats, dogs, and mongoose) nearly caused its extinction. By 1951, there were only 30 left. The Boy Scouts helped reintroduce captive-raised birds into the park. The species remains endangered, but is now protected as the state bird of Hawai'i.

Beyond headquarters are **two scenic overlooks** on the way to the summit; stop at Leleiwi on the way up and Kalahaku on the way back

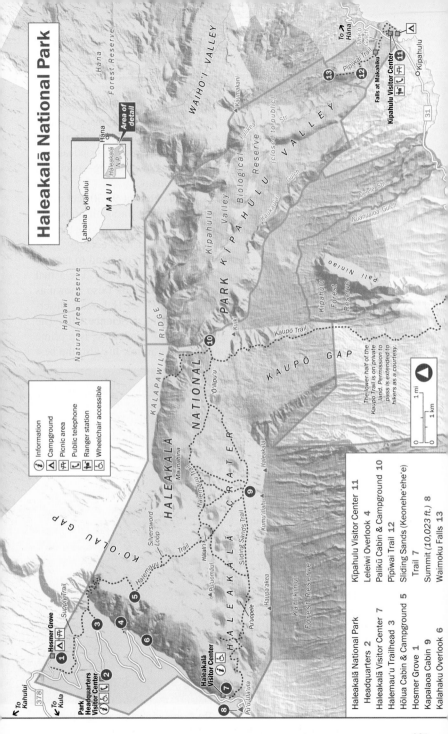

Haleakalā National Park

Area of detail

MAUI

Lahaina o Kahului

Hāna

Haleakalā N.P.

Hāna Forest Reserve

WAIHO'I VALLEY

Hanawi Natural Area Reserve

KO'OLAU GAP

KALAPAWILI RIDGE

Supply Trail

Halemau'u Trail

Silversword Loop

Halemau'u Trail

Pu'uomaui ▲

Pu'u'ula'ula

▲ Pu'uople

Haupa'akea ▲

Kumu'uli'ahi ▲

Halali'i ▲

Sliding Sands Trail

Haleakalā ▲

O'ilipu'u ▲

Maunahina ▲

Kaupō Trail

KAUPŌ GAP

HALEAKALĀ CRATER

HALEAKALĀ NATIONAL PARK

PARK KĪPAHULU VALLEY

Kīpahulu Valley Biological Reserve (closed to public)

Palikea Str.

Kaumakani

Kukui

Kaukukui Gulch

Kahikinui Forest Reserve

Pali Niniao

Kīpahulu Forest Reserve

'Alelele Str.

Nuanualoa Gulch

Oheo Gulch

Pipiwai Trail

Falls at Makahiku

Kīpahulu Visitor Center

Kipahulu

31

To Hāna

To Hāna

To Kahului

To Kula

378

Park Headquarters Visitor Center

Hosmer Grove

Haleakalā Visitor Center

Legend

- ℹ️ Information
- ⛺ Campground
- 🏕 Picnic area
- ☎ Public telephone
- Ranger station
- ♿ Wheelchair accessible

Locations

- Haleakalā National Park **1**
- Headquarters **2**
- Haleakalā Visitor Center **7**
- Halemau'u Trailhead **3**
- Hōlua Cabin & Campground **5**
- Hosmer Grove **1**
- Kapalaoa Cabin **9**
- Kalahaku Overlook **6**
- Kipahulu Visitor Center **11**
- Leleiwi Overlook **4**
- Pipiwai Trail **12**
- Palikū Cabin & Campground **10**
- Sliding Sands (Keoneheʻeheʻe) Trail **7**
- Summit (10,023 ft.) **8**
- Waimoku Falls **13**

The lower half of the Kaupō Trail is on private land. Permission to pass is extended to hikers as a courtesy.

0 1 mi
0 1 km

321

down, if only to get out, stretch, and get accustomed to the heights. Take a deep breath, look around, and pop your ears. If you feel dizzy, or get a sudden headache, consider turning around and going back down.

The **Leleiwi Overlook** is just beyond mile marker 17. From the parking area, a short trail leads to a spectacular view of the colorful volcanic crater. When the clouds are low and the sun is in the right place (usually around sunset), you may witness the "Brocken Spectre"—a reflection of your shadow, ringed by a rainbow, in the clouds below. This optical illusion—caused by a rare combination of sun, shadow, and fog—occurs in just three places: Haleakalā, Scotland, and Germany.

Continue on to the **Haleakalā Visitor Center,** at 9,730 feet, open daily from sunrise (about 5:45am) to noon. Besides a small bookstore with souvenirs, it offers panoramic views, with photos identifying the various features, and exhibits that explain the area's history, ecology, geology, and volcanology. Park staff members are often on hand to answer questions. Restrooms and water are available 24 hours a day. The actual summit is a little farther on, at **Pu'u 'Ula'ula Overlook** (also known as Red Hill), the volcano's highest point, where you'll see Haleakalā Observatories' cluster of buildings—known unofficially as **Science City.** The Pu'u 'Ula'ula Overlook, with its glass-enclosed windbreak, is a prime viewing spot, crowded with shivering folks at sunrise. It's also the best place to see a rare **silversword,** which looks like a silversmith sculpted the top of a pineapple. Silverswords (*'ahinahina,* meaning "very gray") grow only in Hawai'i, take from 4 to 30 years to bloom, and then, usually between May and October, send up a 1- to 6-foot stalk covered in multitudes of reddish, sunflower-like blooms. Don't walk too close to silversword plants, as footfalls can damage their roots.

On your way back down, stop at the **Kalahaku Overlook.** On a clear day you can see all the way across 'Alenuihāhā Channel to the often-snowcapped summit of Mauna Kea on Hawai'i Island. *Tip:* Put your car in low gear when driving down the Haleakalā Crater Road, so you don't destroy your brakes by riding them the whole way down.

The silversword plant grows only in Hawai'i.

GO WITH THE friends

The Friends of Haleakalā National Park is a volunteer organization that leads 1- and 3-day service trips. For the shorter trips, you'll carpool from Pukalani to help the park's horticulturist with tasks in the rare-plant nursery at the summit. For the longer trips, you'll backpack into the heart of Haleakalā, spend a few hours pulling weeds or painting cabins, and gain a deeper appreciation for this magnificent terrain in the company of likeminded volunteers. Trip leaders take care of renting the cabins and supervising rides and meals; the trip is free, though you will pitch in for shared meals. Be prepared for 4 to 10 miles of hiking in inclement weather. Sign up at www.fhnp.org.

East Maui & Heavenly Hāna

Hāna is about as close as you can get to paradise on Earth. In and around Hāna, you'll find a lush tropical rainforest dotted with cascading waterfalls, trees spilling ripe fruits onto the grass, and the sparkling blue Pacific, skirted by gold- and black-sand beaches. Unfortunately, the popularity of driving there before, during, and after the state's tourism lockdown (including when it was supposed to be limited to residents only) has prompted many locals to call for change. If you go, be on your best behavior—more tips on that are below.

THE ROAD TO HĀNA ★★★

Top down, sunscreen on, Hawaiian music playing on a breezy morning—it's time to head out along the Hāna Highway (Hwy. 36), a wiggle of a road that runs along Maui's northeastern shore. The drive takes at least 3 hours from Lahaina or Kīhei, but don't shortchange yourself—take all day. Going to Hāna is about the journey, not the destination. Read the **Hāna Highway Code of Conduct** at www.hanahighwayregulation.com for 20 tips on safe, responsible driving and sightseeing (for example, assume that property is private and do not enter unless there's a sign welcoming visitors, use a pull-off area to let faster commuters go by, park only in legal areas, and so forth). This is a beautiful area, but people still need to get to work, school, or the hospital, and this 50-mile road *from* Hāna is their only access.

The outside world discovered the little village of Hāna in 1926, when pickax-wielding convicts carved a narrow road out of the cliff's edge. Often subject to landslides and washouts, the mud-and-gravel track was paved in 1962, when tourist traffic began to increase; it now sees around 2,000 cars and dozens of vans a day. That translates into half a million people a year, which is way too many. Go at the wrong time, and you'll be stuck in a bumper-to-bumper rental-car parade—peak traffic hours are midmorning and midafternoon year-round, especially on weekends.

In the rush to "do" Hāna in a day, most visitors spin around town in 10 minutes and wonder what all the fuss is about. It takes time to soak up the serene magic of Hāna, including hiking to waterfalls through a

The legendary road to Hāna.

bamboo forest or meandering along a black sand beach. Stay overnight if you can, and head back in similarly leisurely fashion in a day or two. If you really must do the Hāna Highway in a day, leave just before sunrise and return after sunset, or better yet, leave the driving to a professional tour guide.

Tips: Practice aloha. Yield at one-lane bridges; letting four to six waiting cars a time go before you is typical. If the guy behind you blinks his lights, let him pass. Unless you're rounding a blind curve, don't honk your horn—in Hawai'i, it's considered rude.

Safety note: Be aware of the weather when hiking in streams. Flash floods happen frequently in this area. *Do not attempt to cross rising stream waters.*

Guided tours: If you're the driver, you'll only catch glimpses of what your passengers are oohing and aahing about as you white-knuckle around some of the blind curves or feel pressure to speed up from (understandably) impatient local commuters. You may be tempted to park where you shouldn't and get stuck with a $235 fine. So, for those who can afford it, I strongly recommend a small-group or private guided tour. **Temptation Tours** (www.temptationtours.com; ✆ **800/817-1234** or 808/877-8888) uses eight-passenger luxury vans with captain's chairs and full-length windows so everyone can enjoy the views. State-certified guides provide expert but not overly chatty commentary; tours ($299–$449) include a dip in a waterfall pool or swimming at a beach, with options for picnicking, sit-down dining, a cave tour, or return via helicopter. *Tip:* Book direct for a 15% discount.

But for the adventurous and budget-minded:

THE JOURNEY BEGINS IN PĀ'IA Before you start out, fill up on fuel. **Pā'ia ★★** is the last place for gas until you get to Hāna, some 50-plus bridges and 600-plus hairpin turns down the road. Once a thriving sugar-mill town, it lost most of its population to Kahului in the 1950s after the now-skeletal mill closed. Pā'ia nearly foundered, but its beachfront charm lured hippies, followed by adrenaline-seeking windsurfers and, most recently, young families. Today, trendy boutiques and eateries occupy the old ma-and-pa establishments. Pick up breakfast goodies or a picnic lunch at **Hana Picnic Lunch Co.,** 99 Hāna Hwy. (www.hanaheadquarters.com; © **808/579-8686**), whose website conveniently details free and paid parking options in town. Or continue on the road to the little town of **Kū'au,** where a rainbow fence made of surfboards announces **Kū'au Store** 701 Hāna Hwy. (www.thekuaustore.com; © **808/579-8844**), a great stop for smoothies, breakfast panini, and snacks, although parking can be tight.

WINDSURFING MECCA Just before mile marker 9 is **Ho'okipa Beach Park ★★★**, where top-ranked windsurfers come to test themselves against thunderous surf and forceful wind. On nearly every windy day after noon (the board surfers have the waves in the morning), you can watch dozens of windsurfers flying nimbly across the waves. To watch them, go past the park and turn left at the entrance on the far side of the beach. Park on the high grassy bluff or drive down to the sandy beach and park alongside the pavilion. **Green sea turtles** haul out to rest en masse on the east end of the beach; stay at least 15 feet away. Facilities include restrooms, a shower, picnic tables, and a barbecue area, plus a food truck or two.

INTO THE COUNTRY Past Ho'okipa Beach, the road winds down into **Māliko Gulch.** Big-wave surfers use the boat ramp here to launch jet skis

Big wave surfing at Pe'ahi (Jaws).

and head out to **Jaws (Pe'ahi),** one of the world's biggest surf breaks a few coves over; the land is private, however, so you'll have to keep on the highway. For the next few miles, you'll pass through the rural area of **Ha'ikū,** where banana patches and guava trees litter their sweet fruit onto the street.

At mile marker 16, the curves begin, one right after another. Slow down and enjoy the view of fern-covered hills and plunging valleys punctuated by mango and *kukui* trees. After mile marker 16, the road is still called the Hāna Highway, but the number changes from Highway 36 to Highway 360, and the mile markers go back to 0.

TWIN FALLS Not far beyond mile marker 2, you'll see a large fruit stand on the *mauka* (mountain) side of the road—most likely surrounded by lots of cars. This is **Twin Falls** (www.twinfallsmaui.net; © **808/463-1275**), a privately owned piece of paradise with more waterfalls than anyone can count. Parking in one of its 55 spaces is $10; no waiting is allowed if they're full. A gravel footpath leads to the first waterfall pool. Continue up the mountain path to find many more. Swimming is safe as long as it's not raining and you don't have open wounds. (Bacterial infections aren't uncommon.) Be respectful, pack out your trash, and buy something at the Wailele Farm stand. *Note:* The first Saturday of every month is restricted to *kama'āina* (local) visitors.

From here on out, there's a waterfall (and one-lane bridge) around nearly every turn in the road, so be prepared to stop and yield.

WILD CURVES About a half-mile after mile marker 6, there's a sharp U-curve in the road, going uphill. The road is super narrow here, with a brick wall on one side and virtually no maneuvering room. Sound your horn at the start of the U-curve to let approaching cars know you're coming. Take the curve slowly.

Just before mile marker 7, a forest of waving **bamboo** takes over the right-hand side of the road. To the left, you'll see a stand of **rainbow eucalyptus trees,** recognizable by their multicolored trunks. Drivers are often tempted to pull over here, but there isn't any shoulder. Continue on; you'll find many more beautiful trees to gawk at down the road.

AN EASY FAMILY HIKE At mile marker 9, a small state wayside area has restrooms, picnic tables, and a barbecue area. The sign says KOOLAU FOREST RESERVE, but the real attraction here is the **Waikamoi Ridge Trail,** an easy ¾-mile loop. The start of the nature trail is just behind the QUIET: TREES AT WORK sign. The well-marked trail meanders through eucalyptus, ferns, and pandanus trees.

CAN'T-MISS PHOTO OPS Just past mile marker 12 is the **Kaumahina State Wayside Park ★**. This is a good pit stop and great vista point, all the way down the rugged coastline to the jutting Ke'anae Peninsula. (If the parking lot is full, try again on your way back.)

Another mile and a couple of bends in the road, and you'll enter the Honomanū Valley, with its beautiful bay. To get to the **Honomanū Bay,** look for the turnoff on your left, just after mile marker 14, as you begin your ascent up the other side of the valley. The rutted dirt-and-cinder road takes you down to the rocky black-sand beach. There are no facilities here. Because of the strong rip currents offshore, swimming is best in the stream inland from the ocean. You'll consider the detour worthwhile as you stand on the beach, away from the ocean, and turn to look back on the steep cliffs covered with vegetation.

KE'ANAE PENINSULA & ARBORETUM   At mile marker 17, the vintage Hawaiian village of **Ke'anae ★★** stands out against the Pacific like a place that time forgot. Native Hawaiians still grow taro in patches and pound it into poi, the staple of the traditional Hawaiian diet, and they still pluck *'opihi* (limpets) from tide pools along the jagged coast and cast-net for fish. **Ke'anae Congregational Church,** built in 1860 of lava rocks and coral mortar, stands in stark contrast to the green fields surrounding it. Pick up a loaf of still-warm banana bread from **Aunty Sandy's** (10 Ke'anae Rd.). Be wary of the pounding surf on slippery boulders at **Ke'anae Landing;** visitors have drowned after falling in here.

Upland at **Ke'anae Arboretum,** gardens highlight native forest, introduced forest, and traditional Hawaiian plants, food, and medicine. You can swim in the pools of Pi'ina'au Stream or hike the mile-long trail into Ke'anae Valley, where a tropical rainforest waits at the end. Had enough foliage for one day? This is a good spot to turn around.

PUA'A KA'A STATE WAYSIDE   Tourists and locals alike often overlook this convenient stop, a half-mile past mile marker 22. Park by the restrooms; then cross the street very carefully to explore a jade green waterfall pool. Break out your picnic lunch here at the shaded tables. Practice saying the park's name, pronounced *pooh-ah-ah kah-ah,* which means "rolling pig."

An 1860 church in Ke'anae.

Continue on to **Nāhiku,** near mile marker 27.5, where you'll see the rainbow-splashed sign for **Coconut Glen's** ★★ (www.coconutglens. com; ✆ **808/248-4873966**). Pull over for some truly splendid dairy-free ice cream—made with coconut milk. Scoops of chocolate chili, passion fruit, and honey macadamia nut ice cream are served in coconut bowls, with coconut chips as spoons. Open daily 11am to 5pm, this whimsical stand oozes with aloha. From here, you're only 20 minutes from Hāna.

Kahanu Garden & Pi'ilanihale Heiau ★★★   To see one of the most impressive Hawaiian archaeological sites, take a detour off Hāna Highway down 'Ula'ino Road. The National Tropical Botanical Garden maintains the world's largest breadfruit ('*ulu*) collection here—including varieties collected from around the globe. Hawaiian history comes alive in the canoe garden and at the monumental 3-acre Pi'ilanihale *heiau* (temple). Built 800 years ago from stacked rocks hand-carried from miles away, it is a testament to the great chiefdoms of the past. Gaze in wonder at the 50-foot retaining wall and thatched canoe *hale* (house) and imagine steering a war canoe onto the wave-swept shore. If your schedule allows, book the 2-hr. guided tour ($30 for ages 13 and older) available twice weekly.
650 'Ula'ino Rd., Hāna. www.ntbg.org. ✆ **808/248-8912.** Self-guided tour $18 for ages 13 and older (free for children 12 and under). Guided tour $30 for ages 13 and older (free for children 12 and under), Wed and Fri 9:30am. Daily 9am–3pm.

Wai'ānapanapa State Park ★★★   At mile marker 32, on the outskirts of Hāna, the shiny black-sand beach appears like a vivid dream, with bright-green foliage on three sides and cobalt-blue water lapping at its shore. The 120-acre state park on an ancient lava flow includes sea cliffs, lava tubes, arches, and the beach—plus camping, designated sites for camper vans, and a dozen rustic cabins. For nonresidents, reserved, timed passes for entry ($5 per person) and a parking pass ($10 per vehicle) are required, available only online, up to 14 days in advance, at www. gowaianapanapa.com.

   Note: Same-day online bookings are not allowed, so plan in advance. See p. 396 for a review of the cabins. Also see "Beaches," p. 334.
70-200 Wai'ānapanapa Rd., near mile marker 32, Hāna Highway (Hwy. 360), *makai* side. https://dlnr.hawaii.gov/dsp/parks/maui/waianapanapa-state-park. ✆ **808/984-8109** (general info, including camping) or 808/437-8900 (parking and entry passes). $5 timed entry, $10 timed parking pass, both by reservation only, booked minimum of 1 day in advance, at www.gowaianapanapa.com. Daily 7am–6pm.

HĀNA ★★★

Green, tropical, heavenly. A destination all its own, Hāna is a small coastal village in a rainforest inhabited by some 1,300 people, many with Native Hawaiian ancestry. Beautiful Hāna enjoys more than 90 inches of rain a year—more than enough to keep the scenery lush. Banyans, bamboo, breadfruit trees—everything seems larger than life, especially the flowers, like wild ginger and plumeria. Farm stands look like crayon boxes of

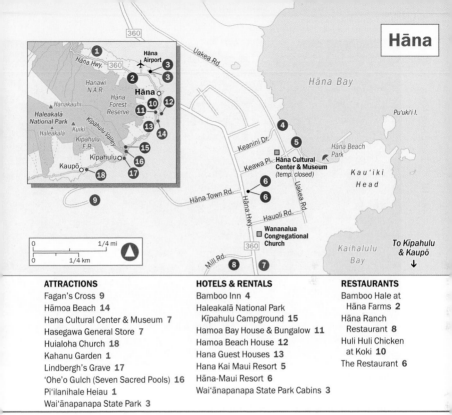

Hāna

ATTRACTIONS
Fagan's Cross **9**
Hāmoa Beach **14**
Hana Cultural Center & Museum **7**
Hasegawa General Store **7**
Huialoha Church **18**
Kahanu Garden **1**
Lindbergh's Grave **17**
'Ohe'o Gulch (Seven Sacred Pools) **16**
Pi'ilanihale Heiau **1**
Wai'ānapanapa State Park **3**

HOTELS & RENTALS
Bamboo Inn **4**
Haleakalā National Park
  Kīpahulu Campground **15**
Hamoa Bay House & Bungalow **11**
Hamoa Beach House **12**
Hana Guest Houses **13**
Hana Kai Maui Resort **5**
Hāna-Maui Resort **6**
Wai'ānapanapa State Park Cabins **3**

RESTAURANTS
Bamboo Hale at
  Hāna Farms **2**
Hāna Ranch
  Restaurant **8**
Huli Huli Chicken
  at Koki **10**
The Restaurant **6**

colorful fruit and flowers. The best of the bunch is **Hāna Farms ★★**, 2910 Hāna Hwy. (www.hanafarms.com; ℭ **808/248-7371;** p. 418).

The last unspoiled Hawaiian town on Maui is, oddly enough, the home of Maui's first resort, which opened in 1946. Paul Fagan, then owner of the San Francisco Seals baseball team, bought an old inn and turned it into what is now called **Hāna-Maui Resort ★★★** (p. 392) and managed by Hyatt. Vacation rentals (p. 391) provide most of the lodging here. Stop at **Hasegawa General Store,** 5165 Hāna Hwy. (https://hasegawastore. com; ℭ **808/248-7079**), a Maui institution open daily, for a T-shirt or bumper sticker and check out their impressive machete display.

On the green hills above Hāna stands a 30-foot-high white cross made of lava rock. Citizens erected the cross in memory of Paul Fagan, who helped keep the town alive. The 3-mile hike up to **Fagan's Cross** provides a gorgeous view of the Hāna coast, especially at sunset, when Fagan himself liked to climb this hill (p. 359).

Tropical Haleakalā: 'Ohe'o Gulch at Kīpahulu

If you're thinking about heading out to the so-called Seven Sacred Pools, past Hāna in Kīpahulu, let's clear this up right now: There are *more* than seven pools—and *all* water in Hawai'i is considered sacred.

At the foot of Waimoku Falls.

'Ohe'o Gulch ★★★ (the rightful name of the pools) is in the Kīpahulu district of Haleakalā National Park (www.nps.gov/hale/planyourvisit/kipahulu.htm), though you can't drive here from the summit district. It's about 30 minutes beyond Hāna town, along Highway 31 (Pi'ilani Hwy.). Expect rain showers on the Kīpahulu coast.

The **Kīpahulu Visitor Station** (℃ **808/248-7375**) is normally staffed daily from 8:30am to 5pm. Here you'll find park-safety information, exhibits, books for sale, restrooms, and a water-bottle refill station. Rangers offer a variety of walks and hikes year-round; check here for current activities. The fee to enter is $30 per car, $25 per motorcycle, or $15 per bicyclist/pedestrian. The Highway 31 bridge passes over some of the pools near the ocean; the others, plus two waterfalls, are uphill, via an often muddy but always rewarding hour-long hike. Tent camping is permitted in the park; see "Camping" (p. 394).

The park has officially closed access to the pools of 'Ohe'o Gulch for safety reasons; many have been injured or drowned here over the years. Floodwaters travel 6 miles down from the Kīpahulu Valley, and the water level can rise 4 feet in less than 10 minutes. You can easily view their burbling beauty instead from the **Kualoa Point Trail.** (If you decide to join the scofflaws swimming anyway, keep in mind that the rainy winter season is the most hazardous.)

From the ranger station, it's just a short hike above the famous 'Ohe'o Gulch to two spectacular **waterfalls.** The **Pīpīwai Trail** begins across the street from the central parking area. Follow the trail a half-mile to the **Makahiku Falls** overlook. This 200-foot-tall beauty is just the beginning. Continue another 1½ miles, across two bridges and through a magical bamboo forest, to reach the dazzling 400-foot-tall **Waimoku Falls.** It's an uphill slog across slippery planks, but worth every step. Beware of falling rocks and never stand beneath the falls.

Beyond 'Ohe'o Gulch

A mile past 'Ohe'o Gulch on the ocean side of the road is **Lindbergh's Grave.** First to fly across the Atlantic Ocean, and later infamous for his anti-Semitic, isolationist views during World War II, Charles A. Lindbergh eventually settled in Hāna, where he died of cancer in 1974. He's buried behind the seaside 1857 **Palapala Ho'omau Congregational Church.**

Adventurers can continue on around Haleakalā, back toward civilization in Kula. The route, Old Pi'ilani Highway (Hwy. 31), is full of potholes and unpaved in parts; most rental-car companies warn you against traveling down this road, but it's really not so bad—just make sure a rockslide hasn't closed it before you go. It winds through ruggedly beautiful territory; about 6 miles (and 60 min.) from 'Ohe'o Gulch, you'll see **Hui-aloha Congregationalist "Circuit" Church,** built in 1859. There's no place for a pit stop until you get to 'Ulupalakua, another hour further, so plan accordingly.

Organized Tours

Blue Hawaiian Helicopters ★★ TOUR   Some of Maui's most spectacular scenery—3,000-foot-tall waterfalls thundering away in the chiseled heart of the West Maui Mountains, say, or Pi'ilanihale, an impressive 3-acre *heiau* (temple) hidden away in Hāna—can only be seen from the air. Blue Hawaiian can escort you there on one of their two types of helicopters: A-star or Eco-Star. Both are good, but the latter is worth the extra cash for its bucket seats (raised in the rear) and wraparound windows. Tours range from 50 to 90 minutes. Be aware that if you visit another island, a good portion of the tour will be over ocean—not much to see. The 65-minute Complete Island Tour ($479) is pricey but stunning, especially if it's been raining and the waterfalls are gushing. After exploring West Maui, your pilot will flirt at the edges of Haleakalā National Park so you can peer into the crater's paint-box colors, and then zip over Oprah's organic farm in Kula. *Tip:* Seats in the back can actually be better for photos, since you can press your camera up to the window. Wear plain, dark colors so your clothing doesn't reflect off the glass.

1 Kahului Airport Rd., Kahului. www.bluehawaiian.com. ⌀ **800/745-2583** or 808/871-8844. Flight times range 50–90 min. and cost $399–$539. Heliport parking $7. Passengers who weigh 240 lb. or more must purchase an additional seat (at 50% off regular price) to balance aircraft safely.

MAUI FARMS: taste & see

Idyllic farms abound across Maui. Many open their doors to visitors and have terrific island-grown products for purchase. To spend the day farm-hopping, join Marilyn Jansen Lopes and her husband, Rick, the sweet, knowledgeable guides of **Maui Country Farm Tours ★★** (www.mauicountryfarmtours.com; ✆ **808/283-9131**). Their 5½-hour Upcountry Farm tour, offered Friday to Sunday at 9am, includes an overview of Valley Isle agriculture with treats and lunch along the way.

If you want to explore Maui's upcountry farms on your own, start by taking a detour on wild Ōma'opio Road to meet the frisky kids at the sweet, off-the-beaten-path **Surfing Goat Dairy ★★**, 3651 Ōma'opio Rd., Kula (www.surfing goatdairy.com; ✆ **808/878-2870**; Tues–Sat 9am–5pm). When you spot the surfboard nailed to the tree, you'll know you're close. Daily, 30-minute farm tours are $25 adults and $18 for ages 3 to 11, with options for feeding kids (the goat kind) December to March at lunchtime ($40 adults, $35 human kids) or just interacting with them ($25 adults, $20 children). Try the goat-milk chocolates, cheese, and other goat goodies for sale, too.

Never heard of a vodka farm? Neither had I until **Ocean Organic Vodka Farm ★★**, 4051 Ōma'opio Rd., Kula (www.oceanvodka.com; ✆ **808/877-0009**), opened just below Surfing Goat Dairy. At this solar-powered distillery on the leeward slope of Haleakalā, sustainable, organically grown sugarcane is blended with ocean mineral water to make fine-quality liquor. Fun, informative tours are $17 a person (ages 12 and up). Those 21 and over can sample various spirits and take home a souvenir shot glass; tours are daily on the half-hour 11am to 5pm. Local farms also supply the cafe, open daily 11:30am to 7pm, with live music from 4:30pm until closing.

Stop and smell the **Ali'i Kula Lavender ★★**, 1100 Waipoli Rd., Kula (www.aliikulalavender.com; ✆ **808/878-3004**), at this gorgeous property set high up on the leeward slope of Haleakalā. The store is chock-full of great culinary products (lavender seasonings, honey, jelly, and teas) and bath and body goodies. General admission is $3, $2 for seniors, free for children 12 and under. *Tip:* Although different varieties of lavender bloom here throughout the year, the purple blossoms are at their peak in July and August. It's open Friday to Monday 10am to 4pm.

Temptation Tours ★ TOUR If you'd rather leave the driving to someone else, this tour company will chauffeur you to Maui's top sites in a comfy deluxe van—much more luxe than the large, crowded buses used by other agencies. Book a pre-dawn trip to the summit of Haleakalā to witness the sunrise (followed by tasting tours at Surfing Goat Dairy and Ocean Organic Vodka; see below) or a picnic out in Hāna. You'll pass numerous waterfalls and stop often, but don't expect to swim or get muddy hiking. The Meet Your Guide to Hāna Tour ($219) is a great value, especially considering your 9-hour narrated tour includes admission to the limited-access Wai'ānapanapa State Park (p. 341) and a stop for lunch. If you're also considering a helicopter tour, opt for the Hana Sky-Trek ($465), a 6-hour

Also on Waipoli Road, **O'o Farm** ★★★, 651 Waipoli Rd., Kula (www.oofarm.com; ☏ **808/856-0141**), hosts scrumptious, 3-hr. breakfast/coffee tours and gourmet lunch tours Monday to Friday. It's pure delight to stroll through the 8½-acre citrus and coffee orchard and biodynamic farm, with stellar views. Pluck your own coffee beans, learn how ripe cherries become drinkable roasts, and then settle under the vine-covered canopy for a feast. The breakfast tour is $135 for adults, $68 for ages 5–12, starting at 8am; the lunch tour costs $150 for adults, $75 for children, starting at 10:30am. Bring sun protection, a light jacket, your favorite beverages (water is provided), and walking shoes.

adventure that starts with a drive (and swim stops) along the lush East Maui coast to Hāna, where you board a helicopter for a scenic flight back home over hidden waterfalls and Haleakalā National Park. The eight-person vans are safe and roomy and tour guides are knowledgeable. www.temptationtours.com. ☏ **800/817-1234** or 808/878-8888. All-day tours $269–$465. Free hotel pickup.

Unique Maui Tours ★★ TOUR If you want to see Maui from a local's perspective with a focus on sustainability, and are traveling with a small group, book a private Haleakalā, Hāna, or birding experience, customized to your wishes. Owner/tour guide Delphine Berbigier hires similarly knowledgeable and friendly guides who share her passion for the island and its unique culture and ecosystems. Lunch usually involves a stop at your choice of food trucks.

www.uniquemauitours.com. © **844/550-6284.** Island tours $1,095 for 1–2 people, $195 per additional guest.

BEACHES

As alluring as Maui's beaches are, don't forget that storms and swells, particularly in winter, can create hazardous surf and undertow. Check https://safebeachday.com/county/maui for current conditions and take advice from lifeguards at one of its 12 beaches with lifeguards before venturing into the water.

West Maui

KĀ'ANAPALI BEACH ★★

Four-mile-long Kā'anapali is one of Maui's most famous beaches. Recent storms have shrunk its sugary golden expanse, though you'll still find somewhere to plunk down a towel. A paved walkway links hotels, open-air restaurants, and the Whalers Village shopping center. Summertime swimming is excellent. The best snorkeling is around Pu'u Keka'a, nick-named Black Rock, in front of the Sheraton Maui, where the water is clear, calm, and populated with clouds of tropical fish. Facilities include outdoor showers; look for restrooms at the hotel pools or Whalers Village. Watersports outfitters and beach vendors line up in front of the hotels. Turn off Honoapi'ilani Highway onto Kā'anapali Parkway in the Kā'anapali Resort. Parking can be a problem—the free public access lots are small and hard to find. Look for the blue shoreline access signs at the Hyatt Regency Maui's southernmost lot, between Whalers Village and the Westin Maui, and just before the Sheraton. Otherwise, park (for top dollar) at the mall or any resort; validated parking may be available with store or restaurant receipts.

Save the Reefs & Your Skin

Since nobody is completely safe from the sun's harmful rays, using sunscreen in Hawai'i is just common sense. However, several ingredients are associated with coral bleaching, which has devastating effects on marine life. Maui County (which includes Lāna'i and Moloka'i) banned the sale, distribution and use of all non-mineral sunscreens in late 2022. Instead, beachgoers should use one of the many commercially available "reef-friendly" sunscreens, which rely on zinc oxide or titanium dioxide to block harmful UVA and UVB rays; some even have tinting to offset any chalky residue. Free samples are often available from hotels, resorts, and even some beach parks and snorkel tour providers. You can also avoid sunscreen altogether by wearing a "rash guard" (lightweight, tight-fitting, long-sleeved swim top) in the water and a wide-brimmed hat, sunglasses, and lightweight, skin-shielding clothes on land.

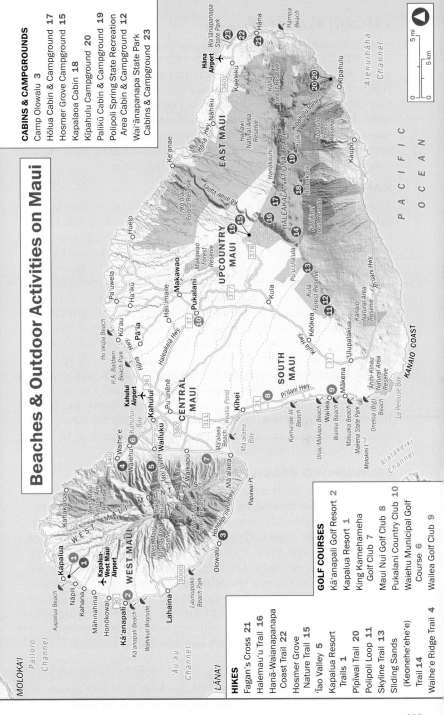

KAHEKILI BEACH PARK ★★★

Often referred to as "North Kā'anapali" or "Airport Beach," this park gets top marks for everything: grassy lawn with a pavilion and palm trees, plenty of soft sand, and a vibrant coral reef a few fin-kicks from shore. Herbivorous fish (surgeonfish and rainbow-colored parrotfish) are off-limits here, so the snorkeling is truly excellent. Facilities include picnic tables, barbecues, showers, restrooms, and parking. On a stretch of coast where parking is scarce, this park with its big shady lot is a gem. Heading north from Kā'anapali on Honoapi'ilani Hwy, turn left at Pu'ukoli'i Road (labeled Kai Ala Rd. on the ocean side of the highway).

KAPALUA BEACH ★★

This beach cove is the stuff of dreams: a golden crescent bordered by two palm-studded points. The sandy bottom slopes gently to deep water at the bay mouth; the water's so clear that you can see it turn to green and then deep blue. Protected from strong winds and currents by the lava-rock promontories, Kapalua's calm waters are ideal for swimmers of all abilities. The bay is big enough to paddle a kayak around without getting into the more challenging channel that separates Maui from Moloka'i. Fish hang out by the rocks, making it decent for snorkeling. The sandy strip isn't so wide that you burn your feet getting in or out of the water, and it's edged by a shady path and lawns. Access the beach via a small tunnel beside **Merriman's** restaurant (p. 405). Parking is limited to about 30 spaces in a lot off Lower Honoapi'ilani Road by Napili Kai Beach Resort, so arrive early. Services include showers, restrooms, lifeguards, and a rental shack.

Note: You can also park here and walk through Napili Kai Beach Resort to **Nāpili Bay** ★★, another attractive beach that has good swimming and snorkeling in calm summer conditions but tends to be more crowded due to the condo resorts lined up on the shore.

LAUNIUPOKO BEACH PARK ★★

The reopening of this beach park 6 weeks after fires devastated Lahaina, just a few miles up the road, brought a welcome bit of cheer to many residents. Families with children love this small park off Honoapi'ilani Highway, thanks to its large wading pool, protected from the surf by giant boulders. Just to the left is a small sandy beach with good swimming when conditions are right. Offshore, the waves are occasionally big enough for surfing; you may spot beginning surfers taking lessons or outrigger surf canoes. The view from the park is one of the best: You can see the islands of Kaho'olawe and Lāna'i. Facilities include a 40-space parking lot, plus 50 spaces across the highway, a restroom and shower, picnic tables, and barbecue grills. *Note:* It's very crowded on weekends.

South Maui

Wailea's beaches may seem off limits, hidden from plain view as they are by a daunting wall of luxury resorts, but all are open to the public. Watch for the shoreline access signs along Wailea Alanui Drive, leading to small parking lots.

KAMA'OLE III BEACH PARK ★★

Three beach parks—Kama'ole I, II, and III—stand like golden jewels in the front yard of suburban Kīhei. This trio is popular with locals and visitors alike because each is easily accessible and all three have shady lawns. On weekends, they're jam-packed with picnickers, swimmers, and snorkelers. The most popular is Kama'ole III, or "Kam-3." It's the biggest of the three beaches, with wide pockets of gold sand, a huge grassy lawn, and a children's playground. Swimming is safe here, but scattered lava rocks are toe-stubbers at the water line. Both the North and South Shores are rocky fingers with a surge big enough to attract fish and snorkelers; the winter waves appeal to bodysurfers. Kam-3 is also a wonderful place to watch the sunset. Facilities include restrooms, showers, picnic tables, barbecue grills, and lifeguards. Plenty of parking is on South Kīhei Road across from the Maui Parkshore condos.

Body boarding on a Maui beach.

KEAWAKAPU BEACH PARK ★★★

You can't see this mile-long beauty from the road, so keep an eye out for the blue shoreline-access signs as you head toward Wailea on South Kīhei Road. The long expanse of white-gold sand has more than enough room for the scores of people who come here to stroll, swim, peer into tidepools at the northern end, or snorkel at the southern end. Clear, aquamarine waves tumble to shore—just the right size for gentle riding, with or without a board. In winter, mama whales come in close to birth and teach their calves the finer points of whale acrobatics. Dip your head underwater to eavesdrop on the humpbacks' songs. At any time of year, soak in the phenomenal sunsets. The beach has three entrances: The first is an unpaved lot just past the Mana Kai Maui hotel, the second is a shady paved lot at the corner of South Kīhei Road and Kilohana Drive (cross the street to the beach), and the third is a large lot at the terminus of South Kīhei Road. Facilities include restrooms and showers.

MALUAKA BEACH ★★

For a less crowded beach experience, head south. Development falls off dramatically as you travel toward Mākena and its wild, dry countryside of thorny kiawe trees. Maluaka Beach is notable for its serene beauty and its views of Molokini Crater, the offshore islet, and Kahoʻolawe, the so-called "target" island (it was used as a bombing target from 1945 until the early 1990s). This sandy, sun-kissed crescent is bound on one end by a grassy knoll and has little shade, so bring your own umbrella. Swimming is idyllic here, where the water is calm and sea turtles paddle by. Facilities include restrooms, showers, picnic tables, and parking. Along Mākena Alanui, turn right on Mākena Road, and head down to the shore.

MĀKENA STATE PARK (BIG BEACH) ★★★

One of the most popular beaches on Maui, Mākena is so vast it never feels crowded. Hawaiians named it *Oneloa,* or Long Sand; residents tend to call it **Big Beach**—it's more than 100 feet wide and stretches out 3,300 feet from Puu Ōlaʻi, the 360-foot cinder cone on its north end to its southern rocky point. The golden sand is luxuriant, deep, and soft, but the shore break is steep and powerful. Many a visitor has broken an arm (or worse) in the surf here. If you're an inexperienced swimmer, better to watch the pros shred waves on skimboards. Facilities are limited to portable toilets, but there's plenty of parking and lifeguards at the first two entrances off Mākena Alanui Road, plus a food truck at the first one. Dolphins often frequent these waters, and nearly every afternoon a heavy cloud rolls in, providing welcome relief from the sun.

If you clamber up Puʻu Ōlaʻi, you'll find **Little Beach** (officially called Puʻu Ōlaʻi) on the other side, a small crescent of sand where assorted nudists work on their all-over tans in defiance of the law (the police do occasionally enforce it). The shoreline doesn't drop off quite so steeply here, and bodysurfing is terrific—no pun intended. About 3¾ miles south of the **Grand Wailea Resort** (p. 385), before you reach the first paved entrance to the park, a dirt road leads to small, well-shaded **Oneuli Beach ★**, whose name means "dark sand" in Hawaiian and understandably is nicknamed Black Sand Beach. It's best for snorkeling or turtle-spotting.

Note: Parking is $10 per vehicle, payable by credit card or phone, available 7am to 6:45pm. Walk-in access is daily 5am to 7pm for Big Beach (Oneloa) and Oneuli; for Little Beach (Puu Ōlaʻi), it's Monday to Friday 5am to 7pm and Saturday and Sunday 5am to 4pm; non-resident admission is $5 per person, free for ages 3 and under. You can pay for parking and entry online at https://dlnr.hawaii.gov/dsp/parks/maui/makena-state-park.

ULUA/MŌKAPU BEACH ★★

The twin beaches of Ulua and Mōkapu, separated by a rocky point, are popular with sunbathers, snorkelers, and scuba divers alike. Some of Wailea's best snorkeling is found on the adjoining reef. The ocean bottom is shallow and gently slopes down to deeper waters, making swimming generally safe. In high season (late Dec to Mar and June–Aug), sunbathers pack the sand and carpet it with beach towels. Facilities include showers and restrooms. Beach gear can be rented at the nearby Wailea Ocean Activity Center. Look for the blue shoreline access sign at Haleali'i Place off on Wailea Alanui Drive near the Wailea Beach Resort.

WAILEA BEACH ★★

Brigades of resort umbrellas and beach chairs make it challenging to appreciate this beach's pristine beauty. It's the front yard of the Four Seasons and the Grand Wailea, and hotel staff makes plenty use of the deep sand. Still, the view out to sea is magnificent, framed by neighboring Kaho'olawe, Lāna'i, and the tiny crescent of Molokini. From shore, you can see Pacific humpback whales in season (Dec–Mar) and unreal sunsets nightly. Facilities include restrooms, outdoor showers, and limited free parking at the blue shoreline access sign, just south of the Grand Wailea on Wailea Alanui Drive.

North Shore & East Maui

H. A. BALDWIN BEACH PARK ★★

This beach park draws lots of locals: dog walkers, yoga enthusiasts, boogie boarders, fishermen, and young families. The far ends of the beach are safest for swimming: "the cove" in the lee of the rocks at the north end, and "baby beach" at the south end, where an exposed reef creates a natural

Windsurfing at Ho'okipa Beach Park.

pool—often with a current that's fun to swim against. Facilities include a pavilion with picnic tables, grills, restrooms, showers, a parking area, and lifeguards. It's busy on weekends and late afternoons; mornings and weekdays are much quieter. Heading east on Hāna Highway (Hwy. 36), turn left at the soccer field just before reaching Pāʻia.

HĀMOA BEACH ★★

James Michener called Hāmoa "a beach so perfectly formed that I wonder at its comparative obscurity." Viewed from above, this half-moon-shaped, gray-sand beach is vision of paradise. The wide stretch of sand (a mix of coral and lava) is three football fields long and sits below 30-foot black-lava sea cliffs. Swells on this exposed beach break offshore and roll in, making it a popular surfing and bodysurfing area. Hāmoa is often swept by rip currents, so take care. The calm left side is best for snorkeling in summer.

Note: The former management of Hāna-Maui Resort once maintained restroom facilities here, but no longer does, due to concerns over ancient burial sites in the area. Instead, there's a portable toilet and an outdoor shower. Street parking is limited. Look for the Hāmoa Beach turnoff from Hāna Highway.

HOʻOKIPA BEACH PARK ★★★

Hoʻokipa means "hospitality," and this sandy beach on Maui's North Shore certainly rolls out the red carpet out for waveriders. Two miles past Pāʻia on the Hāna Highway (Hwy. 36), it's among the world's top spots for windsurfing and kiting, thanks to trade winds that kick up whitecaps. Hoʻokipa offers no less than five surf breaks and daring surfers paddle out to carve waves up to 25 feet tall. Voyeurs are welcome, too; the clifftop

Volcanic black sand at Waiʻānapanapa State Park.

parking lot has a bird's-eye view. On flat days, snorkelers explore the reef's treasure trove of marine life: Gentle garden eels wave below the surface. Green sea turtles haul out here by the dozens to nap on the sand (enjoy from a distance). More than once, a rare Hawaiian monk seal has popped ashore during a surf contest. Facilities include restrooms, showers, pavilions, picnic tables, barbecue grills, and parking.

WAI'ĀNAPANAPA STATE PARK ★★★

A beach of jet-black pebbly sand, a sea arch, a stone temple, blowhole, and historic *hala* (pandanus) groves: This dramatic 120-acre beach park, 4 miles northeast of Hāna, offers many jewels. The Wai'ānapanapa shoreline has hikes and picnicking spots and you can follow the coastal trail for a long distance in both directions from the parking lot. Facilities include picnic tables, barbecue grills, restrooms, showers, tent sites, camper van parking, and 12 cabins (p. 396). *Note:* The state requires timed, paid entry permits ($5 per person) and parking passes ($10 per vehicle), available only online and purchased up to 14 days in advance (no same-day reservations) at https://gostateparks.hawaii.gov/waianapanapa. Slots of 3 or 2½ hours are offered starting at 7am, with the last admission good for 3 to 6pm; you can reserve consecutive slots if available to make a longer day of it. See https://dlnr.hawaii.gov/dsp/parks/maui/waianapanapa-state-park for updates and details.

WATERSPORTS

The watersports options on Maui are mind-boggling—from lazy snorkeling to high-energy kitesurfing and everything in between. Colorful, fish-filled reefs are easily accessible, often from a sandy beach.

You'll find rental gear and ocean toys all over the island. Most seaside hotels and resorts are stocked with watersports equipment (complimentary or rentals), from snorkels to kayaks to Hobies. **Snorkel Bob's** (www.snorkel bob.com) rents snorkel gear for as little as $9 a week, plus boogie boards, wetsuits, and more at several locations: at Napili Village, 5425 C Lower Honoapi'ilani Hwy., Lahaina (℗ 808/669-9603); Kahana Gateway Center, 4405 Honoapi'ilani Hwy., Lahaina (℗ 808/446-3585); in Honokōwai, 3350 Lower Honoapi'ilani Hwy. #201, Lahaina (℗ 808/667-9999); 1217 Front St. (behind Cannery Mall), Lahaina (℗ 808/661-4421); in Azeka II Shopping Center, 1279 S. Kīhei Rd., Kīhei (℗ 808/875-6188); 2411 S. Kīhei Rd., Kīhei (℗ 808/879-7449); and 100 Wailea Ike Dr., Wailea (℗ 808/874-0011). All shops are open daily from 8am to 5pm. If you're island-hopping, you can rent from a Snorkel Bob's on one island and return to a branch on another.

Boss Frog's Dive, Surf, and Bike Shops (www.bossfrog.com) has nine locations for rentals of snorkel sets (starting at $1.50 a day), boogie boards, longboards, paddleboards, and other gear. From West Maui to South Maui, find them in Napili Plaza, 5095 Nāpilihau St., Nāpili (℗ 808/669-4949); in Kahana Manor, 4310 Lower Honoapi'ilani Rd.

(☎ 808/669-6700); in Kā'anapali, 3636 Lower Honoapi'ilani Rd. (☎ 808/665-1200); in Lahaina Cannery Mall, 1221 Honoapi'ilani Hwy. (☎ 808/661-5995); in Mā'alaea Harbor Shops, 300 Mā'alaea Rd. (☎ 808/242-0088); and in Kīhei, 1215 S. Kīhei Rd. (☎ 808/891-0077), 1770 S. Kīhei Rd. (☎ 808/874-5225), Dolphin Plaza, 2395 S. Kīhei Rd. (☎ 808/875-4477), and Kamaole Center, 2463 S. Kīhei Rd. (☎ 808/874-5577). They're open daily 8am to 5pm.

Boating

You'll need a watercraft to visit the crescent-shaped islet **Molokini,** one of the best snorkel and scuba spots in Hawai'i. Trips to the island of **Lāna'i** (see Chapter 8) are also popular for a day of snorkeling. Bring a towel, a swimsuit, mineral sunscreen, and a hat on a snorkel cruise; everything else is usually included. If you'd like to go a little deeper than snorkeling allows, consider trying **SNUBA,** a shallow-water diving system in which you are connected by a 20-foot air hose to an air tank that floats on a raft at the water's surface. Most of these snorkel boats offer it for an additional cost; it's usually around $60 for a half-hour or so. No certification is required for SNUBA. For fishing charters, see "Sport Fishing," below.

Kai Kanani ★★★ TOUR   For more than 30 years, this Native Hawaiian family-owned company has been South Maui's leading tour boat operator. Launching from Maluaka Beach in Mākena, the luxury catamaran *Kai Kanani* has only 3 short miles to cross to Molokini. With a 6:15am departure, its 3-hour **sunrise snorkel** ($280 adults, $229 children ages 2–12) allows you to observe the multihued marine life of Molokini Crater before any other boats arrive, then enjoy a gourmet breakfast. There's also a 9:45am tour with a similarly appetizing lunch, and **sunset** and **whale-watching cruises.**

34 Wailea Gateway Center, Wailea. www.kaikanani.com. ☎ **808/879-7218.** Prices vary by cruise, starting at $140 for a 2-hr whale watch, including pickup from select Wailea lodgings.

Maui Classic Charters ★ TOUR   Maui Classic Charters offers morning and afternoon **snorkel cruises to Molokini** on *Four Winds II,* a 55-foot glass-bottom catamaran. Rates for the 5-hour morning sail are $150 for adults, $115 for children 3 to 12, including breakfast and barbecue lunch. The 3½-hour afternoon sail is a steal at $85 ($70 for children), though the captain usually only visits Coral Gardens, which is accessible from shore. All *Four Winds* trips include beer, wine, and soda; snorkel gear and instruction; and sport fishing along the way. Those hoping to spot dolphins should book a trip on the state-of-the-art catamaran *Maui Magic.* A 5-hour snorkel journey to Molokini and Mākena costs $160 for adults, $125 for children 5 to 12, and includes breakfast; a barbecue lunch; beer, wine, and soda; gear; and instruction.

Mā'alaea Harbor, slip 55 and slip 80. www.mauiclassiccharters.com. ☎ **800/736-5740** or 808/879-8188. Prices vary depending on cruise.

Pacific Whale Foundation ★★ TOUR   This not-for-profit foundation supports its whale research, education, and conservation programs by offering **whale-watch cruises, wild dolphin encounters,** and **snorkel tours,** some to Molokini, Honolua Bay, and Lāna'i. Numerous daily trips are offered out of Mā'alaea Harbor. Two special tours include the **Adult Sunset Sail** ($120, for ages 21 and older only) with drinks, appetizers, and island music, and the **Sunset and Celestial Cruise** ($110 adults, $90 children) with Harriet Witt, a wonderful astronomer and storyteller who highlights stars significant to Hawaiian culture and early navigation. *Note:* Prices reflect 20% discount for booking online.

Shops at Mā'alaea Harbor, 300 Mā'alaea Rd., Wailuku. www.pacwhale.com/ecotours. ✆ **808/249-8811.** Trips from $90 adults, $70 children ages 5–12, free for 1 child ages 4 and under per adult; snorkeling cruises from $160 adults, $110 children ages 5–12.

Teralani Sailing Adventures ★★ TOUR   Passengers board Teralani's fleet of large, stable double-hulled sailing catamarans directly from Kā'anapali Beach, which means all trips start with a splash as the crew tries to time your ascent up its sets with the tidal surge. Its **snorkel sails, whale- and dolphin-watching tours,** and **sunset cruises** have no fixed destinations—the captain simply goes where the best conditions are in West Maui on any given day. Friendly crew members keep the drinks coming and an eye out for wildlife. Formal whale-watching tours take place December 15 to April 15 (you may also spot whales before or after those dates) and range from a premium 2½-hr option with open bar and appetizers ($120 adults, $90 ages 6–12, and $60 children 5 and under), with a maximum of 35 passengers, to a discount, 2-hour cruise with drinks and snacks available for purchase, for up to 49 passengers ($60 adults, $40 ages 6–12, $1 ages 0–5—the $1 is the state's mandatory ocean conservation fee). When whale-watching season ends, the cruises convert to dolphin-watching excursions, primarily spinner and bottlenose dolphins; if you don't see any, you're guaranteed another cruise, but you'll likely think your original time was well-spent.

Note: "Lunch" tours would be better advertised as serving appetizers—typically chips and salsa, cheese and crackers, raw veggies and dip, and meatballs. Parking is available at **Outrigger Kā'anapali Beach Resort** (p. 369) for a flat rate of $8 for up to 5 hours with validation by Teralani. Rates listed below do not include a possible $10 fuel surcharge for ages 6 and older.

Meet on beach in front of Outrigger Kā'anapali Beach Resort, 2525 Kā'anapali Pkwy., Lahaina. www.teralani.com. ✆ **808/400-1638.** Sunset dinner sail $130 adults, $100 children 12 and under; sunset cocktail sail $100 adults, $90 ages 6–12, $60 ages 5 and under; snorkel sails $120 adults, $100 children ages 6–12, $1 for ages 5 and under with paying adult (limit 1 per adult); whale-watching $60–$120 adults, $40–$90 ages 6–12, $1–$60 ages 5 and under; wild dolphin sail $90 adults, $80 ages 6–12, $1 for ages 5 and under with paying adult (limit 1 per adult).

Trilogy Excursions ★★★ TOUR   Trilogy offers my favorite **snorkel-sail trips.** The family-run company prioritizes environmental stewardship—along with ensuring you have a stellar marine adventure. Hop aboard one of Trilogy's fleet of custom-built catamarans, from 54 to 65 feet long, in Mā'alaea or Kā'anapali to sail to **Lāna'i** for a fun-filled day of snorkeling, picnicking, and relaxing. This is the only cruise with rights to take you to Hulopo'e Beach; once you've finished snorkeling in its marine preserve, explore tide pools, hike to Pu'u Pehe (Sweetheart Rock), play beach volleyball, or just nap on the sand. The full-day trip costs $289 for adults, $255 ages 13 to 17, and $190 for kids 3 to 12 (free for younger children).

Trilogy also offers **snorkel-sail trips to Molokini.** This half-day trip leaves from Mā'alaea Harbor and costs $205 for adults, $190 for ages 13 to 17, and $140 for kids 3 to 12. These may be the most expensive sail-snorkel cruises on Maui, but they're worth every penny. Crews are fun and knowledgeable, the boats comfortable and well-equipped. Trips include breakfast and a tasty barbecue lunch. In winter, 2-hour **whale watches** depart right from the sand on Kā'anapali Beach ($85 adults, $69 teens, $50 children).

The **Captain's Sunset Dinner Sail** is a romantic adults-only adventure. Couples enjoy a four-course feast at private, candlelit tables, complete with handcrafted cocktails and cozy blankets ($155 per person). www.sailtrilogy.com. *C* **888/225-MAUI (6284)** or 808/874-5649. Prices and departure points vary depending on cruise.

DAY CRUISES TO LĀNA'I

You can visit the island of Lāna'i by booking a trip with **Trilogy** (see above) or via the **Expeditions** Lāna'i Passenger **Ferry** ★★ (www.go-lanai.com; *C* **800/695-2624** or 808/661-3756), which since the destruction of Lahaina Harbor now runs twice a day from Mā'alaea Harbor. It leaves Mā'alaea at 6:30am and 3:30pm; the return ferry from Lanai's Manele Bay leaves at 8:30am and 5:30pm. Depending on sea conditions, it can take 75 minutes to cross the 'Au'au Channel between the islands. Tickets cost $30 adults, $20 children ages 2 to 11 each way; reservations are strongly recommended, and passengers should be ready to board 30 minutes in advance of departure. In winter, the trip doubles as a whale watch. On Lāna'i, you can walk from the harbor to Hulopoe Beach, but to explore the island further, you'll have to rent a car or book a taxi tour. See p. 465 in Chapter 8 for details.

Ocean Kayaking

Numerous companies launch kayak tours from South and West Maui beaches. Some are better than others—the difference being the personal attention from guides and their level of experience. Kayaking can be a slog if you have to keep up with your guide, rather than paddle alongside someone who shares local knowledge. My favorite, **Hawaiian**

Kayaking on the Maui coast.

Paddle Sports ★★★ (www.hawaiianpaddlesports.com; ℭ **808/442-6436**), launches kayak-snorkel trips from Mākena Landing and Olowalu. Group tours cost $109 per person, while private tours start at $756 for four guests ($189 per person). Guides are ready to spot snowflake eels hiding in the coral, point you to hidden caverns, and snap photos of you swimming with sea turtles. *Note:* If children under 6 are part of your party, you must book a private tour.

    Aloha Kayaks Maui ★★ (www.alohakayaksmaui.com; ℭ **808/250-1114** or 866/308-9361) is also excellent, with snorkel trips for $135 per person (maximum eight people). Professional, informative, and eco-aware guides lead 3-hour trips that launch from Mākena Landing (secluded coves with underwater arches and caves) or Olowalu (vibrant coral reefs and possible manta ray sightings). During whale season, guides can steer you towards the gentle giants for a once-in-a-lifetime encounter; the whale-watching tour is available for ages 10 and older, while kids 5 and up can participate in the other kayak trips.

    The friendly watermen working for **Hawaiian Ocean Sports** ★★ (www.hawaiianoceansports.com; ℭ **808/886-6666**), a Native Hawaiian–owned company, share their cultural as well as marine knowledge. Tours depart Wailea Beach and run 1 to 2 hours, with **snorkeling** and **whale-watching options** ($130–$150).

Ocean Rafting

If you're semi-adventurous and looking for a wetter, wilder experience, try ocean rafting. The inflatable rafts hold 6 to 24 passengers. Tours usually include snorkeling and coastal cruising. Pregnant women and people with back problems are advised to avoid. During winter, these maneuverable boats offer exciting whale-watching tours.

    My favorite operator, the sustainability-minded **Redline Rafting** ★★★ (https://redlinerafting.com; ℭ **808/698-5837**) leads 5-hour tours from the

Kīhei Boat Ramp on zippy, 35-foot canopied rafts. They race over to several snorkeling spots at Molokini (including the backside, where you ride the waves like an elevator over spiraling schools of fish) and then to two or three more sites in South Maui, where you might spot a snoozing monk seal on a rock ledge above swimming green sea turtles. Tours depart daily at 7am, with up to 24 passengers; the $189 price includes drinks and lunch (choice of deli sandwich with pasta salad). A smaller raft zips up to 14 passengers over to Molokini for a 2-hour tour Sunday through Friday at 7am and 9:30am; it costs $129. All passengers must be 8 or older. *Note:* Prices reflect $10 online booking discount.

The owners of **Captain Steve's Rafting Excursions ★★** (www.captainsteves.com; ✆ **808/667-5565**) lost their home as well as their boats in the Lahaina fire. Since then, they have partnered with owners of two other businesses with similar losses to share in the proceeds of small-group **snorkeling** and **whale-watching** tours on temporary vessels, so please book through their website. The two partners are **Hawaii Ocean Rafting,** which use a Zodiac raft or power monohull, both 34 feet and accommodating 18 or fewer passengers, and **Makai Adventures,** which also uses a 34-foot power monohull. Both companies depart from **Māla Boat Ramp** at the northern end of Lahaina, with tours beginning at $64 for adults and $57 for ages 3 to 12 for whale-watching and $149 adults and $129 children for 2.5-hr. snorkel tours. Longer snorkel trips to the waters around **Lāna'i** (you don't actually go on land) that include breakfast and lunch start at $189 adults and $169 children ages 3 to 12.

Maui Reef Adventures ★★★ (www.mauireefadventures.com; ✆ **808/244-7333**) operates out of Mā'alaea Harbor. Its 60-foot *Reef Explorer* zips over to Molokini Crater, allowing a snorkel on the backside, and then to Mākena Landing's Turtle Town on 4-hour tours (Tues–Sat mornings; $159 for ages 12 and older, $139 for ages 4–11, including continental breakfast and lunch).

Outrigger Canoe Paddling

Outrigger canoes are much revered in Hawaiian culture, and several hotels—among them, the Fairmont Kea Lani Maui and the Andaz Maui—offer this wonderful cultural activity right off the beach. If you want to try paddling, expect to work as a team with five other paddlers. Your guide and steersman will show you how to haul the sleek boat into the water, properly enter and exit the boat, and paddle for maximum efficiency. The Native Hawaiian–owned **Hawaiian Ocean Sports ★★★** (www.hawaiianoutriggerexperience.com; ✆ **808/633-2800**) offers the most culturally oriented tours, some with snorkeling, from Wailea Beach Park (1-hour tours start at $130, for ages 5 and older).

Outrigger Canoe Sailing

To get a sense of how ancient Polynesians navigated their way to these remote islands, try a ride on a double-hulled outrigger sailing canoe. Owned and operated by a Native Hawaiian family since 2005, **Maui Sailing Canoe** ★★★ (www.mauisailingcanoe.com; © **808/281-9031**) takes up to eight guests on a 2-hour sail, paddle, and snorkel tour from Wailea's Polo Beach (in front of the Fairmont Kea Lani, p. 384). Tours cost $185 for adults 15 and older, $145 for ages 4 to 14, with daily departures at 8 and 10am. Look for the red-sailed canoe at the west end of the beach.

Scuba Diving

Maui offers plenty of undersea attractions worth strapping on a tank for. Most divers start with **Molokini** (see "Snorkeling," below). In addition to the popular basin, experienced divers can explore the crater's dramatic **back wall** ★★★, which plunges 350 feet and is frequented by larger marine animals and schools of rare butterflyfish. Other top sites include **Māla Wharf,** the **St. Anthony** (a sunken longliner near Keawakapu Beach), and **Five Graves** in Mākena. Don't be scared off by the last site's ominous name, which refers to a nearby family cemetery. Also nicknamed "Five Caves," it's a magical spot with sea caves and arches.

Ed Robinson's Diving Adventures ★★ DIVE COMPANY   Ed Robinson, a widely published underwater photographer, and wife Sue have retired their dive boat after 45 years, but still lead shore dives for certified divers at places like Five Graves, accessed from a small sandy cove known as Chang's Beach (Ulupikunui Beach), next to the Makena Surf condos. Call for current pricing and to arrange a dive. www.mauiscuba.com. © **808/879-3584.**

Island Style Diving ★★★ DIVE COMPANY   Longtime Maui divers Javier and Christina Cantellops took over and renamed the operations of Mike Severns Diving in 2022 but have maintained its reputation for concierge-style diving tours on a spacious boat (the *Pilikai,* which offers a charging station, cupholders for water bottles, and freshwater shower). Formerly of the Maui Ocean Center, divemaster Christina has a background in marine biology and loves to spot rare creatures and share their stories with divers. Captain and dive instructor Javier, who previously operated a dive charter with Christina in Costa Rica, is also the creator of a wetsuit company. Two-tank dives are $229, including mask, wetsuit, and fins, plus snacks and beverages; premium BCD (weights) and regulators can be rented for $30 and snorkelers can join for $159. For $299, experienced divers can use a hip-worn underwater scooter on the first tank for an exhilarating guided ride around the reefs. Island Style Diving also offers one-tank, 3-hour evening shore dives ($150), 2-hour afternoon whale watches (Dec 16–Mar 31, $99), 4-hour line dive training for free divers ($59), and 6-hour private charters for up to 14 people ($1,900–$2,400). Kīhei Boat Ramp, 2988 S. Kīhei Rd., just south of Kamaole Beach Park 3, Kīhei. www.diveislandstyle.com. © **808/879-6596.**

Maui Dreams Dive Company ★★★ DIVE COMPANY Run by husband-and-wife team Rachel and Don Domingo, this is the best full-service dive operation on the island. Stop in at their South Maui shop, and you might just end up scuba certified ($399 for a 2-day course). The skilled dive masters and instructors are so fun that they make every aspect of getting geared up to go underwater enjoyable. You don't need certification for an intro shore dive at Ulua Beach ($169), but you do for a two-tank adventure to **Molokini** aboard the *Maui Diamond II* ($169, with a $149 snorkelers' option). Captain Don regales his passengers with jokes, snacks, and local trivia, while Rachel has a knack for finding camouflaged **frogfish** on the reef.

1993 S. Kihei Rd. www.mauidreamsdiveco.com. (C) **808/874-5332.**

Snorkeling

Snorkeling on Maui is a prime attraction. The island has so many great spots where you can just wade in the water with a mask—avoiding walking on live coral, of course—and look down and see tropical fish. If you haven't snorkeled before, or are a little rusty, practice breathing through your snorkel before you get out on the water. Mornings are best; blustery trade winds kick in around noon. Maui's best snorkeling spots include **Ulua** and **Mokapū Beaches** in Wailea; **Olowalu** along the Honoapi'ilani Highway; **Pu'u Keka'a** (Black Rock) at the north end of Kā'anapali Beach; and, just beyond Black Rock, **Kahekili Beach ★★★**.

These three **truly terrific snorkel spots** are difficult to get to but rewarding for viewing Hawaiian marine life at its best:

Hawaiian green sea turtles.

'Āhihi-Kīna'u Natural Preserve ★★ NATURAL ATTRACTION
This 2,000-acre state natural reserve in the lee of Cape Kīna'u, on Maui's
rugged south coast, is home to bejeweled 'Āhihi Bay. It was here that
Haleakalā spilled its last red-hot lava into the sea, so the entrance to the
ocean is sharp and rocky. Ease into the water to see brilliant corals and
abundant fish. Fishing is strictly forbidden, and the fish know it; they're
everywhere in this series of rocky coves and black-lava tide pools. To get
here, drive south of Mākena and watch for signs. A state naturalist is often
on-site to offer advice.

Note: The Hawai'i Department of Land and Natural Resources has
temporarily restricted access to portions of the popular and heavily used
preserve. See https://dlnr.hawaii.gov/ecosystems/nars/maui/ahihi-kinau-2
for details.

Honolua Bay ★★★ NATURAL ATTRACTION   The snorkeling in
this wide, secluded bay is worth the drive out to West Maui's far corner.
Spectacular coral formations glitter beneath the surface. Turtles, rays, and
a variety of snappers and goatfish cruise along beside you. In the crevices
are eels, lobster, and rainbow-hued fish. Dolphins sometimes come here
to rest. Follow Honoapi'ilani Highway past Kapalua to mile marker 32.
Follow the path through the dense forest to the sea. *Tip:* Don't leave valuables in your car; break-ins have happened in this remote area.

Molokini ★★★ NATURAL ATTRACTION   A sunken crater that sits
like a crescent moon fallen from the sky, almost midway between Maui
and the uninhabited island of Kaho'olawe, Molokini stands like a scoop
against the tide. This offshore site is very popular, thanks to astounding
visibility (you can often peer down 100 ft.) and an abundance of marine
life, from manta rays to clouds of yellow butterflyfish. On its concave
side, Molokini serves as a natural sanctuary and preserve for tropical fish.
Molokini is accessible only by sea, and snorkelers commute here daily in
a fleet of dive boats. See "Boating," p. 342, and "Ocean Rafting," p. 345,
for outfitters that can take you here. Expect crowds in high season.

Sport Fishing

Most of the sport fishing fleet on Maui was destroyed along with Lahaina
Harbor in the 2023 fire. **Sportfish Hawaii** ★ (www.sportfishhawaii.com;
✆ **877/388-1376** or 808/295-8355), which books boats on all the islands,
now only has one option on Maui, departing from Mā'alaea: the 40-foot
power catamaran *Hokua,* which can accommodate up to 10 anglers and
four riders on its **bottom-fishing** trips for delicious snappers. Captain Rob
Elliott will let you keep your catch; tours run $180 per fishing adult ($159
ages 12 and under) and $116 per non-fishing rider.

Stand-up Paddling (SUP) & Surfing

If you want to learn to surf, the best beginners' spots are **Charley Young
Cove** in Kīhei (the far north end of Kalama Beach Park) and several

breaks along Honoapiʻilani Highway, including **Ukumehame Beach Park,** about 3 miles south of Olowalu. The first two are the most convenient, with surf schools nearby. The breaks along Honoapiʻilani Highway tend to be longer, wider, and less crowded—perfect if you're ready to go solo.

In summer, gentle swells roll in long and slow along the South Shore. It's the best time to practice your stance on a longboard. In winter, the North Shore becomes the playground for adrenaline junkies who drop in on thundering waves 30 feet tall and higher. If you want to watch, head to **Hoʻokipa Beach** or **Honolua Bay,** and view the action from a cliff above.

Stand-up paddling (SUP) is one of the oldest and newest Hawaiian ocean sports. Practiced by ancient Hawaiian kings, it's now back in fashion. You can SUP just about anywhere you can surf—and more, since you don't need a swell to get going, just a wide board and paddle, strong arms, and some balance. (And if you lack the latter two, willingness will make up for it.) Gliding over the fish-filled reefs with an unobstructed view of the islands on the horizon is a top-notch experience.

Hawaiian Paddle Sports (www.hawaiianpaddlesports.com; ✆ **808/ 442-6436**) offers combined SUP lessons and tours of Turtle Town in **Mākena** with certified naturalist guides, starting at $189 for two to four paddlers. The company's expert surf instructors, who teach surf etiquette and culture as well as technique, text students where their private lessons will be, based on the wind and water conditions of the day; lessons are $289 for a solo class and $149 per person for two to four students.

Experienced watermen/women can rent a full range of surf, windsurf, and stand-up paddle boards from **Maui Windsurf Company,** 22 Hāna Hwy., Kahului (www.mauiwindsurfcompany.com; ✆ **808/877-4816**).

Maui Stand Up Paddle Boarding ★★ SURF INSTRUCTION   Get up on a board and "walk on water" with a private SUP lesson or guided tour ($249 for one person, $189 for two or more). Adventures start out with an overview of paddling techniques on shore, then you'll launch into the water at Mākena Landing, Olowalu, or Kapalua Bay for 2 salty hours. (Wear a water-friendly hat and sunglasses.) During whale season, you might be surprised by the exhalation of a mighty humpback nearby. Your instructor will snap action shots of you and deliver them by the day's end. 27-B Halekaui St., Kīhei. www.mauistanduppaddleboarding.com. ✆ **808/568-0151.**

Maui Surfer Girls ★★★ SURF INSTRUCTION   Despite its name, MSG offers coed surf and SUP instruction for groms and Betties alike. Owner Dustin Tester is a big-wave surf pioneer; she's among the first women to charge Peʻahi, aka Jaws, one of the planet's biggest breaks, and her commitment to helping others shred waves is inspirational. (She even coached her dog Luna to hang ten alongside her.) Two-hour lessons at Ukumehame Beach Park with Tester or her teammates start at $99. www.mauisurfergirls.com. ✆ **808/214-0606.**

Zack Howard Surf ★ SURF INSTRUCTION Zack is a lifelong waterman who will help you stand up and surf—even on your very first wave. While most surf schools take newbies out into the crowded breaks at Charley Young in Kīhei, Zack and his fellow instructors steer beginning students into the surf at Ukumehame, a gentle, consistent rolling break alongside Honoapiʻilani Highway. They also help intermediate surfers sharpen their skills at world-famous Hoʻokipa. In between swells, Zack offers tips on how to improve your stance and technique. Lessons start at $100 per person for 1½ hours for groups of 3 to 4, $130 per person for two students, or $220 for a private lesson.
www.zackhowardsurf.com. ⓒ **808/214-7766.**

Whale-Watching

Maui is a favorite with Hawaiian humpback whales, who get downright frisky in the surrounding waters from late December to early April (though Jan–Feb are the peak months). Seeing the massive marine mammals leap out of the sea or perfect their tail slap is mesmerizing. You can hear them sing underwater, too! Just duck your head a foot below the surface and listen for creaks, groans, and otherworldly serenades.

WHALE-WATCHING FROM SHORE Look out to sea anytime during the winter months. There's no best time of day, but it seems that when the sea is glassy and there's no wind, the whales appear. Others claim the opposite: that whales are most active when the water is pocked with whitecaps.

Good whale-watching spots on Maui include:

o **McGregor Point** This is a scenic lookout at mile marker 9, just before you get to the Lahaina Tunnel.

o **Olowalu Reef** Along the straight part of Honoapiʻilani Highway, between McGregor Point and Olowalu, you'll sometimes see whales leap out of the water. Their appearance can bring traffic to a screeching halt as people stop their cars and run down to the sea to watch, causing a major traffic jam. Be sure to pull off the road so others can pass.

o **Wailea Beach Resort—Marriott, Maui** On the Wailea coastal walk, stop at this resort to look for whales through the telescope installed by the Hawaiʻi Island Humpback Whale National Marine Sanctuary.

o **Whale-Watching by Raft ★★** I recommend viewing humpback whales from a maneuverable, high-speed raft—you'll be close to the water and that much closer to the cetaceans. Eco-friendly **Redline Rafting ★★★** (www.redlinerafting.com; ⓒ **808/698-5837**) offers 1½-hour excursions ($85) for up to 15 people on its zippy, 35-foot canopied rafts. Tours depart from Kīhei Small Boat Harbor at 7, 9, and 11am (calmer conditions are earlier in the day) during the peak season of January 15 through March 3. *Tip:* Save $10 by booking online.

o **Whale-Watching Cruises** All snorkel and dive boats become whale-watching boats in season; some of them even carry professional naturalists onboard so you'll know what you're seeing and drop hydrophones in the water so you can better hear the whales' song. For options, see "Boating," earlier in this section.

Windsurfing

Maui has the best windsurfing beaches in Hawai'i. In winter, windsurfers from around the world flock to the town of **Pā'ia** to ride the waves; **Ho'okipa Beach ★★★**, known the world over for its brisk winds and excellent waves, is the site of several championship contests. **Kanahā Beach,** west of Kahului Airport, also has dependable winds. When the winds turn northerly, **North Kīhei** is the place to be. **Ohukai Park,** the first beach as you enter South Kīhei Road from the northern end, has good winds, plus parking, a long strip of grass to assemble your gear, and easy access to the water.

EQUIPMENT RENTALS & LESSONS Hawaiian Sailboarding Tech-niques, 425 Kōloa St., Kahului (www.hstwindsurfing.com; © 808/871-5423), offers rentals and 2½-hour lessons (maximum four in class) from $189 at Kanahā Beach, early in the morning before the breeze gets too strong for beginners. Private beginner 3-hour kitesurfing lessons are $325 per person, including gear. **Maui Windsurf Company,** 22 Hāna Hwy., Kahului (www.mauiwindsurfcompany.com; © 808/877-4816), offers gear rental (Goya boards, sails, rig harnesses, and roof racks) from $74.

SURF VAN Since most windsurf gear won't fit into a typical rental car, call **Aloha Rent-a-Car/Al West's Maui Vans** to rent a newish (or old) van by the week. Older vans start at $59 per day, 4-day minimum (www.mauivans.com; © 808/877-0090).

OTHER OUTDOOR ACTIVITIES

Besides the opportunities to explore Maui's great outdoors detailed below, consider helping restore some of its unique ecosystems, which are also trea-sured cultural areas. By volunteering to spend a few hours pulling weeds or planting native vegetation with nonprofit **Kīpuka Olowalu** (www.kipuka olowalu.com), you'll learn the traditional protocol of chanting before you enter a new place; discover the surprisingly lush beauty of a hidden valley south of Lahaina that was historically a place of refuge; "talk story" with botanical and cultural experts; and go for a cooling dip in a mountain stream. Contact the organizers via the website to set up a time to join their ongoing efforts. **Maui Cultural Lands ★★★** (https://mauiculturallands. org; © 808/276-5593) offers similar informative and inspiring volunteer opportunities in verdant Honokōwai Valley (above Kā'anapali) with regu-larly scheduled Saturday morning work trips. Call or email (via the web-site) to confirm your participation, and then meet the group at the former sugar cane train station at 1 Pu'ukoli'i Rd, Lahaina (outside the burn zone).

Biking

CRUISING HALEAKALĀ

Several companies offer the opportunity to coast down Haleakalā, from near the summit to the shore, on basic cruiser bikes. It can be quite a thrilling experience—but one that should be approached with caution. Despite what various companies claim about their safety record, people have been injured and killed during in this activity. If you do choose to go, pay close attention to the safety briefing. Bike tours aren't allowed in Haleakalā National Park, so your van will take you to the summit first, and then drop you off just outside of the park. You'll descend through multiple climates and ecosystems, past eucalyptus groves and flower-filled gulches. But bear in mind: The roads are steep and curvy without bike lanes and with little to no shoulder, and residents also use these roads during their morning commutes. During winter and the rainy season, conditions can be particularly harsh; you'll be saran-wrapped in rain gear. Temperatures at the summit can drop below freezing and 40mph winds howl, so wear warm layers whatever the season.

Mountain Riders Bike Tours (www.mountainriders.com; ℭ **800/706-7700**) offers sunrise rides for $239 (with a shorter option for $145) and midday trips for $115 (self-guided for $112). If you want to avoid the crowds and go down the mountain at your own pace (rather than in a choo-choo train of other bikers), call **Haleakala Bike Company** (www.bikemaui.com; ℭ **808/575-9575**). After assessing your skill, they'll outfit you with gear and shuttle you up Haleakalā for sunrise and morning tours ($109–$220). Guided group and private tours, with or without the bike, are also options—good to know for folks who might feel too sleepy to pedal or drive.

RENTALS

Maui offers dynamic terrain for serious and amateur cyclists. If you've got the chops to pedal *up* Haleakalā, the pros at **Maui Cyclery** ★★★, 99 Hāna Hwy., Pāʻia (www.gocyclingmaui.com; ℭ **808/579-9009**), can outfit you and provide a support vehicle. Tour de France athletes launch their Maui training sessions from this full-service Pāʻia bike shop, which rents top-of-the-line equipment and offers a range of guided tours. Shop owner Donny Arnoult hosts cycling camps and sponsors the annual Cycle to the Sun contest (https://cycletothesun.com); riders travel from around the globe to tackle the 10,023-foot volcano on two wheels.

Note: Currently, all rentals must be reserved in advance by phone; call for pricing, which typically starts at $35 a day for hybrid Scott models and $75 for carbon-fiber road bikes. Car racks and cycling shoes are also available for rent, each for $10 a day.

If **mountain biking** is more your style, hit up **Krank Cycles** ★★★, 270 Dairy Rd., Kahului (www.krankmaui.com; ℭ **808/893-2039**), for a tricked-out bike ($59–$169 a day) and trail directions. They also offer electric-assisted bikes ($45–$100 a day), road bikes ($49–$115), and delivery service, including for beach cruisers (call for rates). Krank Cycles also has a Makawao location, 1120 Makawao Rd. (© **808/572-2299**), an ideal starting point for a ride to the summit of Haleakalā,

Maui County has produced a **full-color map** of the island with various cycling routes, information on road suitability, climate, mileage, elevation changes, bike shops, and safety tips. It's available at most bike shops; download it from www.southmauibicycles.com, the website of **South Maui Bicycles,** 1993 S. Kīhei Rd., Kīhei (© **808/874-0068**), where hybrid city bike rentals start at $30 per day and e-bikes at $60 a day.

Golf

Golfers have many outstanding greens to choose from on Maui, from championship courses to municipal parks with oceanfront views. Greens fees are pricey, but twilight tee times can be a giant deal. Be forewarned: The trade winds pick up in the afternoon and can seriously alter your game.

Note: After they've played the resorts, avid golfers will also want to check out private **King Kamehameha Golf Club** in Waikapu ★★ (www. kamehamehagolf.com; © **808/249-0033**), which offers "guest for a day" access ($279) to its Ted Robinson Jr.–refreshed course with advance booking, and its terraced clubhouse, designed by Frank Lloyd Wright. Those willing to drive a few miles on the winding Kahekili Highway will enjoy scenic but breezy **Waiehu Municipal Golf Course ★** (www.waiehu golf.com; © **808/270-7400**), overlooking shimmering waters and Waiehu Reef, with several holes above the white sand of Waiehu Beach Park; call for a tee time ($65 weekdays, $85 weekends, half-price for twilight hours).

WEST MAUI

Kā'anapali Golf Resort ★ Both courses at Kā'anapali will challenge golfers, from high-handicappers to near-pros. The par-72, 6,305-yard **Royal Kā'anapali (North) Course** is a true Robert Trent Jones, Sr., design: It has an abundance of wide bunkers; several long, stretched-out tees; and the largest, most contoured greens on Maui. The tricky 18th hole (par-4, 435-yard) has a water hazard on the approach to the green. The par-72, 6,250-yard **Kai Kā'anapali (South) Course** is an Arthur Jack Snyder design; although shorter than the North Course, it requires more accuracy on the narrow, hilly fairways. It also has a water hazard on its final hole, so don't tally up your scorecard until you sink the final putt. Facilities include a driving range and putting course. Celebrated chef Roy Yamaguchi runs the clubhouse restaurant.

2290 Kā'anapali Pkwy., Kā'anapali. www.kaanapaligolfcourses.com. © **866/454-4653** or 808/661-3691. Greens fees: Royal Kā'anapali Course $265 ($219 for Kā'anapali guests), twilight rates (starting at 1pm) $159; junior (ages 13–17) $69; Kai Kā'anapali Course $205 ($159 for Kā'anapali guests), twilight rates $109, juniors $55. Both courses: same-day replay $69. Dynamic pricing means rates may vary higher or lower.

Kapalua Resort ★★★ The views from these two championship courses are worth the greens fees alone. Arnold Palmer and Ed Seay designed the par-72, 6,761-yard Bay Course, which is a bit forgiving, with its wide fairways. The greens, however, are difficult to read. The oft-photographed 5th plays over a small ocean cove; even the pros have trouble with this rocky par-3, 205-yard hole. The **Plantation Course,** site of the Century Tournament of Champions, is an updated Ben Crenshaw/Bill Coore design. The 6,547-yard, par-73 course, set on a rolling hillside, is excellent for developing your low shots and precise chipping. Facilities for both courses include locker rooms, a driving range, and great dining. Sharpen your skills at the golf academy, which offers half-day golf school, private lessons, club fittings, and special clinics for beginners. Weekends are your best bet for tee times.

2000 Plantation Dr., Kapalua. www.golfatkapalua.com. © **877/527-2582** or 808/669-8044. Greens fees: Bay Course $279 ($259 for resort guests); Plantation Course $459 ($429 for guests). Club rentals $79, shoe rentals $19.

SOUTH MAUI

Maui Nui Golf Club ★ Unspooling across the foothills of Haleakalā, this Kīhei course is just high enough to afford spectacular ocean vistas from every hole. *One caveat:* Go in the morning. Not only is it cooler, but (more importantly) it's also less windy. In the afternoon, the winds bluster down Haleakalā with gusto. It's a fun course to play, with some challenging holes; the par-5 2nd hole is a virtual minefield of bunkers, and the par-5 8th hole shoots over a swale and then uphill. Amenities include a driving range, pro shop, lessons.

470 Līpoa Pkwy., Kīhei. www.mauinuigolfclub.com. © **808/874-0777.** Greens fees 7:30–11am $99–$109, after 2pm $44–$69.

Wailea Golf Club ★★ You'll have three courses to choose from at Wailea. The **Blue Course,** a par-72, 6,758-yard course designed by Arthur Jack Snyder and dotted with bunkers and water hazards, is for duffers and pros alike. The wide fairways and undulating terrain make it a course for everyone. More challenging is the par-72, 7,078-yard **Gold Course,** designed by Robert Trent Jones, Jr., with narrow fairways and several tricky dogleg holes, plus such natural hazards as lava-rock walls. The **Emerald Course,** also designed by Trent Jones, Jr., is Wailea's most scenic, with tropical landscaping and a player-friendly design. Sunday mornings are the least crowded. Facilities include a golf training center, two pro shops, locker rooms, and two restaurants: the eclectic, oceanview **Gather in Maui ★★** (www.gatheronmaui.com; © **808/698-0555**), by pioneering Hawai'i Regional Cuisine chef Bev Gannon, and **Mulligan's on the Blue ★**, a lively, open-air Irish pub with frequent live entertainment (https://mulligansontheblue.com; © **808/874-1131**).

Blue Course: 100 Wailea Ike Dr., Wailea. www.waileagolf.com. © **808/879-2530.** Emerald and Gold courses: 100 Wailea Golf Club Dr. © **888/328-MAUI (6284)** or 808/875-7450. Greens fees: Blue Course $240 ($210 for Wailea guests, $220 for Maui resort guests), $175 after noon, $150 after 3pm, juniors $60–$120; Gold Course and Emerald Course $299 ($245 for Wailea guests, $265 for Maui resort guests), $185 after noon, $130 after 3pm, juniors $65–$130.

UPCOUNTRY MAUI

Pukalani Country Club ★   This cool par-72, 6,962-yard course at 1,100 feet offers a break from the resorts' high greens fees, and it's really fun to play. The 3rd hole offers golfers two options: a tough (especially into the wind) iron shot from the tee, across a gully (yuck!) to the green, or a shot down the side of the gully across a second green into sand traps below. (Most people choose to shoot down the side of the gully; it's actually easier than shooting across a ravine.) High handicappers will love this course, and more experienced players can make it more challenging by playing from the back tees. Facilities include club and shoe rentals, practice areas, lockers, a pro shop, and a restaurant.

360 Pukalani St., Pukalani. www.pukalanigolf.com. © **808/572-1314.** 18 holes (w/ cart) $69–$99, 11am–1pm $55–$74, 1–2:30pm $44.

Hiking

Over a few brief decades, Maui transformed from a rural island to a fast-paced resort destination, but its natural beauty has remained largely inviolate. Many pristine places can be explored only on foot. Those interested in seeing the backcountry—complete with virgin waterfalls, remote wilderness trails, and quiet, meditative settings—should head to Haleakalā or the tropical Hāna Coast.

For details on Maui hiking trails and free maps, contact **Haleakalā National Park** (www.nps.gov/hale; © **808/572-4400**), the **Hawai'i State Department of Land and Natural Resources** (https://dlnr.hawaii.gov/dsp/hiking/maui; © **808/984-8109**), or the state's **Nā Ala Hele program** (https://hawaiitrails.ehawaii.gov/trails; © **808/873-3508**).

Don't have the time to drive up Haleakalā or all the way to Hāna? The **Kapalua Resort** (p. 354) in West Maui also offers several hiking trails, some maintained better than others. The strenuous, 20-mile round-trip **Mahana Ridge Trail** leads from D. T. Fleming Beach (p. 376) uphill through overgrown former coffee and pineapple fields, with wild *liliko'i* and guava often falling on the path, to the now fenced-in Maunalei Arboretum. Former golf cart paths on the out-of-use Village Golf Course create the moderately challenging 4.2-mile **Village Walking Trail** Lake Loop, which passes by a duck-populated hidden lake and includes a few steep sections; the brushy abandoned links also offer shorter paths. The Village Walking Trails and Mahana Ridge Trail are open daily from 7am to 6pm. The easiest and most scenic Kapalua hike is the 1.75-mile **Coastal Trail,** which runs north from Kapalua Bay to D. T. Fleming Beach; it's open sunrise to sunset. See www.kapalua.com/activities/hiking-trails for maps and parking notes.

In Central Maui, those who are willing to navigate about 3 miles of the narrow, winding Kahekili Highway north of Waiehu Municipal Golf Course (p. 354) can assail the **Waihe'e Ridge Trail.** The 5-mile round-trip hike starts at 1,000 feet elevation and passes through pasture and a guava thicket before delving into native rainforest. If it's not too overcast, the summit at 2,563 feet offers spectacular views; you're sure to see the deep gulches of Waiheʻe and Makamakaʻole along the way.

GUIDED HIKES   Maui's oldest hiking company is **Hike Maui ★★** (www.hikemaui.com; ⓒ **808/879-5270**), headed by Ken Schmitt, who pioneered guided treks on the Valley Isle. Hike Maui offers numerous treks island-wide, ranging from an easy 1-mile, 3-hour hike to two waterfalls ($109) to a strenuous full-day hike in Haleakalā Crater ($199) or kayaking, snorkel and waterfall combo ($249).

The Maui chapter of the **Sierra Club ★★** (www.mauisierraclub.org; ⓒ **808/419-5143**) offers the best deal by far: guided hikes for a $5 donation. Volunteer naturalists lead small groups along historic coastlines and up into forest waterfalls on hikes of varying lengths and difficulty. Some hikes include opportunities to help restore the native landscape.

HALEAKALĀ NATIONAL PARK ★★★

For complete coverage of the national park, see p. 395.

Kīpahulu

All the way out in Hāna, lush and rainy Kīpahulu is one section of Haleakalā National Park that is not accessible from the summit. From the ranger station just off of Hāna Highway, it's a short hike above the famous **ʻOheʻo Gulch** (aka the Seven Sacred Pools, viewable from **Kualoa Trail**) to two spectacular waterfalls. Check with rangers before heading out, to make sure that no flash floods are expected. (Streams can swell quickly, even when it appears sunny. Never attempt to cross flooding waters.) The **Pīpīwai Trail** begins near the ranger station, across the street from the central parking area. Follow it 5 miles to the **Makahiku Falls** overlook. Continue

Peering into the Haleakalā volcanic crater.

on another 1½ miles across two bridges and through a magical bamboo forest to **Waimoku Falls.** It's a challenging uphill trek, mostly shaded and sweetened by the sounds of clattering bamboo canes.

Wilderness Hikes: Sliding Sands & Halemau'u Trails

Hiking into Maui's dormant volcano is an experience like no other. The terrain inside the wilderness area of the volcano, which ranges from burnt-red cinder cones to ebony-black lava flows, is astonishing. There are some 27 miles of hiking trails, two camping sites, and three cabins.

Pools of the 'Ohe'o Gulch.

Entrance to Haleakalā National Park is $30 per car ($25 per motorcycle, $15 per cyclist/pedestrian). The rangers typically offer free guided hikes (usually Mon and Thurs), which are a great way to learn about the unusual flora and geological formations here. Wear sturdy shoes and be prepared for wind, rain, and intense sun. Bring water, snacks, and a hat. Check www.nps.gov/hale or ⓒ **808/572-4400** for the current schedule.

Avid hikers should plan to stay at least 1 night in the park; 2 or 3 nights will allow more time to explore the fascinating interior of the volcano (see below for details on the cabins and campgrounds in the wilderness area of the valley). If you want to venture out on your own, the best route takes in two trails: into the crater along **Sliding Sands (Keonehe'ehe'e) Trail,** which begins on the rim at 9,800 feet and descends to the valley floor at 6,600 feet, and back out along **Halemau'u Trail.** Before you set out, stop at park headquarters to get trail updates.

The trailhead for Sliding Sands is well marked and the path easy to follow over lava flows and cinders. As you descend, look around: The view is breathtaking. In the afternoon, clouds flow into the Kaupō and Ko'olau gaps. Flora is scarce at the top, but the closer you get to the valley floor, the more growth you'll see: bracken ferns, pili grass, shrubs, even flowers. On the floor, the trail crosses rough lava flows, passing silversword plants, volcanic vents, and multicolored cinder cones.

The Halemau'u Trail goes over red and black lava and past native *'ohelo* berries and '¯ohi'a trees as it ascends up the valley wall. Occasionally, riders on horseback use this trail. The proper etiquette is to step aside and stand quietly next to the trail as the horses pass.

Shorter and easier options include the half-mile walk down **Hosmer Grove Nature Trail,** or just the first mile or two of **Sliding Sands Trail.**

(Even this short hike is arduous at the high altitude.) A good day hike is the round-trip **Halemau'u Trail** to Hōlua Cabin, an 8-mile, half-day trip.

HĀNA

The 3-mile hike to **Fagan's Cross,** erected in memory of Paul Fagan, the founder of Hāna Ranch and the Hotel Hāna-Maui, offers spectacular views of the coast, particularly at sunset. The uphill trail starts across Hāna Highway from the hotel. Enter the pastures at your own risk; they're often occupied by glaring bulls with sharp horns and cows with new calves. Watch your step as you ascend this steep hill on a jeep trail across open pastures to the cross.

POLIPOLI SPRINGS AREA ★

At this state recreation area, part of the 21,000-acre Kula and Kahikinui forest reserves on the slope of Haleakalā, it's hard to believe you're in Hawai'i. First, it's cold, even in summer, because the elevation is 5,300 to 6,200 feet. Second, the area, which was overlogged in the 1800s, was reforested in the 1930s with introduced species: pine, Monterey cypress, ash, sugi, red alder, redwood, and several varieties of eucalyptus. The result is a cool area, with muted sunlight filtered by towering trees.

Polipoli Loop

Follow the Skyline trail to its terminus, and you'll reach the Polipoli Spring State Recreation Area. Or you can drive straight there and embark on several cool weather hikes (4WD vehicle is recommended). One of the most unusual hikes is the easy 3.5-mile Polipoli Loop, which takes about 3 hours. Take the Haleakalā Highway (Hwy. 37) to Kēōkea and turn right onto Highway 337; after less than a half-mile, turn on Waipoli Road, which climbs swiftly. After 10 miles, the road ends at the Polipoli Spring State Recreation Area campgrounds. The well-marked trailhead is next to the parking lot near a stand of Monterey cypress; the tree-lined trail offers the best view of the island. Dress warmly.

Polipoli Loop is really a network of three trails: **Haleakalā Ridge, Plum Trail,** and **Redwood Trail.** After .5 mile of winding through groves of eucalyptus, blackwood, swamp mahogany, and hybrid cypress, it joins the Haleakalā Ridge Trail, which, about a mile in, joins with the Plum Trail (named for the plums that ripen in June–July). This trail passes through massive redwoods and by an old Conservation Corps cabin before joining up with the Redwood Trail, which climbs through Mexican pine, tropical ash, Port Orford cedar, and, of course, redwood.

Skyline Trail

This is some hike—strenuous but worth every step if you like seeing the big picture. It's 6.8 miles down, then back up again, with a dazzling 100-mile view of the islands dotting the blue Pacific, plus the West Maui Mountains, which seem like a separate island.

The trail is just outside Haleakalā National Park at Polipoli Spring State Recreation Area; however, you access it by going through the national park to the summit. It starts just beyond the Pu'u 'Ula'ula summit building on the south side of Science City and follows the southwest rift zone of Haleakalā from its lunarlike cinder cones to a cool redwood grove. The trail drops 2,600 feet into the 12,000-acre Kahikinui Forest Reserve. Plan for 8 hours; bring water and extreme weather gear.

WAI'ĀNAPANAPA STATE PARK ★★★

Tucked in a jungle on the outskirts of the little coastal town of Hāna is this state park, a black-sand beach nestled against vine-strewn cliffs.

The **Hāna-Wai'ānapanapa Coast Trail** is an easy 6-mile hike that takes you back in time. Allow 4 hours to walk along this relatively flat trail, which parallels the sea, along lava cliffs and a forest of *hala* (pandanus) trees. The best time to take the hike is either early morning or late afternoon, when the light on the lava and surf makes for great photos. Midday is the worst time; not only is it hot (lava intensifies the heat), but there's also no shade or potable water available.

There's no formal trailhead; join the route at any point along the Wai'ānapanapa Campground and go in either direction. Along the trail, you'll see remains of an ancient *heiau* (temple), stands of *hala,* caves, a blowhole, and hardy *naupaka,* a shrub flourishing along the beach. Upon close inspection, you'll see it only has half-blossoms; according to Hawaiian legend, a similar plant living in the mountains has the other half of the blossoms. Old myths say they are tragically separated lovers, one banished to the mountain and the other to the sea.

Horseback Riding

Maui offers spectacular horse rides through rugged ranchlands and into tropical forests. Join working cowboys and get a rare look at South Maui's pristine Kanaio coast during a private tour on family-owned **Triple L Ranch** (www.triplelranchmaui.com; ✆ **808/280-7070**). You'll traverse scrublands on the back side of Haleakalā, dotted with cinder cones and ancient ruins, as you help ranch hands check on their grazing cattle and keep axis deer and goats out of their pastures. Tours can be booked for any day of the week (the cattle never take a day off, either), for two to six people; choose from the 2-hour Open Range Ranch Tour ($200) or the All-Inclusive Lunch Tour, a 3- to 3½-hour ride with lunch ($300). The views of Kaho'olawe and Molokini Crater are entrancing from the ranch, whose entrance is only a few minutes south of MauiWine (p. 318) in 'Ulupalakua.

Founded by Portuguese immigrants in the late 19th century as Mendes Ranch, **Circle M Ranch ★★**, 3530 Kahekili Hwy., 6¼ miles past Wailuku (https://circlemranchmaui.com; ✆ **808/871-5222**), requires driving on the narrow, winding Kahekili Highway for a few miles, but it's worth it. The 3,000-acre ranch includes waterfalls, palm trees, coral-sand beaches, lagoons, tide pools, a rainforest, and its own volcanic peak (more than a

ESPECIALLY FOR kids

Walk Under Water & Whales While the **Maui Ocean Center** (p. 315) has paused its popular sleepovers (for kids accompanied by adults), a day trip to this incredible aquarium and education center in Māʻalaea Harbor is still in order. With the help of 3D glasses, the Humpbacks of Hawaiʻi Sphere creates an amazing half-hour experience of being surrounded by whales, while the acrylic tunnel through its 750,000-gallon tank allows you to ogle eagle rays, sharks, and other critters at a safe and dry distance.

Zip or Ride Through a Tropical Farm Maui Tropical Plantation ★ (p. 314) is a great place to introduce children 5 and older to **ziplining,** with five lines over an organic farm, lagoon, and lush landscaping (daily; $149; ages 5–10 must be accompanied by an adult). Less exhilarating but still fun is the lively 40-minute **tram tour** ($25 adults, $12.50 ages 3–12), which includes a short coconut husking demonstration, departing hourly Tuesday to Sunday 10am to 4pm.

mile high), visible on 2-hour morning and afternoon trail rides ($180 for ages 7 and older).

Rappelling

Also known as canyoneering, this exhilarating sport lets you safely swing your way down cliffsides using a tethered rope. The expert guides of **Rappel Maui** (www.rappelmaui.com; © **808/270-1500**) lead you through a dry run before coaching you down a 60-foot waterfall and then a 30-foot one, each ending in a refreshing pool lined by thick tropical foliage. The course is in a private botanical garden about halfway along the Road to Hāna, with a short hike on valley trails to the waterfalls; you'll receive directions once you book. The 3-hr. tours cost $230 per person, open to ages 10 and older (weighing a minimum of 70 lb., maximum 250 lb.), with bottled water and snacks provided.

Tennis & Pickleball

Maui has excellent public tennis courts; all are free and available from daylight to sunset (a few are even lit until 10pm for night play). For a complete list of public courts, call **Maui County Parks and Recreation** (© **808/ 270-7383**) or scroll through the park listings at www.mauicounty.gov/287/ maui-county-parks. Courts are available on a first-come, first-served basis; if someone's waiting, limit your play to 45 minutes. Convenient for visitors are the courts in Kīhei (four in Kalama Park on S. Kīhei Rd. and six in Waipualani Park on W. Waipualani Rd. behind the Maui Sunset condos) and Hāna (two in the Hāna Ballpark, 5091 Uakea Rd.).

Private tennis courts are available at most resorts and several hotels on the island. The **Kapalua Tennis Garden,** Kapalua Resort (www.golfat kapalua.com/tennis-garden; © **808/662-7730**), is home to the Kapalua Open, which features the largest purse in the state, held on Labor Day weekend. Rentals for its eight tennis and eight **pickleball courts** are $15 per person for 2 hours. Drop-in play is $20 per player for tennis (Sun and Fri 9–11am, for 3.5-rated players and above) and pickleball (Tues and Sat 9–11am, paddle provided).

In Wailea, try the **Wailea Tennis Club,** 131 Wailea Ike Place (www. waileatennis.com; © **808/879-1958**), with 9 Sportsmaster tennis courts and 10 **pickleball courts.** Court fees are $28 per player for 90 minutes, reservations required. Tennis racket rentals are $10 per day, while paddle rentals are $5 a day, including three pickleballs.

Ziplining

Ziplines offer exhilarating rides through a combination of steel cables, pulleys, and gravity. Be sure to read fine print on minimum ages (typically 7–10), weight restrictions, and other requirements, such as closed-toe shoes.

Flyin' Hawaiian ★★   The most eco-oriented of all Maui's ziplines, this eight-line tour covers 2½ miles from Waikapu to Māʻalaea—the longest on the island, crossing nine different valleys and 11 ridges. You'll not only learn about native plants along the way, but you'll also stop to plant and water some of the rare specimens here. Be aware the experience involves some hiking, as well as a 4×4 drive from the headquarters at **Maui Tropical Plantation** ★ (p. 314), which is also home to its own kid-friendly zipline course ($149).

Check-in at Maui Tropical Plantation, 1670 Honoapiʻilani Hwy., Wailuku. www.flyin hawaiianzipline.com. © **808/463-5786.** Tours $235.

Jungle Zipline Maui ★★   Off the Road to Hāna amid the lush foliage of Hāʻiku, just 25 minutes from the airport, lies this newer 8-line course, which also features an 85-foot-long suspension bridge between two trees, two swinging bridges, and an optional "free fall" ride. After the exhilarating adventure, you can wander through the park below, including a native fern forest and some 400 species of tropical plants. *Note:* Kids receive half-off when booking online with an adult fare; there's also a shorter 5-line option.

50 East Waipiʻo Rd., Hāʻiku. www.junglezip.com. © **808/573-1529.** 8 lines: $148 adults, $74 ages 6–15 (booked online). 5 lines: $128 adults, $64 ages 6–15 (booked online.)

Skyline EcoAdventures ★★   Go on, let out a wild holler as you soar above a rainforest gulch in Kāʻanapali or down the slope of Haleakalā. Pioneers of this internationally popular activity, the Skyline owners brought the first ziplines to the U.S. and launched them from their home, here on Maui. Skyline has two courses, one on the west side and the original, halfway up Haleakalā. Both are fast and fun, the guides are savvy and safety-conscious, and the scenery is breathtaking. In Kāʻanapali, you can even "zip and dip": dropping off your line into a mountain pool. Beyond that, this eco-conscious company is carbon-neutral and donates thousands of dollars to local environmental agencies.

Haleakalā course: 2½ miles up Haleakalā Hwy., Makawao. www.skylinehawaii.com. ✆ **808/878-8400.** Kā'anapali course: Check in at Fairway Shops, 2580 Keka'a Dr. #122, Lahaina. Tours $140–$190.

WHERE TO STAY ON MAUI

Maui has accommodations to fit every kind of vacation, from deluxe oceanfront resorts to homey condos to historic bed-and-breakfasts. "The Island in Brief" (p. 304) section can help you settle on a location.

Prices are typically higher than elsewhere in Hawai'i, even for hotel brands that would be considered moderately priced elsewhere, and you still have to add 17.42% in state and county accommodations and excise taxes. Also, if you're staying at an upscale hotel or resort, you will likely have to pay a "resort fee" ($35–$60 a day), noted below where applicable. (Annoyingly, these fees are also taxed.) Parking is free unless noted; rates listed below are daily. All hotels are non-smoking and pools are outside.

Tip: To mitigate some of the sticker shock when booking a Maui resort hotel, look for the deep discounts offered by Priceline and Hotwire for "hidden" deals, where the name of the property is revealed after you book. See "Internet or Apps for Hawai'i Hotel Discounts," p. 602, for more tips on booking.

Central Maui

KAHULUI

Moderate

Courtyard Marriott Kahului Airport ★ Business travelers and vacationers looking to save on airport drive time will find a comfortable night's sleep here, with soundproofed walls that adequately muffle noise from the neighboring airport. Spacious rooms are attractively furnished, featuring contemporary, island-inspired artwork. Suites come with full kitchens—super convenient considering the lobby has a 24-hour market, and several grocery stores are a 5-minute drive away. The palm-fringed pool deck is nice at night when it's lit by the glow of the fire pit.

532 Keolani Place, Kahului. www.marriott.com. ✆ **808/871-1800.** 138 units. $349–$747 double (2 queens or king with sofa bed); $578–$774 suite; $523–$844 1-bedroom; $620–$808 2-bedroom. Parking $12. Free airport shuttle daily 7am–11pm, on demand. **Amenities:** Deli-style restaurant; fitness center; whirlpool; coin-operated laundry; 24-hr. market; pool; free Wi-Fi.

Maui Beach Hotel ★ Off busy Ka'ahumanu Avenue but backing up onto a small beach, this budget hotel is managed by Springboard Hospitality, which specializes in sprucing up older properties and adding services to make them more appealing yet still affordable, at least by local standards. Enjoy updated tropical hues in spacious rooms with large windows and a mini-fridge with a la carte breakfast. Sunday brunch and dinner buffets in the open-air, second-floor **Rainbow Terrace** restaurant also provide good value if you don't have time to venture off the property, which offers a few tempting ocean-view hammocks. You can find small bites and drinks in **Lokelani Lounge.** *Tip:* Book 2 months in advance for a 25% discount.

170 W. Ka'ahumanu Ave., Kahului. www.mauibeachhotel.com. 🕾 **808/877-0051.** From $299 double, $319 oceanview, $389 oceanfront, $479 suite. Daily "amenity" fee $20. Parking $15. **Amenities:** Free airport shuttle (6am–9pm); ATM; lounge; restaurant; laundry room; pool; Wi-Fi.

WAILUKU

Expensive

The Historic Wailuku Inn ★★   Built in 1928, this estate home with lavish gardens on a side street in old Wailuku has been a gracious inn for many years, but in early 2024 wrapped up renovations under new management that also gave it a new name. The 10 air-conditioned suites still boast native wood or marble floors and high ceilings with crown moldings, but the bedding is modern with crisp white linens, and the art, wallpaper, and other decor reflect a bold Hawaiian palette. Each room has a private, luxurious bathroom stocked with plush towels and either a clawfoot tub, a whirlpool tub, or a deluxe multi-head shower. The inn is located in Wailuku's historic center, just 5 minutes' walk from **Hale Hō'ike'ike** (the Bailey House Museum), Market Street's antique shops, and several good restaurants. 'Īao Valley is a 5-minute drive away.

2199 Kaho'okele St. (at High St.), Wailuku. www.mauiinn.com. 🕾 **808/244-5897.** 10 units. From $499 double, breakfast included. 2-night min. (3-night min. peak periods). **Amenities:** Whirlpool; free Wi-Fi.

West Maui

In addition to the properties mentioned below, check out the vacation rental condos managed by **Maui Beachfront Rentals** (https://mauibeachfront. com; 🕾 **888/661-7200** or 808/661-3500). The listings include 28 updated units at 17 West Maui resorts, and guests receive free admission to local attractions or activities daily.

KĀ'ANAPALI

Don't like driving or hunting for parking? Any Kā'anapali condo or hotel guest can jump on the Kā'anapali Trolley (https://kaanapalitrolley.info; 🕾 **808/667-0648**) daily between 10am and 9:30pm; it stops at all the lodgings on the resort, Whalers Village, the Fairway Shops and Kā'anapali's two golf courses.

You'll find Kā'anapali hotels on the "Lahaina & Kā'anapali Hotels & Restaurants" map (p. 365).

Very Expensive

Sheraton Maui Resort & Spa ★★★   The Sheraton occupies the nicest spot on Kā'anapali Beach, built into the side of Pu'u Keka'a, the dramatic lava rock point (nicknamed Black Rock) at the beach's northern end.

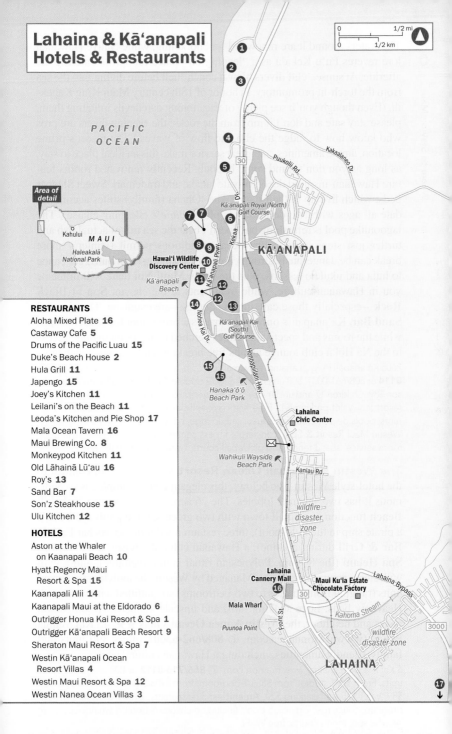

Lahaina & Kāʻanapali Hotels & Restaurants

PACIFIC OCEAN

Area of detail

Kahului

MAUI

Haleakalā National Park

Hawaiʻi Wildlife Discovery Center

Kāʻanapali Beach

Kāʻanapali Royal (North) Golf Course

KĀʻANAPALI

Kāʻanapali Kai (South) Golf Course

Hanakaʻōʻō Beach Park

Lahaina Civic Center

Wahikuli Wayside Beach Park

wildfire disaster zone

Lahaina Cannery Mall

Mala Wharf

Puunoa Point

Maui Kuʻia Estate Chocolate Factory

wildfire disaster zone

LAHAINA

Kakaalaneo Dr.

Puukolii Rd.

Kekaa Dr.

Kāʻanapali Pkwy.

Nohea Kai Dr.

Honoapiilani Hwy.

Kaniau Rd.

Lahaina Bypass

Kahoma Stream

Front St.

RESTAURANTS

Aloha Mixed Plate **16**
Castaway Cafe **5**
Drums of the Pacific Luau **15**
Duke's Beach House **2**
Hula Grill **11**
Japengo **15**
Joey's Kitchen **11**
Leilani's on the Beach **11**
Leoda's Kitchen and Pie Shop **17**
Mala Ocean Tavern **16**
Maui Brewing Co. **8**
Monkeypod Kitchen **11**
Old Lāhainā Lūʻau **16**
Roy's **13**
Sand Bar **7**
Son'z Steakhouse **15**
Ulu Kitchen **12**

HOTELS

Aston at the Whaler on Kaanapali Beach **10**
Hyatt Regency Maui Resort & Spa **15**
Kaanapali Alii **14**
Kaanapali Maui at the Eldorado **6**
Outrigger Honua Kai Resort & Spa **1**
Outrigger Kāʻanapali Beach Resort **9**
Sheraton Maui Resort & Spa **7**
Westin Kāʻanapali Ocean Resort Villas **4**
Westin Maui Resort & Spa **12**
Westin Nanea Ocean Villas **3**

The waters around it are renowned for snorkeling, while Native Hawaiian lore reveres Puʻu Kekaʻa as a "leaping off" place for spirits entering the afterlife. At sunset, cliff divers blow a conch shell before diving into the sea from the torch-lit promontory, in honor of 18th century Maui King Kahekili. (Even though you'll see plenty of vacationing daredevils imitating them, please stay safe and don't jump from the rocks; the evening divers are pros who know how to judge the ebb and flow of waves.) The resort's prime location, ample amenities, and great service make this an ideal place to stay, as long as you don't mind some hubbub. Recently renovated rooms feature Hawaiian-inspired decor, private lanais, and trademark Sweet Sleeper beds, which live up to their name. The ʻOhana (family) suites accommodate all ages with two double beds plus a *pūneʻe* (sleeping chaise). The lagoonlike pool is refreshing but doesn't beat the sea full of actual fish and turtles just steps away, when ocean conditions permit (winter's shore break can be dangerously strong). Activities ranging from outrigger canoe to hula and ukulele lessons, plus the lively **Maui Nui** luau, will immerse you in Hawaiian culture, while treatments at the elegant **Spa at Black Rock**—especially those catering to couples—are exquisite. The elevated **Sand Bar,** Kāʻanapali's only lobby bar, is a prime spot for sunset drinks, while the rooms and spectacular suites perched on the point include access to the Nā Hōkū club lounge and its free breakfast and evening appetizers.

2605 Kāʻanapali Pkwy., Lahaina. www.marriott.com/hotels/travel/hnmsi. ℂ **866/627-8114** or 808/661-0031. 508 units. $674–$1,772 double; $1,604–$3,500 suite. Extra person $89. Children 17 and under stay free in parent's room using existing bedding. $40 resort fee. Valet parking $42 (free first day); self-parking $32. **Amenities:** 5 restaurants; poolside and lobby bars; luau; club lounge; babysitting; children's program (at Westin Maui Resort & Spa); concierge; fitness center; whirlpool; lagoon-style pool; room service; spa; 3 tennis and pickleball courts; watersports rentals; Wi-Fi.

The Westin Kaʻanapali Ocean Resort Villas ★★

In contrast to the hotel-style Westin (see below), this elegant condo complex is so enormous it has two separate lobbies. The 26 acres fronting serene **Kahekili Beach** function as a small town with two grocers, three pools (yes, that's a pirate ship in the kids' pool), three restaurants (hit the sports bar **Pailolo Bar & Grill** during a game), a Hawaiian cultural advisor, the luxurious **Spa Helani** (the 80-min. Polynesian ritual is unforgettable), and a gym with steam rooms and saunas. Managed by Westin, the individually owned units (ranging from studios to two-bedrooms) are outfitted with trademark Heavenly beds, huge soaking tubs, and upscale kitchens. A companion resort and neighbor, the **Westin Nanea Ocean Villas ★★**, 45 Kai Malina Pkwy. (www.westinnanea.com; ℂ **808/662-6300**), offers 390 units and family-friendly amenities, including a Hawaiian cultural center.

6 Kai Ala Dr., Lahaina. www.marriott.com. ℂ **866/716-8112** or 808/667-3200. 1,021 units. From $497 studio; from $554 1-bedroom; from $903 2-bedroom. Extra person $89. Valet $25, self-parking $20. **Amenities:** 3 restaurants; 2 bars; babysitting; kids' program; concierge; 2 gyms; 5 pools (including children's pool); 4 whirlpools; room service; spa; tennis courts; free Wi-Fi.

The Westin Maui Resort & Spa ★★ It's water, water everywhere here, starting with the lobby, where waterfalls spill into pools stocked with flamingos and black swans. The lavish grounds wind around an 87,000-square-foot water wonderland, Kawaiola ("Living Water"), with six pools (including an adults-only pool), waterfalls, garden paths with wildlife, and an extra-speedy 128-foot-long water slide. All the falling water helps drown out some of the echoing noise of happy kids at play. A recent $120-million renovation includes its 217-room hotel-within-a-hotel, the Hōkūpaʻa Tower, featuring neutral-toned, natural materials and mid-century modern accents, plus exclusive access to the infinity-edge "cocktail pool" and breakfast bites on the second floor, oceanview Lānai lounge. All guests can enjoy Hawaiʻi Regional Cuisine legend Peter Merriman's latest concept, the locally sourced breakfast and lunch restaurant **Ulu Kitchen ★★**.

2365 Kāʻanapali Pkwy., Lahaina. www.marriott.com. © **866/627-8413** or 808/667-2525. 759 units. From $794 Kūkahi double; from $1,217 Hōkūpaʻa double; from $1,355 suite. Rates include $45 resort fee. Children 18 and under stay free in parent's room. Extra person $89. Valet parking $50; self-parking $45. **Amenities:** 4 restaurants; 3 bars; babysitting; bike rental; kids' program; concierge; gym; yoga; 6 pools; room service; salon; spa; tennis courts; watersports rentals; Wi-Fi.

Expensive

Aston at the Whaler on Kaanapali Beach ★★ Next door to Whalers Village, this collection of condos feels more formal and sedate than its high-octane neighbors. Maybe it's the koi turning circles in the meditative lily pond, the manicured lawn between the two 12-story towers on the 6-acre grounds, or the lack of a water slide populated by stampeding kids. Decor in the individually owned units varies widely, but most boast full kitchens, upscale bathrooms, and private lanais with views of Kāʻanapali's gentle waves or the emerald peaks of Mauna Kahālāwai. Unit no. 723, in the back corner of the north tower, is exquisite. Guests enjoy free coffee in the newly renovated open-air lobby and complimentary refreshments by the pool, while the beachfront barbecue area is the envy of passersby on the Kāʻanapali Beach walkway.

Note: Aston's fees for mandatory damage waivers, reservation processing, and cleaning add up quickly and may push units into the "very expensive" category.

2481 Kāʻanapali Pkwy., Lahaina. www.astonwhaler.com. © **855/945-4049** or 808/661-6000. 360 units. From $480 studio; from $580 1-bedroom (1 or 2 baths); from $1,507 2-bed/2-bath. Resort fee $33. Damage waiver $79. Cleaning fees: $79 studio; $199 1-bedroom; $319 2-bedroom. **Amenities:** Beach services; concierge; fitness center; laundry; pool; salon; spa; tennis court; Wi-Fi.

Hyatt Regency Maui Resort & Spa ★★ Exotic parrots and South African penguins in the palatial lobby may make you think you're not in Hawaiʻi at this southernmost property on Kāʻanapali Beach, but at least it shares the traditional values of hospitality and cherishing children. Its 40 acres include nine waterfalls, abundant Asian and Pacific artwork, and a waterpark pool with a swim-up grotto bar, rope bridge, and 150-foot lava-tube slide that keeps kids occupied for hours. Spread out among three towers, the resort's ample rooms have huge marble bathrooms, feather-soft platform beds, and private lanais with eye-popping views of the Pacific or Mauna Kahālāwai. Two Regency Club floors offer a private concierge, complimentary breakfast, sunset cocktails, and snacks—not a bad choice for families looking to save on meals.

Activities range from sushi-making classes at **Japengo ★★★**, the resort's superb Japanese restaurant (p. 400), to stargazing on the rooftop. Camp Hyatt offers pint-size guests weekly scavenger hunts, penguin-feedings, and a game room. Oceanfront **Spa Soleil** has 15 treatment rooms, sauna and steam rooms, and a huge menu of hydrafacials, facials, and body treatments. *Bonus:* "Drums of the Pacific" (https://drumsofthepacificmaui.com; ✆ **808/667-4727**), presented 5 to 7 nights a week, offers a Maui-themed show and one of the better buffets, although oddly without the traditional poi and lomi salmon; tickets start at $201 adults, $105 ages 4 to 12.

200 Nohea Kai Dr., Lahaina. www.hyatt.com/hyatt-regency/en-US/oggrm-hyatt-regency-maui-resort-and-spa. ✆ **808/661-1234.** 779 rooms and 31 suites. From $630 double; from $960 Regency Club double; from $1,580 suite. Extra person $80 ($130 in Regency Club rooms). Children 18 and under stay free in parent's room using existing bedding; rollaway $25. Valet parking $40; self-parking $25. **Amenities:** 5 restaurants; 3 bars; luau; babysitting; basketball court; kids' program; stargazing and wildlife tours; concierge; gym and classes; whirlpool; half-acre pool; room service; spa; watersports rentals; free Wi-Fi.

Kaanapali Alii ★★ This oceanfront condo complex sits on 8 landscaped acres in the center of Kāʻanapali Beach. Units are individually owned and decorated—some considerably fancier than others. Both one-(1,500-sq.-ft.) and two-bedroom (1,900-sq.-ft.) units come with the comforts of home: spacious living areas, gourmet kitchens, washer/dryers, lanais, and two full bathrooms. Resortlike extras include bell service, daily housekeeping, and a kids' club (summer only). Views from each unit vary greatly; if watching the sun sink into the ocean is a priority, request a central unit on floor 6 or higher. Mountain-view units are cooler throughout the day. Other amenities include a pool, a kiddie pool, barbecues and picnic areas, yoga classes on the lawn, a spa, and a tennis club with three clay courts, classes, and free use of rackets and balls. Be aware that daily "service" fees ($55) and one-time cleaning and property protection fees, along with taxes, make rates almost double the room rate for a 3-night stay.

50 Nohea Kai Dr., Lahaina. www.kaanapalialii.com. ✆ **866/664-6410** or 808/667-1400. 264 units. From $515 1-bedroom; from $730 2-bedroom. 3- to 5-night minimum. Resort "service" fee $55. Property protection plan $117. Cleaning fee $466. **Amenities:** Babysitting; concierge; fitness center; kids' club (June–Aug); 2 pools; 3 tennis courts; watersports equipment; yoga classes; Wi-Fi.

Kaanapali Maui at the Eldorado ★ It may have been one of Kāʻanapali's first properties in the late 1960s, but this 10-acre condo complex still manages to feel new. Developed in an era when real estate was abundant and contractors built to last, each spacious, individually owned unit has a full kitchen, washer/dryer, central air-conditioning, and outstanding ocean and mountain views. Larger units in the two-story (no elevator) buildings are a great choice for families. It's set on Kāʻanapali Golf Course, not on the beach, but guests have exclusive use of a beachfront pavilion on Kahekili (North Kāʻanapali) Beach, a quick trip by car or golf cart. You're also within walking distance of the Fairway Shops' casual, affordable restaurants—a real bonus in otherwise pricey Kāʻanapali.

Note: Contact info and prices below are for the units managed by Outrigger; other units may be rented via VRBO or other online platforms.
2661 Kekaʻa Dr., Lahaina. www.outrigger.com. ℂ **888/339-8585** or 808/661-0021. 204 units. From $281 studio; from $315 1-bedroom; from $478 2-bedroom. $83 nightly combined resort/condo fees; $165–$275 cleaning fee. **Amenities:** Beach pavilion; concierge; 3 pools; Wi-Fi.

Outrigger Honua Kai Resort & Spa ★★

This North Kāʻanapali Beach resort is a favorite with residents and locals alike. The property sits on Kahekili Beach, immediately north of busier, flashier Kāʻanapali Beach, with a much better reef for snorkeling, and its upscale yet relaxed atmosphere takes a cue from its natural surroundings. Island-inspired artwork in the lobby gives way to colorful koi ponds, landscaped grounds, and meandering swimming pools. Luxe accommodations range from huge 590-square-foot studios to vast 2,800-square-foot three-bedroom units, with top-of-the-line appliances, private lanais, and ocean views.

On the mountain side are the newer **Luana Gardens Villas,** three enclaves (each with its own swimming pool, hot tub, and fire pit) of three-bedroom, three-bath units of 2,000 square feet. The on-site sociable restaurant, **Duke's Maui Beach House ★★**, offers an "ono-licious" breakfast and live music from 3 to 5pm, plus tantalizing nightly seafood specials. Stock up on organic snacks, gelato, and local coffee at **Aina Gourmet Market** in the lobby. **Hoʻila Spa** has the island's only therapeutic Himalayan salt room and uses organic, made-in-Hawaiʻi products in its treatments.
130 Kai Malina Pkwy., North Kāʻanapali Beach. www.outrigger.com/hawaii/maui/honua-kai. ℂ **855/718-5789** or 808/662-2800. 600 units. From $351 studio (king bed and sofa bed, sleeps 4); from $396 1-bedroom (sleeps 4); from $549 2-bedroom (sleeps 6); from $1,029 3-bedroom (sleeps 8). $40 resort fee. Cleaning fee $270–$360. Damage protection waiver $79. **Amenities:** Restaurant; deli; bar; gym; 5 whirlpools; 5 pools; spa; watersports rentals; Wi-Fi.

Outrigger Kāʻanapali Beach Resort ★★

Long the most affordable hotel in Kāʻanapali, and the most dedicated to Hawaiian culture and values in all of Hawaii, this resort recently completed its first major transformation since opening in 1964. Outrigger acquired it just weeks before the August 8, 2023, wildfire in Lahaina. Like many Kāʻanapali properties, it quickly pivoted to hosting its displaced employees and disaster-response crews. Now visitors have returned to the property, where the 180-room, newly renamed Papakua wing—one of three low-rise buildings on the beachfront property—is the best legacy of the $75 million renovation. Rooms in this wing feature midcentury modern-inspired furnishings in a muted palette, botanical prints of indigenous plants, and shadowboxes of employee-made Hawaiian treasures such as fishhooks, leis, and weapons, similar to those already displayed in the lobby.

The 4-acre courtyard between guest rooms and the ocean features indigenous plants, and plumeria trees, the compact but charming whale-shaped pool, and poolside grill. **Maui Brewing Co.** ★★ (p. 403) operates a beachfront, family-friendly restaurant with nightly entertainment.

During the day, the expert watermen and women at the resort's water activity center will teach you to surf or paddle, with a focus on ocean safety and Hawaiian culture. At the excellent cultural center, you can learn how to throw a fish net, stamp patterns on kapa cloth, or play the bamboo nose flute as well as more commonly seen offerings such as weaving a lauhala bracelet or stringing a lei.

2525 Kā'anapali Pkwy., Lahaina. www.kbhmaui.com. © **800/262-8450** or 808/661-0011. 430 units. From $269 double. Extra person $40. Valet parking $26; self-parking $20. Resort fee $35. **Amenities:** Restaurant; bar; breakfast counter; concierge; convenience store; pool grill; babysitting; cultural and family activities; gift shop.

HONOKŌWAI, KAHANA & NĀPILI

Expensive

Napili Kai Beach Resort ★★★   This small resort nestled on Nāpili's white sandy cove feels like a well-kept secret. For 50-plus years, the staff here has been welcoming return guests for a taste of unspoiled paradise. The weekly mai tai and golf putting parties are blasts from the past, but the modern conveniences in each unit and startling ocean views will focus you on the splendid here and now. From the three buildings on the point (Puna, Puna 2, and Lani), you can gaze from your bed at the ocean, which looks like an infinity pool starting at the edge of your lanai. All units (aside from eight hotel rooms) have full kitchens, washer/dryers, flatscreen TVs, king-size beds, and private lanais separated by attractive shoji screens. Hawaiian cultural activities include poi pounding and lauhala weaving workshops, and weekly *keiki* (children's) hula shows and slack key guitar concerts, the latter led by Grammy award–winning musician George Kahumoku, Jr. Kids 12 and under eat for free at the resort's **Sea House** restaurant. As cozy as the rooms are, you'll probably spend most of your time on the beach or in the protected bay paddling past lazy sea turtles. *Bonus:* No resort or cleaning fees.

5900 Honoapi'ilani Rd. (at north end of Nāpili, next to Kapalua), Lahaina. www.napili kai.com. © **800/367-5030** or 808/669-6271. 162 units. $314–$440 double; $485–$710 studio; $740–$1,185 1-bedroom; $1,076–$1,625 2-bedroom; $1,205–$1,805 3-bedroom. **Amenities:** Restaurant; bar; babysitting; children's activities on holidays; concierge; 24-hr. fitness room; 2 putting greens; 4 pools; free Kapalua shuttle; free use of watersports equipment; free Wi-Fi.

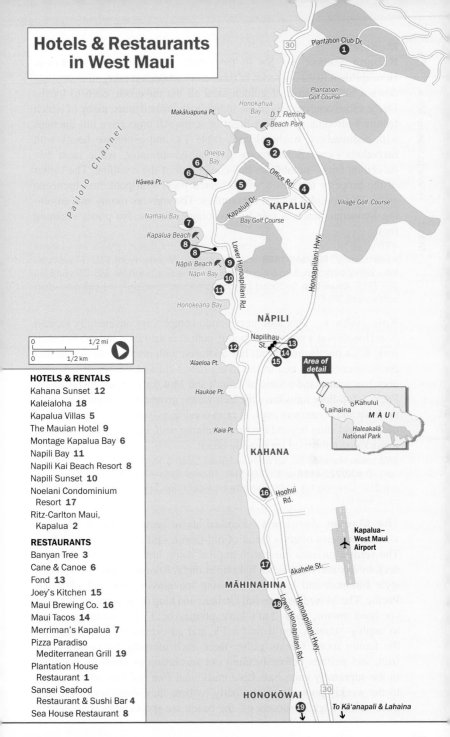

Hotels & Restaurants in West Maui

HOTELS & RENTALS
Kahana Sunset **12**
Kaleialoha **18**
Kapalua Villas **5**
The Mauian Hotel **9**
Montage Kapalua Bay **6**
Napili Bay **11**
Napili Kai Beach Resort **8**
Napili Sunset **10**
Noelani Condominium
  Resort **17**
Ritz-Carlton Maui,
  Kapalua **2**

RESTAURANTS
Banyan Tree **3**
Cane & Canoe **6**
Fond **13**
Joey's Kitchen **15**
Maui Brewing Co. **16**
Maui Tacos **14**
Merriman's Kapalua **7**
Pizza Paradiso
  Mediterranean Grill **19**
Plantation House
  Restaurant **1**
Sansei Seafood
  Restaurant & Sushi Bar **4**
Sea House Restaurant **8**

Moderate

Kahana Sunset ★   Set in the crook of a sharp bend on Lower Honoapiʻilani Road is a series of three-story wooden condos, stair-stepping down a hill to a strip of golden sand all but unknown, even to locals. Decor varies dramatically in the individually owned units, many of which feature bedrooms up a short flight of stairs. All units have full kitchens with dishwashers, washer/dryers, cable TV, and expansive lanais with marvelous views. Some rooms have air-conditioning, while most rely on ceiling fans—suitable on this cooler end of the coastline. The center of the property features a small, heated pool, whirlpool, and barbecue grills. This complex is ideal for families: The units are roomy, and adjoining Keonenui Beach is safe for swimming. *Bonus:* No pricey cleaning fees.

4909 Lower Honoapiʻilani Hwy. (at the northern end of Kahana), Lahaina. www.kahana sunset.com. © **800/669-1488** or 808/633-6816. 79 units. From $267 1-bedroom; from $281 2-bedroom. 3- to 5-night minimum. One-time resort fee $65. Cleaning fee $95–$165. **Amenities:** Secluded beach; barbecues; concierge; 2 pools (including kiddie pool); Wi-Fi.

Kaleialoha ★   This four-story condo complex is conveniently located near Honokōwai's grocery shopping, budget restaurants, and public beach park. Each one-bedroom unit has a kitchen with marble countertops and dishwashers; a sofa bed in the living room; stacked washer/dryers; outdoor barbecues; and a view of Lānaʻi and Molokaʻi across the turquoise Pacific. Top-floor units have the best views; ground-floor units open onto the lawn and oceanfront pool. In calm conditions (summer is best), there's decent snorkeling beyond the rock retaining wall, but you'll have to walk a block down the road for a sandy beach.

3785 Lower Honoapiʻilani Rd. (in Honokōwai), Lahaina. www.mauicondosoceanfront. com. © **800/222-8688** or 808/669-8197. 18 units. $265–$795 1-bedroom. Extra person $15. Cleaning fee $249. Damage protection fee $29. **Amenities:** Concierge; pool; free Wi-Fi.

The Mauian Hotel ★★   Perched above beautiful Nāpili Bay, this vintage property offers a blend of old-time hospitality and modern flair. The verdant grounds burst with tropical color; umbrellas shade the pool deck by day and tiki torches light up at night. Rooms feature Indonesian-style furniture and lanais overlooking the grassy lawn and glittering Pacific. The 38 studios have full kitchens and king or queen beds. Like the six hotel rooms, they don't have phones or TVs—encouraging you to unplug—though you'll find a TV and an extensive DVD library in the family room. Guests gather there each morning for coffee, fresh fruit, and pastries before heading out snorkeling or stand-up paddling in the supremely calm bay. Live music and free mai tais attract guests to the weekly poolside "aloha party," where they share appetizers and travel tales. Nightly sunsets off the beach are spectacular—particularly during winter when whale spouts dot the horizon. Another plus: no resort fee.

5441 Lower Honoapiʻilani Rd. (in Nāpili), Lahaina. www.mauian.com. © **808/669-6205.** 44 units. From $309 double; from $339 studio; from $359 1-bedroom. Extra person $20. **Amenities:** Coin laundry; continental breakfast; pool; shuffleboard courts; free Wi-Fi.

Napili Bay ★ This small two-story condo complex sits on the southern edge of picturesque Nāpili Bay. Fall asleep to the sound of the surf and wake to birdsong. Individually owned studio apartments are compact, with king- or queen-size beds in the oceanfront living room (rather than facing the road like so many on this strip). You'll find a stocked kitchen, beach and snorkeling equipment, and a lanai ideal for sunset views. There's no pool or air-conditioning, but louvered windows and ceiling fans keep the units fairly cool—and why waste time in a pool when you're steps away from one of the island's calmest and prettiest bays? *Note:* Contact and rates info below are for one of the property managers; you'll also find units on VRBO and other rental sites.

33 Hui Dr. (off Lower Honoapiʻilani Hwy., in Nāpili), Lahaina. www.alohacondos.com. © **877/877-5758.** 28 units. $149–$389 double. Cleaning fee $160–$250. Minimum stays may apply. **Amenities:** Barbecue; laundry facility; free Wi-Fi.

Napili Sunset ★★ This humble property hidden down a side street consists of three buildings, two facing spectacular Nāpili Bay and one across the street. At first glance, they don't look like much, and a second glance at dated decor isn't inspiring either, but the prime location, low prices, and friendly staff make up for the plain-Jane exterior. The one- and two-bedroom units are beachfront (with expensive rates to match); the upstairs units have bathtubs, while those downstairs have direct access to the sand. Across the street, overlooking a kidney-shaped pool and gardens, the economical studios feature expansive showers and Murphy beds. All units benefit from daily housekeeping service, full kitchens, and ceiling fans (studios have air-conditioning). Unfortunately, bedrooms in the beachfront buildings face the road, but the ocean views from the lanais are outstanding. The strip of grassy lawn adjoining the beach is an added perk—especially when the sandy real estate is crowded. Several good restaurants are within walking distance, along with Kapalua's tennis courts and golf courses. Room rates have no added cleaning or other fees, either.

46 Hui Rd. (in Nāpili), Lahaina. www.napilisunset.com. © **808/669-8083.** 43 units. $326 studio; $507 1-bedroom; $579 1-bedroom with loft; $825 2-bedroom. **Amenities:** Barbecues; coin laundry; pool; free Wi-Fi.

Noelani Condominium Resort ★★ Whether you book a studio or a three-bedroom unit, everything from the furnishings to the oceanfront pool at this Kahana gem is first class for budget prices. The only caveat: There's no sandy beach attached. Pōhaku Beach Park (good for surfing, not great for swimming) is next door; better beaches are a 5-minute drive away. All units feature full kitchens, daily housekeeping service, panoramic views of passing whales during winter, and sunsets year-round; one-, two-, and three-bedrooms have washer/dryers. My favorites are the Orchid building's deluxe studios, where you can see the ocean from your bed. Units in the Anthurium Building have oceanfront lanais just 20 feet from the water (the nicest are on the ground floor), but the bedrooms face the road. Guests are invited to lei-making and mai tai parties in the poolside cabana and have access to a teeny-tiny gym with a million-dollar view.

4095 Lower Honoapi'ilani Rd. (in Kahana), Lahaina. www.noelanicondoresort.com. ℰ **800/367-6030** or 808/669-8374. 40 units. From $259 studio; from $339 1-bedroom; from $469 2-bedroom; $589 3-bedroom. Extra person $20. Children 17 and under stay free in parent's room. Cleaning fee $165–$275. 3-night minimum. **Amenities:** Concierge; fitness center; whirlpool; laundry center; 2 pools (1 heated); DVD library; free Wi-Fi.

KAPALUA

The beautiful fairways of Kapalua's two golf courses (p. 354) and beaches with gorgeous views of Moloka'i are the big draws of this luxurious enclave. A free, on-call resort shuttle (daily 7am–11pm; ℰ **808/665-9110**) makes it easy to traverse the 22,000-acre compound.

Note: You'll find the following hotels on the "Hotels & Restaurants in West Maui" map (p. 371).

Very Expensive

Montage Kapalua Bay ★★★   Built on the site of the old Kapalua Bay Hotel, this 24-acre compound offers just 50 impeccably furnished rental residences, from one-bedroom to four-bedroom (1,250–4,050 sq.

The ultra-luxe villas at the Montage Kapalua Bay.

ft.). The low density—and astronomical prices—means there's never a crush at the terraced Sunset Pool with gorgeous Lānaʻi and Molokaʻi views, or the more intimate infinity-edged Beach Club Pool, or anywhere else on the beautifully landscaped grounds. It's hard to leave the cocoon of the roomy villas, which offer gourmet kitchens, high-end linens and robes, spalike bathrooms, and lanais or balconies with massive daybeds. Still, you don't want to miss the chance to "talk story" with cultural advisor Silla Kaina over lei-making, ukulele classes, or another of the free Hawaiian-themed activities. The 30,000-square-foot, two-story **Spa Montage Kapalua Bay** includes a vast fitness center with a raft of weekly classes, infinity-edge pool, and well-stocked boutique. The open-air restaurant **Cane & Canoe ★** (p. 405) epitomizes most of the culinary offerings at the resort: expensive, not particularly exciting, but satisfying enough and graciously served. For a magical, over-the-top experience, consider renting the resort's Cliff House perched above Namalu Bay for a private meal.

Note: It's hard to believe at this price level, but room rates do not include the shockingly high $71 daily resort fee.

1 Bay Dr., Kapalua. www.montagehotels.com/kapaluabay. © **808/662-6200.** 50 units. From $1,186 garden view 1-bedroom (sleeps 4), $1,314 oceanview; from $1,696 2-bedroom garden view, $1,894 oceanview; from $1,994 garden view 3-bedroom, $2,121 oceanview; 4-bedroom from $5,635. $71 resort fee. Valet parking (required) $30. **Amenities:** Concierge; 3 restaurants; 2 bars; 2 pools; cultural classes; fitness center; luxury spa; beach services; children's and teen programs; business center; luau; market; resort shuttle; in-room laundry; Wi-Fi.

The Ritz-Carlton Maui, Kapalua ★★★

Perched on a knoll above D. T. Fleming Beach, this resort is a complete universe. The property's intimate relationship to Hawaiian culture began during construction in 1987: When the remains of hundreds of ancient Hawaiians were unearthed, the owners agreed to shift the hotel inland to avoid disrupting the graves. For decades since, Hawaiian cultural advisor Clifford Naeʻole has helped guide resort developments and signature events, such as the Celebration of the Arts—a weeklong Indigenous arts and cultural festival—and **Tales of the Kapa Moe ★★★**, an illuminating and entertaining luau that debuted in 2023. The resplendent accommodations feature dark wood floors, plush beds, marble bathrooms, and private lanais—some with firepits—overlooking the landscaped grounds and mostly undeveloped coast. The sprawling club lounge is the best in the state, serving elaborate buffets at breakfast, lunch, and the cocktail hour, with sweets, snacks, and beverages available 24 hours a day, thanks to a special pantry. A male hula dancer performs a nightly ceremony at sunset.

Additional amenities include several superior restaurants; a 10,000-square-foot, three-tiered pool; and the 17,500-square-foot **Waihua Spa,** with steam rooms, saunas, and whirlpools surrounded by lava-rock walls. Make sure to visit **Jean-Michel Cousteau's Ambassadors of the Environment center** and explore the captivating activities for adults and kids. (You can even feed the resident pot-bellied pigs.) A bit of a hike from the resort proper, **D. T. Fleming Beach** is beautiful but tends to be windier and rougher than the bays immediately south; a 5-minute shuttle ride delivers you to Oneloa or Kapalua beaches. Dining outlets here are excellent, especially the breakfast-only **Ulana Terrace** ★★ and lobby-level **Alaloa Lounge,** both with wonderful ocean views.

1 Ritz-Carlton Dr., Kapalua. www.ritzcarlton.com/en/hotels/kapalua-maui. ✆ **808/ 669-6200.** 466 units. From $1,259 double; from $1,489 club-level; from $1,494 suite; from $2,839 2-bedroom suite. Extra person (ages 9 and older) on club level $100. $50 resort fee. Valet parking $45. **Amenities:** 6 restaurants; 4 bars; babysitting; bike rentals; kids' program; club floor; concierge; cultural tours; fitness room; 2 golf courses; hiking trails; 3-tiered pool; room service; shuttle; luxury spa; tennis/pickleball complex; watersports rentals; Wi-Fi.

Expensive

Kapalua Villas ★★★ The stately townhouses populating the oceanfront cliffs and fairways of this idyllic coast are a (relative) bargain, particularly if you're traveling with a group. Several of the island's best restaurants (Sansei and Merriman's Kapalua) are within walking distance or a quick shuttle trip, and you're granted signing privileges and a discount at the nearby championship golf courses. Outrigger manages the individually owned one-, two-, and three-bedroom units, which feature full kitchens, upscale furnishings, queen-size sofa beds, and large private lanais. You'll enjoy the spaciousness—even the one-bedrooms exceed 1,200 square feet. Of the three complexes (Kapalua Golf, the Ridge at Kapalua, and Kapalua Bay villas), the Bay units are the nicest, positioned on the windswept bluff overlooking Moloka'i on the horizon. In the winter you can whale-watch without leaving your living room.

300 Kapalua Drive. www.kapaluavillasmaui.com. ✆ **800/367-2742** or 808/665-9170. from $328 1-bedroom; from $433 2-bedroom; from $545 3-bedroom. $39 resort fee. $289–$364 cleaning fee. $59 damage protection fee. **Amenities:** Concierge; in-room laundry; golf; tennis; 9 pools; shuttle; Wi-Fi.

South Maui

An enormous number of vacation rental homes and condos in South Maui are on websites such as VRBO.com, Airbnb.com, and even Hotels.com. However, a booking agency with on-island support and multiple units can more easily help you if anything goes wrong during your stay. **Outrigger** (www.outrigger.com; ✆ **866/956-4262** or 303/369-7777), for example, manages units at the **Palms at Wailea** ★★, 3200 Wailea Alanui, as well as at five resorts in West Maui. A one-bedroom, two-bath oceanview villa at the Palms runs 1,022 square feet and starts at $285 a night, plus $264 cleaning fee and $59 damage protection waiver, and taxes, totaling $1,054 for a 2-night stay (the minimum required). Many owners and smaller management companies are putting their units on Vacasa.com, which offers some on-island support to guests.

You'll find these and the following hotels on the "Hotels & Restaurants in South Maui" map (p. 377).

Hotels & Restaurants in South Maui

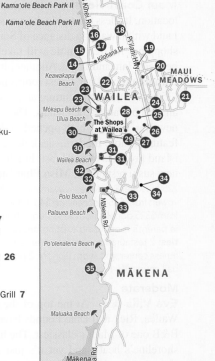

KĪHEI

Kalepolepo Beach

Kulanihakoi St.

S. Kīhei Rd.

Waipuilani Rd.

Pi'ilani Hwy.

Kulanihakoi Gulch

Keonoulu Beach

Lipoa St.

Halama St.

Lahaina ○ Kahului

MAUI

Area of detail

Haleakala National Park

Kalama Beach Park

Kama'ole Beach Park I

Kama'ole Beach Park II

Kama'ole Beach Park III

S. Kīhei Rd.

Pi'ilani Hwy.

Kilohana Dr.

Keawakapu Beach

WAILEA

Mōkapu Beach

Ulua Beach

The Shops at Wailea

Wailea Beach

MAUI MEADOWS

Polo Beach

Palauea Beach

Makena Rd.

Po'olenalena Beach

MĀKENA

Maluaka Beach

Mākena State Park

Makena Rd.

0   1 mi
0   1 km

HOTELS & RENTALS

AC Hotel by Marriott Maui Wailea **28**
Andaz Maui at Wailea **23**
Aston Maui Hill **17**
Dreams Come True on Maui **20**
Eva Villa **21**
Fairmont Kea Lani Maui **33**
Four Seasons Resort Maui at Wailea **32**
Grand Wailea, a Waldorf Astoria Resort **31**
Ho'olei at Grand Wailea Villas **31**
Hotel Wailea **34**
Kohea Kai Resort **3**
Makena Surf **35**
Mana Kai Maui Resort **15**
Maui Coast Hotel **11**
Maui Kamaole **16**
Maui Mango Cottages **14**
Nona Lani Cottages **2**
Palms at Wailea **22**
Pineapple Inn Maui **19**
Punahoa Beach Condominiums **10**
Residence Inn Maui Wailea **25**
Wailea Grand Champions Villas **24**
Wailea Beach Marriott Resort & Spa **30**
What a Wonderful World B&B **18**

RESTAURANTS

Cafe O'Lei Kīhei **13**
Fork and Salad **6**
Humble Market Kitchin **30**
Humuhumunukunuku-āpua'a **31**
Ka'ana Kitchen **23**
Kapa **30**
Kīhei Food Oasis **9**
Kō **33**
Lineage **29**
Matteo's Osteria **27**
Maui Brewing Co. **5**
Maui Tacos **12**
Monkeypod Kitchen **26**
Monsoon India **4**
Morimoto Maui **23**
Nalu's South Shore Grill **7**
The Pint & Cork **29**
Pita Paradise **26**
Restaurant at Hotel Wailea **34**
Spago **32**
Three's Bar & Grill **8**
Ululani's Shave Ice **1**
WowWow Lemonade **7**
Yak and Yeti **8**

KĪHEI

Expensive

Aston Maui Hill ★   This condo complex with Mediterranean-style stucco buildings, red-tile roofs, and three-stories-tall arches marks the border between Kīhei and Wailea—an excellent launching pad for your vacation. Managed by the respected Aqua Aston chain, Maui Hill combines the amenities of a hotel—24-hour front desk, concierge, pool, hot tub, tennis courts, putting green—with the convenience of a condo but no resort or cleaning fees. Units are spacious, with ample kitchens, air-conditioning, washer/dryers, queen-size sofa beds, and roomy lanais—most with ocean views. (For prime views, seek out units #35 and #36.) Two of South Maui's best beaches are across the street; restaurants, shops, and golf are nearby. Check the website for significant discounts.

2881 S. Kīhei Rd. (across from Kamaole Park III, btw. Keonekai St. and Kilohana Dr.), Kīhei. www.astonmauihill.com. ℂ **855/945-4044** or 808/879-6321. 140 units. From $365 1-bed/2-bath; from $490 2-bed/2-bath; from $848 3-bed/3-bath. 2-night minimum. **Amenities:** Concierge; putting green; pool; whirlpool; tennis courts; free Wi-Fi.

Maui Coast Hotel ★   The chief advantage here is location, location, location. It's less than a block from sandy, sun-kissed Kamaole Beach Park I and within walking distance of South Kīhei Road's bars, restaurants, and shopping; its free shuttle will take guests anywhere in Kīhei or Wailea between 7am and 10pm. Another plus: nightly entertainment at the popular **Hanohano** pool bar. Guest rooms in the original Hōkū Tower are smallish (355 sq. ft.), but with sitting areas, sofa beds, huge flatscreen TVs, central air, and private garden lanais. The only rooms with ocean views are in the new Kai Tower, which opened in 2024; they start at 388 square feet and feature a more modern, sleek design. On site, **Kihei Caffe** ★★ provides island favorites at breakfast, lunch, and dinner daily 7am to 9pm, while a new sushi restaurant, **Miso Phat Sushi,** was set to open in fall 2024.

2259 S. Kīhei Rd., Kīhei. www.mauicoasthotel.com. ℂ **808/874-6284.** 427 units. Kai Tower: from $354 (oceanview $401) double; from $895 oceanview suite. Hōkū Tower: from $325 double; from $348 studio; from $372 suite. Children 17 and under stay free in parent's room using existing bedding. Resort fee $41; extra person $30. **Amenities:** 2 restaurants; pool bar w/entertainment; loaner bikes; concierge; rental cars; fitness center; gift shop; laundry; 2 pools; 2 whirlpools; room service; shuttle; pickleball courts; Wi-Fi.

Moderate

Eva Villa ★★   At the top of the Maui Meadows neighborhood above Wailea, Rick and Dale Pounds have done much to make their affordable B&B one of Maui's classiest. The hillside location offers respite from the shoreline's heat—and yet it's just a few minutes' drive to the beaches, shopping, and restaurants of both Kīhei and Wailea. The tastefully designed cottage has a decent-size kitchen and living room, smallish bedroom, washer/dryer, and a sweet outdoor shower. The poolside studio is a single, long room with a huge kitchen and barstool seating. You aren't forced to be social here; continental breakfast (fresh fruit, juice, muffins, coffee) comes stocked in your kitchen. And with just two units, the spacious deck by the renovated heated pool is rarely ever crowded.

815 Kumulani Dr., Kīhei. www.mauibnb.com. ✆ **808/874-6407.** 2 units. $240 studio, $270 cottage, includes continental breakfast. Cleaning fee $125. Extra person $40. 4- to 5-night minimum. No credit cards, PayPal ok. **Amenities:** Laundry facilities (guest cottage only); pool; whirlpool; free Wi-Fi.

Kohea Kai Resort ★ Formerly known as an LGBT resort, this welcoming-to-all, family-friendly boutique property across the street from windswept Sugar Beach in North Kīhei offers standard rooms, studios, or suites sporting bright decor, comfy California king–size beds, wall unit air-conditioners, and spacious ocean- or mountain-view lanais. Studios and suites have kitchens or kitchenettes. The three penthouse suites are fabulous—especially #622, a gorgeous three-bedroom retreat with private two-person hot tub. Rates include a full hot breakfast. Chat with fellow guests over eggs and bagels or in the rooftop hot tub, where you can take in the view of Māʻalaea Bay and Mauna Kahālāwai. Maui's best beaches are a short drive away; the owners supply beach chairs and coolers.

551 S. Kīhei Rd., Kīhei. www.koheakai.com. ✆ **808/879-1261.** 26 units. $347–$404 double; $384–$470 studio; $392–$467 1-bedroom; $537–$900 penthouse suites. Resort fee $25. Extra person $45. **Amenities:** Concierge; 2 whirlpools; pool; Wi-Fi.

Mana Kai Maui Resort ★ Even the views outside the elevator are astounding at this eight-story hotel/condo, which practically has its toes in the sand of beautiful Keawakapu Beach. Every unit in the 1973 building is oceanfront (though many lack views). Most, if not all, have been renovated with contemporary, island-inspired furnishings. The north-facing hotel rooms, which account for half of the units, have no lanais and are small enough to be filled by their king-size beds (or two twins by request) and kitchenettes. The one- and two-bedroom condos have full kitchens, sitting areas, and small lanais that overlook the glittering Pacific and several islands on the horizon; the ones with the best views also have air-conditioning. There's a surf shack on-site, along with a gourmet grocery/deli, yoga studio, and the all-day, oceanfront restaurant **5 Palms** ★★, where guests receive 20% off entrees. *Fun fact:* The lobby's iconic turtle mural appears in the film *Just Go with It.*

2960 S. Kīhei Rd., Kīhei. www.manakaimaui.com. ✆ **800/525-2025** or 808/879-1561. 98 units. From $290 (3-night minimum) double; from $540 1-bedroom; from $650 2-bedroom. Reservation fee 3% of room rate. **Amenities:** Restaurant; bar; barbecues; concierge; coin laundry; pool; watersports equipment rentals; free Wi-Fi.

Maui Kamaole ★ Directly opposite Kamaʻole Beach Park III's sandy beach, enormous lawn, and playground, this comfortable condo complex is ideal for families. Convenience is key here in the center of Kīhei's beach and shopping zone. Each roomy, privately owned and furnished unit comes with a kitchen, central air, two bathrooms, washer/dryer, and two private lanais. The one-bedroom units—which can easily accommodate four—are all on the ground floor, opening onto a grassy lawn, while the two-bedroom units are all on the second floor and include a loft. The attractive property runs perpendicular to the shoreline, and some buildings (indicated by room numbers that start with E, F, K, L, and M) are quite a trek from the beach. Families with small children should seek out units beginning with A, B, G, or H, which are nearest to the beach but off the road. C units are close to both beach and pool.

2777 S. Kīhei Rd., Kīhei. www.mauikamaole.com. ✆ **800/451-5008.** 316 units (not all in rental pool). From $306 1-bedroom; from $338 2-bedroom. 5-night minimum. Reservation, registration and accidental damage fees combined $150. Cleaning fee $200–$230. **Amenities:** 2 pools; 2 whirlpools; 2 tennis courts; free Wi-Fi.

Maui Mango Cottages ★★ Why stay in a condo when you can feel at home in one of these two beautifully updated, vintage cottages? They're shaded by mature mango trees on a 1-acre lot and lie within a short walk to swimmable **Keawakapu Beach** ★★★ (and close to Wailea's 1½-mile beach path)—so take advantage of the complimentary beach chairs, coolers, and boogie boards. Both have fully equipped kitchens, washer-dryers, airconditioning, parking spaces, and decks with tables, chairs, and barbecues; kids can run around the large yard while parents make dinner or drink their morning coffee. Cottage 1 is great for families, with one king bedroom and one with three twin beds, a great room, office, and bathroom with islandstyle private outdoor shower. Plantation-style Cottage 2 is ideal for two couples or larger families, offering two king bedrooms and one with two twin beds, living room, and 1½ small but modern baths. Friendly owners Charlie and Yvonne, who have three boys of their own, chose furnishings with just the right mix of comfort and sturdiness, with fun marine- and beach-themed prints serving as colorful accents to soft pastel walls and neutral upholstery.

Note: The website will direct you to VRBO for booking; that platform charges a varying service fee tied to the room rate, plus a refundable damage deposit of $295.

45 Kilohana Dr., Kīhei. www.mauimangocottages.com. 2 units. $195–$395 Cottage 1 (sleeps 4–5); $395–$445 Cottage 2 (sleeps 6). Cleaning fee $250. Typical VRBO service fee $252. 5-night minimum. **Amenities:** Barbecues; free Wi-Fi.

Nona Lani Cottages ★ Family-owned since the 1970s, this oceanside retreat is one of North Kīhei's sweeter deals. Eight tiny vintage cottages are tucked among the coconut palms and plumeria trees, a stone's throw from Sugar Beach. Inside is everything you'll need: a compact kitchen, a separate bedroom with a queen-size bed, air-conditioning, and a cozy lanai—not to mention updated cabinetry and travertine tile floors. The three suites in the main house are inexpensive but stuffy; stick to the cottages. The charming grounds include a barbecue area and outdoor *hale* for weddings or parties—but no pool. Your hosts, the Kong family, don't offer daily housekeeping service, but they do make fresh flower leis—buy one and fill your cottage with fragrance. Wi-Fi can be spotty here.

455 S. Kīhei Rd. (just south of Hwy. 31), Kīhei. www.nonalanicottages.com. ✆ **808/ 879-2497.** 11 units. From $297 suite; from $397 cottage. Extra person $25. 2-night minimum May to mid-Nov, 4 nights Apr to mid-Nov. **Amenities:** Barbecues; coin laundry; free Wi-Fi.

Punahoa Beach Condominiums ★   This oceanfront condo sits on a large grassy lawn between the Charley Young surf break and Kama'ole I Beach—an ideal headquarters for active sun-seekers. Each unit in the small four-story building boasts a lanai with a marvelous view of the Pacific and islands on the horizon. All are individually owned and decorated, so the aesthetic varies widely. (The website features photos of each.) Studios feature queen-size Murphy beds, full bathrooms, and compact, full-service kitchens, while the three one-bedroom penthouses are the sweetest option. Be aware not all units have air conditioning, but you're able to choose when booking online. Kīhei's shops and restaurants are within walking distance.

2142 'Ili'ili Rd. (off S. Kīhei Rd., 300 ft. from Kama'ole Beach I), Kīhei. www.punahoa beach.com. ℂ **866/786-2462** or 808/879-2720. 13 units. $204–$375 studio; $234–$499 1-bedroom double; $324–$528 1-bedroom penthouse; $335–$556 2-bedroom double (none with A/C). Extra person $15. Cleaning fee $175–$200. 3-night minimum. **Amenities:** Barbecue area; coin laundry; free Wi-Fi.

Inexpensive

Dreams Come True on Maui ★   After several years of vacationing on Maui, Tom Croly and Denise McKinnon moved here to open this dreamy B&B. They offer a stand-alone cottage and two private suites in their house, which is centrally located on a half-acre in the Maui Meadows neighborhood, just a 5- to 10-minute drive from the shopping, restaurants, golf courses, and beaches of Kīhei and Wailea. All units are only for ages 12 and older. Suites have a private entrance and lanai, kitchenette, 42-inch TV, air-conditioning, and use of laundry facilities. Continental breakfasts are offered room-service style: Choose from the menu of freshly baked pastries, mangoes right off the tree, and other treats, and in the morning, it'll be delivered at your chosen time. Rooms are a bit tight, but you're free to use the oceanview deck, living room, and outdoor cooking area. The one-bedroom cottage (which comes with a $175 cleaning fee but no breakfast service) has ocean views from several rooms, vaulted ceilings in the living room, and wraparound decks. Tom is on duty as a personal concierge, doling out beach equipment and suggestions for where to snorkel, shop, or dine.

3259 'Ākala Dr., Kīhei. www.dreamscometrueonmaui.com. ℂ **808/879-7099.** 3 units. No children under age 12. $169–$209 suite (3- to 6-night minimum), including continental breakfast; $50 cleaning fee for stays of 5 nights or less. $240–$285 cottage (6- to 12-night minimum), plus $175 cleaning fee. Extra person $15. Continental breakfast included with suites. **Amenities:** Concierge; free Wi-Fi.

Pineapple Inn Maui ★★   Enjoy a resort vacation at a fraction of the price at this oasis in residential Maui Meadows, luxuriously landscaped with tall coconut palms, dinner-plate-sized pink hibiscus, a lily pond, and—best of all—a saltwater pool that's lit at night. The four guest rooms in the two-story "inn" are equally immaculate: Each has upscale furnishings, a private lanai with a serene ocean view, and a kitchenette that your hosts, Mark and Steve, stock with pastries, bagels, oatmeal, juice, and coffee upon arrival. The bright and airy cottage (two bedrooms, one bath) is one of the island's best deals. Landscaped for maximum privacy, it has a full kitchen, dark wood floors, central air, beautiful artwork, and a private barbecue area. Guests are invited to stargaze from the communal hot tub and make use of the fully equipped outdoor kitchen. Shopping, beaches, restaurants, and golf are minutes away and you can borrow snorkeling equipment, beach chairs, umbrellas, boogie boards, and a cooler to take on your outdoor adventures.

3170 'Ākala Dr., Kīhei. www.pineappleinnmaui.com. ✆ **877/212-MAUI (6284)** or 808/298-4403. 5 units. $239–$339 double; $335–$445 cottage. 3-night minimum for rooms, 6-night minimum for cottage. Breakfast included. **Amenities:** Saltwater pool; watersports equipment; free Wi-Fi.

What a Wonderful World B&B ★   Repeat guests here adore hosts Jim and Eva Tantillo, whose years of experience in the travel industry show in thoughtful touches around their lovely property. Every unit has a private entrance and is air-conditioned with its own unit; all are lovingly furnished with hardwood floors, Hawaiian quilts, and luxurious slate showers. The Guava Suite is smallest and a little dark. The Papaya Suite, with its spacious living room, bathroom, and separate bedroom, is just right. Eva serves continental breakfast on the lanai, with views of the ocean, Mauna Kahālāwai, and Haleakalā. You're also welcome to use the full kitchen or barbecue. For movie nights, the common area has a gigantic TV and a fancy popcorn maker. Although it's in a residential Kīhei neighborhood, it's only about a half-mile from Kamaʻole 3 Beach Park and 5 minutes from Wailea's golf courses, shopping, and restaurants. No cleaning fees mean the rates are very reasonable.

2828 'Ūmalu Place, Kīhei. www.amauibedandbreakfast.com. ✆ **808/870-2191.** 4 units. $195–$245 double, includes breakfast. Children under 12 stay free in parent's room. 5-night minimum in peak seasons. **Amenities:** Beach equipment; barbecue; laundry facilities; free Wi-Fi.

WAILEA

Golfers should note that all Wailea resorts enjoy special privileges at the Wailea Golf Club's three 18-hole championship courses: Blue, Gold, and Emerald. **Aliʻi Resorts** (www.aliiresorts.com; ✆ **855/627-9527**) offers a wide selection of luxury rentals at seven condo resorts in Wailea and Mākena at competitive rates. A 1,000-square-foot one-bedroom, two-bath, partial ocean-view unit at **Wailea Grand Champions Villas ★** (155 Wailea Ike Place), for example, costs $1,940 for a 5-night stay, once all the taxes and fees (including a $60 damage waiver and $340 "guest service fee") are accounted for. It may sound high, but if two couples are splitting costs, that's less than $200 per couple per night. For the most seclusion in busy South Maui, check out the luxurious condo units in **Makena Surf ★★★** on Poʻolenalena Beach and next to the shore-diving favorite spot of Five Graves (also known as Chang's Beach); Aliʻi Resorts manages two dozen ocean-view, oceanfront, or beachfront rentals here, ranging from two-bedroom/two-bath to four-bedroom/five-bath condos. Rates start at $869 a night exclusive of taxes and fees, or about $1,164 with everything factored in.

Marriott's two off-beach properties used to be considered moder-ately priced, relative to the big resorts, but now many visitors will find it a better value to try to use their Marriott points to score a coveted room in them. Opened in 2021, **AC Hotel by Marriott Maui Wailea ★★**, 88 Wailea Ike Place (www.marriott.com; ✆ **808/856-0341**), is a hip, Euro-Hawaiian, art-filled retreat with terrific views of neighboring islands, West Maui, and the ocean. All 110 contemporary-chic rooms have private bal-conies, while the infinity-edge pool sits next to one of Wailea's best bars, the AC Lounge. The open-air AC Kitchen dining area serves locally inspired breakfast, lunch, and dinner. Rates start at $921 doubles, $1,244 suites, plus $30 for parking. **Residence Inn Maui Wailea ★★**, 75 Wailea Ike Dr. (www.marriott.com; ✆ **808/891-7460**), is handsomely built, and a great fit for families, offering kitchens, free breakfast, and a large pool. But keep in mind that, like the AC Hotel, it's a long walk to the beach (take the resort shuttle if available). Current rates—thankfully lower than in recent years, but still pricey for the brand—start at $564 for a studio with king and sofa bed, $580 with two queens and sofa bed, $605 for a one-bedroom suite with king and sofabed, $621 for a one-bedroom suite with two queens and sofa bed, and $1,145 to $1,172 for two-bedroom suites with a king, one or two queens, and a sofa bed. Parking costs $30.

Very Expensive

Andaz Maui at Wailea ★★★ The Andaz boasts a prime beachfront locale, chic decor, apothecary-style spa, and two phenomenal restaurants, including one by superstar chef Masaharu Morimoto. Foodies should look no further: The sushi at **Morimoto Maui ★★★** (p. 410) is a must, while the resort's other restaurant, **Kaʻana Kitchen ★★★** (p. 409), showcases the best from Maui's ranches, farms, and fishing boats. Stan-dard rooms here can seem cramped, but they ramp up the style quotient a notch with crisp white linens, warm wood furniture, and midcentury accents. Wander down past the tiered infinity pools (which look best at night, when lit in a shifting palette of colors) to **Mōkapu Beach** to snor-kel, kayak, or paddle an outrigger canoe. This resort is a dynamic blend of modern and ancient values. Visit with the resident artist in the lobby gallery or learn to braid *ti*-leaf leis and make coconut fiber cordage. What-ever you do, don't miss the **ʻĀwili Spa,** where you can mix your own mas-sage oil and body scrubs. Fitness classes and outrigger canoe excursions are included in the $50 resort fee (which seems a tad exorbitant, given the high rates, plus $48 for required valet parking). If you splurge on one of the resort's two-, three-, or four-bedroom villas (https://villasatandazmaui.

com), you'll have an entire wall that opens to the Pacific, a private plunge pool, and a luxurious kitchen to call your own.

3550 Wailea Alanui Dr., Wailea. www.hyatt.com/andaz/oggaw-andaz-maui-at-wailea-resort. (℅ **808/573-1234.** 321 units. From $933 double; from $1,288 1-bedroom suite; from $4,045 villa. Resort fee $50. Valet parking (required) $48. **Amenities:** 3 restaurants, 24-hr. market; 3 bars; concierge; 24-hr. fitness center; 4 cascading infinity pools; 24-hr. room service; shuttle; **Feast at Mokapū** luau (https://feastatmokapu.com; $280–$340 adults, $140–$180 ages 4–12), luxury spa with pool; watersports rentals; free fitness classes and excursions; free minibar; Wi-Fi.

Fairmont Kea Lani Maui ★★★   At first blush, this blinding-white complex of Arabian turrets looks a tad out of place. But once you enter the recently redesigned lobby—an inviting oasis with waterfalls and tropical gardens, a new Hawaiian cultural center and **Pilina** lobby bar, opened in late 2023—and see the big blue Pacific outside, there's no doubt you're in Hawai'i. For the price of a regular room at the neighboring resorts, you get an entire, newly updated suite here. Each unit in the all-suites hotel has a kitchenette with granite countertop, living room with sofa bed (great for kids), spacious bedroom, marble bathroom (head immediately for the deep soaking tub), and large lanai with views of the pools, lawns, and Pacific Ocean. The two-story beachfront villas are perfect for well-heeled families or couples traveling together: Each of the 37 units has two or three bedrooms, a high-end kitchen, washer/dryer, and private plunge pool just steps from the white sand. They come stocked with complimentary snacks and drinks; breakfast buffet is included, and you can order room service, fixings to barbecue yourself, or a meal prepared by a chef on-site.

    Polo Beach is public but feels private and secluded. Huge murals and artifacts decorate the property, which is home to two top restaurants (**Kō** [p. 409] and **Nick's Fishmarket**), a fun lounge with great cocktails and craft beer, an excellent bakery and gourmet deli/poke shop (**Makana Market**), and the **Willow Stream Spa.** Escape into this heavenly retreat to experience the rain showers, steam rooms, and warm lava-stone foot beds. Youngsters can build volcanoes in the kids' club, while the entire family can get into rhythm paddling a Hawaiian outrigger canoe.

4100 Wailea Alanui Dr., Wailea. www.fairmont.com/kealani. (℅ **866/540-4456** or 808/875-4100. 450 units. From $1,249 suite; from $4,073 villa. $50 resort fee. Valet parking $40; free self-parking. **Amenities:** 5 restaurants, bakery and deli; 4 bars; babysitting; kids' program; concierge; 24-hr. gym; 2 family pools; adults-only pool; water slide and swim-up bar, room service; salon; spa; watersports rentals; Wi-Fi.

Four Seasons Resort Maui at Wailea ★★★   Words fail to describe how luxurious you'll feel rubbing elbows with celebrities in this über-elegant yet relaxed atmosphere. Perched above Wailea Beach, the Four Seasons inhabits its own world, where poolside attendants anticipate your needs: Cucumber slices for your eyes? Mango smoothie sampler? Or perhaps your sunglasses need polishing? The adults-only infinity pool with underwater music, designer cabanas, and a swim-up bar is what all pools aspire to. The roughly 600-square-foot guest rooms feature dream-inducing beds, deep marble bathtubs, walk-in showers big enough for two, and furnished lanais, most with superlative ocean views. If you're in a North Tower room over the parking lot, ask politely to be moved.

The sublime spa offers an incredible array of body treatments, from traditional Hawaiian to craniosacral and Ayurvedic massage. (As nice as the spa facility is, treatments in the oceanside thatched *hale* are even more idyllic.) The resort's restaurants, **Spago** (p. 410), **Ferraro's**, and **DUO**, are consistently superb, if high-priced; the lively lobby lounge has delicious sushi, craft cocktails, and sunset hula. Finally, this might be the island's most kid-friendly resort: Perks include milk and cookies on arrival, toddler-proofing for your room, *keiki* menus in all restaurants, a high-tech game room, and the unmatched, complimentary Kids for all Seasons program from 9am to 5pm. In "Couples Season," September to mid-December, a variety of unique activities (some complimentary) allow adult guests to sharpen skills like photography or cooking, as well as learn new ones, like celestial navigation. Refreshingly, there's no resort fee, although rates are some of the highest on the island. *Tip:* Wedding parties should book #798 or #301—stunning suites with room for entertaining.

3900 Wailea Alanui Dr., Wailea. www.fourseasons.com/maui. © **800/311-0630** or 808/874-8000. 380 units. From $1,320 double; $2,533 club floor; from $2,135 suite; from $3,225 larger suite. Children 17 and under stay free in parent's room. Valet parking $50. **Amenities:** 4 restaurants, 4 bars; babysitting; e-bike rentals; kids' program; cabanas; concierge; concierge-level rooms; putting green; fitness center with classes; 3 pools; room service; shuttle; spa; salon; 2 tennis courts; watersports rentals; free Wi-Fi.

Grand Wailea, a Waldorf Astoria Resort ★★

Built by a Japanese multimillionaire at the pinnacle of creating fantasy megaresorts in Hawai'i, the Grand Wailea opened in 1991 and for years was the grand prize in Hawai'i vacation contests and the dream of many honeymooners—but it's better suited to families and those who like some hustle and bustle. No expense was spared for this resort: Some $30 million of original artwork decorates the grounds, much of it created expressly for the hotel by Hawaiian artists and sculptors. More than 10,000 tropical plants beautify the lobby alone, and rocks hewn from the base of Mount Fuji adorn the Japanese garden. A Hawaiian-themed restaurant floats atop a manmade lagoon.

Guest rooms come with lavish, oversize bathrooms and plush bedding. But for kids, all that matters is the resort's unrivaled pool: an aquatic playground with nine separate swimming pools connected by slides, waterfalls, caves, rapids, a Tarzan swing, a swim-up bar, a baby beach, and allegedly a water elevator that shuttles swimmers back to the top (it just always seems to be out of order these days). If this doesn't satisfy, an actual beach made of real golden sand awaits just past the resort hammocks. The Grand is also home to the state's largest spa, **Kilolani:** a 50,000-square-foot marble compound of mineral soaking tubs, thundering waterfall showers, Japanese *furo* baths, Swiss jet showers, and many other features for its Hawai'i-inspired therapies.

Hydrothermal showers at the Grand Wailea's spa, Kilolani.

Among the dining options are **Humuhumunukunukuāpua'a ★★**, the aforementioned floating restaurant (nicknamed Humu), which features fresh seafood; the newer, coastal Italian-themed **Olivine ★**; and Loulu ★, a wellness-oriented market and cafe.

Tip: Those looking for more room and a bit more privacy should try the adjacent **Ho'olei at Grand Wailea villas** (www.grandwailea.com/stay/hoolei-villas), which offers a free shuttle between its luxurious three-bedroom units (3,400–4,000 sq. ft.) and the hotel.

3850 Wailea Alanui Dr., Wailea. www.grandwailea.com. ✆ **800/888-6100** or 808/875-1234. 832 units. From $1,100 double; from $2,215 suite; from $1,713 Napua Club room; from $2,849 Napua Club suite; from $1,835 Ho'olei villa. Extra person $100. Resort fee $50. Valet parking $65. **Amenities:** 4 restaurants; 4 bars; babysitting; loaner beach cruiser bikes; kids' program; concierge; concierge-level rooms; fitness center with classes; food truck; 5 whirlpools; adults-only pool; 2,000-ft.-long pool with grottoes; room service; scuba clinics; shuttle; spa; salon; watersports rentals; Wi-Fi.

Hotel Wailea ★★★   This ultra-stylish boutique hotel is one of a kind in Wailea, the only Relais & Châteaux property in Hawai'i. An adults-only, hillside haven, with just 72 suites on 15 acres, it's secluded, and serene—an oasis for honeymooners. The pool and cabanas are swank, with free cocktails by the fire pit from 5 to 6pm and mixology classes every Sunday morning. The verdant grounds and koi ponds have been transformed into a meditative garden. Large suites are outfitted with modern luxuries: wide-planked wood floors, Hawaiian *kapa*-inspired prints on plush king-size platform beds, deep soaking tubs, and daybeds on the lanai. Tidy kitchenettes feature Nespresso machines and Sub-Zero refrigerators.

Hotel staff will load up a free tote bag with towels and water and chauffeur you throughout Wailea in the resort's Tesla Model X. It's a 3-minute shuttle to the beach, and the hotel's kiosk at Wailea Beach will supply you with umbrellas and chairs. Take advantage of the free outrigger canoe trip offered on Wednesdays. This isn't a place that nickel-and-dimes guests, and employees come to know you on a first-name basis. Definitely plan to indulge at the **Restaurant at the Hotel Wailea ★★★**

(which may be renamed Ondine, by the time you read this), since the food matches the top-notch views, and quaff cocktails or nibble on sushi under the soaring open-air ceiling of the **Birdcage** lobby bar.

Note: The lawn and gazebo at the hotel's entrance are a fairy-tale venue for weddings and receptions, with special Celebration Suites (from $1,599) that include breakfast and Champagne ideal for honeymooners.

555 Kaukahi St., Wailea. www.hotelwailea.com. © **866/970-4167** or 808/874-0500. 72 units. From $899 garden view suites; from $1,099 oceanview. 2-person max; ages 16 and older only. 2-night minimum stay. $45 resort fee. **Amenities:** 2 bars; concierge; 24-hr. fitness center with Peloton bikes; outrigger canoe trips; pool with whirlpool (ages 18 and older); 2 restaurants; room service; shuttle; yoga; Wi-Fi.

Wailea Beach Marriott Resort & Spa ★★★ Airy and comfortable, this spectacularly renovated resort accentuates rather than overwhelms its sublime environment. Eight buildings, all low-rise except for an eight-story tower, unfold along 22 luxurious acres of lawns and gardens punctuated by coconut palms and Instagram-worthy sculptures. You'll want to spend your entire vacation beneath the cabanas at the exquisite infinity pool. Unless you're age 12 or under—then your parents will have to drag you away from the adventure pool with its four slick slides and animal sculptures that spit water. The resort is ideally positioned on a grassy slope between Wailea and Ulua beaches, so there's plenty of sandy real estate to explore, too. Rooms have tile or wood floors, modern furnishings, and lanais with views of the coastline. The small **Mandara Spa** offers an array of treatments in a very Zen atmosphere. Just downstairs is celebrated chef Roy Yamaguchi's restaurant: **Humble Market Kitchin ★★** (p. 408); a little secret is that the in-house restaurant, **Kapa ★★**, has wonderful island-themed food and views, too. Kids can dig into shave ice at the poolside **Mo Bettah Food Truck ★**.

3700 Wailea Alanui Dr., Wailea. www.waileamarriott.com. © **808/879-1922.** 547 units. From $766 double; from $966 suite. Extra person $75. Resort fee $50. Valet parking $50, self-parking $38. **Amenities:** 2 restaurants; 2 bars; cafe; food truck; luau, babysitting; concierge; gym; 5 pools; room service; spa; free watersports equipment and bikes; Wi-Fi.

Upcountry Maui

Here you'll be (relatively) close to Haleakalā National Park. Makawao is approximately 40 minutes from the entrance to the park at the 7,000-foot level (from there, it's another 3,000 ft. and 45 min. to get to the top). Kula is just 30 minutes from the park entrance.

Note: Temperatures are 5° to 10° cooler than at the coast, and misty rain is common; pack a waterproof jacket or rain poncho.

MAKAWAO
Expensive
Lumeria Maui ★★★ Halfway between Pā'ia and Makawao on the slopes of Haleakalā, a historic women's college (the oldest wooden building on Maui, built in 1910) has been lovingly restored as a boutique resortlike

retreat center. Nestled into 6 landscaped acres are two dozen guest rooms, a resplendent lobby, yoga studio, spa, meditation garden, and farm-to-table restaurant. A small but dazzling pool overlooks a valley full of waving sugarcane as hammocks sway in the ironwood trees. Views of the West Maui Mountains and distant shores are stunning. The crystals, sacred artwork, and *objets d'art* tucked into every corner contribute to the charmed ambiance of this serene retreat. Rooms are small—nearly filled by their plush four-poster beds—but luxurious, with Italian linens, Japanese *tansu* cabinets, and showers with river-rock floors. Ceiling fans and the higher elevation keep the rooms cool. The hitch: You must enroll in the daily classes, such as yoga, meditation, horticulture, or aromatherapy, or be part of an organized retreat to stay here. Still, that's no hardship. The resort's chic, farm-centric restaurant, **Wooden Crate,** serves a complimentary breakfast to guests and also offers prix fixe dinners Tuesday through Saturday ($65). Baldwin Beach is only 2½ miles away; the staff will set you up with a stand-up paddleboard or pack a picnic for an excursion to Hāna. 1813 Baldwin Ave., Makawao. www.lumeriamaui.com. ✆ **808/579-8877.** 25 units. $499–$599 double. Daily retreat fee (mandatory) $34. **Amenities:** Restaurant; spa; concierge; 2 whirlpools; saltwater pool; watersports rental; wellness classes; Wi-Fi.

Moderate

North Shore Lookout ★★   On a working farm just 10 miles from the airport in Kahului, these five private, modern bed-and-breakfast suites do feel like their own world, with private baths and lanais as well as seating and eating areas. Enjoy views of Mauna Kahālāwai and the North Shore and relax in the pool or hot tub in a lava rock deck. When available, order a smoothie or specialty juice or coffee drink to go with the hearty continental breakfast served in the cafe from 7:30am to 9:30am. Couples and surfers will love the handsome Duke's Cottage, which pays tribute to Duke Kahanamoku and offers a kitchenette, swing chair, garden hammock, and lots of room to unwind. 121 Kahakapao Rd., Makawao. www.northshorelookoutmaui.com. ✆ **808/868-1651.** 5 units. $225–$400 suite. Rates include continental breakfast. **Amenities:** Pool; hot tub; free Wi-Fi

KULA

If you can't nab the one suite at G&Z Upcountry Bed & Breakfast (see below), consider one of the five rustic "vacation lodges" at **Kula Lodge** ★, 15200 Haleakala Hwy. (Hwy. 377; www.kulalodge.com; ✆ **808/878-1535**). The wood-paneling, floral curtains, and other dated decor won't wow you—but the ocean views on both sides of distant Central Maui, bracketed by Norfolk pines and brilliantly colored proteas, birds of paradise, and other tropical flowers will. Rates include taxes and fees and start at $379 for a single-story unit with queen bed and $415 for units with a queen bed downstairs and two twin beds or futons in a loft. Bonus: You can make an early start for the summit of Haleakalā from here and have easy access to wood-fired pizzas and other goodies on the tastily reinvigorated

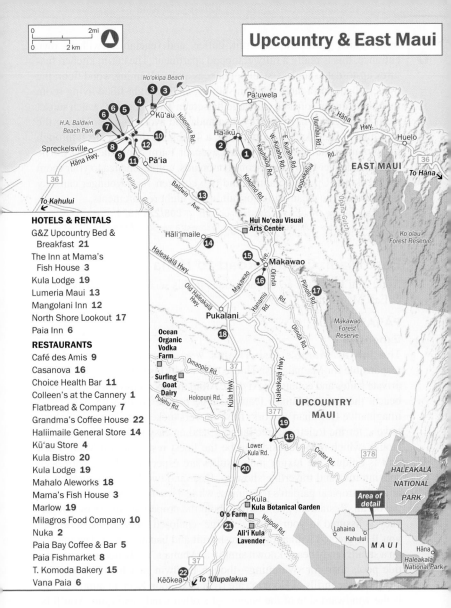

Upcountry & East Maui

HOTELS & RENTALS

G&Z Upcountry Bed & Breakfast **21**

The Inn at Mama's Fish House **3**

Kula Lodge **19**

Lumeria Maui **13**

Mangolani Inn **12**

North Shore Lookout **17**

Paia Inn **6**

RESTAURANTS

Café des Amis **9**

Casanova **16**

Choice Health Bar **11**

Colleen's at the Cannery **1**

Flatbread & Company **7**

Grandma's Coffee House **22**

Haliimaile General Store **14**

Kū'au Store **4**

Kula Bistro **20**

Kula Lodge **19**

Mahalo Aleworks **18**

Mama's Fish House **3**

Marlow **19**

Milagros Food Company **10**

Nuka **2**

Paia Bay Coffee & Bar **5**

Paia Fishmarket **8**

T. Komoda Bakery **15**

Vana Paia **6**

menu of **Kula Lodge Restaurant & Bar** ★★★ (p. 413). The on-site **Kula Marketplace** ★ offers deli fare, gourmet provisions, and an array of Maui-made arts and crafts.

Inexpensive

G&Z Upcountry Bed & Breakfast ★★   Former state tourism director Marsha Wienert has a keen sense of what makes upcountry Maui special, and thankfully she and husband John have decided to share some of that with visitors. Their B&B unit sits on a half-acre next to their 6-acre farm, which grows tropical fruit, coffee, and vegetables; with its own entrance, this is really a fully equipped apartment. The eat-in kitchen features up-to-date stainless-steel appliances and a gleaming wood floor, the modern bath has a large walk-in shower, and the light-filled living room includes a queen sofa bed and large flatscreen TV. Better yet, watch sunset from the large lawn, framed by jacaranda and avocado trees. During the day, hike in Haleakalā National Park, a 45-minute drive, or stroll through the blooming fields at Ali'i Kula Lavender Farm 5 minutes away. The Wienerts deliver fresh fruit, scones or breads, coffee, and tea to your room for breakfast. Up to two adults and two children 18 or younger can stay here. *Bonus:* no cleaning fee or minimum-night requirements.

60 Kekaulike Ave., Kula. www.gandzmaui.com. © **808/224-6824.** 1 unit. $149 double. Rate includes continental breakfast. $25 extra person. **Amenities:** Barbecue; free Wi-Fi.

East Maui: On the Road to Hāna

Note: You'll find the accommodations in this section on the "Upcountry & East Maui" map (p. 389).

PĀ'IA/KŪ'AU
Expensive

The Inn at Mama's Fish House ★★   The Gaudí-esque architect responsible for Mama's Fish House also works his magic on a handful of private suites and cottages next door. Amid the coconuts on a pocket-sized beach, the Inn at Mama's features large private lanais with barbecues; imaginative Hawaiian artwork; fresh flowers tucked into large, fluffy bath towels; terrific toiletries; free laundry; and an easy stroll to Mama's Fish House, which many consider to be the finest restaurant on Maui. Each unit is unique; the luxury junior suites are especially classy, with deep soaking tubs and travertine showers. One- and two-bedroom cottages sit amid the tropical garden's red ginger, while a few two-bedroom units face the ocean. Restaurant guests stroll about the property until 10pm, but privacy is assured in your cottage's large, enclosed lanai. In the morning, you'll be greeted with a tray of fresh fruit and banana bread. The inn sits on a small, sandy beach known simply as Mama's. It's better for exploring tide pools than for swimming—though Baldwin Beach is a short drive away and the thrills of Hookipa are right next-door. Keep in mind that this is the windward side of the island—it's often windy and rainy. You'll be perfectly situated here for a trip to Hāna.

799 Poho Place (off the Hāna Hwy. in Kū'au), Pā'ia. www.innatmamas.com. © **800/ 860-4852** or 808/579-9764. 12 units. $350 studio; $475 1- or 2-bedroom garden cottage; $675 junior suite; $1,050 1-bedroom beachfront suite or 2-bedroom beachfront cottage. **Amenities:** Beach; barbecue; free laundry; restaurant; free Wi-Fi.

Mangolani Inn ★★   A mile from the beach, and within walking distance of Pā'ia's boutiques and cafes, this laidback compound off busy Baldwin Avenue is full of surprises. Mango trees offer shade and privacy to the large yard with hammocks, hot tub, barbecue, and picnic tables, which all guests may use, along with beach gear and laundry. The four recently renovated, air-conditioned studios include stylish touches such as leather couches, bamboo trim, stone-tiled showers, and vessel sinks.

325 Baldwin Ave., Pā'ia. www.mauipaia.com. © **808/579-3000** or 808/298-4839. 3 units. $425–$650 studio. $150 cleaning fee; 3-night minimum. **Amenities:** Barbecue; hammocks; hot tub; laundry facilities; watersports gear; free Wi-Fi.

Paia Inn ★★ Embedded in colorful Pā'ia town, this vibrant boutique inn offers a stylish introduction to Maui's North Shore. The inn comprises several vintage buildings that get progressively closer to the turquoise waters of Pā'ia Bay. The owner's impeccable style seeps into every corner of the inn, from the organic Mālie bath products in the travertine-tiled showers to the antique Balinese drawers repurposed as sink cabinets. The main building rooms hang right over Hāna Highway's restaurants, surf shops, and cafes. The one- and two-bedroom suites in the next buildings are spacious, secluded retreats where you'll feel immediately at home. Couples will appreciate no. 10, which has a private outdoor shower and four-poster daybed. But it can't rival the three-bedroom beach house nestled against the golden, sandy beach. Idyllic in every way, this miniature mansion is outfitted with a Viking stove, whirlpool, gorgeous artwork, and a huge outdoor living room. It's exclusive enough to attract celebrities, who've made it their Maui headquarters. **Vana Paia** ★★ is its courtyard restaurant, serving locally sourced sushi ($12–$28), Japanese-inspired tapas ($10–$25), and cocktails like guava mojitos ($16–$25), open Tuesday through Sunday 5 to 10pm. Massages are available in the upstairs spa rooms.

93 Hāna Hwy., Pā'ia. www.paiainn.com. © **800/721-4000** or 808/579-6000. 17 units. From $399 Petite room; from $499 standard; from $699 deluxe; from $799 junior suite; from $899 1-bedroom suite; from $999 2-bedroom; from $3,999 3-bedroom beach house. **Amenities:** Restaurant; bar; beach access; concierge; spa; laundry services; free use of watersports equipment; free Wi-Fi.

East Maui: Hāna

Note: You'll find Hāna accommodations on the map on p. 329.

VERY EXPENSIVE

Hamoa Beach House ★ Just around the bend from famed Hamoa Beach, this enormous three-bedroom, two-bathroom house is a great option for families or big parties. The rich woods (like koa kitchen cabinetry), earthy tones, and rattan furnishings imbue the spacious interior of this '70s-era house with a cozy, nostalgic feeling. The living room has cathedral ceilings and two-story-tall windows that open up to the ocean. The upstairs bedrooms have vaulted ceilings, ocean-facing lanais, and a total of four king-size beds. A sweet little library is stocked with beach reading. Beneath the coconut palms outside, you'll find hammocks, a barbecue grill, a hot tub, and an outdoor shower—everything you need to enjoy Hāna to the fullest.

487 Haneo'o Rd., Hāna. www.vrbo.com/242599. © **808/248-8277.** 1 unit. $1,075–$1,400 house (sleeps 8). 3-night minimum. $250 "host" fee. VRBO service fee $534. **Amenities:** Beach nearby; beach gear; barbecue; whirlpool; free Wi-Fi.

Hana Kai Maui Resort ★★

"Condo complex" might not mesh with your idea of getting away from it all in Hāna, but Hana Kai is truly special. Set on Hāna Bay, the individually owned units are dotingly furnished and feature many hotel-like extras, such as organic bath products and fresh tropical bouquets. Studios and one- and two-bedroom units have kitchens and private lanais—but the corner units with wraparound ocean views are worth angling for. Gorgeously appointed two-bedroom Ka'ahumanu (#5) has a daybed on the lanai that you may never want to leave. For couples, Popolana (#2) is small but sweet, with woven bamboo walls and a Murphy bed that no one ever puts up. And why would you? You can lie in it and stare out to sea or, at daybreak, watch the sun rise out of the ocean. No air-conditioning or TVs—but they're not necessary. *Note:* Sound can carry here, so bring earplugs if you're a light sleeper.

1533 Uakea Rd., Hāna. www.hanakaimaui.com. © **800/346-2772** or 808/248-8426. 17 units. From $306 studio; from $395 1-bedroom; from $698 2-bedroom. Nightly $25 "service/environmental" fee. Extra person $20. 2-night minimum for beachfront units. Children 6 and under stay free in parent's room. **Amenities:** Beach equipment; barbecue; daily housekeeping; laundry facilities; breakfast (for a charge); free Wi-Fi.

Hāna-Maui Resort ★★★

Ahhh . . . arriving at Maui's oldest resort (now part of the Hyatt brand) is like letting out a deep sigh. The atmosphere is so relaxing you'll forget everything beyond this remote seaside sanctuary. Nestled in the center of quaint Hāna town, the 66-acre resort wraps around Ka'uiki Head, the dramatic point where Queen Ka'ahumanu was born. All of the accommodations here are wonderful, but the Ocean Bungalows are downright heavenly. These duplex cottages with bamboo floors, giant soaking tubs, and plush beds also have floor-to-ceiling windows facing the craggy shoreline, where you might spy horses grazing in misty pastures. Some even include separate living rooms and dining tables. Families or couples traveling together can share one of the one- or two-bedroom Waikoloa residences, which have partial ocean views but boast top-of-the-line kitchens, large living rooms (with cable TV, once a no-no here), and day beds.

The genuinely hospitable staff will set you up with cultural and outdoor activities, often at no charge, while a free shuttle whisks you to renowned **Hāmoa Beach ★★** (p. 340), 8 minutes away. Don't miss a treatment in the serene spa, which has its own basking pool and overlooks Kapueokahi Bay (Hāna Beach Park), or a tropical breakfast on the ocean-view lanai of **the Restaurant.** (Hopefully, the hotel will one day revive its tradition of live music in the bar and dinner service.) You'll also find tasty food and drinks at the main pool bar, grab-and-go gourmet options in the

Hāna Dry Goods Store, and family-friendly, local-style fare at casual Hāna Ranch Restaurant across the street. *Tip:* For a truly relaxing getaway, skip the road to Hāna and fly to Hāna on Mokulele Airlines (p. 302) or the resort's private 10-passenger plane and rely on the resort's airport and beach shuttles on the ground.

5031 Hāna Hwy., Hāna. www.hyatt.com. © **808/400-1234.** 75 units. From $620 garden suite; from $756 bungalows; $1,054 oceanfront with hot tub. Resort fee $45. **Amenities:** Basketball court; beach shuttle; concierge; cultural activities; fitness center with daily yoga and other classes; complimentary clubs and use of the 3-hole practice golf course; 2 pools; room service; spa; tennis/pickleball courts; Wi-Fi.

MODERATE

Bamboo Inn ★ This oceanfront, solar-powered "inn" is really just three suites, all with private lanais overlooking jet-black sand. The accommodations include beds with ocean views, separate living rooms, and either a full kitchen or kitchenette. Naia, the largest unit, sleeps four and has a deep soaking tub on the lanai. (Be aware that you may hear neighbors through the thin walls, and they you; Wi-Fi in this area isn't very strong, either.) The rooms and grounds are decorated with artifacts that knowledgeable host John Romain collected during travels across Asia and Polynesia. Carved Balinese doors, Samoan tapa cloths, coconut wood floors, and a thatched-roof gazebo (where a breakfast basket of coffee, juice, and pastries awaits each morning) add a Pacific polish to a naturally lovely location. Waikoloa isn't great for swimming, but it's an incredible spot to watch the sunrise. All of Hāna is within easy walking distance.

4869 Uakea Rd., Hāna. www.bambooinn.com. © **808/248-7718.** 3 units. $285–$395 double. Extra person $15. 2-night minimum. **Amenities:** Beach, beach equipment; barbecue; free Wi-Fi.

Hamoa Bay House & Bungalow ★★ This Eden-like property has two units: a bungalow and a house. Romance blooms in the 600-square-foot Balinese-style treetop bungalow, a gorgeous one-room studio with a beckoning bamboo bed, full kitchen, and a hot tub that hangs over the garden. The screened lanai and area downstairs function as separate rooms, giving you ample space. The house is just as spacious and lovingly decorated, with a large master bedroom and small second bedroom. Both the house and bungalow have private outdoor lava rock showers and access to tropical fruit trees and flowers. The property is on Hāna Highway, just a 10-minute walk from Hāmoa Beach. *Note:* Cell service is unreliable here, but Wi-Fi is free.

6463 Hāna Hwy., btw. 2 entrances to Haneo'o Rd., 2 miles south of Hāna. www.hamoabay.com. © **808/248-7884.** 2 units. $310–$325 bungalow, 2-person maximum; $100 cleaning fee. $375–$440 house, 4-person maximum; $125 cleaning fee. 3-night minimum. **Amenities:** Barbecue; beach equipment; hammock; outdoor shower; whirlpool; free Wi-Fi.

Hana Guest Houses ★★ Three miles south of Hāna Town lies the glorious compound of Malanai, named for the gentle breezes that cool its leafy, fragrant gardens and two handsomely restored, plantation-style cottages with ocean views. Hale Manu, "Bird House," offers two-bedrooms with vintage rattan furniture; a modern bathroom with a fun mix of bamboo trim, stone floors, shiplap walls, and tiled shower/tub; an airy great room (living, dining, and kitchen) with soaring beamed cupola ceiling; and large deck with recliners and outdoor dining furniture. Hale 'Ulu Lulu, "Breadfruit-Shaded House," was built in the 1900s to house managers of the Hāna Sugar Plantation and sports a mix of charming antique details (clawfoot tub, beadboard cabinets) and contemporary luxuries (Brazilian mahogany floors, granite and koa kitchen counters). Both come with stacked washer-dryers, gas BBQs, and beach gear. Hāmoa Beach is within a 15-minute walk or brief drive.

776 Hāna Hwy., Hāna. https://hanaguesthouses.com. © **808/248-8706.** 2 units. $325–$350 1-bedroom (sleeps 2, adults only) and 2-bedroom (sleeps 4; up to 2 children 12 and older allowed); $45 per extra person. 3-night minimum. $100 cleaning fee. Discounts for weekly stays. **Amenities:** Beach gear; laundry facilities; free Wi-Fi.

Camping

Camping on Maui can be extreme (inside a volcano) or laid back (by the sea in Hāna). It can be wet, cold, and rainy, or hot, dry, and windy—all on the same day! If you're heading for Haleakalā, remember that U.S. astronauts trained for the moon inside the volcano; pack survival gear. You'll need both a swimsuit and raincoat if you're bound for Wai'ānapanapa. You can rent camping gear (3-night minimum) as long as you reserve it in advance from **Maui Camping Company** (www.mauicampingcompany.com; © 808/397-3967), which uses a pickup/drop-off locker close to Kahului airport with day and evening hours. Reservations are necessary for all campsites.

Camp Olowalu ★ Halfway to Lahaina on the Honoapi'ilani Highway, this campground abuts one of the island's best coral reefs. It's perfect for snorkeling and (during winter) whale watching. (You can hear the whales slap their fins against the sea's surface at night—a magical experience.) The 35 tent sites have access to porta-potties and outdoor showers. Closer to the highway, the six mountain-view "tentalows" offer two or four twin beds with linens and private outdoor showers. Large groups can rent the six A-frame cabins with six cots apiece, plus access to private bathrooms, showers, and a 900-square-foot kitchen and mess hall. If you're tent camping, pray that a rowdy wedding party isn't booked that night. Either way, bring earplugs. The camp also offers daily 90-min. **kayak tours** of Olowalu Reef ($80 for adults, $60 ages 7–12).

800 Olowalu Village Rd., Lahaina (off Honoapi'ilani Hwy.). www.campolowalu.com. © **808/661-4303.** 6 cabins, 6 tentalows, 35 tent sites. Tent sites: $32 per night per adult ($11 per night children 9–17). Tentalows: $160 (up to 2 adults) and $210 (up to 4 adults), $25 per child ages 9–17. Cabins: $1,800 for all 6 cabins (sleeps 36, 2-night minimum); $1,500 a night with 7-night minimum.

Haleakalā National Park ★★★ This stunning national park typically has a variety of camping options throughout its diverse landscape: **car camping** at Hosmer Grove halfway up the summit or at ʻOheʻo Gulch in Kīpahulu (the latter closed at press time); **pitching a tent** in the central Haleakalā wilderness; or cozying up in one of the crater's **historic cabins.**

At **Hosmer Grove,** located at 6,800 feet, is a small, open, grassy area surrounded by forest and frequented by native Hawaiian honeycreepers. Trees protect campers from the winds, but nights get very cold; sometimes there's even ice on the ground up here. This is an ideal spot to spend the night if you want to see the Haleakalā sunrise, especially since your camping permit ($5 per campsite) includes a coveted sunrise parking permit. Come up the day before, take a day hike, and then turn in early. After sunrise, enjoy the sound of native birds on the self-guided nature trail. Facilities include a pavilion with picnic tables and grills, chemical toilets, and drinking water. There are now six designated sites; reserve up to 30 days in advance on www.recreation.gov.

On the other side of the island, **Kīpahulu Campground** is in the Kīpahulu section of Haleakalā National Park. Its 15 drive-in and five walk-in sites ($8 per campsite) overlook ocean cliffs and are a short walk from ʻOheʻo Gulch. The campground has picnic tables, grills, and chemical toilets—but no convenient potable water, so bring your own (the ranger station has a refilling station for water bottles). Bear in mind it rains 75 inches a year here. Call the **Kīpahulu Ranger Station** (© **808/ 248-7375**) for local weather.

Inside the volcano are two **wilderness tent-camping** areas: **Hōlua,** just off the Halemauʻu Trail 3.7 miles from its trailhead, and **Palikū,** 10.4 miles away from the trailhead, near the Kaupō Gap at the eastern end of the valley. Both are well over 6,000 feet in elevation and chilly at night. Facilities are limited to pit toilets and non-potable catchment water which must be treated before drinking. Water at Hōlua is limited, especially in summer. No open fires are allowed inside the volcano, so bring a cook stove. Camping is restricted to the signed area and is not allowed in the horse pasture or the inviting grassy lawn in front of the cabins. Mandatory permits (technically free, but requiring $8–$9 reservation per campsite, made online or via a call center) are bookable up to 6 months in advance on www.recreation.gov or by calling © **877/444-6777.**

Also inside the volcano are three **wilderness cabins,** built in 1937 by the Civilian Conservation Corps. Each has 12 padded bunks (bring your own bedding), a table, chairs, cooking utensils, a two-burner propane stove, and a wood-burning stove with firewood. Pit toilets and non-potable water (filter or treat before drinking) are nearby. The cabins are spaced so that each one is a nice hike from the next: **Hōlua** cabin is 3¾ miles down the zigzagging Halemauʻu Trail, **Kapalaoa** cabin is 5½ miles down the Sliding Sands Trail, and **Palikū** cabin (currently closed due to water shortages) is the farthest, at 9⅓ miles down Sliding Sands and across the moonscape to the crater's eastern end. In spring and summer, the endangered Hawaiian dark-rumped petrel can be heard yipping and chortling on their way back home to their cliffside burrows. Some campers and hikers exit through the Kaupō Gap—8½ miles on an unmaintained trail that crosses private property en route to the remote Piʻilani Highway. You can reserve cabins ($75 each) up to 6 months in advance on the park's reservation website (www.recreation.gov; ℂ 877/444-6777). You're limited to 2 nights in one cabin and 3 nights total in the wilderness each month.

Note: All wilderness campers must watch a 10-minute orientation video at the park's visitor center, if open, or on the park's website.

Haleakalā National Park, at top of Crater Rd., and at Kīpahulu Visitor Center, 12 miles past Hāna on Hāna Hwy. www.nps.gov/hale/planyourvisit.camping.htm. ℂ 808/572-4400. 3 cabins, $75; 100-plus tent sites, $5–$9 nightly, by reservation only, www.recreation.gov.

Polipoli Spring State Recreation Area ★

High up on the slope of Haleakalā, at 6,200 feet in elevation, this state park has extensive trails that wind through conifer forests reminiscent of the Pacific Northwest. It's frequently cold and foggy here—be prepared for extra-chilly nights! One eight-bunk cabin is available for $100; it has a cold shower and a gas stove but no electricity or drinking water (bring your own). The cabin can't be booked online; you can reserve by phone and must pick up and return keys to the state parks office in Wailuku. Tent-campers can pitch on the grass nearby, reserve on the website, and print out their permit, which must be displayed. *Note:* The park is only accessible by 4WD vehicles.

9¾ miles up Waipoli Rd., off Kekaulike (Hwy. 377); 4WD vehicle required. By reservation only: c/o State Parks Division, 54 S. High St., Room 101, Wailuku. www.dlnr. hawaii.gov/dsp/camping-lodging/maui. ℂ 808/984-8109. 1 cabin. $100 per night (sleeps 8). $30 for campsites. 5-night maximum.

Waiʻānapanapa State Park ★★

The 12 rustic cabins tucked in the *hala* (pandanus) groves of Waiʻānapanapa State Park are one of the best lodging deals on Maui. Each cabin has three sets of twin bunks (sleeping six), a kitchen (electric hot plate, microwave, and fridge), and a large lanai where you can spend lazy hours watching rainstorms roll in from the sea. Cabins #5 and #6 are closest to the water. They've recently been spiffed up, but they're still frequented by geckos and are fairly spartan; bring your own linens, cookware, and dishes. You can also pitch a tent above the black-sand beach on Pailoa Bay, where undesignated sites for up to 60 permit holders are available, or park a camper van at one of six designated sites. Watch the sun rise out of the ocean and beat the day-trippers to the beach. (Visitors who aren't camping still need to reserve a parking space and entry permits; see www.gowaianapanapa.com for details.) There's an on-site caretaker, along with restrooms, showers, picnic tables, shoreline hiking trails, and historic sites. Bring rain gear and mosquito protection—this is the rainforest, after all. Reserve cabins online at least 7 days in advance and print out your permit, which must be displayed. *Note:* Check in after 2pm, check out by 10am.

End of Waiʻānapanapa Rd., off Hāna Hwy. By reservation only, minimum 7 days in advance: https://dlnr.hawaii.gov/dsp/parks/maui/waianapanapa-state-park. 🕐 **808/ 984-8109.** 12 units. $100 per cabin per night (sleeps up to 6); 2-night minimum. $30 for tent camping (up to 10 people) or camper vans (up to 6 people). 7-night maximum.

WHERE TO EAT ON MAUI

With the loss of so many restaurants in Lahaina, and the loss of so many homes of the people who worked in them, the island's dining scene has been undeniably altered. Many chefs and their staffs put their skills to effective use for months helping feed displaced residents, hosting elaborate fundraising dinners, and in some cases, returning to work at restaurants able to reopen on the fringe of the burn zone. Today, island chefs continue to make memorable meals from the Valley Isle's incredible bounty of produce, seafood, and grass-fed beef and other local meats—there are just fewer choices in West Maui that aren't on a resort, meaning you will pay resort prices.

Luckily, you don't *have* to spend a fortune. Maui does have a few budget eateries, noted below, and a growing fleet of food trucks. For finer dining, make sure you make reservations where possible, and especially well in advance during peak holiday periods.

Note: OpenTable.com allows online reservations for some 50 restaurants on Maui. Some popular restaurants have moved to platforms such as Resy or Tock, which allow hopeful diners to join waitlists.

Central Maui

KAHULUI & WAILUKU

Kahului and Wailuku have a few tasty finds, some quite humble. Minutes outside of the airport in a windy dirt lot across from Costco, you'll find **food trucks** dishing out everything from pork belly sandwiches to poke (seasoned raw fish). Only a few blocks west is the island's best food truck, culinary educator Kyle Kawakami's **Maui Fresh Streatery** ★★ (www. mauifreshstreatery.com; 🕐 **808/344-7929**), which changes menu themes regularly. One of the most popular is Kawakami's Korean-inspired lineup, including boneless fried chicken and fries with Maui beef kalbi and kimchi mayo. Check @mauifreshstreatery on Instagram for current location, hours, and menu. For relatively healthy, affordable tacos, check out the Kahului outlet of **Maui Tacos** ★ (www.mauitacos.com; 🕐 **808/793-3931**) at the Puʻunene Shopping Center, 58 Hoʻokele St. **808/793-3931**); see p. 404 for more on this popular local chain.

More recently, *Top Chef* fan favorite Sheldon Simeon has turned Wailuku into a dining hot spot by revitalizing **Tiffany's** ★★, 1424 Lower Main St. (www.tiffanysmaui.com; 🕐 **808/249-0052**), a former sports bar with a local comfort-food menu. Standouts include honey walnut shrimp and *saimin* from the original menu, plus the James Beard Award nominee's

"Just Like Oxtail" soup, made with silken beef brisket and a heady mix of fragrant spices. People queue up early for dinner and weekend lunch, but you can also join a waitlist on its website. It's open Monday to Friday 4 to 10pm; Saturday 11am to 10pm; and Sunday 11am to 9pm.

Moderate

Cafe O'Lei at the Mill House ★★ ISLAND FUSION   Awe-inspiring views of the West Maui Mountains, lush lakeside gardens, and sugar mill machinery-turned-sculptures create the backdrop for the signature restaurant of **Maui Tropical Plantation** ★, already a destination-worthy attraction for its ziplines, train ride, and organic farm (p. 314). The dining room is now in the capable hands of the chef-owners of Cafe O'Lei, a beloved local chain that started as a five-table cafe in Makawao. They now operate two restaurants (the other is in Kīhei) and a catering company; the Mill House is the more intriguing location. The lunch menu includes wonderful interpretations of local and American fare; try the ahi nachos ($19) or Maui onion soup ($13) before moving on to entrees like tempura mahi mahi and chips ($25) or charbroiled pork belly ($21). At dinner, dig into well-spiced Asian braised short ribs ($44) or the indulgent lobster and sweet corn risotto ($47).

1670 Honoapi'ilani Hwy., Waikapu. www.cafeoleirestaurants.com. © **808/500-0553.** Main courses $18–$28 lunch, $22–$51 dinner. Tues–Sat 11am–2:30pm, 5–8pm. Sat– Sun brunch 9am–2:30pm. Tues–Sun happy hour 3–5pm.

A Saigon Cafe ★★ VIETNAMESE   It's hard to say which is better at this beloved neighborhood restaurant—the delicious Vietnamese cuisine or the hilarious waiters who make wisecracks while taking your order. Whatever you order—the steamed *'ōpakapaka* snapper with ginger and garlic, catfish simmering in a clay pot, or the fragrant lemongrass curry—you'll notice the freshness of the flavors. Owner Jennifer Nguyen grows many of her own vegetables and herbs and even sprouts the mung beans. Try the Buddha rolls dunked in spicy peanut sauce and the Vietnamese "burritos." You make the latter tableside— tricky at first, but fun.

Saimin bowl at Tin Roof.

1792 Main St., Wailuku. www.asaigoncafe. com. © **808/243-9560.** Main courses $20–$36. Daily 11am–8:30pm.

Inexpensive

Tin Roof ★ FILIPINO/PLATE LUNCH   Celebrity chef Sheldon Simeon won the hearts of *Top Chef* fans not just once, but twice, and Maui residents couldn't adore him more. At this to-go (and go-to) spot in an industrial strip mall in Kahului, which he opened with wife Janice, the menu reflects his Filipino

Ululani's Hawaiian Shave Ice

David and Ululani Yamashiro are near-religious about shave ice. At their multiple shops around Maui (www.ululanis hawaiianshaveice.com; 𝄢 **808/877-3700**), these shave-ice wizards take the uniquely Hawaiian dessert to new heights. It starts with the water: Pure, filtered water is frozen, shaved to feather lightness, and patted into shape. This mini-snowdrift is then doused with your choice of syrup—any three flavors from calamansi lime to lychee to red velvet cake. David makes his own gourmet syrups with local fruit purees and a dash of cane sugar. The passion fruit is perfectly tangy, the coconut is free of cloying artificial sweetness, and the electric green kiwi is studded with real seeds. Add a "snowcap" of sweetened condensed milk, and the resulting confection tastes like the fluffiest, most flavorful ice cream ever. Locals order theirs with chewy mochi morsels, sweet adzuki beans at the bottom, or tart *li hing mui* powder sprinkled on top. The Wailuku location also has *manapua* (steamed buns) and chow fun noodles; all are open daily. **Kīhei:** 61 S. Kīhei Rd., 10:30am–6:30pm; **Wailuku:** 50 Maui Lani Pkwy, Unit E1, 10:30am–6pm; **Kahului:** 333 Dairy Rd., 10:30am–6pm.

roots and sense of fun: Buy a 50-cent "dime bag" of furikake to sprinkle on your mochiko chicken. Add a 6-minute egg to your pork belly bowl. Unfortunately, its popularity means it gets unpleasantly packed by lunchtime; you won't be able to see what you're ordering until you're at the very front of the long line.

360 Papa Pl., Kahului. www.tinroofmaui.com. 𝄢 **808/868-0753.** Main courses $9–$20. Tues–Sat 10am–8pm.

West Maui

LAHAINA

Several restaurants and businesses at the northern end of Lahaina's famed Front Street miraculously escaped the flames, although related damage to water and power lines, as well as the devastating effect on the lives of all in the community, meant it was months before any were able to reopen.

Under the same ownership as the equally beloved **Leoda's Kitchen and Pie Shop** (p. 400) and the **Old Lāhaina Lū'au** (p. 427), the affordably priced **Aloha Mixed Plate ★★**, 1285 Front St. (www.alohamixed plate.com; 𝄢 **808/661-3322**), serves the same menu at lunch and dinner—hearty plate lunches, sandwiches (seared fresh fish, crispy marinated chicken sandwiches, kalua pork, and a classic burger), and two types of Asian noodles with pork. The well-shaded, open-air restaurant is open daily 11am to 7pm; reservations (via OpenTable) recommended.

Mala Ocean Tavern ★★★ INTERNATIONAL   When this tiny bistro overlooking Māla Wharf and Lāna'i reopened in early 2024, the owners posted a request that patrons not ask the staff about the fire, and thankfully the wonderful menu and view provide ample distractions from doing so. Maui native Alvin Savella (known on island as the "Kitchen Assassin") took over as executive chef in 2018. At brunch, local flavors are on display in dishes such as French toast with Kula strawberries and *ube* (purple yam) ice cream ($16), and eggs benedict with seared ahi and a kicky wasabi hollandaise ($27). The Greek salad ($20) and Greek pita wrap ($18) are a nod to the restaurant's previous Mediterranean focus and offer a choice of proteins—I recommend the grilled fish ($6–$15 additional). Seared ahi is also one of Savella's signature dinner mains, served with a fragrant shiitake mushroom ginger sauce, Yukon potato mash and green beans ($52), but ask about the catch of the day, accompanied by a creamy kabocha puree and tart pomegranate hibiscus sauce ($45). Flatbreads ($14) and a fresh island fish sandwich ($20), along with $12 cocktails, are the best values at the daily happy hour 2 to 4pm.

1307 Front St., Lahaina. www.malatavern.com. © **808/667-9394.** Main courses $14–$37 brunch; $28–$61 (most $45–$52) dinner. Reservations recommended. Daily: brunch 9am–2pm; dinner 4–9pm; happy hour 2–4pm.

OLOWALU

Leoda's Kitchen and Pie Shop ★★ SANDWICHES/BAKERY
This unexpected oasis in Olowalu, south of the Lahaina bypass, is a must-try, especially for its sweet pies. Banana, coconut, chocolate macadamia nut praline, and other tropical temptations are slathered in whipped cream. Don't have a sweet tooth? The oversize sandwiches ($13–$21) come in tempting combinations like the seared ahi—a hot and juicy mess of sashimi-grade tuna, island pesto, melted Jarlsberg cheese, avocado, and caramelized onions on grilled rye bread. House-made buns and condiments like local *pohā* berry mustard and Maui pineapple chutney mean even hot dogs ($11) are a treat.

820 Olowalu Village Rd. (off Honoapi'ilani Hwy.), Lahaina. www.leodas.com. © **808/662-3600.** Main courses $11–$21; pies $10. Daily 10am–6pm.

KĀ'ANAPALI

In addition to the restaurants below, also see the listings for **Monkeypod Kitchen** ★★ (p. 411) in Wailea and **Joey's Kitchen** ★★ (p. 403) in Nāpili for details on their branches in Whalers Village, 2345 Kā'anapali Pkwy., Kā'anapali.

Expensive

Japengo ★★ SUSHI/PACIFIC RIM The open-air dining room hanging over the Hyatt pool evokes the feel of a Japanese teahouse that happens to witness spectacular tropical sunsets. Superb Japanese-influenced entrees and inspired sushi, sashimi, and hand rolls deservedly keep Japengo at the top of local best-of lists. Depending on what the fishermen reeled in that day, the *moriawase,* or chef's platter, may include achingly red tuna, translucent slivers of Hawai'i Island *hirame* (flounder), poached local abalone, creamy wedges of *uni* (sea urchin), or raw New Caledonia prawn. The sushi wizards at the bar beautifully garnish this bounty with nests of peppery daikon and aromatic shiso leaves. Delicious vegetable sides— kabocha pumpkin, asparagus in Thai chili sauce, and lavender-honey corn—originate on nearby Simpli-Fresh farm. Reserve a table well in advance of your visit.

At Hyatt Regency Maui, 200 Nohea Kai Dr., Kā'anapali. https://kaanapaliresort.com/japengo. ℂ **808/667-4909.** Main courses $28–$65 (most $28–$48). Daily 5–9pm.

Roy's ★★ HAWAI'I REGIONAL CUISINE Roy Yamaguchi, the James Beard award–winning chef and one of the pioneers of Hawai'i Regional Cuisine, has largely divested himself from Roy's restaurants outside of Hawai'i to focus on his home state. Maui boasts his dining room next to the Kā'anapali Golf Course and Wailea's **Humble Market Kitchin** ★★ (p. 408). Memorable dinner menu items include signature rich misoyaki butterfish ($55) and honey mustard–glazed beef short ribs ($59). At lunch, the chicken katsu with rice and macaroni salad ($26) is the best deal as well as a local favorite.

2290 Kā'anapali Pkwy., Kā'anapali. www.royyamaguchi.com/roys-kaanapali-maui. ℂ **808/669-6999.** Main courses lunch $26–$58; dinner $39–$68. Daily 11am–3:45pm and 4–7pm.

Son'z Steakhouse ★ STEAKHOUSE Descend a palatial staircase for dinner at Son'z, where tables overlook a lagoon with resident white and black swans. These are classy digs for a steakhouse; imagine Ruth's Chris with extra flavor and a fairy-tale atmosphere. The juicy filet is on point, as is the New Zealand rack of lamb. Seafood options include catch of the day, often with Moloka'i sweet potato hash browns, and delectable shrimp scampi with baked potato ravioli, mushrooms, and cherry tomatoes. Finish with Portuguese sweet-bread French toast, vanilla gelato, and sweetly tart local bananas set aflame. The wine list is among the best on the island, too.

At Hyatt Regency Maui, 200 Nohea Kai Dr., Kā'anapali. www.sonzsteakhouse.com. ℂ **808/667-4506.** Main courses $36–$125. Daily 5–9pm.

Moderate

Duke's Beach House ★★ PACIFIC RIM There are few more beautiful places to enjoy breakfast than here, facing Kahekili Beach. This restaurant mimics an open-air plantation home, decorated with memorabilia chronicling the life of world-famous Hawaiian surfer, Duke Kahanamoku. It's part of the T S Restaurants family, which includes reliably good Hula Grill and Leilani's on Maui, plus Duke's in Waikīkī and on Kaua'i, and several more. Lunch offers local favorites such as fresh fish tacos on locally made tortillas and kalua pork sandwich, while dinner features sustainable fresh catches, perhaps steamed in banana leaves with shrimp or in a creamy risotto with lobster. The gracious sea-breeze-kissed locale and the kitchen's commitment to serving locally raised beef, eggs, and vegetables also set Duke's apart.

At Honua Kai Resort & Spa, 130 Kai Malina Pkwy., North Kā'anapali Beach. www.dukesmaui.com. ℂ **808/662-2900.** Main courses $15–$21 breakfast, $16–$27 lunch, $20–$69 (most $25–$39) dinner. Daily breakfast 7:30am–11am, lunch 11am–4pm, dinner 4–9pm; bar 4–9pm; pool menu 11am–5pm.

Leilani's on the Beach ★★ STEAK/SEAFOOD   Another outpost of the T S Restaurants empire, Leilani's also highlights sustainable seafood and local produce, sourcing from some 40 Maui farms. Try the mac nut hummus with crudites or Hawaiian big-eye tuna ceviche for starters, and for a main, the seafood hot pot in a rich tomato saffron broth ($37) or herb roasted fresh fish in a port wine gastrique with local green beans and roasted potatoes. The **Beach Bar**—with tables just off Kāʻanapali Beach—features a separate, more casual menu. Here you can people-watch while snacking on sriracha-guava chicken wings or fish tacos and tossing back a guava daquiri. In lieu of the T S trademark Hula Pie, finish with the lighter but still satisfying passion fruit Pono Pie made with local honey, breadfruit, Kula strawberries, and gluten-free nut crust. Its sister restaurant **Hula Grill** ★★ (www.hulagrillkaanapali.com; ✆ **808/667-6636**), also on the ocean side of Whalers Village, offers a similar menu and vibe, with the bonus of a brunch menu Saturday and Sunday from 10am to 2pm.

At Whalers Village, 2435 Kāʻanapali Pkwy., Kāʻanapali. www.leilanis.com. ✆ **808/661-4495.** Reservations recommended for dinner. Main courses $16–$25 at the bar; $28–$54 (king crab $139) dinner. Daily 10:30am–9pm bar and 4:30–9pm dinner.

Inexpensive

Castaway Cafe ★ AMERICAN   Hidden away in the Maui Kaanapali Villas, this little cafe sits right on Kahekili Beach—privy to perfect views and salty breezes. Part of the Cohn Restaurant group, which includes the Plantation House in Kapalua and numerous Southern California favorites, its menu is fairly standard for the island—kalua pork nachos, fish tacos, kalbi chicken, mac nut crusted mahimahi—but it is reliable and well-priced. Breakfast is a mix of classic American and island mains, such as the smoky kalua pork huevos rancheros and eggs benedict with smoked spiral ham.

In the Aston Maui Kaanapali Villas, 45 Kai Ala Dr., Kāʻanapali. www.castawaycafe. com. ✆ **808/661-9091.** Main courses $16–$19 breakfast, $20–$23 (fresh catch $42) lunch, $23–$49 dinner. Daily 8–11:30am breakfast, 11:30am–4pm lunch, 4–8pm dinner.

HONOKŌWAI, KAHANA & NĀPILI

Note: You'll find the restaurants in this section on the "Hotels & Restaurants in West Maui" map (p. 371).

Moderate

Fond ★★ PACIFIC RIM   An acronym for "Feeding Our Neighborhood Daily," Fond is also a French term referring to a base made from the delicious bits of food that stick to the bottom of a pan. Both the name and the menu reflect chef-restaurateur Jojo Vasquez's fondness for his diverse community and his classic training in French techniques. His casual, industrial-chic outpost in Nāpili Plaza is not as ritzy as some of his previous dining rooms, including the Banyan Tree and the Plantation House in Kapalua and the Morimoto restaurants in Waikīkī and Napa, but it's all his own. Dinner offers clever and often spicy twists on casual starters such as adobo brussels sprouts, roasted pork lettuce wraps, and fried chicken bites, with local ingredients bringing fresh appeal to mains such as pork and lentils cassoulet, Maui sirloin steak with broccoli, and seared catch in a Maui onion soubise. Lunch offers tasty burgers ($19–$24) and rice bowls ($14–$18), the latter with choices of local favorites like teriyaki fish, garlic shrimp, tuna poke, and roast pork.

5095 Nāpilihau St., Nāpili. www.fondmaui.com. ✆ **808/856-0225.** Main courses $14–$24 lunch, $23–$32 dinner. Tues–Sat 11am–4pm lunch, 4–9pm dinner; 11am–9pm bar menu.

Joey's Kitchen ★★ FILIPINO/PLATE LUNCH Joey Macadang-dang ran the kitchen at Roy's for many years, winning award after award for his inventive cuisine. Now he's got two eponymous restaurants of his own: an ultra-casual spot in the Whalers Village food court and this slightly fancier eatery in the Napili Plaza shopping center, where Joey and his wife will personally take care of you. If you've never tried Filipino food before, this is your place. Get the savory pork adobo plate, or seafood *sinigang*—a hot and sour medley of fish, clams, and shrimp. You'll find familiar favorites, too: fried Brussels sprouts, fish and chips, and enticing Hawaiian seafood specials, such as ahi salad with octopus or pan-seared shutome with shiitake mushroom risotto.

5095 Nāpilihau St., Nāpili. www.joeyskitchenhimaui.com. ✆ **808/214-5590.** Main courses $13–$25. Daily 10am–2pm and 4–8pm. Also at Whalers Village, 2435 Kāʻanapali Pkwy., Kāʻanapali. ✆ **808/868-4474.** Main courses $11–$25. Daily 9am–11am breakfast, 11am–8pm lunch and dinner.

Maui Brewing Co. ★ BREWPUB Maui's ultra-popular microbrewery has expanded to Oʻahu, but the home is where the heart is. The Kahana brewpub offers beer flights at the bar and excellent pub fare. Local shishito peppers, beer-battered onion rings, ahi poke nachos, and fresh catch ceviche are standout appetizers; the eclectic main dishes lean toward the hearty side, including jambalaya, fish and chips, and loco moco (eggs, rice, burger, and gravy), with flatbreads a slightly lighter option. Try limited-release brews on tap here, along with the company's standards: Bikini Blonde Ale, Big Swell IPA, Pineapple Mana, and a rich and chocolatey coconut porter. Note the cute lamps made from miniature kegs. See the Kīhei listings for details on the main brewery and restaurant (p. 407). An oceanfront Maui Brewing Co. is at the Outrigger Kāʻanapali Beach Resort (p. 369).

At the Kahana Gateway Shopping Center, 4405 Honoapiʻilani Hwy. www.maui brewingco.com. ✆ **808/669-3474.** Main courses $15–$28. Daily 11am–9pm; happy hour 3:30–4:30pm.

Sea House Restaurant ★ PACIFIC RIM Old-fashioned and a bit dated, this oceanfront restaurant at the Napili Kai Beach Resort is a throwback to earlier days. But the view here can't be beat. Breakfast is lovely under the umbrellas outside, overlooking serene Nāpili Bay. The oven-baked Crater pancake is a special treat, made with custard batter. Sunset is a good time to come, too. Sit at the **Whale Watcher's Bar** and order classic cocktails and poke nachos. The happy hour menu (2–4:45pm) is a terrific bargain, with delicious, filling appetizers like Kula onion soup, coconut shrimp, and pork street tacos just $6 to $9. Early birds will appreciate the $44 prix fixe, offered from 5:30 to 6pm, which includes island salad, tiramisu, and a choice of filet mignon, mac nut-covered Hawaiian fish, or shrimp scampi. There's also live Hawaiian music 6:30 to 8:30pm nightly.

At the Napili Kai Beach Resort, 5900 Honoapi'ilani Hwy. www.napilikai.com. © **808/669-1500.** Reservations recommended. Main courses $15–$16 breakfast, $15–$22 lunch, $25–$53 dinner. Daily 7–11am breakfast, 11am–2pm lunch, 5:30–9pm dinner; happy hour 2–4:45pm.

Inexpensive

Maui Tacos ★ MEXICAN   Years ago, chef Mark Ellman launched this restaurant chain, dedicated to Mexican food with "Mauitude." Now it has locations as far away as Minnesota and the late chef's take on healthy fast food continues to satisfy. Choices include fish tacos, chimichangas, and burritos loaded with charbroiled chicken or slow-cooked pork, black beans, rice, and salsa. Other locations are at Kamaole Beach Center, 2411 S. Kīhei Rd., Kīhei (© **808/879-5005**), and at Pu'unēnē Shopping Center, 58 Ho'okele St., Kahului (© **808/793-3931**).

At Napili Plaza, 5095 Nāpilihau St., Lahaina. © **808/665-0222.** $6–$17. Daily 11am–8pm.

Pizza Paradiso Mediterranean Grill ★ ITALIAN/MEDITERRANEAN   The pledge on the wall at this Honokōwai hot spot—to use organic, local ingredients wherever possible and treat employees like family—gives a hint to the quality of food here. The large-ish menu includes gourmet and gluten-free pizzas with terrific toppings (barbecue chicken, smoked Gouda, cilantro), chicken shawarma, lamb gyros, kabobs, pastas, and more. The kitchen makes its own meatballs, out of grass-fed Maui Cattle Company beef, and its own sauces and dressings. But save room for dessert. The tiramisu is an award winner, and the locally made coconut gelato should be. Thursday through Sunday brings open mic, live music, karaoke, and trivia nights, respectively.

At the Honokowai Marketplace, 3350 Lower Honoapi'ilani Rd., Kā'anapali. www.pizzaparadiso.com. © **808/667-2929.** Main courses $12–$19; pizzas $22–$32. Daily 7am–10am breakfast; Mon–Thurs 10am–9:30pm and Fri until 1am.

KAPALUA

Note: You'll find the restaurants in this section on the "Hotels & Restaurants in West Maui" map (p. 371).

Very Expensive

Banyan Tree ★★★ PACIFIC RIM   The ocean views from the sleek open-air bar and contemporary dining room at this outpost on the Ritz's verdant compound are dazzling, while the fresh seafood shines just as bright. The menu highlights local farms and Asian influences. Try the signature seafood red Thai curry brimming with Hokkaido scallops, Kaua'i prawns, and a local white fish ($78), or the Kona kanpachi with tomatoes, kale, and Spam chili crunch ($57). Carnivores will appreciate the grilled steaks ($77–$92) and chicken ($54) emanating from the Josper charcoal oven, imported from Spain. Save room for executive pastry chef Erin Howard's local banana cream pie or trio of warm malasadas (island-style doughnut holes; both $19).

At the Ritz-Carlton Maui, Kapalua, 1 Ritz-Carlton Dr., Lahaina. www.banyantree kapalua.com *Ⓒ* **808/669-6200.** Reservations recommended. Main courses $45–$53. Daily 5–9pm.

Cane & Canoe ★ PACIFIC RIM On the oceanfront side of the intimate Montage Kapalua Bay, tables spill out from under a pointed roof styled like a traditional Hawaiian canoe house. Cane & Canoe offers a striking view of Moloka'i across the resort's terraced pools, and solid interpretations of surf ("canoe") and turf ("cane"), at prices in keeping with the ultra-luxurious resort setting. Chef de cuisine Albert Sandoval focuses on high-quality seafood such as Kona kanpachi with tiger prawns ($64) and prime cuts of meat such as Duroc pork chops ($62) and Jidori chicken breast ($58), the latter served with a Madras curry risotto. Island produce stars in several dishes, such as the Kahuku corn vichyssoise with Moloka'i sweet potato ($18). Go lighter at breakfast with a fresh-pressed juice and egg white frittata ($27) or indulge with the lobster benedict ($39).

On lower level of Montage Kapalua Bay, 1 Bay Dr., Lahaina. www.montagehotels. com/kapaluabay/dining/cane-and-canoe. *Ⓒ* **808/662-6681.** Reservations recommended. Main courses $26–$40 breakfast, $42–$75 dinner. Daily 7–11am and 5–9pm.

Merriman's Kapalua ★★ PACIFIC RIM James Beard award–winning chef Peter Merriman, who helped launch the Hawai'i Regional Cuisine movement in the 1990s, has namesake farm-to-table restaurants on O'ahu, Hawai'i Island, and Kaua'i, but none in such a picturesque location as this, on a rocky point with views of Lāna'i and Moloka'i. Reservations are recommended for the main restaurant and book up quickly, while no reservations are taken for seating on the oceanfront point, which also has a limited menu. Service, while still friendly, can be brisk to handle the nonstop demand. Starters may include the kalua pork quesadilla enlivened with house-made kimchi and a mango-chili sauce and an addictive smoked taro hummus (both $24). Rosemary roasted Colorado lamb chops and harissa spiced diver sea scallops show off the islands' bounty only via their accompaniments, but still merit ordering. For dessert, you can't go wrong with the Waialua flourless chocolate cake, oozing with warm chocolate from O'ahu. The open-air Point is an exceedingly romantic spot; don't be surprised if you see a "Just Maui'd" couple stroll by or witness a neighboring diner propose.

1 Bay Club Place, Kapalua. www.merrimanshawaii.com/kapalua. *Ⓒ* **808/669-6400.** Reservations required; see www.exploretock.com/merrimanskapalua. Main courses $44–$89 (most $68–$72); children's menu $30. Daily 4–8pm.

Moderate

Plantation House Restaurant ★ PACIFIC RIM   This is a dramatic destination for breakfast, lunch, or dinner, sitting amid lush golf greens with panoramic ocean views. Executive chef Jared Krausen's menu is not overly ambitious, but freshly sourced and attractively presented, with a few local touches. At brunch, try an omelet with kalua pork or Kula Farms veggies and local goat cheese. Kung pao calamari and the ahi poke salad are winners at lunch. For dinner, Mary's organic chicken comes with a tasty teriyaki glaze and crunchy cashews; the prime rib-eye and filet mignon are excellent options for meat lovers. *Note:* All food items incur a 3% surcharge (separate from your tip) that is distributed among kitchen staff. Given the high cost of living in the islands, this is a tough place to retain kitchen workers, so every little bit helps.

At the Kapalua Golf Club Plantation Course, 2000 Plantation Club Dr., Kapalua. www.theplantationhouse.com. ℰ **808/669-6299.** Reservations recommended. Main courses $18–$32 brunch and lunch, $33–$97 (most $39–$49) dinner. Daily 8am–8pm.

Sansei Seafood Restaurant & Sushi Bar ★★ PACIFIC RIM/SUSHI With its creative take on sushi (think mango crab hand roll or Cajun seared walu sashimi), Sansei's menu scores higher with adventurous diners than with purists. Expertly sliced sashimi platters and straightforward gobo rolls will please even sushi snobs. Small and big plates are for sharing, though you'll fight over the last bites of misoyaki butterfish and roasted Japanese eggplant. The Dungeness crab ramen is my favorite—its fragrant truffle broth flecked with cilantro, Thai basil, and jalapeños. Save room for Mom Kodama's chocolate brownie sundae or the Granny Smith apple tart with caramel sauce (both $10). *Tip:* On Sunday and Monday, early-bird discounts are up to 50% on many items between 5 and 5:45pm, but line up early, since they don't take reservations then.

600 Office Rd., Kapalua. www.sanseihawaii.com/kapalua. ℰ **808/669-6286.** Reservations recommended. Main courses $20–$77 (most $29–$38); sushi rolls $5–$25. Daily 5–8:30pm.

South Maui

KĪHEI

One of Maui's loveliest, affordable outdoor dining experiences is **Kīhei Food Oasis,** a cluster of 13 food trucks, a bakery, and a coffee shop at either end of the South Maui Gardens nursery, 35 Auhana Rd. (www.southmauigardens.com/foodtrucks). My favorite is **Howzit Eh?** ★★, which offers various twists on Canadian poutine (fries with gravy) and island seafood; check the website for current menus and hours. Indian food lovers will want to visit not only **Monsoon India** ★ (p. 407), but also its Kīhei crosstown rival, **Yak and Yeti** ★, in Kīhei Town Shopping Center, 1881 S. Kīhei Rd. (https://kihei.theyakandyeti.com; ℰ **808/879-7888**). Serving Indian, Nepalese, and Tibetan dishes (many of them gluten-free, with lots of vegan and vegetarian options), it's open daily 11am to 3pm and 5 to 9:30pm.

The sprawling, indoor-outdoor Kīhei location of **Maui Brewing Company ★**, 605 Lipoa Pkwy. (www.mauibrewingco.com; ☏ **808/213-3002**), may be in an office park, but it has plenty of room for kids to stretch their legs and beer lovers to sample drafts where they're made. It also has a family-friendly, moderately priced menu, similar to its two branches in Kahana and Kā'anapali (p. 403).

Note: You'll find the Kīhei restaurants in this section on the "Hotels & Restaurants in South Maui" map (p. 377).

Moderate

Cafe O'Lei Kīhei ★ AMERICAN/PIZZA   The open, airy dining room here is inviting, with hardwood floors, tables separated by sheer curtains, a big circular bar in the center of the restaurant, and a brick oven in back. Call ahead for a table—locals flood this place during their lunch break. For dinner, the Maui onion soup (baked in the wood-burning oven) is a savory treat with fresh thyme and brandy. Groups will do well here, as the diverse menu offers something for everyone, even pizza ($15–$17, with gluten-free crusts $4 more), baked in a brick oven.

In Rainbow Mall, 2439 S. Kīhei Rd., Kīhei. www.cafeoleirestaurants.com. ☏ **808/891-1368.** Reservations recommended. Main courses $16–$27 lunch, $15–$42 dinner. Tues–Sun 11am–3:30pm; dinner 4pm to last seating at 8pm.

Monsoon India ★ INDIAN   If there's one thing Maui could use more of, it's Indian flavors. Thank goodness for Monsoon India, a humble restaurant at the north edge of Kīhei—without it, we'd have to board a plane to enjoy piping-hot naan bread and crisp papadum. The chicken korma ($22) here is creamy and fragrant, the chana masala ($18) spicy and satisfying. With tables that overlook Mā'alaea Bay, this serene spot is lovely just before sunset—particularly in winter when whales are jumping. A newer addition is American-style breakfast of eggs Benedict, bagels, wraps, and fresh organic juices that includes some brunch options like burgers ($24).

Note: The open-air dining room is closed when it rains, and alcohol is bring-your-own.

In the Menehune Shores Bldg., 760 S. Kīhei Rd., Kīhei. www.monsoonmaui.com. ☏ **808/875-6666.** Main courses $19–$27. Daily 8am–1pm breakfast; 11am–2pm lunch; 4–9:30pm dinner; happy hour 4–5pm.

Inexpensive

In addition to the following, try a freshly made limeade, lemonade, or smoothie at **WowWow Hawaiian Lemonade ★**, 1279 S. Kīhei Rd. (in Azeka Shopping Center), Kīhei (☏ **808/344-0319**). It's open daily from 8am to 4pm. Fans of a bargain and fish tacos will also want to check out the Kīhei location of **Maui Tacos ★** in Kamaole Beach Center, 2411 S. Kīhei Rd., Kīhei (https://mauitacos.com; ☏ **808/879-5005**); see the entry under Nāpili (p. 404) for details.

Nalu's South Shore Grill ★ AMERICAN   Casual, noisy, and a lot of fun, this restaurant fills an important niche in Kīhei. Order at the counter, from a wide-ranging menu—everything from chicken and waffles to a commendable Cubano sandwich. It's a great place to bring the family or big groups. Extra touches show that the owners care about customer satisfaction: friendly service, a choice of flavored waters, and terrific live music nightly.

1280 S. Kīhei Rd. (in Azeka Shopping Center–Makai), Kīhei. www.naluskihei.com. © **808/891-8650.** Main courses $11–$18 breakfast; $9–$20 lunch/dinner. Daily 8am–9pm; happy hour 3–6pm.

Three's Bar & Grill ★★ PACIFIC RIM/SOUTHWESTERN   In 2009, culinary school and surfing buddies Travis Morrin, Cody Christopher, and Jaron Blosser figured a catering company would allow them time to catch waves in between kitchen duties. But demand for their varied cuisines—Southwestern, Pacific Rim, and Hawaiian—soon prompted them to open a full-blown casual restaurant, not too far from the surf. Panko-crusted ahi roll (from the huge sushi menu), kalua pork quesadilla, and Hawaiian-style ribs represent satisfying signature dishes, with hot chocolate lava cake a popular finisher. Surfboards, naturally, greet you at the door, with impressive wave photography in the lounge and oil paintings by local artists in the dining room; a large monkeypod tree shades the pleasant outdoor patio.

Note: The chefs' spinoff in Kīhei, the casual **Fork and Salad** ★ in Azeka Shopping Center–Mauka, 1278 S. Kīhei Rd. (https://forkandsalad maui.com; © **808/793-3256**), has also won acclaim, sprouting a second location at the Pu'unēnē Shopping Center, 120 Ho'okele St., Kahului (© **808/793-3256**). In Kīhei, it's open daily from 11am to 8pm and the Kahului location is 10:30am to 8:30pm.

In Kihei Kalama Village, 1945 S. Kīhei Rd., Kīhei. https://threesbarandgrill.com. © **808/879-3133.** Main courses $17–$27 lunch, $24–$45 dinner. Daily 11am–9pm; happy hour 3–6pm.

WAILEA

For memorable drinking and late-night noshing, pop into **the Pint & Cork** ★, in the Shops at Wailea (www.thepintandcork.com; © **808/727-2038**), a kid-friendly tavern that serves gourmet pub grub (lobster salad, grilled cheese with short rib, shishito peppers) and an impressive bevy of alcoholic beverages from noon to midnight Wednesday through Monday. Happy-hour specials and takeout are available from noon to 5pm.

Note: You'll find it and the restaurants in this section on the "Hotels & Restaurants in South Maui" map (p. 377).

Expensive
Humble Market Kitchin ★★ HAWAI'I REGIONAL CUISINE Celebrity chef Roy Yamaguchi pays tribute to summers spent volunteering in his grandfather's general store through this restaurant at the Wailea Beach Resort—Marriott, Maui. The menu features re-imagined Hawaiian comfort foods: poke (raw, seasoned fish), misoyaki butterfish with green tea soba noodles, and ramen loaded with pork belly, dumplings, a sous vide egg, and lip-smacking sesame broth. At breakfast, try the mochi or

coconut pancakes—the latter served with haupia (coconut) cream—or, for the health conscious, avocado toast on house-made focaccia with poached eggs.

At the Wailea Beach Resort—Marriott, Maui. 3700 Wailea Alanui Dr., Wailea. www.hmkmaui.com. © **808/879-4655.** Reservations recommended. Main courses $24–$29 breakfast (hot buffet $49, continental buffet $34, $20 children 12 and under), $42–$70 dinner. Daily 6:30–10:30am breakfast; dinner 5–9:30pm; happy hour 5–6pm.

Ka'ana Kitchen ★ HAWAI'I REGIONAL CUISINE You can hardly tell where the dining room ends and the kitchen begins in this bright restaurant, created by executive chef Isaac Bancaco. Sit ringside where you can watch chef de cuisine Chance Savell and his talented team in action. Start off with a hand-mixed cocktail and the grilled octopus ($29): fat chunks of tender meat tossed with frisée, watercress, and goat cheese. The ahi tataki ($30) is beautiful: ruby-red tuna, heirloom tomato, and fresh burrata decorated with black salt and nasturtium petals. There's only a baker's dozen of appetizers and main courses, divided into garden, ocean, and farm categories, but they're all winners. The downside: A downstairs poolside bar, added later, blocks some of the view and creates ambient noise not conducive to romantic fine dining upstairs. The breakfast buffet is relatively lavish, with several cooked-to-order options.

At the Andaz Maui, 3550 Wailea Alanui Dr., Wailea. www.hyatt.com/andaz/oggaw-andaz-maui-at-wailea-resort/dining. © **808/573-1234.** Breakfast buffet $49 adults, $24.50 children 12 and under; main courses $30–$54 dinner. Daily 6:30–11am and 5:30–8pm.

Kō ★★ GOURMET PLANTATION CUISINE *Kō* is Hawaiian for sugarcane, and this restaurant revives the melting pot of Maui's bygone plantation days. Following in the footsteps of the late Tylun Pang, Kō's founding chef, executive chef Jonathan Pasion pays tribute to Maui's plantation heritage by incorporating the cuisines of the cane fields' labor force—Hawaiian, Filipino, Portuguese, Korean, Puerto Rican, Chinese, and Japanese—into gourmet dishes with elegant presentations. The "ahi on the rock" appetizer features glistening garnet-hued tuna accompanied by a hot rock on which to sear them; once done, dunk it in the delicious orange-ginger miso sauce. Or try Pang's family recipe for Filipino *lumpia* (spring roll with green papaya, chicken, and mushroom, accompanied by a spicy sauce) or pork belly bao buns. Main course standouts include local venison in a black raspberry pineapple compote, seafood *laulau* (fresh catch steamed in *ti* leaf), and lobster tempura. *Note:* Valet parking is free for diners who are staying elsewhere.

At the Fairmont Kea Lani Maui, 4100 Wailea Alanui Dr., Wailea. www.korestaurant.com. © **808/875-2210.** Reservations recommended. Main courses $28–$62. Daily 5–8:30pm; Sunday brunch 10:30am–1:30pm; happy hour 4–5pm.

Lineage ★★ MODERN ISLAND *Top Chef* fan favorite and Hilo native Sheldon Simeon has a long history on the Maui culinary scene but did not have a restaurant of his own until he opened the humble but playful, lunch-only **Tin Roof ★** (p. 398) in Kahului. A few years later he expanded his reach with the dinner-only Lineage in the Shops at Wailea, paying homage to his hometown and the local tradition of family feast. His baby is now in the hands of chef Emmanuel Eng, who continues to apply creativity to family recipes and Asian American cuisine in general. Start with aji tomago, soy-dashi-marinated 6-minute eggs ($16), or the ahi poke salad specials ($23). For the shared dinner plates, go for the crispy noodles with mushroom gravy ($30) or the Cantonese lobster noodles shrimp ($41). Finish with pandan bread pudding ($12) or the milk chocolate and miso ice cream ($13). The full dinner menu is also available at the bar.

At the Shops at Wailea, 3750 Wailea Alanui Dr., Wailea. www.lineagemaui.com. ℗ **808/879-8800.** Reservations recommended. Shared plates $20–$65 (most $31–$42). Tues–Sat dinner 5–9pm.

Morimoto Maui ★★★ JAPANESE/PAN-ASIAN   Iron Chef Masaharu Morimoto's poolside restaurant is simply furnished, directing all of the attention to the culinary fireworks. The immaculate kitchen houses a space-age freezer full of fish bought at auction, and a rice polisher that ensures that every grain is perfect. One revelation is the locally caught fish such as 'ōpakapaka (pink snapper) in Thai curry with *pohole* fern, plump clams, and sushi rice, topped with grilled bananas that balance the curry's heat ($55). For a touch of drama, try the ishi yaki buri bap ($45), yellowtail tuna on rice cooked over a hot stone at your table. You could also make a meal of savory hot appetizers like rock shrimp tempura with wasabi aioli, sticky ribs in a spicy tamarind glaze, grilled kama, or crispy pork gyoza ($11–$19). Lunch prices offer the best value, such as tempura calamari salad ($19) and soft-shell crab bao with fries ($32).

At the Andaz Maui, 3550 Wailea Alanui Dr., Wailea. www.morimotomaui.com.. ℗ **808/573-1234.** Main course $28–$42 lunch, $45–$72 dinner. Daily 12–2:20pm and 5–8:45pm.

Spago ★★★ ASIAN FUSION/NEW AMERICAN   At Wolfgang Puck's restaurant tucked into the posh lobby of the Four Seasons, dishes are flavorful but light—not burdened by heavy sauces. If the chef tried to remove the ahi sesame-miso cones from the menu, fans would probably riot. This appetizer is perfection: bright red spicy ahi spooned into a crunchy, sweet, and nutty cone and topped with flying fish roe. The steamed opakapaka in Chinese black bean sauce is worth the price tag. During truffle season, fragrant shavings of black or white truffles can be added to your dish. Seating hangs over the elegant pool with Pacific views (book tables for no later than 5:45pm for the best vistas), and the bartenders pour handcrafted libations with clever names like the Tequila-based Mo' Money Mo' Problems and Hot Legs, a concoction of Wheatley vodka, guava, ginger, and Thai basil.

At the Four Seasons Resort Maui at Wailea, 3900 Wailea Alanui Dr., Wailea. https://wolfgangpuck.com/dining/spago-maui. ℗ **808/879-2999.** Reservations recommended. Main courses $39–$135. Daily 5–8:30pm.

Moderate

Matteo's Osteria ★★ ITALIAN/SEAFOOD Although Wailea is hardly lacking in Italian eateries, it'd be a shame to miss this gracious restaurant and wine bar, nearly hidden in a small shopping strip near the Residence Inn. Some 30 wines, mostly from Italy and Northern California, are available by the glass, while the 200-plus list of wines by the bottle includes rare Italian varietals from chef-owner Matteo Mistura's personal collection. You don't have to be an oenophile to appreciate his deft blend of Italian cuisine and local ingredients, especially fresh fish. Maui beef appears in his lasagna with homemade pasta, while carnaroli risotto cake, mushroom trifolati, and artichoke-thyme puree adorn the fresh catch plate. For lighter eaters, his salads can't be beat. *Note:* Table time is limited to a maximum of 75 minutes to 2 hours per table, depending on the size of your party; book via OpenTable to confirm an outdoor table.

161 Wailea Ike Place, Wailea. www.matteosmaui.com. ⓒ **808/891-8466.** Main courses $35–$64. Tues–Sat 4:45–8:30pm.

Monkeypod Kitchen ★★ AMERICAN/ISLAND CUISINE Celebrated chef Peter Merriman's casual venture spotlights local, organic produce, pasture-raised beef, and sustainably caught fish—all of which contribute to better tasting food. Pull up a seat at the lively bar here and enjoy *saimin* (soup with locally made noodles), bulgogi pork tacos, or Waipoli Farm greens with beet and chèvre. The expansive drink menu is among the island's best, offering everything from fresh coconut water, kombucha, and "shrubs" (soda or juice with fresh muddled herbs) to award-winning handcrafted cocktails like the signature mai tai. The dessert menu is less inspired; the cream pies are only so-so. A second, similarly hopping location is at the Whalers Village shopping mall in Kāʻanapali. Both typically have live music daily at 1, 4, and 7pm.

In Wailea Gateway Center, 10 Wailea Gateway Place (second floor), Wailea. ⓒ **808/891-2322.** Also in Whalers Village, 2435 Kāʻanapali Pkwy., Kāʻanapali. ⓒ **808/878-6763.** www.monkeypodkitchen.com. Main courses $19–$61 (most $19–$23). Daily 11am–10pm; happy hour 3:30–5pm.

Pita Paradise ★ GREEK/MEDITERRANEAN For fresh, flavorful Greek food cooked to order and served with creamy tzatziki sauce and rice pilaf, head to this oasis in Wailea. Owner Johnny Arabatzis, Jr., catches his own fish, which he prepares in daily specials. The roasted lamb shank with gnocchi and fennel puree ($32) is a delight, if a bit heavy. A trickling fountain serenades the tables in the courtyard, which sometimes hosts musicians. The baklava ice cream cake ($12) is exquisite, and definitely enough to share.

In Wailea Gateway Center, 34 Wailea Ike Dr., Wailea. www.pitaparadisehawaii.com. ⓒ **808/879-7177.** Main courses $15–$26 lunch; $24–$32 dinner. Daily 11am–9pm dinner; happy hour 3–5pm.

Upcountry Maui

Note: You'll find the restaurants in this section on the "Upcountry & East Maui" map (p. 389).

HĀLI'IMAILE (ON THE WAY TO UPCOUNTRY MAUI)
Moderate
Haliimaile General Store ★★★ HAWAI'I REGIONAL/AMERICAN
Bev Gannon, one of the pioneering chefs of Hawai'i Regional Cuisine, brought her gourmet comfort food to this renovated plantation store in rural Hāli'imaile in 1988. It was a gamble then; now it's one of the island's most beloved restaurants. Menu items reflect island cuisine with hints of Texas, Gannon's home state. At lunch, try the kalua pork enchilada pie ($24), layered with homemade mole sauce, cheese, and corn tortillas, or the buttermilk chicken fried sandwich with pickled jalapeño slaw ($19). At dinner, it's best to stick to one rich item like the coconut seafood curry ($44) or blackened seared ahi noodle bowl ($47) rather than ordering several to share. However, that rule does not apply to the sashimi Napoleon ($29). The creamy wasabi vinaigrette that the waiter pours atop your stack of ahi tartare, smoked salmon, and wonton chips *is* rich, but worth it. Sound ricochets in this vintage camp store, with its polished wooden floors, high ceilings, and open kitchen. It's quieter in the back room. The vegetarian menu has tasty options, such as coconut veggie curry ($30) and mixed mushroom bao buns ($18).

900 Hāli'imaile Rd., Hāli'imaile. www.hgsmaui.com. © **808/572-2666.** Reservations recommended. Main courses $18–$36 lunch; $29–$68 dinner. Tues–Sat 11am–2:30pm and 5–8:30pm.

PUKALANI/MAKAWAO

Many come to Makawao just to sate a sweet tooth at **T. Komoda Bakery ★★**, 3674 Baldwin Ave. (© **808/572-7261**), in business for more than a century. Arrive before noon or risk missing out on cream puffs and stick donuts encrusted with macadamia nuts; bring cash. It's open Monday, Tuesday, and Thursday to Saturday 7am to 1pm.

On the outskirts of Makawao, the new **Kulamalu Town Center** in Pukalani is home to a Saturday farmer market, 7am to 11am, and a dependably delicious assortment of food trucks with various hours. It's home as well to the airy, loft-style taproom and brewery of **Mahalo Aleworks ★★**, 30 Kupaoa St. (www.mahaloaleworks.com), which hosts **Upcountry Sausage Co. ★★** cart on its lanai, serving gourmet wurst, burgers, and street tacos. The taproom also allows patrons to bring in the exceptional wood-fired sourdough pizza, charcuterie and cheese plates, and other savory fare from its popular, moderately priced neighbor **Marlow ★★** (www.restaurantmarlow.com), run by esteemed Maui chef Jeff Scheer and Kaili Scheer. Marlow is open daily for breakfast 7 to 11am, lunch 11am to 2pm, and dinner 4:30 to 9pm; reservations are recommended for dinner, with last seating at 8:30pm.

Moderate

Casanova ★ ITALIAN   This upcountry institution serves hearty Italian fare, including brick oven pizzas, homemade pasta, and grilled meats. Snack on freshly baked focaccia with olive oil and balsamic vinegar while waiting for popular main courses such as the pillowy spinach ravioli with sage cream sauce and truffle oil, the chicken parmigiana, or Roman-style grilled lamb chops with potatoes and veggies. Duck lovers should try the duck confit with saffron lemon risotto.

1188 Makawao Ave., Makawao. www.casanovamaui.com. *(*) **808/572-0220.** Reservations recommended. Main courses $30–$50, pizzas $18–$24. Daily 5pm–"close," typically 9pm.

KULA

Moderate

Kula Bistro ★★ HAWAI'I REGIONAL/AMERICAN   Longtime high-end caterer Luciano Zanon, who grew up working a family-owned trattoria in Venice, returned to his roots with wife Chantal by opening this casual bistro. If you can pull your eyes away from the dessert and pastry case, at breakfast you'll find expertly executed eggs Benedict and frittata, plus local favorites like loco moco (eggs/beef patty/rice/gravy) and fried rice with eggs. Lunch and dinner reflects European and Asian techniques and island ingredients, from the calamari steak with lemon beurre blanc to the grilled mahi sandwich with pesto aioli, kalua pork panini, and crowd-pleasers like pasta, pizza, and prime rib. Alcohol is bring your own, with no corkage fee. Seating is walk-in only (no reservations).

4566 Lower Kula Rd., Kula. www.kulabistro.com. *(*) **808/871-2960.** Main courses $12–$21 breakfast, $18–$57 (most $18–$29) lunch and dinner. Daily 11am–8pm; Thurs–Sun 7:30–10:15am.

Kula Lodge Restaurant & Bar ★★★ HAWAI'I REGIONAL/AMERICAN   Junior Ulep, the esteemed former chef of **Meridia** (p. 267) on the Kohala coast of Hawai'i Island, jumped ship to Maui in 2024 and quickly jump-started the menu of this iconic Upcountry restaurant with panoramic views from its dining room and lushly landscaped garden terrace. Here Ulep draws on his talent for creating crusty fresh breads, sourcing flavor-intense local produce and quality proteins, and adding unique flourishes to familiar dishes. The lobster roll ($32) comes on a housemade toasted butter roll that holds up to the delicately creamy lobster salad, made from a whole tail and garnished with tomato bacon jam; it's served with a small salad of local greens and housemade taro and sweet potato chips. Maui onion soup ($15) features the Valley Isle's famous sweet onions in a vegetarian broth with strands of rich Gruyere (vegans can ask for it to be left off) under an impressive dome of flaky puff pastry. If you're sitting in one of the terrace gazebos, where the brick patio has an opening that reveals a babbling stream, you can watch wood-fired brick pizza oven at work ($24–$28, available 11am–8pm). The chewy, buttery braided crust pairs well with hearty toppings like kalua pork, local venison sausage, or island mushrooms. Reservations are recommended and available on OpenTable.

15200 Haleakalā Hwy. (Hwy. 377), Kula. www.kulalodge.com. ✆ **808/878-1538.** Main courses $14–$24 brunch, $20–$32 lunch and dinner. Wed–Sun 8am–9pm.

Inexpensive

Grandma's Coffee House ★ AMERICAN   Alfred Franco's grand-mother started growing and roasting coffee in remote and charming Kēōkea back in 1918. Five generations later, this family-run cafe is still fueled by homegrown Haleakalā beans and frequented by local *paniolo*—one reason why Maui beef is on the menu. Line up at the busy counter for espresso, home-baked pastries, hot oatmeal, scrambled eggs, or, on Sundays, eggs Benedict served on a cornmeal waffle. Plate lunches with proteins like shoyu chicken or meatloaf loco moco and sides of rice and macaroni salad are served all day, as are thickly layered sandwiches. On the scenic lanai, the air is always the perfect temperature for listening to a Hawaiian guitar-ist serenade his bygone sweethearts. Pick up a few lemon squares to go.

9232 Kula Hwy. (Hwy. 37), Kēōkea. www.grandmascoffee.com. ✆ **808/878-2140.** Main courses $9–$27 (most items $15–$17). Daily 7am–2pm.

East Maui

In addition to the ***Pā'ia restaurants below,*** **Choice Health Bar** ★★, 11 Baldwin Ave. (www.choicehealthbar.com; ✆ **808/661-7711**), is notewor-thy for serving organic plant-based cuisine—açai bowls, Buddha bowls, kale salads, vegan soups, and the like—sourced from several Upcountry Maui farms. It's open daily 9am to 4pm. You'll find the restaurants in this section on the "Upcountry & East Maui" map (p. 389).

PĀ'IA
Moderate

Flatbread & Company ★★ PIZZA   This family-friendly Pā'ia out-post embraces a locavore philosophy. The hand-colored menus highlight the best Maui farmers have to offer, particularly where the inventive daily *carne* and veggie specials are concerned. You can watch the chefs hand-toss organic dough, dress it with high-quality toppings—local goat cheese, macadamia-nut pesto, slow-roasted kalua pork, or homemade, nitrate-free sausage—and shovel it into the wood-burning clay oven that serves as the restaurant's magical hearth. Salads come sprinkled with grated green papaya and dressing so delicious that everyone clamors for the recipe. *Note:* A 3% surcharge on food benefits the kitchen staff, while a portion of flatbread sales on Monday go to Maui fire relief.

89 Hāna Highway., Pā'ia. www.flatbreadcompany.com. ✆ **808/579-8989.** Reserva-tions recommended. Main courses $21–$29. Daily 11am–9pm.

Milagros Food Company ★ TEX-MEX   You'll have a prime view of the Pā'ia action from the lanai of this corner restaurant. The kitchen turns out Tex-Mex dishes with Maui flair, such as blackened mahi mahi tacos with salsa, cheese, fresh guacamole, and sweet chili sauce (sounds strange but tastes great). You can also order enchiladas with a house-made four red-chili sauce, fajitas with sautéed vegetables finished in achiote glaze, a variety of burgers, and giant salads. Watch for happy hour: $5 margaritas and mai tais made with local ingredients, $4 Mexican beer (can and draft), and $6 food specials.

3 Baldwin Ave., Pā'ia. www.milagrosfoodcompany.com. © **808/579-8755.** Main courses $14–$22. Daily 11am–9pm; happy hour 3–6pm.

Inexpensive

Café des Amis ★★ MEDITERRANEAN/INDIAN   This sweet, eclectic restaurant serves crepes, curries, and salads that are fresh, tasty, and easy on the wallet. Savory crepes ($15–$18) like the bacon, brie, and avocado combo come with organic local greens and a dollop of sour cream; sweet fillings ($7–$12) include Maui cane sugar with lime and a decadent apple cheesecake. The curries aren't exactly Indian, but they are delicious, especially the fragrant coconut shrimp curry, incorporating a blend of ginger, garlic, cinnamon, and cilantro. Curry wraps ($17–$19) come with cucumber raita and mango chutney; bowls ($19–$26) with basmati rice and optional chutney.

42 Baldwin Ave., Pā'ia. www.cdamaui.com. © **808/579-6323.** Main courses: $15–$26. Mon–Fri 11am–8:30pm, Sat–Sun 9am–8:30pm; daily happy hour 4–6pm.

Paia Bay Coffee & Bar ★ CAFE   Relocated in 2023 just down the road from its original semi-hidden location and expanded to include a bar with craft cocktails and dinner hours, this coffee shop has long been a place for Maui insiders. Most breakfast options are available all day, but order before 1pm if you want to try the savory chicken katsu waffle or the decadent monkey butter waffle, concocted with local banana, pineapple, and coconut. The large salad and starters menu works well for lunch and dinner, with several great half-off deals at happy hour (3–5pm), including the calamari salad, poke bowl, and shrimp ceviche, normally $19 apiece. Heartier entrees ($20–$22) emphasize local flavors, as with the taro burger and pan-roasted mahi mahi.

120 Hāna Hwy., Pā'ia. www.paiabaycoffeeandbar.com. © **808/579-3111.** Main course $17–$21 breakfast; $20–$22 lunch and dinner. Mon 7:30am–8pm, Tues–Fri until 10pm, Sun until 3pm; daily happy hour 3–5pm.

Paia Fishmarket & Restaurant ★★ SEAFOOD   At the corner of Baldwin Avenue and Hāna Highway in Pā'ia, this busy fish market must maintain its own fleet of fishing boats. How else to explain how the cooks can dish out filet after giant fresh filet for little more than it would cost to buy the same at the grocery? Order the fish tacos a la carte ($6 each) or as a plate ($12 with one taco, $15 for two) with cole slaw and choice of Cajun rice, fries, or home potatoes. Fish burgers ($13–$15)—a giant slab of perfectly grilled ahi, ono, or mahi mahi laid out on a bun with coleslaw and grated cheese—are extra satisfying after a briny day at the beach.

(Chicken and beef burgers are also an option.) Also in **Kīhei** at 1913 S. Kīhei Rd., *✆* **808/874-8888.**

100 Hāna Hwy., Pāʻia. https://paiafishmarket.com. *✆* **808/579-8030.** Main courses $12–$25. Daily lunch 11am–9pm.

HAʻIKŪ
Moderate

Colleen's at the Cannery ★ ECLECTIC   This go-to spot for Haʻikū folks serves an excellent breakfast, lunch, and dinner in a loft-style setting. Slide into a booth beside world-famous surfers, yoga teachers, and inspirational speakers: Maui's local celebrities. Wake up with an omelet stuffed with portobello mushroom and goat cheese ($19), accompanied by organic chai or a spicy Bloody Mary, depending on your mood. For lunch, hearty burgers ($15–$23) come with Maui Cattle Company beef or grilled fish, and pizzas ($24–$32) are loaded with creative toppings. For dinner, the local fish specials are spot-on, and portions in general are large. The service is friendly but there can be a wait for your meal to arrive. The dessert case contains some treasures, including extra-rich espresso brownies and sweetly tart *likoʻi* (passion fruit) bars.

At the Haiku Cannery Marketplace, 810 Haʻikū Rd., Haʻikū. www.colleensinhaiku. com. *✆* **808/575-9211.** Main courses $12–$22 breakfast; $15–$23 (most $15–$17) lunch; $17–$36 dinner. Breakfast Mon–Fri 7–11am, Sat–Sun until 11:30am; lunch Mon–Fri 11am–3:30pm, Sat–Sun 11:45am–3:30pm; daily dinner 5:30–9:30pm; daily happy hour 3:30–5:30pm.

Nuka ★★ SUSHI   Executive sushi chef Hiro Takanashi smiles from behind the bar as he turns out beautiful specialty rolls loaded with sprouts, pea shoots, avocado, and glistening red tuna. The garden-fresh ingredients served at this 50-seat sushi restaurant reflect its rural Haʻikū address, but its stylish decor suggests somewhere more cosmopolitan. Start with a side of sweet miso eggplant ($11) or edamame in truffle oil ($13). Then proceed to the sushi menu for excellent nigiri, sashimi, and rolls. Not up for sushi? The wonderful Nuka bowls—your choice of protein piled atop fresh herbs, crushed peanuts, sesame lime dressing, rice, and veggies ($21–$26)—are deeply nourishing. *Tip:* Nuka doesn't take reservations; plan to eat early (before 6pm) or late (after 7:30pm) to avoid crowds.

780 Haʻikū Rd., Haʻikū. www.nukamaui.com. *✆* **808/575-2939.** Main courses $12–$26 lunch, $8–$16 rolls; $21–$26 dinner, $8–$23 rolls. Mon–Fri lunch 10:30am–2:30pm; daily dinner 4:30–9:30pm.

ON THE ROAD TO HĀNA

Before your drive really gets going, stop at **Kūʻau Store** ★, 701 Hāna Hwy. (*✆* **808/579-8844**), for breakfast or lunch to go. The handsome convenience store and deli (items $5–$12) offers gourmet breakfast paninis, smoothies, shoyu chicken plate lunches, pulled pork sandwiches, quinoa salads, and four types of poke. For easier entrance and exit, park on the side street under the bright mural featuring surfers, sharks, and owls. It's open daily from 7am to 7pm.

Expensive

Mama's Fish House ★★★ SEAFOOD   There's a good reason why reservations are often fully booked 6 months ahead at this idyllic spot overlooking Kū'au Cove: It's a Pacific island fantasy come to life. After leaving your car at the valet, you descend into a palm-lined landscape and stroll to the restaurant, where smiling servers wear Polynesian prints and flowers behind their ears. The dining room features curved *lauhala*-lined ceilings, lavish arrangements of tropical flowers, and wide-open windows letting in the ocean breeze. Start your repast with silken ahi *poisson cru* or the savory macadamia nut crab cakes. The menu lists the names of the anglers who reeled in the day's catch and where they found it. As a finale, the Tahitian Pearl dessert is almost too stunning to eat: a shiny chocolate ganache sphere filled with *liliko'i* crème, set in an edible pastry clamshell. Everything is perfect, from the refreshing, umbrella-topped cocktails to the almond-scented hand towels passed out before dessert and squares of creamy coconut haupia delivered with your check.

799 Poho Place, just off the Hāna Hwy., Kū'au. www.mamasfishhouse.com. ✆ **808/ 579-8488.** Reservations strongly recommended 3–6 months ahead. Main courses $22–$95. Daily 11am–8:30pm (last seating).

HĀNA

This is an area renowned for just one resort and many food trucks; the latter come and go with such varying hours that, for the most part, we'll just recommend that you ask your hosts for their favorite or spy the one with the longest line and go for it. Many close before dinner, though, so plan ahead. One other informal dining outlet is the **Bamboo Hale** ★ at the Hāna Farms food stand (see "Groceries & Edible Souvenirs," p. 418), which serves pizzas and salads ($14–$19) Sunday through Thursday 10:30am to 4:30pm and Friday through Sunday 10:30am to 8pm.

Mama's Fish House.

GROCERIES & edible souvenirs

Consider the following shops, markets, and stands to offset some of your culinary splurges—or to stock up on tasty souvenirs to bring back home:

Immediately outside Kahului Airport, the monolith of **Costco,** 540 Haleakalā Hwy. (www.costco.com; (C) **808/877-52451**), offers members numerous local items—including macadamia nuts, Kona coffee, and Maui pineapple. (The discount gas makes this a worthy stop at the end of your vacation.)

You can stock up on quality snacks (at steep prices) for your hotel room at **Whole Foods Market** in the Maui Mall, 70 E. Ka'ahumanu Ave., Kahului (www.wholefoodsmarket.com/stores/maui; (C) **808/872-3310**). The meat selection is superior, and they have Bubbies mochi ice cream (multiple flavors) in bulk. Around the corner, **Down to Earth,** 305 Dairy Rd., Kahului (www.downtoearth.org; (C) **808/877-2661**), serves vegetarian deli items and an assortment of natural foods.

Natural food lovers should seek out **Mana Foods ★★★**, 49 Baldwin Ave., Pā'ia (www.manafoodsmaui.com; (C) **808/579-8078**). The island's best health-food store hides behind an unimposing dark-green facade in the center of the North Shore town. Parking can be a nuisance, but the compact store has a well-priced natural-foods selection and divine tropical fruits, while the deli turns out fresh-made sushi, soups, salads, hot entrees, and raw desserts.

On Saturday, visit the **Maui Swap Meet** (p. 420) or the **Upcountry Farmers Market ★★★** (www.upcountryfarmersmarket.com) from 7 to 11am in the Kulamalu Town Center parking lot in Pukalani (near Longs Drugs). You'll find local honey, fresh-shucked coconuts, pickled veggies, and heaps of bright, Maui-grown produce, plus ready-to-eat foods like açai bowls, vegan wraps, and plate lunches.

On the road to Hāna, you'll pass many tempting fruit stands. The best of the bunch is **Hāna Farms ★★**, 2190 Hāna Hwy. (www.hanafarmsonline.com; (C) **808/248-7371**), a series of thatched *hale* (huts) just outside of Hāna town that overflow with every variety of tropical fruit, Maui-grown coffee, and fresh-squeezed juices and ginger sodas that are just the ticket if the drive has made you queasy. Stock up on coconut candy, hot sauce, jam, and banana butter to slather on top of your choice of six banana breads. Everything is grown nearby. Pizza, salads, and farm sodas are available for a sit-down meal in the Bamboo Hale Sunday to Thursday 10:30am to 4:30pm and Friday, and Saturday to Sunday 10:30am to 8pm.

Maui Coffee Roasters, 444 Hāna Hwy., Kahului (www.mauicoffeeroasters.com; (C) **808/877-2877**), stocks a huge assortment of Hawaiian grown coffees, conveniently located near the airport and cruise terminal. You can also sip a fresh-brewed cup and nosh on a sandwich in the store cafe, open Monday to Friday 7am to 6pm and Saturday 7am to 5pm.

For a taste of plantation-era cuisine, head to **Takamiya Market,** 359 N. Market St., Wailuku (www.takamiyamarket.com; (C) **808/244-3404**). Its unpretentious home-cooked dishes include shoyu chicken, fried squid, kalua pork, Chinese noodles, *pohole* (fiddlehead ferns), plus Western comfort foods such as cornbread and potato salad. The fish counter has fresh sashimi, poke, and *limu* (seaweed). It's great for early birds, too, open Monday to Saturday 5am to 6:30pm.

At the **Hāna-Maui Resort ★★★** (p. 392) the fine-dining restaurant and lounge with oceanview lanai is still evolving under Hyatt management, which unimaginatively has renamed it **the Restaurant.** Call ahead (*℡* **808/400-1234**) for current offerings, limited at press time to breakfast daily 7 to 10am ($16–$26). The resort's **Hāna Dry Goods Store,** open daily 8am to 3pm, carries grab-and-go sandwiches and salads.

Moderate

Hāna Ranch Restaurant ★★ AMERICAN   Owned by the Hāna-Maui Resort, but just across the street, this is a casual, family-friendly spot highlighting local produce and palates, with a nod to West Coast tastes. Seared, fresh island-caught fish is available in a brioche sandwich with lemon caper aioli ($25) or in a fragrant yellow coconut cream curry loaded with veggies ($42). For starters, try the avocado hummus ($21) topped with garlic chili oil and served with sweet potato chips and grilled pita.

2 Mill St. (off Hāna Hwy.), Hāna. www.hyatt.com/en-US/hotel/hawaii/hana-maui-resort/oggal. *℡* **808/270-5280.** Main courses $24–$52 (most $24–$33). Daily 11am–9pm.

Inexpensive

Huli Huli Chicken at Koki ★ PLATE LUNCH/BBQ   This roadside shack just past Koki Beach might be the best place to eat in Hāna—but it's not really a restaurant and we can't vouch that it will be open when you arrive. Grilled over kiawe (mesquite), the chicken often runs out before the end of the day. *Huli* means "turn" as in, turn over the flame; huli huli is mouthwatering Hawaiian barbecue. Place your order for chicken, pork, or ribs, served plate-lunch style. Then, park yourself at the picnic table facing little ʻĀlau Island and count your blessings.

Just past Koki Beach Park, 175 Haneoʻo Rd., Hāna. Plate lunches $18–$23 (cash only). Mon–Fri 10am–5pm and Sat–Sun from 11am.

MAUI SHOPPING

Maui's best shopping is found in the small, independent boutiques and galleries scattered around the island—particularly in Makawao and Pāʻia. (If you're in the market for a bikini, there's no better spot than the intersection of Baldwin Ave. and Hāna Hwy. on Maui's North Shore.) The two upscale resort shopping malls, the **Shops at Wailea** in South Maui and **Whalers Village** in Kāʻanapali, have everything from Louis Vuitton to Sunglass Hut, plus a handful of local designers. If you're looking for that perfect souvenir, consider visiting one of Maui's farms (or farmers markets), most of which offer fantastic value-added products. Take home Kāʻanapali coffee, Kula lavender spice rub, Ocean Vodka (p. 332), Maui Gold pineapple, and other tasty treats that can be shipped worldwide.

Note: Most stores are open Monday to Saturday 10am to 6pm, with shorter hours on Sunday, if they're not closed altogether. Hours can change frequently, so call ahead to confirm.

Central Maui

KAHULUI

Kahului's shopping is concentrated in two malls. The recently updated **Maui Mall Village,** 70 E. Ka'ahumanu Ave. (www.mauimallvillage.com; ℰ 808/877-8952), is home to **Whole Foods Market, Longs Drugs, TJ Maxx,** and local retailers such as surf shop **HIC—Hawaiian Island Creations, Maui Candy Company,** Maui-themed T-shirt and accessories boutique **Makali'i,** and **Tasaka Guri-Guri,** the decades-old purveyor of inimitable icy treats that are neither ice cream nor shave ice, but something in between, plus a 12-screen movie megaplex that features mainly current releases and a **Fun Factory** arcade. **Queen Ka'ahumanu Center,** 275 Kaahumanu Ave. (www.queenkaahumanucenter.com; ℰ 808/877-3369), a 7-minute drive from the Kahului Airport, offers two levels of shops, restaurants, and theaters. It covers the bases, from Maui-designed arts and crafts to **Macy's;** grab a bite at the food court and, by reservation, do yoga or just hang with the adoptable felines at **Cat Café Maui** (https://catcafe maui.com; $20 admission includes coffee and tea), which also has a cute gift shop. The **Maui Friends of the Library** (www.mfol.org; ℰ 808/877-2509) runs a new and used bookstore that is an excellent source for Hawaii reading material; it also has a location in Pu'unēnē and at the South Maui Center in Kīhei. Opened in 1972, **Camellia Seed Shop** (ℰ 808/877-5714) sells "crackseed," sweet-and-sour treats made from pickled plum seeds that are local favorites, as well as other nostalgic candy and boba tea.

Maui Swap Meet ★ For just 75¢, shoppers 13 and older are granted admission to a colorful maze of booths and tables occupying the Maui Community College's parking lot every Saturday from 7am to 1pm. About 200 vendors come from across the island to lay out their treasures: fresh fruits and vegetables from Kula and Ke'anae, orchids, jewelry, ceramics, clothing, household items, homemade jams, hot food, and baked goods. It's fun to stroll around and "talk story" with the farmers, artists, and crafters. At Maui Community College at Kahului Beach Rd. and Wahinepi'o Ave. (access via Wahinepi'o Ave.). www.facebook.com/p/maui-swap-meet-100057250608664. ℰ 808/244-3100.

WAILUKU

Wailuku's vintage architecture, antiques shops, and mom-and-pop eateries imbue the town—rather shabby in comparison with resort areas—with authentic charm. Most stores are closed on Sunday and have shorter weekday hours than elsewhere on the island.

Bird of Paradise Unique Antiques ★ Come here for old Matson liner menus, vintage aloha shirts, silk kimonos, and anything nostalgic that happens to be Hawaiian. Owner Joe Myhand collects everything from 1940s rattan furniture to Depression-era glass and lilting Hawaiian music on vinyl. 56 N. Market St. ℰ 808/242-7699.

Hā Wahine ★★ For out-of-the-ordinary, handmade aloha wear as flattering, flowy tops and dresses in bold, modern Hawaiian prints, stop by this small downtown boutique. 52 N. Market St. ℂ **808/344-1642.**

Hale Hōʻikeʻike (Bailey House Museum) ★ The small gift shop at the entrance of this excellent museum (hours currently limited to Mon–Fri 10am–2pm) offers a trove of authoritative Hawaiiana, from hand-sewn feather hatbands to traditional Hawaiian games, music, and limited-edition books. Make sure to stroll through the gracious gardens and view Edward Bailey's paintings of early Maui. 2375-A Main St. www.mauimuseum. org. ℂ **808/244-3326.**

Native Intelligence ★★★ This wonderful shop feels like a museum or gallery—only you can take the marvelous artifacts home with you. The store's owners are committed to supporting Native Hawaiian artisans, who come here both to shop and stock the shelves with artwork of the highest craftsmanship. Browse the truly Hawaiian keepsakes and gifts: locally designed Kealopiko clothing silkscreened with Hawaiian proverbs, *kukui* nut spinning tops, soaps scented with native herbs, and *lei o manu*—fierce war clubs fringed with shark teeth. You can also buy bags of fresh poi and precious leis made of feathers, shells, or fragrant flowers. 1980 Market St., #2. www.native-intel.com. ℂ **808/249-2421.**

West Maui

LAHAINA

After the loss of so many prized art galleries, boutiques, and surf shops in the August 2023 fire, the reopening in March 2024 of **Lahaina Cannery Mall,** 1221 Honoapiʻilani Hwy. (www.lahainacannerymall.com; ℂ **808/ 661-5304**), was very welcome news. Formerly a pineapple cannery, the handsomely renovated shopping center not only hosts necessities such as a **Safeway** grocery store, **Longs Drugs,** and **ABC** convenience and souvenir store, but also island-based boutiques such as **Maui Toy Works** (www.mauitoyworks.com; ℂ **808/661-4766**); **Serendipity Maui** (www. facebook.com/SerendipityMaui; ℂ **808/661-7621**), known for sarongs, dyed silk ponchos, and other tropical wear; and jeweler **Maui Island Creations** (www.mauislandcreations.com; ℂ **808/661-3824**). Free hula shows take place Sunday at 1pm in the recently renovated courtyard and the **Lahaina Art Society** presents an art show every Saturday and Sunday from 9am to 4pm on the lawn by the parking lot.

KĀʻANAPALI

Honolua Surf ★ Gear up for a day on the water at this local franchise named for one of Maui's best surf breaks. You'll find cute beach cover-ups, rash guards, bikinis and surf trunks, sweatshirts, sandals, hats, and even duffle bags to carry it all. www.honoluasurf.com. Kāʻanapali: at Whalers Village, 2345 Kāʻanapali Pkwy. ℂ **808/661-1778.** Kīhei: 2411 S. Kīhei Rd. ℂ **808/874-0999.**

Wailea: at Shops of Wailea: 3750 Wailea Alanui. ☏ **808/891-8229.** Pā'ia: 115 Hāna Hwy. ☏ **808/579-9593.**

Mahina ★★ For moderately priced, carefree, and casual women's fashion, head to this popular boutique with locations throughout Hawai'i. You can dress up one of the billowy or body-hugging dresses with thin gold bangles, gold necklaces with tiny pineapple pendants, and other island-chic accessories. www.shopmahina.com. Kā'anapali: at Whalers Village, 2345 Kā'anapali Pkwy. ☏ **808/793-2231.** Kīhei: at Kihei Kalama Village, 1913 S. Kīhei Rd. ☏ **808/879-3453.** Wailea: at Shops at Wailea, 3750 Wailea Alanui Dr. ☏ **808/868-4717.** Pā'ia: 23 Baldwin Ave. ☏ **808/579-9131.**

Whalers Village ★★ Right on Kā'anapali Beach, this landmark mall offers everything from **Louis Vuitton** to **Tommy Bahama,** with a few island designers in the mix. Find classy aloha wear at **Tori Richard** (www.toririchard.com; ☏ **808/667-7762**) and men's and women's batik clothing at **Blue Ginger** (www.blueginger.com; ☏ **808/667-5793**); downstairs is **Blue Ginger Kids** (☏ **808/661-1666**). The **Totally Hawaiian Gift Gallery** (www.totallyhawaiian.com; ☏ **808/667-4070**) carries N'iihau shell jewelry, Norfolk pine bowls, and Hawaiian quilt kits. Many stores remain open until 9pm. Check the website's Events page for the current calendar of weekly classes in hula, palm frond weaving, and ukulele, plus a workout at athletic wear boutique **Lululemon** (☏ **808/861-5323**) and a presentation by the **Hawai'i Wildlife Discovery Center** (p. 315). Parking is expensive; be sure to get validation. 2435 Kā'anapali Pkwy. www.whalersvillage.com. ☏ **808/661-4567.**

HONOKŌWAI, KAHANA & NĀPILI

Those driving north of Kā'anapali toward Kapalua will notice the **Honokowai Marketplace,** 3350 Lower Honoapi'ilani Road, only minutes before the Kapalua Airport (www.honokowaimarketplace.com; ☏ **808/667-9216**). It houses restaurants and coffee shops, a shave ice place, snorkel gear rentals, and the flagship **Times Supermarket,** among other stores and service providers.

KAPALUA

Village Galleries ★★ This well-regarded gallery sadly lost its main storefronts in Lahaina, but still displays top regional artists at the two hotels in Kapalua. At the Ritz-Carlton Maui, Kapalua (p. 375), look for Maui-themed paintings and giclées by Tracy Dudley, Betty Hay Freeland, and Suzy Papanikolas, among others, in Ulana restaurant, the Lobby Bar, the spa, and other public areas. Check the gallery's website for available art at Montage Kapalua Bay (p. 374). www.villagegalleriesmaui.com. Kapalua: at the Ritz-Carlton Maui, Kapalua, 1 Ritz-Carlton Dr. ☏ **808/669-6200;** and at Montage Kapalua Bay, 1 Bay Dr. ☏ **808/662-6600.**

South Maui
KĪHEI

Kīhei is one long stretch of strip malls. The busiest are **Azeka Place Shopping Center** and **Azeka Place II** across from each other on South Kīhei Road, brimming with mid-priced restaurants and activity outlets. Maui-based **KaiAloha Supply** (www.kaialohasupply; ✆ **808/727-2007**), which celebrates the ocean and supports its conservation through sporty clothing lines for men and women, lost two storefronts in Lahaina but still has a branch at Kihei Kalama Village, 1945-A S. Kīhei Rd., as well as in Kā'anapali at Whalers Village (p. 419; ✆ **808/868-0315**) and at the Shops at Wailea, below (✆ **808/793-3302**).

WAILEA

Shops at Wailea ★★   This elegant high-end mall features luxury brands (**Prada, Tiffany & Co., Gucci,** and so forth), but some unique gems are hidden amid the complex's 70-odd shops and restaurants. **Martin & MacArthur** (https://martinandmacarthur.com; ✆ **808/891-8844**) sells luminous, curly koa bowls and keepsake boxes—or you could bring home a beautiful handmade Hawaiian musical instrument from **Mele Ukulele** (www.meleukulele.com; ✆ **808/879-6353**). Also see the listings for **Honolua Surf Co., Mahina,** and **Maui Hands** in Kā'anapali for details on their Shops at Wailea outposts. Grocery/deli/souvenir stop **Island Gourmet Markets** offers affordable dining options lunch: everything from pastries to sushi, burgers, sandwiches, and gelato. 3750 Wailea Alanui. www.theshopsatwailea.com. ✆ **808/891-6770**.

Upcountry Maui
MAKAWAO

Makawao has several gorgeous boutiques and galleries to browse, plus a well-curated grocery. **Rodeo General Store,** 3661 Baldwin Ave. (www.rodeogeneralstore.com; ✆ **808/572-1868**), offers ready-made items, dry goods, and a fine deli with poke bar. A superior wine selection is housed in a temperature-controlled cave at the back of the store. Fuel up with stick donuts from one of Maui's oldest and most beloved mom-and-pop shops, **T. Komoda Store & Bakery** (p. 318).

Driftwood ★★   One-stop shopping for a glamorous life: Browse the shelves for slinky crocheted tops, flowy maxi or body-hugging mini dresses, and jaunty fedoras. The Home by Driftwood goods are equally stylish, but if you want to travel light, just cruise the Hawaiian-themed stationery and pearl-accented jewelry 1152 Makawao Ave. www.driftwoodmaui.com. ✆ **808/573-1152**.

Hot Island Glassblowing Studio & Gallery ★★   Watch glass blowers transform molten glass into artwork in this Makawao Courtyard studio. If you didn't witness it happening, you might not believe that the kaleidoscopic vases and charismatic marine animals were truly made out of the fragile, fiery-hot medium. Several artists show their work here; prices range from under $30 for small, pretty plumeria-shaped bowls in jewel tones to over $4,000 for sculptural pieces. In the middle range are luminescent jellyfish floating in glass. 3620 Baldwin Ave. www.hotislandglass.com. © **808/572-4527.**

Hui No'eau Visual Arts Center ★★ This marvelous gallery's gift shop spills into the foyer and sunroom. The Hui is a hub for local art and education and more than 75 inspired artists contribute their work to the shop here. Browse the shelves for whimsical jewelry, paintings, wood block prints, children's toys, and much more. 2841 Baldwin Ave. www.huinoeau.com. © **808/572-6560.**

Maui Hands ★★ This collective of some 300 artists has several consignment shops/galleries around the island, each teeming with hand-crafted treasures by local artisans. You'll find Ni'ihau shell necklaces, vivid paintings of local beaches and tropical flowers, carved koa bowls and rocking chairs, screen-printed textiles, and one-of-a-kind souvenirs for every budget. The artists are on hand and happy to discuss their work. www.mauihands.com. Makawao: 1169 Makawao. © **808/572-2008.** Pā'ia: 84 Hāna Hwy. © **808/579-9245.** Wailea: at the Shops at Wailea, 3750 Wailea Alanui Dr. © **808/667-7997.**

The Mercantile ★★ Every texture in this boutique is sumptuous, from the cashmere sweaters to the tooled leather belts. In addition to upscale men's and women's clothing, you'll find yoga wear, Maui Vera mineral sunscreen and other locally made body products, eye-catching jewelry, and an assortment of French soaps and luxurious linens. 3673 Baldwin Ave. www.instagram.com/the_maui_mercantile. © **808/572-1407.**

Viewpoints Gallery ★★ Tucked into Makawao Courtyard, this small gallery features the museum-quality work of 40 established Maui artists. The front half is dedicated to revolving solo shows and invitational exhibits—always worth a look. The gallery's back half features works by collective artists, including prints and paintings by Maui native Judy Bisgard, the glowing turned-wood bowls and other Norfolk Island pine artworks by Honolulu-born Todd Campbell, vocative watercolor landscapes by Diana Lehr, and the painted flax capes of Pam Peterson, inspired by her Native Hawaiian heritage. 3620 Baldwin Ave. www.viewpointsgallerymaui.com. © **808/572-5979.**

East Maui

PĀ'IA

In addition to these stores, see the listings for **Mahina** and **Honolua Surf** in Ka'anapali and Maui Hands in Makawao, above, for details on their **Pā'ia** branches.

Maui Crafts Guild ★★ On the corner of Hāna Highway and Baldwin Avenue, this artists' collective features distinctive, high-quality arts and crafts. Formally established in 1983, the guild gives a showcase to 30 or so juried artists who must be full-time residents; you can see a different artisan at work each day in this gallery. Look for the intricate woven artwork by Maui native Fiama von Schuetze and Debra Lumpkins' traditional Japanese *gyotaku,* colorful prints made by rubbing tropical fish in ink. 120 Hāna Hwy. www.mauicraftsguild.com. ⓒ **808/579-9697.**

Pearl ★★ This chic housewares shop in Pā'ia can supply everything necessary for beach cottage living: Turkish spa towels, vintage hardware, embroidered cover-ups, and Indonesian furnishings. Stylish shop owner Malia Vandervoort collects treasures from around the globe that match her soulful, simple aesthetic, including supporting fair trade and environmentally sensitive small businesses. 71 Baldwin Ave. www.pearlbutik.com. ⓒ **808/579-8899.**

Wings Hawaii ★ Handmade on Maui's North Shore from sustainable and comfortable materials like organic cotton, bamboo-based fabrics, and recycled vintage clothes, the beautiful and relaxed women's clothing line founded by best friends Samantha Howard and Melody Torres in 2003 has expanded to include men's and children's apparel, plus jewelry and home goods such as blankets and curtains. 100 Hāna Hwy. www.wingshawaii.com. ⓒ **808/579-3110.**

Maui's North Shore Is Bikini Central

Pā'ia's many clothing boutiques are the best place to browse for Maui's sun-kissed beach uniform: the bikini. Head here for everything from Brazilian thongs to full-figured, mix-and-match-your-own suits. The best place to start is in **Maui Girl,** the bright blue boutique at 12 Baldwin Ave. (https://maui-girl.com; ⓒ **808/579-9266).** Founded in 1985 by designer Debbie Kowalski Wilson, who moved to the islands in 1969 after being inspired by the surfing documentary *Endless Summer,* Maui Girl now sells swimsuits and beach apparel for all sizes and shapes, including some one-of-a-kind suits hand sewn by Makawao designer Pam Winans.

HĀNA

Hana Coast Gallery ★★★ Found in the posh **Hāna-Maui Resort** (p. 392), this critically acclaimed, 3,000-square-foot gallery is a cultural experience to savor. You won't find pandering sunsets or jumping dolphins here. Known for its quality curatorship and commitment to Hawaiian culture, this art haven is almost entirely devoted to Hawaiian artists, including *plein air* painter Michael Clements, the virtuoso weavers Maui Feather Artists, and woodworker Kapahikaua Haskell. If you're considering buying a koa wood bowl or piece of furniture, look here first; you'd be hard-pressed to find a better selection under one roof. At Hāna-Maui Resort. www.hanacoast.com. ⓒ **808/248-8636.**

Hasegawa General Store ★ This humble, family-run mercantile has been serving the Hāna community since 1910 with just about anything it might need. (Check out the assortment of machetes above the office window.) Harkening back to the days when stores like these were islanders' sole shopping outlet, the aisles are packed with books and music, fishing poles, Hāna-grown coffee, diapers, fridge magnets, garden tools, fresh vegetables, dry goods, and ice cream. Boast you were here with a Hasegawa T-shirt or baseball cap. Open daily 7am to 6pm, this is Hāna's equivalent of a 24-hour convenience store. 5165 Hāna Hwy. https://hasegawastore.com. ✆ **808/248-8231.**

MAUI NIGHTLIFE

Maui tends to turn out the lights by 10pm, but you'll find a few later diversions listed below. Many lobby lounges in the major hotels offer Hawaiian music, soft jazz, or hula shows beginning at sunset.

West Maui

Every Wednesday and Saturday night, the Napili Kai Beach Resort's indoor amphitheater showcases slack key guitar masters in the **Masters of Hawaiian Slack Key Guitar Series** ★★★ (www.slackkeyshow.com; ✆ **888/669-3858**). The intimate shows present a side of Hawai'i that few visitors get to see. Host George Kahumoku, Jr., introduces a different slack key master every week. Not only is there incredible Hawaiian music and singing, but George and his guest also "talk story" about old Hawai'i, music, and local culture. Not to be missed. The price is $60 for reserved seating in first four rows, $40 for open seating behind that. Doors open at 6pm, the show starts at 6:30pm.

Other venues for music in West Maui include:

- **Hula Grill,** on the beachfront side of Whalers Village, Kā'anapali (www.hulagrillkaanapali.com; ✆ **808/667-6636**), has live Hawaiian music daily from 5:30 to 8pm, accompanied by hula 6:30 to 7:30pm.

- **Leilani's on the Beach** (www.leilanis.com; ✆ **808/661-4495**), across the way from Hula Grill, features live Hawaiian and pop music daily from 3 to 5pm and 6 to 8pm.

South Maui

Kīhei and Wailea in South Maui also feature music in a variety of locations:

- **Kahale's,** 36 Keala Place, Kīhei (www.kahales.com; ✆ **808/215-9939**), is a self-proclaimed dive bar with live music Tuesday at 7:30pm.

- **Life's a Beach,** 1913 S. Kīhei Rd., Kīhei (www.mauibars.com; ✆ **808/891-8010**), typically has karaoke Saturday through Thursday 7pm to midnight. See www.facebook.com/hauikihei808 for updates.

luau, **MAUI-STYLE**

Most of the larger hotels in Maui's major resorts offer luaus on a regular basis. You'll pay anywhere from $120 to $240 to attend, but don't expect it to be a homegrown affair prepared in the traditional Hawaiian way. There are, however, commercial luaus that capture the romance and spirit of the luau (*lū'au*, in Hawaiian) with quality food and entertainment.

Maui's best and most inspiring choice is the **Old Lāhainā Lū'au ★★★** (www.oldlahainaluau.com; ✆ **808/667-1998**), located at the edge of the off-limits fire zone, ocean-side of the Lahaina Cannery, at 1251 Front St. Its owners made the decision to reopen in March 2024, in consultation with employees, as a way to support local nonprofits focused on rebuilding Lahaina. Despite all the challenges its staff still face, the luau has kept its high standards in offering locally sourced, chef-prepared food and authentic hula in a lovely enclave only a few feet from the waves.

Seating is private for your group up to 8 people. You can sit on cushions at low tables closest to the stage for those who wish to dine much as the traditional Hawaiians did, or at regular tables and chairs, all with a good view. Servers bring dinner and top-shelf cocktails and other beverages to your seat—no queuing in a long line. Starters included Maui breadfruit (*'ulu*) hummus, taro and sweet potato chips, haupia (coconut pudding), and *kūlolo*, a taro-coconut fudgy treat, while the mains and sides come in a traditional Hawaiian course (two kinds of roasted pork, ahi poke, *lomi* salmon, fiddlehead fern salad, pounded taro), followed by gourmet preparations of fresh fish, steak, chicken, and vegetables. For dessert, a pineapple sponge cake topped with a chocolate petroglyph appears with coffee and tea. The cost is $230 for adults, $140 for children ages 3 to 12, taxes and gratuity included.

○ **Mulligan's on the Blue,** 100 Kaukahi St., Wailea (www.mulligans ontheblue.com; ✆ **808/874-1131**), offers live music (rock, country, soul) Wednesday to Sunday, with varying start times. **Wailea Nights Luau** (www.waileanightsluau.com; ✆ **808/874-1234**) takes over Tuesday at 5pm with dinner and a show ($80–$220).

○ **South Shore Tiki Lounge,** 1913 S. Kīhei Rd., Kīhei (https://south shoretiki.com; ✆ **808/874-6444**), has live music nightly from 4 to 6pm, with additional shows some nights 8:30 to 10:30pm, and DJs with dancing Thursday through Saturday from 9:30pm to midnight.

Central Maui & Upcountry

The island's most prestigious entertainment venue is the $32-million **Maui Arts & Cultural Center** in Kahului (www.mauiarts.org; ✆ **808/ 242-7469**), which includes a visual arts gallery, outdoor amphitheater, a 300-seat theater for experimental performances, and a 1,200-seat main theater. Check the website for schedules and buy your tickets in advance.

MOLOKA'I

by Jeanne Cooper

"Don't try to change Moloka'i. Let Moloka'i change you." That's the mantra on the least developed of the major Hawaiian Islands. No luxury hotels, no stoplights, and "no rush" are points of pride for some 7,000 residents, nearly half of whom are of Native Hawaiian descent. The island is famously apprehensive about mass tourism. So, it was a relief for some that when tourism resumed in earnest in 2021 after the COVID-19 pandemic, many potential visitors were dissuaded by newly limited airline access and the ongoing closure of Kalaupapa National Historical Park and its famed cliffside trail. Still, for spiritual pilgrims and other low-key travelers willing to tread lightly and rightly, Moloka'i may enchant with its untrammeled beauty and unhurried ways.

Known as "the child of the moon" in Native Hawaiian lore, Moloka'i remains a place apart, luminous yet largely inaccessible to the casual visitor. Tourism, and modern conveniences in general, have only a small footprint here. Although the island is just 38 miles long by 10 miles wide, it takes time to see what it has to offer. As the sign at the airport reads: ALOHA, SLOW DOWN, THIS IS MOLOKAI.

Patience and planning reward travelers with a compass of superlatives. The world's tallest sea cliffs stand on the North Shore; on the South Shore, historic fishponds line the state's longest fringing reef. The island's most ancient settlement sits within gorgeous Hālawa Valley on the East End, while the West End offers one of the most impressive stretches of golden sand in Hawai'i, the more than 2-mile-long (and often empty) Pāpōhaku.

The percentage of people of Native Hawaiian descent is also higher on Moloka'i than on the other major islands. Many have maintained or revived Hawaiian traditions such as growing taro, managing fishponds, and staging games for Makahiki, the winter festival. "Sustainability" isn't a buzzword here but a way of life, and one that eyes modern innovations with caution—many islanders are fiercely opposed to growth.

In front of a house along the main road just outside of Kaunakakai, home to nearly half of the island's population, a hand-painted sign that once read "Visit, spend, go home" now has the words "visit" and "spend" crossed out. I once spotted a sign on the East End saying, "Aloha is not an invitation to move here." These are not personal attacks so much as desperate pleas from people hoping to avoid the loss of public access, affordable

FACING PAGE: **The vibrant plumeria flowers of Moloka'i.**

The Moloka'i coastline.

housing, and traditional lifestyles that they've seen occur on more populated and developed islands in Hawai'i. Stay in licensed vacation rental condos or the lone hotel, sample its small restaurants and shops, enjoy its public parks and beaches (rather than trespassing), and you'll generally be welcomed, particularly if you take the time to smile and "talk story" (chat) with all you meet.

> ### Moloka'i or Molokai?
>
> Many longtime residents, including some Native Hawaiians, prefer to write and say "Molokai" (rhymes with "bolo tie") over the standard Moloka'i ("mow-low-kah-ee"), believing that the former name refers to the turning (*molo*) waters (*kai*) surrounding the island. However, traditional expressions such as *Moloka'i nui a Hina* ("Great Moloka'i, child of the moon goddess Hina") justify the latter pronunciation.

Residents and visitors alike take inspiration from the stories of saints Damien and Marianne, and all others who cared for the suffering exiles of Kalaupapa. Once a natural prison for those diagnosed with leprosy, the remote North Shore peninsula is now a national historical park with very limited access but much to teach the few who may visit—much like Moloka'i itself.

ESSENTIALS
Arriving

BY PLANE   Often just called Moloka'i Airport, **Ho'olehua** (airport code: MKK) is about 7½ miles from the center of Kaunakakai town. *Note:* Make sure to book your flight for daylight hours and get a window seat. The views of Moloka'i from above are outstanding, no matter which way you approach the island.

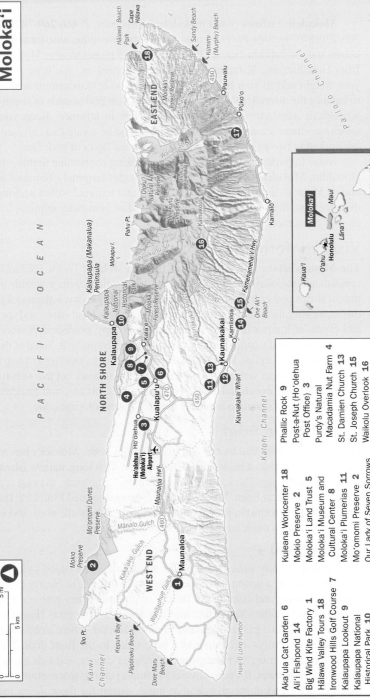

Moloka'i

PACIFIC OCEAN

NORTH SHORE

WEST END

EAST END

Kalaupapa (Makanalua) Peninsula

Kalaupapa National Historical Park

Ho'olehua

Ho'olehua (Moloka'i) Airport

Kualapu'u

Kaunakakai

Kaunakakai Wharf

Maunaloa

Kepuhi Bay

Papohaku Beach

Dixie Maru Beach

Kamiloloa

Kamalō

One Ali'i Beach

Pūko'o

Pauwalu

Hālawa Beach Park

Cape Hālawa

Sandy Beach

Kumimi (Murphy) Beach

Moloka'i Forest Reserve

'Oloku'i Natural Area Reserve

Pelekunu Preserve

Pahu Pt.

Mōkapu I.

Mo'omomi Dunes Preserve

Mokio Preserve

Mānalo Gulch

Kalae

'Īlio Pt.

Hale O Lono Harbor

Maunaloa Hwy

Kamehameha V Hwy

Kalohi Channel

Kaiwi Channel

Pailolo Channel

Waialua Str.

Hālawa Str.

Waikolu Str.

Wailau Str.

Kamakou

Waikolu Gulch

Kaunakakai Gulch

Oloku'i

Honomuni Gulch

Pelekunu Str.

Kawela Gulch

Waikaluhlue Gulch

Manawainui Gulch

Kakahaiʻa Gulch

Inset map: Hawaiʻi — Kauaʻi, Oʻahu, Honolulu ★, Moloka'i, Lānaʻi, Maui, Hawaiʻi

0 — 100 mi / 0 — 100 km

0 — 5 mi / 0 — 5 km

Aka'ula Cat Garden **6**
Ali'i Fishpond **14**
Big Wind Kite Factory **1**
Hālawa Valley Tours **18**
Ironwood Hills Golf Course **7**
Kalaupapa Lookout **9**
Kalaupapa National Historical Park **10**
Kamakou Preserve **16**
Kapuāiwa Coconut Grove **12**

Kuleana Workcenter **18**
Mokio Preserve **2**
Moloka'i Land Trust **5**
Moloka'i Museum and Cultural Center **8**
Moloka'i Plumerias **11**
Mo'omomi Preserve **2**
Our Lady of Seven Sorrows Church **17**
Pāiāʻau State Park **9**

Phallic Rock **9**
Post-a-Nut (Ho'olehua Post Office) **3**
Purdy's Natural Macadamia Nut Farm **4**
St. Damien Church **13**
St. Joseph Church **15**
Waikolu Overlook **16**

Mokulele Airlines (www.mokuleleairlines.com; ☏ **866/260-7070** or 808/270-8767 outside the U.S.) uses mostly single-engine, nine-passenger planes and several twin-engine, 30 to 36 passenger planes to serve Moloka'i from Honolulu and Kahului, Maui. *Note:* At check-in, you'll be asked your weight and all your bags will be weighed, to help determine seating to balance the aircraft; those who weigh more than 350 pounds or require wheelchair assistance must contact the airline in advance. Keep your shoes on—there are no security screenings—and be aware that carry-ons are limited to two small items that can fit on your lap or at your feet.

Note: Important to consider if you're booking connecting flights—in Honolulu, Mokulele operates from the commuter terminal (Terminal 3) and on Maui, it departs from the small commuter terminal within walking distance from the main Kahului airport. The Maui commuter terminal has its own convenient parking lot.

Visitor Information

The **Maui Visitors and Convention Bureau website** (www.gohawaii. com/islands/molokai) includes Moloka'i information, with a wealth of practical tips and cultural insights. *Molokai Dispatch* (www.themolokai dispatch.com), the island's weekly newspaper, covers local issues and special events of interest to visitors; pick up a free copy, published Wednesdays, for the island's current dining specials and entertainment. Some of the practical information on **VisitMolokai.com** (slogan: EVERYTHING ABOUT MOLOKAI, BY FOLKS WHO LIVE ON MOLOKAI) is outdated, but the website still has a useful events calendar, sightseeing tips, photos, and insights. These sources all maintain regularly updated Facebook pages, too.

The Island in Brief

Only 38 miles from end to end and just 10 miles wide, Moloka'i has an east side, a west side, a back side, and a top side. This long, narrow island is like yin and yang: The south and west are dry scrublands; the east is a lush, green, tropical Eden. Three volcanic eruptions formed Moloka'i; the last produced a peninsula jutting out of the steep cliffs of the north shore, like a punctuation mark on the island's geological story.

KAUNAKAKAI ★

This central, usually sunny town on the south side is the island's closest approximation to a downtown, albeit one out of the 1920s. Nearly every restaurant, store, and community facility on the island lies within a few blocks of one another. You'll find a public library with a great Hawaiian history section, two gas stations, and Friendly Market, where aloha spirit is required for entry—according to a note taped to the front door. The state's longest pier serves fishing boats, outrigger canoes, and kids enjoying a dip in the ocean. It's typically easy to find a parking space among the pickup trucks, and absolutely dead at night, except for those doing the after-hours **"hot bread run"** ★★ at Kanemitsu Bakery.

CENTRAL UPLANDS & NORTH SHORE ★★

Upland from Kaunakakai, Hawaiian homesteaders in **Hoʻolehua** tend small plots near the state's largest producer of organic papaya and the main airport. In the nearby plantation town of **Kualapuʻu,** rows of coffee trees grow near one of the island's best restaurants and a small cat sanctuary.

The forest grows denser and the air cooler as Kalaʻe Highway (Hwy. 470) passes the island's lone golf course and a small cultural museum, then ends at **Pālāʻau State Park ★★,** known for its phallic rock and dramatic overlook of **Kalaupapa National Historical Park ★★★,** which lies some 1,700 feet below and is currently off-limits to visitors. Generations of people diagnosed with leprosy (now called Hansen's disease) were exiled to lonely settlements on the isolated North Shore peninsula, guarded by the world's tallest sea cliffs, 3,600 to 3,900 feet.

The plantation-era village of **Maunaloa** at the end of the Maunaloa Highway (Hwy. 460) has barely held on with a general store, gift shop, post office, and modest cottages, while the decaying buildings of Kaluakoi Hotel (closed in 2001), above **Kepuhi Beach ★★,** look like a set from *Lost.* Summer is the best time to explore the shoreline here, although the crash of winter waves provides a convenient sleep aid for inhabitants of the three still-open condo developments on the overgrown **Kaluakoi** resort. Look out for axis deer when driving here at night; wild turkeys rule the roost by day.

THE EAST END ★★★

From Kaunakakai, the two-lane King Kamehameha V Highway (Hwy. 450) heads 27 miles east past coastal fishponds and sculpted hillsides to **Hālawa Valley ★★★.** This stunning, culturally significant enclave is only accessible by guided tour, though anyone may drive to the road's end and explore **Hālawa Beach Park ★★.** Before the road makes its final dip to

Looking over the Hālawa Valley.

the valley, pull over for a distant view of 500-foot **Hīpuapua Falls** and 250-foot, two-tiered **Moʻoula Falls** (also known as Moaʻula Falls). Before you arrive, though, you'll pass pocket beaches, a mom-and-pop grocery/take-out counter, two churches built by Saint Damien, and picturesque **Puʻu O Hōkū,** a working cattle ranch and biodynamic farm that also serves as a reserve for nēnē, the endangered state bird. Stop here for local honey and fresh produce. This is the rainier half of the island, with more frequent showers January through March, but be careful: The sun still blazes here, too.

GETTING AROUND

Getting around Moloka'i isn't easy without a rental car, which you should reserve as early as possible. During special events and holiday weekends (see "When to Go" in chapter 3), rental agencies run out of vehicles. Stay alert to invasive axis deer darting onto the highway, especially at night. *Note:* **Molokai Outdoors** (www.molokaioutdoors.com; ✆ **808/633-8700**), based at **Hotel Moloka'i** (www.hotelmolokai.com; ✆ **808/553-5347**), can arrange shuttles from the airport to the hotel and from the hotel to downtown Kaunakakai.

BY CAR   The international chain **Alamo Rent a Car** (www.alamo.com; ✆ **888/826-6893**) has both an office and cars at the airport in Ho'olehua. **Molokai Car Rental** (www.molokaicars.com), based at **All Things Molokai Travel,** 61 Ala Malama Ave. (Kaunakakai; ✆ **619/713-6198** or 808/553-3299), has rates starting at $420 a week, but you'll need to hire a taxi from the airport (see below) to pick up your vehicle. If you're renting for a week or longer, consider reserving a lightly used but perfectly adequate car, van, or SUV from **Mobettah Car Rentals** (✆ **808/308-9566**). The company will drop vehicles at the airport, or you can pick up your rental at its office at Mahana Gardens, 2 miles west on the Maunaloa Highway; note that driving on long unpaved roads such as those accessing Moloka'i Forest Preserve or Mo'omomi Dunes is not allowed. **Molokai Outdoors** (www.molokaioutdoors.com; ✆ **808/633-8700**) can also arrange reasonable car and Jeep rentals with advance notice, with surcharges for off-road use. For more budget-friendly car-rental options, contact Phillip Kikukawa of **Moloka'i Bicycles** (www.mauimolokai bicycle.com; ✆ **808/747-3760**).

BY TAXI   Per county law, taxis charge $3 a mile plus a "drop charge" of $3.50, or about $32 from the airport to the Hotel Moloka'i in Kaunakakai and $42 to a West End condo. Try to arrange rides a day or two in advance, either with the friendly folks at **Hele Mai Taxi** (www.molokaitaxi.com; ✆ **808/336-0967**), **Molokai Club** (✆ **808/284-6971**), or **Midnight Taxi** (✆ **808/658-1410**).

[FastFACTS] MOLOKA'I

Note: All addresses are in Kaunakakai unless noted.

ATMs/Banks   Both **Bank of Hawai'i,** 20B Ala Malama Ave. (www.boh. com; ✆ **808/553-3273**), and **American Savings Bank,** 40 Ala Malama St. #101 (www.asbhawaii.com;

✆ **808/627-6900**), have 24-hour ATMs.

Cellphones   The island has only a few cellphone towers; Verizon clients seem to have the strongest signal, but overall the best reception is in Kaunakakai, so plan phone use accordingly.

Dentists/Doctors   The **Moloka'i Community Health Center,** 30 Oki Place (www.molokaichc.org; ✆ **808/553-5038** for medical care, **808/553-4511** for dental care), provides dental services Monday through Thursday from 7am to noon and 1 to 6pm, and medical services Monday through Friday from 7am to noon and 1 to 5pm.

Emergencies   Call 𝐶 **911** in life-threatening situations. Otherwise, contact the **police** at 𝐶 **808/553-5355** or the **fire department** at 𝐶 **808/553-5601.**

Hospital   **Moloka'i General Hospital,** 280 Home Olu Place (www.queens.org/locations/hospitals/Molokai; 𝐶 **808/553-5331**), has 15 beds, a 24-hour emergency room open daily, and an outpatient clinic open Monday to Friday 7am to 5:30pm.

Internet Access   **Moloka'i Public Library,** 15 Ala Malama Ave. (www.librarieshawaii.org; 𝐶 **808/553-1765**), offers free Wi-Fi and computers by reservation. **Moloka'i General Hospital** also offers free Wi-Fi in public areas, including its cafeteria.

Pharmacy   The family-run **Molokai Drugs,** 28 Kamoi St. (www.facebook.com/molokaidrugs; 𝐶 **808/553-5790**), carries everything from greeting cards to hospital-grade medical equipment and is open Monday to Friday 8:45am to 5:45pm, and Saturday until 2pm.

Post Office   The **central office** at 120 Ala Malama Ave. is open Monday to Friday 9am to 3:30pm and Saturday until 11am. The **Ho'olehua branch,** just off Farrington Avenue (Hwy. 480), at 69-2 Pu'upe'elua Ave., offers the popular "Post-a-Nut" service (p. 437); it's open Monday to Friday 8:30am to noon and 12:30 to 4pm.

EXPLORING MOLOKA'I

Note: You'll find the following attractions on the "Moloka'i" map on p. 431.

Attractions & Points of Interest

Most of the island's attractions are of the natural variety, but a few man-made sights are worth adding to your itinerary. For the quaint "topside" churches related to St. Damien, see "The Saints of Moloka'i," p. 439.

KAUNAKAKAI

Molokai Plumerias ★★ FARM   Hundreds of plumeria trees produce fragrant white, yellow, pink, and scarlet blooms virtually year-round here, just off the main highway between the airport and town. Drop in to purchase lei or make a weekday appointment for an informative blossom-gathering tour that ends with a lesson on how to string your own lei. The perfume is intoxicating.

1342 Maunaloa Hwy. (Hwy. 460), across the road from 'Ulili St., 2½ miles west of Kaunakakai. www.molokaiplumerias.com. 𝐶 **808/553-3391.** Tours $25 (Mon–Fri by appointment 8am–noon).

CENTRAL UPLANDS & NORTH SHORE

Aka'ula Cat Garden ★ ANIMAL SHELTER   You're bound to see a few homeless (not necessarily feral) cats on the island, but thanks to this indoor-outdoor shelter—the only animal sanctuary on the island and welcoming to visitors—more of the island's felines stand a chance of finding homes. Founder Carol Gartland enlists the help of students at neighboring Aka'ula School to care for the cats and will even pay the costs of flying a kitty home with you, should you be so smitten. Or stop by **Desi's Island**

Gifts (p. 458) across the parking lot to buy cute cat-themed items with proceeds benefiting the sanctuary.

Next to Aka'ula School, 900 Kala'e Hwy. (Hwy. 470), just south of Farrington Rd., Kualapu'u. www.akaulacatgarden.org. ✆ **808/658-0398.** By appointment only.

Mokio Preserve ★★★ NATURE PRESERVE   The only way to visit this rugged but beautiful 1,718-acre preserve on the northwest shore is to sign up for one of the frequent half-day volunteer excursions with Moloka'i Land Trust, but it's more than worth it. Home to numerous archaeological sites like an adze quarry and fishing shrine, it also hosts rare native flowering plants like red-blossomed *'akoko* and an endemic morning glory in a dune ecosystem with dramatic views of North Shore sea cliffs, West End beaches, and wetlands. On one bluff pockmarked with shearwater burrows stand pairs of wooden Laysan albatross (*mōlī*). They're designed to attract live breeding pairs with the help of a recording of their eerie cries that plays nonstop through a speaker. But first you'll pass many acres of scrubby kiawe (mesquite) trees shading a carpet of pink and yellow lantana and canary-yellow golden crownbeard flowers—all highly invasive—lining the long, bumpy, red-dirt road to the dunes. Luckily, you won't be doing the driving; instead, you'll leave your car at the Moloka'i Land Trust headquarters and nursery in Ho'olehua and hop in a roomy, air-conditioned van for the narrated hour's drive to Mokio. After about 2 hours of actual hands-on work, such as pulling weeds from the dunes, you'll break for a bring-your-own picnic lunch and a short hike to the seabird habitat. After the drive back, you can learn more about indigenous plants in the small but abundant nursery, which also offers regular volunteer opportunities.

Meet at Moloka'i Land Trust, 1800 Farrington Ave. Kualapu'u. www.molokailandtrust. org. ✆ **808/553-5626.** Volunteer excursions available most weekdays, starting at 9am, but call ahead or email molokailandtrust@gmail.com to confirm and register. Free admission.

Moloka'i Museum and Cultural Center ★ MUSEUM/HISTORIC SITE   This small museum on the site of a restored sugar mill has a large gift shop of local arts and crafts (look for *liliko'i* butter) and eclectic exhibits from petroglyphs to plantation-era furnishings. Lining the walls are the poignant portraits of Kalaupapa residents, including a granddaughter of mill founder Rudolph W. Meyer, a German surveyor who married Kalama, a Hawaiian of chiefly rank. Kalaupapa's historic buildings are the subject of one of two 10-minute videos shown on a TV; the other focuses on the ingenuity of the mill, built in 1878. Walk a few yards uphill from the museum (the Meyers' former home) to see the barnlike mill and outdoor pit where circling mules once powered cane-crushing machinery.

West side of Kala'e Hwy. (Hwy. 470), near mile marker 4 (just past turnoff for the Ironwood Hills Golf Course), Kala'e. www.kalaupapaohana.org/molokai-museum. ✆ **808/567-6436.** $5 adults; $1 children and students. Mon–Sat 10am–2pm.

Send a coconut-gram with Post-a-Nut.

Post-a-Nut ★ ICON A few minutes' drive from the airport awaits a unique opportunity to say "Aloha" by mailing someone a Moloka'i coconut that you've decorated yourself. At the tiny Ho'olehua post office, you may pick out a coconut from the bin, if available, or bring your own (look outside the fence of Kapuāiwa Coconut Grove) or—the most reliable option—go to Molokai Deconut inside Desi's Island Gifts (p. 458) and, for $10, pick out one that has been especially washed and dried for this purpose. The post office may offer colored felt-tip pens to write a message on one side and an address on the other, but it's best to either bring your own or use the variety of brushes and paint available from Molokai Deconut. In any case, the postmaster will fill the third side with a kaleidoscopic array of stamps to mail it to the continental U.S. Postage averages $20 for a medium coconut.

Ho'olehua Post Office, 69-2 Pu'upe'elua Ave. (Hwy. 480), near Maunaloa Hwy. (Hwy. 460). ✆ **808/567-6144.** Mon–Fri 8:30am–noon and 12:30–4pm.

Purdy's Natural Macadamia Nut Farm ★★ FARM Hawaiian homesteaders Kammy and Tuddie Purdy offer free tours in the shade of their macadamia nut orchard, planted more than a century ago. Moloka'i native Tuddie is a wealth of information and passionate about his crop; this isn't a casual stop-and-shop experience. After an educational spin around the 5-acre family farm, he'll ply you with samples of delicious nuts—raw, salted, or air-dried—and macadamia blossom honey. They can ship home whatever you buy, too.

2240 Lihi Pali Ave., above Moloka'i High School, Ho'olehua. www.molokai-aloha.com/macnuts. ✆ **808/567-6601.** Mon–Fri 9:30am–3:30pm, Sat 10am–2pm; Sun and holidays by appointment.

EAST END

Ancient Fishponds ★ HISTORIC SITE The rock walls of dozens of ancient fishponds—a pinnacle of Pacific aquaculture—can be seen for

Viewing the restored 15th-century Ali'i Fishpond.

miles along the shoreline from the highway between Kaunakakai and the East End. The U-shaped lava rock and coral walls contain *mākāhā* (sluice gates) that allowed smaller fish to enter but trapped them as they grew larger. Some are still in use today; join volunteers with **Ka Honua Momona** (www.kahonuamomona.org; © **808/553-8353**) in restoring the 15th-century **Ali'i Fishpond,** a half-mile west of One Ali'i Beach Park (p. 443) and once reserved for kings, or **Kaloko'eli Pond,** another 3½ miles east, generally on the third Saturday of the month. **Ka Honua Momona** also offers a 45-minute tour of the Ali'i Fishpond at various times for a recommended donation of $25 per person (two-person minimum); book online. *Note:* Please don't swim, wade, or kayak in any fishpond, or walk on fishpond walls.

Parks & Preserves

For information on the relatively inaccessible Kamakou and Mo'omomi preserves, managed by the Nature Conservancy, see "Fragile Beauties," p. 447.

Kapuāiwa Coconut Grove ★ HISTORIC SITE Planted in the 1860s by King Kamehameha V (born Prince Lot Kapuāiwa), this royal grove of 1,000 coconut trees (unfortunately, many now frondless) on 10 oceanfront acres is closed for safety and preservation reasons, but still presents a side-of-the-road photo op. Across the highway stands Church Row: seven churches, each of a different denomination—clear evidence of the missionary impact on Hawai'i.

Ocean side of Maunaloa Hwy. (Hwy. 460), 1 mile west of Kaunakakai.

CENTRAL UPLANDS & NORTH SHORE

Kalaupapa National Historical Park ★★★ HISTORIC SITE
Before the COVID-19 pandemic, only 100 people a day, age 16 and older, could visit this isolated peninsula below the North Shore's soaring sea

cliffs, and then only by reservation (see "Organized Tours," on p. 441). It's been closed ever since, with no sign of tours resuming.

The area properly known as the Makanalua Peninsula was once home to the Native Hawaiian villages of Kalawao and Kalaupapa, on either side of 443-foot Kauhakō Crater. Residents were evicted and the naturally isolated peninsula turned into a place of exile. In 1865 King Kamehameha V signed the Act to Prevent the Spread of Leprosy, which ultimately sent some 8,000 people with the dreaded disease to live in Kalawao and Kalaupapa. The exiles' suffering was particularly acute before the arrival in 1873 of now-canonized Father Damien (see "The Saints of Moloka'i," below), who worked tirelessly on their behalf until his death from the disease in 1889.

THE saints OF MOLOKA'I

Tiny Moloka'i can claim two saints canonized by the Roman Catholic church in recent years, both revered for years of devotion to the outcasts of Kalaupapa (see "Kalaupapa National Historical Park," below). Born in Belgium as Joseph de Veuster, **Father Damien** moved to Hawai'i in 1864, building churches around the islands until 1873, when he answered a call to serve in the infamous leper colony (a now-discouraged term). He tended the sick, rebuilt St. Philomena's church, and pleaded with church and state officials for better care for the exiles, the earliest of whom had been thrown overboard and left to fend for themselves. Damien ultimately died of Hansen's disease, as leprosy is now known, in Kalaupapa in 1889. Caring for him at the end was **Mother Marianne,** who came to Hawai'i with a group of nuns from New York in 1883. She spent 30 years serving the Kalaupapa community, before dying in 1918 at age 80, without contracting Hansen's disease. (It's only communicable to a small percentage of people.)

You'll see many images of both saints in Kalaupapa as well as "topside" (the nickname for the rest of Moloka'i). Three topside churches are worth peeking into: in Kaunakakai, the modernist, concrete **St. Damien of Moloka'i Church ★**, 115 Ala Malama Ave. (https://damienchurch molokai.org; ✆ **808/553-5220**), features four lovely mosaics depicting scenes from Damien's life. Inside, you'll find a life-size wooden sculpture of the eponymous saint, canonized in 2009. Turn around to see the large banners bearing his photograph and one of Marianne, canonized in 2012.

Ten miles east of Kaunakakai, on the ocean side of Highway 450, **St. Joseph's Mission Church ★★** is a diminutive wood-frame church built by Damien in 1876. A lava-rock statue of the sainted Belgian priest stands in the little cemetery not far from the newer, 7-foot marble sculpture of Brother Dutton, a Civil War veteran and former alcoholic inspired by Damien to serve at Kalaupapa for 45 years, until his death in 1931. This church no longer hosts regular services.

Another 4 miles east, set back from the large cross on the mountain side of the highway, is the larger but still picturesque **Our Lady of Seven Sorrows ★**, the first church Damien built outside Kalaupapa. Inside both East End churches hang colorful iconic portraits of the saints by local artist Linda Johnston. It hosts a regular Sunday morning service. Doors at both East Side churches are typically unlocked; please feel free to enter, but close doors when you leave.

Other than during the COVID-19 era, residents with Hansen's disease have been to come and go freely since the 1960s, with only a few elderly patients and their family members still living on site. But many buildings and ruins remain, and the park service is kept busy restoring them.

Note: A private landowner currently does not allow access to the trailhead in Kala'e for the Kalaupapa Pali Trail, 3 steep downhill miles with 26 switchbacks once traversed by tourist-toting mules and much earlier by Saint Damien. If the national park reopens, you'll need to fly to Kalaupapa to meet a required tour.

Kalaupapa. www.nps.gov/kala. © **808/567-6802.**

Pālā'au State Park ★★ PARK   This 234-acre forest park literally puts visitors between a rock and a hard place. From the parking lot, go left on the short but steep dirt trail through an ironwood grove to the **Phallic Rock** ★; go right on the paved path, and the **Kalaupapa Lookout ★★★** offers a panoramic view of the peninsula that was once a place of exile (see "Kalaupapa National Historical Park," above). Interpretive signs identify the sights some 1,700 feet below and briefly relate the tragic history that also spawned inspirational stories. As for that unmistakably shaped 6-foot-tall boulder, one legend holds that it's the fertility demigod Nānāhoa, turned to stone after he threw his wife over a cliff during an argument. It's also believed that a woman wishing to become pregnant need only spend the night nearby. (Treat this cultural site with respect, as signs urge.) *Note:* Restrooms are near the overlook and at a small pavilion

Statue of St. Damien at St. Joseph's Mission Church, Moloka'i.

Moloka'i: Place of Powerful Prayer

Moloka'i emits a deep spirituality, earning it the nickname Moloka'i *pule ō'ō*, "place of powerful prayer." In ancient times, the island was an epicenter of religious practices and home to a school of sorcery. According to legend, powerful sorcerers could pray away attacking armies, summon fish into nets, and control the weather at will. Modern residents still put a lot of stock in prayer. Churches of every denomination line the rural roads. You can count eight on the way from the airport into Kaunakakai, and a dozen more on the way to Hālawa Valley. More hidden but still revered are the ruins of ancient stone temples, known as *heiau*.

before the parking lot; there is no potable water. Tent camping is allowed with permit (see "Camping," p. 453).

At the northern end of Kala'e Hwy. (Hwy. 470), Pālā'au. dlnr.hawaii.gov/dsp/parks/molokai/palaau-state-park. Free admission. Daily 7am–7pm.

Organized Tours

Although Moloka'i attracts independent travelers, a few guided tours are essential—they're the only way to see the island's most awe-inspiring sights up close. For other guided hikes in Moloka'i Forest Reserve and Mo'omomi Dunes, see "Fragile Beauties," p. 447, and "Hiking," p. 448.

HĀLAWA VALLEY TOURS   On the East End, a guided tour or authorized escort is required to go beyond Hālawa Beach Park into breathtakingly beautiful Hālawa Valley, home to the island's earliest settlement and 250-foot Mo'oula Falls. Mentored by his cultural practitioner father Pilipo Solatorio, **Greg Solatorio**'s 4½-hour tours ($75 adults, $45 ages 4–12) start with traditional Hawaiian protocol before hiking 1¾ miles past cultural sites to the waterfall for a dip and your packed lunch. Advance booking is necessary, with a minimum of two guests per tour, Monday to Saturday at 9am; contact **Hālawa Valley Falls Cultural Hike** (https://halawavalleymolokai.com; ✆ **808/542-1855**). **Kalani Pruet** pairs a hike to the waterfall with a visit to his flower farm, known as the **Kuleana Workcenter** (www.molokaiflowers.com; Tues–Sat 10am–4pm, Sun by appointment; e-mail him several days in advance at kuleanaworkcenter@yahoo.com). His 4-hour tours cost $60. It's more expensive but easier to book with Molokai Outdoors (www.molokaioutdoors.com; ✆ **808/633-8700**), which charges $75 for adults, $55 ages 14 and younger; tours are on Wednesday and Saturday. *Note:* The valley is privately owned—trespassers may be prosecuted, and almost certainly hassled, if caught.

ISLAND TOURS   Just have a day to spend on Moloka'i? The friendly drivers of **Molokai Outdoors** (www.molokaioutdoors.com; ✆ **855/208-0811** or 808/633-8700) will take you on a private, nearly 8-hr tour in an air-conditioned car (or 15-passenger van, depending on the size of your group), with airport pickup and drop-off available. The tour ($199 adults,

$104 ages 14 and younger) starts by heading to the East End for an overlook of **Hālawa Valley** and its waterfalls (p. 441) and a stop at **St. Joseph's Mission Church** (p. 439), one of the quaint churches built by St. Damien. You'll then head to the central uplands for stops at **Pālā'au State Park** (p. 440), including short walks to the **Kalaupapa Overlook** (p. 440) and a phallic rock, and the guided tour of **Purdy's Macadamia Nut Farm** (p. 437). A picnic lunch at a scenic spot is included and, time permitting, a trip to **Pāpōhaku Beach** (p. 444) and the West End hamlet of **Maunaloa** (p. 433). Departure is typically at Monday and Wednesday 8am, returning to Hotel Moloka'i (p. 450) in Kaunakakai or the airport in Ho'olehua at 4pm. Call about customized options. *Tip:* Book online for a 10% discount.

KALAUPAPA TOURS   The only way to explore the spectacular, haunting Kalaupapa peninsula is on an authorized guided tour, if available. **Father Damien and Marianne Cope Molokai Tours** (molokaidaytour@hawaii.

rr.com; ℰ **808/895-1673**) was hoping to resume tours in 2024 but the National Park Service had not committed to a timeline. Stops on the tour previously included the original graves of Father Damien and Mother Marianne (see "The Saints of Moloka'i," p. 439); St. Philomena Church, where the Belgian priest carved holes in the floor so patients could discreetly spit during services; a cash-only snack shop and bookstore; and a small museum with heart-rending photos and artifacts, such as a spoon reshaped for a disfigured hand. Prepare to be deeply moved by the landscape and the stories of those exiled here. Restricted to ages 16 and older, the 4-hour tour previously cost $149, including picnic lunch; add another $200 or more for the flight from Maui or Honolulu.

A historic church on Moloka'i.

WHALE-WATCHING TOURS   If you're on island in winter (Dec–Mar), don't miss the chance to see humpback whales from Alaska frolic in island waters, often with clingy calves in tow, or boisterous pods of males competing for a female's attention. Though you may spot whales spouting or breaching from the shore, a whale-watching cruise from Kaunakakai skirts the fringing reef to provide front-row seats. Veteran outfitter **Molokai Fish & Dive** (www.molokaifishanddive.com; ℰ **808/553-5926**) offers 2- to 3-hour tours for $109 ($89 ages 7–12, $75 ages 3–6) on its comfortable

31-foot power twin-hulled catamaran *Ama Lua* or its 38-foot, two-level *Coral Queen* dive boat. **Molokai Ocean Tours** (www.molokaiocean tours.com; ✆ **808/553-3290** or 808/336-6291) leads humpback-spotting hunts on its 40-foot power catamaran *Manu Eleʻele* for $95 (minimum two adults, maximum six passengers).

BEACHES

Because of the South Shore's extensive shallows, hemmed by a fringing reef and fishponds, and the general inaccessibility of the North Shore, the best Molokaʻi beaches for visitors are on the East or West Ends. There are no lifeguards; on weekdays, you may even be the sole person on the sand. So enter the water only in calm conditions (which rarely occur in winter), and even then be cautious: If you get into trouble, help may take longer to arrive than you expect. *Note:* You'll find relevant sites on the "Molokaʻi" map on p. 431.

Kaunakakai

Local kids swim off the wharf, but if you just want to dip your feet in the water, head 3 miles east along the Kamehameha V Highway (Hwy. 450) to the sandy shore of **One Aliʻi Beach Park** ★. Pronounced *"oh-nay ah-lee-ee,"* it has a thin strip of golden *one* (sand) once reserved for the *aliʻi* (high chiefs). Although the water is too shallow and murky for swimming, the spacious park (with two entrances) is a picnic spot and attracts many

families on weekends. Facilities include outdoor showers, picnic areas, a playground, and restrooms; tent camping allowed with permit (see "Camping," on p. 453).

East End

At mile marker 20, palm-fringed **Kūmimi Beach** ★★, also known as Murphy Beach Park or 20-Mile Beach, provides a small, shaded park with picnic tables, white sand, and good swimming, snorkeling, and diving in calm conditions. Look for **Sandy Beach** ★★ between mile markers 21 and 22—the last beach before you head uphill en route to lush Hālawa Valley. It has no facilities, just winsome views of Maui and Lānaʻi and generally safe swimming; stay out of high surf.

Pāpōhaku Beach Park has a long, wide strand of blond sand.

At the narrow end of the winding highway, 28 miles east of Kaunaka-kai, lies **Hālawa Beach ★★**. Tucked between sea cliffs, the wide rocky bay is beautiful but not safe for swimming. Behind it, the gray sand cove adjacent to the river is a serene option for those willing to ford the stream. Avoid this during winter or after heavy rains. Look back into Hālawa Valley (accessible only via cultural tours; see p. 441) for distant waterfall views. The **Hālawa Park** picnic pavilion has a portable toilet, shower, and water tap; it's 100 yards from the shore, across from **Ierusalema Hou,** a tiny green church built in 1948.

West End

Much of the shoreline here is for sightseeing only, thanks to dangerous currents and fierce surf—especially in winter. But solitude, sunsets, and clear-day vistas of Diamond Head on O'ahu across the 26-mile Kaiwi Channel make it worth the trek. From Kaunakakai, take Maunaloa Highway (Hwy. 460) almost 15 miles west, turn right on Kaluako'i Road, and drive 4½ miles until you see the sign on your right pointing to Ke Nani Kai; turn right for public beach access parking at the end of the road. Walk past the eerily decaying, closed hotel to gold-sand **Kepuhi Beach ★★**, and watch surfers navigate the rocky break. A 15-minute walk north along the bluff leads to the Pōhaku Māuliuli cinder cone, which shares its name with two sandy coves better known as **Make Horse Beach ★**, pronounced *"mah-kay"* and meaning "dead horse" (don't ask). You can snorkel and explore the tide pools in calm conditions, but do keep an eye on the waves. Hiking several miles north on a rugged dirt road leads to the white crescent of **Kawākiu Beach ★**, the original launch site of the Moloka'i to O'ahu outrigger canoe race. It's relatively safe in summer, but be wary whenever surf is up. Unfortunately, locals now complain that a private hunting company with land backing up to Kawākiu has taken to giving beachgoers menacing looks, despite Hawai'i state laws protecting public beach access.

Continue on Kaluako'i Road 2 miles south from the resort to the parking lot for **Pāpōhaku Beach Park ★★★**, where the light-blond sand is more than 2 miles long and 300 feet wide. Enjoy strolling the broad expanse but beware the water's ferocious rip currents. County facilities—restrooms, water, picnic, and campsites (see "Camping," on p. 453)—are at the northern end, a third of a mile past the intersection with Pā Loa Loop Road (a shortcut back to upper Kaluako'i Rd.).

From Pāpōhaku, follow Kaluako'i Road 1¾ miles south to the T at Pōhakuloa Road; turn right and head another 1¾ miles. Just before the road ends, turn seaward at the beach access sign. Park in the small lot and follow a short path to cozy **Dixie Maru Beach ★★★** (formerly Kapuka-hehu, but renamed after a Japanese shipwreck). Popular with families, this sheltered cove is the island's best, safest spot to swim. Facilities are minimal: a trash can and outdoor shower.

WATERSPORTS

The miles-long, untrammeled South Shore reef is home to curious turtles and Hawaiian monk seals, billowing eagle and manta rays, and giant bouquets of colorful fish, but because it lies a half-mile or more offshore, it's easiest to explore via watercraft of some kind. Surfers, stand-up paddleboarders, and boogie boarders can find waves to entertain themselves, just as sport fishers have numerous near-shore and deep-sea options; since conditions are variable by day as well as by season, consult one of the Kaunakakai-based outfitters below before venturing out.

Diving, Fishing & Snorkeling

Molokai Fish & Dive, 61 Ala Malama Ave. (www.molokaifishanddive. com; ⓒ **808/553-5926**), carefully selects the day's best sites for its **snorkel tours** ($119 adults, $95 ages 7–12, $85 ages 3–6) and two-tank **scuba dives** ($219 divers, $99 passengers). Owner, captain, and certified dive master Tim Forsberg runs tours on a Coast Guard–inspected boat: the twin-hulled, 31-foot power catamaran *Ama Lua.* When conditions permit, he also offers three-tank dives ($365) along the remote North Shore; you can also take introductory dives ($275) or lessons (call for pricing). Half-day **deep-sea fishing charters** start at $695. All kinds of dive and fishing gear, along with snacks and gifts, are for rent or sale at the downtown headquarters.

Among several other charter operators, Captain Tim Brunnert of **Captain's Gig Charters** (www.captaintcharters.com; ⓒ **808/552-0390** or 808/336-1055) books **sport-fishing, snorkel, sunset,** and **sightseeing cruises** on the comfortable 31-foot *Hapa Girl.* You can also book a

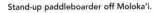

Stand-up paddleboarder off Moloka'i.

fishing charter to hunt for ono, mahimahi, marlin, and other deep-sea fish, $495 to $895 for 4 to 8 hours for the entire boat; he'll filet your catch to take home to grill. Captain Tim is also a certified dive master.

Molokai Ocean Tours, 40 Ala Malama Ave., above American Savings Bank (www.molokaioceantours.com; © 808/553-3290 or 808/336-6291), uses its six-passenger power catamaran to offer 3-hour **troll fishing** ($850 for the boat up six people) and a half-day **deep-sea fishing charter** (call for current rates). Charter sunset cruises with appetizers and water for two to six passengers ($480–$660) are also a possibility.

While you can also charter his 2013 Prima Sea 18-foot flats boat, made specifically for fly fishing and running skinny water, Captain Clay of **Hallelujah Hou Fishing** (www.hallelujahhoufishing.com; © 808/336-1870) specializes in catch-and-release fishing for Moloka'i's enormous bonefish from a skiff in the shallow flats. An advocate for sustainability, Captain Clay is also a longtime resident and minister who considers fishing here "almost a spiritual journey." The 4- to 6-hour bonefishing trips cost $800 for one to two anglers, plus $150 for extra anglers, up to four.

For **whale-watching tours** (Dec–Mar), see "Organized Tours," p. 441.

Paddling

Molokai Outdoors ★★ (www.molokaioutdoors.com; © 808/633-8700) leads a fantastic downwind sunrise 3-mile **kayak or stand-up-paddleboard (SUP)** tour ($95 adults, $51 ages 14 and younger) and a pleasant 8- to 8½-mile downwinder that takes about 4 hours ($115 adults, $60 for children). *Note:* SUP is only available with a 1-foot or higher tide. Owner and former world champion windsurfer Clare Seeger Albino occasionally guides the tours, as does her husband, Moloka'i native Gordon Albino. Based in Hotel Moloka'i (p. 450), their company can also arrange kayak and SUP rentals (starting at 24 hr. for $65 to 10–14 days for $552) and help experienced paddlers arrange a self-guided North Shore kayak excursion that starts in Hālawa Valley, including gear and pickup by boat. *Tip:* Book online for a 10% discount.

Surfing & Bodyboarding

This isn't a place to learn surfing—the currents and waves may be too strong for beginners—but experienced riders may enjoy good, uncrowded breaks off Kaunakakai Wharf, Kepuhi Beach, and Dixie Maru, depending on the time of year and the wave conditions. Be sure to show courtesy to the local surfers, who are sensitive to even small increases in their lineups.

Moloka'i native and avid surfer Zach Socher is happy to dispense advice and offer inexpensive surfboard rentals (though no more than four at a time, to keep breaks uncrowded) from the **Big Wind Kite Factory,** 120 Maunaloa Hwy., Maunaloa (www.bigwindkites.com; © 808/552-2364); it's open Monday to Saturday 10am to 5pm and Sunday until 2pm.

OTHER OUTDOOR ACTIVITIES

Biking

Moloka'i is a great place to see by bicycle, with lightly used roads and, on the East End, inviting places to pull over for a quick dip. **Moloka'i Bicycle,** 80 Mohala St., Kaunakakai (www.mauimolokaibicycle.com; © **808/747-3760** or 808/553-5740), offers mountain, road, and hybrid bike rentals for $35 to $50 a day, or $75 to $180 a week, including helmet, lock, and car rack. Trailers rent for $12 to $25 a day, $60 a week. Because owner Phillip Kikukawa is a schoolteacher, the store is open only Wednesday (2–5pm) and

FRAGILE BEAUTIES: MOLOKA'I nature reserves

The Nature Conservancy of Hawai'i helps preserve two of the island's most fragile landscapes: the windswept dunes in the 920-acre **Mo'omomi Preserve** on the north-west shore, and the cloud-ringed forest named after the highest peak on Moloka'i, the 2,774-acre **Kamakou Preserve** on the island's East End.

About 8½ miles northwest of Ho'olehua, Mo'omomi is one of the most intact beach and sand dune area in the main Hawaiian Islands, harboring jewel-like endemic plants, nesting green sea turtles, and fossils of now-extinct flight-less birds.

Towering over the island's eastern half, 4,970-foot Kamakou is the summit of the extinct volcano that formed East Moloka'i, which provides 60% of the island's fresh water. Its namesake pre-serve shelters rare native species, such as happy-faced spiders and deep-throated lobelias, and includes the **Pēpē'opae Trail boardwalk ★★★**. The 1.5-mile boardwalk (3 miles round-trip) winds through a bog of miniature 'ōhi'a trees and silver-leaved lilies that evolved over millennia; it leads to a view of pristine Pelekunu Valley on the North Shore. But it is very difficult for off-island partici-pants to take part in the Conservancy's free monthly hikes (Mar–Oct), which give preference to residents and are booked months in advance. It's still possible to access the preserves on your own, but you'll need a rugged four-wheel-drive (4WD) vehicle, clear weather, and dry roads for Mo'omomi, or in the case of

Kamakou Preserve, to rent a mountain bike from Moloka'i Bicycle (see "Biking," above) or—the best option—to book the services of Molokai Outdoors (see "Hik-ing," p. 448). Please be extremely careful to stay on designated roads and trails.

Check in first at the **Nature Conser-vancy field office,** open Monday to Friday 8am to 3pm, north of Kaunakakai in Moloka'i Industrial Park, 23 Pueo Place, near Highway 460 (© **808/553-5236**). Ask for detailed directions and current road conditions. For Kamakou, you'll begin by driving or biking 10 miles up mostly unpaved Maunahui Road start-ing from its unmarked intersection with Maunaloa Highway (Hwy. 460) near mile marker 4 (look for HOMELANI CEMETERY sign); leave your bike locked at the Waikolu Lookout campsite (which has restrooms but no drinking water) and hike 2.2 miles to the start of the mile-long Pēpē'opae boardwalk. In the case of Mo'omomi, you'll also need to ask the field office for a pass for its locked gate. Clean your shoes and gear before visiting either preserve to avoid bringing in invasive species. If driving, do so cautiously—a tow job from Mo'omomi can easily cost $1,000. Cell-phone service may be nonexistent.

Saturday (9am–2pm); call to set up an appointment for other hours. Drop-off and pickup in or near Kaunakakai is free, with charges for runs to the airport ($30 each way) or Kaluako'i Resort and Wavecrest condos ($45 each way).

Golf

Take a swing back into golf history at **Ironwood Hills Golf Course** (© **808/567-6000**). Built in 1929 by the Del Monte Plantation for its executives, the 9-hole, undulating course with uneven fairways lies a half-mile down an unpaved road off Highway 470 in Kala'e, between the Coffees of Hawai'i farm in Kualapu'u and the Kalaupapa Lookout. Gorgeous mountain and ocean views, some filtered by tree growth, also compensate for the challenging course, which has no pro on-site. Greens fees are $20 for 9 holes, $36 for 18, including cart; club rentals are $10.

Hiking

With most land privately held, the only real hiking opportunities currently available on Moloka'i are in Hālawa Valley by guided tour only (p. 441), in two hard-to-access Nature Conservancy preserves (see "Fragile Beauties," p. 447), and along the West End's wide beaches and their bluffs (p. 444).

Fortunately, **Molokai Outdoors** (https://molokaioutdoors.com; © **808/633-8700**) offers a terrific hiking package ($199 adults, $104 children ages 14 under) that includes a 4WD shuttle to the spectacular **Waikolu Lookout** in the Moloka'i Forest Preserve, sack lunch, and tips on how and where to hike from the driver, usually Moloka'i native Gordon Albino. He will share intriguing stories on the hour-plus drive to the overlook, where he'll await your return. If you're in good hiking condition, it's an ideal way to access the Nature Conservancy's Kamakou Preserve and its unique bog and boardwalk (see "Fragile Beauties," below). Before you go, clean your shoes and gear of any previous hikes' soil or plant matter, and tread lightly in this treasured place. *Note:* Rental cars are not allowed on the forest road and there is no cellphone service, hence the need for a shuttle (or a mountain bike) to access trails. Bring a phone with satellite service or VHF radio for added safety.

WHERE TO STAY ON MOLOKA'I

With only one small hotel on the island, the majority of the island's approximately 24,000 annual visitors stay in vacation rentals, which are only allowed in the five condo communities on the island and a few individually owned units at Hotel Moloka'i. The decor and upkeep of condo units vary widely in taste and quality, leaning heavy on rattan styling. Don't expect air-conditioning or elevators in the two- and three-story buildings, either.

You'll find some 36 well-managed properties through **Vacasa** (www.vacasa.com/usa/Molokai). *Note:* If using Airbnb, VRBO, or other rental websites, be sure to check for the Maui County license and tax ID numbers to verify they're legitimate. Don't forget to calculate cleaning and booking fees when comparing rates.

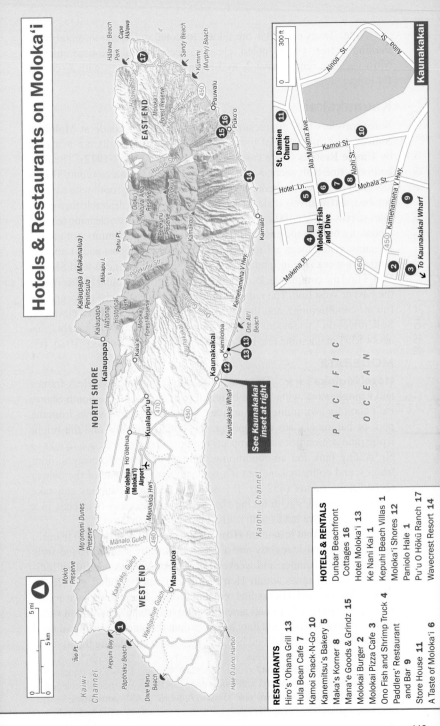

Hotels & Restaurants on Moloka'i

RESTAURANTS

Hiro's 'Ohana Grill **13**
Hula Bean Cafe **7**
Kamoi Snack-N-Go **10**
Kanemitsu's Bakery **5**
Maka's Korner **8**
Mana'e Goods & Grindz **15**
Molokai Burger **2**
Molokai Pizza Cafe **3**
Ono Fish and Shrimp Truck **4**
Paddlers' Restaurant
and Bar **9**
Store House **11**
A Taste of Moloka'i **6**

HOTELS & RENTALS

Dunbar Beachfront
Cottages **16**
Hotel Moloka'i **13**
Ke Nani Kai **1**
Kepuhi Beach Villas **1**
Moloka'i Shores **12**
Paniolo Hale **1**
Pu'u O Hōkū Ranch **17**
Wavecrest Resort **14**

Kaunakakai

St. Damien Church **11**

Molokai Fish and Dive **4**

← To Kaunakakai Wharf

449

Note: Taxes of 17.5% are added to hotel and vacation rental bills. Parking is free. Unless noted, cleaning fees refer to one-time charges. Most vacation rentals have 2- to 3-night minimum stays, with discounts for longer stays.

Kaunakakai

Some travelers may appreciate the convenience of a condo at **Moloka'i Shores** ★, 1 mile east of town, where many of the units are managed by **Castle Resorts** (www.castleresorts.com; ✆ **877/367-1912**). The one-bedroom, one-bath, second-story unit **A304** (www.vacasa.com/unit/51479) has great ocean views, bedroom with queen bed, living room with a queen sofabed, and relatively updated decor that make it more desirable than most; rates start as low as $100 a night, excluding damage waiver, cleaning fee, and a booking fee that increases with the length of stay and number of guests. Dynamic prices mean a 3-night stay in October could cost a total of $613 while a 1-week stay in January (the required minimum) can total $1,385. Still, I find the complex lacks the ambience and privacy found further out on the East or West End. The rather compact condos can also be noisy and hot (no air-conditioning), and the three-story buildings don't have elevators. Still, prices on Vacasa.com for other units start as low as $110 a night (plus about $331 in one-time fees) for one-bedroom, one-bath units (510 sq. ft.).

MODERATE

Hotel Moloka'i ★★   This retro collection of Polynesian-style A-frames and a single-story wing face a beach that, like most on the South Shore, isn't good for swimming. The upsides: Sunset and sunrise views from the pool or hammocks are outstanding, the staff is friendly, and the bright white (and sometimes very compact) remodeled rooms are cool, thanks to big ceiling fans and air-conditioning units. All have microwaves, mini fridges, and coffeemakers, but it's better to spring for one of the deluxe second-floor rooms (432 sq. ft.) with kitchenettes. Families can take advantage of suites with a king-size bed downstairs and twin beds in a loft. All units have lanais with a small table and chairs, too.

The oceanfront restaurant **Hiro's 'Ohana Grill** ★★ (p. 455) features live Hawaiian music nightly and a delicious, locally sourced island-style menu for lunch, dinner, and weekend breakfast. *Note:* A handful of individually owned units within Hotel Moloka'i can be found on VRBO, Airbnb, Vacasa, and other online rental platforms. These units have access to the pool but no other hotel amenities and may require minimum stays. Still, rates in a given period may be lower than the hotel's; you'll just need to consider cleaning rates and booking fees when comparing them.

1300 Kamehameha V Hwy. (Hwy. 450), 2 miles east of Kaunakakai. www.hotel molokai.com. ✆ **877/553-5347** or 808/553-5347. 40 units. $154–$346 double. $15 daily resort fee includes snorkel and beach gear, DVD library. Airport shuttle available through **Molokai Outdoors** (see "Getting Around," p. 434). **Amenities:** Restaurant, bar; coin laundry; computer kiosk; gift shop; pool; activity desk; free Wi-Fi.

West End

MODERATE

Kaluakoi Resort ★ Developed and managed separately, the three condo complexes in this long-faded resort near Maunaloa have much in common. Negatives include a remote location, varying quality of furnishings and decor, and the slightly haunted ambience thanks to the shuttered hotel next door. Positives: inexpensive to moderate prices, easy access to Kepuhi and other West End beaches (see "Beaches," p. 443), large lanais, and serene silence.

The 120-unit, two-story **Ke Nani Kai** ★★ (50 Kepuhi Place) is set back farthest from Kepuhi Beach but boasts the nicest pool and the only hot tub and tennis courts of the bunch; units are two-bedroom, two-bathroom (880–990 sq. ft.) or one-bedroom, one-bathroom (680 ft.). One of the best Ke Nani Kai units available on Vacasa is **No. 239** (www.vacasa.com/unit/51455; $125–$155), an oceanview unit on the second floor with a roomy sun deck, stone tiled floors, two queen beds, and cheery blue Mexican tiles in the kitchen and two bathrooms, plus $383 in one-time fees for cleaning, booking, and limited damage waiver.

The diverse condos of **Kepuhi Beach Villas** ★, 255 Kepuhi Beach Rd., are closest to the sand, with a generous oceanview pool on the grounds of the abandoned Kaluakoi Hotel. Built in 1978, the 148 units are spread among two-story buildings with shared laundry facilities (and thin walls), and eight duplex cottages with individual washer/dryers; the largest units have a ground floor (642 sq. ft.) with a master bedroom and bathroom, and a small loft with a second bedroom and bathroom. **Cottage 2B** perhaps the nicest of the units on Vacasa (www.vacasa.com/unit/51457), has a two-story, two-bedroom, two-bath floorplan in a setting as close to the waves as you can get. It offers a queen bed, twin beds, 1 sofa bed with a private washer-dryer, and free Wi-Fi ($144–$200, plus $342 in one-time fees for cleaning, booking, and limited damage waiver).

Nearly hidden in tropical foliage, the 78-unit **Paniolo Hale** ★, 100 Lio Place, means "cowboy house," and the screened lanais and wooden floors give it a hint of the Old West. Built in 1980, the 21 two-story buildings come in a host of floor plans, from studios (548 sq. ft.) to two-bedroom, two-bathroom units (1,398 sq. ft.), some with lofts and sleeping quarters in the living room. Of the units on Vacasa, brightly updated **studio I2** may have the best ocean view; it's also just a few steps up to the pool and barbecue area ($130–$150, plus $279 in one-time fees for cleaning, booking, and limited damage waiver).

Kaluakoi Resort, Maunaloa. 346 units in 3 complexes. Units are all privately owned and may be listed on various rental platforms, including Vacasa, Airbnb, and VRBO. Rates, fees, and minimum-night requirements vary widely, but expect to pay a minimum of $150–$200 above the daily rate and book a minimum of 2 nights. **Amenities:** Barbecues; Jacuzzi; pools; tennis courts (Ke Nani Kai only); Wi-Fi (varies by unit).

East End

Note: Mailing addresses for these lodgings use Kaunakakai, but they are miles from the actual town.

MODERATE

Dunbar Beachfront Cottages ★★★

Although Moloka'i has banned single-family vacation rental homes, these two attractive, green-and-white, plantation-style cottages have a permit valid through 2030—making them even more sought after. Both cottages sit on hidden beaches, with year-round swimming and snorkeling (in calm conditions). Each has two bedrooms (one with twin beds), one bathroom, a full kitchen, washer and dryer, and attractive furnishings. The family friendly Pauwalu cottage is at ocean level, with a queen-size bed in the master and an ancient fishpond out front. The Pu'unana cottage has a king-size bed in its master bedroom and sits one flight of stairs above the beach.

9750 Kamehameha V Hwy. (Hwy. 450), past mile marker 18, Kainalu. www.molokai beachfrontcottages.com. ✆ **808/336-0761.** 2 cottages (each sleeps 4). $270; $150 cleaning fee. 3-night minimum. No credit cards (PayPal accepted). **Amenities:** Barbecue with picnic table; free Wi-Fi.

Pu'u O Hōkū Ranch ★★★

Its name means "hill of stars," which accurately describes this 14,000-acre cattle ranch and biodynamic farm on a cloudless night. You'll stay in **Sunrise Cottage,** a secluded, 1930s-era bungalow, which offers a panoramic view of green bluffs and the blue sea. Thoughtfully decorated with rustic Hawaiian and Balinese furnishings, it has a double bed in the master bedroom and two twins in the second, plus two bathrooms and a small lanai. The cottages' farm-style kitchen is perfect for taking advantage of the ranch's freshly harvested venison, its organic beef, honey, and produce; ask about deliveries when

Dunbar Beachfront Cottages.

making reservations. Only ranch guests have access to its numerous hiking trails, which pass ocean bluffs, an ancient grove, and a nursery for nēnē (the endangered state bird). *Note:* Groups (a minimum of 14 people) may book the handsome 12-room lodge, with a private pool, yoga deck, and fireplace; it previously rented for $185 per person a night, including meals, but contact info@puuohoku.com for current pricing.

Main entrance off Kamehameha V Hwy. (Hwy. 450) at mile marker 25. www.puuohoku. com. © **808/558-8109.** $425 (for up to 4) cottage; $195 cleaning fee. **Amenities:** Store (daily 9am–3pm); free Wi-Fi at select hotspots (none in cottage).

Wavecrest Resort ★★   Halfway to Hālawa Valley from Kaunakakai, this three-story condo complex on 6 green acres is a convenient, clean home base. Your best bet is Building A, the closest to the ocean. Vacasa's seven listings on the resort include a third-floor, remodeled beauty (**A309;** www.vacasa.com/unit/51494) with, a king bed in the bedroom, queen sofabed in the living room, and a deluxe kitchen with stainless appliances ($135–$150 a night, with a 3-night stay starting at $750, including all fees and taxes). Top floors offer the best views of Maui, Lānaʻi, and uninhabited Kahoʻolawe, but keep in mind that the resort has no elevators (or air-conditioning). Bottom floor units aren't bad, and open straight to the grass and plumeria trees. Bedrooms face the parking lot, so you'll hear traffic. Units are individually owned and decorated; scrutinize photos and amenity lists closely. The gated pool and cabana with barbecues are well maintained, and the front desk has free tennis equipment to use on its two courts.

7148 Kamehameha V Hwy. (Hwy. 450), ʻUalapuʻe, 13 miles east of Kaunakakai. 128 total units. Units are all privately owned and may be listed on various rental platforms, including Vacasa, Airbnb, and VRBO. Rates, fees, and minimum-night requirements vary widely, but expect to pay a minimum of $125–$150 above the daily rate and book a minimum of 2 nights. **Amenities:** Barbecues; coin laundry; pool; tennis courts; Wi-Fi (varies by unit).

Camping

All campgrounds are for tents only and permits for county and state sites must be purchased in advance. You'll have to bring your own equipment or plan to buy it on the island, as there are no rentals.

County Campgrounds ★   The family friendly **One Aliʻi Beach Park ★★** (p. 443) provides restrooms, barbecues, outdoor showers, drinking water, picnic tables, and electricity, but little shade; **Pāpōhaku Beach Park ★★** (p. 444) has much the same, minus electricity and plus the shade of kiawe trees with plenty of sharp thorns. *Note:* The NO CAMPING signs near the Pāpōhaku parking lot apply only to the lawn to the right of the restrooms.

Permits Mon–Thurs $50 adults, $6 ages 17 and under; Fri–Sun and holidays $100 adults, $12 ages 17 and under (discounts for state residents). 4-night maximum (max. 8 days per month). Permits available Mon–Fri in person 8am–1pm and 2:30–4pm at the Maui County parks office, Mitchell Pauole Community Center, 90 Ainoa St., Kaunakakai, HI 96748. © **808/553-3204.**

State Campgrounds ★★   The state manages two campgrounds at high, often cool and misty elevations: **Pālā'au State Park** ★★ (p. 440) and the remote **Waikolu Overlook** ★ in the Moloka'i Forest Reserve. Both have restroom and picnic facilities, but no drinking water or barbecues. *Note:* Waikolu, which has just two campsites, has spectacular views, but requires a 4WD vehicle to drive 10 miles up mostly unpaved Maunahui Road starting from its unmarked intersection with Maunaloa Highway (Hwy. 460) near mile marker 4 (look for HOMELANI CEMETERY sign); do not attempt in muddy or rainy conditions. Rental cars are not allowed on the road, so you'll have to figure out a shuttle or brave it on a mountain bike. If the area is not covered in clouds, you'll be rewarded with views of the pristine Waikolu Valley and the Pacific, and be that much closer to the **Kamakou Preserve** ★★★ (p. 447).

Permits $30 per campsite (up to 10 persons). 5-night maximum. Available online at https://dlnr.hawaii.gov/dsp/camping-lodging/molokai. *©* **808/984-8100** or 808/281-0189.

WHERE TO EAT ON MOLOKA'I

Gourmands looking for fine dining will be disappointed on Moloka'i, but with a little strategizing you can eat well. Plan on cooking most of your meals if you are staying any distance from Kaunakakai, but be prepared for sticker shock in the grocery store, since so much is imported here. See p. 456 for where to stock up before heading out to your accommodations. You can only join the Facebook group "What's the Happenings Moloka'i????" if you live on the island, but anyone can browse its posts, which frequently include sales of plate lunches, notices of pop-up snack stands, and other foodie news.

Note: If you arrive on a Sunday, bring snacks! Most restaurants and groceries are only open Monday through Saturday. Find the restaurants noted below on the "Moloka'i" map on p. 431.

Kaunakakai

Modern innovations often take a while to reach Moloka'i, but the island has two food trucks now. The **Ono Fish and Shrimp Truck** ★★ sits outside of Molokai Fish & Dive, 53 Ala Malama Ave. (https://ono-fish-shrimp-truck.edan.io; *©* **808/553-8187**), with a few outdoor seats available; try its garlic shrimp, fresh poke, or fish tacos with mango salsa ($12–$15, including soda). It's open Monday to Friday 11am to 2:30pm. **A Taste of Moloka'i** ★★, near Friendly Market Center, at 82 Ala Malama Ave. (www.instagram.com/a.taste.of.molokai; *©* **808/658-1726**), serves açai bowls ($7–$12) for breakfast and delectable fresh poke bowls from one truck and specials like kalua pork nachos ($8–$14) from another for lunch. The poke and açai truck is open weekdays 10am to 3pm and Saturdays 9am to 2pm, while the black hot-food truck is open Monday 8:30am to 2pm, and Tuesday to Friday 7am to 2pm.

HOT ITEM: hot bread

Moloka'i may not have much to do after hours, but the late-night **"hot bread run"** ★★ at **Kanemitsu's Bakery**, 79 Ala Malama Ave., Kaunakakai (© 808/553-5585), is one tasty option. Facing the family-run bakery, follow well-lit Hotel Lane at the right to a left at the awning marked "hot bread." Soon you'll see a window where patrons are queuing for pillowy loaves of warm, fresh bread with "toppings" slathered inside—cream cheese, jelly, butter, cinnamon, or sugar ($11 for two toppings, $15 for the works, plus 50¢ for a paper bag). The window is open Tuesday through Thursday and Sunday 7:30 to 10pm and Friday and Saturday until 11pm.

The oceanfront restaurant at Hotel Moloka'i, **Hiro's 'Ohana Grill** ★★ (www.hirosohanagrill.com; © 808/660-3400), is a family affair, with several generations stepping in to serve island-inspired dishes. The locally sourced fish entrees, fresh pesto chicken sandwiches, and the bananas lumpia Foster dessert have already won diners' devotion. It's open for lunch and dinner Tuesday to Sunday, with nightly entertainment and breakfast service on Sunday. **Paddlers Restaurant and Bar** ★★, 10 S. Mohala St., Kaunakakai, on the ocean side of Highway 450 (www.paddlersrestaurant.com; © 808/553-3300), is the only other restaurant in town that serves alcohol (including draft beer), but its casual-gourmet menu is now the star of the show. The eclectic entrees ($10–$23) include pastas, sandwiches, burgers on brioche buns, and heartier fare like steak Marsala and chili pork (roasted pork in garlic vinegar sauce with chili oil). It's open Tuesday to Saturday 11am to 8pm, with happy hour weekdays 2 to 5pm.

On the corner of Highway 450 and Ala Malama Avenue, **Molokai Burger** ★★ (www.facebook.com/molokaiburgerHI; © 808/553-3533) offers burgers ($5–$12) and dinner plates ($9–$17), such as fried chicken or kalbi ribs. It's open Monday to Saturday 7am until 8:30pm, with egg dishes and pancakes ($3–$10) available Saturday until 10:30am, plus free Wi-Fi. Next door, **Molokai Pizza Cafe** ★, 15 Kaunakakai Place, off Wharf Road (© 808/553-3288), has been serving standard pizza, salads, and burgers since 1992 (daily 10am–9:30pm). Cash only and no delivery.

Locals flock to **Maka's Korner** ★, 35 Mohala St. (© 808/553-8058), for plate lunches (try the mahi mahi) and more burgers ($6–$12). It has a handful of outdoor tables with counter service. One plus: It's open Monday to Friday 7am to 8:30pm and Saturday and Sunday 8am to 2pm. The same family owns **Molokai Minimart** (p. 456) and **Hula Bean Cafe** in the same shopping strip. The latter is open Monday to Saturday 6:30am to 4pm and Sunday from 7:30am, a real boon to visitors. This is the best (and apparently the only) place to get your macchiatos and lattes; fortunately, they're quite tasty, as are smoothies and breakfast paninis.

The quaint **Store House** ★, 145 Ala Malama St. © 808/553-5222), has an array of tropical lemonades, smoothies, pastries, salads, and sandwiches. It's a great place to stock up before heading out on an adventure,

GROCERIES, MARKETS & treats

Nearly every storefront in Kaunakakai sells groceries of some sort and you'll want to visit several to stock up on specialty items. Start at **Friendly Market,** 90 Ala Malama Ave. (www.friendlymkt.com; © **808/553-5595**), which has a variety of dry goods and a small produce section open Monday to Saturday 8am to 6pm. A few doors down, **Misaki's Grocery Store,** 78 Ala Malama Ave. (© **808/553-5505**), features fresh poke (seasoned, raw fish) and a few more vegetables; open Monday to Saturday 8:30am to 8:30pm and Sunday hours are 9am to noon. Across the street, tiny **C. Pascua Store,** 109 Ala Malama Ave. (© **808/553-5443**), stays open Monday to Friday from 5:30am until 10pm, and on Saturday and Sunday it opens at 6:30am. It often has ripe fruit and jumbo frozen prawns farm-raised on O'ahu—perfect for pairing with a crisp Sauvignon Blanc from **Molokai Wines N Spirits,** 77 Ala Malama Ave. (https://kualapuumarket. wixsite.com/kmltd; © **808/553-5009;** Mon–Fri 10am–5:30pm, Sat until 4pm). Aside from an excellent array of adult beverages, you'll also find gourmet cheeses and crackers here. For organic and health-food brands, head to **The Planter Box,** 145 Ala Malama Ave #103 St. (www.facebook.com/theplanterboxkkai; © **808/560-0010;** Mon–Fri 6am–3pm and Sun from 9am). The convenience store **Molokai Minimart,** 35 Mohala St. (© **808/553-4447**), helpfully stays open daily 7am to 11pm.

Sustainable Molokai (www.facebook. com/sustainablemolokai) hosts a lively night market with music, ready-to-eat food, produce, and more, one Saturday a month from 4 to 7pm at Molokai Community Health Center, 30 Oki Place.

Grocery shopping is very limited outside of Kaunakakai. On the West End, thirsty beachgoers will be glad to discover **A Touch of Molokai** (© **808/552-0133**), inside the otherwise-empty Kaluakoi Hotel. Also called "Da Store," it's open daily 9am to 5pm, with snacks, sodas, many canned and boxed groceries, and frozen fare. The **Maunaloa General Store,** 200 Maunaloa Hwy., Maunaloa (© **808/552-0005**), has a somewhat larger grocery selection, though still heavy on tempting snacks and sweets, plus gifts and sundries. It's open Monday to Friday 9am to 6pm and Saturday and Sunday 8am to 2pm.

In the central uplands, **Kualapuu Market,** 311 Farrington Rd. (Hwy. 480), at Uwao Street, Kualapu'u (https://kualapuu market.wixsite.com/kmltd; © **808/567-6243**), offers essentials, beer and wine, and even ready-to-grill steaks; it's open Monday to Saturday 9am to 5pm. The **Ho'olehua Saturday Market,** weekly 9am to noon at Grace Episcopal Church, 2210 Farrington Ave., Ho'olehua, is a festive affair where several vendors sell homegrown fruits and vegetables and baked goods, along with arts and crafts. **Kumu Farms ★★**, 9 Hua 'Ai Rd., 1 mile south of Highway 460, near the airport (https://kumufarms.com; © **808/280-3262**), is famed for luscious, GMO-free papayas. The farm stand also sells organic herbs, vegetables, banana bread, and other treats. It's open Tuesday through Friday 9am to 4pm.

and has a small Moloka'i history exhibit, too. Open Sunday to Friday 6am to 3pm.

Sweets lovers have several temptations. At **Kamoi Snack-n-Go ★**, 28 Kamoi St. (www.facebook.com/kamoisnack; © **808/553-3742**), choose from more than 31 flavors of Dave's Hawaiian Ice Cream from Honolulu, including local favorites such as *kulolo* (taro-coconut custard), haupia (coconut pudding), and *ube* (purple yam); it's open daily 10am to 6pm. You can't miss the lime-green storefront of **Kanemitsu's Bakery** ★, 79 Ala Malama Ave. (✆ **808/553-5585**), a throwback to the 1960s that churns out pies, pastries, and cookies as well as sweet and savory breads (see "Hot Item: Hot Bread," p. 455). During breakfast and lunch hours, the attached restaurant serves typical American fare with local touches such as kimchi fried rice with eggs ($13) and local organic papaya (for just $3). Don't miss anything made with taro, including pancakes and doughnuts. It's open Thursday and Friday 6am to noon and Saturday to Monday and Wednesday until 2pm (closed Tues).

On the East End, the "Goods" (convenience store) half of **Mana'e Goods & Grindz,** 8615 Kamehameha V Hwy., Puko'o, near mile marker 16 (✆ **808/558-8498**), is open daily 8am to 3:30pm (deli counter/grill closed Wed). At mile marker 25, the **Pu'u O Hōkū Ranch Store** ★★ (https://puuohoku.com; ✆ **808/558-8109**) sells organic produce, honey, fresh herbs, and free-range organic beef—all produced at the ranch.

Elsewhere on the Island

On the East End, the takeout counter at **Mana'e Goods & Grindz,** 8615 Kamehameha V Hwy., Puko'o, near mile marker 16 (✆ **808/558-8498**), is the area's lone dining option. Hearty portions of loco moco, açai bowls, plate lunches, burgers, and specials like spicy poke bowls ($5–$14) arrive through a counter window; enjoy at one of a few shaded picnic tables. The counter is open Thursday through Tuesday 8am to 3:30pm.

On the West End, besides packaged food at the Maunaloa General Store (p. 456) or a possible pop-up stand outside it, the only available food is the array of snacks at **A Touch of Molokai** ★, by the pool at the closed Kaluakoi Hotel, 1121 Kaluakoi Rd., Maunaloa (✆ **808/552-0133**).

MOLOKA'I SHOPPING

Unless noted, stores listed here are closed on Sunday, so plan accordingly. You'll receive an extra welcome by asking for locally produced art, apparel, and jewelry, which Moloka'i residents create with special flair.

Gifts & Souvenirs

KAUNAKAKAI

The artist cooperative **Molokai Art From the Heart** ★★, also at 64 Ala Malama Ave. (www.molokaigallery.net; ✆ **808/553-8018**), features works by some 150 artists, virtually all from Moloka'i. **Something For Every-body** ★★★, 61 Ala Malama Ave. (www.allthingsmolokai.com; ✆ **808/553-3299**), showcases well-priced, locally designed, Hawaiian-inspired T-shirts and caps (some with slightly racy slogans), sarongs, other apparel, and jewelry; its lunch counter/smoothie stand also features local produce. **Imports Gift Shop** ★★, 82 Ala Malama Ave. (https://molokai imports.com; ✆ **808/553-5734**), carries a huge array of aloha and surf wear, jewelry, Hawaiian quilts, body lotions, and other gifts—just be aware, as the name implies, that much of the inventory is made on Moloka'i. Next to Molokai Pizza, **Makana Nui Hawaiian Gift Shop ★★**, 15 Kaunakakai Place (www.facebook.com/makananuimolokai; ℂ **808/553-8158**), offers Hawaiian and Polynesian jewelry, sarongs, clothing, jewelry, gourd bowls, and other home decor; it's only open Tuesday to Friday 11am to 4pm.

The island's sole pharmacy, the venerable **Molokai Drugs ★**, 28 Kamoi St. (www.facebook.com/molokaidrugs; ℂ **808/553-5790**), also holds a cache of cute souvenirs and sundries, including greeting cards and gift wrap. T-shirts with original island-inspired designs, hats, aloha shirts, sporting goods, and various souvenirs can be found at **Molokai Fish & Dive ★★**, 53 Ala Malama St. (www.molokaifishanddive.com; ℂ **808/553-5926**); it's open daily. Live music, jewelry, clothing, crafts, and local produce attract shoppers to the **Ho'olehua Saturday Market,** weekly 9am to noon at Grace Episcopal Church, 2210 Farrington Ave., Ho'olehua. The church's **Grace Thrift Shop** (Fri–Sat 9am–1pm) is a must for bargain hunters and fans of vintage clothing.

ELSEWHERE ON THE ISLAND

Stop by **Desi's Island Gifts ★★**, 900 Kala'e Hwy. (Hwy. 470), Kualapu'u (www.facebook.com/DesisIslandGifts), and you'll find not only an array of affordable gifts such as Hawaiian print potholders and scrunchies, island-style jewelry, and Moloka'i-made lip balm, but also a number of items whose sales benefit the nearby **Aka'ula Cat Garden** (p. 435). You might also be greeted by a few cats. You can also pick up one of Moloka'i Deconut's dried coconuts for $10 to decorate on-site or later, and if you wish, mail it from the Ho'olehua Post Office (see Post-a-Nut, p. 437).

North of Kualapu'u, near mile marker 4 of the Kala'e Hwy. (Hwy. 470), is the **Moloka'i Museum Gift Shop ★★** (ℂ **808/567-6436**), a trove of crafts, fabrics, cookbooks, quilt sets, and other gift items. There's also a modest selection of cards, T-shirts, coloring books, and, at Christmas, handmade ornaments made of lauhala and koa. Its hours are limited, like the museum's, to Monday to Saturday 10am to 2pm.

In 1980, Daphne Socher and her late husband Jonathan founded the colorful **Big Wind Kite Factory & Plantation Gallery ★★**, 120 Maunaloa Hwy., Maunaloa (www.bigwindkites.com; ℂ **808/552-2364**), chock-full of Balinese furnishings, stone and shell jewelry, Kalaupapa memoirs, and

---

The Perfect Moloka'i Souvenir

Found in nearly every Moloka'i store, the dozen varieties of local sea salts from **Pacifica Hawaii** (www.pacificahawaii.com) make ideal gifts. Taking over from the late salt master Nancy Gove, Michelle Naeole now practices the ancient Hawaiian tradition of evaporating seawater in elevated pans. She then infuses colors and flavors via ingredients such as local clay ('alaea), Kaua'i-made rum, and Maui sugar.

ancient CELEBRATIONS

During **Ka Hula Piko ★★★** (www.facebook.com/kahulapiko), an intimate celebration of the ancient art of hula, practitioners offer powerful chants and dance, not as performance but as gifts to their ancestors. This hula is unlike anything you'll see elsewhere: dances mimicking mythological turtles, honoring taro farmers, and proclaiming ancient prophecies. Festivities typically occur in early June and include an all-day *ho'olaule'a* (festival), during which troupes from as far as Japan and Europe share their skills.

Ka Moloka'i Makahiki ★★★ (search "Ka Molokai Makahiki" on Facebook) is another not-to-miss event. Islanders celebrate the rainy season—a time of peace and prosperity in ancient Hawai'i, associated with the god Lono—with traditional crafts, hula, chanting, games, and competitions. All of Moloka'i gathers for the daylong event, held on a Saturday in late January at the Mitchell Pauole Center in Kaunakakai, while a 4-day procession takes the banner of Lono to every *ahupua'a* (district) on the island.

other books on Moloka'i. Their son Zach Socher has added surf and beach gear, as well as his gorgeous large-format island photography to the inventory. Test-fly one of the handmade Big Wind kites at the nearby park. It's open Monday to Saturday 10am to 5pm, and Sunday until 2pm. **A Touch of Molokai ★**, widely known as "Da Store," overlooks the pool at the closed Kaluakoi Hotel, 1121 Kaluakoi Rd., Maunaloa (✆ **808/552-0133**). It carries a small sampling of apparel, crafts, and souvenirs of its Kaunakakai motherhouse, **Imports Gift Shop ★★** (p. 457).

MOLOKA'I NIGHTLIFE

The few choices for evening entertainment at least mean a lively crowd is guaranteed wherever you go. **Paddlers Restaurant and Bar,** 10 S. Mohala St., Kaunakakai, on the ocean side of Highway 450 (www.paddlersrestaurant.com; ✆ **808/553-3300**), is the island's primary watering hole as well as one of its top restaurants. Happy hour is Monday to Friday 2 to 5pm (the restaurant is closed Sun–Mon). The spacious indoor-outdoor restaurant and bar also hosts live music—predominantly local acts in various genres—and dancing most nights. **Hiro's 'Ohana Grill,** the oceanfront/poolside bar and slightly more refined restaurant at Hotel Moloka'i (p. 450), hosts live Hawaiian music Tuesday to Sunday.

LĀNA'I

by Jeanne Cooper

8

Lāna'i is deliciously remote: The island's tiny airport doesn't accommodate direct flights from the continental U.S., and its closest neighbor is a 70-minute ferry ride away. It's almost as if this quiet, gentle oasis—known for both its small-town feel and luxurious appeal—demands that visitors go to great lengths to get here to better appreciate its beauty.

ESSENTIALS
Arriving

BY PLANE   The tiny but quite modern Lāna'i Airport (LNY) sits in the vast scrubland of Pālāwai Basin, once the world's largest pineapple plantation. There's no nonstop service from the continental U.S., but two airlines with small aircraft offer interisland flights, primarily from Honolulu and Kahului (Maui).

Lāna'i Air (www.lanaiair.com; © **833/486-8397**) has six daily flights from Honolulu to Lāna'i City, and vice versa, aboard luxurious Pilatus PC-12 aircraft that seat eight. Fares start at $160 per person, each way, and flights are included in nightly rates at the Sensei Lāna'i, a Four Seasons Resort. All guests of that hotel or the Four Seasons Resort Lāna'i traveling to or from Honolulu can take advantage of a private lounge on the second floor of Terminal 2. The airline also offers charter service between Lāna'i City and Honolulu, Kahului, Līhu'e (Kaua'i), and Kona (Hawai'i Island).

Mokulele Airlines (www.mokuleleairlines.com; © **866/260-7070**) offers up to three daily flights from Maui's Kahului airport (a 35-min. flight) and six from Honolulu (50 min.) on its nine-passenger Cessna 280EX Grand Caravan plane. Carry-on space is limited, and passengers' self-reported weights are determine the seating balance. Two larger aircraft are now occasionally in service, which reduces time in the air.

From the airport, it's about 10 minutes by cab or shuttle service to Lāna'i City, 15 minutes to Kō'ele, and 25 minutes to Mānele Bay.

BY BOAT   Relocated from Lahaina Harbor after the 2023 fire, **Expeditions Lāna'i Passenger Ferry** (https://go-lanai.com; © **800/695-2624** or 808/661-3756) now shuttles between Ma'alaea, Maui, and Lāna'i's Mānele Bay with two daily round-trips (down from four). The ferry departs Maui at 6:30am and 3:30pm and Lāna'i at 8:30am and 5:30pm. The cost is $30 per adult and $20 per child each way. Arrive 30 minutes early for the channel crossing, which takes about 70 minutes, depending on sea conditions (the ride can be longer and bumpier in winter). Reservations

FACING PAGE: **Hiking the Koloiki Ridge Trail.**

THERE'S an app FOR THAT

The Lāna'i Culture & Heritage Center partnered with Pūlama Lāna'i (the company created by the island's main landowner, Oracle cofounder Larry Ellison) to produce the **Guide,** a frequently updated GPS-enabled app that directs you to historic sites and trails replete with detailed maps, old photos, aerial videos, and chants. Download the app for free from iTunes.

are strongly recommended; call or book online. Baggage is limited to two checked bags and one carry-on for free; fees apply for excess baggage, dogs, and bulky items, such as bicycles, kayaks, sailboards (with bag and mast), and surfboards over 7 feet long. You'll also need to complete a shipping form at the harbor an hour before boarding. ***Bonus:*** During the winter months, taking the ferry can turn into a value-added opportunity to whale watch, while spinner dolphins may accompany the ship anytime.

Four Seasons Resort Lāna'i guests may also charter private passage with **Lāna'i Ocean Sports** (https://lanaioceansports.com; ✆ **808/866-8256**), which has two catamarans accommodating 49 passengers each. Contact the outfitter for current rates.

Visitor Information

The **Maui Visitors and Convention Bureau** (www.gohawaii.com/lanai; ✆ **800/525-6284** or 808/244-3530) provides info on Lāna'i. Download a travel planning brochure from the site, or request one be mailed to you.

The Island in Brief

Lāna'i is pronounced *"lah-nuh-ee,"* in contrast with *lanai* (meaning "deck or balcony"), pronounced *"luh-nye."* Most of the island is still wilderness;

Live music at the Hotel Lāna'i.

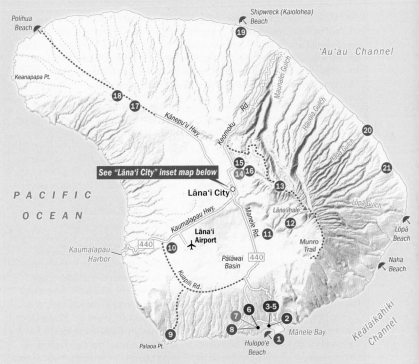

Lānaʻi

0	2 mi
0	2 km

Polihua Beach

Shipwreck (Kaiolohea) Beach **19**

Keanapapa Pt.

ʻAuʻau Channel

Maunalei Gulch

Hauola Gulch

Hulopoe Gulch

18 **17**

Kānepuʻu Hwy.

Keōmoku Rd.

Hau.a Gulch

20

21

See "Lānaʻi City" inset map below

15 **14** **16**

13

Lōpā Gulch

Lānaʻi City

Lānaʻihale

PACIFIC OCEAN

Kaumalapau Hwy.

Manele Rd.

12

Lōpā Beach

Lānaʻi Airport

11

Munro Trail

440

10

Naha Beach

Kaumalapau Harbor

Pālāwai Basin

440

Kuanili Rd.

Kealaikahiki Channel

6 **3-5**

7 **2**

8 **1**

9

Mānele Bay

Palaoa Pt.

Hulopoʻe Beach

Lānaʻi City

4th St.
5th St.
Lānaʻi Ave.
Ilima Ave.
Jacaranda St.
Nani St.
6th St.
Puʻuhanai Pl.

22

23 **25** **26**
24

Dole Park

7th St.
8th St.
9th St.

28
28

27

10th St.
Queens St.
Olapa St.
Lānaʻi Ave.
Ilima Ave.
11th St.

29

Gay St.
Houston St.
Fraser Ave.
12th St.
13th St.

30

31

ghosts **TO GOLF COURSES**

Lānaʻi hasn't always been so welcoming. Early Hawaiians believed the island was haunted by Pahulu (the god of nightmares) and spirits so wily and vicious that no human could survive here. But many have, for the past 800 or so years. Remnants of ancient Hawaiian villages, temples, fishponds, and petroglyphs decorate the Lānaʻi landscape. In the late 18th century, King Kamehameha started spending his summers here at a cliffside compound overlooking the sunny southern coast.

The island's arid terrain was once native forest—patches of which persist on the 3,379-foot summit of **Lānaʻihale**—along with native birds, insects, and jewel-like tree snails. But the 1800s brought foreign ambitions and foreign strife to Hawaii: Disease took more than half of the native populace, and Western commerce supplanted the islanders' subsistence culture. Exotic pests such as rats, mosquitos, and feral goats and cattle decimated the native ecosystem and the island's watershed. Various entrepreneurs tried to make their fortune here, farming sugarcane, cotton, sisal, or sugar beets. All failed, mostly for lack of water.

Jim Dole was the first to have real commercial success. In 1922, he bought the island for $1.1 million. He built Lānaʻi City, blasted out a harbor, and turned the island into a fancy fruit plantation. For 70 years, the island was essentially one big pineapple patch. Acres of prickly fields surrounded a tiny grid of workers' homes. Life continued pretty much unchanged into the 1980s.

Ultimately, cheaper pineapple production in Asia brought an end to Lānaʻi's heyday. In 1985, self-made billionaire David Murdock acquired the island in a merger (well, 98% of it anyway; the remaining 2% is owned by the government or longtime Lānaʻi families).

Murdock built two grand hotels, and almost overnight the plain, red-dirt pineapple plantation became one of the world's top travel destinations. Murdock's grand maneuver to replace agriculture with tourism never proved quite lucrative enough, however. In 2012, after years of six-figure losses, he sold his share of the island to the then-third-richest person in the United States, Larry Ellison.

The software tycoon made important moves to endear himself to the tiny, tight-knit community, including reopening the movie theater and the public swimming pool, renovating dilapidated homes, creating an organic farm, and hiring Lānaʻi natives to run Pūlama Lānaʻi, a company tasked with creating a sustainable future for the island. Longtime residents, who have lived through several island makeovers, appreciate the improvements while worrying about those whose businesses are unable to compete with Ellison's focus on luxury, not to mention his unlimited wealth. The resurgence of tourism in 2020 after the long COVID-19 lockdown also prompted moves to restrict camping and limit the number of nonresidents at Hulopoʻe Beach, long the island's jewel in the crown.

Visitors will find an island still in flux, but worth seeking out.

there's one town, barely 30 miles of paved road, and not a single stoplight. Silicon Valley billionaire Larry Ellison owns 98% of Lānaʻi, including its two Four Season resorts and the humbler Hotel Lānaʻi, all of which have undergone extensive renovations (and price hikes) since his purchase of the 140-square-mile island in 2012.

Inhabited Lāna'i is divided into two regions: Lāna'i City, up on the mountain where the weather is cool and misty, and Mānele, on the sunny southwestern coast where the weather is hot and dry.

Lāna'i City (pop. 3,400) sits at the heart of the island at 1,645 feet above sea level. Nearly all businesses are based here, including the island's only gas station, and the airport is just outside of town. Built in 1924, this village is a tidy grid of quaint tin-roofed cottages in bright pastels, with gardens of banana, passion fruit, and papaya. Many of the residents are the children and grandchildren of Filipino immigrants who once toiled in the island's pineapple fields. Their modest homes, now worth $500,000 or more (for a 1,500-sq.-ft. home, built in 1935, on a 6,000-sq.-ft. lot), are excellent examples of historic preservation; the whole town looks like it's been kept under a bell jar.

Around **Dole Park,** a charming village square lined with towering Norfolk and Cook pines, plantation buildings house general stores, a post office (where people stop to chat), two banks, a half-dozen restaurants, an art gallery, an art center, a few boutiques, a fantastic cultural center, the rustic-chic **Hotel Lāna'i** (a rare and popular source of live music), and a coffee shop that easily outshines any Starbucks. The historic one-room police station displays a "jail" consisting of three padlocked, outhouse-size cells as a throwback to earlier times. The new station—a block away, with regulation-size jail cells—probably sees just as little action.

Just up the road from Dole Park in Kō'ele, the **Sensei Lāna'i, a Four Seasons Resort,** is an ultra-luxurious, all-inclusive, and very private wellness retreat. Standing on a knoll overlooking green pastures and the sea at the edge of a misty forest, the hotel allows only guests in its elaborate gardens, spa and fitness facilities, and elegant dining room and bar. **Lāna'i Adventure Park,** however, is open to the public; it offers ziplines and an "aerial adventure" ropes course on 2 holes of the former Kō'ele golf course, plus guided tours on electric mountain bikes.

Mānele is directly downhill—comprising Mānele Bay (with its small boat harbor and general store), Hulopo'e Beach, and the island's other bastion of extravagance, the **Four Seasons Resort Lāna'i.** You'll see more of "typical" Hawai'i here—sandy beach, swaying palms, and superlative sunsets—plus the towering landmark of Lāna'i, Pu'u Pehe, also known as **Sweetheart Rock.**

With such a small population, everybody knows everybody. The minute you arrive, you'll feel the small-town coziness. People wave to passing cars, residents stop to talk with friends, and fishing and gardening are considered top priorities in life. Leaving the keys in your car's ignition is standard practice.

GETTING AROUND

The island has little infrastructure, so you'll need to plan your transportation in advance. **Rabaca's Limousine Service,** also known as the **Lāna'i**

City shuttle (© **808/559-0230**) will retrieve you from the airport or harbor for $10 per person; they meet each ferry. A complimentary shuttle bus will retrieve guests of the Four Seasons Resort Lānaʻi; if arriving by Lānaʻi Air, shuttle by Tesla Model X is included. (Lānaʻi Air and shuttle are included in the room rate for guests at the Sensei Lānaʻi, a Four Seasons Resort.)

If you're camping at Hulopoʻe Beach, you can walk over from the harbor—a 5-minute stroll. Farmer and former newspaper publisher **Alberta de Jetley** also runs the island's lone taxi service, **Lanai Taxi** (www.facebook.com/lanaitaxi; © **808/649-0808**), with drivers who can double as impromptu tour guides; it's best to arrange all rides in advance, though.

Once you've arrived at your lodging, it's entirely possible to enjoy Lānaʻi without getting behind the wheel. Lānaʻi City is easily walkable and if you're staying at one of the Four Seasons, you'll hardly want to stray from the luxurious property. But if you plan to explore the island's remote shores (which I highly recommend), you'll need a four-wheel-drive (4WD) vehicle for at least a day, or plan to hire a driver.

Reserve your ride far in advance; cars are in short supply here. Thanks to subsidizing by Larry Ellison, gas is less expensive on Lanai—about $4 a gallon—compared to other islands' rates, but remember off-road vehicles get lousy mileage. Spending $40 to $50 per day on gas isn't unheard of. *Tip:* Rent only for the day (or days) you want to explore the island's hinterlands. Keep in mind that rainy weather makes many roads impassable. Check with your rental agent to see which roads are open—and whether renting that day is worth your money.

The island's lone national-brand rental car agency, Dollar, closed its doors in 2019. In its place are several local options:

Artist Judi Riley's **808 Day Trip** (https://808daytrip.com; © **808/649-0664,** text 24 hr.) offers cars for paved roads only. Four options include delivery: four-door Nissan hatchback ($175 per calendar day, plus taxes), Ford Escape SUV ($195), and Grand Cherokee ($250) can each seat five; and six passengers can fit in a four-door Ram 1500 V-6 cylinder Big Horn/Lone Star Quad Cab 4×2 pickup truck ($249; sixth seat is small front middle bench seat; no passengers are permitted in truck bed). If you pick up and drop off your rental in Lānaʻi City, city special rates are $135 (per calendar day, plus taxes) for a five-passenger hatchback, and $200 for a six-passenger pickup truck. Rates may increase during high season (Nov 15–Mar 15). A $300 refundable deposit and use of a credit card with comprehensive car rental insurance is required; be prepared to pay a $1,000 fee if you go off-roading.

Owned by Larry Ellison, **Lānaʻi Car Rental** (https://lanaicarrental.com; © **808/565-3100**) offers older Jeep Wrangler Saharas that can go off-road ($200 a day), and a Tesla 3 for $95. You'll need to arrange a taxi or shuttle ride, though, to pick up your car at its office in town (949 Lānaʻi Ave.). Ask about discount rates if you're staying at the Hotel Lānaʻi.

Despite not actually being cheap, **Lana'i Cheap Jeeps** (https://lanai cheapjeeps.com; © **808/563-0630**) may have the best vehicles for unpaved roads, with new and late-model 4×4 trucks and Jeeps (both $225 per day). Driving on sand, the Munro Trail, and on the deteriorated road to Polihua Beach, however, are not allowed. Pick up your vehicle at the **Hula Hut** boutique, 418 8th St., Lāna'i City, and ask about guided tour options.

Guests of either of the **Four Seasons** (p. 480) can rent four-door, fully loaded Jeep Wranglers for $225 per 24 hours, including gas, directly from the Island Activities desk at the Four Seasons Resort Lāna'i in Mānele Bay (www.fourseasons.com/lanai/experiences; © **808/565-2072**); Toyota Land Cruisers and 4Runners, better suited to remaining on paved roads, are also available.

If you'd rather leave the driving to someone else, **Rabaca's Limousine Service** (p. 465) is a terrific option for a short romp around the island. Knowledgeable local drivers will navigate the rough roads for you, visiting Shipwreck Beach (Kaolohia), Keahiakawelo ("Garden of the Gods"), and the ghost town of Keōmoku in roomy Suburbans. Trips run 3½ hours and cost $80 per person (minimum two guests). If you've got a larger group, Rabaca's will chauffeur the lot of you around in a six-person SUV for $110 per hour. Fifteen-passenger vans go for $150 per hour; they stay on paved roads. Shared rides between town and Mānele Bay, or the cat sanctuary and town, are $10 per person, one-way ($2 tips appreciated).

Whether or not you rent a car, sooner or later you'll find yourself at another Ellison-owned property, **Lāna'i Service Station**, 1036 Lāna'i Ave. (© **808/565-7227**, ext. 3). Get directions, maps, and all the local gossip at this all-in-one grocery, gourmet deli, shave ice stand, gas station, and souvenir shop. It's also a good place to fill your water jugs: A reverse-osmosis water dispenser is just out front.

[Fast FACTS] LĀNA'I

Note: Lāna'i is part of Maui County.

Doctors & Dentists

All services are in Lāna'i City. For over-the-counter prescriptions and vaccines, head to **Rainbow Pharmacy** right by Dole Park, 431 Seventh St. (© **808/565-9332;** Mon–Fri 9am–6pm, Sat until 1pm). If you need a doctor, make an appointment at the **Straub Medical Center Lāna'i Clinic,** 628-B Seventh St.

(© **808/565-6423**). The clinic does not accept walk-ins, but is open Monday and Thursday 8am to 7pm; Tuesday, Wednesday, and Friday 8am to 5pm; on some Saturdays until noon. Open 24 hours a day, the **Lāna'i Community Hospital,** 628 Seventh St. (© **808/565-8450**) offers emergency and urgent care. Next door to the Lāna'i Cultural & Heritage Center, **Hawai'i Dental Clinic,**

730 Lāna'i Ave., Suite 101 (© **808/565-6418**), offers emergency and standard services from Monday to Friday 8am to 6pm; it's best to call ahead.

Emergencies
In case of **emergencies,** call the police, fire department, or ambulance services at © **911,** or the **Poison Control Center** at © **800/222-1222.** For non-emergencies, call the **police** at © **808/565-6428.**

Post Office The island's lone post office is at 620 Jacaranda St., Lāna'i City (© **808/565-6517**). It's open Monday to Friday 9am to 3pm and Saturday 9:30am to 11:30am.

Weather For both land and sea conditions, visit the **National Weather Service** website (www.weather.gov/hfo) and type "Lanai, HI" in the search box.

EXPLORING LĀNA'I

You'll need an off-road vehicle to reach the sights listed below. Four-wheel-drive rentals on Lāna'i are expensive—but worth it for a day or two of adventure. See "Getting Around," above.

Your first stop on Lāna'i (perhaps after a dip at Hulopo'e Beach) should be the **Lāna'i Culture & Heritage Center ★★**, 730 Lāna'i Ave. (www.lanaichc.org; © **808/565-7177**), in the heart of town. Orient yourself to the island's cultural and natural history at this tiny, well-curated museum. Learn how Polynesian voyagers navigated thousands of miles of Pacific Ocean to settle Hawai'i, see relics of the Dole plantation years, and get directions to the island's petroglyph fields. Even better, ask the docents to recount local legends passed down in their families. It's open Monday to Friday 1 to 3pm.

Note: You'll find the following attractions on the "Lāna'i" map on p. 463.

Kanepu'u Preserve ★★ This ancient grove on the western plateau of Lāna'i is the island's last remaining dryland forest, containing 48 native species. A self-guided hike through some of its 590 acres reveals several of the rare trees and shrubs that once covered the dry lowlands of all the main Hawaiian Islands, with well-illustrated interpretive signage. Elsewhere these species have succumbed to axis deer, agriculture, or "progress." Protected by the Nature Conservancy (www.nature.org) and a Native Hawaiian land trust, the reserve's botanical marvels include *olopua* (Hawaiian olive), *lama* (Hawaiian ebony), and *ma'o hau hele* (a Hawaiian hibiscus). Kanepu'u is easily reached via 4WD. Head west from Kō'ele on Polihua Road; in about 1¾ miles, you'll see the fenced area on the left. It's open daily sunrise to sunset.

Kaunolū Village ★★ Out on the nearly vertical sea cliffs of Lāna'i is an old royal compound and fishing village, now a national historic landmark and one of the most treasured ruins in Hawai'i. King Kamehameha the Great considered it a prime spot for fishing and relaxation, but the village was eventually abandoned after 1880.

It's a hot, dry, 3-mile 4×4 drive from Lāna'i City to Kaunolū; if the road is passable (ask your rental agent), the mini-expedition is worth it. Take plenty of water and wear a sun-blocking hat and sturdy shoes. Signs explain the site's importance. Ruins of 86 house platforms and 35 stone shelters have been identified on both sides of Kaunolū Gulch. The residential complex also includes the **Halulu Heiau,** a rock temple named

Keahiakawelo, nicknamed Garden of the Gods.

after a mythical man-eating bird. Rebuilt in the early 1800s by Kamehameha I after his conquest of the island, the heiau was the only *puʻuhonua,* or place of refuge, on Lānaʻi for those who had violated the *kapu* system. The king's royal retreat is thought to have stood on the eastern edge of Kaunolū Gulch, overlooking the rocky shore facing **Kahekili's Leap.** Chiefs leapt from the 62-foot-high perch as a show of bravado. Nearby are **burial caves,** a **fishing shrine,** a **lookout tower,** and boulders with **petroglyphs.** Just offshore stands the telltale fin of little **Shark Island,** a popular dive spot that teems with bright tropical fish and, frequently, sharks.

From Lānaʻi City, take Kaumalapau Highway past the airport. Look for a carved boulder on the left side of the road. Turn left onto a dirt road (Kaupili Rd.) and drive east until you see another carved boulder. Turn right, toward the ocean. *Tip:* On your way out, turn right to continue on Kaupili Road. It meets with Hulopoʻe Drive, a shortcut to Mānele Bay.

Keahiakawelo (Garden of the Gods) ★★★   A four-wheel-drive dirt road leads out of Lānaʻi City, through fallow pineapple fields, past the Kanepuʻu Preserve (see above) to Keahiakawelo. Punctuated by boulders strewn by volcanic forces and sculpted by the elements, the rugged beauty of this place is in its varying shapes and colors—brilliant reds, oranges, ochers, and yellows.

Modern visitors nicknamed this otherworldly landscape "the Garden of the Gods," but its ancient Hawaiian name, Ke-ahi-a-kawelo, means "the fire of Kawelo." According to legend, it's the site of a sorcerers' battle. Kawelo, a powerful *kahuna* (priest), noticed that the people and animals of Lānaʻi were falling ill. He traced their sickness to smoke coming from the neighboring island of Molokaʻi. There, an ill-intentioned priest, Lanikāula, sat chanting over a fire. Kawelo started a fire of his own, here at Keahiakawelo, and tossed some of Lanikāula's excrement into the flames. The smoke turned purple, Lanikāula perished, and health and prosperity returned to Lānaʻi.

Paws for Reflection: Lanai Cat Sanctuary

Abandoned and feral cats used to roam freely around the island, unless someone called animal control, which promptly euthanized them. Lāna'i City resident Kathy Carroll decided there must be a better way and so cajoled Castle & Cooke, then the island's owners, into donating 3 acres near the airport for the island's first shelter, **Lanai Cat Sanctuary ★★★**, 1 Kaupili Rd. (https://lanaicatsanctuary. org; ✆ **808/215-9066**). The cleverly arranged, brightly painted open-air compound, which also protects the island's rare native and migratory birds from predation, now hosts more than 600 "Lāna'i lions" and cats relocated from West Maui after the Lahaina fire of 2023. Visitors drop by daily between 10am and 3pm to frolic with the healthy, spayed and neutered felines (senior cats and those needing medical care are lovingly tended in separate areas). Sporting gleaming ginger, gray, tuxedo, and tabby coats, residents here love to perch on visitors' laps. You are welcome to adopt favorites or donate on their behalf. **Rabaca's Limousine** (p. 465) offers a shuttle from the harbor, airport, or hotels for $10 each way.

Take the bumpy drive out to Keahiakawelo early in the morning or just before sunset, when the light casts eerie shadows on the mysterious lava formations. Drive west from Kō'ele on Polihua Road; in about 2 miles, you'll see a hand-painted sign pointing left down a one-lane, red-dirt road through a kiawe forest to the large stone sign. Don't stack rocks or otherwise disturb this interesting site; leave everything as you found it.

Visiting with the residents of the Lanai Cat Sanctuary.

Luahiwa Petroglyphs Field ★★   Lāna'i is second only to Hawai'i Island in its wealth of prehistoric rock art, but you'll have to search a little to find it. Some of the best examples are on the outskirts of Lāna'i City, on a hillside site known as Luahiwa Petroglyphs Field. The characters incised on 13 boulders in this grassy 3-acre knoll include a running man, a canoe, turtles, and curly-tailed dogs. You may spot some modern-day carvings but please do not add your own.

To get here, take Mānele Road from Lāna'i City toward Hulopo'e Beach. About 2 miles out of town, you'll see a pump house on the left. Look up on the hillside for a cluster of dark boulders—the petroglyphs are there, but you'll have to zigzag to get to them. Two dirt roads lead off of Mānele Road, on either side of the pump house. Take the first one, which leads straight toward the hillside. After about 1 mile, you'll come to a fork. Head right. Drive another ½ mile. At the first V in the road, take a sharp left and double back the way you came, this time on an upper road. After about ¼ mile; you'll come to the large cluster of boulders on the right. It's just a short walk up the cliffs (wear sturdy shoes) to the petroglyphs. Exit the same way you came. Go between 3pm and sunset for ideal viewing and photo ops. Don't touch the petroglyphs or climb on the rocks; these cultural resources are very fragile.

Munro Trail ★   In the first golden rays of dawn, when owls swoop silently over the abandoned pineapple fields, take a peek at **Mount Lāna'ihale,** the 3,366-foot summit of Lāna'i. If it's clear, and your rental contract allows it, hop into a 4×4 and head for the Munro Trail, the narrow, winding ridge trail that runs across Lāna'i's razorback spine to its peak. From here, you may get a rare treat: On a clear day, you can see most of the main islands in the Hawaiian chain.

But if it's raining, forget it. On rainy days, the Munro Trail becomes slick and boggy with major washouts. Rainy-day excursions often end with a rental Jeep on the hook of the island's lone tow truck—and a $250 tow charge. You could even slide off into a major gulch and never be found, so don't try it. But when trade winds stop blowing and the air over the islands stalls in what's called a *kona* condition, the suddenly visible summit becomes an irresistible attraction.

Look for a red-dirt road off Mānele Road (Hwy. 440), about 5 miles south of Lāna'i City; turn left and head up the ridgeline. No sign marks the peak, so you'll have to keep an eye out. Look for a wide spot in the road and a clearing that falls sharply to the sea. From here you can also see silver domes of Science City atop the summit of Haleakalā on Maui; Pu'u O Moa'ulanui, the summit of Kaho'olawe; the tiny crescent of Molokini; and, looming above the clouds, Mauna Kea on Hawai'i Island. At another clearing farther along the thickly forested ridge, all of Moloka'i, including the 4,961-foot summit of Kamakou and the faint outline of O'ahu of (more than 30 miles across the sea), are visible. For details on hiking the trail, see "Hiking" on p. 477.

off the tourist trail: **EASTSIDE LĀNAʻI**

If you've got good weather and a trusty 4×4 vehicle (or even if you'd rather leave the driving to **Rabaca's Limousine Service,** p. 465), go find adventure on the untamed east side of on Lānaʻi. Bring snacks and extra water; there are no facilities out here and cell service is scarce. Follow Keōmoku Road for 8 miles to the coast. Here the road turns to dirt, mud, or sand; proceed with caution. Head left to find **Shipwreck (Kaiolohia) Beach** and the **Kukui Point petroglyphs** (p. 474).

Venture right to explore a string of empty beaches and abandoned villages, including **Keōmoku**—about 5¾ miles down the rough-and-tumble dirt road. This former ranching and fishing community of 2,000 was home to the first non-Hawaiian settlement on Lānaʻi. A ghost town since the mid-1950s, it dried up after droughts killed off the Maunalei Sugar Company. Check out **Ka Lanakila,** the sweetly restored church that dates back to 1903.

Continue another 2 miles to the deserted remains of **Club Lanai.** A lonely pier stretches into the Pacific from a golden-sand beach populated by coconut palms, a few gazebos, and an empty bar floating in a lagoon. You can pretend you're on the set of *Gilligan's Island* here. The area's Hawaiian name, **Halepalaoa,** means "whale ivory house." Historians speculate that the teeth and bones of a sperm whale—rare in these waters—once washed ashore here. If you have time, press on to **Lōpā Beach** (good for surfing, not for swimming). The road ends at empty **Naha Beach** with its ancient fishponds. Return the way you came, taking any trash with you.

Beaches

If you like big, wide, empty, gold-sand beaches and crystal-clear, cobalt-blue water full of bright tropical fish—and who doesn't?—Lānaʻi is your place. With 18 miles of sandy shoreline, Lānaʻi has some of Hawaii's least crowded and most interesting beaches. *Note:* For descriptions of the remote east side's beaches, see "Off the Tourist Trail," p. 472.

Hulopoʻe Beach ★★★   Hulopoʻe is one of the loveliest beaches in all of Hawaiʻi. Palm-fringed golden sand is bordered by black-lava fingers, which protect swimmers from ocean currents. The bay at the foot of the Four Seasons Resort Lānaʻi is a protected marine preserve, with schools of colorful fish, spinner dolphins, and humpback whales that cruise by in winter and often stop to put on a show. The water is perfect for snorkeling, swimming, or just lolling about; the water temperature is usually in the mid-70s (mid-20s Celsius). Swells kick up slightly in winter. Hulopoʻe is also the island's premier beach park,

Shipwreck Beach.

Polihua Beach.

with a grassy lawn, picnic tables, barbecue grills, restrooms, showers, and ample parking.

Hulopoʻe Tide Pools ★★   Some of the best **tide pools** in Hawaiʻi are found along the south shore of Hulopoʻe Bay. These submerged pockets of lava rock are full of strange creatures such as asteroids (sea stars) and holothurians (sea cucumbers), not to mention spaghetti worms, barber pole shrimp, and a favorite local delicacy, the *ʻopihi,* a tasty morsel also known as a limpet. Youngsters enjoy swimming in the enlarged tide pool at the eastern edge of the bay. *A few tips:* When you explore tide pools, do so at low tide. Never turn your back on the waves. Wear running shoes or reef walkers, as wet rocks are slippery. Collecting specimens or souvenirs in this marine preserve is forbidden.

Polihua Beach ★   According to legend, a mythical sea turtle once hauled herself out of the water to lay her eggs in the deep sand at Polihua, or "egg nest." This deserted beach lies at the end of Polihua Road, a challenging, 4-mile Jeep trail (check that your contract allows access). When it isn't windy, this huge, empty stretch on the northwestern shore of Lānaʻi is ideal for beachcombing, fishing, or indulging fantasies of being marooned on a desert island. When the wind *is* blowing, beware—you'll be sandblasted. Look for treasures in the flotsam and (during winter months) whales on the horizon. The beach has no facilities except fishermen's huts and driftwood shelters. Bring water and reef-safe sunscreen. Strong currents and undertow make the water unsafe for swimming.

Shipwreck (Kaiolohia) Beach ★★   This 8-mile-long windswept strand on the island's northeastern shore—named for the rusty ship *Liberty* stuck on the coral reef—is a sailor's nightmare and a beachcomber's dream. The strong currents yield all sorts of sea debris, from glass fishing floats and paper nautilus shells to lots of junk. Shipwreck is not a place to go swimming, but is a great place to spot humpback whales December through March. The road to the beach is paved most of the way, but you really need a 4×4 to get down here. At the end of the road, a trail leads about 200 yards inland to the **Kukui Point petroglyphs;** follow the stacked rock *ahu* (altars) to the large boulders. Respect this historic site by not adding anything to it or taking anything away. Most important, do not touch these fragile, irreplaceable petroglyphs.

Watersports

Because Lānaʻi lacks major development and experiences very little rainfall/runoff, it typically boasts Hawaii's best water clarity. The coast is washed clean daily by strong sea currents, which can wash you away, too, if you aren't careful where you jump in. Most aquatic adventures—swimming, snorkeling, scuba diving—are centered on the somewhat protected west coast, particularly around Hulopoʻe Bay. Spinner dolphins often cruise this coast, traveling in large pods and leaping from the water to twirl mid-air. Green sea turtles, humpback whales, and monk seals make appearances, too. For surf breaks, head to the untamed east shore.

Unfortunately, only guests of one of the two Four Seasons resorts on Lānaʻi can currently book the scheduled, daily snorkeling tours and sunset sails offered by **Lānaʻi Ocean Sports** (www.lanaioceansports.com; ✆ **808/866-8256**). If you *are* a guest there, do take advantage of the opportunity to spend some time on the company's *Lānaʻi II,* a decked-out 65-foot sloop-rigged catamaran built in 2020.

KAYAKING

The south and west coasts of Lānaʻi offer spectacular vistas: dramatic sea cliffs punctuated by hidden caves, quiet coves, and mysterious sea stacks. If your vacation rental provides a kayak, or you're able to shlep your own inflatable, you can put kayaks in at **Mānele** or **Kaumalapau Harbor.** Both are working harbors, but not very busy. From Kaumalapau, paddle roughly 2½ miles north to reach **Nānāhoa,** a cluster of needlelike sea stacks. This picturesque lunch stop has a shady cave and rocky apron to pull up onto for a landing. The snorkeling around these islets can be magical. Check weather conditions and currents before you go.

SAILING & WHALE-WATCHING

Every evening, **Lānaʻi Ocean Sports** (www.lanaioceansports.com; ✆ **808/866-8256**) offers a 2-hour **sunset sail,** available only to guests at the island's two Four Seasons resorts. Cruise past sea cliffs and unspoiled coastline while spinner dolphins and flying fish dart ahead of the bow. You'll arrive at Puʻu Pehe, Sweetheart Rock, just in time for the best sunset shots. The trip costs $180 ($90 for ages 3–12), including appetizers (such as shrimp cocktail and marlin dip with taro chips), an open bar, and Dramamine for those prone to seasickness. The 65-foot *Lānaʻi II* catamaran can seat 49 passengers, but the tour is limited to 30 guests.

During whale season (typically late Dec to Mar), migratory humpback whales put on impressive shows, breaching, slapping their pectoral fins, and singing complex melodies underwater. You can view them from just about any spot on Lāna'i, particularly on the eastside, looking toward Maui, but being on the water provides even better opportunities to see the magnificent creatures up close.

Private sunset and whale-watching charters aboard the 50-foot sailing catamaran *Lāna'i I* are available for $2,400; call for capacity.

SCUBA DIVING

Two of Hawaii's best-known dive spots are found in Lāna'i's clear waters, just off the south shore: **Cathedrals I** and **II,** so named because the sun lights up an underwater grotto like a magnificent church. **Shark Fin Rock** also teems with coral and a rainbow of reef fish. Sadly, the on-island scuba options have shrunk over the years. **Lāna'i Ocean Sports** (www.lanai oceansports.com; © **808/866-8256**) offers private, two-tank dives to Four Seasons guests who are certified divers. The excursion aboard the *Lāna'i I,* a 50-foot sailing catamaran, costs $1,800 for up to four divers.

SNORKELING TOURS

To snorkel on your own, simply strap on a mask and head out from **Hulopo'e Beach.** The marine-life conservation area is Lāna'i's best snorkeling spot; fish are abundant in the bay and marine mammals regularly swim by. Try the lava-rock points at either end of the beach and around the tide pools. *Note:* The Four Seasons' beachside stand offers complimentary gear, including prescription masks, for guests.

Four Seasons guests may venture further afield with **Lāna'i Ocean Sports** (www.lanaioceansports.com; © **808/866-8256**) aboard its 65-foot sailing catamaran, *Lāna'i II.* The captains will steer you alongside the island's dramatic southern coast to a site near the Kaunolū lighthouse. Limited to 30 guests, the daily **3-hour snorkel trips** cost $250 ($125 ages 3–12), including a simple lunch (wraps, chips, fruit, and cookies), cocktails, and local microbrews; help yourself to the stand-up paddleboards. Private group snorkel charters (from $4,100 for up to 36 passengers on the *Lāna'i II* or $3,800 aboard the smaller *Lāna'i I*) are also available.

Note: If you're staying on Maui, **Trilogy** (https://sailtrilogy.com; © **888/225-6284** or 808/874-5649) offers two excellent day trips to Lāna'i. The Discover Lāna'i package includes snorkeling at Hulopo'e, onshore recreational and cultural activities, and a barbecue lunch ($289 adults, $255 ages 13–17, and $190 ages 3–12).

SPORT FISHING

To go for the big fish—including Hawaiian grouper, trevally, amberjack, barracuda, and more—charter *Lāna'i I,* a 50-foot sailing catamaran, from **Lāna'i Ocean Sports** (www.lanaioceansports.com; © **808/866-8256**). The private tours ($3,800) can accommodate up to six passengers (at least one must be a Four Seasons guest); your catch can be delivered to the Nobu or One Forty restaurants at the Four Seasons Lāna'i to be prepared for your dinner.

Other Outdoor Activities

Lāna'i has a surprising number of outdoor activities for visitors, including unusual-for-Hawai'i options such as archery and sporting clays, but nearly all of them must be booked through the **Island Activities desk** at the Four Seasons Resort Lāna'i at 1 Mānele Bay Rd., Lāna'i City (www.four seasons.com/lanai/services-and-amenities/adventure-center; 𝄌 **808/565-2072**). Located next door to the resort's tennis courts, it's open daily 8am to 5pm; you'll need to call or visit in person, since it does not offer online bookings (or current rates). *Note:* Those who aren't guests of the Four Seasons resorts in Mānele or Kō'ele may book activities no more than 24 hours in advance.

AERIAL CHALLENGE COURSES

Children as young as 6 years old and adults have their own ropes, ladders, and other aerial challenge courses at the **Lāna'i Adventure Park** (www.lanaiadventurepark.com; 𝄌 **808/563-0096**) just below the Four Seasons Hotel Lāna'i at Kō'ele, 1 Keōmoku Hwy., Lāna'i City. The two-story Aerial Adventure Tower, which features several dozen obstacles for adults and older children to attempt in a 2-hour span, sits in a large pond surrounded by pines. Ages 8 to 12 need to have a parent on the tower with them, while ages 13 to 18 can test their skills as long as a parent is onsite; it's $85 per participant. Children ages 3 to 8 can do an easier set of challenges through the woods if accompanied by an adult on the course; it's $50 per participant.

ARCHERY & SPORTING CLAYS

Sharpen your shooting skills in two different modes at the **Lāna'i Archery and Shooting Range,** booked through the Four Seasons Resort Lāna'i's **Island Activities desk** (𝄌 **808/565-2072**). Both sharpshooters and novices will enjoy the 14-station shooting clay course in the Lāna'i uplands, zipping from station to station beneath the whispering ironwood trees in their own golf cart. Each target mimics the movement of a different bird or rabbit; shots grow increasingly difficult as the course progresses. Private, 1-hour shooting lessons run $110 per person ($100 for Four Seasons guests). Aspiring archers can aim at 3D animal targets or traditional paper bullseyes ($55 per person per hour, $50 for Four Seasons guests). Wear closed-toe shoes and bring a jacket.

BIKING

The relatively car-free paved roads around Lāna'i City are ideal for cyclists, but note that biking from the harbor up to Lāna'i City or down to Shipwreck (Kaiolohia) Beach and back require excellent fitness. Open to the public, **Lāna'i Adventure Park** (www.lanaiadventurepark.com; 𝄌 **808/563-0096**) offers guided bike tours ($120) on Kona electric bikes on four different scenic routes for ages 14 and older (ages 14–18 must be accompanied by an adult).

GOLF

Cavendish Golf Course ★ This quirky par-36, 9-hole public course lacks not only a clubhouse and club pros, but also tee times, scorecards, and club rentals. To play, just show up, put a donation into the little wooden box next to the first tee, and hit away. The 3,071-yard, E. B. Cavendish–designed course was built by the Dole plantation in 1947 for its employees. The greens are a bit bumpy, but the views of Lāna'i are great and the temperatures usually quite mild. *Note:* You'll need to bring your own clubs; you can't rent them from the Four Seasons golf shop to use here.
Off Kauna'oa Dr., Kō'ele. By donation.

Manele Golf Course ★★★ Designed by Jack Nicklaus, this target-style, desert-links course is one of the most challenging courses in the state—hence its original name, the Challenge at Manele—and unfortunately limited to Four Seasons guests. This starkly beautiful oceanfront course, routed among lava outcroppings, archaeological sites, and kiawe groves, offers five sets of staggered tees that pose a challenge to pro and casual golfer alike. The staff hands out complimentary Bloody Marys and screwdrivers, while carts come with Bluetooth to stream your own music. The clubhouse's well-named if pricey **Views restaurant** ★★—which unlike the golf course is open to the public—is a destination in its own right (daily 11am–3pm; main courses $26–$38). Facilities include a clubhouse, pro shop, rentals, practice area, lockers, and showers.
1 Challenge Dr. (next to the Four Seasons Resort Lāna'i), Lāna'i City. www.fourseasons. com/lanai. ☏ **808/565-2222.** Four Seasons guests only: $385 for 18 holes ($175 ages 12–17, free for kids 11 and under), $215 for 9 holes ($95 ages 12–17, free for kids 11 and under). Juniors also play free after noon with each paying adult. Club rentals $85 for 18 holes, $55 for 9 holes. Daily 8am–6pm.

HIKING

For more information on these trails and others, such as the 1-mile **Keālia-Kapu Kaunolū Trail** near the ancient village of Kaunolū (p. 468), or the scenic **Naha Overlook** spur off the **Munro Trail** (see below), download the Lāna'i Guide app, by the **Lāna'i Culture & Heritage Center.** The **Four Seasons' Island Activities** desk (☏ **808/565-2072**) can provide maps for the **Pōhakuloa Gulch** hiking trail near the Mānele resort and for **Koloiki Ridge** (see below) near Sensei Lāna'i.

Kapiha'a Trail ★★ An old fisherman's trail starts at Mānele Bay and snakes along the scenic coastline. This easy hike will expose you to the unique geography of Lāna'i and many unusual native Hawaiian coastal plants. The back-and-forth trek takes around 90 minutes.

Koloiki Ridge Hike ★★★ The leisurely 2-hour self-guided hike starts behind the Sensei Lāna'i, a Four Seasons Resort, and takes you on a 5-mile loop through Norfolk Island pines, into Hulopo'e Valley, past wild ginger, and up to Koloiki Ridge, with its panoramic view of Maunalei Valley and the islands of Moloka'i and Maui in the distance. Go in the morning; by afternoon, the clouds usually roll in, marring visibility at the top and increasing your chance of being caught in a downpour. It's considered moderate, with some uphill and downhill hiking.

Munro Trail ★★   This tough, 11-mile (round-trip) uphill climb through groves of Norfolk pines is a lung-buster, but if you reach the top, you'll be rewarded with a breathtaking view of Moloka'i, Maui, Kaho'olawe, and Hawai'i Island. Plan for 7 hours. The trail begins at Lāna'i Cemetery (interesting in its own right) along Keōmoku Road (Hwy. 44) and follows the island's ancient caldera rim, ending up at the island's highest point, **Lāna'ihale.** Go in the morning for the best visibility. After 4 miles, you'll get a view of Lāna'i City. The weary retrace their steps from here, while the more determined go the last 1.25 miles to the top. Diehards head down the island's steep south-crater rim to join the highway to Mānele Bay.

Pu'u Pehe ★   Skirt along Hulopo'e Bay to scale the cliff on its southern edge (it's a gentle slope, not a steep climb). This 20-minute hike leads above the turquoise-gray waters of Shark's Cove to the dramatic point overlooking Pu'u Pehe, or Sweetheart's Rock. The picturesque islet rises 80 feet from the sea and is home to nesting seabirds. Look closely to see an *ahu,* an altar of rocks at the top. According to legend, a young Lāna'i warrior hid his beautiful wife in a sea cave at the base of the cliffs here. One day a storm flooded the cave and she drowned. Grief-stricken, her beloved climbed the sheer face of the islet, carrying her body. He buried her, then jumped to his death in the pounding surf below.

HORSEBACK RIDING

Get a taste of the *paniolo* (cowboy) life on a horseback tour. Sign up for an upland trail ride at the **Island Activities desk (** © **808/565-2072)** at the Four Seasons Resort Lāna'i, which can also arrange a shuttle up to Kō'ele to meet your steed. On horseback, you'll meander through guava groves and past ironwood trees; catch glimpses of spotted deer, wild turkeys, and quail; and end with panoramic views of Maui and Lāna'i. The trails are dusty and rain is frequent; wear clothes you don't mind getting dirty and bring a light jacket. Long pants and closed-toe shoes are required. Daily tours (9am, 11am, and 1pm) last 1½ hours and cost $180 per person. Private rides are available for $275 per person; for children, a private ride lasts 30 minutes and costs $75 per child. A private horse and carriage that seats up to four can be rented for $400 per person; a customized equine experience is $325 per person (ages 9 and up). (For an enjoyable and safe excursion, riders must weigh less than 195 lb.)

Even if you don't book a ride, you may want to visit the stables to "Meet the Minis." Parents can arrange half-hour visits for their children to meet the miniature horses, donkeys, and goats daily 10am to 3pm, with shuttle service for resort guests.

SWIMMING

Palm trees and lounge chairs line the outdoor, heated, Olympic-sized Lānaʻi Community Pool at the Lānaʻi Recreation Center, near the intersection of Caldwell Avenue and Fifth Street in Lānaʻi City. This well-maintained pool is open for lap swimming by reservation Monday to Friday 8am to noon (✆ **808/215-1075**) and open swimming 12:30 to 5pm and Saturday and Sunday from 8am to 3pm.

TENNIS & PICKLEBALL

Three public tennis courts, lit for night play, are available at Lānaʻi Recreation Center, near the intersection of Caldwell Avenue and Fifth Street in Lānaʻi City; call ✆ **808/565-6979** for reservations, at no charge. If you're staying at the Four Seasons in Mānele, you can take advantage of the **Tennis Garden** (www.fourseasons.com/lanai/services-and-amenities/tennis; ✆ **800/321-4666**), which offers two Plexi-Pave cushion courts (which can be configured into pickleball courts by reservation) and a Har-Tru green clay court—the same as used by the pros. Court access ($65 per person

per hour) comes with complimentary use of tennis or pickleball rackets, balls, and bottled water—even shoes if you need them; clinics and lessons for adults and kids are also available.

ZIPLINING

Soar over a deep green valley surrounded by Cook pines on the dauntingly steep ziplines at **Lānaʻi Adventure Park** (www.lanaiadventurepark.com; ✆ **808/563-0096**) near Sensei Lānaʻi, 1 Keōmoku Hwy., Lānaʻi City. The two-zip tour, flying seated or prone like Superman, is $100 per person for 2 rides, open to ages 8 and older; height, weight, and ability restrictions also apply.

The ropes course at Lānaʻi Adventure Park.

WHERE TO STAY ON LĀNAʻI

Like nearly everything on Lānaʻi, lodging options are very limited. You can go for broke at one of the luxurious Four Seasons resorts, or spring for a pricey vacation rental (30-day minimum) along its golf course. In the "village," as residents call Lānaʻi City, book a more moderately priced but stylishly renovated room at the plantation-era Hotel Lānaʻi, or a short-term rental in a similarly updated vintage cottage.

Note: VRBO and Airbnb offer plenty of vacation rentals; to avoid legal conflicts, look for the Maui County license number in the listings. Hotel and state taxes will add 17.962% to all lodging bills; don't forget to calculate cleaning and booking charges added to vacation rentals.

Very Expensive

Four Seasons Resort Lāna'i ★★★   It's only in recent years that its "Love Lāna'i" Hawaiian cultural program—with hands-on activities like throw-net fishing and *kapala* (bamboo stamping), and performances of Hawaiian music and hula—has thankfully become a more prominent feature of this opulent oasis. Under Larry Ellison's ownership, the island's sole beachfront resort has long reflected the latest in tech-savvy luxury, from wristband room keys to bidet toilets; but without Hawaiian touchstones, it seemed out of place.

Lobby of Four Seasons Resort Lāna'i.

Service is impeccable: The concierge texts you when dolphins or whales appear in the bay. Beach attendants set up umbrellas in the sand for you, spritz you with Evian, and deliver popsicles. Guest rooms are large and luxurious, with blackout shades that you can control with a flick of your hand. Suites have Japanese cedar tubs and views that stretch on forever. The resort's two wings overlook Hulopo'e Beach with lush landscaping of waterfalls, koi-filled lotus ponds; you'll find artwork tucked into every corner. Rare Polynesian artifacts purchased from the Bishop Museum decorate the main lobby's lower level, which is home to two superb restaurants: **Nobu Lāna'i ★★★** and **One Forty ★★★**. Other amenities include the **Break ★★**, an excellent if expensive coffee, pastry, and panini outlet; **Malibu Farm ★★**, the poolside casual California-style restaurant; a first-rate adventure center; adults-only and family pools; and an 1,100-square-foot yoga pavilion with free classes and a killer ocean view (*Namaste!*). Inspired by indigenous healing traditions, the resort's **Hawanawana Spa** offers traditional *lomi lomi* Hawaiian massages, seaweed body wraps, facials, and salon services in serene treatment rooms. The free "Kids for All Seasons" childcare activities are excellent, but you'll probably have trouble pulling your youngsters away from the beach and tide pools. Give

Where to Stay on Lāna'i

LĀNA'I

480

Building a volcano at Four Seasons Resort Lāna'i.

Ellison extra credit for providing long-term housing to rescued exotic birds, which have their own caretaker, large aviaries, and daily outings at the beach.

1 Mānele Bay Rd., Lāna'i City. www.fourseasons.com/lanai. © **800/321-4666** or 808/565-2000. 168 rooms, 45 suites. From $1,928 garden-view double, $2,323 partial oceanview, $2,753 oceanview; from $4,550 suite. **Amenities:** 3 restaurants; cafe; 2 bars; babysitting; kids' program; concierge; gym w/classes; Jack Nicklaus–designed golf course; whirlpools; 2 pools; Jeep rentals; room service; full spa; 3 tennis courts; free use of watersports equipment; free Wi-Fi.

Sensei Lāna'i, a Four Seasons Resort ★★★   A $75 million meta-morphosis of a former Anglo-Hawaiian country lodge in Kō'ele, this first-ever Sensei Retreat is the brainchild of billionaire (and Lāna'i's majority landowner) Larry Ellison, who's famously obsessed with Japanese aesthetics, and Dr. David Agus, with whom Ellison co-founded a wellness company called Sensei. You can choose all-inclusive or a la carte rates, but the atmosphere is ultra-exclusive; very rarely are non-guests allowed on the property. Guests (restricted to ages 16 and up) can opt for private wellness and nutrition consultations from "Sensei Guides," who use high-tech diagnostics to help them choose from the variety of daily classes (yoga, core, resistance, meditation, and so forth). Elaborate tropical gardens surround Japanese *onsen* (hot tubs), free-form pools, airy movement studios, and house-sized, private spa cottages with their lush landscaping and water features. Sourced from Ellison's Sensei Organic Farm and local fish and meat suppliers, the cuisine at gracious **Sensei by Nobu ★★★** is exquisite, with a nightly five-course *omakase* (chef's choice) menu. The somewhat sterile though

481

spacious rooms and sprinkling of voluptuous nude sculptures by Fernando Botero seem a little off; still, it's hard to fault anything but the high price. 1 Keōmoku Hwy., Lāna'i City. www.fourseasons.com/sensei. ℂ **800/505-2624** or 808/650-7451. 96 rooms. Adult-only, all-inclusive stays (lodging, meals, drinks, consultations, fitness and wellness classes, 2 spa treatments, private air service to/from Honolulu, Tesla Model X airport shuttle) start at $1,010 a night (3-night minimum); room with only Honolulu flight and yoga class included from $980 ($1,200 suite). **Amenities:** Restaurant; bar; concierge; fitness center, yoga pavilion, and movement studio w/classes; free access to Lāna'i Adventure Center; Onsen Garden with 10 whirlpools; 2 large free-form pools with whirlpools; room service; 10 private spa cottages; Wi-Fi.

Expensive

The well-landscaped two-bedroom, two-bath **Artists House ★★**, 1243 Queens St., Lāna'i City (www.airbnb.com/rooms/17501056), was lovingly renovated by longtime Lāna'i artist Jordanne Weinstein, now based on Maui. Her bright paintings of pineapples adorn the well-insulated walls, the kitchen gleams with stainless steel kitchen and granite counters, and the master bath includes a leafy outdoor shower. Rates start at $490 a night (sleeps six), plus a $175 cleaning fee and Airbnb service fee of $163; inquire with the property manager about car rentals.

Hotel Lāna'i ★★   Also part of Larry Ellison's empire, this plantation-era hotel in the heart of town boasts modern style and comforts, including immense flatscreen TVs, phones, air-conditioning, electric window shades, and bidet-style toilets. Two holdovers from the plantation era: Guest rooms are small, and noise travels. Still, it's a bargain compared with either of the Four Seasons resorts, and its stand-alone cottage offers more space and privacy. The popular lanai units are slightly larger than garden units and share a furnished lanai (deck) that faces Dole Park; families or couples traveling together can book garden units as adjoining rooms. All of Lāna'i City is within walking distance. The in-house restaurant, **Lāna'i City Bar & Grill ★★**, is not only an excellent dining choice with innovative island cuisine, but also a lively social spot where visitors mingle with locals in the bar, talking or playing the ukulele long into the night. *Tip:* Weekday room rates are cheaper. 828 Lāna'i Ave., Lāna'i City. www.hotellanai.com. ℂ **800/795-7211** or 808/565-7211. 11 units. $315–$365 garden room; $370–$420 lanai room; $685–$735 cottage; includes continental breakfast. Free parking. **Amenities:** Restaurant; bar; free Wi-Fi.

Moderate

Families and small groups may appreciate the roominess and cost of a vacation rental in town. Among the nicer options, owned by a Lāna'i native who now lives on O'ahu, **444 Lanai ★★**, 444 Lāna'i Ave., Lāna'i City (www.airbnb.com/rooms/13657322), is a smartly renovated 3-bedroom, 1½-bath cottage with a beautifully updated kitchen, modern bathrooms, large white-paneled living room with full-size sofabed and single daybed, one queen bed apiece in the three bedrooms, washer/dryer, and

Wi-Fi; rates start at $295 a night (minimum 2 nights) for up to seven people, plus a $95 cleaning fee and $98 Airbnb service fee.

Inexpensive

Dreams Come True ★ Susan and Michael Hunter have operated this bed-and-breakfast off what passes for a busy road on Lāna'i for more than 35 years. Although they no longer serve a full breakfast (just muffins and coffee), their nicely renovated 1925 plantation house is roomy and quaint, with four bedrooms, four bathrooms, and a backyard orchard of papaya, banana, and avocado trees. Among the many perks: marble bathrooms, a well-equipped kitchen with mountain views, and proprietors who love the island.

1168 Lāna'i Ave., Lāna'i City. https://dreamscometrueonlanai.com. ✆ **808/565-6961** or 808/565-7211. 4 rooms, or entire house. $200 double; $800 entire house. **Amenities:** Barbecue; laundry; free Wi-Fi.

WHERE TO EAT ON LĀNA'I

Lāna'i offers dining experiences on two ends of the spectrum, from humble ma-and-pa eateries to world-class culinary adventures, although both are few in number. Expect to pay more at either kind of establishment than on larger islands.

Note: You'll find the restaurants reviewed in this chapter on the "Lāna'i" map on p. 463.

Expensive

Nobu Lāna'i ★★★ JAPANESE Most of celebrity chef Nobu Matsuhisa's acclaimed Japanese-Peruvian restaurants lie in more glamorous, bustling locales such as Milan, Malibu, and Miami. Luckily for Lāna'i, Matsuhisa agreed to Larry Ellison's request to open an outpost here. Under O'ahu-born chef Christopher Texeira, who trained at Nobu Waikīkī, every dish is as delicious as it is artful: the smoked Wagyu gyoza with jalapeño miso, the immaculate plates of nigiri sushi, and the lobster salad with spicy lemon. A teppanyaki tasting menu—15 courses for $295 per person—is available at the two teppan tables (book in advance); there's also an intimate sushi bar for perfectly executed sushi and sashimi. The wine and cocktail list is top-notch, including exclusive Hokusetu sake and a sassy caipirinha with Pisco, lime, ginger beer, and sprigs of shiso.

At the Four Seasons Resort Lāna'i, 1 Mānele Bay Rd., Lāna'i City. www.fourseasons.com/lanai/dining. ✆ **808/565-2832.** Sushi rolls $7–$30; main courses $28–$76; 15-course teppanyaki tasting menu $295. Daily 5:30–9:30pm.

One Forty ★★★ BREAKFAST/STEAK & SEAFOOD Named for the number of miles in the radius in which the restaurant tries to source most of its ingredients (that is, within the state of Hawaii), this restaurant shines day and night. Breakfast is via a delicious a la carte menu and dinner is decidedly sumptuous: Look for the pan-seared Hawaiian catch of

Hulopo'e Beach Park, with the Four Seasons Resort Lāna'i in the background.

the day ($120) or the lobster saffron risotto with caviar ($76). Ocean views and excellent service help make up for the nondescript decor.

At the Four Seasons Resort Lāna'i, 1 Mānele Bay Rd., Lāna'i City. www.fourseasons. com/lanai/dining. ☎ **800/321-4666.** Main courses $28–$70 (lighter fare $15–$25) breakfast; $56–$145 dinner. Daily 6:30–11am and 5:30–9:30pm.

Moderate

Lāna'i City Bar & Grill ★★ AMERICAN   This Lāna'i mainstay has three handsome dining areas to choose from. Your options are a rustic-chic dining room with plank-topped tables and wooden chairs with carved-pineapple backs; an airy bar with woven chairs and leather booths; or an outdoor patio with sturdy tables and chairs, plus living room-style heat lamps, so you can stay warm while listening to Hawaiian musicians croon under the stars. Trofie pasta with a rich ragout of local venison may be the star of a menu, but you'll also find fresh-caught seafood, hearty burgers made with grass-fed beef, and specialty cocktails. *Note:* The restaurant serves continental breakfast for Hotel Lāna'i guests.

At the Hotel Lāna'i, 828 Lāna'i Ave., Lāna'i City. https://lanaicitybarandgrill.com. ☎ **808/565-7212.** Main courses $14–$39. Tues–Sat 5:30–9pm; happy hour Tues–Thurs 4–5:30pm and Fri–Sat 9–10pm.

Malibu Farm ★ AMERICAN   The poolside restaurant at the Four Seasons Resort Lāna'i—open only for resort guests, alas—offers the healthful/comfort fare favored by the Hollywood set for lunch and cocktail hour. If you skipped breakfast, start with an açai bowl or fried egg sandwich with Havarti cheese and bacon; for lunch, black quinoa and white rice accompany grilled local fish, while one of the four salads pairs burrata and papaya. At dusk, pull up a seat at the bar for a craft cocktail and watch the sun melt into the sea.

At the Four Seasons Resort Lāna'i, 1 Mānele Bay Rd., Lāna'i City. www.fourseasons. com/lanai/dining. ☎ **808/427-8690.** Main courses $20–$33. Daily 11am–5pm.

Inexpensive

Blue Ginger Café ★ COFFEE SHOP   With its cheery curtains and oilcloth-covered tables, this humble eatery welcomes visitors and locals alike for eggs and Spam (a beloved breakfast meat in Hawaii), bowls of *saimin,* epic plates of fried rice, fried chicken katsu, and grilled mahi sandwiches. The kitchen staff bakes all the breads and pastries, so burgers and sandwiches taste especially fresh. The blueberry turnovers, cinnamon buns, and cookies are local favorites.

409 Seventh St. (at Ilima St.), Lāna'i City. www.bluegingercafelanai.com. © **808/565-6363.** Main courses $10–$13 breakfast; $11–$24 dinner; $7–$11 sandwiches. Cash only. Mon and Thurs–Fri 6am–8pm; Tues–Wed 6am–2pm; Sat–Sun 6:30am–8pm.

Coffee Works ★ COFFEEHOUSE   A short stroll from Dole Park, this cozy coffeehouse in a restored plantation house churns out excellent espresso drinks, plus "small kine" breakfast and lunch items: amply loaded lox and bagels, açai bowls, omelets, sandwiches, and ice cream. It's also Lāna'i City's local watering hole—expect to see your server from dinner last night chatting away with the shuttle driver on the wide wooden deck. As you wait for your cappuccino, browse the gift items: T-shirts, tea infusers and pots, and Hawai'i coffee beans.

604 Ilima St. (at Sixth St.), Lāna'i City. www.coffeeworkshawaii.com. © **808/565-6962.** Most items under $15. Tues–Fri 7am–2pm and Sat until noon.

Lāna'i Service Station ★ DELI   The island's sole gas station includes the Plantation Store, a souvenir shop, and deli with refreshing shave ice, tasty sandwiches, soups, and a few more hot items—all more gourmet than you might expect. Grilled cheese comes with Boursin, Swiss, provolone, and avocado, while the crab cake hoagie comes with wasabi black pepper mayo. Check the Facebook page for specials.

1036 Lāna'i Ave., Lāna'i City. www.facebook.com/lanaiservicestation. © **808/565-7227.** Lunch items $10–$12. Deli daily 6am–2pm; store until 9pm.

Pele's Other Garden ★ DELI/BISTRO   The checkered floor and vanity license plates decorating the walls set an upbeat tone at this casual bistro in a cheery yellow cottage. For lunch, dig into an avocado and feta wrap, an Italian hoagie, or the thin-crusted four-cheese pizza—a gooey medley of mozzarella, Parmesan, feta, and provolone. During happy hour, nosh on onion rings and coconut shrimp at one of Lāna'i City's few bars. Enjoy cocktails, wine by the glass, or one of the dozen brews on tap. The atmosphere grows slightly more romantic after sundown, with white linens on the tables and twinkle lights over the outdoor seating.

811 Houston St., Lāna'i City. https://pelesothergarden.com. © **808/565-9628.** Main courses $11–$17 lunch, $17–$20 dinner; pizza from $11. Mon–Fri 11am–2pm and 5–8pm; happy hour Mon–Fri 4:30–6:30pm.

LĀNA'I SHOPPING

Lāna'i has limited shopping, but you can find some gems here, whether strolling around Dole Park or shopping in the Four Seasons' well-curated boutiques. A barge delivers groceries only once a week (Thurs), so if you're in a vacation rental, plan your shopping accordingly. Shops are typically open Monday to Saturday 9am to 6pm, and Sundays with more limited hours.

Art

Lāna'i Art Center ★★ Established in 1989, the Lāna'i Art Center showcases works by Lāna'i residents, including evocative watercolor paintings of local landmarks, silkscreened clothing, and necklaces of polished shells and bone, plus inexpensive keepsakes. Often, the artists are at work in back. It's open Monday to Saturday 10am to 4pm. 339 Seventh St., Lāna'i City. www.lanaiartcenter.org. © **808/565-7503.**

Mike Carroll Gallery ★★★ Oil painter Mike Carroll left a successful 20-year career as a professional artist in Chicago for a distinctly slower pace on Lāna'i in 2001. His gorgeous, color-saturated interpretations of local life and landscapes fill the walls of his eponymous gallery, which also sells original work by other artists. Sales of Carroll's charming

The lively Mike Carroll Gallery.

"Cats in Paradise" oils, photos, and prints help support the **Lanai Cat Sanctuary ★★★** (p. 470), which wife Kathy Carroll founded. It's open Monday to Friday 10am to 5pm and Saturday and Sunday until 6pm—one of the rare Sunday options. 443 Seventh St., Lāna'i City. www.mikecarroll gallery.com. ✆ **808/565-7122.**

Local Treats & Grocery Staples

Pine Isle Market ★ The Honda family has operated this grocery for 7 decades. Three doors down from Richard's (see below), it carries everything that its competition doesn't. Pine Isle specializes in locally caught fresh fish, but you can also find ice cream, canned goods, fresh herbs, toys, diapers, and other essentials, including every imaginable fishing lure. Open Monday to Saturday 8am to 6pm. 356 Eighth St., Lāna'i City. ✆ **808/565-6488.**

Richard's Market ★★ Since 1946, this small grocery store has also been the go-to for dry goods, frozen food, liquor, paper products, cosmetics, and other miscellany. Courtesy of new owners Larry Ellison and Pūlama Lāna'i, it now resembles a miniature Whole Foods with an array of fancy chocolates and fine wines, plus poke, aloha shirts, and beach mats. Don't faint when you see that milk costs $9 a gallon; that's the price of paradise. Open daily 6am to 9pm. 434 Eighth St., Lāna'i City. ✆ **808/565-3781.**

Gifts & Souvenirs

In addition to the Dole Park shops below, adults will find elegant splurges on swimwear, jewelry, and housewares at the **Makamae** and **Pilina** boutiques in the Four Seasons Resort Lāna'i (p. 480); the resort's sundries store **Mua Loa** carries cute children's items and beach gear.

The Local Gentry ★★ Jenna (Gentry) Majkus manages to outfit her small but wonderful boutique with every wardrobe essential, from fancy lingerie to stylish chapeaux, for the whole family. If you need sunglasses, come here for polarized Maui Jims. It's open Monday to Friday 10am to 6pm, Saturday until 5pm and Sunday until 2pm. 363 Seventh St., Lāna'i City. www.facebook.com/thelocalgentrylanai. ✆ **808/565-9130.**

Rainbow Pharmacy ★★ Like so many island institutions, this pharmacy plays dual roles. It's not just a place to fill your prescription or stock up on earplugs and sunburn gel; you'll also find quality locally made souvenirs, including Cory Lovejoy's coin purses and clutches made with vintage Hawaiian fabric. From the counter in back, you can order an assortment of medicinal Chinese teas and—unpredictably—shave ice. *Note:* The pharmacy is officially open Monday to Friday 9am to 6pm, but the staff takes off for lunch from 1 to 2pm; on Saturday it's open 9am to 1pm. 431 Seventh St., Lāna'i City. www.facebook.com/rainbowpharmacylanai/. ✆ **808/565-9332.**

LĀNA'I NIGHTLIFE

Guests at the **Four Seasons Resort Lāna'i,** 1 Mānele Bay Rd. (www. fourseasons.com/lanai), may enjoy small plates, cocktails, or dessert while shooting pool or playing table games in the **Break,** open daily till 11pm; the public may join them in the open-air lounge by reservation (© **808/808-4178**). The resort's intimate **Nobu Bar,** which serves a variety of sakes and small bites daily from 5:30 to 9:30pm, is open only to guests. Welcoming all comers, the heated outdoor patio at **Lāna'i City Bar & Grill ★★**, part of the Hotel Lāna'i, 828 Lāna'i Ave. (www.lanai citybarandgrill.com; © **808/565-7212**), hosts weekend jam sessions by local musicians under the stars.

Part of Ellison's island overhaul, the wonderfully renovated **Hale Keaka ★**, 465 Seventh St., Lāna'i City (www.lanai96763.com/movies), opened in 1926 as the Lanai Theater. The cinema underwent a $4-million update that kept the vintage feel while adding air-conditioning, digital sound, two stages and screens, cushy seats, and more. It usually screens two movies, including one for kids, each week. Tickets are $10 adults, $9 seniors and students ages 12 to 18, $7 children ages 3 to 11.

KAUA'I

by Jeanne Cooper

9

T ime has been kind to Kaua'i, the oldest and northern-most of the Hawaiian Islands. Millions of years of erosion have carved fluted ridges, emerald valleys, and glistening waterfalls into the flanks of Wai'ale'ale, the extinct volcano at the center of this near-circular isle. Similar eons have created a ring of enticing sandy beaches and coral reefs. Its wild beauty sometimes translates to rough seas and slippery trails, but with a little prudence, anyone can safely revel in the natural grandeur of Kaua'i—and many, many have. That has prompted concerns about overtourism, with the future likely to bring more entry fees and paid parking at popular natural attractions. But I've found the slight cost and crimp on spontaneity worth it to experience serenity amid the gorgeous sands and reefs in Hā'ena, where the island's first visitor reservation system began in 2018. By planning your adventures carefully, adopting the island's laidback attitude, respecting its distinctive culture, and showing consideration for residents as well as the environment, you can maximize everyone's enjoyment of unique Kaua'i.

ESSENTIALS

Arriving

BY PLANE A number of North American airlines offer regularly scheduled, nonstop service to the island's main airport in Līhu'e (airport code: LIH) from the continental U.S., nearly all from the West Coast. (*Note:* From California, flights take about 5½ hr. heading to Kaua'i, but only 4½ hr. on the return, due to prevailing winds.)

United Airlines (www.united.com; © **800/864-8331**), flies nonstop to Kaua'i daily from Los Angeles, San Francisco, and Denver; **Delta Airlines** (www.delta.com; © **800/221-1212**) also flies nonstop from Los Angeles and Seattle. **American Airlines** (www.aa.com; © **800/433-7300**) has year-round nonstop services from Los Angeles and Phoenix. **Alaska Airlines** (www.alaskaair.com; © **800/252-7522**) flies nonstop to Līhu'e several times a week from San Diego, San Jose, and Seattle, as well as seasonally from Portland, Oregon. **Hawaiian Airlines** (www.hawaiianairlines.com; © **800/367-5320**) flies nonstop to Līhu'e from Los Angeles, Oakland, and Sacramento. **Southwest Airlines** (www.southwest.com; © **800/367-5320**)

PREVIOUS PAGE: **Mākua Beach is the best snorkeling and diving site on Kaua'i.**

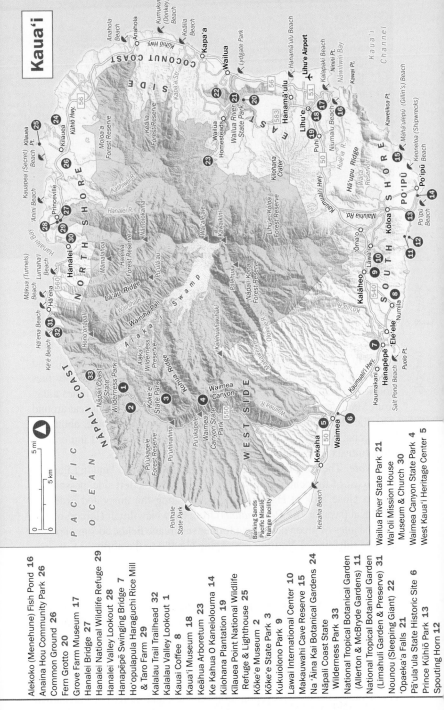

Kaua'i

491

A horseback ride through the Kaua'i countryside.

offers nonstop service from Oakland, San Jose, and Las Vegas, as well as seasonally from Los Angeles. **WestJet** (www.westjet.com; ⓒ **888/937-8538**) offers nonstop flights between Vancouver and Līhu'e from late October through early April.

You can also travel to Līhu'e via Honolulu; Kahului, Maui; and Kona, on Hawai'i Island. **Hawaiian Airlines** (see above) typically flies nonstop to Kaua'i 16 to 20 times a day from Honolulu, four times a day from Maui, and once from Kona. All using Boeing 717s that seat around 120, the Honolulu flight is about 35 minutes; the Maui route, about 45; and Kona, about 50. Southwest (see above) also flies to Līhu'e from Honolulu six times daily, using Boeing 737s that seat 175.

Note: The view from either side of the plane as you land in Līhu'e, 2 miles east of the center of town, is arresting. On the left side, passengers have a close look at Hā'upu Ridge, separating the unspoiled beach of Kīpū Kai (seen in *The Descendants*) from busy Nāwiliwili Harbor; on the right, shades of green demarcate former sugarcane fields, coconut groves, and the ridgeline of **Nounou** ("Sleeping Giant") to the north.

Visitor Information

Before your trip begins, visit www.gohawaii.com/islands/kauai, the website of **Kaua'i Visitors Bureau** (ⓒ **800/262-1400** or 808/245-3971), and download or view the free "Kaua'i Official Travel Planner." (*Note:* The bureau's Līhu'e office at 4473 Pahe'e St., Suite F, is open Mon–Fri 8am–4:30pm.) Click on the "Visitors" link of **Kaua'i County**'s homepage (www.kauai.gov), for links to the Visitors Bureau, bus schedules, camping information, park and golf facility listings, a festival and events calendar, farmers market schedules, recycling drop-off sites, and more. For lifeguarded beaches, including descriptions of amenities and potential hazards, plus

Beaches & Outdoor Activities on Kaua'i

BEACHES & BEACH PARKS
*Anahola Beach Park 20
'Anini Beach Park 17
Brennecke's Beach 34
*Hā'ena Beach State Park 11
*Hanalei Bay Beach Parks 14
Kalapaki Beach 29
Kauapea (Secret) Beach 18
*Keālia Beach Park 22
*Kē'ē Beach (Haena State Park) 10
Kekaha Beach Park 39
Keoneloa (Shipwrecks) Beach 32
Kumukumu (Donkey) Beach 21
Lumaha'i Beach 13
*Lydgate Park 26
Māhā'ulepū (Gillin's) Beach 31
Mākua (Tunnels) Beach 12
*Po'ipū Beach Park 34
Polihale State Park 1
*Salt Pond Beach Park 38

CABINS & CAMPGROUNDS
'Anini Beach Park 17
Hā'ena Beach Park 11
Hanakoa Valley 9
Kalalau Valley 7
Kōke'e State Park 3
Kōke'e Cabins 4
Lydgate Park 26
Polihale State Park 1
YWCA of Kaua'i Camp Sloggett 3

GOLF COURSES
Hōkūala Golf Club 30
Kiahuna Golf Club 35
Kukuiolono Golf Course 37
Kukui'ula Golf Course 36
Makai Golf Club 16
Poipu Bay Golf Course 33
Puakea Golf Course 28
Wailua Golf Course 27

HIKES
'Awa'awapuhi Trail 5
Canyon Trail 2
Kalalau Trail 8
Kuamo'o/Nounou West Trail 25
Kuilau/Moalepe Trails 23
Māhā'ulepū Heritage Trail 32
Nounou East Trail 24
Nualolo Cliff Trail 5
'Okolehao Trail 15
Pihea/Alaka'i Swamp Trails 6
Powerline Trail 23
Wai Koa Loop Trail/Stone Dam 19

updated daily reports on winds, waves, and ocean temperature, visit https://oceansafety.hawaii.gov/list-of-lifeguarded-beaches.

The website of **Po'ipū Beach Resort Association** (www.poipu beach.org) highlights accommodations, activities, shopping, and dining in the Po'ipū area.

Check out the latest entertainment listings online at *Midweek Kauai* (www.midweekkauai.com) before you arrive. Once you're on Kaua'i, look for a free copy, distributed on Wednesdays. *The Garden Island* daily newspaper (www.thegardenisland.com) publicizes concerts and other events online under the "Entertainment" link.

First-time visitors with smartphones may enjoy the four **Shaka Guide** driving tour apps for Kaua'i at www.shakaguide.com. The apps for the North Shore, Waimea & Na Pali, and Wailua Valley & Waterfalls are $20 each, Poipu and Koloa Town is $10.

The Island in Brief

EAST SIDE

Home to the airport, the main harbor, most of the civic and commercial buildings on the island, and the majority of its residents, the East Side of Kaua'i has nevertheless preserved much of its rural character, with green ridges leading to the shore, red-dirt roads crossing old sugarcane fields, and pretty-as-a-postcard waterfalls. Heading east from Līhu'e into the Coconut Coast strip of Wailua and Kapa'a, the main highway changes its name and number from the Kaumuali'i Highway (Hwy. 50) to Kūhiō Highway (Hwy. 56). More noticeable are the steady trade winds that riffle the fronds of hundreds of coconut palms, part of the area's royal legacy; a long and broad river (by Hawai'i standards) and easily accessed waterfalls; and the chock-a-block low-rise condos, budget hotels, and shopping centers—all adding to the East Side's significant rush-hour traffic jams.

LĪHU'E Bargain hunters will appreciate the county seat's many shopping, lodging, and dining options, but Līhu'e also boasts cultural assets, from the exhibits at the **Kaua'i Museum ★★** to hula shows, concerts, and festivals at the **Kaua'i War Memorial Convention Hall** and **Kaua'i Community College's Performing Arts Center.** Nearby outdoor attractions include **Kalapaki Beach ★★**, next to the cruise port of Nāwiliwili; ATV, ziplining, hiking, and tubing, the latter on old sugarcane irrigation flumes; and kayaking on Hulē'ia River past the historic **Alekoko (Menehune) Fishpond ★**, an ancient feat of aquaculture.

WAILUA **Wailua Falls ★** (seen in the opening credits of *Fantasy Island*), the twin cascades of **'Opaeka'a Falls ★★**, and a riverboat cruise to **Fern Grotto ★★** are highlights of this former royal compound, which includes remains of stone-walled *heiau* (places of worship), birthstones, and other ancient sites. Kayakers flock to Wailua River, which also offers wakeboarding and water-skiing opportunities; the municipal **Wailua Golf Course ★★** is routinely ranked as one of the tops in the state; and hikers

MOA BETTER: chickens & roosters

One of the first things visitors notice about Kaua'i is the unusually considerable number of wild chickens. Mostly rural, Kaua'i has always had plenty of poultry, including the colorful jungle fowl known as *moa*, but after Hurricane 'Iniki blew through the island in 1992, they soon were everywhere, reproducing quickly and, in the case of roosters, crowing night and day. Although resorts work tirelessly to trap or shoo them away, it's impossible to ensure you'll never be awakened by a rooster; if you're staying outside a resort, it's pretty much guaranteed you will be. Light sleepers should bring earplugs; some hotels provide them at the front desk or on demand.

can choose from three trailheads to ascend **Nounou** (Sleeping Giant) mountain. Highway 56 also passes by the iconic Coco Palms resort, featured in Elvis Presley's *Blue Hawaii*. Closed after being damaged by Hurricane 'Iniki in 1992, it has seen continual decay and some demolition during long-running disputes over insurance, permitting, and ownership; still, some signs of construction had appeared by early 2023. The family-friendly **Lydgate Park ★** connects with one leg of **Ke Ala Hele Makalae coastal path ★★★**, popular with cyclists and walkers.

KAPA'A The modern condos, motels, and shopping strips of Wailua and Waipouli along the Kūhiō Highway eventually segue into **Old Kapa'a Town,** where funky boutiques and cafes share plantation-era buildings with mom-and-pop groceries and restaurants. Clusters of food trucks serving a rainbow of cuisines and treats such as shave ice can be found along the main road, too. Sandy beaches are hidden from the highway until the road rises past **Keālia Beach Park ★**, a boogie-boarding destination along the northern leg of the coastal hike/bike path.

ANAHOLA Just before the East Side becomes the North Shore, the highway dips and passes through this predominantly Native Hawaiian community near Kalalea Mountain, more widely known as **King Kong Mountain,** or just Kong, for its famous profile. Farm stands and a convenience store with homemade goodies can supply provisions for a weekday picnic at **Anahola Beach Park ★**; weekends draw local crowds.

NORTH SHORE

On a sunny day, there may be no more beautiful place on earth than North Shore Kaua'i. It's not half-bad even on a rainy day (more frequent in winter) when waterfalls almost magically appear on verdant mountains; once the showers stop, rainbows soar over farms, taro patches, and long, curving beaches. The speed limit, and pace of life, slow down dramatically as the Kūhiō Highway traverses a series of one-lane bridges; if you have a parking permit or shuttle pass, you can proceed all the way to a suitably show-stopping beach and the trailhead for the breathtaking **Nāpali Coast.** The quaint towns of Hanalei and Kīlauea—the latter home to a lighthouse and a seabird preserve—plus the island's most luxurious hotel provide ample lodging, dining, and shopping options. But it's far enough from the South Shore (minimum 1½ hr. away) that day-trippers may wish they had relocated for a night or two.

KĪLAUEA A right turn going north on Kūhiō Highway brings you to this village of quaint stone buildings and the plantation-vintage **Historic Market Center ★**, a cozy den of cafes, crafts makers, and boutiques. Across the street lies the newer **Ahuimanu Shopping Center** with some notable restaurants and shops. Kīlauea Road heads *makai* (seaward) to **Kīlauea Point National Wildlife Refuge ★★★**, a sanctuary for nēnē (the gooselike state bird) and other endangered species, and home to the stubby, red-topped **Kīlauea Lighthouse,** built in 1913. Shortly before the preserve is the turnoff for scenic but not-so-secret **Kauapea (Secret) Beach ★★**, a 15-minute hike from

Kīlauea Lighthouse.

a dirt parking lot. Actor Ben Stiller owns a home on the cliffs here; numerous farms, the island's only mini-golf course, and the extensive **Na 'Āina Kai Botanical Gardens & Sculpture Park ★★** are the immediate area's other claims to fame. Two miles north, a 5-minute detour off the highway leads to **'Anini Beach ★★★**, where a 2-mile fringing reef—the longest on Kaua'i—creates a shallow, pondlike setting for swimmers, snorkelers, and (when conditions permit) windsurfers.

PRINCEVILLE This 11,000-acre resort and residential development is home to two 18-hole golf courses, steep trails to pocket beaches, and gorgeous views of crescent-shaped Hanalei Bay and iconic **Makana,** the mountain that portrayed Bali Hai in *South Pacific.* The **Princeville Center** holds a few bargain eateries as well as supplies for those staying in one of the many condo or timeshare units. Opened in early 2023, **1 Hotel Hanalei Bay,** formerly the Princeville Resort, is the island's most luxurious and sustainability-minded hotel, with elevator service to the beach below. Just before the highway drops into Hanalei Valley, a vista point offers a photo-worthy panorama of the Hanalei River winding through wetland taro patches under towering green peaks.

HANALEI Waiting to cross the first of nine one-lane bridges on the northern stretch of the Kūhiō Highway (now Hwy. 560) is a good intro-duction to the hang-loose ethos of the last real town before road's end. The fringing green mountains share their hue with the 1912 **Wai'oli Hui'ia Church ★** and other vintage wooden buildings, some of which house unique shops and moderately priced restaurants. Nearby, the beaches along 2-mile-long, half-moon **Hanalei Bay ★★★** attract surfers year-round; during the calmer summer conditions, children splash in the water while parents lounge on the sand. Three county beach parks offer various facilities and lifeguard stations.

HĀ'ENA Homes modest and grand hide in the lush greenery of Hā'ena on either side of the Kūhiō Highway as it undulates past rugged coves, tranquil beaches, and immense caves. The road dead-ends at **Kē'ē Beach ★★★**, gateway to the Nāpali Coast and a popular destination for snorkel-ers (surf permitting) and campers. *Note:* A parking permit or shuttle bus ticket is now required to access the beach and environs; book well in advance. **Limahuli Garden and Preserve ★★★**, the northern outpost of the National Tropical Botanical Garden, explains Hā'ena's legends, rich cultural heritage, and ecological significance to visitors able to navigate its steep terraces in the shadow of Mount Makana. Food trucks at **Hā'ena Beach Park ★★★** supplement the meager if delicious dining options, such as **Opakapaka Grill and Bar ★** at the **Hanalei Colony Resort ★★** (p. 564), the only North Shore resort with rooms on the sand.

Hanalei, on the North Shore of Kaua'i.

NĀPALI COAST ★★★　Often written as Nā Pali ("the cliffs"), this dramatically crenellated region that bridges the North Shore and West Side begins close to where the road ends. Hardy (and some foolhardy) hikers will cross five valleys as they follow the narrow, 11-mile Kalalau Trail to its end at beautiful **Kalalau Valley,** with tempting detours to waterfalls along the way. The less ambitious (or more sensible) will attempt shorter stretches, such as the 2-mile hike to Hanakāpi'ai Beach; all will need the new permit to park near the trailhead at Hā'ena Beach or take a shuttle. Physically fit kayakers can still spend a summer's day exploring Nāpali's pristine reefs, sea caves, and hidden coves, which also come into view on catamaran and motorized raft tours (almost all departing from the West Side, with a few great options from 'Anini Beach); helicopter tours from Līhu'e, Port Allen, or Princeville offer the quickest if most expensive way to explore Nāpali's stunning topography (p. 551).

SOUTH SHORE

After a short drive west from Līhu'e on Kaumali'i Highway, a well-marked left turn leads to a mile-long **tree tunnel** of eucalyptus trees, planted in 1911. The well-shaded Maluhia Road is ironically the primary entrance to the sunniest of Kaua'i resort areas, Po'ipū. The South Shore also generally has the calmest ocean conditions in winter. Among outdoor attractions are the geyserlike **Spouting Horn** ★★, the restored **Kaneiolouma cultural complex** ★★, multiple gardens at the **National Tropical Botanical Garden** ★★, family-friendly **Po'ipū Beach Park** ★★★, and other sandy beaches, including those in rugged **Māhā'ulepū** ★★, where **Makauwahi Cave Reserve** ★★ reveals the island's fascinating prehistory. Pocket coves, surf breaks, and diving sites also make the area ideal for watersports. The only downside: The North Shore is at least 1½ hours away.

PO'IPŪ & KUKUI'ULA　Four of the best hotels on Kaua'i—the lavish **Grand Hyatt Kauai Resort & Spa** ★★★, the family-friendly **Sheraton Kauai Resort** and **Kōloa Landing Resort** ★★★, and the luxury boutique **Ko'a Kea Hotel & Resort** ★★★—punctuate the many low-rise condos and vacation homes in **Po'ipū Beach Resort.** Landlubbers can enjoy tennis, 36 holes of golf, and numerous options for dining and shopping, including those at the **Shops at Kukui'ula,** part of the nearby luxury Kukui'ula development, which includes roomy rental bungalows.

KŌLOA　Before the Kōloa Bypass Road (Ala Kinoiki) was built, nearly every South Shore beachgoer drove through the oldest sugar plantation town in Hawai'i, founded in 1835. It would be a shame not to visit at least once, to browse the shops and restaurants in quaint storefronts under towering monkeypod trees. Historical plaques on each building give glimpses into the lives of the predominantly Japanese American families who created the first businesses there. Those staying in South Shore condos may find themselves making multiple trips, especially to stock up on produce at the "sunshine market" at noon Mondays, to buy fresh seafood from the **Koloa Fish Market** ★, or to purchase other groceries from two local

On the road to Kōloa.

supermarkets; several food trucks also hang out here. Opened in 2023, the one- and two-story cottages of **Village Marketplace** also host a rainbow of enticing places to eat and shop.

KALĀHEO & LĀWAʻI These more residential communities on either side of the main highway are just a 15-minute drive from Poʻipū Beach Park. On the way, you'll pass through the green fields of rural ʻŌmaʻo along Kōloa Road (Hwy. 530); stop at **Warehouse 3540 ★** for intriguing shops, coffee, and food trucks. Visitors going to or from Waimea Canyon often refuel at the locally oriented restaurants here; others find lodgings in relatively inexpensive (but often unlicensed) B&Bs. (Keep in mind that higher elevations are mistier, and have more wild chickens, than beachfront resorts.) Savvy golfers savor the views and discount fees at upcountry **Kukuiolono Golf Course ★★**. Others find serenity amid the 88 Buddhist shrines and golden temple of the **Lawai International Center ★★**. On the west edge of Kalāheo, look for the turnoff for **Kauai Coffee ★★**, where the 3,100-acre farm yields a dizzying variety of coffees, with free samples at the visitor center.

WEST SIDE

This arid region may have the fewest lodgings, destination restaurants, or swimmable beaches, but the twin draws of **Waimea Canyon State Park ★★★** (hailed as the "Grand Canyon of the Pacific") and the **Kalalau Lookout ★★★** in Kōkeʻe State Park make up for the long drive (80 min. to the latter from Poʻipū). Most Nāpali snorkel tours are also based here, not to mention two swinging bridges, a weekly art festival, and other good excuses to pull over. Those who manage the bumpy, unpaved 5-mile road to **Polihale State Park ★★** are rewarded with views of Niʻihau and Nāpali, as well as a 17-mile stretch of sand (including the restricted-access **Nohili [Barking Sands] Beach** on the Pacific Missile Range Facility).

'ELE'ELE & PORT ALLEN The main highway from Kalāheo passes by plantation homes of 'Ele'ele and several miles of Kauai Coffee's orchards before the intersection with Waialo Road. Turn *makai* (seaward) and the road dead-ends a few blocks later at Port Allen, the island's second largest commercial harbor; nearly all boat tours launch from here. Although the area is fairly industrial, the affordable dining and shopping options in Port Allen and adjacent **'Ele'ele Shopping Center** are worth exploring post-snorkel or pre-sunset cruise.

HANAPĒPĒ An easy detour off Kaumali'i Highway, Hanapēpē looks like an Old West town, with more than two dozen art galleries and quaint stores, plus a fantastic bakery and Japanese restaurant, all behind rustic wooden facades that inspired Disney's *Lilo & Stitch.* Musicians, food trucks, and other vendors truly animate the quiet town during the Friday night festival and "artwalk" from 6 to 9pm. The other daytime attraction is the **swinging footbridge ★** over Hanapēpē River (rebuilt after 1992's Hurricane 'Iniki and marked by a large sign off Hanapēpē Rd.). Across the highway, family-friendly **Salt Pond Beach ★★** is named for the traditional Hawaiian salt pans in the red dirt, which gives the salt its distinctive color and flavor.

WAIMEA The modern history of Hawai'i officially begins here with the landing of British explorer Capt. James Cook on Jan. 20, 1778, 2 days after his ships sailed past O'ahu. Despite Cook's orders to the contrary, his sailors quickly mingled with native women, introducing venereal disease to a long-isolated population. Foreigners kept coming to this enclave at the mouth of the Waimea ("reddish water") River, including a German doctor who tried to claim Kaua'i for Russia in 1815, and American missionaries in 1820. The bronze statue of Kaumuali'i, the last king of Kaua'i, and

Colorful Waimea Canyon.

views of **Niʻihau,** 17 miles across the ocean, are the main reasons to stop at **Pāʻulaʻula State Historic Site ★**, formerly Russian Fort Elizabeth State Historical Park. Today Waimea is attuned to its more recent history of plantation and *paniolo* (cowboy) culture, as well as its Native Hawaiian roots, all of which can be explored at the **West Kauaʻi Heritage Center ★**. Waimea Canyon and Kōkeʻe State Park hikers flock to Waimea's shave ice stands and budget dining choices in the late afternoon, while locals seek out **Waimea Theater,** one of the island's few places to catch a movie or concert.

KEKAHA   Travelers heading to or from Waimea Canyon may be tempted to go via Kōkeʻe Road (Hwy. 55) in Kekaha as a change of pace from Waimea Canyon Road. Don't bother. Unless you're a cyclist looking for less traffic and fewer blind spots, or have the active or retired military ID that lets you into the beach club of the Pacific Missile Range Facility at Barking Sands (the English nickname for Nohili Beach), there's not much to see in this former sugar town, whose mill operated for 122 years before shutting down in 2000. You do have to pass through Kekaha on the way to **Polihale State Park ★★★**; if the latter's access road is impassable, stop by **Kekaha Beach Park,** a long, narrow strand with often-rough waters, for a striking sunset and view of Niʻihau.

NIʻIHAU   Just 17 miles across the Kaulakahi Channel from the West Side of Kauaʻi lies the arid island of Niihau (pronounced *"nee-ee-how"*), nicknamed "The Forbidden Island." Casual visitors are not allowed on this privately owned isle, once a cattle and sheep ranch that now supports fewer than 200 full-time residents, all living in the single town of Puʻuwai, and nearly all Native Hawaiians. Nonresidents can visit on hunting safaris (starting at $3,300 for feral pig and sheep) and half-day helicopter tours including lunch and beach time ($630 per person, five-person minimum), departing from the West Side (www.niihau.us; © **877/441-3500**). You're more likely to see the endangered Hawaiian monk seal than you are Niihauans, which is how they like it.

GETTING AROUND

Unless you're on a fairly leisurely schedule, you'll need a car or other motorized vehicle to see and do everything on Kauaʻi, which has one major road—one lane in each direction in most places—that rings the island except along the Nāpali Coast. During rush hour, from about 6 to 9am and 3 to 6pm, the road between Līhuʻe and Kapaʻa—the central business district—can turn into a giant parking lot, even with a third, "contraflow" lane whose direction is determined by time of day. Traffic flows into Līhuʻe and Kapaʻa in the morning and out in the late afternoon. Bypass roads in Kīpū (when heading north from Poʻipū) and Kapaʻa (when heading south) can alleviate some of the stress, but plan accordingly.

Note: The top speed is 50mph, with many slower sections in residential and business areas. Addresses in this chapter will use Kaumaliʻi

Addresses in Po'ipū Beach

The official mailing address of sites in and around Po'ipū Beach is Kōloa, which GPS devices may require. This chapter lists them as "Po'ipū" to distinguish them from Old Kōloa Town and environs.

Highway for Highway 50 and Kūhiō Highway for Highway 56/560, following local convention. Some addresses use a single number before a dash, which simply indicates one of five island divisions. Since highway addresses can be hard to spot (if marked at all), directions may be given with mile marker numbers, cross streets, and/or the descriptors *mauka* (toward the mountains) and *makai* (toward the sea).

BY CAR   All of the major car-rental agencies are represented on Kaua'i. At the airport baggage claim, cross the street to catch one of the frequent shuttle vans to the rental lots. If you just want a car for a day trip, **Avis** (www.avis. com; ℂ **800/879-2847**) also rents cars from the Grand Hyatt Kauai, while **Hertz** (www.hertz.com; ℂ **800/654-3131**) has additional offices at the Hilton Garden Inn in Kapa'a, Outrigger Kaua'i Beach Resort near Līhu'e and Sheraton Kauai in Po'ipū. Be sure to book early for peak periods. You may find cheaper options at **Discount Hawaii Car Rental** (www.discounthawaii carrental.com; ℂ **800/292-1930**), especially for last-minute bookings; it also offers free pickup for cruise passengers. **Turo.com**, a "car share" system like Airbnb, has its own airport shuttle to a convenient nearby parking lot.

BY MOTORCYCLE, MOPED, OR SCOOTER   Riders 21 and older with a heavyweight motorcycle license can rent a "hog" from **Kauai Harley-Davidson** (www.kauaimotorsports.com; ℂ **808/241-7020**) outside Līhu'e. Rates for a Sportster typically start at $137 for 24 hours, with unlimited mileage; bigger rides start at $203 to $241. **Kauai Mopeds** (www.kauai-mopeds.com; ℂ **808/652-7407**) in Līhu'e offers two-person scooters with similar age and license restrictions; daily rates start at $155 for models with a top speed of 65mph, and $200 for those reaching 75mph or higher. Those 18 or older with a driver's license can cruise back roads on a single person moped (top speed 30mph) for $110 a day.

BY TAXI, RIDESHARE, OR SHUTTLE   Set by the county, taxi meter rates start at $3, with an additional $3 per mile; from the airport, it's about $65 to Po'ipū and $117 to Princeville, plus 40¢ per item of luggage, and $4 per bulky item. You can also arrange private tours by taxi starting at $120 for 2 hours. Call **Kauai Taxi Company** (www.kauaitaxico.com; ℂ **808/246-9554**) for taxi, limousine, or airport shuttle service. Ride-sharing apps Uber and Lyft also operate on Kaua'i, but homegrown app **Holoholo** (www.rideholoholo.com) is easy to use, too; pricing varies by demand, but a typical rate from the airport to Po'ipū is $34 and to Princeville, $63.

Solo travelers who don't use ridesharing will save money taking **SpeediShuttle** (www.speedishuttle.com; ℂ **877/242-5777**) from the airport ($54 to Po'ipū, $93 to Princeville), but be aware it may make multiple stops; allow plenty of extra time.

Once in Po'ipū, book a free ride on the **Aloha Spirit Shuttle** ℂ **808/ 651-9945**); Doug Bean's 12-person open-air tram—a former Disneyland people-mover built in 1965—shuttles locals and visitors around resorts and restaurants daily from 5 to 10pm; tips are appreciated.

BY BUS   Kaua'i Bus (www.thekauaibus.com; ℂ **808/246-8110**) has daily service between Kekaha and Hanalei, including stops near several Po'ipū and Līhu'e hotels, the central Kapa'a hotel corridor, the Princeville Center, and Hanalei. *Note:* The bus also has an airport stop, but suitcases, large backpacks, and surfboards are not allowed. The white-and-green buses, which have small bike racks in front, run Monday to Friday more or less hourly from 5:15am to 10:50pm, and Saturdays and holidays 6am to 8:45pm (no service on Sun). The fare is $2 for adults and $1 for seniors 65 and older and children ages 7 to 18, exact change required.

BY BIKE   Due to narrow (or nonexistent) shoulders along much of the main highway, relying on bicycles for transportation is generally unsafe. For recreational routes, including the **Ke Ala Hele Makalae** coastal path on the East Side, see "Biking," p. 543.

[FastFACTS] KAUA'I

Dentists   For emergency dental care, go to **Baird Dental,** 4-976 Kūhiō Hwy. (at Keaka Rd.), Kapa'a (ℂ **808/822-9393;** Mon–Fri 8am–4:30pm), or **Līhu'e Dental,** 4414 Kukui Grove St., Ste. 103, Līhu'e (www. lihue-dental.com; ℂ **808/ 378-4754;** Mon–Fri 8:30am–5pm).

Doctors   Walk-ins are accepted daily from 8am to 7pm (except Jan 1, Thanksgiving, and Dec 25) at the **Kaua'i Urgent Care Clinic,** 4484 Pahe'e St., Līhu'e (ℂ **808/245-1532**). The non-urgent-care **Kaua'i Medical Clinic,** part of the Wilcox Medical Center complex at 3-3420 Kūhiō Hwy., *makai* side (at 'Ehiku St.), Līhu'e (ℂ **808/245-1500**), is open for appointments Monday to Friday 8am to 5pm and Saturday

8am to noon. Kaua'i Medical Clinic also has branches, with varying hours, in **Kōloa,** 5371 Kōloa Rd. (ℂ **808/742-1621**); **Kapa'a,** 4-1105 Kūhiō Hwy., *mauka* side, in the Kapa'a Shopping Center (ℂ **808/822-3431**); and **'Ele'ele,** 4382 Waialo Rd. (ℂ **808/ 335-0499**).

Emergencies   Dial ℂ **911** for police, fire, or ambulance service.

Hospitals   Wilcox Medical Center, 3-3420 Kūhiō Hwy. *makai* side (at 'Ehiku St.), Līhu'e (ℂ **808/245-1100**), has emergency services (ℂ **808/245-1010**) available 24 hours a day, as do the smaller **Mahelona Memorial Hospital,** 4800 Kawaihau Rd., Kapa'a (ℂ **808/822-4961**), and **Kaua'i Veterans Memorial Hospital,** 4643 Waimea

Canyon Dr., Waimea (ℂ **808-338-9431**).

Internet Access   Many cafes (including **Starbucks** outlets in Po'ipū, Līhu'e, and Kapa'a; www.starbucks. com) offer free Wi-Fi hotspots; most hotels offer free Wi-Fi in public areas and, if not free, for a fee in rooms. All Hawai'i public libraries have free Wi-Fi but require a library card ($10 nonresidents, good for 3 months). Local branches are in Hanapēpē, Kapa'a, Kōloa, Līhu'e, Princeville, and Waimea; all closed Sunday. Go to www.librarieshawaii.org and click on "How Do I ..." for locations, hours, and details on reserving a PC with Wi-Fi.

Police   For non-emergencies, call ℂ **808/241-1711**.

Post Office   The **main** post office is at 4441 Rice St., Līhu'e, open Monday to Friday 8am to 4pm and Saturday 9am to 1pm; hours vary at the 14 other offices across the island. To find the one nearest you, visit www.usps.com or call ☎ **800/275-8777.**

Weather   For current weather conditions and forecasts, call the National Weather Service at ☎ **808/245-6001.** For the daily ocean report, including high surf advisories and other alerts, visit **www.kauai.gov/surf**.

EXPLORING KAUA'I

Attractions & Points of Interest

EAST SIDE

Alekoko (Menehune) Fishpond ★★ CULTURAL SITE   While you can glimpse this magnificent example of Hawaiians' ingenuity in aquaculture from a helicopter tour or a kayak ride on the Hulē'ia River, it's easiest to stop at the scenic overlook on Hulemalu Road, about a half-mile inland from Nāwiliwili Small Boat Harbor. There you can gaze at the Hulē'ia River and the 900-foot-long, 5-foot-tall lava rock wall that for 6 centuries or so has separated the river from the fishpond. Legend holds it was constructed overnight by the unseen and presumably mythical little people known as *menehune,* who passed boulders hand to hand from 25 miles away. To get an even closer look and learn more about this *wahi pana* (special place), sign up for one of the community workdays organized by Mālama Hulē'ia, the nonprofit that began restoring the wall and removing invasive mangroves 3 years before it acquired ownership of the site (which it calls Alakoko) in 2021. The view of Hā'upu mountain range, where the remains of ancient Hawaiian chiefs lie hidden in caves, is enchanting, as is watching fish frolic in the cool, clear waters. Register online a week in advance for the workday, held the third Saturday of the month from 8am to noon, with lunch provided; you can also sign up for an email reminder of when registration opens. *Note:* The fishpond is not normally open to the public except on workdays or when Mālama Hulē'ia brings school groups to the site. It lies next to the Hulē'ia National Wildlife Refuge (www.fws.gov/refuge/huleia), which is not open to the public and also bans the use of drones, which can disturb endangered birds.

Alekoko (Menehune) Fishpond Scenic Overlook, off Hulemalu Rd., 7 miles west of its intersection with Niumalu Rd. near Nāwiliwili Small Boat Harbor, Līhu'e. Register online for free monthly community workdays, 3rd Sat of the month 8am–noon, at www.malamahuleia.org.

Fern Grotto ★★ NATURAL ATTRACTION   The journey as much as the destination has kept this tourist attraction popular since 1946, when the Smith family first began offering boat trips 2 miles up the Wailua River to this lava-rock cave with lush ferns hanging from its roof. The barge cruises past royal and sacred sites of antiquity, arriving at a landing that's a short walk from the grotto. Ancient Hawaiians knew it as Ma'ama'akualono, a site dedicated to the god Lono, who is associated with agriculture and

The lush greenery of the Fern Grotto.

healing. Although you can no longer enter the cave, an observation deck provides a decent view, as well as the stage for a musician and hula dancer to perform the "Hawaiian Wedding Song" (made famous by Elvis Presley's 1961 film *Blue Hawaii,* filmed nearby at the Coco Palms). The tour, a total of 80 minutes, includes music and hula on the return trip down the state's longest navigable river (see "Wailua River State Park," below).

Note: Kayakers may visit Fern Grotto on their own, as long as their arrival or departure doesn't overlap with the tour boats; see "Kayaking" on p. 535 for rental information.

2 miles inland from Wailua Marina State Park, south side of Wailua River off Kūhiō Hwy. Smith's Motor Boats (www.smithskauai.com; *©* **808/821-6895**) tours Mon–Fri at 9:30am and 11am, and 2 and 3:30pm. $30 adults, $15 children ages 2–12. Free shuttle from Wailua area.

Grove Farm Museum ★ HISTORIC SITE/MUSEUM   AOL cofounder Steve Case may own Grove Farm now, but little else has changed at the 100-acre homestead of George N. Wilcox. The son of missionaries in Hanalei, Wilcox bought the original 900-acre Grove Farm from a German immigrant in 1864 and turned it into a successful sugar plantation. Two-hour guided tours start at the original plantation office and include the two-story main home, still furnished with vintage decor and Hawaiiana, plus extensive gardens and intriguing outbuildings, such as a Japanese teahouse built in 1898. *Note:* Tours may be canceled on rainy days. Contact the museum about its occasional free rides on a restored, plantation-era diesel train near the old Līhu'e Sugar Mill.

4050 Nāwiliwili Rd. (Hwy. 58), at Pīkaka St., Līhu'e. www.grovefarm.org. *©* **808/245-3202.** $20 adults, $10 children ages 5–12. Open only for guided tours Mon, Wed, Thurs at 10am and 1pm; reservations required.

Kaua'i Museum ★★ MUSEUM   The fascinating geological and cultural history of Kaua'i and Ni'ihau on display in this museum may inspire a return visit. Visitors enter through the Wilcox Building, the former county library built in 1924 with a Greco-Roman facade on its lava rock exterior. Inside, Evelyn Ritter's portraits of Hawaiian royalty hang over koa wood-trimmed cases with intriguing artifacts from their reigns. Also on display are some of the hundreds of items recovered from *Haaheo O Hawaii* ("Pride of Hawai'i"), King Kamehameha II's luxurious barge, which sank off the North Shore in 1824. In the Heritage Gallery to the rear await exquisite Ni'ihau shell lei, feather work, glossy wooden bowls (*'umeke*) and other items that once belonged to royalty.

The adjacent Rice Building, a two-story lava rock structure opened in 1960, tells "The Story of Kaua'i," with exhibits on the island's volcanic origins, the arrival of Polynesian voyagers, the missionary and plantation eras, up to the island's contemporary surf stars. Head upstairs to Waimakua gallery for rotating exhibits on Kaua'i and Ni'ihau arts and culture. Don't forget to bring a smartphone to take advantage of the "extended reality" experiences that overlay digital content, including animated historical figures, on top of specific exhibits marked by a QR code. Though the cost of admission has jumped to $15, the fee allows you to come back within a week. The small gift shop has an extensive book selection and handmade items from Kaua'i and across the Pacific.

4428 Rice St., Līhu'e. www.kauaimuseum.org. © **808/245-6931.** $15 adults, $12 seniors, $10 students ages 8–17, free for children 7 and under. Free docent-led 1-hr. tour Mon, Wed, and Sat 10am. Check "Events" listings online for crafts workshops, music, and festivals. Mon–Fri 9am–4pm and Sat until 2pm.

Keāhua Arboretum ★ GARDEN   Part of the vast Līhu'e–Kōloa Forest Reserve, this grove of rainbow eucalyptus (named for its colorful bark), monkeypod, and mango trees may not be well maintained from an arborist's standpoint, but it's a nifty, family-friendly place to picnic and dip in a cool stream, particularly after a hike on the **Kuilau Ridge Trail** (p. 547). A short loop trail leads to a swimming hole with a rope swing. Facilities include picnic tables, pavilions, and toilets. Be sure to wear mosquito repellent. Part of the fun is getting here: The parking area and picnic tables are across a spillway at the paved end of Kuamo'o Road, about 5 miles inland from 'Opaeka'a Falls. (Please use good judgment when deciding if it's safe to ford the stream.) This is where adventurers will find the trailhead for the 13-mile **Powerline Trail** (p. 548), which ends near Princeville, and the extremely rugged, unpaved Wailua Forestry Management Road, the start of much more challenging, all-day treks to the *Jurassic Park* gates (just poles now) and the "Blue Hole" inside Wai'ale'ale, normally seen via helicopter only; for details on those hikes and updates on current conditions, consult https://alltrails.com.

End of Kuamo'o Rd., Kapa'a. 7 miles inland from Kūhiō Hwy., Wailua. https://dlnr. hawaii.gov/forestry/frs/reserves/kauai/lihue-koloa. © **808/274-3433.** Free admission. Daily dawn to dusk.

Kilohana Plantation ★★ FARM/ATTRACTIONS   This 105-acre portion of a former sugar plantation has long been known for the unique shops tucked into a handsome 1930s mansion and the **Plantation House by Gaylords** ★★ restaurant in its courtyard, named for original owner Gaylord Wilcox. But more recent additions are also memorable. Tipplers ages 21 and up can create their own mini mai tai or other tropical cocktail around a gleaming wood bar in the **Koloa Rum Co. tasting room** ★★ (www.koloarum.com; ℂ **808/246-8900**). A $5 booking fee applies per party of up to 6 guests; there's a 20-person maximum for tastings Tuesday to Saturday starting on the hour from 10am to 4pm, and everyone needs a reservation, whether they are tasting or not. The all-ages store sells locally made spirits and non-alcoholic gifts, with no reservations needed. Ages 21 and up can also book Kilohana's **Rum Safari** ($78), a 2-hour excursion by open-air truck and walk through the estate's tropical fruit orchards and Kahanu Nui valley, where you'll taste Koloa Rum and sip on a mai tai before feeding some wild goats, pigs, and a donkey. Another freshly made, farm-sourced cocktail awaits at the taro field.

All ages can take a ride on the **Kauai Plantation Railway** ★★ (ℂ **808/245-7245**), which uses a restored diesel locomotive to pull open-sided cars with trolley-style bench seats around a 2½-mile track. The train passes by Kilohana's gardens growing 50 varieties of fruit and vegetables and through flowering fields and forest on a 40-minute narrated tour that includes a stop to feed goats, sheep, and wild pigs (watch your hands). It departs daily between 10am and 2pm, plus on Tuesdays and Fridays at 4:30 and 5:30pm. Tickets are $22 for adults, $19 seniors 62 and older, and $16 for kids 3 to 12. Providing more all-ages entertainment with a Hawaiian cultural angle is **Lūʻau Kalamakū** ★★★ (www.luaukalamaku.com; ℂ **808/833-3000**), a 3½-hour theatrical show with luau-style dinner presented three times a week in a specially built theater-in-the-round near the

Kayaking on Wailua River.

Wilcox mansion. Tickets are $159 adults, $98 ages 13 to 17, $59 ages 3 to 12, with various upgrades and packages available.

3-2087 Kaumali'i Hwy., Līhu'e, just north of Kaua'i Community College. www.kilohana kauai.com. © **808/245-5608.** Mansion daily 11am; restaurant, lounge, and shop hours vary.

Lydgate Park ★ PARK   This is one of the rare beach parks in Hawai'i where the facilities almost outshine the beach. In front of the Hilton Garden Inn Kauai Wailua Bay, **Lydgate Beach** ★ (p. 525) offers two rock-walled ponds for safe swimming and snorkeling. But many families also gravitate to the 58-acre, half-mile-long park for the immense **Kamalani Playground,** a sprawling wooden fantasy fortress decorated with ocean-themed ceramics. Stroller pushers, joggers, and cyclists also pick up the 2½-mile southern leg of the **Ke Ala Hele Makalae coastal path** here; Lydgate's northern end abuts **Hikinaakalā Heiau,** part of Wailua River State Park (see below). Facilities include picnic tables, restrooms, showers, pavilions, and campgrounds.

Leho Dr. at Nalu Rd., Wailua. Free admission. Daily dawn to dusk.

Wailua River State Park ★★ PARK/HISTORIC SITE   Ancients called the Wailua River "the river of the great sacred spirit." Seven temples once stood along this 20-mile river, the longest in Hawai'i, fed by the 450 inches of rain that fall annually on Wai'ale'ale at the island's center. The entire district from the river mouth to the summit of Wai'ale'ale was once royal land, originally claimed by Puna, a Tahitian priest said to have arrived in one of the first double-hulled voyaging canoes to come to Hawai'i.

Cultural highlights include the remains of four major temples; royal birthing stones, used to support female royalty in labor; a stone bell used to announce such births; and the ancient stone carvings known as petroglyphs, found on boulders near the mouth of the Wailua River when currents wash away enough sand. Many sites have **Wailua Heritage Trail** markers; go to www.wailuaheritagetrail.org for map and details. The **Hawai'i State Parks website** also has downloadable brochures (https://dlnr.hawaii.gov/dsp/brochures) for two *heiau* (temples) that each enclosed an acre of land: Just north of Lydgate Park, next to the mouth of the Wailua River, **Hikinaakalā Heiau** is known for its use in sunrise ceremonies; its name means "rising of the sun." Now reduced to its foundation stones, it's part of a sacred oceanfront complex that was also likely a place of refuge (*pu'uhonua*). Two miles up Kuamo'o Road (Hwy. 580) from the main highway, **Poli'ahu Heiau** shares its name with the goddess of snow (admittedly, a weather phenomenon more common to Hawai'i Island). The 5×5-feet lava rock walls—attributed to *menehune,* and most likely erected by the 1600s—may have surrounded a *luakini,* used for human sacrifice. (Don't stand on the rock walls, enter the center of the heiau, or—unless you're a Native Hawaiian cultural practitioner—leave "offerings," all of which are considered disrespectful.)

Across the road from Poli'ahu is an ample parking lot and sidewalk leading to the overlook of 40-foot-wide, 151-foot-tall **'Opaeka'a Falls** ★★.

Named for the "rolling shrimp" that were once abundant here, this twin cascade glistens under the Makaleha ridge—but don't be tempted to try to find a way to swim beneath it. The DANGER KEEP OUT signs and wire fencing are there because two hikers fell to their deaths from the steep, slippery hillside in 2006 (among others injured here).

You're allowed to wade at the base of the 100-foot **'Uluwehi Falls ★★**, widely known as Secret Falls, but first you'll need to paddle several miles to the narrow right fork of the Wailua River, and then hike about 30 to 45 minutes on a trail with a stream crossing. Many kayak rental companies offer guided tours here (see "Kayaking," p. 535).

Also part of the state park, but at the end of Mā'alo Road (Hwy. 583), 4 miles inland from the main highway in Kapaia, is equally scenic **Wailua Falls ★**. Pictured in the opening credits of *Fantasy Island,* this double-barreled waterfall drops at least 80 feet (some say 113) into a large pool. Go early to avoid crowds and enjoy the morning light. *Note:* The state has also installed fencing here to block attempts at a hazardous descent—please don't risk your life trying to find a way around it.

'Opaeka'a Falls and **Poli'ahu Heiau:** Off Kuamo'o Rd., 2 miles *mauka* of intersection with Kūhiō Hwy. just north of Wailua River Bridge. **Hikinaakalā Heiau:** South side of Wailua River mouth; access from Lydgate Park (p. 508). **Wailua Falls:** End of Mā'alo Rd. (Hwy. 583), 4 miles north of intersection with Kūhiō Hwy. in Kapaia, near Līhu'e. https://dlnr.hawaii.gov/dsp/parks/kauai. ℂ **808/274-3444.** Free admission. Daily 7am–7:45pm.

NORTH SHORE

Anaina Hou Community Park ★ ATTRACTION   Anywhere else, a mini-golf park might be easily dismissed as a tourist trap. On Kaua'i, it's a wonderful introduction for families to the Garden Island's tropical flora and cultural history, and just one of several visitor attractions in this inviting park. The 18-hole **Anaina Hou Mini Golf & Gardens** showcases native species, Polynesian introductions, plantation crops, Japanese and Chinese gardens, and modern plantings. It's quite popular on weekends, although it may close early in inclement weather or slow periods. Donated by the founder of E-Trade and his wife, Bill and Joan Porter, the 500-acre community park also offers a playground, skateboard ramps, dog park, the open-air **Sunset Lanai ★** bar and family-friendly **Silvercloud Eatery ★**, and farmers markets (p. 596).

5-2723 Kūhiō Hwy. (*mauka* side), Kīlauea. North from Līhu'e, pass the gas station at the Kolo Rd. turnoff to Kīlauea; entrance is 500 yards farther on the left at the Kaua'i Mini Golf sign. www.anainahou.org. ℂ **808/828-2118. Anaina Hou Community Park:** Free admission. **Mini Golf:** $18.50 adults, $15 ages 4–12, free for children 3 and under; Wed–Sun 10am–4pm. **Silvercloud Eatery:** Thurs–Sat 11:30am–3pm and 4–7:30pm; Sat 9–11:30am, noon to 3pm, and 4–7:30pm. **Sunset Lanai:** Wed–Sat 4:30–8:30pm, Sun until 6pm.

Common Ground ★ FARM/ATTRACTION   On the site of a former sugar cane plantation and guava orchard, this farm and educational center puts the spotlight on community-building regenerative agriculture. Its twice-weekly farm and food tours ($115 adults, $65 ages 6–12) are the only way to visit, unless there's a special event. After an informative walk through the "food forest," tours end with a light, family-style meal in the Common Ground Lounge that includes seasonal tropical fruits, roasted farm-raised chicken with breadfruit, and a Meyer lemon and ginger blossom lemonade; beer and wine are available for purchase. You're allowed to arrive an hour early to make the 1-mile (1.6km) round-trip hike along the **Wai Koa Loop** trail (see "Hiking," p. 547) to the pretty waterfall created by **Stone Dam,** built during the property's plantation days of the 19th century and now protected and publicly accessible through the Hawai'i Land Trust. A marketplace featuring island-made foods and other items is also open during the pre-tour hour.

4900 Kuawa Rd., *mauka* side of Kūhiō Hwy., Kīlauea. https://commongroundkauai. com. ✆ **808/828-6368.** Tours Tues–Fri 4–6pm, by reservation only; $115 adults, $65 ages 6–12, free for children ages 5 and under. Tour participants may arrive an hour early to hike to Stone Dam or shop in Common Ground Marketplace.

Hā'ena State Park ★★ NATURAL ATTRACTIONS Besides snorkeling at pretty **Hā'ena Beach** ★★★ (p. 529), in the shadow of jutting Makana (Bali Hai) mountain, or camping, the main allure of this state park is that it's at the end of the road, the perfect place to witness sunset after a leisurely drive to the North Shore. It's also the start of the spectacularly challenging 11-mile **Kalalau Trail** (p. 549).

The overwhelming popularity of both the beach and trail have led to a reservation system that limits visitor numbers to 900 a day. Nonresidents must reserve a permit ($10) for one of 70 parking spaces available to them (residents have use of another 30), or, if planning to bike or walk into the park, reserve an entry voucher ($5). You can choose from morning, midday, or sunset time periods; to stay all day, you'll need three permits or vouchers. All passes are available on https://gohaena.com; you

---

Ho'opulapula Haraguchi Rice Mill & Taro Farm

Many of the green taro patches seen from the **Hanalei Valley Lookout** ★★★ belong to the 30-acre **Haraguchi Farm,** where fifth-generation farmer Lyndsey Haraguchi-Nakayama, family members, and other laborers tend the revered Hawaiian staple by hand. When the Haraguchis bought the farm in 1924, the wetlands were rice paddies, planted by Chinese immigrants in the 1800s. With the purchase came a wooden rice mill that stayed in operation until 1960, the only such structure left in the state but badly battered by flooding in 2018. Part of **Hanalei National Wildlife Refuge** (www.fws.gov/refuge/hanalei), a wetlands oasis for many endangered birds, the farm is closed to visitors but offers virtual tours via the website (www. haraguchiricemill.org; ✆ **808/651-3399**). The family's **Hanalei Taro & Juice** ★★ food truck at 5-5070 Kūhiō Hwy., *makai* side, Hanalei (1¼ miles west of Hanalei Bridge; Fri–Sun 10am–4pm), sells delicious hummus, pork-based plates, mochi cake, and fruit smoothies all made with taro, as well as savory plate lunches with poi on the side.

can't buy them at the kiosk. You can avoid driving by reserving a spot on the new shuttle system ($40 ages 16 and older, $25 ages 4–15, younger free if seated on laps; https://gohaena.com), which includes entry to the park and makes a stop at **Hā'ena Beach Park ★★**, where parking has become very tight. The shuttle departs from the Waipā Park & Ride (just north of Hanalei Town); a Princeville terminus is expected to reopen after additional landslide repairs are completed.

Note: The parking lot with shuttle stop near Hā'ena Beach requires a leisurely 10-minute walk on a boardwalk through taro fields and a path through the ironwood forest.

Northern end of Kūhiō Hwy., Hā'ena. https://dlnr.hawaii.gov/dsp/parks/kauai (shuttle and permit info at https://gohaena.com). ℂ **808/274-3444.** Parking permit $10, shuttle pass $40 adults, $25 ages 4–15, children ages 4 and under are free when seated on a lap, walk-in/bike-in entry voucher $5; buy online up to 30 days in advance. Daily 7am–6:45pm.

Kīlauea Point National Wildlife Refuge & Lighthouse ★★★

NATURE PRESERVE/LIGHTHOUSE   Two miles north of the historic town of Kīlauea is a 200-acre headland habitat—the island's only wildlife refuge open to the public (online reservations required)—that includes cliffs, two rocky wave-lashed bays, and a tiny islet serving as a jumping-off spot for seabirds. Even from a parking area outside the gate that's accessible without a reservation, you can easily spot red-footed boobies, which nest in trees and shrubs, and wedge-tailed shearwaters, which burrow in nests along the cliffs between March and November (they spend winters at sea). Scan the skies for the great frigate bird, which has a 7-foot wingspan, and the red-tailed tropicbird, which performs aerial acrobatics during the breeding season of March through August. Endangered nēnē, the native goose reintroduced to Kaua'i in 1982, often stroll close to visitors, but please don't feed them. Telescopes and loaner binoculars may bring into view the area's marine life, from spinner dolphins, Hawaiian monk seals, and green sea turtles year-round to humpback whales in winter. Still, the primary draw for many of the half-million annual visitors is the 52-foot-tall, red-capped **Daniel K. Inouye Kīlauea Point Lighthouse,** built in 1913 and renamed in memory of the state's late senator. Listed on the National Register of Historic Places, the beacon boasts a 7,000-pound Fresnel lens, whose beam could be seen from 20 miles away before it was deactivated in 1976. (Check www.kauairefuges.org for updates on lighthouse tours, which were temporarily suspended at press time.)

Note: The refuge is an immensely popular attraction, so make your reservation as early as possible; tickets for hourly timed-entry slots for adults ages 16 and older are available up to 2 months in advance online (no fee or reservations for younger visitors).

End of Kīlauea Rd., Kīlauea. www.fws.gov/refuge/kilauea-point. ℂ **808/828-1413.** $10 ages 16 and older, plus $1 reservation fee; free admission and no reservation required for ages 15 and under. Wed–Sat 10am–4pm.

Limahuli Garden and Preserve ★★ GARDEN Beyond Hanalei and the last wooden bridge is a mighty cleft in the coastal range where ancestral Hawaiians lived in what can only be called paradise. Carved by a waterfall stream known as Limahuli, the lush valley sits at the foot of steepled cliffs that Hollywood portrayed as Bali Hai in *South Pacific*. This small, almost secret garden, part of the National Tropical Botanical Garden, is ecotourism at its best. Here botanists hope to save endangered native plants, some of which grow in the 1,000-acre Limahuli Preserve behind the garden, which is off-limits to visitors. The self-guided tour encourages visitors to walk slowly up and down the .75-mile loop trail (resting places provided) to view indigenous and "canoe" plants, which are identified in Hawaiian and English, as well as plantation-era imported flowers and fruits. From taro to sugarcane, the plants brought over in Polynesians' voyaging canoes (hence their nickname) tell the story of the people who cultivated them for food, medicine, clothing, shelter, and decoration. The tour booklet also shares some of the fascinating legends inspired by the area's dramatically perched rocks and Makana mountain, where men once hurled firebrands (*'oahi*) that floated far out to sea.

5-8291 Kūhiō Hwy. (*mauka* side), Hāʻena, ½-mile after mile marker 9. www.ntbg.org/gardens/limahuli. ℓ **808/826-1053.** Self-guided tour: $30 ages 13 and older; free for children 12 and under with adult. Tues–Sat 8:30am–3:15pm. Guided tour: $60 ages 13 and older (younger not allowed); Tues and Thurs 9am. Credit card required to book guided tours.

Na ʻĀina Kai Botanical Gardens & Sculpture Park ★★ GARDEN Off the North Shore's beaten path, this magical garden and hardwood plantation covers 240 acres, sprinkled with 70 life-size (some larger-than-life-size) whimsical bronze statues. It's the place for avid gardeners, as well as people who think they don't like botanical gardens. It has something for everyone: a poinciana maze, an orchid house, a lagoon with spouting fountains, a Japanese teahouse, a streamside path to a hidden beach—even re-creations of traditional Navajo and Hawaiian compounds. A host of different tours is typically available, from a self-guided stroll through the formal gardens ($20) open to all ages to guided walks from 90 minutes to 3 hours ($45–$60) for ages 13 and older; some include rides in small, covered trams to treks or a moderately challenging hike down to deserted Kaluakai Beach. Bird watchers can join special tours ($70) in winter and early spring that may visit sites not normally open to the public for spotting Laysan albatross during their courting and nesting season, other migratory seabirds, and year-round endangered native species. One Saturday a month, the garden offers a Splash and Play session ($10, by reservation only) in its children's garden with fountain, tree house, and other fun structures; bring a towel, snacks, and drinks.

4101 Wailapa Rd., Kīlauea. www.naainakai.org. ℓ **808/828-0525.** $20–$85 tours Tues–Fri at 9 or 9:30am; some repeat at 1 or 1:30pm. $60 bird-watching tours; Dec–Apr Wed 8:30am. $10 Splash and Play ages 2 and older; 1 Sat a month 9am–1pm (last entry at noon; see website for schedule). Reservations required.

Na 'Āina Kai Botanical Gardens.

Nāpali Coast State Wilderness Park ★★★ PARK   This 15-mile-long crown of serrated ridges and lush valleys is the most impressive of the island's natural features—and its most inaccessible. Only hardy, well-equipped hikers with permits should attempt the full length of the 11-mile **Kalalau Trail,** which begins at Hā'ena Beach and plunges up and down before ending at **Kalalau Valley.** Nāpali's last Hawaiian community lived in this 3-mile-wide, 3-mile-deep valley until the early 1900s. The valley, which can also be viewed from an overlook in **Kōke'e State Park ★★★** (p. 519), is the setting for Jack London's 1912 short story "Koolau the Leper." Like the 2022 film *The Wind & the Reckoning,* it's based on the gripping true story of a Native Hawaiian man and his family, who hid from authorities determined to exile him to Moloka'i. (Today, rangers diligently shoo illegal campers out to protect the valley's cultural treasures.) Most visitors just hoof it 4 miles round-trip from Hā'ena Beach to scenic but dangerously unswimmable **Hanakāpi'ai Beach** or make it a day's adventure by adding a 4-mile, boulder-hopping slog to Hanakāpi'ai Falls (see "Hiking," p. 547). A state camping permit ($35, only 60 issued per day, up to 90 days in advance) is required to go any farther, with sites available in Hanakoa and Kalalau valleys.

Note: A parking permit, shuttle pass or entry voucher to Hā'ena Beach is required to access the Kalalau trailhead; see "Hā'ena State Park," above, or https://gohaena.com for details. Limited overnight parking at Hā'ena Beach is available for those with camping permits, which must be secured first.

In late spring and summer, kayakers may explore the sea caves and oceanside waterfalls of Nāpali, but landing is only allowed at **Kalalau** and **Miloli'i beaches;** visiting Kalalau requires a camping permit ($35, available up to 30 days in advance), while Miloli'i allows both camping and day use (see "Kayaking," p. 535). **Nualolo Kai,** the lower, seaside portion of another valley, has many archaeo-logical sites, some under restoration, but only motorized raft (Zodiac) tours may land here (see "Boat & Raft [Zodiac] Tours," p. 533). The natural arch at **Honopū Beach** is a highlight of the snorkel cruises passing by but may be examined closely only by the few capable of swimming here from Kalalau or a moored kayak—a dicey proposi-tion much of the year.

The easiest, and most expen-sive, way to survey Nāpali's stun-ning land- and seascape is by helicopter (see "Helicopter Tours," p. 551). However you experience it, you'll understand why Nāpali remains the star of countless calen-dars, postcards, and screen savers.

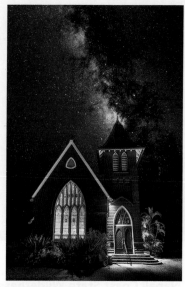
Waiʻoli Huiʻia Church.

Btw. Hāʻena Beach and Polihale State Park. https://dlnr.hawaii.gov/dsp/parks/kauai/napali-coast-state-wilderness-park. © **808/274-3444.**

Waiʻoli Mission House Museum and Church ★ HISTORIC SITE/ MUSEUM

Many visitors passing through Hanalei pull over for a photo of **Waiʻoli Huiʻia Church** (www.waiolihuiiachurch.org; © **808/826-6253**), a 1912 American Gothic wooden church with a steep roof, forest-green walls, and belfry reflecting the shape and hues of the mountains behind it. Nearby is the timber-and-plaster **Mission Hall,** built in 1841 and the oldest surviving church building on Kauaʻi. Hidden by a grove of trees behind it is the two-story **Mission House,** erected in 1837 by the area's first missionaries, who traveled from Waimea via outrigger canoe. Teachers Abner and Lucy Wilcox and their four sons moved to this two-story, surprisingly airy home in 1846; four more sons were born here while the Wilcoxes instructed native students in English and the newly transliterated Hawaiian language. The homespun Americana—well-thumbed Bibles, braided rugs, and a spinning wheel—is complemented by Hawaiian elements such as ʻōhiʻa wood floors, a lava rock chimney, and lanais. Restored in 1921, the house is open for drop-in, first-come, first-served guided tours 3 days a week; you'll leave your shoes on the lanai and stay about 30 minutes.

5-5363 Kūhiō Hwy., Hanalei. www.grovefarm.org/waiolimissionhouse. © **808/245-3202.** Free admission to church. Mission House tour donation requested $10 adults, $5 children ages 5–12. Tours on demand Tues, Thurs, and Sat 9am–3pm. Heading north from Waiʻoli Huiʻia Church, turn left on the dirt road just before Hanalei School. A dirt parking area is about 150 yards on the left, with a footpath to the house.

SOUTH SHORE

Kauai Coffee ★★ FARM   Some 4 million coffee trees grow on 3,100 acres of former sugarcane fields from Lāwa'i Valley to 'Ele'ele, making Kauai Coffee the largest producer of coffee in Hawai'i—and the United States. Kona coffee fans might sniff at the fact that the beans are machine-harvested, but it's surprisingly sustainable for such massive production, with 2,500 miles of drip-irrigation tubes, water recycling, cherry-pulp mulching, and other practices. You can learn all about the coffee-growing and roasting process on a free short, self-guided walking tour, on the per-sonalized, hourlong Coffee on the Brain walking tour ($25), or on the bumpy but entertaining 1-hr. Farm Tour in an open-air truck ($45). Or just watch the video and read displays in the free tasting area behind the gift shop on a covered porch. Everyone heads to the latter first: How better to determine the difference between coffee varietals such as Blue Mountain, yellow catuai, or red catuai beans in an equally wide array of roasts and blends? A small snack bar in the tasting room helps take the edge off all that caffeine.

870 Halewili Rd. (Hwy. 540), Kalāheo. www.kauaicoffee.com. © **808/335-0813.** Free admission; free self-guided tours. Coffee on the Brain Tour $25 Sun–Fri 10am. Farm Tour $45, $40 children ages 8–18 (ages 7 and under not allowed); Mon–Fri 9:30am. Daily 9am–5pm.

Ke Kahua O Kaneiolouma ★★ CULTURAL SITE   It's impossible to miss the four towering tiki on a stone platform by the main turnoff for Po'ipū Beach Park, but you're doing yourself a disservice if you just drive by. Still under restoration, and unfortunately threatened by flooding from nearby development, this rock-walled, centuries-old complex contains a navigation-themed *heiau* (temple), fishpond and taro patches, home sites, and a large games arena used during the winter season of *Makahiki.* Entry isn't permitted, but well-designed signs explain the site's cultural and his-torical significance.

Po'ipū Rd., *makai* side (at Ho'owili Rd.), Po'ipū. www.kaneiolouma.org.

Kukuiolono Park ★ HISTORIC SITE/GARDEN   Hawaiians once lit signal fires atop this Kalāheo hillside, perhaps to aid seafarers or warn of invaders. Most visitors are still in the dark about this unusual park, created by pineapple magnate Walter McBryde and then bequeathed to the public after his death in 1930. A mile off the main highway it includes the 9-hole **Kukuiolono Golf Course** ★★ (p. 499); the clubhouse sports bar and res-taurant, **Paco's Tacos Cantina** ★, which serves bargain cocktails and tasty tacos; a Japanese garden; a collection of intriguing Hawaiian lava rock artifacts; a 9-hole mini-golf course ($5); and several miles of jogging paths. A meditation pavilion and stone benches also provide excuses to enjoy the views.

854 Pu'u Rd., Kalāheo. https://kukuiolonogolf.com. © **808/332-9151.** Free admis-sion. Daily 7am–6pm. **Paco's Tacos Cantina:** Daily 8am–5pm; happy hour 3–5pm.

Lawai International Center ★★ BUDDHIST SHRINE/HISTORIC SITE   Although you'll hear some noise from the unseen highway, the serenity of this historic 32-acre valley is unshakable, especially once you ascend the former Hawaiian *heiau* (temple) to the **Hall of Compassion,** a gleaming wooden structure in the style of a 13th-century Buddhist shrine. You're expected to keep silent there and on the hillside path marked by 88 diminutive Shingon Buddhist shrines, a replica of a 900-mile temple route in Shikoku, Japan. Built in 1904 by young plantation workers from Japan, the shrines beckoned pilgrims for decades until the local cannery closed, workers moved away, and the site became overgrown. An all-volunteer, nondenominational effort restored the shrines; you'll hear that inspiring story over a cup of tea and cookies first before quietly heading up the steep hill (walking staff included). *Note:* It's only open for free guided tours two Sundays a month, but if your visit coincides with the first Saturday of the month, you can join volunteers in grounds upkeep from 9am to 1pm; tools and lunch are provided.

End of Wāwae Rd., off Kaumali'i Hwy., *makai* side, Lāwa'i. www.lawaicenter.org. © **808/639-5952.** Tours by reservation the 2nd and last Sun of each month at 10am, noon, and 2pm. Free admission; donations welcomed.

Makauwahi Cave Reserve ★★ ARCHAEOLOGICAL SITE   The Pacific's greatest cache of fossils, including those of enormous, long-extinct waterfowl, may lie in the depths of the largest limestone cave in Hawai'i. Exposed by a sinkhole thousands of years ago, the cave is managed by paleo-archaeologists and conservationists David and Lida Pigott Burney, who have opened it for fascinating tours. After a slow, bumpy drive through former cane fields near the Grand Hyatt Kauai, a short walk takes you to the small entrance to the cave—stay hunched until you see sky overhead. Non-native tortoises, abandoned as house pets, help keep the vegetation down; visit their sanctuary outside the cave, where the Burneys are restoring native plants. Admission is free, but please donate toward upkeep and research. *Tip:* Rough roads may make it easier to park near the arena at CJM Stables (p. 552) and follow signposts north.

Near Māhā'ulepū (Gillin's) Beach, Māhā'ulepū. www.cavereserve.org. © **808/631-3409** or 808/212-1710. Tours daily 10am–4pm. Free admission; donations welcomed. From Po'ipū, take Po'ipū Rd. east past the Grand Hyatt Kauai onto dirt road. Follow 2 miles to crossroads, turn right, then right again just past green gate and shack. Follow road along edge of field and park on left just past signpost 18. Cross trail over footbridge, turn right, and head to signpost 15; cave entrance is small hole. Tortoise rescue is left of parking area.

National Tropical Botanical Garden ★★★ HISTORIC SITE/GARDEN   Formerly owned by the McBryde Sugar Company, which bought the land from Queen Emma in 1886, this lush swath of Lāwa'i Valley contains two major gardens worth visiting, as well as the headquarters and research facilities of the National Tropical Botanical Garden. The 186-acre **McBryde Garden** boasts the largest collection of rare and endangered Hawaiian plants in the world, plus numerous varieties of palms, fruit trees, heliconias, orchids, and other colorful flowers, growing along mostly unpaved trails. Its Spice of Life trail, which includes cacao and allspice trees, meanders past picturesque Maidenhair Falls. The accessible Diversity Trail follows a 450-million-year timeline as it passes through a misty tunnel and ends at a pavilion with restrooms. The self-guided tour ($30 adults, $15 ages 6–12) requires a reservation but allows you up to 2 hours to explore. ***Tip:*** Sign up at https://ntbg.org/support/

Fig tree trunks at Allerton Garden.

volunteer for a unique, 3-hour volunteer experience on Wednesday mornings in the **McBryde Nursery,** where you'll first get a guided tour of some of the world's rarest plants growing there and then help coax tiny seedlings into new pots or complete other easy tasks while seated in the shade. As a bonus, you're allowed to drive to the nursery by making a short but scenic descent into the valley from Kalāheo, via a private road.

Open only to guided tours, the captivating formal gardens of adjacent **Allerton Garden** are the legacy of wealthy Chicagoan Robert Allerton and his companion John Gregg, whom Allerton later adopted. Allerton bought the land from McBryde in 1938 and with Gregg designed a series of elegant outdoor "rooms," where fountains and European statuary bracket plants collected from Southeast Asia and the Pacific. Garden tours last about 2½ hours; 3-hour sunset tours begin in the afternoon and end with a peek inside the oceanfront Allerton estate (normally off-limits), plus a chef-prepared bento box dinner and drinks on the lanai. Twice a week, live Polynesian music and dance, including fire knife, is added to the dinner portion of the tour ($175 adults, $150 ages 2–12), for an intimate, unique luau-style experience called "Allerton by Fire." The "Best of Both Worlds" 2¾-hour guided tour visits select areas in Allerton Garden and McBryde Garden ($60 adults).

All valley garden tours require a tram ride and reservations by credit card. It's free, however, to tour the **Southshore Visitors Center Garden,** where the trams depart. Its several acres include separate areas for ornamental flowers and trees, a plantation-era home garden, Hawaiian native plants, and the profusion of color and textures known as the Gates Garden at the entrance. The visitors center hosts an **Aloha Market** with vendors

A prince OF A PRINCE

With his name gracing half of the main Kauaʻi highway as well as a popular beach and busy avenue in Waikīkī, you could say **Prince Jonah Kūhiō Kalanianaole** is all over the map, just as he was in life. The nephew of Queen Kapiʻolani, who with King David Kalākaua adopted him, Prince Kūhiō studied in California and England before the American-backed overthrow of the monarchy in 1893. He spent a year in prison after being arrested in 1895 for plotting to restore the kingdom and later fought with the British in the Boer War. In 1903, he was elected as a territorial delegate to the U.S. Congress, where he served until his death in 1922, at age 50.

Along the way, Prince Kūhiō founded the first Hawaiian Civic Club, restored the Royal Order of Kamehameha, created the Hawaiian Home Lands Commission (which awards long-term leases to Native Hawaiians), established national parks on Maui and Hawaiʻi Island, opened his Waikīkī beachfront to the public, and popularized outrigger canoe racing—just to name a few of the reasons "the people's prince" is so revered. His March 26 birthday is a state holiday, which his home island of Kauaʻi and others mark with various festivities.

His birthplace in Poʻipū is part of **Prince Kūhiō Park,** a small, grassy compound off Lāwaʻi Road, not far from where surfers navigate "PK's," a break also named for the prince. The park holds the foundations of the family home, a fishpond that's still connected by a culvert to the sea, the remains of a *heiau* (shrine), and a monument that still receives floral tributes. **Note:** It's considered disrespectful to sit on the rock walls, as tempting as it might be to picnic or don snorkel gear there.

of crafts, gifts, and local produce Thursday 10am to 2pm, and a hula show at 12:30pm; admission is free.

4425 Lāwaʻi Rd. (across the street from Spouting Horn), Poʻipū. www.ntbg.org. ✆ **808/ 742-2623. Visitors Center Garden:** Free admission; self-guided tours Tues–Sat 9am–4:30pm, with Aloha Market Thurs 10am–2pm (hula show 12:30pm). **McBryde Garden:** Self-guided tours by reservation $30 adults, $15 children 2–12; Tues–Sat 9:30am–5pm; trams leave hourly on the half-hour, last tram 3:30pm. **Allerton Garden:** $65 adults; guided tours daily 9:30am, 11:30am, and 1:30pm. Sunset tours $100 adults, $60 children 6–12, $25 for ages 2–5, free for children 4 and under; Wed and Fri–Sat 4:30pm. Allerton by Fire (sunset tour, meal, Polynesian live entertainment) $175 adults, $150 ages 2–12, free (but no meal) for children 1 and under; Tues and Thurs 4pm. **Best of Both Worlds (both gardens):** Guided tour $65 adults Tues–Sat varying times. All tours require reservations and check-in 30 min. prior. **Twilight Tour** available dependent on lunar phase, guided by moonlight among Allerton and/or McBryde Gardens; adults $8). **Volunteer sessions:** Wed 8am; must sign up in advance at https://ntbg.org/support/volunteer.

Spouting Horn ★★ NATURAL ATTRACTION   The Hawaiian equivalent to Old Faithful—at least in regularity, if not temperature—is an impressive plume of seawater that shoots anywhere from 10 to 50 or so feet into the air above the rocky shoreline (fenced for safety reasons). The spout comes from the force of ocean swells funneling waves through a lava tube, with the most spectacular displays in winter and other high-surf days. The *whoosh* of the spraying water is often followed by a loud moaning sound, created by air being pushed through another nearby hole. There's an ample parking lot (as well as restrooms) on the site, but if you spot tour buses, don't try to compete with the crowds for a Spouting Horn photo. Instead, browse the vendors of arts, crafts, and jewelry (from $5 bangles to Ni'ihau shell leis costing hundreds of dollars) under the tents along the bluff, or watch the wild chickens put on a show. When the buses will leave 15 to 20 minutes later, take your photo op. Keep an eye out for whales in winter.

Lāwa'i Rd., *makai* side, Po'ipū, 2 miles west of the traffic circle with Po'ipū Rd. Free admission. Daily dawn to dusk.

WEST SIDE

Kōke'e State Park ★★★ PARK   It's only 16 miles from Waimea to Kōke'e, but the two feel worlds apart: With 4,345 acres of rainforest, Kōke'e is another climate zone altogether, where the breeze has a bite and trees look quite continental. This is a cloud forest on the edge of the Alaka'i Swamp, the largest swamp in Hawai'i, on the summit plateau of Kaua'i. Days are cool and wet, with intermittent bright sunshine, not unlike Seattle on a good day. Bring your sweater, and, if you're staying over, be sure you know how to light a fire (overnight lows dip into the 40s/single-digit Celsius).

Although invasive foreign plants such as strawberry guava, kahili ginger, and Australian tree ferns have crowded out native plants, the forest still holds many treasures, including several species that only grow on Kaua'i: *mokihana* shrubs, whose anise-scented green berries adorn the island's signature lei; *iliau,* a spiky plant similar to Maui's silversword; and the endangered white hibiscus, one of the few with a fragrance.

Mist and sunshine mix to create rainbows over Kōke'e State Park.

Before exploring the area, though, be sure to stop by the **Kōke'e Museum ★★** (www.kokee.org; ✆ **808/335-9975;** daily 9am–4:30pm). It's right next to the restaurant/gift shop of the Lodge at Kōke'e, in the meadow off Kōke'e Road (Hwy. 550), 5 miles past the first official Waimea Canyon lookout. Admission is free, but it deserves at least the $1 donation requested per person. The museum shop has great trail information as well as local books and maps, including the official park trail map. A .1-mile nature walk with labeled plants starts just behind the museum.

Another 2.7 miles up the road from Kōke'e Lodge is **Kalalau Lookout ★★★**, the spectacular climax of your drive through Waimea Canyon and Kōke'e—unless the gate is open to the Pu'u O Kila Lookout 1 mile farther, the true end of the road. The latter lookout is usually closed in the frequent inclement weather: Nearby Wai'ale'ale is playing catch for clouds that have crossed thousands of miles of ocean. The view from Kalalau Lookout can be Brigadoon-like, too, but when the mists part, it's breathtaking. Shadows dance across the green cliffs dappled with red and orange, white tropicbirds soar over a valley almost 4,000 feet below, and the turquoise sea sparkles on the horizon. Just below the railing, look for the fluffy red honeycreepers (*'apapane*) darting among the scarlet-tufted 'ōhi'a lehua trees. Mornings tend to offer the clearest views.

With so many trails to hike up here, including the boardwalk through the Alaka'i Swamp (p. 551), some choose to stay overnight, either by pitching a tent in one of several campsites (by permit only) or opting for one of the cabins run by West Kauai Lodging or the YWCA's Camp Sloggett (p. 573). You'll need to plan carefully, though, when it comes to food and drink: The **Kōke'e Lodge Restaurant** (p. 588) is the only game in town, although a good one, so check its hours carefully. Otherwise, it's a slow, 15-mile drive down to Waimea.

Note: Visitors need to pay an entrance fee ($5 per person for ages 4 and older) as well as for parking ($10 per vehicle) at Kōke'e and Waimea Canyon state parks but can visit both with the same permit.

Kōke'e Rd., 7 miles north of its merge with Waimea Canyon Rd. (Hwy. 550). https://dlnr.hawaii.gov/dsp/parks/kauai/kokee-state-park. ✆ **808/274-3444.** Nonresident parking $10 per vehicle; entry $5 per person ages 4 and older. Daily dawn to dusk.

Pā'ula'ula State Historic Site ★ HISTORIC SITE To the list of those who tried to conquer Hawai'i, add the Russians. In 1815, a German doctor tried to claim Kaua'i for Russia. He even supervised the construction of a fort on this site in Waimea, naming it Fort Elizabeth for the wife of Czar Alexander I. However, Kamehameha I expelled the doctor and his handful of Russian companions a couple of years later. Only the walls remain today, built with stacked lava rocks in the shape of a star. You can easily follow a path around the fort's perimeter to the oceanside entrance to the interior; see the interpretive signs by the parking lot. Leis typically adorn the 8-foot bronze statue of the last king of Kaua'i, Kaumuali'i, who avoided bloodshed by ceding control of his kingdom (including Ni'ihau)

Pāʻulaʻula State Historic Site.

to Kamehameha in 1810. The site also provides panoramic views of the west bank of the Waimea River, where Captain Cook landed, and the island of Niʻihau. *Note:* Tidy restrooms and a picnic table make this a convenient pit stop.

Ocean side of Kaumaliʻi Hwy., Waimea, just after mile marker 22, east of Waimea River. https://dlnr.hawaii.gov/dsp/parks/kauai/paʻulaʻula-state-historic-site. © **808/ 274-3444.** Free admission. Daily dawn to dusk.

Waimea Canyon State Park ★★★ PARK/NATURAL ATTRACTION

Often called the Grand Canyon of the Pacific—an analogy attributed to Mark Twain, although there's no record he ever visited—Waimea Canyon is indeed spectacular, albeit on a smaller scale. A mile wide, 3,600 feet deep, and 14 miles long, depending on whom you ask, this counterpart to Arizona's icon deserves accolades for its beauty alone. A jumble of red-orange pyramids, striped with gray bands of volcanic rock and stubbled with green and gold vegetation, Waimea Canyon was formed by a series of prehistoric lava flows, earthquakes, and erosion from wind and water, including the narrow Waimea River, still carving its way to the sea. You can stop by the road and look at the canyon, hike into it (p. 547), admire it from a downhill bicycle tour (p. 543), or swoop through it in a helicopter (p. 551).

By car, there are two ways to visit Waimea Canyon and reach Kōkeʻe State Park, 15 miles up from Waimea. From the main road of Kaumaliʻi Highway, it's best to head up Waimea Canyon Drive (Hwy. 550) in Waimea town. You can also pass through Waimea and turn up Kōkeʻe Road (Hwy. 55) at Kekaha, but it's steeper—one reason the twice-daily downhill bike tours prefer that route—and its vistas, though lovely, are not as eye-popping as those along Waimea Canyon Drive, the narrower rim road. The two routes merge about 7 miles up from the highway and continue as Kōke'e Road.

The first good vantage point is **Waimea Canyon Lookout ★★★**, between mile markers 10 and 11 on Kōke'e Road; there's a long, gently graded, paved path for those who can't handle the stairs to the observation area. Far across the canyon, two-tiered **Waipo'o (*"why-poh-oh"*) Falls** cascades 800 feet; you might spot a nimble mountain goat clambering on the precipices just below. From here, it's about another 5 miles to Kōke'e. A few more informal and formal lookout points along the way also offer noteworthy views. **Pu'u Ka Pele Lookout ★★**, between mile markers 12 and 13, reveals the multiple ribbons of water coursing through Waipo'o Falls. **Pu'u Hinahina Lookout ★**, between mile markers 13 and 14, actually has two different vista points, one with a sweeping view of the canyon down to the Pacific, and another of Ni'ihau, lying 17 miles west. Waimea Canyon Drive (Hwy. 550) and Kōke'e Road (Hwy. 55), Waimea. https://dlnr. hawaii.gov/dsp/parks/kauai/waimea-canyon-state-park. (©) **808/274-3444.** $5 ages 4 and older, parking $10 per vehicle, paid at entrance to Kōke'e State Park. Daily dawn to dusk.

West Kaua'i Heritage Center ★ MUSEUM   Although its hours are limited, this center's small but well-curated cultural exhibitions merit a stop before or after your Waimea Canyon expedition. The **"Keepers of the Culture"** displays include vintage photos, artifacts, and panels on Waimea's natural and cultural history, from traditional Hawaiian practices such as salt-making and herbal medicine to the arrival of Captain Cook, the sugar plantation era, *paniolo* (cowboy) culture, and the modern Pacific Missile Range Facility. Call for the current schedule of weekly programs

Waipo'o Falls in Waimea Canyon.

such as a lei making class ($10), guided motor tour, and 2-hour *kani kapila* (jam session) led by local seniors.

9565 Kaumali'i Hwy. (*mauka* side) at Waimea Canyon Rd., Waimea. Park at rear of building, but lot entrance is only from Kaumali'i Hwy. www.wsmmuseum.org. © **808/338-1332**. Free admission. Tues–Fri 9am–3pm.

BEACHES

Note: You'll find relevant sites on the "Beaches & Outdoor Activities on Kaua'i" map, p. 493.

Beaches

Kauai's nearly 70 beaches include some of the most beautiful in the world, and all are open to the public, as required by state law. They are also in the middle of the vast, powerful Pacific, where currents and surf patterns are often quite different from Mainland beaches. The North Shore sees the highest surf in winter (Oct–Apr), with swells originating in the Arctic that can wrap around the West Side and turn the East Side's waters rough. In summer, Antarctic storms can send large swells to the South Shore that may also wrap around the West Side and churn up the East Side.

The good news is there's almost always a swimmable beach somewhere: You just need to know where to look. Start by asking your hotel concierge or check the daily ocean report for lifeguarded beaches at **https://oceansafety.hawaii.gov**. Nine beaches—all of them county or state parks—have lifeguards, who are keen to clue you in on safety.

Below are highlights of the Garden Isle's more accessible beaches. For detailed listings, including maps and videos, of virtually all strands and coves, see **www.kauaibeachscoop.com**.

EAST SIDE

Anahola Beach ★ Anahola is part of the Hawaiian Home Lands federal program, meaning that much of the land here is reserved for lease by

Nāpali Coast viewed from a helicopter.

Native Hawaiians; you'll pass their modest homes on the road to this secluded, mostly reef-protected golden strand. The 1½-acre **Anahola Beach Park** on the south end feels like the neighborhood's back yard, particularly on weekends, with kids learning to surf or bodyboarding, a hula class on the grass, and picnickers. It's better to explore here during the week, when you might share it with just a few local fishermen (give their poles and nets a wide berth) and campers. There are sandy-bottomed pockets for swimming and reefy areas for snorkeling, safe except in high surf. The Anahola River, usually shallow enough to walk across, bisects the beach. Facilities include picnic tables, restrooms, campsites, and lifeguards. From Kūhiō Hwy. heading north, turn right on Anahola Rd. (btw. mile markers 13 and 14) and head ¾-mile to the beach park. Or park north of the Anahola River by taking a right on 'Aliomanu Rd. ½-mile past Anahola Rd.

Safe Swimming on Kaua'i

"When in doubt, don't go out" is the mantra of local authorities, who repeat this and other important safety tips in public service announcements. That refers to going into unsafe waters, walking on slippery rocks and ledges that may be hit by high surf, or other heedless acts, such as disregarding "Beach Closed" signs in winter. Many of the unguarded beaches have waters that should only be enjoyed from the sand or during calm conditions, which can change rapidly; large waves may come in sets as much as 20 minutes apart. Although you might see residents seemingly ignoring the warning signs that note hazards such as strong currents, steep drop-offs, dangerous shorebreak, and the like, keep in mind they've had years to acclimatize. Don't be afraid to ask for their advice, though, since they'll tailor it for newcomers—no one wants injuries or worse in their home waters.

Kalapaki Beach ★★   This quarter-mile-long swath of golden sand may seem like a private beach, given all the lounge chairs on its border with the Royal Sonesta Kaua'i Resort, which towers behind. But there's plenty of room to find your own space to sunbathe, while the jetty stretching across much of Kalapaki Bay offers a protected area to swim or paddle; bodysurfing and surfing are also possible at a small break. The view of the mossy-green Hā'upu Ridge rising out of Nāwiliwili Bay is entrancing, as is watching massive cruise ships and Matson barges angle their way in and out of the nearby harbor. The water is a little murkier here, due to stream runoff. Facilities include restrooms and showers, with shops and restaurants a short walk away. From Līhu'e Airport, turn left onto Hwy. 51, then turn left on Rice St., and look for the Royal Sonesta Kaua'i Resort entrance on the left. Free beach access parking is in the upper lot, past the hotel's porte cochère.

Keālia Beach ★   Only very experienced surfers and bodyboarders should try their skill on the usually powerful waves here, but everyone else can enjoy the show from the broad golden sand, a picnic table, or the nearby coastal multiuse path. The lifeguards can advise you if it's calm enough to go for a swim and where to do it. When the wind is up, you might see kite flyers. The 66-acre **Keālia Beach Park** is just off the main highway, often with food trucks and coconut vendors in the parking lot, making it a good spot for an impromptu break. Facilities include restrooms and picnic shelters. Off Kūhiō Hwy. in Kapa'a, just north of Kapa'a River and Mā'ilihuna Rd.

Kumukumu (Donkey) Beach ★★   When the only way to reach this beach was by a downhill hike through sugarcane fields near a donkey pasture, nude sunbathers took full advantage of its seclusion. Now it's bordered by luxury estates and the **Ke Ala Hele Makalae** coastal path; the 10-minute walk down to the ocean is mostly paved and starts at a parking lot with restrooms. So keep your clothes on while enjoying the soft golden sand at this tree-lined beach, also known as Paliku ("vertical cliff") and Kuna Bay. The water is too rough for swimming or snorkeling, but you may see advanced surfers and bodyboarders here. The north side has a shallow cove that's safe for wading in calm conditions. From Kapa'a, take Kūhiō Hwy. north past mile marker 11; parking is on right, marked by sign with 2 hiking figures on it. Footpath to beach starts near parking lot entrance.

Lydgate Beach ★   Part of the family oasis of 58-acre **Lydgate Park** ★ (p. 508) on the south side of the Wailua River mouth, Lydgate Beach has two rock-walled ponds that create the safest swimming and best snorkeling on the East Side—unless storms have pushed branches and other debris into the pond. Families also gravitate here for the immense wooden play structure known as the **Kamalani Playground** and access to a 2½-mile stretch of the **Ke Ala Hele Makalae coastal path,** suitable for strollers and bikes. Be aware there may be long-term campers in some corners;

affordable housing is extremely tight on the island. Facilities include a pavilion, restrooms, outdoor showers, picnic tables, barbecue grills, lifeguards, campsites, and parking. Leho Dr. at Nalu Rd., Wailua.

NORTH SHORE

'Anini Beach ★★★   'Anini is usually the safest beach on Kaua'i for swimming and windsurfing, thanks to one of the longest, widest fringing reefs on the island, among the largest in Hawai'i. With shallow water 4 to 5 feet deep, it's also a good snorkel spot for beginners (although the coral and varieties of fish are sparse closer to shore). In summer months, divers are attracted to the 60-foot drop-off near the channel in the northwest corner of the nearly 3-mile-long reef. In winter, this channel creates a very dangerous rip current, although the near-shore waters generally stay calm; it can be fun to watch breakers pounding the distant reef from the bathlike lagoon. The well-shaded, sinuous beach is very narrow in places, so just keep walking if you'd like more privacy. The 13-acre **'Anini Beach Park** on the southwestern end has restrooms, picnic facilities, a boat-launch ramp, campsites, and often a food truck or two. From Kīlauea, head north on Kūhiō Hwy. to the 2nd Kalihiwai Rd. exit on right (the first Kalihiwai Rd. ends at Kalihiwai Beach). Head downhill ½-mile then left on 'Anini Rd.

Hā'ena Beach ★★★   The road ends here at this iconic tropical beach in **Hā'ena State Park** (p. 510), hugged by swaying palms and sheltering ironwoods, its pale dunes sloping into a cozy lagoon brimming with a kaleidoscope of reef fish. You used to feel like a sardine during summer

Waiting for the perfect set at Wai'oli Beach Park.

(when the ocean is at its most tranquil), and spectacular sunsets often packed the sands, too. But it's much more tranquil now, thanks to a permit system that limits the total number of daily nonresident visitors to 900, including campers and hikers on the nearby **Kalalau Trail** (p. 549) as well as beachgoers. Permits ($10) to park in the 70 spaces reserved for nonresidents are spread across three time brackets a day, so if you want to spend the whole day, you'll need to purchase three permits. Everyone in the car will need an entry permit ($5 per person). You can also buy a shuttle pass ($40) from Hanalei, which includes park entry. ***Tips:*** Reservations for parking and entry passes, which are available 30 days in advance, sell out quickly, but you can always check the website 5 to 6am and 5 to 6pm daily for any openings due to cancellations. The parking lot and shuttle stop are no longer at the end of the road, but require a short walk on a boardwalk through taro fields—please don't take a shortcut through these wetlands—and a forest, where you'll find restrooms and showers. **Kē'ē** (pronounced *"keh-eh"*) is also subject to high surf in winter when rogue waves can grab unwitting spectators from the shoreline and dangerous currents form in a channel on the reef's western edge. Always check with the lifeguards about the safest areas for swimming or snorkeling. About 7½ northwest of Hanalei off Kūhiō Hwy. Before visiting, you must purchase a parking permit ($10), entry voucher ($5 per person), or shuttle pass including entry ($40 adults, $25 ages 4–15, younger children free if seated on laps) from https://gohaena.com. Purchases are allowed up to 30 days in advance.

Hanalei Beach ★★★ Easily one of the most majestic settings in Hawai'i, and unbelievably just a few blocks from the main road, Hanalei Beach is a gorgeous half-moon of golden-white sand, 2 miles long and 125 feet wide. Hanalei means "lei-shaped," and like a lei, the curving, ironwood-fringed sands adorn Hanalei Bay, the largest inlet on Kaua'i. While the grass-topped roofs of Princeville's 1 Hotel Hanalei Bay help it blend more into the eastern vista, the view west is even more lush and green; behind you, emerald peaks streaked with waterfalls rise to 4,000 feet. Renowned for experts-only big surf in winter (Sept–May), Hanalei attracts both beginners and old hands with steady, gentler waves the rest of the year. In summer, much of the bay turns into a virtual lake. The county manages three different beach parks here, two with lifeguards.

Black Pot Beach Park, near the historic, 300-foot-long **Hanalei Pier,** is particularly good for swimming, snorkeling, surfing, and fishing, so it's very popular on weekends and holidays. Fortunately, there's a newer overflow parking lot across from the main one with 50 spaces; facilities include restrooms, showers, and picnic tables. **Hanalei Pavilion Beach Park,** in the center of the bay, has wide-open swimming (in calm weather), surfing, and boogie boarding under the watchful eyes of lifeguards; facilities include restrooms, showers, and pavilions. "Pine Trees" is the widely used moniker for **Wai'oli Beach Park,** shaded by ironwood trees towards the western edge of the bay. It's another popular surf spot—champions Andy and Bruce Irons grew up riding the waves here and started the children's Pine Trees Classic held here every April. Check with lifeguards in winter about possible strong currents; facilities include showers and restrooms. From Kūhiō Hwy. in Hanalei, turn makai on Aku Rd., then right on Weke Rd. Hanalei Pavilion Beach Park is on your left; the road ends at Black Pot Beach Park. For Wai'oli Beach Park (Pine Trees): Aku Rd. to a left on Weke Rd.; right on He'e Rd.

Kauapea (Secret) Beach ★★ Not exactly secret, but still wonderfully secluded, this long, broad stretch of light sand below forested bluffs lies snugly between rocky points, with only a few cliff-top homes and Kīlauea Point Lighthouse to the east providing signs of civilization. Although strong currents and high surf, especially in winter, make the water unsafe, tide pools at the west end invite exploration when the surf is low, creating beguiling mini-lagoons; a small artesian waterfall to the east is perfect for washing off salt water. *Note:* Despite its reputation as a safe haven for nudists (who hang out at the more remote eastern end), Kaua'i County does occasionally enforce the "no public nudity" law here. And as with all rural destinations where your car will be out of sight for extended periods, plan to take your valuables with you. It's a 15-minute walk downhill to the beach. Heading north on Kūhiō Hwy. from Kīlauea, take 1st Kalihiwai Rd. turnoff on right. Drive about 50 yards, then turn right on unmarked dirt road, and follow to parking area. Trail at end of lot leads downhill to beach, about a 15-min. walk.

Lumaha'i Beach ★ Between lush tropical jungle of pandanus and ironwood trees and the brilliant blue ocean lie two crescents of inviting golden-sand beach, separated by a rocky outcropping. This beautiful beach is Kaua'i at its most captivating—and where you must exercise the most caution. Locals have nicknamed it "Luma-die," reflecting the sad tally of those drowned or seriously injured here every year. With no reef protection and a steeply sloping shore, the undertow and shorebreak are exceptionally strong, while the rocky ledges that invite exploration are often slapped by huge waves that knock sightseers into the tumbling surf and sharp rocks. Flash floods can also make the Lumaha'i River, which enters the ocean from the western beach, turn from a wading pool into a raging torrent. Plus, it has neither lifeguards nor facilities; parking is in a bumpy, unpaved area or along the narrow highway. So why would one even go here? When summer brings more tranquil surf, it's a gorgeous setting to stretch out on the sand—not too close to the shorebreak—and soak in the untamed beauty. *Note:* The eastern beach, reached by a short, steep trail from the highway, is where Mitzi Gaynor sang "I'm Gonna Wash That Man Right Outta My Hair" in *South Pacific*. From Hanalei, follow Kūhiō Hwy. about 2½ miles west. Look for pull-off on makai side, near mile marker 4, for trail to eastern beach. For western beach, continue west (downhill) to larger, unpaved parking area on makai side by mile marker 5.

Mākua (Tunnels) Beach ★★★ & Hāʻena Beach ★★★ Mākua Beach earned the nickname of "Tunnels" from the labyrinth of lava tubes that wind through its inner and outer reef, making this Kauai's premiere snorkeling and diving site year-round. But as fascinating as the rainbow of tropical fish and the underwater tunnels, arches, and channels may be, they're more than matched by the beauty above water. The last pinnacle in a row of velvety green mountains, Makana ("Bali Hai") rises over the western end of a golden curved beach with a fringe of ironwood trees. The only problem: The few parking spots on dirt roads fill up instantly, and residents vigilantly enforce "no parking" zones.

Fortunately, a quarter mile up the sand is **Hāʻena Beach Park,** a county facility with a bit more parking—plus restrooms, showers, picnic tables, campsites, and lifeguards. During calm conditions, most frequent in summer, Hāʻena Beach offers good swimming and some snorkeling, though not as enticing as at Makua. Winter brings enormous waves, rip currents, and a strong shorebreak; leave the water then to local surfers. Walk across the road for a gander at **Maniniholo Dry Cave ★★**, where you can stroll for many yards inside before it gets too dark and low (watch your noggin). Hāʻena Beach is also a stop on the new **Kauaʻi North Shore Shuttle** ($40; https://gohaena.com), which allows purchases up to 30 days in advance and includes entry to **Hāʻena Beach** (p. 529) up the road. From Hanalei, Mākua (Tunnels) is just past mile marker 8 on Kūhiō Hwy., not visible from the road. Continue ½-mile to Hāʻena Beach Park's parking lot on right.

SOUTH SHORE

Keoneloa (Shipwrecks) Beach ★ Makawehi Point, a lithified sand dune, juts out from the eastern end of this beach, whose Hawaiian name means "the long sand." Harrison Ford and Anne Heche jumped off Makawehi in *Six Days, Seven Nights* (don't try it yourself), while body-surfers and boogie-boarders find the roiling waters equally exhilarating. Novices should stick to the shore or follow the ironwood trees to the path to the top of Makawehi Point, which is also the start of the **Māhāʻulepū Heritage Trail** (p. 549). A paved beach path in front of the Grand Hyatt Kauai leads west past tide pools to the blustery point at Makahūʻena, perfect for photographing Makawehi Point. Restrooms and showers are by the small parking lot on ʻĀinakō Street. Public access from ʻĀinakō St., off Poʻipū Rd., just east of Grand Hyatt Kauai.

Māhāʻulepū Beaches ★★ Close to the well-groomed resorts of Poʻipū is a magical place to leave the crowds—and maybe the last few centuries—behind. To reach the three different beaches of Māhāʻulepū, framed by lithified sand dunes, former sugarcane fields, and the bold Hāʻupu ridge, you'll have to drive at least 3 miles on an uneven dirt road through private land (gates close at 6pm) or hike the fascinating Māhāʻulepū Heritage Trail (p. 549). The first tawny strand is **Māhāʻulepū Beach,** nicknamed Gillin's Beach after the former Grove Farm manager

Kaua'i has many kid-friendly beaches.

whose house is the only modern structure you'll see for miles (the house is available for rent from $900 a night with 1-week minimum; www.the gillinbeachhouse.com). Windsurfing is popular here; the strong currents prevent swimming or snorkeling. Around the point is **Kawailoa Bay,** also a windsurfing destination, with a rockier shoreline great for beachcombing and fishing. Wedged between dramatically carved ledges, **Hā'ula Beach** is a picturesque pocket of sand with a rocky cove, best for solitude; access may be restricted. *Note:* The coastline here can be very windy and subject to high surf in summer. **By car:** From Po'ipū Rd. in front of Grand Hyatt Kauai, continue on unpaved road 3 miles east, past the golf course and stables. Turn right at the T intersection, go 1 mile to the big sand dune, turn left, and drive ½-mile to a small lot under the trees to reach **Māhā'ulepū Beach.** Continue on the dirt road (high-clearance 4WD recommended) another ¼-mile to **Kawailoa Bay,** and then, if it's open, drive another ½-mile to a short trail to **Hā'ula Beach. By foot:** Follow Māhā'ulepū Heritage Trail (www.kauai.com/mahauleu-beach-trail) 2 miles from east end of Keoneloa (Shipwrecks) Beach; limited public parking is just east of Grand Hyatt Kauai on 'Āinakō Street.

Po'ipū Beach ★★★   A perennial "best beach" winner, the long swath of Po'ipū is two beaches in one, divided by a tombolo, or sandbar point. On the left, a lava-rock jetty protects a sandy-bottom pool that's perfect for children most of the year; on the right, the open bay attracts swimmers, snorkelers, and surfers. (If the waves are up, check with the lifeguards for the safest area to swim.) The sandy area is not all that large, but it's become famous in recent years for the number of Hawaiian green sea turtles that come ashore daily at twilight, as well as the occasional Hawaiian monk seal (please observe the law by staying well back and not harassing, touching, or feeding them). **Po'ipū Beach Park** offers a lawn for kids to run around in, plus picnic shelters, play structures, restrooms, and showers on its 5½ acres. Though palm trees are plentiful, they don't offer much shade; bring a beach umbrella. Given the lodgings nearby, Po'ipū understandably stays busy year-round, and on New Year's Eve, it becomes Kauai's version of Times Square with fireworks. It's on the county's radar for becoming accessible by permit. *Note:* A third sandy strand, to the west in front of Kiahuna Plantation Resort, is known as **Kiahuna** or **Sheraton Beach;** swimming and surfing are possible, but there are no lifeguards here. A short walk east is **Brennecke's Beach,** a sandy cove beloved by bodysurfers and boogie-boarders; be forewarned that waves can be large, especially in summer, and the rocky sides are always hazardous. Injuries do occur at Brennecke's, which also has no lifeguard. From Kōloa, follow Po'ipū Rd. south to traffic circle and then east to a right turn on Ho'owili Rd. Parking is on the left at intersection with Ho'one Rd. Additional public parking closer to Kiahuna Beach is opposite the Sheraton Kauai at the eastern end of Po'ipū Beach Rd.

WEST SIDE

Polihale Beach ★★   This mini-Sahara on the western end of the island is the biggest beach in Hawai'i: 17 miles long and as wide as three football fields in places. This is a wonderful place to get away from it all, but don't forget your flip-flops—the midday sand is hotter than a lava flow. The pale golden sands wrap around the northwestern shore of Kaua'i from Kekaha to the ridges of Nāpali. For military reasons, access is highly restricted for a 7-mile stretch along the southeastern end near the Pacific Missile Range Facility, including the famed **Nohili (Barking Sands) Beach.** If you have a military ID, visit the beach club onsite or try to score one of a handful of beach cottages, booked up to a year in advance.

Polihale State Park.

Civilians still have miles of sand to explore in 140-acre **Polihale State Park,** provided you (or your car) can handle the 5-mile, often very rutted dirt road leading there; four-wheel-drive is recommended. (Avoid driving on the car-trapping sand, too.) The sheer expanse, plus views of Ni'ihau and the first stark cliffs of Nāpali, make the arduous trek worth it for many. Although strong rip currents and a heavy shorebreak make the water dangerous, especially in winter, **Queen's Pond,** a small, shallow, sandy-bottom inlet, is generally protected from the surf in summer. The park has restrooms, showers, picnic tables, campsites, and drinking water (usually; vandalism is sadly frequent), but no lifeguards or any other facilities nearby, so plan accordingly. As in all remote areas, don't leave any valuables in your car. From Kekaha, follow Kaumali'i Hwy. 7 miles northwest past Pacific Missile Range Facility to fork at Ka'o Rd., bear right, and look for sign on left to Polihale. Follow dirt road 5 miles to unpaved parking area, bearing right at forks.

Salt Pond Beach ★★   The only traditional salt ponds in Hawai'i that are still in production lie across from Salt Pond Beach, just outside Hanapēpē. The area's original Hawaiian name, Waimakaohi'iaka, refers to a legend that the demigoddess Hi'iaka shed tears (*waimaka*) here, which later became salt; a mural depicts the tale. Generations of Hawaiians have carefully tended the beds in which the sun turns seawater into salt crystals. Tinged with red clay, *'alae,* the salt is used as a health remedy as well as for seasoning food and drying fish, but may only be given, not purchased. Although the salt ponds are off-limits to visitors, 6-acre **Salt Pond Beach Park** is a great place to explore, offering a curved reddish-gold beach between two rocky points, a protective reef that creates lagoonlike conditions for swimming and snorkeling (talk to the lifeguard first if waves are up), tide pools, and a natural wading pool for kids. Locals flock here on weekends. Facilities include showers, restrooms, a campground, and picnic areas. From Kaumali'i Hwy. in Hanapēpē, cross Hanapēpē Bridge, and look for Lele Rd. ½-mile ahead, makai side. Turn left and follow Lele Rd. to a right turn on Lokokai Rd. Salt Pond Beach parking lot is 1 mile ahead.

WATERSPORTS

Several outfitters on Kaua'i not only offer equipment rentals and tours, but also dispense expert information on weather forecasts, sea and trail conditions, and other important matters for adventurers. Brothers Micco and Chino Godinez at **Kayak Kaua'i** (www.kayakkauai.com; ⓒ **888/596-3853** or 808/826-9844) are experts on paddling Kauai's rivers and coastline (as well as hiking and camping), offering guided tours and equipment rentals at their store in the Wailua River Marina. You can also learn about ocean and reef conditions and recommended boat operators at **Snorkel Bob's** (www.snorkelbob.com), with two locations in Kapa'a and Po'ipū (see "Snorkeling," later). *Note:* Plan to tip $20 in cash per person in your party for the crew or guides on any tours; prices exclude tax.

Boat & Raft (Zodiac) Tours

One of the most spectacular natural attractions in all of Hawai'i is the **Nāpali Coast.** Unless you're willing to make an arduous 22-mile round-trip hike (see "Hiking," on p. 547), there are only two ways to see it: by helicopter (see "Helicopter Tours," on p. 551) or by water. Cruising to Nāpali may involve a well-equipped yacht under full sail, a speedy powerboat, or for the very adventurous, a Zodiac inflatable raft, with which you can explore Nāpali's sea caves or even land at one of Nāpali's pristine valleys—be prepared to hang on for dear life (it can reach speeds of 60mph) and get very wet.

You're almost guaranteed daily sightings of pods of spinner dolphins on morning cruises, as well as Pacific humpback whales during their annual visit from December to early April. In season, both sailing and powerboats combine **whale-watching** with their regular adventures. **Sunset cruises,** with cocktails and/or dinner, are another way to get out on the water and appreciate Kauai's coastline from a different angle.

Unfortunately, very few tours leave from the North Shore, meaning you'll miss seeing some of the most beautiful portions of Nāpali, including Kalalau Valley, from the water. That is why I highly recommend booking with **North Shore Charters ★★★** (www.kauainorthshorecharters. com). Their custom-built 32-foot power catamaran leaves right from 'Anini Beach on a 4-hour tour ($250, lunch and snorkel at Nualolo Kai included, limited to 18 passengers). You'll zip past Hanalei Bay and dip into sea caves while learning modern and ancient Hawaiian lore of the area from friendly local guides. Don't forget to wave to the beleaguered hikers on the Kalalau Trail.

Note: In addition to Captain Andy's (details below), only two other companies have permits to land at Nualolo Kai, home to the ruins of an 800-year-old Hawaiian village below an elevated Nāpali valley. All trips are on rigid-hull inflatables, which, unlike larger boats, can pass through the reef opening, and include snorkeling, picnic lunch, and drinks. **Blue Ocean Adventure Tours ★★** (www.napaliexplorer.com; ✆ **808/338-9999**) departs from Kekaha mornings year-round and afternoons March to October ($189 adults, $169 ages 6–12). **Kauai Sea Tours ★★** (www. kauaiseatours.com; ✆ **800/733-7997** or 808/335-5309) operates from Port Allen ($190 adults, $180 ages 7–12; weight limit 250 lb.) and offers a wide variety of other Zodiac and catamaran cruises.

Captain Andy's Sailing Adventures ★★   Captain Andy has been sailing to Nāpali since 1980, with a fleet that now includes two sleek 55-foot custom catamarans, the *Spirit of Kauai* and *Akialoa;* two luxurious 65-foot catamarans, the *Southern Star* and the *Northern Star;* and the zippy 24-foot Zodiac, which holds about a dozen thrillseekers. The 5½-hour **Nāpali catamaran cruise** costs $215 for adults and $195 for children ages 3 to 12, and it includes a continental breakfast, a deli-style lunch, snorkeling, and drinks; aboard the Southern Star ($245 adults, $225 children ages 3–12), a barbecue lunch replaces the deli fare. A 4-hour Nāpali Coast dinner cruise—which sails around the South Shore when Nāpali's waters are too rough, most often in winter—costs $245 for adults and $225 for children ages 3 to 12 ($215/$195 on the *Southern Star*), with no snorkeling; all Nāpali catamaran cruises leave from Port Allen. **Napali Zodiac cruises** depart from Kīkīaola Small Boat Harbor in Kekaha; the 4-hour version ($224 adults, $199 children ages 6–12) includes snorkeling and snacks, while the 6-hour version ($295/$255) adds a landing at Nualolo Kai (depending on conditions) and expands snacks to a picnic lunch. www.napali.com. (*) **800/535-0830** or 808/335-6833.

Holo Holo Charters ★★★ A leader in ecotourism, Holo Holo asks all clients to take its "Pono Pledge" to travel responsibly and safely while embracing the aloha spirit. The company models the same principles aboard its two gleaming catamarans, which depart Port Allen. The 50-foot *Leila,* licensed for 45 passengers but limited to just 37, serves Holo Holo's 5-hour, year-round **Nāpali snorkel sails:** They're $240 for adults and $220 for children ages 5 to 12, including a continental breakfast and deli lunch, and post-snorkel beer and wine. The 65-foot *Holo Holo* power catamaran, the island's largest, was built specifically to handle the channel crossing between Kauaʻi and Niʻihau, where passengers snorkel in stunningly clear water after Nāpali sightseeing on 7-hour trips, also with two meals and post-snorkel libations ($310 adults, $290 children ages 5–12). The 3½-hour **Nāpali Sunset Dinner Tour** ($210 adults, $190 children ages 5–12), also aboard the *Holo Holo,* offers dinner and drinks on its way back to port, while the 4-hour **Napali Sunset Dinner Sail** ($210 adults, $190 children ages 5–12) aboard the *Leila* serves the same fare but motors upwind and sails downwind. Holo Holo also runs seasonal Nāpali snorkel tours conveniently from Hanalei on comfortable inflatable "rafts," really speedboats with fiberglass hulls, twin motors, stadium seats, and a freshwater shower. The 4-hour trip, including drinks and lunch, costs $315 for ages 5 and older (younger not allowed), and runs April through October, as conditions allow. www.holoholokauaiboattours.com. (*) **800/848-6130** or 808/335-0815.

Liko Kauai & Makana Charters ★★ Born and raised on Kauaʻi, in a Native Hawaiian family that once farmed taro in Kalalau Valley, Captain Liko Hoʻokano offers more than just typical cruises; instead, they're a 5-hour combination Nāpali Coast tour/snorkel/cultural history class/seasonal whale-watching extravaganza with lunch. Snorkeling is typically at Nualolo Kai. Choose from four different catamarans, all with restrooms, shaded areas, snorkel gear, and a limit on passengers below the official capacity, for greater comfort. The 49-foot *Na Pali Kai III* power catamaran, limited to 32 passengers, is narrow enough to go in the sea caves normally only visited by inflatable craft, and can carry children as young as 4, as does the *Amelia K,* a comfy catamaran limited to 36 passengers. The 32-foot, twin-engine *The Makana,* which can also access sea caves, is limited to 12 passengers ages 9 and up, while *Seiko,* a custom-built

34-foot boat with zippy twin engines, is limited to 16 passengers ages 9 and above. Tours on *Na Pali Kai III* and *Amelia K* cost $169 adults and $139 for children ages 4 to 12; tours on the other watercraft cost $189 for adults and $159 for children 4 to 12. Most tours depart daily at 8:30am and 2pm from Kīkīaola Small Boat Harbor in Kekaha; check in at 4516 Alawai Rd., Waimea (from Kaumaliʻi Hwy., turn right at Alawai Rd., just west of the Waimea River). *Amelia K* tours depart from Port Allen in ʻEleʻele.
www.tournapali.com. ℭ **808/338-9980.**

Bodysurfing & Boogie Boarding

The best places for beginners' bodysurfing and boogie boarding are **Kalapaki Beach** and **Poʻipū Beach;** only the more advanced should test the more powerful shorebreaks at **Keālia, Shipwrecks (Keoneloa),** and **Brennecke's** beaches (see "Beaches," p. 523). Boogie-board rentals are widely available at surf shops (see "Surfing," p. 541) and beachfront activity desks. On the South Shore, **Nukumoi Surf Shop** (www.nukumoi. com; ℭ **808/742-8019**), right across from Brennecke's Beach at 2080 Hoʻone Rd., Poʻipū, has the best rates and selections ($10 a day, $30 a week). On the North Shore, **Hanalei Surf Co.** (www.hanaleisurf.com; ℭ **808/826-9000**) rents boogie boards for $10 a day, $28 a week; it's in Hanalei Center (the old Hanalei School Building), 5-5161 Kūhiō Hwy., *mauka* side, Hanalei. You can also rent from **Pedal N Paddle** (www. pedalnpaddle.com; ℭ **808/826-9069**) for $6 daily or $20 weekly; it's in Ching Young Village Shopping Center, 5-5190 Kūhiō Hwy., *makai* side, in Hanalei.

Kayaking

With the only navigable river (some would say rivers) in Hawaiʻi, numerous bays, and the stunning Nāpali Coast, Kauaʻi is made for kayaking. The most popular kayaking route is up the Wailua River to Uluwehi (Secret) Falls, limited to permitted kayaks Monday to Saturday. You can also explore the Huleʻia and Hanalei rivers as they wind through wildlife reserves, go whale-watching in winter along the South Shore, or test your mettle in summer with an ultra-strenuous, 17-mile paddle from Hanalei to Polihale. *Note:* Tipping for kayak tour guides of 10% to 15% of the cost is expected, or a minimum of $10 per person.

For the most intimate and informative kayak tours on the Wailua River, including a hike to Uluwehi (Secret) Falls, book with **Wailua Kayak Adventures ★★★** (www.wailuakayakadventure.com; ℭ **808/ 639-6332**), which controls the most kayaking permits on the river but deliberately doesn't use them all. Tours cost $100 per adult and $50 for children 12 and under; its double kayaks can hold two adults and one small child, with single kayaks available when needed. Prices include organic snacks and use of a dry bag and hiking sticks (you'll want them). You can also rent double kayaks for $100 a day and single kayaks for $50.

Kayak Kaua'i (www.kayakkauai.com; ☎ **888/596-3853** or 808/826-9844) is the island's overall top outfitter for paddling, with a range of rentals and tours from its store in Wailua River Marina, 3-5971 Kūhiō Hwy., Kapa'a (just south of Wailua River Bridge, *mauka* side). River kayak rental starts at $130 per day for a two-person kayak, with just six available that are permitted for the Wailua River (and launched only Mon–Sat 8:30–11:30am due to regulations). Rates include paddles, life vests, back rests, and car rack; rent a dry bag or cooler for $6 more per day. The 5-hour guided **Wailua River tours** with a Secret Falls hike/swim and picnic lunch, offered four times a day, cost $130 for everyone ages 6 and up. The 4-hour **Blue Lagoon tour** from the Hanalei River mouth includes a shuttle to/from the Wailua River Marina, snorkeling, birdwatching, and beach time; it's $125 for all ages.

Kayak Kaua'i typically runs **Nāpali tours** ($245, including lunch) mid-April through mid-October, are only for the very fit who also aren't prone to seasickness; the 11-hour tour requires 5 to 6 hours of paddling, often through large ocean swells, in two-person kayaks. Co-owner Micco Godinez calls it "the Everest of sea kayaking." Trips depart Hā'ena Beach and end at Polihale, with lunch and a rest stop at Miloli'i Beach, and shuttle to/from Wailua. Guided tours to Miloli'i for those with camping permits (see "Camping & Cabins," p. 572) are also available, with guide fees starting at $385 per trip, drop-off/pickup fees at $140 round-trip per person, and double kayak rental for $65 to $75 a day (two-person, 2-day minimum). Shuttle service to Hā'ena (from $65) and Polihale (from $70) is also available separately.

Headquartered in Po'ipū, **Outfitters Kauai** (www.outfitterskauai.com; ☎ **888/742-9887** or 808/742-9667) offers two well-organized kayak tours. The **Wailua kayak/waterfall hike** ($135 adults, $125 children ages 5–17, including lunch) follows the usual route to a hike at 'Uluwehi Falls. The kid-friendly Hidden Valley Falls tour heads 2 miles downwind on the **Hulē'ia River** through a national wildlife refuge and includes a short hike to a swimming hole and a picnic by a small waterfall, with the bonus of a motorized canoe ride back ($150 for adults, $140 for children ages 3–17, younger free.)

Family-owned **Kayak Hanalei** (www.kayakhanalei.com; ☎ **808/826-1881**) offers relaxed, informative guided tours of Hanalei River, with snorkeling in Hanalei Bay, Monday to Friday at 8:30am for $149 for ages 5 and older. Daily rentals start at $45 half day for a single kayak to $70 full day for a double, all gear included, with $10 to $15 discounts for rentals after 1pm. No hauling is required; you launch under the colorful "Dock Dynasty" sign behind the store, 5-5070A Kūhiō Hwy., *makai* side (behind Hanalei Taro & Juice Co.), Hanalei.

Outrigger Canoe Paddling

The state's official team sport, outrigger canoe paddling epitomizes Hawaiian culture's emphasis on collaboration, understanding of the ocean, and ability to have fun when the opportunity presents itself—that is, to catch a wave. **Kauai Beach Boys** (www.kauaibeachboys.com; ✆ **808/246-6333**) hosts 45-minute outrigger canoe paddling/surfing from Kalapaki Beach for $69 per person Monday, Tuesday, and Thursday to Saturday at 9am and 10am; paddlers must be at least 6 years of age. **Hoku Water Sports** (www.hokuwatersports.com; ✆ **808/639-9333**) offers 1-hour paddles ($55) from Kalapaki and Po'ipū beaches; a steersman helps you spot sea life and, if conditions permit, ride a few exhilarating waves. The rides, which must be booked in advance, depart Monday to Friday at 5pm, allowing you to return just in time for sunset; riders must be 10 years or older and weigh no more than 225 pounds.

Scuba Diving

Diving, like all watersports on Kaua'i, is dictated by the weather. In winter, when heavy swells and high winds hit the island, it's generally limited to the more protected South Shore. The best-known site along the South Shore is **Sheraton Caverns,** located off the Po'ipū Beach resort area. This site consists of a series of lava tubes interconnected by a chain of archways. A constant parade of fish streams by (even shy lionfish are spotted lurking in crevices), brightly hued Hawaiian lobsters hide in the lava's tiny holes, and turtles often swim past.

In summer, the magnificent North Shore opens up, and you can take a boat dive locally known as the **Oceanarium,** northwest of Hanalei Bay, where you'll find a kaleidoscopic marine world in a horseshoe-shaped cove. From the rare (long-handed spiny lobsters) to the more common (ta'ape, conger eels, and nudibranchs), the resident population is one of the more diverse on the island. The topography, which features pinnacles, ridges, and archways, is covered with cup corals, black-coral trees, and nooks and crannies enough for a dozen dives. Summer is also the best time to go deep in the crystal-clear waters off Ni'ihau, although the afternoon ride back across the channel can still be bumpy.

Seasport Divers ★★★ (www.seasportdivers.com) leads two daily South Shore boat trips; mornings are for experienced divers ($219 plus $45 for gear rental), early afternoons for novice or rusty divers ($219 certified, excluding gear; $270 noncertified, including gear). Its twice-weekly, all-day, 3-tank boat dives for just six divers head to less visited places like Kipu Kai or the Mānā Crack ($310; fall to spring). Seasport operates two stores, in Po'ipū, from where South Shore trips depart (2827 Po'ipū Rd., across from the fire station; ✆ **808/742-9303**) and Kapa'a (4-976 Kūhiō Hwy., at Keaka Rd.; ✆ **808/823-9222**).

Also highly rated, and based on the South Shore, **Fathom Five Ocean Quest Divers** (www.fathomfive.com; ✆ **800/972-3078** or 808/742-6991) offers customized boat dives for up to six passengers, starting at $199 for a two-tank dive up to $425 for a three-tank Ni'ihau dive ($43 more for gear rental). The latter uses a custom-built 38-foot boat limited to just six passengers.

Bubbles Below Scuba Charters (www.bubblesbelowkauai.com; © 808/332-7333) specializes in highly personalized, small-group dives with an emphasis on marine biology. Based in Port Allen, the 36-foot *Kaimanu* is a custom-built Radon dive boat complete with a hot shower, accommodating up to eight passengers; the 31-foot, catamaran-hulled *Dive Rocket,* also custom-built, takes just six. Standard two-tank boat dives cost $180 (if booked directly); it's $2,700 to charter the boat for a private two-tank dive along the Mānā Crack, as well as a Nāpali cruise. Bubbles Below also offers a three-tank trip, for experienced divers only, to more challenging locations such as the "forbidden" island of Ni'ihau, 90 minutes by boat from Kaua'i, and its nearby islets of Lehua and Ka'ula; locations vary by season and conditions (from $400, including weights, dive computer, lunch, drinks, and marine guide). You should also be willing to share water space with the resident sharks. Ride-alongs for nondivers and crustacean-focused twilight/night dives, as well as bottles of Nitrox, are also available.

GREAT SHORE DIVES Spectacular shoreline dive sites on the North Shore include beautiful **Hā'ena Beach,** where the road ends and the drop-off near the reef begs for underwater exploration (check with lifeguards first). **Cannons,** east of Hā'ena Beach Park, has lots of vibrant marine life in its sloping offshore reef. Another good bet is the intricate underwater topography off **Mākua Beach,** widely known as Tunnels. The wide reef here makes for some fabulous snorkeling and diving, especially during the calm summer months. (See "Beaches," on p. 523.)

On the South Shore, head right of the tombolo (sand bar) splitting **Po'ipū Beach** if you want to catch a glimpse of sea turtles; it's officially known as Nukumoi Point but nicknamed Tortugas (Spanish for "turtles"). The former boat launch at **Kōloa Landing,** also known as Whalers Cove, is considered one of the top sites in the Pacific for shore dives for its horseshoe-shaped reef teeming with tropical fish. It's off Ho'onani Road, about a quarter mile south of Lāwa'i Road near the Po'ipū traffic circle.

If you want a guided shore dive, **Fathom Five Ocean Quest Divers** (see above) will take you out daily to Kōloa Landing for a variety of two-tank dives ($152–$202). Spring through fall, it also offers a variety of shore dives at Tunnels/Mākua ($162–$235). **Seasport Divers** (see above) leads twice-daily shore dives from Kōloa Landing for both certified divers (one-tank $135, two-tank $155) and noncertified (one-tank $169, two-tank $199). Noncertified divers' rates include gear rental charges; certified divers can rent gear for $35 as needed.

Snorkeling

You can buy snorkel gear at any number of stores on the island, but with luggage fees going up, I find it easier just to rent. **Kauai Bound** (www. kauaiboundstore.com; © 808/320-3779) provides top-quality snorkel sets—including carrying bags, fish ID card, and no-fog drops—for $12.50

a day or $42 a week (child's version $7.50 daily, $30 weekly). You can also rent pro-level underwater cameras ($25–$30 a day), camera accessories, golf clubs, and other gear at its store, in Anchor Cove Shopping Center, 3486 Rice St., Līhuʻe.

Robert Wintner, the quirky founder of the statewide chain **Snorkel Bob's** (www.snorkelbob.com; ℂ **800/262-7725**), is a tireless advocate for reef protection through his Snorkel Bob Foundation. His two stores here rent top snorkel gear for $68 a week per adult set, while a budget option costs $44 a week; masks with corrective lenses and premium children's sets (from $30 a week) are also available. The stores also allow 24-hour and interisland drop-offs, and offer discounts on reputable snorkeling cruises. The East Side location is at 4-734 Kūhiō Hwy., Kapaʻa, just north of Coconut Marketplace (ℂ **808/823-9433**), while the South Shore outlet is at 3236 Poʻipū Rd., just south of Old Kōloa Town (ℂ **808/742-2206**).

On the North Shore, **Pedal N Paddle** (www.pedalnpaddle.com; ℂ **808/826-9069**) rents adult snorkel sets for $6 a day ($20 weekly) and children's sets for $5 ($15 weekly); it's in Ching Young Village Shopping Center, 5-5190 Kūhiō Hwy., *makai* side, in Hanalei.

In general, North Shore snorkeling sites are safest in summer and South Shore sites in winter, but all are subject to changing conditions; check daily ocean reports such as those on **https://oceansafety.hawaii. gov** before venturing out. See "Boat & Raft (Zodiac) Tours" for snorkel cruises to the reefs off Nāpali and Niʻihau. The following shoreline recommendations apply only in times of low surf (see "Beaches," on p. 523, for more detailed descriptions).

EAST SIDE The two rock-walled ponds at **Lydgate Park** south of the Wailua River are great for novices and children, if it hasn't rained heavily, which makes it too cloudy to see much.

NORTH SHORE **Hāʻena Beach,** located at the end of Kūhiō Hwy., and **Mākua (Tunnels) Beach,** about a mile before in Hāʻena, offer the greatest variety of fish; surf is often dangerously high in winter. *Note:* See https://gohaena.com for information on the required permit ($5 per person, plus $10 parking) to enter Hāʻena State Park, home of Hāʻena Beach, and optional shuttle service ($40 entry included) to Mākua and Hāʻena beaches; bookings can (and should) be made up to 30 days in advance. **ʻAnini Beach,** off the northern segment of Kalihiwai Road, between Kūhiō Hwy. mile markers 25 and 26, south of Princeville, has the most protected waters; avoid the channel in the reef.

SOUTH SHORE The right side of the tombolo, the narrow strip of sand dividing **Poʻipū Beach** into two coves, has good snorkeling but can be crowded. You can also follow the beach path west past the Waiʻohai Marriott to the pocket cove in front of Koʻa Kea Hotel. A boat ramp leads into the rocky cove of **Kōloa Landing** (see "Scuba Diving," above), where on clear days you'll spot large corals, turtles, and plenty of reef fish. (*Note:* Rain brings in stream runoff, which turns the water murky.) Tour groups often visit rock-studded **Lāwaʻi Beach** off Lāwaʻi Road, next to the Beach House Restaurant; watch out for sea urchins as you swim among parrotfish, Moorish idols, and other reef fish.

WEST SIDE **Salt Pond Beach,** off Kaumaliʻi Hwy. near Hanapēpē, has good snorkeling amid schools of tropical fish around two rocky points. Check with the lifeguard if you're unsure about the conditions.

Sport Fishing

DEEP-SEA FISHING Kauai's fishing fleet is smaller than others in the islands, but the fish are still out there, and relatively close to shore. All you need to bring is your lunch (no bananas, per local superstition) and your luck. **Sportfish Hawaii** (www.sportfishhawaii.com; ✆ 877/388-1376 or 808/295-8355), which inspects and books boats on all the islands, has prices starting at $1,100 for a 4-hour exclusive charter (six passengers maximum), up to $1,700 for 8 hours; shared trips start at $220 per person. Rates may be better, though, booking directly through local operators such as Captain Lance Keener at **Ohana Fishing Charters** (www. fishingcharterskauai.com; ✆ **808/635-8442**); excursions on the wide and stable 30-foot *Hoʻo Maikai* out of Kapaʻa start at $195 per person for a 4-hour shared trip ($155 if you're not fishing), up to $1,400 for a private 8-hour trip (up to six passengers).

FRESHWATER FISHING Freshwater fishing is big on Kauaʻi, thanks to dozens of reservoirs full of largemouth, smallmouth, and peacock bass (also known as *tucunare*). The **Puʻu Lua Reservoir,** in Kōkeʻe State Park, also has rainbow trout and is stocked by the state every year, but has a limited season, in recent years mid-June to late September.

Sportfish Hawaii (www.sportfishhawaii.com; ✆ **877/388-1376** or 808/295-8355) offers guided bass-fishing trips starting at $365 for one or two people for a half-day ($500 for three people) and $475 for one person for a full day ($550 for two, $675 for three), starting at 6:30am in Kapaʻa. Gear, bait, and beverages are included; gratuity and 4% state tax are not.

Whatever your catch, you're required to first have a **Hawaiʻi Freshwater Fishing License,** available online through the **State Department of Land and Natural Resources** (https://freshwater.ehawaii.gov) or through fishing-supply stores such as **Walmart,** 3-3300 Kūhiō Hwy., Līhuʻe (✆ **808/246-1599**), or **Umi's Store,** 4485 Pōkole Rd., Waimea (https://umistorekauai.com; ✆ **808/338-0808**). A 7-day tourist license is $11 (plus a $1 convenience fee if purchased online).

Stand-Up Paddleboarding (SUP)

Like everywhere else in Hawaiʻi, stand-up paddleboarding (SUP) has taken off on Kauaʻi. It's easily learned when the ocean is calm, and still easier than traditional surfing if waves are involved. Lessons and equipment are generally available at all beachfront activity desks and the island's surf shops (see "Surfing," below), while Kauaʻi's numerous rivers provide even more opportunities to practice. Kaua'i native and pro surfer Chava Greenlee runs **Aloha Stand Up Paddle Lessons** (www.alohasurflessons.com; ☎ **808/639-8614**) at Kalapaki Beach, where he first learned to stand-up paddle; the bay offers a large, lagoonlike section ideal for beginners, plus a small surf break for more advanced paddlers. He and his fellow instructors (all licensed lifeguards) also teach SUP in Po'ipū, just south of the Sheraton Kauai. Two-hour group lessons (eight-person maximum) cost $75 and include 15 minutes on land and 1 hour on water, both with instructor; sessions are offered four times a day, with private lessons $300 per person. Walk-ups are welcome, but reservations are recommended.

Kauai Beach Boys (www.kauaibeachboys.com) gives 90-minute lessons four times a day at Kalapaki Beach (☎ **808/246-6333**) and Po'ipū (☎ **808/742-4442**); the $99 fee includes a rash guard, which also helps prevent sunburn. Rental gear costs $35 an hour, $50 for 2 hours, $80 a day. Also in Po'ipū, **Hoku Water Sports** (www.hokuwatersports.com; ☎ **808/639-9333**) gives twice-daily 90-minute group lessons ($90); semi-private and private classes are an option ($250–$300). Once you've got the hang of it, rent a board from **Nukumoi Surf Shop,** across from Brennecke's Beach (www.nukumoi.com; ☎ **808/742-8019**), for $20 an hour, $60 for a full day, or $250 a week, including wheels for easy transport.

Some kayak outfitters based at the Wailua River Marina also rent paddleboards for use there, including **Wailua Kayak Adventures** ($30 a day, $150 a week www.wailuakayakadventure.com; ☎ **808/639-6332**) and **Kayak Kaua'i** ($65 a day; www.kayakkauai.com; ☎ **888/596-3853** or 808/826-9844).

In Hanalei, launch directly into the river and head to the bay from **Kayak Hanalei,** 5-5070A Kūhiō Hwy., *makai* side (www.kayakhanalei.com; ☎ **808/826-1881**), behind Hanalei Taro & Juice. Rental boards are $50 daily, $45 half-day, offered daily; 90-minute lessons are available Monday through Saturday, with group classes $85 for ages 10 and up (semi-private, $95 for ages 8 and up; private, $130 for ages 5 and up). Based in Hanalei Beach Boys Surf Shop, 5-5134 Kūhiō Hwy., **Hawaiian Surfing Adventures** (www.hawaiiansurfingadventures.com; ☎ **808/482-0749**) offers 90-minute private group classes for $150 to $300 for ages 13 and up. Rentals start at $30 for up to 4 hours, $40 for 24 hours. **Pedal N Paddle** (www.pedalnpaddle.com; ☎ **808/826-9069**) rents stand-up paddleboards for $50 a day, $175 a week; it's in Ching Young Village Shopping Center, 5-5190 Kūhiō Hwy., *makai* side, in Hanalei.

Surfing

With the global expansion in surfing's popularity, the most accessible breaks around the island have plenty of contenders. Practice patience and courtesy when lining up to catch a wave and ask for advice from local surf shops before heading out on your own. **Hanalei Bay**'s winter surf is the most popular on the island, but it's for experts only. **Kalapaki** and **Po'ipū beaches** are excellent spots to learn to surf; the waves are generally smaller, and—best of all—nobody laughs when you wipe out. To find out where the surf's up, check **https://oceansafety.hawaii.gov** or call the **Weather Service** (✆ **808/245-3564**).

In addition to SUP lessons, pro surfer and Garden Island native **Chava Greenlee** (www.alohasurflessons.com; ✆ **808/639-8614**) offers surfing lessons at Po'ipū, just south of the Sheraton Kauai (look for the Aloha Surf Lessons sign). Group lessons, offered four times a day, cost $75 and include a short briefing on land, an hour in the water with an instructor; private lessons cost $300, but you can include up to four people if you choose. Rates include a rash guard and reef walkers. Reservations are recommended.

In Po'ipū, rent a board from **Nukumoi Surf Shop,** right across from Brennecke's Beach at 2100 Ho'one Rd. (www.nukumoi.com; ✆ **808/742-8019**); soft boards cost $10 an hour, $30 a day, or $90 a week; hard (epoxy) boards, for experienced surfers, cost $12 an hour, $40 a day, or $120 a week. Surf at either Kalapaki or Po'ipū with a rental from **Kauai Beach Boys** (www.kauaibeachboys.com; ✆ **808/246-6333**) for $15 an hour, $35 a day.

If you're staying on the North Shore, consider a lesson from **Hawaiian Surfing Adventures** (www.hawaiiansurfingadventures.com; ✆ **808/482-0749**), which offers smaller group lessons (four students max) that include 90 minutes of instruction, up to an hour of practice, and soft boards for $150 for a private class. The exact surf spot in Hanalei will vary by conditions; check-in for lessons is at the **Hanalei Beach Boys Surf Shack,** 5-5134 Kūhiō Hwy., *makai* side (just before Aku Rd. when heading north; https://hanaleisurfboardrentals.com). Daily rentals start at $20 for soft boards and $25 for the expert epoxy boards, with discounts for longer periods; rent for $24 and $29, respectively, at **Hanalei Surf Co.,** 5-5161 Kūhiō Hwy. (*mauka* side, in Hanalei Center), Hanalei (www.hanaleisurf.com/rentals; ✆ **808/826-9000**). **Pedal N Paddle** (www.pedalnpaddle.com; ✆ **808/826-9069**) rents 8-foot foam boards for $15 a day, $60 weekly; it's in Ching Young Village Shopping Center, 5-5190 Kūhiō Hwy., *makai* side, in Hanalei.

Tubing

Back in the days of the sugar plantations, Kaua'i kids would grab inner tubes and jump in the irrigation ditches crisscrossing the cane fields for an exciting ride. Today you can enjoy this (formerly illegal) activity by "tubing" the flumes and ditches of the old Līhu'e Plantation with **Kaua'i Backcountry Adventures** (www.kauaibackcountry.com; ✆ **855/846-0092** or 808/245-2506). Passengers are taken in 4WD vehicles high into the mountains above Līhu'e to look at vistas off-limits to the public. At the flumes, you will be outfitted with a giant tube, gloves, and headlamp (for the long passageways through the tunnels, hand-dug ca. 1870). Jump in the water, and the gentle flow will carry you through forests, into tunnels, and finally to a mountain swimming hole, where a picnic lunch is served. The

3-hour tours are $156, open to ages 5 and up (minimum height 43 in., maximum weight 300 lb.). Swimming is not necessary—all you do is relax and drift downstream—but do wear a hat, swimsuit, sunscreen, and shoes that can get wet, and bring a towel, change of clothing, and insect repellent. Tours are offered up to 24 times a day, from 8am to 4pm. *Tip:* The water is always cool, so starting midday, when it's warmer, may be more pleasant.

Windsurfing & Kite Surfing

With a long, fringing reef protecting shallow waters, the North Shore's 'Anini Beach is one of the safest places for beginners to learn windsurfing. Celeste Harzel, owner of **Windsurf Kauai** (© **808/482-1217**) has been teaching windsurfing on 'Anini Beach for decades, with special equipment to help beginners learn the sport. A 2-hour lesson is $175 and includes equipment and instruction (maximum four students per class). Refresher and advanced classes offered by request. *Note:* Celeste prefers mornings for the best conditions.

Serious windsurfers and kitesurfers (that is, those who travel with their own gear) will want to check out **Hā'ena Beach** and **Mākua (Tunnels) Beach** on the North Shore, and the **Māhā'ulepū** coastline on the South Shore. See "Beaches," p. 523, for details.

OTHER OUTDOOR ACTIVITIES
Biking

Although the main highway has few stretches truly safe for cycling, Kaua'i has several suitable places for two-wheeling. The **Po'ipū** area has wide, flat paved roads and several dirt cane roads (especially around Māhā'ulepū), while the **East Side** has completed nearly 7 miles and two segments of the **Ke Ala Hele Makalae** multi-use trail (www.kauaipath.org/kauaicoastalpath), eventually intended to extend from Anahola to the airport in Līhu'e. For now, the 2½-mile Lydgate Park loop connects with Wailua Beach; restrooms and parking are off Nalu Road at the northern end of Lydgate Park, home of Kamalani Playground and Lydgate Beach (p. 525) connects it with Wailua Beach. To the north, the 4.1-mile leg in Kapa'a links Lihi Park to 'Āhihi Point, just past Kumukumu (Donkey) Beach, 1½ miles north of Keālia Beach Park; parking and restrooms are available at Waipouli Beach at the Lihi Boat Ramp, end of Kaloloku Road, and Kapa'a Beach, at the end of Niu Street.

Several places, nearly all in Kapa'a, rent mountain bikes, road bikes, and beach cruisers, including helmets and locks, with sizeable discounts for multiday rentals. Routes include choices for both adventurers itching to explore the single-track trails in the mountains and vacationers just wanting to pedal the coastal path for a couple of hours. **Hele On Kauai Bike Rentals** (www.kauaibeachbikerentals.com; © **808/822-4628**) has the best bargains for beach cruisers and children's trailers, at $20 for 2 hours, $35 for 4 hours or $45 for 24 hours; e-bikes, tandem cycles, and tricycles are also available. Its main store is at 4-1302 Kūhiō Hwy., Kapaʻa, between Pono Market and Wailua Shave Ice, with satellite locations in Princeville and Kapaʻa.

On the North Shore, **Pedal N Paddle** in Hanalei (www.pedalnpaddle. com; ✆ **808/826-9069**) rents beach cruisers for $20 a day ($80 weekly); reservations are recommended during holidays and summer months. It's in the Ching Young Village Shopping Center, 5-5190 Kūhiō Hwy., *makai* side.

Birding

Kauaʻi is home to more than 80 species of birds—not counting the "wild" chickens seen at every roadside attraction. Coastal and lowland areas, including the wildlife refuges at Kīlauea Point (p. 511) and along the Hanalei River, are home to introduced species, endangered native waterfowl, and migratory shorebirds; the cooler uplands of Kōkeʻe State Park shelter native woodland species, who were able to escape mosquito-borne diseases that killed off lowland natives. David Kuhn of **Terran Tours** (✆ **808/335-0398**) leads custom bird-watching excursions that spot some of the rarest birds in Hawaiʻi, using a four-wheel-drive vehicle to access remote areas. Rate start at $300 for a half-day, with longer periods available; e-mail info@soundshawaiian.com for details.

Many pairs of endangered nēnē, the endemic state bird, call Princeville's **Makai Golf Club** home, as do mating and nesting Laysan albatross in winter; for $120 a cart, you can ogle them, their carefully marked nests, and spectacular scenery on a self-guided, six-stop **sunset golf cart tour ★★★** (www.makaigolf.com; ✆ **808/826-1863**). Reserve in advance; start times vary seasonally for the weekday tours.

In Kīlauea, the woods and shoreline of **Na ʻĀina Kai Botanical Gardens** are the setting for seasonal bird-watching tours (2 hr., $70); see "Attractions & Points of Interest," p. 504.

Golf & Disc Golf

It's no wonder that the exceptional beauty of Kauaʻi has inspired some exceptionally beautiful links. More surprising is the presence of two lovely, inexpensive public courses: the 9-hole **Kukuiolono** on the South Shore, and the even more impressive 18-hole **Wailua Golf Course** on the East Side; see details below. On the North Shore, fans of disc golf (also known as Frisbee golf) also have a beautiful 18-hole course to play, either walking or riding a cart, at Princeville's **Makai Golf Club.** *Note:* Greens fees listed here include cart rentals unless stated otherwise.

Value-seekers who don't mind occasionally playing next to a Costco and suburban homes—amid panoramas of several soaring green ridges—will appreciate **Puakea** (www.puakeagolf.com; ✆ **808/977-3777**), part of AOL founder Steve Case's portfolio. Greens fees for 18 holes are $179 before noon, $139 after. The links are centrally located, at 4150 Nuhou St., off Nāwiliwili Road, Līhuʻe.

To play the newest course on the Garden Island, you'll need to be a guest in one of the Lodge at Kukui'ula cottages, bungalows, or villas, starting at $944 per night, with a 3-night minimum (www.lodgeatkukuiula.com; ✆ 866/901-5204). Along with members of **Kukui'ula** (www.kukuiula.com; ✆ 808/742-8000), Lodge guests have exclusive access to Tom Weiskopf's 18-hole, rolling course through gardens, orchards, and grasslands, and a practice facility. Guest tee times Monday to Friday start at 12:40pm and Saturday and Sunday at 11:40am; greens fees are $250, plus $25 for a cart, $30 for a Golfboard. Wherever you play, money can't buy your way out of dealing with trade winds, so start early for the best scores.

All courses listed below are open daily, with first tee times generally around 7am and last tee times around 4pm, depending on the season.

EAST SIDE

Hōkūala Golf Club ★★★   The former Kauai Lagoons Golf Club is now part of the Timbers Resort development, Hōkūala, which includes luxurious vacation residences available for nightly rental. Jack Nicklaus originally designed the 18-hole, oceanfront Kiele Course (since renamed the **Ocean Course**) in the late 1980s, returning in 2011 to create even more spectacular links with views of Ninini Point Lighthouse, Kalapaki Bay, and Hā'upu Mountain. Timbers renovated and reopened the course, and it's as stunning as ever. Facilities include a driving range, snack bar, pro shop, practice greens, clubhouse, and rentals.

3351 Hoolaulea Way, Līhu'e, btw. Marriott's Kauai Lagoons–Kalanipu'u and Royal Sonesta Kaua'i Resort. www.golfhokuala.com. ✆ **808/241-6000.** Greens fees start at $279. Check website for discounts or packages.

Wailua Golf Course ★★   Highly rated by both *Golf Digest* and the Golf Channel, this coconut palm-dotted, seafront course in windy Wailua has hosted three U.S. amateur championships. Along the *makai* (ocean) side of the main highway, the first 9 holes were built in the 1930s; the late Kaua'i golf legend Toyo Shirai designed the second 9 in 1961. Nonresident greens fees start at just $80, half-price after 2pm, for 18 holes. Facilities include a locker room with showers, driving range, practice greens, and club rentals ($20).

3-5350 Kūhiō Hwy., *makai* side, Wailua, 3 miles north of Līhu'e airport. www.kauai.gov/golf. ✆ **808/241-6666.** Greens fees Mon–Fri $80, Sat–Sun/holidays $100, half-price after 2pm. $24 motorized cart ($14 for 9 holes), $7 pull cart ($5 for 9 holes).

NORTH SHORE

Makai Golf Club ★★★   This gem of a course—the first on the island to be designed by Robert Trent Jones, Jr.—has extra luster now that the nearby Prince Course has gone private. It's already gained favor with non-golfers by offering self-guided **sunset golf cart tours** ★★★ ($120 per cart; ✆ 808/826-1863), with a map to memorable vistas, flora, and fauna (including nesting Laysan albatross in winter), plus **sunrise yoga** on the 7th hole Monday, Wednesday, and Friday at 7:15am ($25; book online).

For golfers, it's worth noting that Jones returned in 2009 to remake the 27 holes he created here in 1971. The resulting 18-hole championship Makai Course winds around ocean bluffs and tropical forest with compelling sea and mountain views, including Mount Makana. There's a "time par" of 4 hours, 18 minutes here, to keep golfers on track (otherwise, they might be gawking at the scenery all day). Disc golfers can take advantage of the highly rated championship **Mauka Disc Golf Course ★★★**, an 18-hole course with sand traps, ponds, etc.; you can toss your disc for 6 or 18 holes, or all day, for $30; a 5-day pass costs $100. Other facilities include a clubhouse, pro shop, practice facilities, the **Makai Grill ★** restaurant (with many locally sourced and organic ingredients), and club rentals.

Note: "Dynamic" pricing means greens fees vary by time, season, and demand—all guests of a Kaua'i hotel are eligible for a $275 rate.

4080 Lei O Papa Rd., Princeville. www.makaigolf.com. 📞 **808/826-1912. Makai Course** greens fees vary, but standard rate is $359; $705 3-round pass. Non-renovated **Woods Course,** $53 9 holes. **Mauka Disc Golf Course** $30 day pass, $100 5-day pass. **Makai Grill:** Daily 8am–4:30pm.

SOUTH SHORE

Kiahuna Golf Club ★   This par-70, 6,353-yard course designed by Robert Trent Jones, Jr. is a veritable wildlife sanctuary, where black-crowned night herons, Hawaiian stilts, and moorhens fish along Waikomo Stream, and outcroppings of lava tubes by the second fairway hold rare blind spiders. Keep your eyes peeled for remains of a stone-walled *heiau* (temple) and a Portuguese home from the early 1800s, whose former inhabitants lie in a nearby crypt—and watch out for the mango tree on the par 4, 440-yard hole 6. Facilities include a driving range, practice greens, club rentals, and **Paco's Tacos Cantina ★**, offering a lovely view and Mexican fare for breakfast and lunch, with American dishes also on the breakfast menu.

2545 Kiahuna Plantation Dr. (off Po'ipū Rd.), Kōloa. www.kiahunagolf.com. 📞 **808/742-9595.** $140 greens fees, $80 for 9 holes or after 3pm, $65 for juniors 17 and under w/paying adult. **Paco's Tacos Cantina:** Daily 8am–9pm.

Kukuiolono Golf Course ★★   Although not on a resort, this 9-hole hilltop course has unbeatable views to match an unbeatable price: $15 for all day, plus $15 for every 9 holes for an optional cart. The course is part of woodsy **Kukuiolono Park ★** (p. 515), which includes a Japanese garden, Hawaiian rock artifacts, and trails; both the garden and the course were developed by pineapple tycoon Walter McBryde, who bequeathed it to the public in 1930. The course is well maintained, given the price, with relatively few fairway hazards (barring a wild pig now and then). Facilities include a newer 9-hole mini-golf course ($5), driving range (just $2), practice greens, club rental, and a **Paco's Tacos Cantina ★** restaurant with well-priced tacos and cocktails.

Kukuiolono Park, 854 Puu Rd., Kalāheo. https://kukuiolonogolf.com. 📞 **808/332-9151.** $15 greens fees, $15 optional cart rental; cash only. **Paco's Tacos Cantina:** Daily 8am–5pm.

Poipu Bay Golf Course ★★   This 7,123-yard, par-72 course with a links-style layout was, for years, the home of the PGA Grand Slam of Golf. Designed by Robert Trent Jones, Jr., the challenging course features undulating greens and water hazards on 8 of the holes. The par-4 16th hole has the coastline weaving along the entire left side. The most striking hole is the 201-yard par-3 on the 17th, which has an elevated tee next to an ancient *heiau* (place of worship) and a Hawaiian rock wall along the fairway. Facilities include a restaurant, lounge, locker room, pro shop, club and shoe rentals, and practice facilities (off grass).

2250 'Āinakō St. (off Po'ipū Rd., across from the Grand Hyatt Kauai), Po'ipū. www. poipubaygolf.com. ✆ **800/858-6300** or 808/742-8711. Greens fees (includes $5 resort fee): Mid-Dec to Mar $275 before noon; $235 after noon; Apr to mid-Dec: $250 before noon, $225 after noon. $140 for the back 9, 7–8am; $110 first 7 holes anytime.

Hiking

As beautiful as Kauai's drive-up beaches and waterfalls are, some of the island's most arresting sights aren't reachable by road: You've got to hoof it. Highlights are listed below; for descriptions of the 37 trails in Kauai's state parks and forestry reserves, check out **Nā Ala Hele Trail & Access System** (https://hawaiitrails.ehawaii.gov; ✆ **808/274-3433**).

Note: When heavy rains fall on Kaua'i, normally placid rivers and streams overflow, causing flash floods on some roads and trails. Check the weather forecast, especially November through March, and avoid dry streambeds, which flood quickly. Always bring ample drinking water; stream water is unsafe to drink due to the risk of leptospirosis.

For guided hikes, Micco Godinez of **Kayak Kaua'i** (www.kayak kauai.com; ✆ **888/596-3853** or 808/826-9844) is just as expert on land as he is at sea. He and his savvy guides lead trips through Waimea Canyon to Waipo'o Falls ($146) and through Kōke'e to dazzling overlooks of Nāpali via the Nualolo or 'Awa'awapuhi trails ($156). In Kapa'a, they lead clients up Nounou, or Sleeping Giant ($125), and Kuilau Ridge ($115). Departing from Po'ipū Beach Park, naturalists with **Kauai Nature Tours** (www.kauainaturetours.com; ✆ **888/233-8365** or 808/742-8305) lead similar day hikes, focusing on the geology, environment, and culture of Kaua'i; they're $155 to $195 adults and $135 to $175 for children ages 7 to 12 (5–12 for Māhā'ulepū hike), including lunch.

The Kaua'i chapter of the **Sierra Club** (www.sierraclubkauai.org) typically offers four to seven different guided hikes around the island each month, varying from easy 2-milers to 7-mile-plus treks for serious hikers only; they may include service work such as beach cleanups and trail clearing. Listings on the online calendar include descriptions and local phone contacts; requested donation per hike is $5 adults and $1 for children under 18 and Sierra Club members. *Note:* The Sierra Club advises solo women travelers not to camp or hike remote trails on Kaua'i.

9

KAUA'I | Other Outdoor Activities

The dappled green wooded ridges of the Līhu'e-Kōloa and Nounou forest reserves provide the best hiking opportunities here. From Kuamo'o Road (Hwy. 580) past 'Opaeka'a Falls, you can park at the trailhead for the easy, 2-mile **Kuamo'o Trail,** which connects with the steeper, 1.5-mile **Nounou West Trail;** both have picnic shelters. Stay on Kuamo'o Road until just before the Keāhua Arboretum to pick up the scenic, 2.1-mile **Kuilau Trail,** often used by horses, which can link to the more rugged, 2.5-mile **Moalepe Trail,** ending at the top of Olohena Road in Kapa'a. In the arboretum, you'll find the trailhead for the challenging **Powerline Trail,** an unmaintained path that follows electric lines all the way to Princeville's Kapaka Street, on the *mauka* side of Kūhiō Highway; avoid if it's been raining (the mud can suck your sneakers off, or worse). A steady climb, but worth the vista at the top, is the 2-mile **Nounou East Trail,** which takes you 960 feet up the mountain known as Sleeping Giant (which does look like a giant lying down); the trail ends at a picnic shelter and connects with the west leg about 1½ miles in. The east trailhead, which has parking, is on Hale'ilio Road in Kapa'a; turn inland just past mile marker 6 on Kūhiō Highway and go 1.25 miles uphill.

NORTH SHORE

There are two ways to access Kīlauea's gently rolling and mostly shaded **Wai Koa Loop** trail, a wide, 4.5-mile path that passes lagoons with water lilies and leads through the largest mahogany plantation in North America en route to the always-running waterfall at handsome **Stone Dam.** Built

Hiking the Kalalau Trail.

in the 1880s to provide irrigation during the plantation era, the dam and surrounding forest are now protected by Hawai'i Land Trust. Access the trailhead from the North Shore Dog Park on the Wai Koa Plantation, 5445 Kahililolo Rd., Kīlauea. It's open dawn to dusk. *Note:* If you book one of the twice-weekly farm tours at **Common Ground** (see "Attractions & Points of Interest," p. 504), you're allowed to arrive an hour early to make a 1-mile round-trip hike along the Wai Koa Loop Trail.

Traversing Kauai's amazingly beautiful Nāpali Coast, the 11-mile (one-way) **Kalalau Trail** is the definition of breathtaking: Not only is the scenery magnificent, but even serious hikers will huff and puff over its extremely strenuous up-and-down route, made even trickier to negotiate by winter rains. It's on every serious hiker's bucket list, and a destination for seemingly every young backpacking bohemian on the island. That's one reason a camping permit ($35 per night; https://camping.ehawaii.gov) is required for those heading beyond Hanakāpi'ai Beach; limited to 60 a day, permits often sell out up to a year in advance (see "Camping & Cabins," p. 572).

People in good physical shape can tackle the 2-mile stretch from the trail head at Hā'ena Beach to Hanakāpi'ai, which starts with a mile-long climb; the reward of Nāpali vistas starts about a half-mile in. You may see a barefoot surfer on the first 2 miles but wear sturdy shoes (or hiking boots) and a hat, and carry plenty of water. The trail can be very narrow and slippery; don't bring children who need carrying. Sandy in summer and mostly rocks in winter, Hanakāpi'ai Beach has strong currents that have swept more than 80 visitors to their deaths; best just to admire the view. Those able to rock-hop can clamber another 2 miles inland to the 120-foot Hanakāpi'ai Falls, but only when it has not been raining heavily. Allow 3 to 4 hours for the round-trip trek to the beach, and 7 to 8 hours with the falls added in. *Note:* Unless you have a Kalalau camping permit, which includes entry (but not parking) to Hā'ena State Park, you'll need to purchase an entry permit (one included with parking pass, $15) or shuttle pass ($40, including entry) from www.gohaena.com, available 1 month in advance.

Nearly as beautiful, but less demanding and much less crowded, is the 2.5-mile **'Okolehao Trail** in Hanalei, which climbs 1,232 feet to a ridge overlooking Hanalei Bay and the verdant valley. (Avoid during or after heavy rain; it gets slippery fast.) The trail starts at a parking area off 'Ōhiki Road, inland from Kūhiō Hwy.; take an immediate left just past the **Hanalei Bridge** and look for the parking lot on the left and the trailhead across a small bridge to the right. Be sure to brake for nēnē (geese) and do not venture into the privately owned taro fields, which are part of the otherwise-closed Hanalei National Wildlife Refuge.

SOUTH SHORE

At the end of Keoneloa (Shipwrecks) Beach, in front of the Grand Hyatt Kauai, the limestone headland of Makawehi Point marks the start of the **Māhā'ulepū Heritage Trail,** an easy coastal walk—after the first few

Gain a unique perspective of two hidden waterfalls—by walking down them. Technically, you're rappelling on the 30- and 60-foot cataracts, with help from guide Charlie Cobb-Adams of **Da Life Outdoors** (www.dalifeoutdoors.com; © **808/246-6333**). A Native Hawaiian nicknamed "Hawaiian Dundee," Cobb-Adams leads a practice session on a 25-foot wall before a 15-minute hike near the Hulē'ia National Wildlife Refuge to the otherwise off-limits falls. The 4-hour tour ($224 person, ages 12 and older) departs from Līhu'e Monday through Saturday at 8:30am and 1pm. A more family-friendly, 2-hour hike to both waterfalls (with time to swim at one) departs Monday, Wednesday, and Friday at 11am and 1pm ($89 adults, $69 children ages 8–12).

minutes uphill—along lithified sand dunes, pinnacles, craggy coves, and ancient Hawaiian rock structures. Inland lie the green swath of Po'ipū Bay Golf Course, Makauwahi Cave Reserve (p. 516), and the Hā'upu summit. Keep a safe distance from the fragile cliff edges and give the green sea turtles and endangered Hawaiian monk seals a wide berth, too. It's 1½ miles to the overlook of Māhā'ulepū (Gillin's) Beach, and then—if the landowner permits access—another 2 miles to windy Hā'ula Beach.

WEST SIDE

Some of the best hikes in Hawai'i are among the 45 miles of maintained trails in **Kōke'e State Park** (p. 519), 4,345 acres of rainforest with striking views of the Nāpali Coast from up to 4,000 feet above, and the drier but no less dazzling **Waimea Canyon State Park** (p. 521). Pick up a trail map at the **Kōke'e Museum** (www.kokee.org; © **808/335-9975**), which also describes a number of trails in the two parks on its website. *Note:* It costs nonresidents ages 3 and older $5 to enter either Kōke'e or Waimea Canyon state parks, and $10 per vehicle for parking.

The best way to experience the bold colors and stark formations of Waimea Canyon is on the **Canyon Trail,** which starts after a .8-mile forested walk down and up unpaved Halemanu Road, off Kōke'e Road (Hwy. 550) between mile markers 14 and 15. From there, it's another mile to a small waterfall pool, lined with yellow ginger, that lies above the main cascade of 800-foot **Waipo'o Falls;** you won't be able to see the latter, but you can hear it and gaze far across the canyon to try to spot the lookout points you passed on the way up. On the way back, check out the short spur called the **Cliff Trail** for more vistas. (*Note:* Families can hike this trail, but be mindful of the steep drop-offs.)

Two more challenging hikes beckon in dry conditions. The 6.2-mile round-trip **'Awa'awapuhi Trail** takes at least 3 hours—1 hour down, 2 hours coming back up, depending on your fitness level—but it offers a jaw-dropping overlook for two Nāpali valleys: 'Awa'awapuhi (named for the wild ginger blossom) and Nualolo. Usually well maintained, it drops about 1,600 feet through native forests to a thin precipice with a guardrail at the overlook. The trailhead is just past mile marker 17 on Kōke'e Road at a clearing on the left. The 2-mile **Nualolo Cliff Trail** connects the 'Awa'awapuhi Trail with the even more strenuous 8-mile Nualolo Trail.

Slippery mud can make the **Pihea Trail** impassable, but when the red clay is firm beneath your feet, it's another must-do for fit hikers. Starting at the end of the Pu'u O Kila Lookout at the end of Kōke'e Road (Hwy. 550), the trail provides fantastic views of Kalalau Valley and the distant ocean before turning into a boardwalk through a bog that connects with the **Alaka'i Swamp Trail,** which you'll want to follow to its end at the Kilohana Overlook; if it's not socked in with fog, you'll have an impressive view of Wainiha Valley and the North Shore. The Pihea-Alaka'i Swamp round-trip route is 8.6 miles; allow at least 4 hours and be prepared for drizzle or rain. If you go, just imagine trekking here in the fog on horseback from Lāwa'i, as Queen Emma did in January of 1871, accompanied by hula dancers and her court chanter. Kōke'e State Park celebrates her feat every October with the Eō E Emalani I Alaka'i festival, including hula; click on "Events" at www.kokee.org for details.

Helicopter Tours ★★★

If you forgo touring Kaua'i by helicopter, you'll miss seeing the vast majority of its untouched ridgelines, emerald valleys, and exhilarating waterfalls. Yes, the rides are expensive (most are $280–$390 per person), but you'll take home memories—not to mention photos, videos, and/or a professional DVD—of the thrilling ride over Waimea Canyon, into Kalalau Valley on Kauai's wild Nāpali Coast, and across the green crater of Wai'ale'ale, laced with ribbons of water.

Most flights depart from Līhu'e, last about 55 to 75 minutes, and, regardless of advertising, offer essentially the same experience: narrated flights, noise-canceling headphones with two-way communication, and multicamera videos of your ride or a pre-taped version (often a better souvenir). Ask when booking if an instrument-rated pilot is available, meaning the pilot can still fly safely by instruments even if visibility is suddenly poor, as can happen on Kaua'i. In late 2019, a Safari Helicopters tour flown by a non-instrument-rated pilot crashed in inclement weather on the Nāpali Coast, killing all aboard. (Regardless of their rating, all pilots are, of course, concerned about their safety as well as yours, so if yours chooses to bypass Mount Wai'ale'ale or curtail a tour due to bad weather, know that it's for a very good reason.)

Given the noise inflicted on wildlife, residents, and tranquility-seeking hikers by flights that hover as low as 500 feet, I recommend touring with the most eco-friendly of the bunch, and most luxurious: **Blue Hawaiian ★★★** (www.bluehawaiian.com; ✆ **800/745-2523** or 808/245-5800). Its American Eurocopter Eco-Star choppers have a unique tail design that reduces noise and fuel use, while the roomy interior has six business-class-style leather seats with premium views. The best seats are the two next to the pilot, but the raised row of rear seats won't disappoint (keep in mind that seating is usually determined by weight distribution). Its 50-minute Eco Adventure ride from Līhu'e costs $389.

Sunshine Helicopters ★★ (www.sunshinehelicopters.com; ☎ **866/ 501-7738** or 808/270-3999) flies out of Līhu'e in quiet, roomy Whisper Star models (similar in design to Blue Hawaiian's Eco-Stars) and less expensive FX Stars. Its 50-minute FX Star flights begin at $294, or $369 if you want to reserve an even roomier "first class" seat in the front row; it's $349 open seating and $424 reserved for Whisper Star flights. *Tip:* Book a flight before 8:30am or after 2pm for $20 off.

Although their aircraft are not as quiet as those of Blue Hawaiian and Sunshine, three other companies have unique itineraries deserving of consideration. **Island Helicopters** (www.islandhelicopters.com; ☎ **800/829-5999** or 808/245-8588) has exclusive rights to land at remote 350-foot Manawaiopuna Falls, nicknamed "Jurassic Falls" for its movie cameo. During your 25 minutes on the ground, you'll hear about the geological history and rare native plants in this area of Hanapēpē Valley, which like Ni'ihau is owned by the Robinson family. In part due to added landing fees and fuel costs, the 75-minute **Jurassic Falls Tour** ★★ costs $404; you'll see the falls but not land there on the 50-minute Grand Circle Tour ($250). Both leave from Līhu'e Airport; add 4% to prices for credit card use. The 90-minute **Canyon Landing Safari Tour** ★★ of **Safari Helicopters** (www.safarihelicopters.com; ☎ **800/326-3356** or 808/246-0136) includes a 30-minute stopover at an otherwise inaccessible Robinson-owned site overlooking vast Olokele Canyon; Keith Robinson is occasionally on hand to explain his efforts to preserve rare, endemic plants here (which your landing fees subsidize). The tour costs $359 and departs from Līhu'e.

Mauna Loa Helicopter Tours (www.maunaloahelicoptertours.com; ☎ **808/245-7500**) offers private tours, with a thrilling doors-off option, starting at $359 for 1 hour (two-passenger minimum.)

Note: Minimum ages and maximum weights may apply; read fine print before booking.

Horseback Riding

Riding horses will let you see parts of Kaua'i many have missed, while helping preserve its treasured *paniolo* (cowboy) culture; just be sure to pack a pair of jeans or long pants and closed-toe shoes.

CJM Country Stables ★★   A trail ride through the rugged Māhā'ulepū region, passing through former plantation fields and natural landscape to the untrammeled sandy beaches under the shadow of Haupu Ridge, may well be the highlight of your trip. CJM's standard rides both include 2 hours of riding, but the **Secret Beach Picnic Ride** ($229) adds an hour for lunch and beach exploration; reserve early. Private rides, which allow paces faster than a walk, are also available for a minimum of two riders, starting at $289 per rider for a 90-minute ride. *Note:* CJM also hosts rodeos throughout the year that are open to the public; click "Events" on the website for details.

Off Poʻipū Rd., Poʻipū. From Grand Hyatt Kauai, head 1½ miles east on unpaved Poʻipū Rd. and turn right at sign for stables. www.cjmstables.com. ✆ **808/742-6096. 2-hr. Māhāʻulepū Beach Ride:** $195; Tues–Sat 9:30am and 2pm. **3-hr. Secret Beach Picnic Ride:** $229; Wednesdays 1pm.

Princeville Ranch Adventures ★★   The tourism options at this 2,500-acre working cattle ranch, owned by descendants of the area's first missionaries, are limited now to 1-hour English and Western horseback riding lessons in an arena ($150 for ages 4 and older, or $450 for a series of four lessons). It's still a beautiful North Shore experience, with mountain and ocean views. Wear closed-toe shoes and long pants, and bring water and a rain jacket.

Check in *makai* side of Kūhiō Hwy., just north of mile marker 27, Princeville. www.princevilleranch.com. ✆ **808/826-7669.** 1-hr. riding lessons $150 for ages 4 and older; $450 for 4 lessons. Weight limit 250 lb.

Tennis & Pickleball

Public tennis and pickleball courts are managed by the **Kauaʻi County Parks and Recreation Department** (www.kauai.gov; ✆ **808/241-4460**). Its website (click on "Parks and Recreation," then "Facilities") lists some of the 24 public tennis courts around the island, 20 of which are lighted and all of which are free. Although not listed online, some have striping for pickleball courts, such as the two tennis courts at Līhuʻe County Park at 4200 Hardy St. *Note:* Lights are shut off September 15 to December 15 to protect endangered shearwater fledglings, which may be misdirected by them.

Other tennis courts open to the public include the eight courts (four hard court, four artificial turf) at the Peter Burwash International Facility of **Hanalei Bay Resort,** Princeville (www.hanaleibayresort.com/tennis; ✆ **808/821-8225**). Court fees for non-guests are $15 per person per day; the resort also offers private lessons, daily clinics, and a pro shop.

The South Shore is brimming with resort courts—including **Grand Hyatt Kauai, Poipu Kai Resort, Nihi Kai Villas,** and **Kukuiʻula**—but they're restricted to overnight guests. Guests in **Kiahuna Plantation** units managed by Castle or Outrigger, among many individual units elsewhere, have access to the otherwise members-only four tennis courts, two pickleball courts, resort pool, and other facilities at the **Poipu Beach Athletic Club.** Check https://poipuclub.com/vacation-rental-partnerships to see if your rental is included in the program.

On the East Side, **Timbers Kauaʻi** offers the use of two tennis and three pickleball courts, remodeled in 2023, exclusively to its guests.

Yoga

While yoga classes are widely available at resorts and studios across the island, **Kauai Yoga on the Beach** (https://kauaiyogaonthebeach.com) is unique in its combination of daily hourlong classes, weekly and full-moon sound healing sessions, and island tours, all outdoors and on the East Side. Sunrise yoga classes ($25 if reserved online; drop-in is $20, cash only) take place at 7am daily on the oceanfront lawn of **Outrigger Kaua'i Beach Resort** (p. 562) in Līhu'e, while **Kauai Shores Hotel** (p. 563) in Kapa'a hosts a beachside class ($25 reserved online, $20 cash drop-in) at 8:30am. Līhu'e's **Kalapaki Beach** (p. 525) provides the backdrop for Thursday night sound healing ($100) by Anya, a Russian-trained ballet dancer and longtime yoga instructor on the island who uses crystal bowls tuned to specific frequencies to relax you. She also leads a 1-hr. restorative yoga mini-workshop with sound healing ($199) at 8:30am Sunday at Kauai Shores. Spiritual- and yoga-themed tours ($45–$80) showcase Kadavul Hindu Temple above Kapa'a and its Rudraksha Forest, a grove of Himalayan *rudraksha* trees (www.himalayanacademy.com; ✆ **808/822-3012**), along with other sites; they're available Wednesday and Friday by advance request.

Ziplining

Kaua'i apparently has Costa Rica to thank for its profusion of ziplines, the metal cable-and-pulley systems that allow harness-wearing riders to "zip" over valleys, forests, and other beautiful but inaccessible areas. After reading about Costa Rica's rainforest canopy tours, Outfitters Kauai co-founder Rick Haviland was inspired to build the Garden Isle's first zipline on Kōke'e Ranch in 2003. Others soon followed, with ever longer, higher, and faster options. It may seem like a splurge but remember that ziplines not only offer an exhilarating rush and breathtaking views; they also help keep the verdant landscape gloriously undeveloped.

Be sure to book ahead, especially for families or groups—because of the time spent on harness safety checks, tour sizes are limited—and read the fine print about height, age, and/or weight restrictions. Tours usually go out rain or shine, except in the most severe weather, and include a snack. As with all excursions, plan to tip your guides ($10–$20 per rider).

SOUTH SHORE A 2,500-foot swoop over the Waita Reservoir is the highlight of the eight-line course ($159) at **Koloa Zipline** (www.koloa zipline.com; ✆ **877/707-7088** or 808/742-2734). Its custom Flyin' Kauaian harness allows you to soar headfirst over most of the lines on the 3½- to 4-hour tour. Check in at the office at 3477-A Weliweli Rd., Kōloa, in the Kauai ATV office behind the Old Kōloa Town shops. **Shaka Zipline** (formerly Skyline Eco Adventures; www.shakazipline.com; ✆ **808/855-8124**) opened its eight-line course above Po'ipū in 2013 and shares a different legend of Kaua'i for each of the progressively longer, faster lines on the 2½- to 3-hour tour. The cost is $160 for eight zips, $130 for five, for ages 10 and older. Check in at the office at Shops at Kukui'ula, 2829 Ala Kalanikaumaka St., Po'ipū.

EAST SIDE   Lush, 4,000-acre Kipu Ranch hosts the nine lines of **Outfitters Kauai** (www.outfitterskauai.com; *✆* **888/742-9887** or 808/742-9667), including suspension bridges, tandem lines, and a "zippel" (a zipline/rappelling combo) over picturesque streams and waterfalls. The scenery will be familiar from hit movies such as *Jurassic Park, Raiders of the Lost Ark*, and *The Descendants*. The latest addition is the longest zipline in Hawai'i, the 4,000-foot FlyLine, which also boasts the tallest launchpad at 50 feet high; you ride it prone like a superhero on tandem lines. At $55 for a 1-hour tour, the FlyLine is ideal for those on a budget or tight schedule.

You can also try the FlyLine on the four-zip, 2½-hour **AdrenaLine Kauai Zipline Tour** ($170 adults, $160 ages 7–14), which starts with an 800-foot zipline and also includes an 1,800-foot tandem line and a zip that ends at a swimming hole; the **Powerline Tour** offers the same rates and itinerary, minus the swim. Check in for these zips at the Kipu Ranch visitor center, 230 Kīpū Rd., Līhu'e. My favorite, the all-day **Kipu Zipline Safari** ($255 adults, $245 children ages 3–17), includes three ziplines (open to ages 7 and up), an easy 2-mile kayak on the Hulē'ia River, a short hike, wagon ride, swimming, and lunch. Check-in for most zip tours is at the Outfitters Kauai store, 2827 Po'ipū Rd., across from the fire station, in Po'ipū. One exception: Those staying on the East Side or North Shore may check in for the Kipu Zipline Safari at Outfitters Kauai's shack at the Nāwiliwili Small Boat Harbor.

Kaua'i Backcountry Adventures (www.kauaibackcountry.com; *✆* **855/846-0092** or 808/245-2506) offers excursions through 17,000 acres of former sugarcane fields above Līhu'e. In addition to its unique tubing

ESPECIALLY FOR kids

Climbing the Wooden Jungle Gyms at Kamalani Playground (p. 508)   Located in Lydgate Park, Wailua, this unique playground has a maze of jungle gyms for kids of all ages, including an actual labyrinth. Spend an afternoon whipping down slides, exploring caves, hanging from bars, and climbing all over.

Exploring a Magical World (p. 512) **Na 'Āina Kai Botanical Gardens** sits on some 240 acres, sprinkled with around 70 life-size (or larger-than-life-size) whimsical bronze statues, hidden off the beaten path of the North Shore. The tropical children's garden features a gecko maze, a tropical jungle gym, a treehouse in a rubber tree, and a 16-foot-tall Jack-and-the-Beanstalk giant with a 33-foot

wading pool below. Regular tours remained on hold at press time, but check online for dates of the monthly Splash and Play sessions ($10), held on a Saturday.

Riding an Open-Sided Train (p. 507) The **Kauai Plantation Railway** at Kilohana Plantation is a trip back in time (albeit on new tracks and replica cars) to the sugarcane era, with younger kids exhilarated just by the ride. Parents can justify it as an informal botany class, since passengers learn about the orchards, gardens, and forests they pass along the 2½-mile journey. Children of all ages will enjoy the stop to feed goats, chickens, and wild pigs (as long as they watch their fingers).

Kaua'i offers many opportunities to go ziplining.

ride (see "Tubing," p. 542), the company has a seven-line zip course leading from the lush mountainside to a bamboo grove, where you can take a dip in a swimming hole; the 3-hour tour leaves Monday to Friday at 8am, 10am, noon, and 2pm ($156). Check in at the office at 3-4131 Kūhiō Hwy., Hanamā'ulu, between Hanamā'ulu Rd. and Laulima St.

WHERE TO STAY ON KAUA'I

To avoid long drives, it pays to base your lodgings on the kind of vacation you envision and consider dividing your time among locations. The island's East Side makes the most sense for those planning to divide their time equally among island sights; however, the best resorts for families and winter weather are on the South Shore. The most gorgeous scenery and best ocean conditions in summer are on the North Shore. If you plan to hike more than a day in Waimea Canyon or Kōke'e, or want to experience the island's low-key lifestyle, the West Side will suit.

Taxes totaling 17.962% are added to all hotel bills. Parking is free unless otherwise noted; all pools are outdoors. Applicable parking, Wi-Fi, and resort fees are charged daily; "cleaning" fees refer to one-time charges for cleaning after your stay, not daily housekeeping—the latter often available for an additional fee for condos and other vacation rentals.

Tip: To mitigate some of the sticker shock when booking a Kaua'i resort hotel, look for the deep discounts offered by Priceline and Hotwire for "hidden" deals (where the name of the property is revealed after you book). Even better, install the TravelArrow extension (www.travelarrow. io) to your Chrome browser first, and it will reveal the exact location of the bargain you're considering booking. See also "Internet or Apps for Hawai'i Hotel Discounts," p. 602.

East Side

Convenient to all parts of the island (except during rush hour), Līhu'e and the Coconut Coast have the greatest number of budget motels and moderately priced beachfront hotel rooms and condos, along with a couple of posh resorts. Rural Anahola and upcountry Kapa'a are outside the official "visitor destination area," so their vacation rentals may not be licensed. *Note:* Much of the East Side's most iconic hotel, the **Coco Palms** (of *Blue Hawaii* fame), was demolished in 2017, 25 years after Hurricane 'Iniki forced its closure. Despite much local opposition, in 2024 a developer began building a new 350-room hotel on the culturally and ecologically significant site.

In addition to the properties below, consider a condo at one of two oceanfront complexes in Kapa'a. At the 84-unit **Kapa'a Shore ★**, 4-900 Kūhiō Hwy., the nine condos managed by Garden Island Properties (www.kauaiproperties.com; *✆* **800/801-0378** or 808/822-4871) start at $314 a day for a one-bedroom, one-bath oceanview unit to $375 for a two-bedroom, two-bath oceanfront unit (plus $178–$220 cleaning and $85 in other fees). At the more upscale **Lae Nani ★★**, 410 Papaloa Rd. (off Kūhiō Hwy.), Outrigger (www.outrigger.com; *✆* **866/956-4262** or 808/823-1401) manages about a quarter of the 83 one- and two-bedroom units (from $254; cleaning $264–$288); perks include a lighted tennis court, pool, and beach with child-friendly, rock-walled swimming area.

---

sensitive issue: **VACATION RENTALS**

With a median housing price of over $1.5 million, Kaua'i became the least affordable island for homeowners in 2023, which increased sensitivity over vacation rentals in areas not zoned for tourism. Be aware all licensed lodgings must display their permit number (often starting with TVR or TVNC) in any online advertising and post a sign on the premises listing that number, plus the name and phone number of an on-island emergency contact. You can also find a list of permitted rentals outside resort areas at www.kauai.gov/planning; click on "Transient Vacation Rentals" and then "List of Approved Homestays & Non-Conforming TVRs."

The Kaua'i Visitors Bureau also urges special caution when booking a vacation rental online from sources other than licensed agencies such as those listed here, to avoid unscrupulous scammers with phantom accommodations. For condos, be aware that companies that manage multiple properties in a complex may be able to find you another unit if you're dissatisfied with your view or problems arise during your stay. Happily, more management companies are now advertising their listings on VRBO.com, Airbnb.com, and other DIY sites—but they are eliminating daily housekeeping service and other niceties to remain competitive. Always read the fine print before you arrive to know what to expect, including steep one-time cleaning charges.

For more privacy, check out the two elegantly furnished cottages in a leafy setting known as **17 Palms Kauai Vacation Cottages ★★** (www.facebook.com/17PalmsKauai; © **888/725-6799**), a block away from Wailua Bay. Rates for the one-bedroom, one-bathroom Hale Iki (sleeps two adults, plus a small child) start at $378 a night, plus $200 cleaning and $78 damage protection fee; the two-bedroom, one-bathroom Meli Meli (sleeps four adults, plus a small child) starts at $499, plus $250 cleaning and $78 damage protection fee. Tucked off busy Kuamo'o Road in Kapa'a, but with easy access to the Wailua River (kayaks provided), the pleasant **Fern Grotto Inn ★** (www.kauaicottages.com; © **808/821-9836**) has nine quaint cottage units (most sleeping two), for $250 to $600 a night, plus $175 to $275 cleaning, and the more upscale, three-bedroom, three-bath **'Ohana House ★★** (sleeps six), starting at $500 a night with a $300 cleaning fee. Book within 10 days of arrival for 10 to 30% discount.

VERY EXPENSIVE

Timbers Kaua'i Ocean Club & Residences ★★★ The centerpiece of the 450-acre Hōkūala Resort (next to the Royal Sonesta Kaua'i Resort), this luxurious enclave of residential villas and townhomes overlooks Kalapaki Bay, the Ninini Point lighthouse, and the Jack Nicklaus-designed Ocean Course. It also allows nightly guests to experience the same kind of cossetting owners and vacation club members receive. That includes sumptuously furnished suites with lavishly stocked kitchens—though you'll be tempted to dine poolside at **Hualani's ★★★** (p. 576) for all your meals—and an array of customizable, exclusive excursions, such as private waterfall hikes and beach outings, and unique voluntourism opportunities at sites such as **Alekoko (Menehune) Fishpond** (p. 504). All this comes at a price, of course; also, the closest beach with services is Kalapaki (in front of the Royal Sonesta, a 10-min. walk along Kalapaki Circle to an elevator), though the tiered infinity-edge oceanfront pool—one of two pools at the resort—is stunning. The small, organic-themed spa is exceptional, too.

3770 Ala'oli Way, Līhu'e. www.hokualakauai.com. © **808/320-7400**. 47 units. From $765 (special) to $1,500 2-bedroom, 2½-bath residence (sleeps 4); $1,600 3-bedroom, 3½-bath residence (sleeps 6); $2,900 4-bedroom, 4-bath residence (sleeps 10). 2-night minimum. Rates include daily breakfast for 2. **Amenities:** 2 restaurants; bar; loaner bikes; business center; fitness room; 18-hole championship golf course; whirlpools; 2 pools; pickleball; spa; tennis; free Wi-Fi.

EXPENSIVE

Royal Sonesta Kaua'i Resort ★★★ Rebranded in 2021 from a Marriott resort, this 10-story, multi-wing hotel—the tallest on Kaua'i—may be what prompted the local ordinance that no new structures be higher than a coconut tree. Still, it would be hard to imagine Kaua'i without it. Superlatives include the island's largest swimming pool, a sort of Greco-Roman fantasy that would fit in at Hearst Castle; its location on

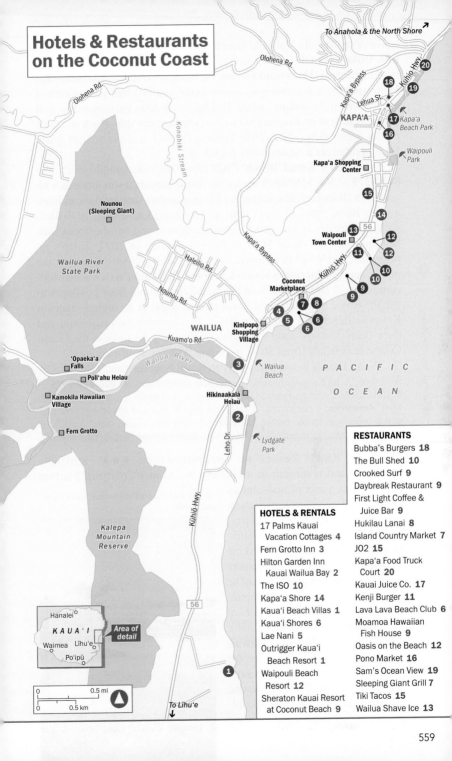

Hotels & Restaurants on the Coconut Coast

To Anaholo & the North Shore ↗

Olohena Rd.

Olohena Rd.

Kapa'a Bypass

Kūhiō Hwy.

Lehua St.

KAPA'A

Kapa'a Beach Park

Waipouli Park

Konohiki Stream

Nounou (Sleeping Giant)

Kapa'a Shopping Center

Wailua River State Park

Kapa'a Bypass

Haleilio Rd.

Kapa'a Bypass

56

Waipouli Town Center

Kūhiō Hwy.

Nounou Rd.

Coconut Marketplace

WAILUA

Kinipopo Shopping Village

Kuamo'o Rd.

Wailua River

Wailua Beach

'Opaeka'a Falls

Poli'ahu Heiau

Kamokila Hawaiian Village

Fern Grotto

Hikinaakala Heiau

Leho Dr.

Lydgate Park

P A C I F I C

O C E A N

Kalepa Mountain Reserve

Kūhiō Hwy.

56

KAUA'I

Hanalei

Waimea   Līhu'e

Po'ipū

Area of detail

0   0.5 mi
0   0.5 km

To Līhu'e ↓

HOTELS & RENTALS

17 Palms Kauai Vacation Cottages **4**
Fern Grotto Inn **3**
Hilton Garden Inn Kauai Wailua Bay **2**
The ISO **10**
Kapa'a Shore **14**
Kaua'i Beach Villas **1**
Kaua'i Shores **6**
Lae Nani **5**
Outrigger Kaua'i Beach Resort **1**
Waipouli Beach Resort **12**
Sheraton Kauai Resort at Coconut Beach **9**

RESTAURANTS

Bubba's Burgers **18**
The Bull Shed **10**
Crooked Surf **9**
Daybreak Restaurant **9**
First Light Coffee & Juice Bar **9**
Hukilau Lanai **8**
Island Country Market **7**
JO2 **15**
Kapa'a Food Truck Court **20**
Kauai Juice Co. **17**
Kenji Burger **11**
Lava Lava Beach Club **6**
Moamoa Hawaiian Fish House **9**
Oasis on the Beach **12**
Pono Market **16**
Sam's Ocean View **19**
Sleeping Giant Grill **7**
Tiki Tacos **15**
Wailua Shave Ice **13**

559

watersports-friendly Kalapaki Beach; and the popular beachfront restaurant, **Duke's Kauai** (p. 574), among other dining choices. The long escalator to the central courtyard lagoon, the immense statuary, and handsome lobby sporting a koa outrigger canoe make you feel like you've arrived somewhere truly unique, while Hōkūala's 18-hole championship golf course is next door. Rooms tend to be on the smaller side. Book at least a partial ocean view—Nāwiliwili Harbor, the bay, and the rugged green Hā'upu ridge are a mesmerizing backdrop.

Marriott's Kauai Beach Club (www.marriott.com/lihka; © **800/ 845-5279** or 808/245-5050) shares the Royal Sonesta resort grounds with access to all its facilities, including the free airport shuttle. You can book a guest room, "parlor" room with wall bed and kitchenette, or "villas" with kitchenettes in one-bedroom/two-bathroom and two-bedroom/two-bathroom layouts (from $611 nightly), renovated in 2024. There's no resort fee, and Wi-Fi is included, but valet parking is $40. Guests at the newer, nearby **Marriott's Kauai Lagoons—Kalanipu'u** (www.marriott.com/lihkn; © **800/845-5279** or 808/632-8202) do *not* have privileges to use the Royal Sonesta's pool (renovated in 2024) or its lounge chairs at Kalapaki Beach, but it offers roomier, two-bedroom/two-bathroom and three-bedroom/three-bathroom villas overlooking the links of the Ocean Course at Hōkūala (from $646, including Wi-Fi and self-parking).

Note: Details below apply only to Royal Sonesta Kaua'i Resort. 3610 Rice St. (at Kalapaki Beach), Līhu'e. www.sonesta.com. © **800/220-2925** or 808/245-5050. 356 units. From $479–$919 double. $40 resort fee. $30 parking; $40 valet. **Amenities:** 4 restaurants; 2 bars; free airport shuttle; babysitting; kids' program; concierge; fitness center; salon; spa; 5 Jacuzzis; "Hawaii Alive" luau (Mon 6pm; $160 adults, $56 ages 6–12); pool; room service; watersports rentals; Wi-Fi.

Sheraton Kauai Resort at Coconut Beach ★★★

Strikingly remodeled and rebranded in mid-2019, this former Courtyard Marriott now features a mix of mid-century modern and contemporary Hawaiian decor and firepits around a large, beachfront pool. The locale is ultra-convenient to kayaking and hiking adventures, shopping, and prolific dining options, but guests would be remiss if they didn't linger in house for poke and artisanal cocktails at the **Crooked Surf** pool bar (p. 576), seafood dinner at **Moamoa Hawaiian Fish House** (p. 576), or the twice-weekly luau in a new pavilion, staged by Leilani Rivera Low, one of the island's most popular recording artists (www.luaukahikina.com;

Sunset over the pool at Sheraton Kauai Coconut Beach.

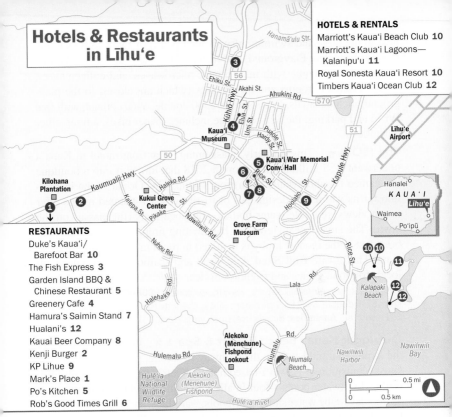

Hotels & Restaurants in Līhuʻe

KAUAʻI
Hanalei
Līhuʻe
Waimea
Poʻipū

ⓒ **800/822-3455**; $189 adults, $115 ages 7–13, $75 ages 3–6). Off the lobby, the **First Light Coffee & Juice Bar** has the perfect nitro cold brew for a warm morning, while adjacent **Daybreak Restaurant** serves a la carte island-style breakfasts as well as a hearty buffet. A well-manicured lawn hosting yoga classes separates the hotel from golden-sand Makaiwa Beach, which is too reefy for swimming, but just the ticket for long walks. Rooms, most of which are still just 320 square feet, have lanais with cinnamon-wood shutters and wall-size photos of ocean waves; two-thirds have at least partial ocean views. For more space, book a premium oceanfront room (528 sq. ft.). The comprehensive $40 resort fee includes self-parking, Wi-Fi, two cocktails, yoga class, and more.

650 ʻAleka Loop, Kapaʻa. www.marriott.com/lihsk. ⓒ **888/236-2427** or 808/822-3455. 311 units. $392–$629 double; $518–$1,039 premium double. Extra person $25. Children 17 and under stay free in parent's room. $40 resort fee, including valet parking. **Amenities:** 3 restaurants; coffee shop; luau; 2 bars; business center; fitness center; Jacuzzi; luau; pool; room service; spa; Wi-Fi; yoga.

MODERATE

In addition to the below, families and Hilton Honors members may want to consider **Hilton Garden Inn Kauai Wailua Bay** ★ (www.hilton.com/en/hotels/lihwbgi-hilton-garden-inn-kauai-wailua-bay; ⓒ **808/823-6000**) next to the protected swimming/snorkeling ponds of Lydgate Beach, the fanciful Kamalani Playground, and historic Hawaiian sites by the Wailua River. All units come with minifridges, microwaves, and coffeemakers; some oceanview rooms and all cottages (which are closest to the playground) include lanais. Rates start at $360 double, $460 cottage, with free Wi-Fi and parking; the $25 resort fee includes loaner bikes, among other amenities.

The ISO ★★   This formerly unassuming oceanfront motel in Kapa'a underwent a $5 million renovation in 2018 that turned it into a boutique inn named (in abbreviated form) for "Island, Sky, Ocean"—the inspiration for its whimsical design. All of its rustic-beach-themed rooms offer ocean views, reusable water bottles, and yoga mats (for classes on the lawn). The small oceanview pool has inviting firepits, while continental breakfast in the modest lobby is included in room rates—a rarity in these parts. The on-site **Bull Shed ★**, a steak and seafood spot popular with locals for good values and friendly service.

4-796 Kūhiō Hwy. (*makai*), Kapa'a. www.theiso.com. ✆ **808/822-3971.** 79 rooms. From $249 double; $429 for 1-bedroom with kitchenette (sleeps 4). $30 extra person. $30 resort fee. **Amenities:** Bicycle use; pool; yoga classes; Wi-Fi.

Outrigger Kaua'i Beach Resort & Spa ★★   Only 5 minutes from the airport, but hidden from the highway by a long, palm-lined drive, the latest acquisition of Hawai'i-based hotelier Outrigger features beautifully sculpted saltwater pools—four in all, with adult and children's options, a 75-foot lava-tube water slide, whirlpools, waterfalls, and a sandy-bottomed beachfront lagoon. Decorated in a Balinese wood/Hawaiian plantation motif, rooms in the hotel itself are on the small side, and some "mountain view" (odd-numbered rooms) units overlook parking lots, where wild chickens may congregate. No matter: You can linger by the pool, walk for miles along the windswept beach (not recommended for swimming), which passes by the Wailua Golf Course, or indulge in a spa treatment onsite. *Note:* Rates may rise after Outrigger's planned renovations.

A number of hotel rooms are also individually owned "condos;" you'll find lower daily rates when booking through an owner, but you'll pay an extra $80 in resort/cleaning fees, with maid service upon request ($15–$30 daily). The 25-acre resort is also home to the **Kauai Beach Villas,** one- and two-bedroom condos operated as timeshares or privately owned rentals, all with access to the hotel facilities, for a daily resort fee; rates vary widely. Details below apply only to the Outrigger Kaua'i Beach Resort & Spa.

4331 Kaua'i Beach Dr., Līhu'e. From the airport, drive 2½ miles northeast on Hwy. 51 (Kapule Hwy.) to Kūhiō Hwy. and ½ mile later, turn right on Kaua'i Beach Dr. www.outrigger.com/hawaii/kauai/outrigger-kauai-beach-resort-spa. ✆ **888/805-3843** or 808/245-1955. 350 units. $235–$417 double; $430–$1,079 suite. $45 extra person. $20 rollaway. $35 resort fee. **Amenities:** 2 restaurants; lounge; pool bar; babysitting; concierge; fitness center; 2 Jacuzzis; laundry facilities; 4 pools; rental cars; room service; spa and salon; Wi-Fi.

Waipouli Beach Resort ★★   Although its namesake beach is not good for swimming, kids and quite a number of adults are happy to spend all day in the heated fantasy pool here. Stretching across two of the resort's 13 lushly landscaped acres, the pool offers a lazily flowing river, sandy-bottomed hot tubs, a children's area, twin water slides, and waterfalls. The individually owned condos (mostly two-bedroom/three-bathroom) in the $200-million complex boast high-end kitchen appliances and luxe finishes such as granite counters, Travertine tiles, and African mahogany cabinets. There's room for the whole family, too: Most of the two-bedroom units are 1,300 square feet, while a few corner penthouses are 1,800 square feet; all have washer/dryers and central air-conditioning. The resort lies across the street from a grocery store and close to shops and restaurants—but avoid the cheaper units facing the parking lot due to noise. Outrigger manages the most units here and operates the front desk but be sure to compare rates (which vary widely by view) and cleaning fees with those of independently rented condos; see www.waipoulibeachresort.net for additional listings.

4-820 Kūhiō Hwy., Kapa'a. https://hawaiivacationcondos.outrigger.com. ⓒ **877/418-0711** or 808/823-1401. 196 units. From $267 studio; $303–$430 1-bedroom/2-bath; $359–$754 2-bedroom/3-bath. $165–$300 cleaning fee. $30 resort fee. 2-night minimum. **Amenities:** Oasis on the Beach restaurant (p. 577); fitness center; pool; day spa; 3 whirlpools; Wi-Fi.

INEXPENSIVE

Kauai Shores Hotel ★   This beachfront bargain features small but functional rooms with slightly quirky, IKEA-style furnishings, bright blue geometric-patterned rugs, and very compact bathrooms. No need to hole up in your room, though: The oceanview pool is inviting, while the ocean-front **Lava Lava Beach Club** ★★ (p. 576) serves three meals daily, with a full bar, indoor/outdoor seating, and nightly live entertainment. Children can splash in the rock-walled ocean pool in front of Lae Nani next door. Yoga classes take place on the oceanfront lawn 3 mornings a week. *Note:* Request a second-floor room for more privacy (if you can carry your own bags) and a room not adjacent to the parking lot.

420 Papaloa Rd. (off Kūhiō Hwy.), Kapa'a. www.kauaishoreshotel.com. ⓒ **877/220-1468** or 808/822-4951. 206 rooms. $161–$269 double; studio w/kitchenette from $279. $25 extra person. $22 resort fee (includes yoga classes, Wi-Fi, bicycle rentals, and parking). **Amenities:** 2 pools; bar; business center; coin laundry; restaurant; Wi-Fi.

North Shore

Despite this magical region's popularity with visitors, Princeville is its only official "visitor destination area." So if you're not staying in a hotel, I recommend booking through one of the following agencies, which manage only licensed vacation rentals, or checking closely for the permit number in online listings on VRBO.com or other platforms.

   Kauai Vacation Rentals (www.kauaivacationrentals.com; ⓒ **800/367-5025** or 808/245-8841) has managed well-maintained, well-priced homes and condos across the island since 1978, with some 67 at press time on the North Shore. Most have a 3- to 5-night minimum that expands to 1 week or 2 weeks from December 15 to January 6, when rates also rise. For all rentals, you'll also pay a $50 non-refundable reservation fee and one-time cleaning fee, anywhere from $125 for a studio condo to as high as $700 for a five-bedroom house.

Parrish Collection Kauai (www.parrishkauai.com; © **800/325-5701** or 808/742-2000) represents some 50 properties (nearly all condos) in Princeville. Many of the latter are in the **Hanalei Bay Resort ★★**, which has spectacular views rivaling those of the Princeville Resort, air-conditioning in units, and a recently redone fantasy pool with waterfalls, slides, and so forth; rates start at $295 a night (3-night minimum) for an oceanview hotel suite, plus nightly $22 resort and $17 parking fees. If you can forgo an ocean view, Parrish's best values are in the **Plantation at Princeville ★**, roomy two- and three-bedroom air-conditioned units in a complex built in 2004 with a pool, spa, barbecues, and fitness center; rates start at $302 for a two-bedroom, two-bathroom unit. Not included in any of Parrish's rates are the $97 "processing" fee and cleaning fees, starting at $150 for a studio and increasing by size.

VERY EXPENSIVE

A complete overhaul of the faded but formerly luxurious Princeville Resort, **1 Hotel Hanalei Bay ★★**, 5520 Haku Rd., Princeville (www.1 hotels.com/hanalei-bay; © **833/623-2311**), focuses on sustainability and wellness in sumptuous fashion, with prices to match. A waterfall garden and open-air, living room-style lobby now welcome guests, who can pick up free local fruit on their way to the guest rooms, which descend over several stories down the bluff to a narrow beach. The 252 rooms (including 51 suites) feature rustic, island-inspired furnishings of reclaimed wood and woven fibers and neutral or earth-toned hues—all the better to let the beautiful blue Hanalei Bay and the North Shore's green mountains shine. An elevated, adults-only infinity pool overlooks the peak-framed bay, while the natural-looking family pool provides easy access to the beach. The cutting-edge spa, oversized fitness center, and roster of wellness classes should satisfy any health devotee, while the multiple dining outlets are "plant-forward" and locally sourced where possible. Rooms start at $1,218 with advance purchase—but at least there's no resort fee or charge for the mandatory valet parking.

EXPENSIVE

Hanalei Colony Resort ★★   With two bedrooms (separated by louvered wooden doors), one-and-a-half to two bathrooms, full kitchens, and living rooms, these 48 individually owned, updated condos are perfect for families—or anyone who can appreciate being as few as 10 feet from the beach in the shadow of green peaks near the end of the road. It has no TVs, phones, or entertainment systems, although the Wi-Fi means guests don't disconnect completely. The beach is generally not safe for swimming, but you're less than a mile from Mākua (Tunnels) Beach, and the barbecue area by the small pool boasts lush landscaping and a koi pond. The resort operates a shuttle to Hanalei, Princeville, and various beaches; the independently run Ayurvedic-themed **Hanalei Day Spa** and Hawaiian fusion **Opakapaka Grill and Bar** ★★ (p. 582) restaurant, with excellent cocktails, are on site.

5-7130 Kūhiō Hwy., *makai* side, Hā'ena, about 5 miles west of Hanalei. www.hcr.com. C **800/628-3004** or 808/826-6235. 48 units. $359–$611 suite. 2-night minimum; 7th night free. 4th person $50. Resort fee $30. **Amenities:** Restaurant; coffee bar/art gallery; babysitting; barbecues; concierge; Jacuzzi; coin laundry; pool; spa; Wi-Fi.

Westin Princeville Ocean Villas ★★   A "vacation ownership" property that nonetheless offers nightly rentals, this 18½-acre bluffside resort is a winner with families and couples seeking condo-style units with resort furnishings and amenities. Besides Westin's justly famed "Heavenly Beds," the roomy studios and one-bedroom suites (which can be combined into two-bedroom units) have immaculate, well-stocked kitchens, washer/dryers, and huge bathrooms with separate glass showers and deep whirlpool tubs. Playful statuary and fountains mark the centrally located children's pool next to the main pool; adults will appreciate the quieter, bluff-side plunge pools. **Nanea Restaurant and Bar** ★ has substantial discounts for children 11 and under. *Note:* Since the nearby unmaintained trail to 'Anini Beach is steep and often muddy, most guests opt to take the free shuttle to the public beach access next to 1 Hotel Hanalei Bay, where they walk down nearly 200 steps to Pu'u Poa Beach or drive themselves to 'Anini or another beach.

3838 Wyllie Rd., Princeville. www.marriott.com/en-us/hotels/lihwp-the-westin-princeville-ocean-resort-villas. C **808/827-8700.** 346 units. From $607 studio; $744 1-bedroom; $1,124 2-bedroom. Parking $25. **Amenities:** 2 restaurants; bar; deli/store; barbecues; car rentals; kids' program; concierge; fitness room w/steam room and sauna, use of lap pool and fitness center, 1 mile away; golf and tennis access; 4 pools; free resort shuttle; spa; free Wi-Fi.

MODERATE

The best values on the North Shore can be found among Princeville's many condo complexes, which vary widely in age and amenities; check the listings of the brokers mentioned above. Larger groups should consider splitting costs in the new, oceanfront **Orchid Point** triplex; rates average $475 a night, plus $225 cleaning fee and $142 VRBO fee. Also peruse updated units at the dramatically perched, 22-acre **Hanalei Bay Resort** ★★ (www.hanaleibayresort.com; C **877/344-0688**), known for its fantasy pool. It participates in timeshare and rental programs but offers direct bookings, too, from $149 for a studio (512 sq. ft.) with kitchen, lanai, and pull-out sofa bed (but no other bed); one-bedroom suites (1,091 sq. ft.) sleep four and start at $329. Rates exclude the $20 daily resort fee and $6 daily parking fee.

Tip: Request a ground-floor unit if you have a problem with stairs, as there are no elevators here, although a shuttle service around the resort is available for guests with mobility issues.

Cliffs at Princeville ★★★   This may not be the poshest place in Princeville, but it's among the most serene, with nearly 22 verdant acres, including a massive lawn on the ocean bluff with views toward Hanalei and Makana. It's definitely the greenest, having won numerous sustainability awards. Spread across three-story buildings with lush garden views in rental units (timeshare and full-ownership units claim the ocean views), the mostly renovated condos are ultra-roomy: 900 square feet for one bedroom and two bathrooms, and 1,200 square feet for two-story units with full kitchens, large living rooms, and lanais with room to dine outside. There are no elevators or air-conditioning, but units do have excellent ceiling and standing fans; the well-tended grounds include two tennis and pickleball courts, an attractive fitness center, tropically landscaped pool with waterfalls and two hot tubs, and a mini putting green. A variety of food trucks visit over the course of a week, as do a mini farmers market and fresh fish vendors. The onsite concierge and management team go out of their way to ensure the best experiences.

3811 Edward Road, Princeville. www.cliffsatprinceville.com. ✆ **808/826-6219.** 202 units. From $289 1-bedroom (sleeps 4), $389 1-bedroom with loft (sleeps 6), $575 for 4-bedroom (sleeps 6). Resort fee $20. Parking $15. **Amenities:** Barbecue grills; basketball half-court; bike rentals; business center; concierge; fitness center; pool; 2 hot tubs; playground; mini putting green; shuffleboard; 2 tennis and pickleball courts; Wi-Fi; yoga.

South Shore

The most popular place to stay year-round, the resort area of Poʻipū Beach is definitely a "visitor destination area," with hundreds of rental condos, cottages, and houses vying with Kauai's best luxury resorts for families and a romantic boutique hotel. Upcountry Lāwaʻi and Kalāheo offer more modest (not necessarily licensed) B&Bs and vacation rentals.

VERY EXPENSIVE

The luxuriously appointed villas, cottages, and bungalows of the heavenly **Lodge at Kukuiʻula** ★★, 2700 Ke Alaula St., Kōloa (www.lodgeat kukuiula.com; ✆ **866/901-5204**), give a taste of the good life at Kukuiʻula, the island's most exclusive resort, with a private, ultra-posh spa, championship golf course, large pool, farm, ocean activities, and clubhouse dining. Now part of Destination by Hyatt, unit categories begin with a golf-view, 1,275-square-foot one-bedroom bungalow for $984 a night ($1,480 for a golf-view three-bedroom cottage and $1,704 for a three-bedroom cottage). All lodgings here incur a $150 reservation fee, $42 nightly resort fee, and damage waiver fee of $149, too.

Grand Hyatt Kauai Resort & Spa ★★★   The island's largest hotel aims to have one of the smallest carbon footprints. Its 604 luxurious rooms feature not only pillow-top beds and Toto toilets, but also eco-friendly elements such as recycled-yarn carpets and plush robes made from recycled plastic bottles. Grass-covered roofs and solar panels reduce

Massage at the Grand Hyatt Kauai's Anara Spa.

emissions, a hydroponic garden grows produce for its dining outlets (such as the thatched-roof **Tidepools** restaurant), and used cooking oil becomes biodiesel fuel. But that's just green icing on the cake of this sprawling, family-loving resort where the elaborate, multi-tiered fantasy pool and saltwater lagoon more than compensate for the rough waters of Keoneloa (Shipwrecks) Beach. The 45,000-square-foot indoor/outdoor **Anara Spa** and adjacent **Poipu Bay Golf Course** (p. 547) offer excellent adult diversions. To feel even more virtuous about splurging on a stay, check out the hotel's volunteer programs with the National Tropical Botanical Garden and Kaua'i Humane Society, among others.

1571 Po'ipū Rd., Po'ipū. www.grandhyattkauai.com. © **800/233-1234** or 808/742-1234. 602 units. $586–$772 double; from $868 Grand Club; from $1,671 suite. $55 resort fee includes self-parking, Wi-Fi, fitness classes, and more. Children 17 and under stay free in parent's room. Valet parking $40. **Amenities:** 5 restaurants; 4 bars; babysitting; bike and car rentals; kids' program; club lounge; concierge; fitness center; 3 whirlpools; saltwater swimming lagoon; luau; 2 pools; room service; spa; 2 tennis courts; watersports rentals; Wi-Fi.

EXPENSIVE

Ko'a Kea Hotel & Resort ★★★ This oceanfront jewel box hides between the sprawling Kiahuna Plantation Resort and the densely built Marriott Waiohai Beach Club. A chic boutique inn with arguably the island's best hotel restaurant, **Red Salt ★★★** (p. 586), it takes its name from Hawaiian words for "white coral," which inspires the white and coral accents in the sleek, modern decor. All rooms feature lanais, many with views of the rocky coast (a short walk from sandy beaches). Nespresso coffee makers and L'Occitane bath products suggest Europe, but the staff resounds with pure Hawaiian aloha. *Note:* At these prices, the "garden view" may disappoint—best to spring for an ocean view.

2251 Po'ipū Rd., Po'ipū. www.koakea.com. © **888/898-8958** or 808/828-8888. 121 units. From $456 garden view double; $544–$748 oceanview; $760–$1,098 oceanfront; from $1,209 oceanview suite. $45 resort fee includes valet parking, fitness center and classes, and more. **Amenities:** Restaurant; 2 bars; bike and watersports rentals; concierge; fitness room; whirlpool; pool; room service; spa; Wi-Fi.

A PERFECT PLACE IN Po'ipū

The best way to find a high-quality, licensed vacation rental in Po'ipū is through **The Parrish Collection Kauai** (www.parrishkauai.com; 📞 **800/325-5701** or 808/742-2000). Parrish manages more than 300 units for 25 different island-wide condo developments, plus dozens of vacation houses ranging from quaint cottages to elite resort homes; about three-quarters are in Po'ipū. The company maintains resortlike standards, classifying its lodgings into four categories ("premium plus" is the highest, for new or completely renovated units), sending linens for professional laundering, and providing luxe bathroom amenities. It staffs a concierge desk at **Waikomo Stream Villas ★**, **Nihi Kai Villas ★★**, and **Po'ipū Kapili ★★**, where the company manages about half the condos (100 in total), with no kickbacks for referrals, according to owner J.P. Parrish. "Our staff knows the island really well and has no agenda; we only recommend what works for each guest," he notes.

Each well-equipped rental offers a full kitchen, washer/dryer, TV/DVD, phone, and free Wi-Fi; you'll pay a one-time cleaning fee that varies by size of unit, plus a reservation fee that varies by price of unit (typically $50–$107) for condos. At Nihi Kai Villas, which has a heated pool (a rarity here) and large floor plans, off-peak nightly rates start at $215 for a garden view two-bedroom condo (sleeps six), plus $250 cleaning; at Waikomo Stream Villas, a garden view one-bedroom condo (sleeps four) starts at $230 a night, plus a $175 cleaning fee and $49 damage protection fee. The more luxurious Poipu Kapili, overlooking the ocean, offers a saltwater pool and two tennis courts; one-bedroom, two-bath units (sleeps four) start at $425 a night, plus $250 cleaning, while two-bedroom, three-bath units start at $485 plus a $275 cleaning fee. The recently built **Nalo Bungalow**, a cheerily decorated 3-bedroom, 3½-bath, two-story cottage with golf-course view and private pool, is perfect for large family or group rentals, starting at $840 a night, plus a $450 cleaning fee and $192 reservation fee.

Condos typically have a 3-night minimum stay; houses are typically 5 nights. Stays of a week or longer may be eligible for discounts; sign up online for specials, such as a $50 gas card with rentals, or other perks.

Kōloa Landing Resort ★★★   It may not have the best, or any, beachfront, but otherwise this brilliantly transformed 25-acre resort (now part of Marriott's Autograph Collection) deals in several superlatives. Among them are the largest residential-style hotel villas in Kaua'i—studios to three-bedrooms, with Wolf and SubZero appliances. Kōloa Landing also has the best pool complex, including a water slide, sprawling main pool with terraces, grottos, and undulating rock walls, plus two outlying pools, all with Jacuzzis. Renowned restaurateur Sam Choy designed the enticing menus for its casual **HoloHolo Grill** (p. 583). It's a short walk to shops and a 5-minute drive to Po'ipū Beach.

Note: Rooms with "resort views" may overlook the parking lot, but there's generally some greenery.

2641 Po'ipū Rd., Po'ipū. www.koloalandingresort.com. 📞 **808/240-6600.** 306 units. From $597 double; $669 studio; $729 1-bedroom; $1,079 2-bedroom; $1,229 3-bedroom. $35 resort fee includes self-parking, beach shuttle, and more. Valet parking $12. **Amenities:** Restaurant; 2 bars; fitness room; 3 pools; 3 whirlpools; food market with cafe; spa; Wi-Fi.

Sheraton Kauai Resort ★★ This appealingly low-key resort lives up to its ideal beachfront location, where the western horizon sees a riot of color at sunset and rainbows arc over a rocky point after the occasional shower. The oceanfront pool—with rock-lined whirlpool and luxurious bungalows and cabanas (for rent)—provides an inviting place for a dip; the traditional pool in the Mauka garden wing, where rooms have been converted to timeshare units, is a quieter spot. Nights here are lively, too, thanks to large fire pits in the oceanview courtyard and the tasty libations and wine-tasting social hours at **RumFire Poipu Beach** ★★ (www.rum firekauai.com; ✆ **808/742-4786**), an ambitious, island-inspired restaurant/lounge with walls of glass. The beachfront luau (details below) is also worth booking.

2440 Ho'onani Rd., Po'ipū. www.sheraton-kauai.com. ✆ **866/716-8109** or 808/742-1661. 391 units. $479–$725 double; from $903 suite. $30 resort fee includes self-parking, fitness center, bicycles, and more. Extra person $70. Valet parking $30. **Amenities:** 3 restaurants; bar; babysitting; concierge; cultural lessons, fitness room; whirlpool; luau (www.auliiluau.com; Mon and Wed $190 adults, $140 ages 13–17, $115 ages 4–12); 2 pools; room service; spa services; watersports rentals; torch lighting; Wi-Fi.

MODERATE

In addition to the hotels below, consider the 35-acre, green-lawned **Kiahuna Plantation Resort** ★★, on the sandy beach next to the Sheraton; some rates now fall in the expensive category but are still a good value. Its 333 individually furnished, one- and two-bedroom condos vary widely in taste; they also rely on ceiling fans (and trade winds) for cooling, and there's no elevator in the three-story buildings. The nearly 60 units available from **Castle Resorts** (www.castleresorts.com; ✆ **800/367-5004** or 877/367-1912) receive daily housekeeping; prices start at $179 for a one-bedroom, one-bath garden view unit, plus $255 cleaning fee and $30 reservation fee. **Outrigger** (www.outrigger.com; ✆ **808/742-6411**) manages

Kōloa Landing Resort's 350,000-gallon main pool.

more than half of the units; its nightly rates for a one-bedroom garden view unit start at $337, plus $264 cleaning. Castle includes free Wi-Fi and parking in their rates, and access to the tennis courts and resort-style pool of the Poipu Beach Athletic Club across the street.

Also consider the one-bedroom/one-bathroom, partial oceanview units in the **Kahala ★** condominium on the 70-acre, verdant Poipu Kai resort, managed by **Suite Paradise** (www.suite-paradise.com; ☎ **800/367-8020**), starting at $269 a night, plus $250 cleaning and $20 daily resort fee. *Note:* You can filter Suite Paradise searches by air-conditioning—a strongly recommended unit feature—among its Poipu listings.

Kauai Cove ★★ Honeymooners and other romance seekers find a serene oasis on a quiet lane close to the cove at Kōloa Landing, and a short walk to a sandier cove known as Baby Beach. The bright Plumeria and Hibiscus cottages provide a four-poster canopy queen-size bed under high vaulted ceilings, private bamboo-walled lanai with barbecue grill, flatscreen TV with DVD player, and full kitchen. Since it can get hot in Poʻipū, the wall-unit air-conditioner (along with ceiling fan) is a nice touch. Helpful owners E.J. and Diane Olsson live nearby in Poʻipū Kai, where they also rent the one-bedroom Pool Cottage (a suite in their house with private entrance and full kitchen, plus use of the pool and hot tub).
Plumeria and Hibiscus cottages: 2672 Puʻuholo Rd., Poʻipū. www.kauaicove.com. ☎ **808/651-0279.** $179–$279 double; $150 cleaning fee. **Pool Cottage:** 2367 Hoʻohu Rd., Poʻipū. **Amenities:** Grill; beach gear; use of Poipu Kai pool and hot tub; free Wi-Fi.

Marjorie's Kauai Inn ★ Keeping with its hilltop setting in Lāwaʻi, this three-room, purpose-built B&B prides itself on green touches: energy-efficient appliances, eco-friendly cleaning products, and local organic produce (some grown on-site) in lavish breakfasts. You're more likely to notice the sweeping valley views from the private lanais. All rooms have private entrances and kitchenettes, while Sunset View, the largest, boasts its own hot tub in a gazebo and a foldout couch for extra guests. Any guest can use the 50-foot-long saltwater pool and hot tub, down a long flight of stairs (this isn't the best place for young children). Rooms include TV with cable and DVD player, but guests are encouraged to explore the island with a booklet of helpful tips and free use of bikes, a surfboard, a kayak, and beach gear.
Off Haʻilima Rd., Lāwaʻi. www.marjorieskauaiinn.com. ☎ **800/717-8838** or 808/332-8838. 3 units. $350–$395 double, includes breakfast (Mon–Sat). Extra person $20. No cleaning fees. **Amenities:** Barbecue; free use of bikes, kayak, and beach gear; Jacuzzi; laundry; pool; free Wi-Fi.

Poipu Plantation B&B Inn and Vacation Rentals ★★★ This ultra-tranquil compound almost defies description. It comprises four adults-only, B&B suites of various sizes in a lovingly restored 1938 plantation house and nine vacation rental units in three modern cottage-style wings behind the B&B. The B&B suites feature handsome hardwood floors, vintage furnishings, bright tropical art, and modern bathrooms; the 700-square-foot Alii

Suite also includes a wet bar, two-person whirlpool tub, and private lanai. The one- and two-bedroom cottage units on the foliage-rich 1-acre lot have less character but offer more space (plus full kitchens); some have ocean views across the rooftops of Sunset Kahili condos across the street. Innkeepers Chris and Javed Moore and their friendly staff delight in offering travel tips. *Note:* When comparing rates, consider that the units here have air-conditioning but no cleaning, resort, parking, or Wi-Fi fees; plus, breakfasts for the B&B units include Kauaʻi coffee, hot entrees, and fresh island fruit.

1792 Peʻe Rd., Poʻipū. www.poipubeach.com. ✆ **808/742-6757.** 12 units. Inn suites: $300, includes breakfast and daily housekeeping; adults only (2 max.), 3-night minimum (7 for winter holidays). Rental units: $330–$450 1-bedroom; $495–$637 2-bedroom. Extra person $20. **Amenities:** Use of beach gear; laundry facilities; free Wi-Fi.

INEXPENSIVE

In pricey Poʻipū, staying anywhere under $200 a night—especially if fees and taxes are included—can be a challenge. **Kauai Vacation Rentals** (www.kauaivacationrentals.com; ✆ **800/367-5025** or 808/245-8841) manages 14 oceanview studios and one-bedroom units in the well-kept **Prince Kuhio ★★** complex, 5061 Lāwaʻi Rd., across from Lāwaʻi Beach (and overlooking Prince Kūhiō park) that start at $165 and $195 a night (3-night minimum), respectively, plus $50 reservation and $100 to $200 cleaning fees.

West Side

MODERATE

Waimea Plantation Cottages ★★★   Serenity now: That's what you'll find at this 30-acre oceanfront enclave of 61 restored vintage cottages, spread among large lawns dotted with coconut palms, banyan trees, and tropical flowers. The 2-mile-long, black-sand beach is not good for swimming (there's a small pool for that), but it offers intriguing driftwood for beachcombers and mesmerizing sunset views; claim a hammock or a lounge chair. The charmingly rustic but newly renovated and airy cottages feature full kitchens, lanais, and modern perks such as Wi-Fi, air-conditioning (window units), and flatscreen TVs. The one- and two-bedroom units have one bathroom, while the three-bedroom versions offer two baths, perfect for families; a few larger houses are also available. Owned by the heirs of Norwegian immigrant Hans Peter Faye, who ran a sugar plantation, it's now managed by a Canadian firm, Coast Hotels, which has poured money into tasteful upgrades. *Tip:* Local barbecue chain **Chicken in a Barrel ★** (www.chickeninabarrel.com; ✆ **808/320-8397**) now operates the in-house restaurant; it's a brightly painted spot with numerous beers on serve-yourself taps, open daily 8:30am to 9pm, with breakfast until 11:30am.

9400 Kaumaliʻi Hwy., *makai* side, west of Huaki Rd., Waimea. www.coasthotels.com. ✆ **808/338-1625.** 60 units. From $313 1-bedroom; $428 2-bedroom; $433 3-bedroom. $30 resort fee. Children 17 and under stay free in parent's room. Check for online specials. **Amenities:** Barbecue grills; beach chairs; bocce ball and shuffleboard; DVD and game rentals; gift shop; free laundry facilities; pool; restaurant; Wi-Fi.

The West Inn ★ The closest thing the West Side has to a Holiday Inn Express, the West Inn offers clean, neutral-toned rooms with bright accents, stone counters, and Serta Perfect Sleeper mattresses. One two-story wing of medium-size rooms is just off the highway across from Waimea Theater; some second-story rooms have an ocean view over corrugated metal roofs from the long, shared lanai, and all units have refrigerators, microwaves, air-conditioning, coffeemakers, and cable TV. Another wing of one- and two-bedroom suites, designed for longer stays with full kitchens and living rooms, is tucked off to the side. *Note:* There's no elevator; call ahead to arrange check-ins after 6pm.

9690 Kaumali'i Hwy., *makai* side (at Pōkole Rd.), Waimea. www.thewestinn.com. ⓒ **808/338-1107.** 20 units. $198–$325 king or double. 3- to 5-night min. for larger rooms: $319 king w/kitchen, $325–$349 1-bedroom suite, $489–$519 2-bedroom suite. Longer minimum stays may apply. $30 extra person. **Amenities:** Barbecue grills; coin laundry; free Wi-Fi.

INEXPENSIVE

Inn Waimea/West Kauai Lodging ★★ If you're looking for accommodations with both character and modern conveniences, check out the small lodge and three vacation rentals managed by West Kauai Lodging. A former parsonage that's also known as Halepule ("House of Prayer"), **Inn Waimea** is a Craftsman-style cottage in the center of quaint Waimea, with simple, tropical-tinged, plantation-era decor in its four wood-paneled suites, some with separate living areas and air-conditioning; all have flatscreen TVs, Wi-Fi, private bathrooms with pedestal sinks, coffeemakers, mini-fridges, and ceiling fans. West Kauai Lodging also manages a moderately priced, vintage two-bedroom cottage in Waimea plus the newly built five-bedroom, five-bathroom **Hale Lā** beach house in Kekaha, all with full kitchen and laundry facilities ($595 a night, plus $395 cleaning). The homey, Craftsman-inspired **Ishihara Home** is above town, with sweeping views of ridges and the distant sea, three bedrooms with queen beds, and one bathroom ($269 a night, plus $125 cleaning). *Note:* Manager Patrick McLean, who owns Hale Lā, is a former Kaua'i B&B pro who loves to help visitors plan their days. He also manages the upgraded cabins in Kōke'e State Park (see "Camping & Cabins," below).

4469 Halepule Rd. (off Kaumali'i Hwy.), Waimea. www.akamaihawaiiproperties.com/wkl-2020. ⓒ **808/652-6852.** Inn (4 units) $139–$159 ($25 for 3rd person). **Ishihara Home** (3-bedroom, 1-bath): $379, plus $195 cleaning fee. **Hale Lā** beach house (5-bedroom, 5-bath) $695, plus $495 cleaning. **Amenities:** Free Wi-Fi.

Camping & Cabins

Kaua'i offers tent camping in four county-run beach parks and, for extremely hardy and self-sufficient types, several state-managed, back-country areas of the **Nāpali Coast** and **Waimea Canyon.** Tents and simple cabins are available in the cooler elevations of **Kōke'e State Park,** and minimal campgrounds at **Polihale State Park;** you have to be well equipped for the rugged conditions in the latter. With the exception of

Kōke'e cabins, all camping requires permits, which must be purchased in advance; camping in vehicles is not allowed.

County campsites, often busy with local families on weekends, close 1 day each week for maintenance. **'Anini** and **Lydgate** beach parks are recommended. Go to **www.kauai.gov**, hover over "Government," click on "Parks and Recreation," then "Permit Applications" to find the link for camping schedules, online permit applications, and regulations. Permits for nonresidents cost $3 per adult (free for children 17 and under, with adult), except for Lydgate, which is $25 per site (up to five campers).

For camping in state parks and forest reserves, the **Department of Land & Natural Resources** (https://camping.ehawaii.gov; © **808/274-3444**) only issues online permits; its office in Līhu'e, 3060 'Eiwa St., Suite 306, is open Monday to Friday 8am to 3:30pm. **Nāpali Coast State Wilderness Park** allows camping at two sites along the 11-mile Kalalau Trail—**Hanakoa Valley,** 6 miles in, and **Kalalau Valley,** at trail's end—for a maximum of 5 nights (no more than 1 consecutive night at Hanakoa). Camping is also permitted at Miloli'i, for a maximum of 3 nights; it's reached only by kayak or authorized boats mid-May through early September. There's no drinking water, trash must be packed out, and composting toilets are not always in good repair, yet permits ($35 per night) sell out quickly, available only 30 days in advance. *Note:* Rangers conduct periodic permit checks here, so make sure yours is handy. Don't forget you'll also need an overnight parking permit for the trailhead ($15 per day, including entrance to **Hā'ena State Park,** p. 510, purchased from www.gohaena.com). Limited parking may be available at Ali'i Kai Resort, 3830 Edward Rd., Princeville; call © **808/826-9988.**

Permits for primitive campsites in eight backcountry areas of Waimea Canyon and nearby wilderness preserves cost $18 per night for up to six people (additional people $3 each), with a 5-night maximum; see https://camping.ehawaii.gov for detailed descriptions.

In **Kōke'e State Park,** which gets quite chilly on winter nights, **West Kauai Lodging** (www.akamaihawaiiproperties.com/wkl-2020; © **808/652-6852**) manages 11 cabins ($89–$169 a night, 2-night minimum) that sleep two to six people; each has fully equipped kitchens and linens. Be sure to book well in advance. Less than a mile away, down a dirt road, the YWCA of Kaua'i runs **Camp Sloggett** (https://ywcakauai.org/camp-sloggett; © **808/245-5959**), offering a cottage that sleeps up to four ($165) and two buildings designed for groups. The bunkhouse ($215) and two-bedroom lodge ($265) both sleep up to 15. Tent camping remained suspended at press time.

Kayak Kaua'i (www.kayakkauai.com; © **888/596-3853** or 808/826-9844) offers camping rentals, supplies, and car and luggage storage at its Wailua River Marina shop, 3-5971 Kūhiō Hwy., Kapa'a. **Pedal N Paddle** (www.pedalnpaddle.com; © **808/826-9069**) rents backpacks and sleeping bags; it's in Ching Young Village, 5-5190 Kūhiō Hwy., Hanalei.

WHERE TO EAT ON KAUA'I

Thanks to a proliferation of hamburger joints, plate-lunch counters, and food trucks, you'll find affordable choices (by local standards) in every town. At the gourmet end of the spectrum, Kauai's very expensive restaurants—both on and off the resorts—provide swank service and more complex but reliably executed dishes. And nearly every place trumpets its Kauai-grown ingredients, which help keep the Garden Island green and the flavors fresh.

The challenge is finding exceptional value in the moderate to expensive range—and more recently, booking a table. Costs are indeed higher here, and service is often slower; it's best not to arrive anywhere—even at one of the many food trucks—in a state of starvation. Patience and pleasantness on your part, however, will usually be rewarded. During peak holiday and summer seasons, avoid stress by booking online with **Open Table** (www.opentable.com), currently available for around 30 Kaua'i restaurants and dinner shows. The listings below, not all of which are on Open Table, will note where reservations are recommended.

For those with access to a kitchen (or even just a mini-fridge), check out "Kaua'i Farmers Markets" (p. 596). You're guaranteed farm-to-table cuisine at a good price—and at your own pace.

East Side

This populous area yields several unique, fairly priced dining experiences. In Kapa'a, for happy hour appetizers and cocktails with a dazzling ocean view, head to **Sam's Ocean View** ★, 4-1546 Kūhiō Hwy. (www.samsoceanview.com; ✆ **808/822-7887**); **Wailua Shave Ice** ★★, 4-831 Kūhiō Hwy. (www.wailuashaveice.com; ✆ **808/634-7183**), serves gourmet varieties of the fluffy island treat daily noon to 9pm.

In Līhu'e, microbrew lovers will find hearty, island-grown food pairings on tap at the expanded **Kauai Beer Company** ★★, 4265 Rice St. (www.kauaibeer.com; ✆ **808/245-2337**); try a 4-ounce brew for $3, and snack on fries ($7–$12) in special renditions like taro or *okonomiyaki* (Japanese blend of mayo, eel sauce, and nori-sesame seasoning). It's open Monday to Saturday 11am to 9pm. For lunch Monday through Friday (and breakfast Thurs–Fri), the **Greenery Cafe** ★★ (www.thegreenerycafe.com; ✆ **808/246-4567**), in the rear cottage at 3146 'Akahi St., will delight health and soul food fans alike with Kaua'i-grown collard greens, organic rosemary chicken, ahi wraps, and fresh cornbread (main courses $10–$14).

Note: The restaurants in this section are on either the "Hotels & Restaurants on the Coconut Coast" map (p. 559) or the "Hotels & Restaurants in Līhu'e" map (p. 561).

EXPENSIVE

Duke's Kauai ★★ STEAK/SEAFOOD   The view of Kalapaki Beach, an indoor waterfall, koi pond, and a lively beachfront bar, rivals the food at this popular outpost of the California–Hawai'i T S Restaurants chain. The menu offers fresh seafood, plus a vast salad bar, and the belt-straining Hula Pie (an ice cream confection with classic and rotating versions). The downstairs **Duke's Barefoot Bar ★★**, which has frequent live music (see "Kaua'i Nightlife," p. 597), offers the best values, with burgers, sandwiches, and salads for lunch and dinner, but the dinner-only upstairs dining room shows local flair with Lāwa'i mushroom gnocchi and seared ahi with papaya mustard sauce—among satisfying but less ambitious dishes such as macnut-crusted mahi-mahi. A trip to the island's biggest salad bar costs $4 with any entree upstairs or $18 as a stand-alone meal. It's paired with prime rib (Wed and Sat) and surf and turf (Sun) as a dinner buffet option.

At west end of Royal Sonesta Kaua'i Resort, 3610 Rice St., Līhu'e. www.dukeskauai. com. ✆ **808/246-9599.** Reservations recommended for dinner. Bar main courses $19–$27 lunch and dinner; $27–$57 in dining room. Bar daily 11am–9pm; dining room daily 4:15–9pm; Sun brunch 9am–noon.

Hukilau Lanai ★★ SEAFOOD/ISLAND FARM   Although his restaurant is hidden inside the nondescript Kauai Coast Resort at the Beachboy, off the main highway in Kapa'a, chef/owner Ron Miller has inspired diners to find their way here in droves since 2002. The lure: a hearty menu that's virtually all locally sourced—from Kaua'i whenever possible, and other islands when not—as well as expertly prepared and presented. Four to five seafood specials, incorporating local produce, are offered nightly; try the coffee-spiced candied ahi, or the *hebi* (short-billed spearfish) when available. The mushroom meatloaf also packs a savory punch, thanks to grass-fed beef and Hawai'i Island mushrooms. Value-conscious diners should try the $45 five-course tasting menu ($65 with wine pairings) offered from 5 to 5:45pm. Reservations are strongly recommended, especially for oceanview seating. *Note:* The gluten-free menu includes variants of the five-course tasting menus.

In the Kauai Coast Resort at the Beachboy, 520 'Aleka Loop, Kapa'a. www.hukilau kauai.com. ✆ **808/822-0600.** Reservations recommended. Main courses $26–$50. Tues–Sat 5–9pm.

JO2 ★★★ ASIAN/FRENCH   A Hawai'i Regional Cuisine co-founder and six-time nominee for a James Beard Foundation Award, Jean-Marie Josselin's latest victory is JO2, an island-sourced, "natural cuisine" restaurant with Asian-influenced dishes prepared using classic French techniques. The tiny but chic dining room has a neutral palette that makes the artful presentations of brightly hued greens, sauces, and glazes pop. Among the small plates, try the lamb dumpling or organic tomato sampler; for larger dishes, seared Hokkaido scallops or the locally caught blackened opah; don't skip the yuzu lemon cheesecake. The early-bird three-course prix fixe is a bargain at $45; it's available from 5 to 6pm, when signature cocktails are $10, except during holiday periods.

4-971 Kūhiō Hwy., *mauka* side, Kapa'a. www.jotwo.com. ✆ **808/212-1627.** Reservations recommended. Main courses $39–$56; small plates $14–$36. 3-course prix fixe 5–6pm $45 (not offered during holidays). Tues–Mon 5–9pm.

MODERATE

In addition to the listings below, seek out **Hualani's ★★** (© 808/320-7399) in Timbers Kaua'i Ocean Club & Residences (p. 578) for outstanding but casual oceanfront dining with a lighthouse view on Līhu'e's Hōkūala Resort. The truly farm-to-table menu showcases produce grown on the resort and island seafood—often on the same dish, as with local coconut shrimp at dinner ($20). Thursday tasting dinners ($40) sell out quickly; reservations are recommended. It's open daily, with a la carte and breakfast buffet options ($17–$29) served 8 to 10am; lunch is a great time to savor the ocean vistas over poke, salads, and sandwiches ($14–$24), served 11am to 3pm; and happy hour 3 to 5pm precedes dinner 5 to 8:30pm (mains $39–$63).

Another casual oceanfront/poolside restaurant with superior food, **Crooked Surf ★★** (© 808/320-3651) takes its name from the surf break just offshore from the **Sheraton Kauai Resort at Coconut Beach** (p. 560) and serves island favorites like firecracker shrimp and the huli huli chicken sliders with kewpie mayo (both $16); tropical cocktails are also excellent, with a lively happy hour from 4 to 6pm daily. It's open for lunch and dinner daily 11am to 10pm and shares some seating with the hotel's more upscale but still informal **Moamoa Hawaiian Fish House ★★**, typically open for dinner Sunday to Wednesday 5:30 to 9pm. Naturally, it shines at seafood, including the locally raised prawns ($24); meat dishes such as Kurobuta pork chop ($42) push prices into the expensive category, but show equal flair.

KP Lihue ★ ITALIAN The last remaining outpost of one of the island's best Italian restaurants emphasizes homemade pasta standards, such as chicken parm and fettuccine Alfredo, and meat specials, such as osso buco or sous vide pork. The truffle-parmesan fries with three dipping sauces ($9) and meatballs made with local beef ($10) are great starters. Thankfully, it recently relocated to a new dining room (next to Kuhio Ford) that not only has twice the space but also plenty of parking.

4028 Rice St., Līhu'e. www.kplihue.com. © **808/245-2227.** Main courses $18–$27 lunch; $16–$32 dinner. Mon–Thurs 11am–8:30pm; Fri–Sat until 9pm.

Lava Lava Beach Club ★ AMERICAN/ISLAND On the ocean side of Kauai Shores Hotel, Lava Lava Beach Club has the island's only "toes-in-the-sand" dining area, on comfy wicker sofas facing Wailua Bay. It also offers plenty of other oceanview indoor and outdoor seating, a full bar with zippy tropical cocktails and a dozen beers (seven local), and an attentive staff serving American and island-flavored specialties including the mango tango naan pizza ($18) and coconut shrimp with ginger guava sauce ($39). Food quality can vary, but otherwise this is a beachy-Hā'enan hideaway, with live music nightly.

At Kauai Shores Hotel, 420 Papaloa Rd., Kapa'a (off Kūhiō Hwy., *makai* side, south of Coconut Marketplace). www.lavalavabeachclub.com. © **808/241-5282.** Main courses $20–$49. Light fare 3–4:30pm, dinner 4:30–9pm, happy hour 3–5pm. Dinner reservations recommended. Free valet parking (required).

Oasis on the Beach ★★ SEAFOOD/ISLAND FARM   Though not actually on the sand, the open-air, oceanfront setting at the Waipouli Beach Resort is still memorable, as are the daily fresh-catch (grilled or pan-seared), the caprese-style tomato salad with house-made ricotta, and braised short ribs with bacon-truffle fried rice. Executive chef Sean Smull proudly notes that 90% of ingredients come from Kaua'i. Save room for the apple banana spring roll with gelato. The handsome canoe bar and sounds of ocean surf make the occasional wait worthwhile.

In the Waipouli Beach Resort, 4-820 Kūhiō Hwy., Kapa'a (across from Safeway). www.oasiskauai.com. ℭ 808/822-9332. Reservations recommended. Main courses $29–$42. Mon–Sat 4–9pm; happy hour Wed 3–5pm.

INEXPENSIVE

In addition to these listings, and the many in "Plate Lunch, Bento & Poke" and "Cheeseburgers in Paradise," below, check out **Tiki Tacos** ★★, 4-971 Kūhiō Hwy., *mauka* side, in the Waipouli Complex. Billed as "Mexican food with a Hawaiian heart," the latter features sizable tacos ($8–$11) with island fish, kalua pork, and other fillings on handmade tortillas. It's open daily 11am to 7pm. For fresh-pressed juices of island-grown fruits and veggies, plus quinoa salad, kelp noodles, and veggie burritos ($7–$12), visit the Kapa'a branch of **Kauai Juice Co.,** 4-1384 Kūhiō. Hwy., *makai* side behind Java Kai (www.kauaijuiceco.com; ℭ 808/631-3893), open daily 8am to 5:30pm. Food trucks are popping up all over Kapa'a, including the multi-ethnic, often changing lineup at **Kapa'a Food Truck Court** ★, 4-1620 Kūhiō. Hwy., *makai* side; picnic tables offer ocean views.

Hamura's Saimin Stand ★★★ JAPANESE NOODLES   Honored by the James Beard Foundation in 2006 as one of "America's Classics," this hole-in-the-wall has been satisfying local palates since 1952. Visitors have also now caught on to the appeal of *saimin:* large bowls of ramen noodles in salty broth with green onion, cabbage, and slices of fish cake, hard-boiled eggs, and pork, for starters. Here the housemade noodles are served al dente, and sometimes brusquely; figure out what you're going to order before seating yourself at one of the U-shaped counters. The "special regular" includes wontons and diced ham; top off any dish with a barbecued chicken skewer. If your appetite isn't large, order a to-go slice of the ultra-fluffy *liliko'i* (passion fruit) chiffon pie, just as renowned as the *saimin.* Shave ice is also delicious, but its separate counter isn't always open. ***Note:*** There's often a line inside and out; it moves fast, so stay put.

2956 Kress St., Līhu'e (1 block west of Rice St. in small blue building on left; park farther down the street). ℭ 808/245-3271. Most items under $15. No credit cards. Daily 10am–9:30pm.

North Shore

In addition to the following, consider **The Dolphin** ★★, 5-5016 Kūhiō Hwy., Hanalei (https://hanaleidolphin.com; ℭ 808/826-6113), widely known as Hanalei Dolphin and a landmark since the 1970s, with spacious

PLATE LUNCH, BENTO & poke

If you haven't yet tried the Hawaii staples of plate lunch, bento, or poke (seasoned, raw fish), Kauai's inexpensive eateries are a good place to start.

EAST SIDE In Kapa'a, the indispensable **Pono Market ★**, 4-1300 Kūhiō Hwy. (*makai* side), Kapa'a (www.pono marketkauai.com; *©* 808/822-4581), has enticing counters of sashimi, poke, sushi, and a diverse assortment of take-out fare. The roast pork and the potato-macaroni salad are top sellers, but it's also known for plate lunches, including pork and chicken *laulau* (steamed in *ti* leaves), plus flaky *manju* (sweet potato and other fillings in baked crust). It's open Monday to Friday 6am to 2pm. Kapa'a also has **Sleeping Giant Grill ★**, a renamed branch of Kilauea Fish Market (see "North Shore," below) at 440 'Aleka Place (*©* 808/822-3474; Mon–Fri 1–8pm); try the mochi ono tacos (battered in rice flour) for a deliciously crisp take on fish tacos.

In Līhu'e, **Po's Kitchen ★**, 4100 Rice St. (*©* 808/246-8617), packs a lot of goodies in its deluxe bento boxes ($11), including shrimp tempura, chicken katsu, chow fun noodles, macaroni salad, hot dog, ham, and rice balls. It's hidden behind Ace Hardware and open Monday to Saturday from 6am to 2pm (cash only). A block away, **Garden Island BBQ & Chinese Restaurant ★**, 4252 Rice St. (www.gardenisland barbecue.com; *©* 808/245-8868), is the place for Chinese plate lunches, as well as soups and noodle dishes; it's open Monday to Saturday 10am to 9pm, and Sunday until 8:30pm. Across from Walmart, **The Fish Express ★**, 3-3343 Kūhiō Hwy. (*©* 808/245-9918), draws crowds for its range of poke (the ahi with spicy crab in a light mayo sauce is a favorite), pork laulau, Spam musubi, bentos, and plate lunches, including lighter options such as Cajun blackened ahi and smoked fish. The downside: no seating. It's open daily 10am to 4pm, with kitchen hours 10:30am to 2:30pm.

Mark's Place ★★, in Puhi Industrial Park at 1610 Haleukana St., Līhu'e (www.marksplacekauai.com; *©* 808/245-2522 and 808/245-2722), fashions daily salad and entree specials with a California-healthy bent: shrimp and grilled-vegetable quinoa salad, say, or cornmeal-crusted mahi with chipotle

grounds on the Hanalei River as you enter town. It doesn't take reservations, so you'll always see crowds milling outside, but the fresh sushi and seafood ($26–$36) are worth the wait—and the Dolphin's fish market makes it easy to grab some hot chowder or other prepared foods to go if you're in a rush. It's open daily for dinner 5 to 9pm (no reservations, but waitlist starts at 4:30pm). In Kīlauea, stop by **Kauai Juice Co.,** 4270 Kīlauea Rd. (www.kauaijuiceco.com; *©* 808/631-5529), for fresh-pressed juices, salads, and vegan noodles ($7–$12); it's open Monday to Saturday 8am to 5:30pm and Sunday until 4:30pm.

Note: The Dolphin and other restaurants in this section are on the "Hotels & Restaurants on Kaua'i's North Shore" map (p. 581).

EXPENSIVE

Bar Acuda ★★★ TAPAS   Named one of *Food & Wine* magazine's "Top 10 New American Chefs" in 1996, when he was still working in San aioli. But it also serves island standards such as Korean-style chicken, beef stew, and chicken katsu and is famed for its baked goods, including butter mochi and bread pudding; you can even pick up an entire dinner for four (menu changes daily). It's open Monday to Friday 11am to 4pm, with a handful of picnic tables for seating.

NORTH SHORE Everything is pricier on the North Shore. **Sushigirl Kauai ★★**, in the Kong Lung Center, 2484 Keneke St., Kīlauea (www.sushi girlkauai.com; ⓒ **808/320-8646**), offers gluten-free takeout, from ahi poke bowls with rice or local organic greens ($15–$16) to seafood and veggie sushi rolls and nori-wrapped "burritos" ($16–$17). It's open daily 11am to 3pm and 4 to 8pm (check Instagram for updates). At **Kilauea Fish Market ★**, 4270 Kīlauea Rd., Kīlauea (enter from Keneke St.; www.kilaueafishmarket.com; ⓒ **808/828-6244**), skip the pricey poke and opt for Korean BBQ or grilled teriyaki chicken plates ($16–$17); the ahi wrap ($19) is a messy but filling alternative. It's open Monday to Saturday 11am to 8pm, with outdoor seating only.

In Hanalei, head to **Village Snack Shop and Bakery ★**, across from Puka Dog inside Ching Young Village, 5-5190 Kūhiō Hwy. (ⓒ **808/826-6841**), for loco moco (eggs, meat, and gravy on rice) at breakfast and chili pepper chicken at lunch; everyone loves the chocolate haupia (coconut cream) pies, malasadas (doughnut holes), and other pastries. It's open Thursday to Tuesday 8am to 4pm.

SOUTH SHORE The **Koloa Fish Market ★★**, 3390 Po'ipū Rd. (https://koloafishmarket.com; ⓒ **808/742-6199**), in Old Town Kōloa, offers excellent fresh poke, plate lunches, or seared ahi to go; you can also pick up raw seafood to grill. Don't forgo decadent desserts such as Okinawan sweet potato haupia pie on macadamia nut crust. It's open Monday to Wednesday, Friday, and Saturday 10am to 3pm. **Sueoka's Snack Shop ★** (ⓒ **808/742-1112**), the cash-only window counter of Sueoka grocery store, 5392 Kōloa Rd. (www.sueokastore.com; ⓒ **808/742-1611**), offers a wide selection of meat-based lunch plates, such as shoyu chicken or kalua pork for $10 or less; cheeseburgers are just $4. It's open daily 6am to 8pm.

Francisco, chef/owner Jim Moffatt later decided to embrace a lowkey lifestyle in Hanalei. But he never relaxed his standards for expertly prepared food, in this case tapas—small plates inspired by several Mediterranean cuisines. Enjoy them on the torch-lit veranda or in the sleek, warm-toned dining room. Given Bar Acuda's deliciously warm, crusty bread, ordering one hearty and one light dish per person, plus a shared starter of spiced olives or crostini, should suffice for a couple; ask the server which are suitable for sharing. The menu changes to reflect seasonal tastes and availability but usually includes seared fresh fish and grilled beef skewers. Note that the crowd here tends to be more smartly dressed than anywhere else on Kaua'i.

In Hanalei Center, 5-5161 Kūhiō Hwy., Hanalei. www.cudahanalei.com. ⓒ **808/826-7081.** Reservations strongly recommended (up to 1 month in advance). Hearty tapas $9–$30. Tues–Sat 5:30–9:30pm.

MODERATE

Bar Acuda's busy chef-owner James Moffatt serves five kinds of silky Japanese ramen bowls ($19) plus grilled fish and meat skewers ($12) with housemade kimchi at **Ama ★★** (© **808/826-9452**), next door to his Bar Acuda (see above) in Hanalei Center's rear courtyard. It's only open Tuesday through Sunday 5 to 9pm; the mountain (and occasional waterfall) views as well as the food are worth any wait. Moffatt also runs **Hanalei Bread Company ★★**, a bakery and coffee house in Hanalei Center, 5-5161 Kūhiō Hwy (© **808/826-6717**). It's open daily 7am to 12:30pm. Patrons line up early for chocolate chip scones, *liliko'i* cinnamon rolls, avocado toast, and other goodies to go with their espresso drinks; don't be in a rush when you arrive.

Tiki 'Iniki ★ (www.tikiiniki.com; © **808/431-4242**), tucked behind Ace Hardware in Princeville Center (p. 496), is a moderately priced, cheeky tiki bar/restaurant owned by Michele Rundgren and her rock-musician husband, Todd. It's open Tuesday to Saturday from 11am to 11pm, with lunch 11am to 3pm and dinner 4:30 to 9pm. **Tahiti Nui ★★** in Hanalei is similarly renowned for nightlife (p. 597) but reasonably priced; appealing appetizers such as coconut shrimp, fresh seafood specials, and pizza make it worth a stop for lunch or dinner. It's open Tuesday to Friday 11am to 9pm and Sunday 9am to 9pm.

Avalon Gastropub ★★★ GOURMET PUB/COCKTAIL BAR   A favorite of fans of whiskey, craft cocktails, and Scotch eggs since it first opened in Kapa'a in 2018, this appropriately named gastropub has become even more beloved since moving to a larger, indoor-outdoor space in Kīlauea in late 2023. Belly up to the long, handsome bar for pre-Prohibition or modern mixologist cocktails, or chow down on attractively presented small and shared plates ($8–$24) of fried green tomatoes, veggie or fig and prosciutto pizzetta, truffle fries, and other savory temptations. Main dishes such as mole Kurobota pork chop, a thick burger, or fresh-caught fish are multilayered in flavor, too.

In 'Āhuimanu Shopping Center, 2555 Ala Namahana Pkwy., Kīlauea. www.avalon gastropub.com. © **808/828-0275.** Reservations strongly recommended. Main courses $24–$43. Wed–Sat 5–9pm.

The Bistro ★★ CONTEMPORARY AMERICAN/ISLAND FARM John-Paul Gordon is yet another Kaua'i chef taking inspiration from the bounty of local fields and fishing grounds, with an admirably inventive palate and a well-practiced eye for presentation. Although his menu is largely seasonal, the "fish rockets" starter of seared ahi in lumpia wrappers with wasabi aioli is a signature dish; Kaua'i beef sirloin and grilled pork chops are standards. If you crave something lighter, order a salad with local goat cheese and almonds or the grilled fresh catch, perhaps with a baby spinach ragu. Lunch includes simpler but satisfying options such as a Kaua'i beef burger or fish and chips. The wine list is reasonably priced; ask about the $5 daily, all-day happy hour specials, which you can

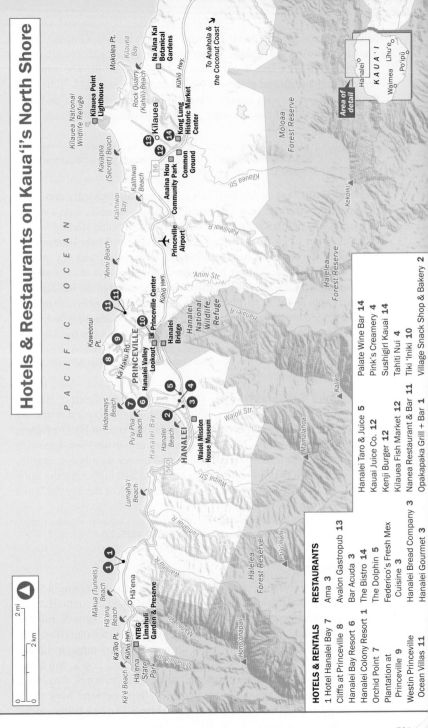

Hotels & Restaurants on Kaua'i's North Shore

HOTELS & RENTALS

1 Hotel Hanalei Bay **7**
Cliffs at Princeville **8**
Hanalei Bay Resort **6**
Hanalei Colony Resort **1**
Orchid Point **7**
Plantation at Princeville **9**
Westin Princeville Ocean Villas **11**

RESTAURANTS

Ama **3**
Avalon Gastropub **13**
Bar Acuda **3**
The Bistro **14**
The Dolphin **5**
Federico's Fresh Mex Cuisine **3**
Hanalei Bread Company **3**
Hanalei Gourmet **3**
Hanalei Taro & Juice **5**
Kauai Juice Co. **12**
Kenji Burger **12**
Kilauea Fish Market **12**
Nanea Restaurant & Bar **11**
Opakapaka Grill + Bar **1**
Palate Wine Bar **14**
Pink's Creamery **4**
Sushigirl Kauai **14**
Tahiti Nui **4**
Tiki 'Iniki **10**
Village Snack Shop & Bakery **2**

Map labels

PACIFIC OCEAN

Mākua (Tunnels) Beach
Hā'ena Beach
Ke'ē Beach
Hā'ena State Park
Kā'ilio Pt.
Limahuli Garden & Preserve
NTBG
Lumaha'i Beach
Wainiha R.
Hā'ena
Mānoa Str.
Hanalei Bay
Puʻu Poa Beach
Hideaways Beach
Kaweonui Pt.
PRINCEVILLE
Hanalei Valley Lookout
Ka Haku Rd.
HANALEI
Waioli Str.
Waioli Mission House Museum
Waipa Str.
Māmālāhoa
Kaliko
Hanalei R.
Hanalei Bridge
Kūhiō Hwy.
Hanalei National Wildlife Refuge
Halelea Forest Reserve
Pōhakumō'ī'ī
Honono'āpali
'Anini Beach
'Anini Str.
Princeville Airport
Kalihiwai Bay
Kalihiwai Beach
Kauapea (Secret) Beach
Kīlauea National Wildlife Refuge
Kīlauea Point Lighthouse
Mokolea Pt.
Kīlauea Bay
Na Aina Kai Botanical Gardens
Rock Quarry (Kahili) Beach
Kīlauea
Kong Lung Historic Market Center
Anaina Hou Community Park
Common Ground
Kūhiō Hwy.
Kīlauea Str.
Moloaa Forest Reserve
Kekoiki
Halelea Forest Reserve
To Anahola & the Coconut Coast

Area of detail
KAUA'I
Hanalei
Līhu'e
Waimea
Po'ipū

0   2 mi
0   2 km

581

pair with live slack-key guitar Thursday and soft jazz on Saturday. *Note:* The owners also run **Palate Wine Bar** ★★ (www.palatewinebar.net; ✆ **808/212-1974**) a few doors down at 2474 Keneke St. The wine bar serves small and shared plates ($14–$33) and flatbreads ($18–$28) daily from 5 to 8:30pm, with quality wine and beer starting at $11 and $5 a glass, respectively. If you like what you drink, buy more at the Palate Market next door.

In Kong Lung Historic Market Center, 2484 Keneke St., Kīlauea. www.thebistro hawaii.com. ✆ **808/828-0480.** Reservations recommended for parties of 6 or more. Main courses $22–$72. Daily 5:30–8:30pm.

Hanalei Gourmet ★ AMERICAN   This casual, decidedly non-gourmet spot offers the best values (by local standards) at lunch, with a variety of burgers and ample sandwiches on freshly baked bread starting at $10; order the latter to go from the deli. The market-priced beer-battered fish and chips, accompanied by a suitably tart Asian slaw and soy wasabi sauce, is also notable. Dinner has higher aspirations, not always met, as well as higher prices, but you can still order from much of the lunch menu. The atmosphere tends to be lively if not downright noisy, thanks to wooden floors, the popular bar, TV, and live music Wednesday to Friday, drawing an enthusiastic local crowd. Service is laidback but friendly.

In Hanalei Center, 5-5161 Kūhiō Hwy., *mauka* side, Hanalei. www.hanaleigourmet. com. ✆ **808/826-2524.** Main courses $8–$13 lunch, $10–$29 dinner. Mon–Fri 11am–7pm; daily happy hour from 5pm.

Opakapaka Grill and Bar ★   On the oceanfront grounds of Hanalei Colony Resort in Hāʻena (p. 564), this relaxed, locally sourced restaurant is the last sit-down restaurant before the end of the road at Hāʻena Beach. Lunch options are simple but satisfying, such as a grilled fish sandwich ($17), fish and chips ($18), and a half-pound burger with bacon, cheese, and sriracha aioli ($19). Dinner prices are about $10 higher for the same items, with a slightly wider selection, including catch of the day ($42) and a 12-oz. ribeye steak ($48).

5-7132 Kūhiō Hwy., *makai* side, Wainiha (shared parking lot with Hanalei Colony Resort). www.opakapakagrillandbar.com. ✆ **808/378-4425.** Main courses $13–$19 lunch; $22–$48 dinner. Daily 11am–8pm.

INEXPENSIVE

Other than places offering plate lunches (p. 578), the best bargains in North Shore dining usually come from food trucks, often found at ʻAnini, Hanalei, and Hāʻena beach parks, but with fickle hours. **Hanalei Taro & Juice** ★ (www.hanaleitaro.com; ✆ **808/651-3399**), *makai* side of Kūhiō Highway, a mile west of the Hanalei Bridge, is open only Friday through Sunday 10am to 4pm. Kalua pork appears in plate lunches, rice bowls, and tacos, with a side of poi, macaroni salad, and other local favorites; taro-based hummus, wraps, and smoothies are good vegetarian options. Most items are under $10. Be sure to sample the banana bread–like taro butter mochi.

Nearby, the tiny storefront **Pink's Creamery** ★, 4489 Aku Rd. (www. pinkscreamerykauai.com; ✆ 808/212-9749), is as justifiably renowned for its grilled-cheese sandwiches on Hawaiian sweet bread with Muenster cheese and optional pineapple and kalua pork ($10–$11, including chips) as it is for 17 flavors of luscious tropical ice cream made on Maui; it's open Tuesday through Saturday 11am to 8pm.

Federico's Fresh Mex Cuisine ★ (✆ 808/320-8394) lives up to its name with no-frills but appealing burritos ($11–$18) and tacos ($6–$7) made with fresh seafood, New Zealand beef, natural chicken, vegan refried beans, and local avocados and tomatoes. It has a tiny dining room at Hanalei Center, 5-5161 Kūhiō Hwy., *mauka* side, Hanalei, open daily 11am to 8pm. Cash only.

South Shore

Sometimes gems truly are hidden. The best poolside restaurant is tucked inside **Kōloa Landing Resort** (p. 568), where Hawaii Regional Cuisine cofounder and "godfather of poke" Sam Choy helped craft the Hawaiian-infused menu at casual **HoloHolo Grill** ★★ (www.holohologrill.com), open for breakfast ($10–$23), lunch ($17–$24), and dinner ($24–$55). The ahi and ginger poke bowl ($24) is a must. In bland Poipu Shopping Village, 2360 Kiahuna Plantation Dr., Po'ipū, **Keoki's Paradise** ★★ (www. keokisparadise.com; ✆ 808/742-7534) is a lively tropical oasis with lush

CHEESEBURGERS IN paradise

Delicious as fresh Hawaiian seafood is, sometimes what you're really looking for—in the words of Jimmy Buffett—is a cheeseburger in paradise. Luckily, Kaua'i boasts several joints bound to satisfy.

Famed for its sassy slogans (WE CHEAT TOURISTS, DRUNKS & ATTORNEYS, among them) as much as for its burgers ($6–$13) made from grass-fed Kaua'i beef, **Bubba's Burgers** ★ (www.bubbaburger.com) claims to have been around since 1936. It's certainly had time to develop a loyal following, even while charging $1.50 for lettuce and tomato. It also offers a vegan Maui taro burger, hot dogs, and chili rice. The original Bubba's is in **Kapa'a,** 4-1421 Kūhiō Hwy. (✆ 808/823-0069), where the deck has a view of the ocean across Kapa'a Beach Park. The **Po'ipū** location is on the *makai* end of the Shops at Kukui'ula, 2829 Ala Kalanikamauka (✆ 808/742-6900), and both are open Tuesday to Saturday 10:30am to 8pm.

From its original location in a small Kapa'a cottage, **Kenji Burger** ★★, 4-788 Kūhiō Hwy., *makai* side (www.kenji burger.com; ✆ 808/320-3558), churns out a surprisingly diverse menu of burgers (including beef, misoyaki fish, and chicken katsu), rice bowls ($10–$14), and only-in-Hawai'i sushi burritos ($15). Don't skip the furikake fries ($5). You can also find the menu at three newer branches: in Līhu'e, at 4454 Nuhou St. (✆ 808/320-8989); in Kīlauea, in the 'Āhuimanu Shopping Center, 2255 Ala Namahana Pkwy. (✆ 808/378-4455); and in Old Town Kōloa, at 5404 Kōloa Rd. (✆ 808/431-4770). All four locations open at 11am and close at 8:30am or 9pm; check website for details or to order online.

garden seating. Part of the same family of restaurants as **Duke's** (p. 574), it serves similarly fresh seafood with local touches, like panko crumbs and furikake seasoning, casual fare like fish tacos and Korean fried chicken sandwiches, and massive pies. It's open Monday to Friday for lunch and dinner 11am to 10pm (main courses $18–$44) and opens at 9am for weekend brunch (main courses $15–$27), with lunch and dinner also till 10pm.

Note: You'll find the restaurants in this section on the "Hotels & Restaurants on Kaua'i's South Shore" map (p. 585).

EXPENSIVE

The Beach House Restaurant ★★ HAWAI'I REGIONAL CUISINE Call it dinner and a show: As sunset approaches, diners at this beloved oceanfront restaurant start leaping from their tables to pose for pictures on the grass-covered promontory, while nearby surfers try to catch one last wave. The genial waiters are as used to cameras being thrust upon them as they are reciting specials featuring local ingredients—a staple here long before "farm to table" became a catchphrase. But there are other good reasons to dine at this restaurant, co-owned by iconic Hawai'i Regional Cuisine chef-restaurateur Peter Merriman. Among them: coconut corn chowder with island kale, tomato, and lemongrass; and the grilled fresh catch with citrus brodo, Parmesan polenta, candied fennel, and local arugula; and the Monkeypod Mai Tai ($19) with *liliko'i* (passion fruit) foam. 5022 Lāwa'i Rd., Kōloa. www.the-beach-house.com. ✆ **808/742-1424.** Reservations recommended. Main courses $35–$63. Daily 3:30–9pm; happy hour 3:30–4:30pm.

Eating House 1849 ★★★ GOURMET PLANTATION Hawai'i Regional Cuisine co-founder Roy Yamaguchi, known for his Roy's chain, created this casual concept inspired by the multicultural plantation era (and named for the islands' first restaurant, founded in Honolulu in 1849). The throngs heading up to this second-story, open-walled dining room in

Butterfish "Kamameshi" (hot pot rice bowl) at Eating House 1849.

Hotels & Restaurants on Kaua'i's South Shore

KAUA'I

Hanalei
Waimea   Līhu'e
Po'ipū

Area of main map

Koula River
Kaumuali'i Hwy.
To Līhu'e
520
'Ōma'o
Kalāheo
Kaumuali'i Hwy.
50
Papalina Rd.
Lāwa'i International Center
Lāwa'i
540
Kukuiolono Park
Hailima Rd.
Kōloa Rd.
Maluhia Rd.
Waita Reservoir
Kaua'i Coffee
Nomilo Fishpond
NTBG Allerton McBryde Gardens
Kōloa
Weliweli Rd.
Ala Kalanikaumaka
Kōloa Bypass Rd.
Haula Beach
Kawaile Bay
Lāwa'i Bay
Spouting Horn
Kukui'ula Bay
Po'ipū Rd.
Po'ipū
Māhā'ulepū (Gillin's) Beach
Makauwahi Cave
Po'ipū Beach
Makawehi Pt.
Keoneloa (Shipwrecks) Beach
Makahuena Pt.

0   2 mi
0   2 km

See detail map below

Ala Kalanikaumaka
Po'ipū Rd.
Prince Kuhio Park
Shops at Kukui'ula
Kiahuna Golf Club
Lāwa'i Rd.
Baby Beach
Ho'onani Rd.
Kapili Rd.
Kiahuna Dr.
Po'ipū Rd.
Kipuka St.
Ala Kinoiki (Kōloa Bypass)
Po'ipū Rd.
PO'IPŪ
Kiahuna Beach
Kānei'olouma
Po'ipū Beach Park
Hoone Rd.
Brennecke's Beach
Hoohu Rd.
Pe'e Rd.
Keoneloa (Shipwrecks) Beach
Makahuena Pt.

0   1/2 mi
0   1/2 km

PACIFIC OCEAN

HOTELS & RENTALS

Grand Hyatt Kauai Resort & Spa **27**
Kahala (Poipu Kai Resort) **26**
Kauai Cove **12**
Kiahuna Plantation Resort **21**
Ko'a Kea Hotel & Resort **23**
Kōloa Landing Resort **16**
Lodge at Kukui'ula **9**
Marjorie's Kaua'i Inn **5**
Nihi Kai Villas **24**
Po'ipū Kapili **17**
Po'ipū Plantation B&B Inn & Vacation Rentals **25**
Prince Kuhio **11**
Sheraton Kauai Resort **18**
Waikomo Stream Villas **15**

RESTAURANTS

Anuenue Cafe **20**
The Beach House Restaurant **10**
Break+Feast **6**
Brick Oven Pizza **3**
Bubba's Burgers **13**
Craving Thai **6**
Da Crack **14**
Eating House 1849 **13**
The Fresh Shave **4**
HoloHolo Grill **16**
Kalāheo Café & Coffee Co. **2**

Kenji Burger **6**
Kiawe Roots **4**
Keoki's Paradise **20**
Koloa Fish Market **8**
La Spezia **7**
Little Fish Coffee **22**
Merriman's Fish House **13**
Paco's Tacos Cantina **1, 19**
Red Salt **23**
RumFire Poipu Beach **18**
Savage Shrimp **13**
Sueoka's Snack Shop **5**

the Shops at Kukui'ula know the food is predictably excellent. Executive chef Clinton Nuyda's culinary finesse and local beef, fish, and produce ensure excellent preparations of "humble" fare such as pork and crab pillows ($16), Hapa burger made of grass-fed Kaua'i beef and wild boar ($27), and *kamameshi* (hot-pot rice bowl) with butterfish ($45).

In the Shops at Kukui'ula, 2829 Ala Kalanikaumaka St., Poipu. www.royyamaguchi.com/eating-house-koloa. ℂ **808/742-5000.** Reservations recommended. Main courses $20–$68. Daily 5–9pm; happy hour 4–5pm; Sat–Sun brunch 10:30am–2pm.

Merriman's Fish House ★★ AMERICAN/ISLAND FARM A pioneer in Hawai'i Regional Cuisine, Maui-based chef Peter Merriman first expanded onto Kaua'i with this fine-dining restaurant, an airy space on the second floor of the plantation-style Shops at Kukui'ula, before joining the Beach House operation. This setting may be less scenic, but the emphasis on fresh, locally sourced ingredients—such as sweet Kaua'i shrimp and Kona lobster, smoked taro, wok-charred ahi, and juicy tomatoes—and the expertise in preparing them are equally memorable. Live music (roughly 5:30–8pm) adds to the ambience Monday, Tuesday, and Thursday.

In the Shops at Kukui'ula, second floor, 2829 Ala Kalanikaumaka St., Po'ipū. www.merrimanshawaii.com. ℂ **808/742-2856.** Main courses $36–$69 (most $48–$46). Daily 4:30–8:30pm; happy hour 4–5pm.

Red Salt ★★★ HAWAI'I REGIONAL CUISINE One of the best hotel restaurants on Kaua'i, this is also one of the smallest and hardest to find, tucked inside the discreetly located **Ko'a Kea Hotel & Resort** (p. 567). Although rivals offer more dramatic ocean views in plusher settings (and with less chilly air-conditioning), Red Salt has consistently executed elegantly presented dishes from a menu first designed by El Bulli–trained chef Ronnie Sanchez in 2009. Kaua'i native Noelani Planas, who trained under Joel Robuchon and Wolfgang Puck, became executive chef in 2016. Her furikake-crusted ahi steak ($52) shines with yuzu beurre blanc and coconut milk-infused black rice, while her Kona lobster risotto ($62) is plump with leeks, asparagus, and mushrooms; the latter is on Planas' four-course tasting menu ($145). Beef lovers can also splurge on a Wagyu beef burger with lobster and truffle fries ($60) or filet mignon ($75). The adjacent sushi bar serves exquisite sashimi and sushi, along

Sushi at Red Salt at Ko'a Kea Hotel & Resort.

with small plates such as kalua pork potstickers and crab cakes. Red Salt is also open for breakfast; the house specialty, lemon-pineapple souffle pancakes drizzled with caramel, take 20 minutes, but are worth the wait, if not the cost ($29).

Koa Kea Hotel & Resort, 2251 Po'ipū Rd., Po'ipū. www.koakea.com/red-salt. **808/ 742-4288.** Dinner reservations recommended. Main courses $24–$35 breakfast; $32–$85 dinner (most $48); sushi rolls $25–$32. Daily 7–11am breakfast; 5:30–8:30pm dinner and sushi bar.

MODERATE

For a breakfast reflecting the many cultures of Kaua'i—curry veggie scramble, kalbi bibimbap, loco moco, and pork hash are among the rib-sticking entrees ($17–$26)—book a table at **Break+Feast** ★★ (www. breakandfast.com; © **808/431-4508**), in the Village at Koloa Village, 5640 Kōloa Rd. It's open Tuesday to Sunday 8am to 1pm.

Two former food trucks that morphed into restaurants are worth taking a seat. **Savage Shrimp** ★, at the Shops at Kukui'ula, 2829 Ala Kalani-kaumaka St., Po'ipū (www.savageshrimp.com; © **808/320-3021**), churns out affordable shrimp plates ($17) with minimal ambience. Savage Shrimp's former upstairs neighbor **Kiawe Roots** ★★, 2-3687 Kaumali'i Hwy., Lāwa'i (www.eatatkiawe.com; © **808/855-5055**), continues to have a devoted following for its Filipino, Asian, and Latin American dishes flavored by kiawe (mesquite) barbecue. It's now open Tuesday through Saturday for dinner ($15–$45) 4 to 8:30pm. Try the brisket plate with peppered guava sauce and calamansi slaw ($24).

La Spezia ★★★ ITALIAN   The definition of charming, this much-needed stylish but cozy bistro in Old Kōloa Town doesn't accept reservations for parties of fewer than six—reason enough to make a few friends at the pool to join you for dinner. Still, walk-ins will find it worth the possible wait for a table, handmade from wine crates by co-owner Dan Seltzer; don't hesitate to sit at the small but handsome bar either. Stalwarts on the seasonal, homestyle menu include rib-sticking lasagna Bolognese, chicken scaloppini with fettucine and pancetta rosemary cream, and eggplant Parmesan arrabbiata with pesto linguine.

5492 Kōloa Rd., Kōloa (across from the post office). www.laspeziakauai.com. © **808/742-8824.** Reservations accepted for parties of 6 or more. Main courses $21–$38. Tues–Sat 5–9pm.

INEXPENSIVE

In addition to the listings below, pop into **Little Fish Coffee** ★★ (www. littlefishcoffee.com; © **808/742-2113**) in Po'ipū for fresh pastries, salads, panini, and beautifully swirled coffee and tea drinks. It's at the entrance to the Poipu Beach Athletic Club, 2290 Po'ipū Rd., and open daily 7:30am to 1pm. **Anuenue Cafe** ★ © **808/469-7000**) in Poipu Shopping Village opens daily at 8am, serving locally sourced omelets, macnut pancakes, and kalua pig sandwiches, among other treats, until noon. In the Kukui'ula strip mall, 2827 Po'ipū Rd., **Da Crack** ★ (www.dacrackkauai.com; © **808/742-9505**) is a takeout window where a line often forms for fish tacos with wasabi cream and the massive but relatively healthy burritos (vegan beans, brown rice); it's open daily 11am to 8pm.

In Old Town Kōloa, check out **Craving Thai** ★, 3477 Weliweli Rd., next to Koloa Zipline (© **808/634-9959**), dishing out noodles and curries Monday to Friday 11:30am to 3pm and 4 to 7pm. Nearby, **the Fresh Shave** ★★, 5356 Kōloa Rd. (www.thefreshshave.com; © **808/631-2222**), serves fluffy, artisanal shave ice topped with the freshest of natural syrups.

Brick Oven Pizza ★ PIZZA   This local favorite is relatively easy on the budget—the 12-slice pizzas, featuring hand-tossed crusts, are genuinely large. Pastas, subs, and salads are basic but well priced; decadent dessert pizzas come topped with Snickers and the like. For island flavors, order the kimchi tofu or guava-glazed smoked pork appetizers at the bar, which has a broad beer list. *Note:* Gluten-free crusts are available for a $4 surcharge.
2-2555 Kaumali'i Hwy., *mauka* side, Kalāheo (across the street from Kalāheo Cafe). www.brickovenpizzahawaii.com. © **808/332-8561.** $12–$22 sandwiches; $22–$24 pastas; $22–$31 medium (10-slice) pizzas, $28–$41 large (12-slice). Wed–Mon 11am–9pm.

Kalaheo Café & Coffee Co. ★★ BAKERY/ISLAND CAFE   Whether you just grab a freshly baked cookie and cup of Kaua'i coffee to go or make a full meal of it, you'll quickly discover why visitors and locals jockey for parking spots at this casual restaurant and bakery with counter service. Early hours and hearty breakfasts (including convenient wraps) make it a popular stop on the way to snorkel cruises or Waimea Canyon. About a 15-minute drive from Po'ipū, the cafe also offers a great alternative to high-priced resort dining. Greens grown nearby dominate the extensive salad list, while the rustic housemade buns pair nicely with grass-fed Kaua'i beef, veggie, or turkey burgers, among other plump sandwiches. Breakfast portions are huge and delicious. Dinner is on the pricier side, but fresh seafood—such as blackened ahi with kale Caesar—and the Hunan-style pork ribs shine.
2-2560 Kaumali'i Hwy., *makai* side, Kalāheo (across from Brick Oven Pizza). www.kalaheo.com. © **808/332-5858.** Main courses $8–$19 breakfast; $8–$18 lunch; $17–$41 dinner. Breakfast Wed–Sun 7am–11:30am; lunch Wed–Sat 11am–8pm; dinner Wed–Sat 5–8pm; Sun breakfast available until closing.

West Side

With fewer hotels, the West Side offers mostly unassuming food options with limited hours (typically closed Sun). Many visitors just stop in Waimea for shave ice, especially **Jo-Jo's Shave Ice** ★ at 9734 Kaumali'i Hwy., *makai* side, across from the high school (© **808/378-4712**).

Near Waimea Canyon, visit the **Kōke'e Lodge** ★★, 3600 Kōke'e Rd. (www.kokee.com; © **808/335-6061**), for locally inspired breakfast and lunch entrees ($13–$21) from 9:30am to 4:30pm daily (kitchen closes at 4pm). Hikers will appreciate the hearty Portuguese bean soup ($13) or chili (beef or veggie, $15), or a pick-me-up slice of *liliko'i* chiffon or warmed coconut chocolate macadamia pie with an espresso or pour-over coffee from Kaua'i Roastery. Anything made with Hanapēpē's Midnight Bear sourdough is delicious, too. *Note:* The in-house Koa Bar's cocktails ($11–$13) are also tasty. Enjoy a tipple with live music Tuesday, Wednesday and Friday to Sunday 1 to 3pm. Once you've driven down from the canyon, **Chicken in a Barrel ★** (*©* **808/320-8397**) at Waimea Plantation Cottages (p. 571) in Waimea makes a convenient stop for barbecue (plates $15–$20) or a brew from its self-serve beer wall; it's also one of the rare restaurants in this area that's open daily (and for all three meals)—in this case, 8:30am to 8pm Monday to Thursday and Friday to Sunday until 9pm.

Hanapēpē can claim the island's best bakery, **Midnight Bear Breads ★★★**, 3830 Hanapēpē Rd. (www.midnightbearbreads.com; *©* **808/335-2893**), which makes crusty European loaves, flaky croissants, and other island-sourced, organic baked goods, including pizzas and sandwiches. It's open Wednesday to Saturday 8am to 3pm but be aware it may be cleaned out hours before closing. Spacious courtyard seating and excellent, organic Japanese and island-style dishes (including sushi, $9–$22) make for a wonderful lunch or dinner at **Japanese Grandma's Cafe ★★**, 3871 Hanapēpē Rd. (www.japanesegrandma.com; *©* **808/855-5016**). It's open Thursday to Monday for lunch 11:30am to 2:30pm, cocktails and pupus 2:30 to 5pm, and dinner 5 to 8pm. Not a fan of fish? Try the avocado poke with sea asparagus ($18) with an order of sauteed mushroom tacos with yuzu wasabi aioli ($14) or seared tofu with tamari garlic ginger sauce ($15).

MODERATE

Kaua'i Island Brewery & Grill ★★ BREWPUB   The founders of the former Waimea Brewing Company opened this snazzy industrial/loft-style microbrewery and restaurant in Port Allen in 2012. The *liliko'i* ale—one of up to 10 house brews on tap—flavors the batter on fish and chips, but I prefer the silken ahi poke with seaweed salad or the blackened grilled catch of the day. The menu includes fish tacos, burgers (with a falafel veggie option), and other sandwiches. The open-air mezzanine provides an angled view of sunset over the harbor—and it can be mobbed when snorkel boats return midafternoon. *Note:* The kitchen closes at 9pm, but the bar may stay open later.

4350 Waialo Rd., Port Allen. www.kauaiislandbrewing.com. *©* **808/335-0006.** Main courses $11–$17. Daily 11am–9pm; happy hour 3–5pm.

Wrangler's Steakhouse ★ STEAK/SEAFOOD   Like a steer in a rodeo, service here can be poky or lightning fast, but as the only full-service restaurant in town, it's often worth it even if you have to sit a spell. Steaks ($33–$43) come in a variety of cuts and preparations, including grilled over kiawe (mesquite), topped with red wine peppercorn gravy, or glistening in garlic butter. There's even Cowboy Poke ($15), cubes of sauteed prime rib, onions, bell peppers, and mushrooms under a dollop of creamy horseradish. This isn't a place to take vegetarians, but seafood eaters have a couple of options, including shrimp scampi over linguine ($23); specials often include BBQ pork ribs ($25). The cozy **Saddle Room** ★★ next door serves burgers and fish sandwiches, but with a more ambitious cocktail menu, such as the Kōke'e Mule with passion fruit vodka ($10).

9852 Kaumali'i Hwy., *makai* side, Waimea (at Halepule Rd.). ℂ **808/338-1218. Wrangler's:** Main courses $21–$68 dinner. **Saddle Room** burgers and small plates $8–$18. Tues–Sat 5–9pm.

INEXPENSIVE

In Waimea, go to **Gina's Anykine Grinds Cafe** ★, 9691 Kaumali'i Hwy., *mauka* side by the theater (ℂ **808/338-1731**), for casual breakfast and lunch ($5–$12), or just killer handheld coconut pies ($3). It's open Tuesday to Thursday 8am to 2pm, Friday 7am to 1pm, and Saturday 8am to 1pm. For lunch or early dinner, shrimp platters ($20) are the stars at **the Shrimp Station** ★, 9652 Kaumali'i Hwy., Waimea, *makai* side, at Mākeke Rd. (www.theshrimpstation.net; ℂ **808/338-1242**). If you don't want to get your hands messy peeling shrimp, order the chopped shrimp tacos, a fried shrimp burger, or the fried coconut shrimp with a zesty papaya ginger tartar sauce. The open-air picnic tables do attract flies, so consider making yours a to-go order. It's open daily 11am to 5pm.

KAUA'I SHOPPING

Kaua'i has more than a dozen open-air shopping centers and historic districts well suited to browsing, so souvenir and gift hunters are unlikely to leave the island empty-handed. To find something unique to the Garden Isle, look for the purple KAUA'I MADE logo. The image of a *ho'okupu,* the *ti*-leaf wrapping for special presents, means the county certifies that these handicrafts and food items were made on the island using local materials where possible, and in relatively small batches. Search for them by type of product or region at **www.kauaimade.net**.

Below are some of the island's more distinctive shopping stops. *Note:* Many stores are closed Sunday and at least one weekday; hours change frequently, but tend to be shorter than on the mainland, too.

East Side

LĪHU'E

The island's largest mall, **Kukui Grove Center,** 3-2600 Kaumali'i Hwy., *makai* side at Nāwiliwili Road (www.kukuigrovecenter.com), lost its flagship department store, **Macy's,** in 2024. Still, residents and visitors appreciate the competitively priced, locally made foodstuffs (coffees, jams, cookies, and the like) as well as necessities at **Longs Drugs** (ℂ **808/245-8871**). The mall's family-run **Déjà Vu Surf Hawaii** (www.dejavusurf. com; ℂ **808/320-7169**) has a full selection of local and national brands.

Parents should stop by **Small Fry Kauai** (https://smallfrykauai.com; ✆ **808/212-1794**), conveniently by the mall's Keiki Korner Playground, for island-made T-shirts and other kids' clothing, plus toys, children's books, and nursery decor.

Anchor Cove, 3416 Rice St., and **Harbor Mall,** 3501 Rice St. (www.harbormall.net), two small shopping centers near Nāwiliwili Harbor, mostly offer typical T-shirts, aloha wear, and souvenirs. Harbor Mall has a free trolley shuttle for cruise ship passengers to their dock.

The Shops at Kilohana lie within the graceful 1930s mansion of Kilohana Plantation, 3-2087 Kaumali'i Hwy., *mauka* side, south of Kaua'i Community College (www.kilohanakauai.com). It's a handsome setting for a half-dozen boutiques selling locally made, Hawaiian-inspired artwork, jewelry, clothing, and vintage Hawaiiana. Don't miss the handmade guava and sea salt caramels at **Kauai Sweet Shoppe** (✆ **808/245-8458**) or the stand-alone **Koloa Rum Co.** (www.koloarum.com; ✆ **808/246-8900**), which carries six kinds of its locally made rum, rum-based treats, and nonalcoholic goodies. Adults 21 and older can book one of the hourly tasting sessions at the handsome bar (Mon–Sat 10am–4pm) that sample four rums in various combinations.

Near the turnoff for Wailua Falls, the **Koa Store,** 3-3601 Kūhiō. Hwy. (www.thekoastore.com; ✆ **808/245-4871**), showcases boxes, picture frames, and other small pieces by local woodworkers. Nearby, you'll find tropical-print fabrics and clothes, batiks, and Hawaiian quilts at **Kapaia Stitchery,** 3-3351 Kūhiō Hwy., *mauka* side at Laukini Road (www.kapaiastitchery.com; ✆ **808/245-2281**).

COCONUT COAST

The flagship of the open-air **Coconut MarketPlace,** 4-484 Kūhiō Hwy., *makai* side, Kapa'a (www.coconutmarketplace.com), is **Island Country Markets** (✆ **808/821-6800**), an upscale souvenir store, deli, and supermarket. To see Stephanie Deng's elegant jewelry created with brilliantly hued shells and pearls, peek inside **Kauai Handmade** (www.kauaihandmadejewelry.com; ✆ **808/482-9245**). At **Kauai Pottery** (✆ **505/919-9813**), Reda Awadallah's jewelry and ceramic tiles, mugs, and other pottery gleam like a rainbow. The center also presents frequent and free live entertainment in the courtyard (see website for calendar), plus a farmers market every Tuesday and Thursday 9am to 1pm.

In the tiny Kinipopo Shopping Village, 4-369 Kūhiō Hwy., *makai* side, **Pagoda** (www.pagodakauai.com; ✆ **808/821-2172**), ably fills its niche with Chinese antiques and curios, Hawaiiana, Asian-inspired decor, candles, soaps, and other gifts. Hidden behind a Taco Bell, **Nani Moon Meadery,** 4-939 Kūhiō Hwy., *mauka* side (https://nanimoonmead.com; ✆ **808/651-2453**), recommends reservations for tastings ($30, for ages 21 and up, maximum of six people) of its naturally produced honey-based wines, or mead. Akin to tropical sun in a bottle, the silky wines come in six varieties with fragrant notes such as starfruit, passion fruit, cacao, ginger, pineapple, and lime. Shipping (assuming your place of residence allows) is a flat $15, or free with $100 purchase.

The historic (and hippie) district of Old Town Kapaʻa (www.ourkapaa.com) offers an intriguing mix of shops, cafes, and galleries. Natural fibers rule the day at **Island Hemp & Cotton,** 4-1373 Kūhiō Hwy., *mauka* side (at Huluʻili St.; ✆ **808/821-0225**), featuring stylish clothing, backpacks, home items, and gifts. Flowy harem pants, earth-toned coverups, daring bikinis, mineral sunscreen, and other beach apparel and necessities, many locally made, are in good supply at **Salt+Sea,** 4-1435 Kūhiō Hwy., *mauka* side (at Lehua St.; www.saltandseakauai.com; ✆ **808/378-4554**). Learn to play *kōnane,* an indigenous game similar to checkers, and buy a take-home set at **Sole Mates,** 4-1286 Kūhiō Hwy., *makai* side (at rear of building off Inia St.; ✆ **808/822-2180**). Co-owners John and Juliet Kaʻohelauliʻi are happy to "talk story" about Hawaiian cultural practices, too, or help you find a stylish pair of "slippahs" (flip-flops) in their store.

North Shore

ANAHOLA

The Native Hawaiian-operated **Anahola Marketplace,** 4523 Iaone Rd. (www.anaholamarketplace.org; ✆ **808/431-4067**), offers locally made food, clothes, accessories, and other goods and services in a collection of humble buildings just off the *mauka* side of Kūhiō Highway, amid fertile farms in the shadow of green mountains.

KĪLAUEA

On the way to Kauapea (Secret) Beach and the lighthouse, **Kong Lung Historic Market Center,** 2484 Keneke St., deserves its own slot on the itinerary, with a bakery, bistro, and a half-dozen chic shops in vintage buildings with historical markers. Of the stores, the flagship **Kong Lung Trading** (www.konglung.com; ✆ **808/828-1822**) is a showcase for Asian-themed ceramics, jewelry, books, and home accessories, including hand-turned wood bowls.

Across the road from Kong Lung is **Ahuimanu,** 2555 Ala Namahana Pkwy. (www.ahuimanu.com; ✆ **808/664-8333**), a cluster of modern plantation-style cottages with mostly restaurants and service providers. The retail options are good ones, though: **Sway Island Living** (✆ **808/278-8816**), a companion home goods store to Sway Hanalei boutique (p. 593); **Island Soap & Candle Works** (www.islandsoap.com; ✆ **808/828-1955**), which creates luscious, tropically scented candles and body products; and the luminous Tahitian pearls, Australian opals, and other adornments at family-owned **Kilauea Fine Jewelry** (www.kilaueafinejewelry.com; ✆ **808/431-4100**).

PRINCEVILLE

Although **Princeville Center,** 5-4280 Kūhiō Highway, *makai* side, north of the main Princeville entrance (www.princevillecenter.com), is mostly known for its inexpensive dining and resident-focused businesses, the **Hawaiian Music Store** kiosk outside Foodland grocery has good deals on a wide selection of CDs. **Magic Dragon Toy & Art Supply** (© 808/826-9144) has a compact but cheery array of rainy-day entertainment for kids. The equally petite but packed-to-the gills **Princeville Wine Market** (https://princevillewinemarket.com; © 808/826-0040) has a well-curated selection of alcoholic drinks and locally made items such as Lydgate Farms Chocolate and Kauai Nectar Co. honey. Look for "Lilikoicello" (passion fruit limoncello) and other products from **Hanalei Spirits** (https://hanaleispirits.com; © 808/977-0663), which distills premium craft vodka, rum, gin, and other spirits from island ingredients—some grown at its lovely farm in Kīlauea, where tours are available by appointment. *Note:* Princeville Center hosts a free hour-long hula show in the open-air food court Saturdays at 1:30pm; a night market with live music and local vendors is the second Sunday of the month 4 to 8pm.

HANALEI

Two eclectic shopping and dining complexes in historic buildings face each other on Kūhiō Highway in the center of town. In the two-story rabbit warren of **Ching Young Village Shopping Center** (www.chingyoungvillage.com; © 808/826-7222), **Divine Planet** (www.divine-planet.com; © 808/826-8970) brims with beads, star-shaped lanterns, silver jewelry from Thailand and India, and Balinese quilts; it also has stores in Old Kōloa Town (© 808/742-0281) and Kapaʻa (© 808/212-0999). **Sway Hanalei** (© 808/826-7360) stocks cute cropped T-shirts, beach coverups, straw hats, filmy sundresses, faded jeans, ocean-inspired body products, and other "beach lifestyle" items.

Across the street, the old Hanalei Schoolhouse now serves a retail role as the **Hanalei Center,** 5-5161 Kūhiō Hwy.; poke around it to find **Yellowfish Trading Company** (www.yellowfishtradingcompany.com; © 808/826-1227) and **Havaiki Oceanic and Tribal Art** (www.havaikiart.com; © 808/826-7606). At Yellowfish, retro hula girl lamps, vintage textiles and pottery, and collectible Hawaiiana mingle with reproduction signs, painted guitars, and other beach-shack musts in ever-changing inventory. The owners of Havaiki have sailed across the Pacific many times to obtain their museum-quality collection of gleaming wood bowls and fishhooks, exotic masks, shell jewelry, and intricately carved weapons and paddles; they also sell CDs, handmade cards, and other less-expensive gifts.

South Shore

KŌLOA

Between the tree tunnel road and beaches of Poʻipū, **Old Kōloa Town** (www.oldkoloa.com) has the usual tourist trinkets and a few chain apparel shops like **Billabong** and **Crazy Shirts,** but it's worth a stop to peruse the historic photos and signs on the vintage plantation buildings. Try a gourmet shave ice at the **Fresh Shave** (www.thefreshshave.com), sample locally roasted nuts at **Kauai Gourmet Nuts** (www.kauaigourmetnuts.com), or pick up a bottle at the island's best wine shop, **the Wine Shop** (www.thewineshopkauai.com; © **808/742-7305**). The latter also sells high-quality, locally made treats such as Monkeypod Jam. A cluster of modern cottages designed to look old, **the Village** at Koloa Village (www.koloavillage.com/the-village) opened in 2023 and continues to add shops and restaurants, including an outpost of Honolulu's **Ali'i Coffee** (www.aliicoffee.com; © **808/724-1707**) and the national chain **Flip Flop Shops.**

LĀWA'I

On the road between Kōloa and Kalāheo, **Warehouse 3540,** 3540 Kōloa Rd. (www.warehouse-3540.com), provides a rustic-industrial space for moderately priced, pop-up style boutiques selling gifts, jewelry, home decor, and art. The limited hours of Monday to Saturday 10am to 4pm are offset by delicious coffee from Kind Koffee (available 8am–3pm) and treats from other vendors (most open 11am–7pm).

Just up the road, at the intersection with Kaumali'i Highway, is **Hawaiian Trading Post,** 3427 Kōloa Rd. (https://hawaiiantradingpostkauai.com; © **808/332-7404**), a family operation founded in 1985. It looks kitschy on the outside (and has a fair amount of kitsch inside), but also sells black pearls, Ni'ihau shells, and other well-made jewelry, gifts, and clothes at decent prices; shop carefully, because returns are not allowed.

PO'IPŪ

Besides browsing the two main shopping centers here, bargain hunters should check to see if crafts and jewelry vendors are in residence at Spouting Horn (p. 518). The entrance to the **National Tropical Botanic Garden's South Shore Visitor Center,** 4425 Lāwa'i Rd. (www.ntbg.org; © **808/332-7324**), is just across the street from Spouting Horn; head up the driveway to check out the gift shop where people check in for their tour.

Poipu Shopping Village, 2360 Kiahuna Plantation Dr. (www.poipushoppingvillage.com), hosts gift shops, independent boutiques, and Hawai'i–based resort and surfwear chains; it also presents a free hula show Monday and Thursday at 5pm, and a farmers market with craft demonstrations and live music the first and third Tuesday of each month from 4 to 7pm.

The plantation-style cottages of the **Shops at Kukui'ula,** just off the Po'ipū Road roundabout (www.theshopsatkukuiula.com), have even more intriguing—and often expensive—boutiques spread among flowering hibiscus. Amid all the high-end chic, surfers will feel right at home in **Poipu Surf** (www.poipusurf.com; © **808/742-8797**) and **Quiksilver** (run by Déjà Vu Surf Hawaii; www.dejavusurf.com; © **808/320-7178**). The open-air center is also home to the flagship store of **Mālie Organics Lifestyle Boutique** (www.malie.com; © **808/339-3055**), renowned for its bath and beauty products based on distillations of island plants, including mango, plumeria, and the native, lightly spice-scented *maile* vine. Regular activities include lawn games, a Wednesday culinary market from 3:30 to 6pm, and a Hawaiian music concert Fridays 5:30 to 7:30pm.

KALĀHEO

The crisp, tropical-flavored butter cookies of **Kauai Kookie** (www.kauai kookie.com) are ubiquitous in Hawai'i. Even better than a trip to the factory store in Hanapēpē (1-3529 Kaumali'i Hwy., *makai* side; Mon–Fri 8am–5pm) is a stop at the **Kauai Kookie Kalaheo Marketplace, Bakery & Cafe** in Kalāheo, 2-2436 Kaumali'i Hwy., *makai* side (✆ **808/631-6851**). It includes a small cafe selling specialty baked goods as well as a variety of "kookies" and a gift shop, with long hours: Monday to Friday 6am to 8pm and Saturday and Sunday 6:30am to 8pm.

West Side

HANAPĒPĒ

Known for its Friday-night festival (see "Kaua'i Nightlife," p. 597), the historic town center of Hanapēpē and its dozen-plus art galleries and shops are just as pleasant to peruse by day. Don't miss the playful tiles, prints, and beautifully illustrated children's books at **Banana Patch Studio,** 3865 Hanapēpē Rd. (www.bananapatchstudio.com; ✆ **808/335-5944**), or the bold, textured canvases of Tess Sieradzki at **Kalakoa Kaua'i Fine Arts Gallery,** 3848 Hanapēpē Rd., across from the Swinging Bridge path (https://kalakoakauai.com; ✆ **808/335-6468**).

If the door is open, the store is open at tiny **Taro Ko Chips Factory,** 3940 Hanapēpē Rd. (✆ **808/335-5586**), where dry-land taro farmer Dale Nagamine slices and fries his harvest—along with potatoes, purple sweet potatoes, and breadfruit—into delectable chips for $6 a bag (cash only). You might not get a friendly greeting—the owner is strictly business—but his potato chips sprinkled with *li hing mui* are worth the possibly terse exchange. The wares of **Aloha Spice Company,** 3857 Hanapēpē Rd. (www.alohaspice.com; ✆ **808/335-5960**), include grill-ready seasonings with a base of Hawaiian sea salt, and Hawaiian cane sugar infused with hibiscus, vanilla, or passion fruit. **Talk Story Bookstore,** 3785 Hanapēpē Rd. (www.talkstorybookstore.com; ✆ **808/335-6469**), boasts the island's biggest trove of new, used, and out-of-print books. It's also a reliable source for locally designed tote bags, T-shirts, and humorous stickers, including a line based on Celeste, the bookstore's famously bossy feline who died in 2022.

PORT ALLEN

Chocolate fiends need to try the luscious handmade truffles, fudge, and "opihi" (chocolate-covered Kauai Kookie shortbread, caramel, and macadamia nuts in the shape of a shell) at **Kauai Chocolate Company,** 4353 Waialo Rd. (https://kauaichocolate.com; ✆ **808/335-0448**). You can watch them being made on-site, too.

Kaua'i FARMERS MARKETS

A trip to one of the two county-sponsored **Sunshine Markets** is a fun glimpse into island life, with shoppers lined up before the official start—listen for a yell or car honk—to buy fresh produce at rock-bottom prices. On Wednesdays, head to **Kapa'a** for the Sunshine Market in the New Town Ball Park parking lot, 4600–4999 Kahau St., from 3 to 4:30pm. On Thursday **Hanapēpē** hosts a market from 3 to 4pm at Hanapēpē Park, 4481 Kona Rd.

For an even more abundant farmers market, with many chef-prepared foods, head to **Kaua'i Community Market,** at Kaua'i Community College, 3-1901 Kaumali'i Hwy., Līhu'e, Saturdays 9:30am to 1pm (www.kauaicommunitymarket. org). Līhu'e also has another, smaller farmers market Monday 3 to 4:30pm in the south side parking lot at Kukui Grove Center, 3-2600 Kaumali'i Hwy. (at Nāwiliwili Rd.).

A free hula show at 12:30pm adds to the enchanting atmosphere of the **Aloha Market** (https://ntbg.org/events/aloha), Thursday 10am to 2pm at the South Shore Visitor Center of the National Tropical Botanic Garden, 4425 Lāwa'i Rd., Kōloa. It's a great spot to pick up lunch after a garden tour, too (p. 594).

North Shore farmers markets offer the most organic produce. In **Kīlauea,** that includes the **Anaina Hou Farmers Market** at Anaina Hou Community Park in Kīlauea, *mauka* side of Kūhiō Highway (www.anainahou.org; ✆ **808/828-2118**), Saturday 9am to noon. The popular **Waipā Farmers Market** (www.waipa foundation.org; ✆ **808/826-9969**) takes place Tuesdays from 2pm to dusk at its farm site on the western end of **Hanalei,** *mauka* side of Kūhiō Highway, between the one-lane Wai'oli and Waipā bridges. Vendors sell baked goods, jewelry, and other crafts. A similar market is Saturdays 9am to noon at the bustling **Hanalei Farmers Market** at Hale Halawai ballpark, 5-5299 Kūhiō Hwy., *mauka* side at Mahimahi Road, next to the green church in Hanalei (www.halehalawai.org; ✆ **808/826-1011**). The market also hosts an all-levels yoga class from 10:30am to noon ($1–$25 sliding-scale donation).

WAIMEA

Like Kauai Kookies, the passion fruit (*liliko'i*) products of **Aunty Lilikoi** (www.auntylilikoi.com; ✆ 808/338-1296)—including jellies, mustards, syrups, and salad dressings—are often found around the state, but the factory store at 9875 Waimea Rd., across from the Captain Cook statue, offers shipping and in-store-only delicious baked goods, such as scones, bars, and fudge.

In Kōke'e State Park (p. 519), the **Kōke'e Museum** (www.kokee. org; ✆ 808/335-9975) sells Kaua'i- and nature-themed books, maps, and DVDs, plus hiking sticks, T-shirts, and Kaua'i-made gifts, while **Kōke'e Lodge** (www.kokeelodge.com; ✆ 808/335-6061) offers a few souvenirs, island foods, and locally made crafts in a shop that has the same hours as its bar (daily 9:30am–4:30pm). The restaurant closes a half-hour earlier, so be sure to eat first, then shop.

KAUA'I NIGHTLIFE

Local nightlife is more suited to moonlight strolls than late-night partying. Most venues feature gentle Hawaiian music and close before 9pm.

Inside the Royal Sonesta Kaua'i Resort (p. 558) in Līhu'e, **Duke's Barefoot Bar** (www.dukeskauai.com; ℭ **808/246-9599**) draws a crowd of visitors and locals, especially at *pau hana* (end of work) on Friday. The downstairs bar offers live Hawaiian music from 6 to 8pm daily, plus Monday to Saturday 3:30 to 5:30pm and Sunday brunch 9:30 to 11:30am.

At **Hukilau Lanai** (www.hukilaukauai.com; ℭ **808/822-0600**), inside the Kauai Coast Resort at the Beachboy, 520 'Aleka Loop, Kapa'a, a rotating roster of musicians plays in its lounge, known as Wally's Lobby Bar, Wednesday through Saturday 5:30 to 8:30pm. It's typically Hawaiian music on weeknights and pop standards on Saturday; you're in luck if recording artist Mike Keale is playing because his wife Linda often accompanies him with hula.

In Po'ipū, the **Grand Hyatt Kauai** (www.grandhyattkauai.com; ℭ **808/741-1234**) offers live Hawaiian entertainment with sunset views in **Seaview Terrace** Sunday to Friday from 5 to 7pm and 7:30 to 9pm; the earlier Friday entertainment begins with a torch-lighting ceremony. The innovative Euro-Asian pop duo Falling Down Romance performs most Saturdays from 6:30 to 9:30pm.

In Princeville, head to the oceanview **Happy Talk Lounge** at Hanalei Bay Resort, 5380 Honoiki Rd. (www.happytalklounge; ℭ **808/431-4084**), which hosts live music from 6 to 9pm. Mike Keale holds the fort on Sundays, Falling Down Romance takes Mondays, and Hawaiian music artists fill up the rest of the week. It's also a restaurant, but no reservations are taken, making it easier to find a seat.

You'll meet more residents—and pay a lot less for your drinks—by leaving the resort hotels. Here are highlights from around the island:

EAST SIDE   A combination sports bar, family restaurant, and nightclub, **Rob's Good Times Grill,** in the Rice Shopping Center, 4303 Rice St., Līhu'e (www.kauaisportsbarandgrill.com; ℭ **808/246-0311**), bustles with live music Wednesday, Friday, and Saturday 4 to 10pm, plus a trivia night Thursday for teams of up to six (call to reserve). The first Saturday of the month, Old Kapa'a Town's partylike **Ho'olaulea Multi-Cultural Event** (https://kbakauai.org/first-saturday-art-walk) includes live music from 5 to 9pm, plus food and crafts vendors; many stores stay open late, too. Look for the copious free parking at Restore Kauai, 4451 Lehua St., within a short walk of Old Town.

NORTH SHORE   Opened in 1963, and still family run, **Tahiti Nui,** 5-5122 Kūhiō Hwy., Hanalei (www.thenui.com; ℭ **808/826-6277;** Sun– Fri 11am–9pm), morphs from a kid-friendly restaurant with delicious island-style fare into a locals' lounge with nightly live music 6:30 to 8:30pm. In the Old Hanalei Schoolhouse, **Hanalei Gourmet,** 5-5161 Kūhiō Hwy. (www.hanaleigourmet.com; © **808/826-2524**), cranks up live music Wednesday to Friday 5 to 7pm.

SOUTH SHORE Popular with visitors for dining, too, **Keoki's Paradise** (p. 583) in Poipu Shopping Village usually features Hawaiian music performers Monday to Thursday 5:30 to 8:30pm and Saturday and Sunday 5 to 7pm, but check www.keokisparadise.com for the monthly lineup and occasional altered hours. **The Shops at Kukui'ula** (www.theshopsat kukuiula.com) hosts a *kani kapila* (jam) Friday from 6:30 to 8:30pm.

WEST SIDE The *tūtū kāne* (granddaddy) of local art events, the **Hanapēpē Friday Art Night** (www.hanapepe.org) features food trucks, live music, and extended hours for art galleries and shops every Friday from 5 to 8pm.

PLANNING YOUR TRIP TO HAWAI'I

H awai'i is rich in natural and cultural wonders, and each island has something unique to offer. With so much vying for your attention, planning a trip can be bewildering. And with so many people traveling to Hawai'i these days, reservations for certain scenic wonders as well as cars, hotels, and restaurants are essential. Here we've compiled everything you need to know before escaping to the islands.

The first thing to do: **Decide where you want to go.** Read through each chapter to see which islands fit the profile and offer the activities you're looking for. We strongly recommend that you limit your island-hopping to one island per week. If you decide to visit more than one in a week, be warned: You could spend much of your precious vacation time in airports and checking in and out of hotels. Not much fun!

Our second tip is to **fly directly to the island of your choice;** doing so can save you a 2-hour layover in Honolulu and another plane ride. O'ahu, Hawai'i Island (also known as the Big Island), Maui, and Kaua'i all receive direct flights from the continental United States.

Our third tip: Once you've decided on the island, **make reservations for a rental car** as soon as possible and book permits for unforgettable experiences like sunrise atop Maui's Haleakalā volcano or sunset in Kaua'i's Hā'ena State Park. (Each island's specific chapter will inform you of sights requiring permits and/or admission fees.)

For pertinent facts and on-the-ground resources in Hawai'i, turn to "Fast Facts: Hawai'i," on p. 609 of this chapter.

GETTING THERE
By Plane

Most major U.S. and many international carriers fly to Honolulu's **Daniel K. Inouye International Airport** (HNL) on O'ahu. Some also offer non-stop flights to **Kahului Airport** (OGG) on Maui, **Līhu'e Airport** (LIH) on Kaua'i, and **Kona International Airport** (KOA) and **Hilo Airport** (ITO) on Hawai'i Island. If you can fly directly to the island of your choice, you'll be spared a 2-hour layover in Honolulu and another plane ride. If you're heading to **Moloka'i Airport** (MKK), you'll need to connect in Honolulu or Kahului; for **Lāna'i Airport** (LNY), you'll have to fly from Honolulu or Kahului. See island chapters for detailed information on nonstop flights to each island.

PREVIOUS PAGE: Pu'uhonua O Hōnaunau National Historical Park, Hawai'i Island.

Hawaiian Airlines offers flights from more mainland U.S. and international gateways than any other airline, including numerous West Coast cities and long-haul flights from Austin, Boston, New York, and Salt Lake City. Most land in Honolulu, but several of Hawaiian's West Coast hubs also boast nonstop flights to Maui. Hawaiian's easy-to-navigate website makes finding the cheapest fares a cinch. Its closest competitor is **Alaska Airlines,** which offers frequent nonstop flights from West Coast cities, including Anchorage, Seattle, Portland, Oakland, San Francisco, San Jose, Los Angeles, San Diego, and Las Vegas. **Southwest Airlines** is worth checking out for deals to Honolulu, Maui, Kaua'i, and Hawai'i Island from California—Oakland, Los Angeles, Long Beach, Sacramento, San Diego, and San Jose—plus Phoenix and Las Vegas. From the West Coast and points farther east, **United, American,** and **Delta** all fly to Hawai'i with nonstop service to Honolulu and most neighbor islands; United has the most flights. If you're having difficulty finding an affordable fare, try routing your flight through Las Vegas. It's a huge hub for traffic to and from the islands. Travelers from Canada can find a variety of routes from major cities to Hawai'i's main airports on **Air Canada** and **WestJet.**

> ### Flying from Beyond the U.S. or Canada
>
> For nonstop international service to the islands, check these airlines: Air Asia, Air New Zealand, ANA (All Nippon Airways), Asiana Airlines, China Airlines, China Eastern Airlines, Fiji Airways, Jin Air, Qantas Airways, Japan Airlines, Jetstar Airways, Korean Air, Philippine Airlines, Qantas, and Zipair Tokyo. Hawaiian Airlines also flies nonstop to Australia, New Zealand, American Samoa, Tahiti, the Cook Islands, South Korea, and Japan.

ARRIVING AT THE AIRPORT

IMMIGRATION & CUSTOMS CLEARANCE International visitors arriving by air should cultivate patience before setting foot on U.S. soil. U.S. airports have considerable security practices in place. Clearing Customs and Immigration can take as long as 2 hours.

AGRICULTURAL SCREENING AT AIRPORTS Inbound passengers must fill out a form during their flight that says they are not bringing in any fresh fruit, vegetables, raw seeds, or plants; if you forgot to eat that banana in the bottom of your purse, use the disposal bin just before the exit to baggage claim. Fines of up to $500,000 and jail time may apply to violators, including those who try to smuggle in live animals—Hawai'i closely guards its rabies-free status. Passengers heading for the U.S. continent must have their baggage and carry-ons screened by agriculture officials. Officials will confiscate fresh local produce like bananas and mangoes in the name of fruit-fly control. Pineapples, coconuts, and papayas inspected and certified for export; boxed flowers; most leis without seeds; and processed foods (macadamia nuts, coffee, dried fruit, and the like) will pass.

internet or apps **FOR HAWAI'I HOTEL DISCOUNTS**

Hawai'i hotels and resorts know they have a captive audience, and high prices reflect that. And while it's not impossible to get a good deal by calling a hotel, you're more likely to snag a discount online or with a mobile app. Here are some strategies:

1. **Bid for lodgings without knowing which hotel you'll get.** You can do so on **Priceline.com** and **Hotwire.com,** and both sites can be money-savers, particularly if you're booking within a week of travel (according to a recent study of billions of hotels bookings, that's when the hotels resort to deep discounts to get beds filled). As these companies use only major chains, you can rest assured that you won't be put up in a dump. For Priceline, you can install the browser extension **Hotel Canary** for free on your computer, and it will tell you the name of the hotel Priceline is trying to hide from you. There's not as easy a hack for Hotwire, but if you search for it on Frommers.com you'll find a four-step method we figured out for correctly guessing which hotel you're being shown.

2. **Make a reservation you can cancel.** As the date of your stay approaches, hotels start to play "chicken" with one another, dropping the price a bit one day to try to lure customers away from a nearby competitor. So search again the week you're traveling, and then within 48 hours of arrival. This strategy takes vigilance and persistence, but since your credit card won't usually be charged until 24 hours before check-in, little risk is involved and it's paying off more often than ever before, thanks to current conditions. These discounts are always better than the book-ahead-discounts that require you to lock in a price.

3. **Use the right hotel search engine.** They're not all equal, as we at Frommers.com learned in 2024 after putting the top 20 sites to the test in 20 cities around the globe. We discovered that HotelsCombined.com and Google/Hotels both listed the lowest rates for hotels in 20 out of 20 times—the best record, by far, of all the sites we tested.

4. **Review discounts on the hotel's website.** Hotels tend to give the lowest rates to those who book through their sites rather than through a third party. But you'll only find these truly deep discounts in the loyalty section of these sites—so join the club.

5. **Consider joining** Room Steals, Travel + Leisure's Go, or one of the travel clubs associated with many professional organizations. These clubs have access to the "fire sales" of the hotel industry: room rates that are slashed to a level the hotels would never want to surface on a Google search. These clubs work best for frequent travelers, as there are initial membership fees. Another alternative is @Hotels on Instagram, which unlocks the same types of discounts, but with no membership fee (it does have a slightly more cumbersome research and booking method, involving messaging @Hotels for access). But all these entities unlock wholesale prices that consistently shave 25% off the nightly rate at hotels, more for really pricey ones.

Honey and jam are typically considered liquids or gels, so don't pack them in carry-on luggage to avoid the disappointment of having TSA screeners dispose of them.

GETTING AROUND HAWAI'I

For additional advice on travel within each island, see "Getting Around" in the individual island chapters.

Interisland Flights

Hawaiian Airlines (www.hawaiianairlines.com; ℂ **800/367-5320**) offers the most flights between the four major islands (Kaua'i, O'ahu, Maui, and Hawai'i Island) and flies 128-passenger, wide-body jets. **Southwest Airlines** (www.southwest.com; ℂ **800/435-9792**) uses jets for flights between O'ahu, Kaua'i, Maui, and Hawai'i Island; its hubs are in Honolulu and Kahului, Maui.

Even before merging with Makani Kai Air in 2020, the commuter airline **Mokulele Airlines** (www.mokuleleairlines.com; ℂ **866/260-7070**) served the most airports in Hawai'i, primarily using nine-passenger prop planes that you board on the tarmac, with no security screening. In addition to the larger airports of Kona, Honolulu, and Kahului, it offers flights to Hana and Kapalua on Maui, Waimea (Kamuela) on Hawai'i Island, "topside" Ho'olehua and historic Kalaupapa on Moloka'i, and Lāna'i's sole airport, Lāna'i City. In 2023, it introduced its second 34-passenger Saab 340 plane to help serve Lāna'i and Moloka'i, which have the fewest air options. *Note:* Mokulele "cannot accept a Customer of Size (COS) whose body weight exceeds 350 pounds."

Check-in at least 90 minutes before your flight—especially in Honolulu or during holidays, when arriving 2 hours in advance is recommended if you're heading to the mainland and especially if checking bags. During non-holiday periods, you can generally get by with 60 to 75 minutes at other island airports if you have TSA PreCheck security clearance, and a mere 30 minutes for Mokulele flights.

> ### A Weeklong Cruise Through the Islands
>
> If you're looking for a taste of several islands in 7 days, consider **Norwegian Cruise Line** (www.ncl.com; ℂ **866/234-7350**), the only cruise line that operates year-round in Hawai'i. NCL's 2,186-passenger ship *Pride of America* circles Hawai'i, starting and ending at Honolulu and visiting ports on Maui, Hawai'i, and Kaua'i (in that order) in between; rates start at $1,499 per person. Prefer something smaller? The 36-passenger Safari Explorer yacht of **UnCruise Adventures** (www.uncruise.com; ℂ **888/862-8881**) visits Maui, Lāna'i, Moloka'i, and Hawai'i Island on weeklong trips November to April. Rates start at $5,795 per person.

By Shuttle

Roberts Hawai'i Express Shuttle (www.robertshawaii.com/airport-shuttle; ℂ **800/439-8800**) offers curb-to-curb shuttle service to and from the airports on O'ahu, Hawai'i, Maui, and Kaua'i. Booking is a breeze (and 15% cheaper) on their website. Shared shuttles start at $25 per person, varying by island and drop-off destination; private shuttles from $96.

SpeediShuttle (www.speedishuttle.com; © 877/242-5777) services all of the major airports plus cruise terminals; varying rates start at $17.60. For an extra fee, you can request a fresh flower lei greeting.

By Bus

Public transit is spotty—Oʻahu has adequate bus service, but even so, it's set up for residents, not tourists carrying suitcases or beach toys (all carry-ons must fit on your lap or under the bus seat). **TheBus** (www.thebus.org; © 808/848-5555) delivers you to destinations around the island for $3; buy a reusable Holo Card for easy payment (see www.holocard.net for details). If you're traveling on a shoestring and have the patience of a saint, this could be a transportation option for you. Bus no. 20 travels regularly between the airport and Waikīkī; the trip takes about an hour.

The neighbor-island buses are even less visitor-friendly. One-way rides on Kauaʻi and Maui cost $3. The **Kauaʻi Bus** (www.kauai.gov/Government/Departments-Agencies/Transportation/Bus-Schedules; © 808/246-8110) stops at Līhuʻe Airport twice every hour, but connections to towns outside of Līhuʻe are few and far between. Buses no longer run on Sundays. On the Valley Isle, the **Maui Bus** (www.mauicounty.gov/605/Bus-Service-Schedule-Information; © 808/871-4838) picks up at Kahului Airport every 90 minutes and delivers riders to a transfer station at Queen Kaʻahumanu Mall. The free **Hele-On Bus** (www.heleonbus.org; © 808/961-8744) on Hawaiʻi Island visits the Hilo Airport every 60 minutes, Monday through Saturday, and every 90 minutes on Sundays. Two bus routes each stop at Kona Airport approximately hourly.

By Car

Bottom line: Rent a car. You will need your own wheels to get around the islands, especially if you plan to explore outside your resort—and you absolutely should. As discussed above, public transit is unreliable and taxis are obscenely expensive. While ride-sharing platforms **Uber** and **Lyft** are widely available in Waikīkī, expect longer waits elsewhere (and remember remote areas have poor cellphone signals). **Holoholo** (www.rideholoholo.com), a ride-sharing platform based in Hawaiʻi, has drivers on Oʻahu, Maui, Kauaʻi, Hawaiʻi Island, and Lānaʻi.

That said, Hawaiʻi has some of the priciest car-rental rates in the country, and that was even before the mass sell-off of rental cars during the months-long effective ban on tourism in 2020 and an exacerbating dearth of new rental cars due to supply chain issues. The most expensive is the island of Lānaʻi, where four-wheel-drive (4WD) vehicles cost a small fortune. Rental cars are often at a premium on Kauaʻi, Hawaiʻi Island, Molokaʻi, and Lānaʻi, and may be sold out on any island over holiday weekends or during special events. Be aware that rates on **Turo.com,** the Airbnb of rental cars, can be higher than the national chains, although you'll find more trucks, Jeeps, and minivans through them; most airports in Hawaiʻi do not allow onsite pickups, so you'll need to check with your

Turo host on what services they provide. We recommend reserving your car as soon as you book your airfare.

To rent a car in Hawai'i, you must be at least 25 years old and have a valid driver's license and credit card. *Note:* If you're visiting from abroad and plan to rent a car in the United States, keep in mind that foreign driver's licenses are usually recognized in the U.S., but you should get an international one if your home license is not in English.

At the Honolulu and most neighbor-island airports, you'll find many major car-rental agencies, including **Alamo, Avis, Budget, Dollar, Enterprise, Hertz, National, Sixt,** and **Thrifty.** Most of the islands have independent rental companies that operate outside of the airport, often for cheaper rates; check individual island chapters. If you're traveling with windsurfing or other sports gear on Maui, check out **Aloha Rent a Car** (www.aloharentacar.com; ✆ **877/452-5642** or 808/877-4477). We highly recommend AutoSlash.com over other online car rental services. It applies every available coupon on the market to the booking, yielding surprisingly low daily rates. And if the cost of a rental drops, it automatically rebooks renters, again lowering the price.

GASOLINE Gas prices in Hawai'i, always much higher than on the U.S. mainland, vary from island to island. Expect to pay at least $5 a gallon, higher in resort areas, and more than $6 a gallon on Moloka'i. The one exception is Lāna'i, where billionaire Larry Ellison has subsidized rates at the local gas station, keeping them closer to $4. Check www.gasbuddy.com to find the cheapest gas in your area. Costco (www.costco.com) is usually a good bet, although membership is required; there are three locations on O'ahu and one apiece on Maui, Kaua'i, and Hawai'i Island.

INSURANCE Hawai'i is a no-fault state, which means that if you don't have collision-damage insurance, you are required to pay for all damages before you leave the state, whether or not the accident was your fault. Your personal car insurance may provide rental-car coverage; check before you leave home. Bring your insurance identification card if you decline the optional insurance, which usually costs from $9 to $45 a day. Obtain the name of your company's local claim representative before you go. Some credit card companies also provide collision-damage insurance for their customers; check with yours before you rent.

DRIVING RULES Hawai'i state law mandates that all car passengers must wear a **seatbelt** and all infants must be strapped into a car seat. You'll pay a $102 to $112 fine if you're caught unbuckled. **Pedestrians** always have the right of way, even if they're not in the crosswalk. You can turn **right on red** after a full and complete stop, unless otherwise posted. Handheld cellphones and similar devices are prohibited while driving.

ROAD MAPS The best and most detailed maps for activities are published by **Franko Maps** (www.frankosmaps.com/collections/hawaii); they feature a host of island maps, plus a terrific "Hawaiian Reef Creatures Guide" for snorkelers curious about those fish they spot underwater. Free

Talking on a cellphone, texting, or using any handheld device (like a navigation system) while driving in Hawai'i is a big no-no. Fines start at $297 and increase in school or construction zones. Save yourself the money; if you *have* to take a photo of that rainbow, pull over.

road maps are published by *This Week* magazine (www.thisweekhawaii.com), a visitor publication available on O'ahu, Hawai'i Island, Maui, and Kaua'i.

Another good source is the **University of Hawai'i Press maps,** which include a detailed network of island roads, large-scale insets of towns, historical and contemporary points of interest, parks, beaches, and hiking trails. If you can't find them in a bookstore near you, contact **University of Hawai'i Press** (www.uhpress.hawaii.edu/product-category/map; © **888/UH-PRESS** [847-7377]). For topographic maps of the islands, go to the **U.S. Geological Survey** site (pubs.er.usgs.gov).

SPECIAL-INTEREST TRIPS & TOURS

This section presents an overview of special-interest trips, tours, and outdoor excursions in Hawai'i. See individual island chapters for detailed information on the best local outfitters and tour-guide operators—as well as tips for exploring on your own. Each island chapter discusses the best spots to set out on your own, from the top offshore snorkel and dive spots to great daylong hikes, as well as the federal, state, and county agencies that can help you with hikes on public property. For your safety, always use the resources available to inquire about weather, trail, or surf conditions, access to drinking water, and other conditions before you take off on your adventure.

Air Tours

Nothing beats getting a bird's-eye view of Hawai'i. Some of the islands' most stunning scenery can't be seen any other way. You'll have your choice of aircraft here: **helicopter, small fixed-wing plane,** or, on O'ahu, **seaplane.** For wide-open spaces such as the lava fields of Hawai'i Volcanoes National Park, a fixed-wing plane is the safest and most affordable option. But for exploring tight canyons and valleys, helicopters have an advantage: They can hover. Only a helicopter can bring you face to face with waterfalls in remote places like Mount Wai'ale'ale on Kaua'i and Maui's little-known Wall of Tears, up near the summit of Pu'u Kukui.

Today's pilots are part historian, part DJ, part amusement-ride operator, and part tour guide, sharing anecdotes about Hawai'i's flora, fauna, history, and culture. *Tip:* Although accidents are rare, I prefer to fly with pilots who are instrument certified, meaning they know how to operate their craft in poor visibility, which can occur in rain and fog (most common in winter). Also, be kind to residents and wildlife by looking for companies that advertise quieter helicopters, such as EcoStars.

Top trips include:

o **Nāpali Coast,** Kaua'i, where you soar over the painted landscape of Waimea Canyon, known as the "Grand Canyon of the Pacific," and visit the cascading falls of Mount Wai'ale'ale, one of the wettest spots on Earth (p. 513).

o **Haleakalā National Park and West Maui,** where you skirt the edges of Haleakalā's otherworldly crater before plunging into the deep, pristine valleys of the West Maui Mountains (p. 395).

o **Hawai'i Volcanoes National Park and Hilo Waterfalls** on Hawai'i Island, where you stare into massive craters, cross vast lava fields with pockets of rainforest, and revel in the web of waterfalls above Hilo (p. 209).

Farm Tours

Overalls and garden spades might not fit your image of a Hawai'i vacation, but a tour of a lush and bountiful island farm should be on your itinerary. Agritourism has become an important income stream for farmers in Hawai'i, who often struggle with the rising costs of doing business in paradise. Farm tours benefit everyone: The farmer gets extra cash, visitors gain an intimate understanding of where and how their food is produced, and fertile farmlands stay in production—preserving Hawai'i's rural heritage. The islands have many diverse and inspiring farms to choose from: **100-year-old Kona coffee farms, bean-to-bar chocolate plantations, vanilla and orchid farms,** an award-winning **goat dairy,** and even a **vodka farm** (distilled from sugarcane).

With its massive cattle ranches, tropical flower nurseries, and coffee-covered hillsides, Hawai'i Island is the agricultural heart of Hawai'i. But each of the islands has farms worth visiting. Many agri-tours include sumptuous tasting sessions, fascinating historical accounts, and tips for growing your own food at home. See each island's "Exploring" section for details on visiting local farms.

National Parks

Hawai'i boasts some of the oldest national parks in the system—and the only one with two recently erupting volcanoes. The National Park Service manages nine sites on four islands: the **Pearl Harbor National Memorial** on O'ahu, **Haleakalā National Park** on Maui, **Kalaupapa National Historic Park** on Moloka'i, and **Hawai'i Volcanoes National Park, Pu'ukoholā Heiau National Historic Site, Kaloko-Honōkohau** and **Pu'uhonua O Hōnaunau** national historical parks, and the **Ala Kahakai National Historic Trail** on the island of Hawai'i. O'ahu's **Honouliuli National Historic Site,** where ethnic Japanese and other citizens were interned during WWII, is not yet open to the public but has its own gallery at the Japanese Cultural Center of Hawai'i in downtown Honolulu. Similarly, you can vicariously visit the **Papahānaumokuākea Marine National**

Monument—the largest protected marine area in the world—at the Mokupapapa Discovery Center in Hilo.

Volunteer Vacations & Ecotourism

If you're looking to swap sunbathing for something more memorable on your next trip to Hawai'i, consider volunteering while on vacation. Rewards include new friends and access to spectacular wilderness areas that are otherwise off-limits.

If you're looking for eco-friendly tour operators, the **Sustainable Tourism Association of Hawai'i** (www.sustainabletourismhawaii.org; © 808/800-3531) is a good place to start.

The **Surfrider Foundation** organizes beach and reef cleanups and has several active chapters throughout the islands: O'ahu (https://oahu.surfrider.org); Maui (https://maui.surfrider.org); Kaua'i (https://kauai.surfrider.org); and, on Hawai'i Island, Kona (https://kona.surfrider.org) and Hilo (https://hawaii.surfrider.org). And what could be more exciting than keeping watch over nesting sea turtles? Contact the **University of Hawai'i Sea Grant College Program** (© 808/956-7031) and the **Hawai'i Wildlife Fund** (www.wildhawaii.org; © 808/643-3567) to see if they need help monitoring marine life.

A great alternative to hiring a private guide is taking a trip with the **Nature Conservancy** or the **Sierra Club.** Both organizations typically offer guided hikes in preserves and special areas during the year, as well as day- to week-long volunteer work trips to restore habitats and trails and root out invasive plants. It's a chance to see the "real" Hawai'i—including wilderness areas that are ordinarily off-limits.

The Sierra Club's half- or all-day hikes reach beautiful, remote spots on O'ahu, Kaua'i, Hawai'i Island, and Maui. Knowledgeable volunteers lead the trips and share a wealth of cultural and botanical information. Hikes are classified as easy, moderate, or strenuous; some (but not all) incorporate a few hours of volunteer work. Donations of $1 for Sierra Club members and $5 for non-members (bring exact change) are recommended. Contact the **Hawai'i Chapter of the Sierra Club** (https://sierraclubhawaii.org/outings; © 808/538-6616).

The Nature Conservancy hikes and work trips are free (donations appreciated). However, you have to reserve a spot, with hikes offered once a month on Maui and Moloka'i, and occasionally on O'ahu. Contact the **Nature Conservancy of Hawai'i** (www.nature.org/hawaii; © 808/537-4508 on O'ahu; © 808/572-7849 on Maui; © 808/553-5236 on Moloka'i; and © 808/587-6257 on Kaua'i).

See the chapters for each island for other voluntourism opportunities.

Watersports Excursions

The same Pacific Ocean surrounds all of the Hawaiian Islands, but the varying topography of each shoreline makes certain spots superior for watersports. If **surfing** is your passion, head to O'ahu. You'll find gentle waves at Waikīkī and adrenaline-laced action on the famed North Shore. Maui has plenty of surf breaks, too; plus, it's the birthplace of **windsurfing** and a top **kitesurfing** destination. Beginners and pros alike will find perfect conditions for catching air off of Maui's swells.

Kayaking is excellent statewide, particularly on Kaua'i, which offers scenic river opportunities as well as the adventurous Nāpali Coast challenge, and on Moloka'i, where you can lazily paddle downwind past ancient fishponds. Unless very experienced, kayakers should go with guides on the open ocean—currents are strong here! Paddlers will also enjoy opportunities for stand-up paddling (SUP) and outrigger canoeing.

Sport fishing fans should head to Hawai'i Island's Kona Coast, where billfish tournaments have reeled in monster Pacific blue marlins.

The deep blue Kona waters are also home to giant manta rays, and **scuba diving** among these gentle creatures can be a magical experience; go with the smallest group possible. Scuba diving is also spectacular off Lāna'i, where ethereal caverns have formed in the reefs, and on Maui, on the back wall of Molokini Crater.

All of the islands have great **snorkeling** spots, but Maui's small boat harbors offer the widest range of snorkel and dive tours. Book a half-day cruise out to Molokini or an all-day adventure over to Lāna'i.

During the winter months, typically December through March, **whale-watching** tours launch from every island, but Maui's Mā'alaea Bay is the premier spot for seeing breaching and spouting whales. **Dolphin-spotting** is most reliable on Lāna'i at Mānele Bay and on Hawai'i at Kealakekua Bay, where the charismatic spinner dolphins come to rest. *Note:* Avoid operators that promise "swimming with dolphins," because it's illegal to approach dolphins for that purpose.

Go to each island's "Watersports" sections for detailed information on watersports outfitters and tour providers.

[FastFACTS] HAWAI'I

Agricultural Inspections Due to its remote location and unique environment, Hawai'i strictly limits what can be brought to the islands. Fresh fruit and vegetables and most plants are not allowed; you'll see a courtesy waste bin when deplaning. Pets and service animals require extensive health screening and advance documentation; a quarantine at the owner's

expense may also be required. See the regulations posted by the **Animal Industry Division** (© 808/483-7151) at https://hdoa.hawaii.gov/ai/aqs/aqs-info.

You also cannot take most fruits and vegetables on planes leaving the state; specially marked pineapples and papayas are exceptions. *Note:* Your carry-on and checked bags will be screened for such items.

Area Codes Hawai'i's area code is 808; it applies to all islands. Use the area code when calling from one island to another; there is a long-distance charge.

Customs Only international arrivals in Honolulu or Kona will need to pass through customs and passport control. In addition to Hawai'i's restrictions (see "Agricultural Inspections," above), there may be limits on what types of **food, alcohol,** and other items you may bring based on your country of origin; consult your nearest U.S. embassy or consulate or see the U.S. Customs' page www.cbp.gov/travel/international-visitors/know-before-you-visit. For information on what you're allowed to bring home, contact one of the following agencies, or the customs agency in your home country, if not listed here:

Canadian Citizens: Canada Border Services Agency (www.cbsa-asfc.gc.ca; ☎ **800/461-9999** in Canada, or 204/983-3500).

U.K. Citizens: HM Customs & Excise (www.gov.uk/government/organisations/hm-revenue-customs; ☎ **0300/322-9434**).

Australian Citizens: Australian Customs Service (www.homeaffairs.gov.au; ☎ **131-881** in Australia or 61/2-6196-0196 from abroad).

New Zealand Citizens: New Zealand Customs (www.customs.govt.nz; ☎ **0800/428-786** or 64/9-927-8036 outside of NZ).

Electricity   Like Canada, the United States uses 110 to 120 volts AC (60 cycles), compared to 220 to 240 volts AC (50 cycles) in most of Europe, Australia, and New Zealand. Downward converters that change 220–240 volts to 110–120 volts are hard to find in the U.S., so bring one with you if you're traveling to Hawai'i from abroad.

Embassies & Consulates   All embassies are based in Washington, D.C., a full day's travel from Hawai'i, but many have consulates in major West Coast cities—just a half-day away—and Australia and New Zealand both offer consular services in Honolulu. (For a full list of embassies, visit **www.embassy.org.**)

Australia: Its embassy (www.usa.embassy.gov.au; ☎ **202/797-3000**) has a consulate in Honolulu, 1000 Bishop St. (☎ **808/529-8100**).

Canada: The embassy (www.canadianembassy.org; ☎ **202/682-1740**) provides services to Canadians in Hawai'i through its consulate in San Francisco, 580 California St. #1400 (☎ **844/880-6519**).

Ireland: Embassy The nearest consulate for this embassy (www.ireland.ie/en/usa/washington; ☎ **202/462-3939**) is in San Francisco, 1 Post St., Suite 2300 (www.ireland.ie/en/usa/sanfrancisco; ☎ **415/392-4214**).

New Zealand: The embassy (www.mfat.govt.nz/en/embassies; ☎ **202/328-4800**) has a consulate in Honolulu, 733 Bishop St. (☎ **808/675-5555**).

United Kingdom: The embassy (www.gov.uk/world/usa; ☎ **202/588-6500**) provides services to citizens in Hawai'i via its consulate in Los Angeles, 2029 Century Park East, Suite 1350 (☎ **310/789-0031**).

Family Travel   With beaches to build castles on, calm water to splash in, and amazing sights to see, Hawai'i is paradise for children. Take a look at "The Best of Hawai'i for Kids" in chapter 1, p. 13.

The larger hotels and resorts offer supervised programs for children and can refer you to qualified babysitters. By state law, hotels can accept only children ages 5 to 12 in supervised activities programs but can often accommodate parents with younger kids by hiring babysitters to watch over little ones. **People Attentive to Children (PATCH)** can refer you to babysitters who have taken a training course in childcare. On O'ahu, call ☎ **808/839-1988;** on the Hawai'i Island, call ☎ **808/322-3500** in Kona or ☎ **808/961-3169** in Hilo; on Maui, call ☎ **808/242-9232;** on Kaua'i, call ☎ **808/246-0622;** on Moloka'i and Lāna'i, call ☎ **800/498-4145;** or visit www.patchhawaii.org. The **Nanny Connection** (www.thenannyconnection.com; ☎ **808/875-4777**) is a reputable business that sends Mary Poppins–esque nannies to resorts and beaches on O'ahu, Maui, and Lāna'i to watch children ($20 per hour and up, with a 3-hr. minimum and a $30 booking fee, $50 booking fee on Lāna'i).

Baby's Away (https://babysaway.com) rents cribs, strollers, highchairs, playpens, infant seats, and the like on O'ahu (☎ **800/496-6386** or 805/453-0303), Maui (☎ **800/942-9030** or 808/298-4647), and Hawai'i

Island (☏ **800/996-9030** or 808/854-7630). The staff will deliver whatever you need to wherever you're staying and pick it up when you're done.

Health   **Mosquitoes**

Mosquito-borne diseases are rare in Hawai'i, though an outbreak of dengue fever did affect remote areas of Hawai'i Island in 2016. The Hawai'i State Health Department recommends travelers: a) choose lodging with screens or sleep under a mosquito net; b) cover up in long sleeves and pants; and c) use EPA-registered insect repellent. In the last decade, a few people on Maui and Hawai'i Island have contracted **rat lungworm,** a parasitic disease, by accidentally consuming part of an infected snail or slug. Among other symptoms, it can cause painful headaches, fever, and nausea, but generally clears up without treatment. You can avoid it by thoroughly washing any produce you buy, especially from farm stands in remote, rainy areas. There's no cure, but some doctors believe taking over-the-counter anti-pinworm medication after suspected snail or slug ingestion can prevent rat lungworm from developing.

Centipedes, Scorpions & Other Critters   Although insects can get a little close for comfort in Hawai'i (expect to see the occasional ant, cockroach, or other little critter indoors, even in posh hotels), few cause serious trouble. Giant centipedes—as long as 8

inches—can be seen on occasion, as can scorpions in drier areas. Now detected on every populated island except Moloka'i and Niihau, little red fire ants can rain down from trees and sting unsuspecting passersby. If you're stung or bitten by an insect and experience extreme pain, swelling, nausea, or any other severe reaction, seek medical attention right away. Geckos—the little lizards circling your porch light and making tiny clucking sounds at night—are harmless and considered good luck in Hawai'i's homes. Yes, even *inside* homes, where they munch on intruding insects. Cane toads, imported for insect control decades ago, can reach 9 inches in length; do not touch their bumpy olive-brown skin, which secretes a toxin that can kill a dog. Also known as bufo frogs, cane toads are nocturnal and are frequently flattened in the road due to their tendency to freeze in headlights. Much-smaller coqui frogs are widespread on Hawai'i Island (p. 199) and a growing presence on Maui; their all-night, shrill mating call may disturb your sleep, so pack earplugs.

Hiking Safety   Before you set out on a hike, let someone know where you're heading and when you plan to return; too many hikers spend cold nights or hot days in the wilderness because they don't take this simple precaution. It's always a good idea to hike with a pal. Select your route

based on your own fitness level. Check weather conditions with the **National Weather Service** (www.weather.gov/hfo; ☏ **808/973-5286** on O'ahu), even if it looks sunny: The weather here ranges from blistering hot to freezing cold (at high elevations) and can change in a matter of hours or miles. Do *not* hike if rain or a storm is predicted; flash floods are common in Hawai'i and have resulted in many preventable deaths. Plan to finish your hike at least an hour before sunset; because Hawai'i is so close to the equator, it does not have a twilight period, and thus it gets dark quickly after the sun sets. Wear sturdy shoes, a hat, clothes to protect you from the sun and from getting scratches, and high-SPF sunscreen on all exposed areas. Take plenty of water, a basic first-aid kit, a snack, and a bag to pack out what you pack in. Watch your step. Loose lava rocks are famous for twisting ankles. Don't rely on cellphones or Wi-Fi; service isn't available in many remote places.

Vog   Whenever molten lava appears on Hawai'i Island, as happens nearly every year, the gases that are released can result in *vog,* a gray haze that hovers at the horizon, sometimes as far away as O'ahu. Although there's no evidence that vog causes lingering damage to healthy individuals, it can irritate airways, especially for those with existing respiratory issues. You can minimize the effects of vog by closing your windows and using an air-conditioner indoors. **A word of caution:** If you're pregnant or have heart or breathing problems, avoid exposure to the sulfuric fumes in and around Hawai'i Volcanoes National Park.

Ocean Safety The range of watersports available here is astounding—this is a prime water playground with conditions for every age and ability. But the ocean is also an untamed wilderness; don't expect a calm swimming pool. Many people who visit Hawai'i underestimate the power of the ocean. With just a few precautions, your Pacific experience can be a safe and happy one. Before heading out for the day, always check **Hawai'i Beach Safety** (https://safebeach day.com/state/hawaii), which offers real-time conditions, maps, and detailed info for beaches on O'ahu, Maui, Kaua'i, and Hawai'i Island. When you arrive at the beach, talk to a lifeguard if present before entering the water; if it's an unguarded beach, observe any warnings or closure signs, and take a few minutes to watch where others are swimming, how the waves are breaking, and where reefs and rocks lie. If others aren't swimming, take that as a sign to enjoy the sea from the shore. Keep in mind that currents may be much stronger here and conditions may change quickly, especially during storms and winter swells.

If you're snorkeling, take a moment to familiarize yourself with your equipment. Make sure you feel at ease breathing and clearing water from the snorkel. Look for landmarks so you can orient yourself once in the water, and not drift too far away. Go with a buddy. It may be prudent to wait a few days after your flight before snorkeling, especially if you are a male more than 50 years old, due to the possibility of ROPE—rapid-onset pulmonary edema—which may be the cause of drowning in snorkelers who were capable swimmers and otherwise healthy.

If you get caught in big surf, dive underneath each wave until the swell subsides. Never turn your back to the ocean; rogue waves catch even experienced water folk unaware. Be realistic about your fitness—more than one visitor has ended their vacation with a heart attack in the water. Don't go out alone, or during a storm.

Note that sharks are not a big problem in Hawai'i; in fact, local divers look forward to seeing them. Only 2 of the 40 shark species present in Hawaiian waters are known to bite humans, and then usually it's by accident, and rarely very close to shore. But here are the general rules for avoiding sharks: Don't swim at dawn, dusk, or in murky water—sharks may mistake you for one of their usual meals—and swim close to the beach. It should be obvious not to swim where there are bloody fish in the water, as sharks become aggressive around blood.

Seasickness The waters in Hawai'i range from calm as glass to downright turbulent (in storm conditions) and usually fall somewhere in between. In general, expect rougher conditions in winter than in summer and on windward coastlines versus calm, leeward coastlines. If you've never been out on a boat, or if you've been seasick in the past, you might want to heed the following suggestions:

- The day before you go out on the boat, avoid alcohol, caffeine, citrus and other acidic juices, and greasy, spicy, or hard-to-digest foods.

- Get a good night's sleep the night before.

- Take or use whatever seasickness prevention works best for you—medication, an acupressure wristband, ginger tea or capsules, or any combination. But do it **before you board;** once you set sail, it's generally too late.

- While you're on the boat, stay as low and as near the center of the boat as possible. Avoid the fumes (especially if it's a diesel boat); stay out in the fresh air and watch the horizon. Do not read.

- If you start to feel queasy, drink clear fluids like water, and eat something bland, such as a soda cracker.

Stings The most common stings in Hawai'i come from **jellyfish** (more properly known as jellies) particularly Portuguese man-of-war and box jellyfish. The latter occur mostly on south-facing beaches on O'ahu (including Waikīkī) and on Kaua'i.

A bluish-purple floating bubble with a long tail, the **Portuguese man-of-war** is responsible for some 6,500 stings a year on O'ahu alone. Although painful and a nuisance, these stings are rarely harmful; fewer than 1 in 1,000 requires medical treatment. The best prevention is to watch for these floating bubbles as you snorkel (look for the hanging tentacles below the surface). Get out of the water if anyone near you spots these jellyfish. Reactions to stings range from mild burning and reddening to severe welts and blisters. Most jellyfish stings disappear by themselves within 15 to 20 minutes if you do nothing at all to treat them. *All Stings Considered: First Aid and Medical Treatment of Hawai'i's Marine Injuries,* by Craig Thomas, M.D., and Susan Scott (University of Hawai'i Press, 1997), recommends the following treatment: First, pick off any visible tentacles with a gloved hand or a stick; then, rinse the sting with salt- or fresh water, and apply ice to prevent swelling. Avoid applying vinegar, baking soda, or urine to the wound, which may actually cause further damage. See a doctor if pain persists or a rash or other symptoms develop.

Transparent, square-shaped **box jellyfish** are nearly impossible to see in the water. Fortunately, they seem to follow a monthly cycle: 8 to 10 days after the full moon, they appear off the leeward side of each island (most prominently on O'ahu and Kaua'i) and hang around for about 3 days; check the Waikīkī Aquarium's calendar noting days of "high probability" for box jellyfish at www.waikiki aquarium.org/interact/box-jellyfish-calendar. They also seem to sting more in the morning, when they're on or near the surface. The stings from a box jellyfish can cause hivelike welts, blisters, and pain lasting from 10 minutes to 8 hours. *All Stings Considered* recommends the following treatment: First, pour regular household vinegar on the sting; this will stop additional burning. Do not rub the area. Pick off any vinegar-soaked tentacles with a stick and apply an ice pack. Seek medical treatment if you experience shortness of breath, weakness, palpitations, or any other severe symptoms.

Punctures Most sea-related punctures come from stepping on or brushing against the needlelike spines of sea urchins (known locally as *wana*). Be careful when you're in the water; don't put your foot down (even if you are wearing booties or fins) if you can't clearly see the bottom. Waves can push you into *wana* in a surge zone in shallow water. The spines can even puncture a wet suit. A sea urchin puncture can result in burning, aching, swelling, and discoloration (black or purple) around the area where the spines entered your skin. The best thing to do is to pull out any protruding spines. The body will absorb the spines within 24 hours to 3 weeks, or the remainder of the spines will work themselves out. Again, contrary to popular thought, urinating or pouring vinegar on the embedded spines will not help.

Cuts Stay out of the ocean if you have an open cut, wound, or new tattoo. The high level of bacteria present in the water means that even small wounds can become infected. Staphylococcus, or "staph," infections start out as swollen, pinkish skin tissue around the wound that spreads and grows rather than dries and heals. Scrub any cuts well with fresh water and avoid the ocean until they heal. Consult a doctor if your wound shows signs of infection.

Also see "Fast Facts" in the individual island chapters for listings of local **doctors, dentists, hospitals,** and **emergency numbers.**

Internet & Wi-Fi On every island, branches of the **Hawai'i State Public Library System** have free computers with Internet access. To find the closest, check www.librarieshawaii. org/visit/branches/all-branches. Computer use is free with a Hawai'i library card, which is free to

Hawai'i residents and members of the military. Visitors can visit any branch to purchase a $10 visitor card that is good for 3 months.

The state also supports 100 Wi-Fi "hotspots" that offer 1 free hour of service a day; check the map on https://cca.hawaii.gov/broadband. Every **Starbucks** (www.starbucks.com) in Hawai'i also has free Wi-Fi, as do many other cafes and most **hotel lobbies.**

The airport in Honolulu, as well as those in Hilo and Kailua-Kona (Hawai'i Island), Kahului (Maui), and Līhu'e (Kaua'i) all provide free Wi-Fi.

LGBTQ Travelers

The number of gay- or lesbian-specific accommodations on the islands is limited, but lively gay bars are in every major population center, and Hawai'i welcomes all people with aloha. Since 1990, the state's capital has hosted the **Honolulu Pride Parade and Celebration** (but typically in Oct, not in June as on the mainland). See **https://honolulupride.com** for information on upcoming events. **Pride Guide Hawai'i** (www.gogayhawaii.com) features LGBTQ news, blogs, business recommendations, and other information for the entire state.

Mail

At press time, domestic postage rates for 2025 were 53¢ for a postcard and 68¢ for a letter. For international mail, a first-class postcard or letter up to 1 ounce costs $1.55. For more information go to **www.usps.com**.

If you aren't sure what your address will be in the United States, mail can be sent to you, in your name, c/o General Delivery at the main post office of the city or region where you expect to be. (See www. usps.com or call ℂ **800/275-8777** for information on the nearest post office.) The addressee must pick up mail in person and must produce proof of identity (driver's license, passport, and the like). Most post offices will hold mail for up to 1 month and are typically open Monday to Friday from 9am to 4pm, and some also Saturday from 9am to noon.

Always include zip codes when mailing items in the U.S. If you don't know the zip code, visit https://tools.usps.com/zip-code-lookup.htm.

Medical Requirements

Unless you're arriving from an area known to be suffering from an epidemic (particularly cholera or yellow fever), inoculations or vaccinations are not required for entry into the United States.

Mobile Phones

Cellphone coverage is decent throughout Hawai'i but can be inconsistent in the more remote and mountainous regions of the Islands. AT&T and Verizon tend to get the best reception.

If you are traveling from outside of the U.S., you may want to purchase an international SIM card for your cellphone or buy a prepaid cellphone with local service.

Do *not* use your cellphone while you are driving. Strict laws and heavy fines ($297 and up) are diligently enforced.

Money & Costs

Frommer's lists exact prices in the local currency. The currency conversions quoted below were correct at press time. However, rates fluctuate, so before departing, consult a currency exchange website such as www.oanda.com or www.xe.com to check up-to-the-minute rates.

THE VALUE OF US$ VS. OTHER POPULAR CURRENCIES

US$	Can$	UK£	Euro €	Aus$	NZ$
$1	C$1.36	£.79	€.93	A$1.55	NZ$1.65

ATMs (cashpoints) are everywhere in Hawai'i—at banks, supermarkets, Long's Drugs, major airports, most resorts and shopping centers, as well as some gas stations.

Note: Many banks impose a fee every time you use a card at another bank's ATM, and that fee is often higher for international transactions (up to $5 or more) than for domestic ones (rarely more than $4).

WHAT THINGS COST IN HAWAI'I	US$
Hamburger	6.00–22.00
Movie ticket (adult/child)	10.00–15.00/10.00
Taxi from Honolulu airport to Waikīkī	40.00–45.00
Entry to Bishop Museum (adult/child)	33.95/25.95
Entry to Honolulu Zoo (adult/child)	21.00/13.00
Entry to Maui Ocean Center (adult/child)	44.95/34.95
Luau at Hilton Waikoloa Village (adult/child)	198.00/99.00
Entry to Hawai'i Volcanoes National Park (car)	30.00
Moderately priced three-course dinner without alcohol	70.00 per person
20-ounce soft drink at convenience store	2.75
16-ounce apple juice	3.50
Cup of coffee	4.00
Moderately priced Waikīkī hotel room (double)	200.00–300.00

In addition, the bank from which you withdraw cash is likely to charge its own fee. Visitors from outside the U.S. should also find out whether their bank assesses a 1 to 3% fee on charges incurred abroad.

Credit cards are accepted everywhere except on the public buses and some taxicabs, vendors at farmers markets and roadside stands, and food trucks or smaller restaurants, although more and more are using mobile phones to accept credit card payments.

Packing Tips Hawai'i is very informal. Clean shorts, T-shirts, and sandals will get you by at most restaurants and attractions; a casual dress or a polo shirt and long pants are fine even in the most expensive places. (Only restaurants at the Halekulani hotel in Waikīkī have a more formal dress code—collared shirts for men and no jeans or sandals—although some report having worn just a nice aloha shirt with long, non-denim pants.) Aloha wear is acceptable everywhere, so you may want to plan on buying an aloha shirt or a Hawaiian-style dress while you're in the islands. Closed-toe shoes are required for horseback riding or ziplining, and strongly recommended for hiking. Bringing a pair of jeans or long pants is also advised for various activities and cool weather.

The tropical sun poses the greatest threat to anyone who ventures into the great outdoors, so pack **sun protection:** a good pair of sunglasses, strong reef-friendly, mineral sunscreen (meaning its active ingredients are only zinc oxide or titanium dioxide), a light hat, and a water bottle. Dehydration is common in the tropics.

One last thing: **It can get really cold in Hawai'i.** If you plan to see the sunrise from the top of Maui's Haleakalā Crater, venture into Hawai'i Island's Hawai'i Volcanoes National Park, or spend time in Kōke'e State Park on Kaua'i, bring a warm jacket. Temperatures "upcountry" (higher up the mountain) can sink to 40°F (4°C), even in summer when it's 80°F (27°C) at the beach. Bring a windbreaker, sweater, or light jacket. And if you'll be in Hawai'i between November and April, or staying on the Windward Side of the islands in any season, toss a **rain jacket** or poncho into your suitcase, too.

Passports Virtually every air traveler entering

615

the U.S. is required to show a passport. Children 15 and under may continue entering with only a U.S. birth certificate, or other proof of U.S. citizenship. Bring a photocopy of your passport with you and store it separately. If your passport is lost or stolen, the copy will facilitate the reissuing process at your consulate.

Safety   Although tourist areas are generally safe, visitors should always stay alert, even in laidback Hawai'i (and especially in Waikīkī). Avoid deserted areas, especially at night. Don't go into any city park at night unless there's an event that attracts crowds—for example, the Waikīkī Shell concerts in Kapi'olani Park. Generally speaking, you can feel safe in areas where there are many people and lots of open establishments.

Avoid carrying valuables with you on the street, and don't display expensive cameras or electronic equipment. Hold on to your purse, and place your billfold in an inside pocket. In theaters, restaurants, and other public places, keep your possessions in sight. Remember also that hotels are open to the public and that security may not be able to screen everyone entering, particularly in large properties. Always lock your room door—don't assume that once inside your hotel you're automatically safe.

Burglaries of tourists' rental cars in hotel parking structures and at beach or

hiking parking lots have become more common. Park in well-lit and well-traveled areas, if possible. Never leave any packages or valuables visible in the car, and in remote areas, leave nothing in your trunk. In the unlikely event that someone attempts to rob you or steal your car, do not try to resist the thief or carjacker—report the incident to the police immediately. Ask your rental car agent about any specific areas to avoid.

In the even more unlikely event that you experience serious crime or misfortune (a medical crisis or death of a traveling companion, for example), the local branches of the **Visitor Aloha Society of Hawai'i** can provide some helpful services and referrals as well as compassion. **O'ahu:** www.visitoralohasocietyofhawaii.org, ℂ **808/926-8274; Kaua'i:** www.visitoralohasociety.org, ℂ **808/482-0111; Maui:** www.hvcb.org/about-hvcb/island-chapters/maui-visitors-convention-bureau, ℂ **808/244-3530; Hawai'i Island:** https://vashbigisland.org, East Hawai'i ℂ **808/756-1472,** West Hawai'i ℂ **808/756-0785.**

Senior Travel   Getting older pays off! Discounts for seniors are available at almost all of Hawai'i's major attractions and occasionally at hotels and restaurants. The Outrigger hotel chain, for instance, offers travelers ages 50 and older at least a 20% discount on regular published rates—and an

additional 5% off for members of AARP. Always ask when making hotel reservations or buying tickets and carry proof of your age with you—it can really make a difference. Members of **AARP** (www.aarp.org; ℂ **866/654-5572** or 202/434-2277) are usually eligible for hotel or car rental discounts. AARP also puts together organized tour packages at moderate rates. Some great, low-cost trips to Hawai'i are offered to people 55 and older through **Road Scholar** (www.roadscholar.org; ℂ **800/454-5768**), a nonprofit group that arranges travel and study programs around the world.

If you're planning to visit Hawai'i Volcanoes or Haleakala National Park, you can save sightseeing dollars if you're 62 or older with a **Senior Pass,** available at https://store.usgs.gov/lifetime-senior-pass. This lifetime pass has a one-time fee of $80 ($20 for annual pass) and provides free admission to all of the parks in the system, plus a discount on some fees at many sites.

Smoking   Smokers will be hard-pressed to find places to light up. It's against the law to smoke or vape in public buildings (including airports, malls, stores, buses, movie theaters, banks, convention facilities, and all government buildings and facilities). There is no smoking in restaurants, bars, and nightclubs. Neither can you smoke at public beaches or parks. Essentially, you'll be relegated to the tiny smoking section on the edge of your hotel property. Smoking is prohibited within 20 feet of a doorway, window, or ventilation intake (so no hanging around outside a bar to smoke—you must go 20 feet away). Smoking **marijuana (cannabis)** is illegal for non-registered medical users; if you attempt to buy it or light up without a Hawai'i state-issued medical marijuana card, you can be arrested. While it's illegal to purchase products including CBD (cannabidiol) without a medical marijuana card, they are widely available in Hawai'i.

Sunscreen State law prevents the sale of sunscreen with oxybenzone or octinoxate, which harm coral reefs and fish. Maui, Moloka'i, Lāna'i and Hawai'i Island have stricter bans, allowing use of only mineral-based sunscreens. Please don't bring sunscreen with you that includes these chemicals, and instead look for brands that only list zinc or titanium oxide as active ingredients. Raw Elements, Alba Botanica, and All Good (available at Costco) are among brands of mineral-based sunscreens widely available in the islands as well as mainland stores and online.

Taxes The United States has no value-added tax (VAT) or other indirect tax at the national level. Every state, county, and city may levy its own local tax on all purchases, including hotel

and restaurant checks and airline tickets. These taxes will not appear on price tags.

Hawai'i state general excise tax is 4.166%, which applies to all items purchased (including hotel rooms and resort fees). O'ahu, Kaua'i, and Hawai'i Island are allowed to levy a surcharge that brings it up to 4.712%. On top of that, the state's Transient Accommodation Tax (TAT) is 10.25%, with another 3% added by each county, both applying to room rates and the hefty resort fees ($30–$40 a day), too. All together, these taxes and resort fees can elevate a moderately priced hotel's base rate of $250 a night to $333 or more. Do the math before booking and budget accordingly.

Telephones All calls on-island are local calls; calls from one island to another via a landline are long distance and you must dial 1, then the Hawai'i area code (808), and then the phone number. Convenience stores sell **prepaid calling cards** in denominations up to $50. Hawai'i still has a few public pay phones. Those at airports now accept American Express, MasterCard, and Visa. **Local calls** made from most pay phones cost 50¢. Most long-distance and international calls can be dialed directly from any phone. **To make calls within the United States and to Canada,** dial 1, followed by the area code and the seven-digit number. **For other international calls,** dial

011, followed by the country code, city code, and the number you are calling.

Calls to area codes **800, 888, 877,** and **866** are toll-free. However, calls to area codes **700** and **900** (chat lines, bulletin boards, "dating" services, and so forth) can be expensive—charges of 99¢ to $3 or more per minute. Some numbers have minimum charges that can run $15 or more.

For **reversed-charge or collect calls,** and for person-to-person calls, dial the number 0, then the area code and number; an operator will come on the line, and you should specify whether you are calling collect, person-to-person, or both. If your operator-assisted call is international, ask for the overseas operator.

For **directory assistance** ("Information"), dial 411 for local numbers and national numbers in the U.S. and Canada. For dedicated long-distance information, dial 1, then the appropriate area code plus 555-1212.

Time The continental United States is divided into **four time zones:** Eastern Standard Time (EST), Central Standard Time (CST), Mountain Standard Time (MST), and Pacific Standard Time (PST). Alaska and Hawai'i have their own zones. During Standard Time, when it's 7am in Honolulu (HST), it's 9am in Los Angeles (PST), 10am in Denver (MST), 11am in Chicago (CST), noon in New York City (EST), 5pm in

London (GMT), and 2am the next day in Sydney.

Daylight Saving Time, in effect in most of the United States from 2am on the second Sunday in March to 2am on the first Sunday in November, is **not observed** in Hawai'i. Daylight Saving Time moves the clock 1 hour ahead of standard time, that is, 9am (PDT) in Los Angeles will be only 6am (HST) in Honolulu.

Tipping   Tips are a major part of certain workers' income, and gratuities are the standard way of showing appreciation for services provided. (Tipping is certainly not compulsory if the service is poor!) In hotels, tip **bellhops** at least $2 per bag (and a minimum of $5) and tip the **housekeepers** $2 to $3 per person per day (more if you've left a disaster area for them to clean up or have a larger suite). Tip the **door attendant** or **concierge** only if he or she has provided you with some specific service (such as calling a cab for you or obtaining hard-to-get dinner reservations). Tip the **valet-parking attendant** $3 to $5 every time you get your car.

In general, tip service staff such as **waiters, bartenders, and hairdressers** 18% to 20% of the bill before tax. Tip **cab drivers** 15% of the fare. Tip **guides** for tours and activities, including ziplines, kayaks, horseback rides, and snorkeling, $10 to $20 per person in your party, depending on the length and quality of their services.

Toilets   You won't find public toilets on the streets in Hawai'i, but you can find them in hotel lobbies, restaurants, museums, department stores, service stations, and beach parks (where you'll find showers, too). Large hotels and fast-food restaurants are often the best bet for clean facilities. Restaurants and bars in heavily visited areas may reserve their restrooms for patrons.

Travelers with Disabilities   Travelers in wheelchairs will find more than 2,000 ramped curbs in O'ahu alone and many hotels equipped with wheelchair-accessible rooms and pools. Tour companies may also provide special services. Beach wheelchairs are available at one beach park on Maui (Kama'ole I; ask lifeguard), three on Kaua'i (Po'ipū, Lydgate, and Salt Pond), and five on O'ahu (another nine have wheelchair-friendly beach mats). See www.honolulu.gov/parks/beach-parks/beach-wheelchair-access.html or call ✆ **808/768-3027** for locations.

For tips on accessible travel in Hawai'i, go to the **Hawai'i Tourism Authority** website, www.gohawaii.com/trip-planning/accessibility. The **Statewide Independent Living Council of Hawai'i** (www.hcoahawaii.org; ✆ **808/585-7452**) can provide additional resources about accessibility throughout the Islands. On Maui and Kaua'i, **Gammie**

Homecare (www.gammie.com; Maui: ✆ **808/877-4032;** Kaua'i: ✆ **808/632-2333;** O'ahu: ✆ **808/597-8087**) rents everything from motorized scooters to shower chairs.

Travelers with disabilities who wish to do their own driving can request free assistive devices such as hand controls, spinner knobs, and swivel seats from all major rental car agencies, although **Avis** (www.avis.com; ✆ **800/331-1212**) and **Budget** (www.budget.com; ✆ **800/214-6094**) offer the most options. Hawai'i recognizes other states' windshield placards indicating that the driver of the car is disabled, so bring yours with you. Vision-impaired and other travelers who use a service dog need to present documentation that the dog is a trained service animal and has had rabies shots, among other health information. For details, see the regulations posted by the **Animal Industry Division** (https://hdoa.hawaii.gov/ai/aqs/aqs-info; ✆ **808/483-7151**).

Visas   The U.S. State Department has a **Visa Waiver Program (VWP)** allowing citizens of numerous nations to enter the United States without a visa for stays of up to 90 days. Consult **https://travel.state.gov/content/travel/en/us-visas.html** for the most up-to-date list of countries in the VWP. Citizens of all other countries must have (1) a valid passport that expires at least 6 months later than the scheduled end of their visit to the U.S., and (2) a tourist visa.

Even though a visa isn't necessary for travelers from VWP countries, in an effort to help U.S. officials check travelers against terror watch lists before they arrive at U.S. borders, visitors from VWP nations must register online through the Electronic System for Travel Authorization (ESTA, go to https://esta.cbp.dhs.gov/esta) before boarding a plane or a boat to the U.S.

The Department of Homeland Security recommends filling out the online application ($21), which asks for basic personal and travel information, at least 3 days before traveling. Authorizations will be valid for up to 2 years or until the traveler's passport expires, whichever comes first. VWP travelers must also present an **E-passport,** which contains a computer chip capable of storing biometric information, such as the required digital photograph of the holder. Citizens of VWP nations also need to present a round-trip air or cruise ticket upon arrival.

Water   The water in your hotel or at public drinking fountains is safe to drink (depending on the island, it may have more chlorine than you like). Do not drink water from waterfalls, rivers, or streams without boiling or treating it first, and don't swim in fresh water with open cuts, since infections from leptospirosis and giardia could result.

Index

Accommodations

PHOTO CREDITS